HISTORY OF INDIA

HISTORY OF INDIA

FROM THE EARLIEST PERIOD TO THE CLOSE OF THE EAST INDIA COMPANY'S GOVERNMENT

JOHN CLARK MARSHMAN

GYAN

Published by

Gyan Publishing House
5, Ansari Road
Daryaganj, New Delhi-110002
Phone: 011-47034999, 9811692060
E-mail: books@gyanbooks.com

Distribution Network
gyanbooks.com
India, USA, Canada, UK, Australia, France

ISBN: 978-81-212-8880-4 (PB)
First Published, 1876

2nd Impression 2023

Printed at: Gyan Press, Delhi.

HISTORY OF INDIA

AUTHOR: JOHN CLARK MARSHMAN

ABRIDGMENT

OF THE

HISTORY OF INDIA

HISTORY OF INDIA

FROM THE EARLIEST PERIOD TO THE CLOSE OF THE EAST INDIA COMPANY'S GOVERNMENT

ABRIDGED FROM THE AUTHOR'S LARGER WORK

BY

JOHN CLARK MARSHMAN

C.S.I.

EDINBURGH AND LONDON

WILLIAM BLACKWOOD AND SONS

CALCUTTA SCHOOL BOOK SOCIETY, CALCUTTA

1876

INTRODUCTION

I HAVE BEEN ADVISED that an Abridgment of the History of India which has been in use by the students of the University of Calcutta for eight years would be welcome to them, and I have endeavoured to compress the substance of the three volumes into one, which, although scanty in detail, will suffice to give them a view of the salient events of the different periods.

The space allotted to the Mahomedan period has been abbreviated to make room for a fuller narrative of the progress of British power, in which the Queen's Indian subjects are more particularly interested. This will not be considered a matter of regret, as Elphinstone's classical and standard History of India, which treats exclusively of the Musulman dynasties, is included in the student's curriculum of study.

The present abridgment has been brought down to the close of the administration of the East India Company, and the annexation of the empire of India to the crown of Great Britain, which forms one of the most important epochs in Indian history. A brief notice of events from that date to the death of Lord Mayo has been added.

Since the publication of the original work a new system of spelling Indian names, designated the trans-literal, has been introduced in India, which in some cases differs so materially from that which has hitherto been in vogue, that it is not easy to identify the places or persons. I have adhered to the old form of orthography, as the student may have occasion to refer to the records and despatches of Government, to Parliamentary papers, to previous histories, and to current English journals, in which it has been, and continues to be, used. There are some cases in which names have been variously spelled by different writers, but the diversities are neither important nor embarrassing. On the principle of preferring general usage to philological nicety, I have in every such instance collated diverse authors, and, to the best of my ability, made choice of that mode which appeared to have the preponderance. For the convenience of the native student, the two forms of spelling are placed in juxtaposition in the following table.

JOHN CLARK MARSHMAN.

LONDON: *October*, 1873.

NOTE TO THE PRESENT EDITION.

THE hand which wrote the above lines no longer holds the pen: John Clark Marshman died in London on the 8th of July 1877, and India lost in him a zealous worker, and a most conscientious and faithful historian. During a long life, his efforts were unceasingly directed to the study of her interests, and the welfare of her people, and it was his highest aim and proudest title to be considered "the Friend of India." In the present edition, the summary of important events, from the death of Lord Mayo in 1872 to the close of the year 1879, has been briefly chronicled by a member of the author's family.

LONDON, *April* 1880.

TABLE OF ORTHOGRAPHY

CUSTOMARY	TRANSLITERAL
Abdalee	Abdáli
Abdoolla	Abdullah
Aboo	Abú
Abul Fazil	Abul Fazl
Acharjyu	Achárya
Afzool Khan	Afzal Khán
Agra	Agrah
Ahmed	Ahmad
Ahmedabad	Ahmadábád
Ahmednugur	Ahmadnagar
Ajeet	Ajit
Ajmere	Ajmír
Aliverdy	Alivardi
Alla-ood-deen	Alá-ud-dín
Alliwal	Aliwal
Allygurh	Aligarh
Alum	Alam
Alumgeer	Alamgír
Aluptugeen	Alptigin
Ambajee	Ambaji
Amboor	Ambur
Ameer	Amír
Amercote	Amarkot
Amrut	Amrita
Anglia	Inglia
Anund	Anand
Anwar-ood-deen	Anwar-ud-din
Argaum	Argáon
Arracan	Arakán
Aseergurh	Asirgahr
Asof Khan	Asaf Khán
Assye	Assai
Aurungabad	Aurangábád
Aurungzebe	Aurangzeb
Aylah	Ahalyá
Azim	Azam
Azimgurh	Azimgarh
Baber	Bábar
Baboo	Bábú
Bagdad	Baghdád
Bahadoor	Bahádur
Bahminee	Bahmani
Bajee Rao	Báji Rao
Balaghaut	Bálaghát
Ballajee	Báláji
Bandoo	Banda
Bapoo	Bápú
Barcelore	Barcelor
Bareilly	Bareli
Beder	Bidar
Bednore	Bednor
Beejanuger	Bijanagar
Beejapore	Bijapur
Beema	Bhima
Begum	Begam
Behar	Bihár
Bellals	Ballálas
Bellary	Ballary
Beloch	Bilúch
Belochistan	Bilúchistán
Beloli	Buhlol
Berar	Barár
Beyas	Beya
Bharutu	Bharata
Bhawulpore	Bháwálpur
Bheem	Bhíma
Bhonslay	Bhonslé
Bhoobaneshur	Bhuvaneshwar
Bhurtpore	Bhartpur
Biana	Biánah
Bithoor	Bithour
Bokhara	Bukhara
Boohddha	Buddha
Booddhism	Buddhism
Booddhist	Buddhist
Boorhanpore	Burhánpur
Bootwul	Bhútwál
Brahmin	Bráhman
Brumhapooter	Brahmaputra
Budgebudge	Baj-Baj
Budukshan	Badakshán
Bukhtijar	Bakhtiár
Bulbun	Balban
Bullabhis	Vallabhis
Bundlecund	Bandelkhand
Burdwan	Bardwán
Burmah	Barmah
Buxar	Baxar
Bye	Bái
Byram	Bairám
Cabul	Kábul
Cachar	Kachár
Calicut	Calicát
Caliph	Khalif
Callinger	Kálinjar
Calpee	Kalpi
Cambay	Kambáy
Cambuksh	Kámbaksh
Camran	Kámrán
Candahar	Kandahár

CUSTOMARY	TRANSLITERAL	CUSTOMARY	TRANSLITERAL
Candesh	Khándesh	Fyzabad	Faizábád
Carrical	Kárikal	Furruckabad	Farakhábád
Cashmere	Kashmir	Gawilgurh	Gawilgarh
Cauvery	Kaveri	Geriah	Gheriah
Cawnpore	Cawnpur	Ghauts	Gháts
Chanderee	Chanderi	Ghazee	Ghází
Chandernagore	Chandernagar	Ghazeepore	Gházipur
Cheetoo	Chitu	Ghiljie	Khilji
Chenab	Chináb	Gholam	Ghulám
Cheyt Sing	Chait Singh	Ghore	Ghor
Chillumbrum	Chilambram	Ghuzni	Ghazni
Chittore	Chitor	Gingee	Gingi
Choule	Choul	Godavery	Godávari
Choute	Chauth	Gogra	Ghoghra
Chumbul	Chambal	Gohud	Gohad
Chumpanere	Champánir	Gohur	Gauhár
Chunar	Chanár	Golab	Gulab
Chunda	Chandá	Golconda	Golkandah
Chundergiree	Chandragiri	Goomsoor	Gumsur
Chundragooptu	Chandragupta	Gooptu	Gupta
Chuttanuttee	Chattanatty	Goorkha	Ghurká
Chutter	Chattar	Gooroo	Guru
Coimbatoor	Coimbator	Goruckpore	Gorakhpur
Colapore	Kohlapur	Gour	Gaur
Coles	Kols	Gukkers	Gakkhars
Coorg	Kúrg	Gungadhur	Gangádhar
Corah	Korah	Guntoor	Guntur
Cossim	Kásim	Guzerat	Guzarát
Cossimbazar	Kasimbazár	Gwalior	Gwáliár
Cuddalore	Cuddalor	Gya	Gaya
Cuddapa	Kadapa	Hafiz Ruhmut	Hafiz Rahmat
Cunouge	Kanauj	Hajee	Haji
Curumnassa	Karmanasa	Hamed	Hahmid
Cutch	Kach	Hejira	Hijrah
Cuttack	Cattack	Hemu	Himú
Daniel	Dányál	Herat	Harát
Daood Khan	Daud Khán	Hindee	Hindi
Deccan	Dakkin	Hindoo	Hindú
Deeg	Dig	Hindoo Coosh	Hindú Kush
Deogaum	Deogaon	Hindostan	Hindústán
Deogurh	Deogiri	Hooghly	Hugli
Devicotta	Devikotta	Hoosen Ali	Husian Ali
Dewan	Diwán	Hoshungabad	Húshangábád
Dewanee	Diwáni	Humayoon	Humayún
Dholpore	Dholpur	Hnooman	Hanumát
Dhriturastu	Dhritarástra	Hussun Gunga	Hasan Gango
Dhuleep Sing	Dhúlip Singh	Hustinapore	Hastinápura
Dhyan	Dian	Hyderabad	Haidarábad
Delawur	Deláwar	Hyder Ali	Haidar Ali
Dilere	Dilir	Indore	Indor
Dindigul	Dindigal	Irrawaddy	Irawádi
Doondhoo Punt	Dhandu Pant	Jain	Jaina
Dooranees	Duranis	Jaulna	Jálna
Doorjun Sal	Durjan Sál	Jaut	Ját
Dooryudhun	Duryodhana	Jehander	Jahándár
Dowlut	Daulat	Jehangeer	Jahángir
Drupudee	Draupudi	Jehan Lodi	Jahán Lodi
Dumdum	Damdam	Jellalabad	Jalálábad
Dushuruthu	Dasaratha	Jellal-ood-deen	Jalál-ud-din
Eldoze	Ilduz	Jenghis Khan	Changiz Khán
Ellichpore	Ilichpur	Jeswunt	Jeswant
Emamgurh	Imangurh	Jeypore	Jaipur
Eusufzies	Yúsufzais	Jey Sing	Jai Singh
Ferokshere	Farrukh Siyar	Jhelum	Jhelam
Feroze	Firúz	Joudhpore	Jodhpur
Ferozepore	Firúzpur	Jounpore	Jaunpur
Firman	Farmán	Juggut Sett	Jagat Set
Furnavese	Farnavis	Jullunder	Jallandar
Futteh Khan	Fathkhán	Jummoo	Jammu
Futtehpore	Fathpur	Jumna	Jamnah

CUSTOMARY	TRANSLITERAL	CUSTOMARY	TRANSLITERAL
Junkojee	Jankoji	Moslem	Muslim
Junuku	Janaka	Mozuffer	Muzaffar
Katmandoo	Khátmandu	Muazzim	Muazzam
Kharism	Khwarizm	Muckwanpore	Makwánpur
Khelat	Kalát	Mugudu	Maghada
Khizir	Khizr	Muhabharut	Mahábhárata
Khojah	Khwájah	Muhanudee	Mahánadi
Khoond	Khond	Mulhar	Malhár
Khorasan	Khurásán	Mundel	Mandal
Khosroo	Khusrau	Muneepore	Manipur
Khurruk	Karak	Munoo	Manu
Khyber	Khaibar	Musulman	Musalmán
Khyrpore	Khairpur	Muttra	Mattra
Kineyree	Kineri	Mysore	Maisúr or Mysor
Kirkee	Kharki	Nabob	Nawáb
Kistna	Krishna	Nagarcote	Nagarkot
Koh-i-noor	Koh-i-nur	Nagpore	Nagpúr
Kolapore	Kolhapur	Nahapan	Nahápána
Koombho	Khumbo	Nalagurh	Nalagarh
Kooroos	Kurus	Nanuk	Nának
Koorookshetru	Kurukshetra	Narrain	Náráyana
Kootúb	Kutb	Nazir Jung	Nasir Jang
Korygaum	Koregám	Nepaul	Nepál
Krishnu	Krishna	Nerbudda	Narbaddah
Kshetriyus	Kshatriyas	Nizam-ool-moolk	Nizám-ul-mulk
Kuloosha	Kulusha	Noor Jehan	Núr Jahán
Kulyan	Kalian	Nuddea	Naddea
Kureem	Kharim	Nundu	Nanda
Kurnool	Karnúl	Nunkoomar	Nandakumár
Kurrachee	Karáchi	Nuzeeb-ood-dow-lah	Nazib-ud-daulah
Kootub	Kutb	Omar	Umar
Lahore	Lahor	Omichund	Umáchánd
Lall	Lal	Omrah	Umará
Leswaree	Laswari	Ooch	Uchh
Lohanee	Lohání	Oodypore	Udaipur
Loodiana	Lúdhiánah	Oody Sing	Udai Singh
Lucknow	Lakhnau	Oojein	Ujjain
Lucknowtee	Laknauti	Oude	Oudh
Lucksmunu	Lacksmana	Palghaut	Pálkkát
Madhoo	Mádu	Pandoos	Pándavas
Mahmood	Mahmúd	Pandyas	Pandics
Mahomed	Muhammad	Paniani	Ponáni
Mahomedan	Muhammadan	Paniput	Panipat
Mallojee	Malloji	Pataus	Patháns
Malown	Maloun	Peelajee	Pilaji
Mama Sahib	Mama Saheb	Persajee	Parsaji
Mandoo	Mándú	Pertab Sing	Pratáb Singh
Mangalore	Mangalor	Peshawur	Pesháwar
Mawulees	Máwalis	Pindarees	Pindáris
Meeanmeer	Mianmír	Plassy	Plassey
Meeanee	Miani	Poona	Púna
Meer	Mir	Pooranus	Puránas
Meer Jaffier	Mirjáfar	Pooree	Puri
Meer Joomla	Mir Jamla	Poornea	Púrniah
Meerun	Miran	Pooroosram	Purasu Rama
Meerut	Mirat	Poorundur	Púrandhar
Mehidpore	Mahidpur	Punchala	Panchála
Melown	Mellún	Punderpore	Pandharpur
Merdan	Mardán	Punjab	Panjáb
Mewar	Maiwár	Punt	Pant
Mednapore	Midnapur	Purwandurra	Parwándurra
Mobarik	Mubarak	Prithee	Prithvi
Mogul	Mughul	Qwettah	Kettah
Monghyr	Monghir	Raiseen	Raisin
Moodkee	Múdki	Raigurh	Raigarh
Moolraj	Mulráj	Rajpoot	Rajpút
Mooltan	Multán	Rajpootana	Rajpútáná
Moorshedabad	Murshidábád	Ramayun	Rámáyana
Morad	Murad	Ramnugger	Ramnagar
Morteza	Múrtazá		

CUSTOMARY	TRANSLITERAL
Ramraj	Rámrájá
Ramu	Ráma
Ranu Sunga	Ráná Sanga
Rangoon	Rangún
Ravee	Rávi
Ravunu	Rávana
Rawul-pindee	Ráwal-pindi
Rezia	Raziah
Rhotas	Rahtás
Rinthimbore	Rantambhor
Robilcund	Rohilkhand
Roopur	Ropar
Rughoojee	Raghuji
Rughoonath	Raghunáth
Runjeet Sing	Rangit Singh
Sa'adut	Sa'adat
Sahoo	Sáhu
Salabut Jung	Salábat Jung
Salbye	Salbai
Sambajee	Sambaji
Satgang	Sátgawn
Satpoora	Sátpurá
Saugor	Ságar
Savanoor	Sávanur
Savendoorg	Suvarnadrúg
Secunder	Sikandar
Seeta	Sita
Seetabuldee	Sitábaldi
Seeva	Siva
Selim	Salim
Seljuks	Saljúks
Sen	Sena
Seoraj	Siorój
Setts	Sets
Sevajee	Sevaji
Shah Alum	Shah Alam
Shahee	Sháhhi
Shahjee	Sháji
Shah Jehan	Shah Jahán
Shahpooree	Shahpúri
Shariar	Shahryár
Shastur	Sastra
Shustree	Sahstri
Sheah	Shiah
Sheiks	Shaikhs
Shere	Sher
Shirjee	Shirji
Shunkur	Sankara
Sikkim	Sikhim
Sinde	Sind
Sing	Singh
Sipree	Sipra
Sircars	Circars
Sirhind	Sarhind
Sirjee Angengaum	Sir ji Angengaon
Soane	Son
Soliman	Sulaimán
Soobah	Súbah
Soobadar	Súbahdar
Sooder	Sudra
Shoojah	Shujá
Soor	Súr
Sooruj Mull	Suráj Mall
Subuktugeen	Sebaktigin
Succaram	Sakaram
Suddaseo-rao-bhow	Sivadás ráo bhao
Suddoosain	Suddosam
Sufder	Safdar
Suraj-ood-dowlah	Siráj-ud-daulah
Surat	Saurashtra
Sutlej	Satlaj
Sutnaramees	Satnurámis
Suttee	Sati
Syhadree	Syhadri
Syuds	Sayyids
Tallikotta	Talikot
Talpooras	Talpúrs
Tamul	Támil
Tanjore	Tanjor
Tanna	Thána
Taptee	Tápti
Tara-bye	Tara-bái
Tartar	Tatár
Tellicherry	Tellicheri
Teloogoo	Telugu
Teraee	Tarái
Thanesur	Thuneswar
Tinnevelly	Tinnevelli
Tippoo	Tippú
Tirhoot	Tirhút
Toder Mull	Todar Mall
Toghluk	Tughlak
Tokajee	Tukaji
Tonk	Tank
Toolsee-bye	Tulsí-bái
Toombudra	Tumbadra
Travancore	Travancor
Trichinopoly	Trichinápalli
Trimbukjee Dunglia	Trimbakji Dainglia
Tumlook	Tamluk
Ugni-Kools	Agnikulas
Umritsir	Amritsar
Urjoon	Arjuna
Vedic	Vaidik
Vellore	Vellor
Vencajee	Venkáji
Vikrumadityu	Vikramáditya
Vishnoo	Vishnu
Vizier	Vazir
Warungul	Warangal
Wassil	Wasil
Wishwanath	Vishwanáth
Wiswas	Viswas
Wurda	Warda
Wurgaum	Wargám
Wuzeerabad	Vazirábád
Yoodistheer	Yudhisthira
Zabita	Zabitah
Zeman	Zamán
Zemindar	Zamindár
Zoolfikar	Zulfikár

TABLE OF CONTENTS

CHRONOLOGICAL AND HISTORICAL

CHAPTER I.

Section I.

Section II.

CHAPTER II.

Section I.

Section II.

SECTION III.

SECTION IV.

SECTION V.

CHAPTER III.

SECTION I.

SECTION II.

SECTION III.

SECTION IV.

CHAPTER IV.

Section I.

Section II.

Section III.

Section IV.

CHAPTER V.

SECTION I.

CHAPTER VI.

SECTION I.

SECTION IV.

SECTION V.

CHAPTER VII.

SECTION I.

SECTION II.

SECTION III.

CHAPTER VIII.

SECTION I.

SECTION II.

SECTION III.

SECTION IV.

SECTION V.

CHAPTER IX.

Section I.

Section II.

Section III.

Section IV.

CHAPTER X.

Section I.

Section II.

Section III.

Section IV.

CHAPTER XI.

Section I.

SECTION II.

SECTION III.

CHAPTER XII.

SECTION I.

SECTION II.

SECTION III.

SECTION IV.

CHAPTER XIII.

SECTION I.

SECTION III.

SECTION IV.

CHAPTER XIV.

SECTION I.

SECTION II.

SECTION III.

SECTION IV.

CHAPTER XV.

SECTION I.

Section II.

Section III.

Section IV.

Section V.

ABRIDGMENT

OF THE

HISTORY OF INDIA

CHAPTER I.

SECTION I.

EARLY HISTORICAL NOTICES.

INDIA is bounded on the north and the east by the Himalaya mountains, on the west by the Indus, and on the south by the sea. Its length from Cashmere to Cape Comorin is 1900 miles; its breadth from Kurrachee in Sinde to Sudiya in Assam, 1500 miles. The superficial area is 1,287,000 miles, and the population under British and native rule is now estimated at 240,000,000. It is crossed from east to west by the Vindhya chain of mountains, at the base of which flows the Nerbudda. The country to the north of this river is generally designated Hindostan, and that to the south the Deccan. Hindostan is composed of the basin of the Indus on one side, and of the Ganges on the other, with the great sandy desert on the west, and an elevated tract now called Central India. The Deccan has on its northern boundary a chain of mountains running parallel with the Vindhya, to the south of which stretches a table-land of triangular form, terminating at Cape Comorin, with the western ghauts on the western coast, and the eastern ghauts, of minor altitude, on the opposite coast. Between the ghauts and the sea lies a narrow belt of land which runs round the whole peninsula.

Boundaries and divisions of India.

India has no authentic historical records before the era of

the Mahomedans. The notices of the earliest period can only be gleaned from the two great epics, which were composed ten or twelve centuries after the events which they celebrate, and are so overlaid with the vagaries of an oriental imagination that it is difficult to extract a few grains of truth from a vast mass of fable. Between the era of the Muhabharut and the Ramayun and the arrival of the Musulmans, the rise and fall of dynasties is to be traced exclusively from coins and inscriptions, through the researches of antiquarians, whose conjectures differ so widely from each other that their theories cannot as yet be accepted with implicit confidence. The chronology of the Hindoos consists of astronomical periods, and the successive ages of the world are made to correspond with the conjunctions of the heavenly bodies, and are divided into four periods. The first, or *sutyu* joog, is therefore, said to have extended to 1,728,000 years; the second, or *treta* joog, to 1,296,000; the third, or *dwapur* joog, to 864,000; and the fourth, or *kulee* joog, is predicted to last 432,000 years; of which 4500 have already expired. The periods of the first three joogs may therefore be dismissed as altogether imaginary, while the commencement of the fourth, or present age, corresponding, as it does to a certain extent, with the authenticated eras of other nations, is entitled to greater consideration.

Early history and chronology.

Of the original inhabitants of India there is not the faintest record. To distinguish them from their Aryan conquerors it is usual to designate them Turanians, who came from across the Indus. By Hindoo writers they are described as rakshusus, usoors, pisaches, hobgoblins and monsters, and it is therefore natural to suppose that they must have offered a stern resistance to the invaders. Some of them doubtless made their submission, and it is conjectured that they may have formed the basis of the soodra, or servile caste, which was probably recruited also from the issue of intercourse with the victors. But the great body of them retreated to the forests of the Sone, the Nerbudda, and the Muhanudee, and to the hills of Sirgooja and Chota Nagpore, and they are identified with the Bheels, the Meenas, the Coles, the Santals, the Gonds, and other tribes. In those inaccessible fastnesses they have continued to maintain their primitive barbarism of habits, their language, and their crude religious observances, with little change amidst the revolutions which have convulsed India for thirty centuries.

The aborigines, and the Aryan invasion.

At the present time they are supposed to number 12,000,000. The 'fair complexioned Aryans,' the ancestors of the present Hindoo communities, are believed to have emigrated in a remote age from some undefined region in Central Asia, from which other tribes swarmed westward, and spreading over Europe, laid the foundation of its present nationalities. The only notices we obtain of them are derived from the Vedus, the most ancient and sacred of the Hindoo writings, and more especially from the Rig Vedu, which, however, consists chiefly of the hymns and invocations which were traditionally handed down. From them we gather that the original Aryans crossed the Hindoo Coosh and the Indus in search of a settlement, bringing with them their own language, the Sanscrit, and settled in the Punjab, the cradle of Hindooism. They were devoted to pastoral and agricultural pursuits, worshipped Indra, the god of the firmament, as the sovereign of the gods, and inferior deities as the personification of the powers of nature. They do not appear to have had either idols or temples, and there was no distinction of castes.

Rise of Brahminism.

The age of the Vedus was succeeded by what has been termed the heroic age, when the Aryans extended their conquests beyond the narrow limits of the Punjab, and, expanding to the south and the east, established kingdoms at Hustinapore, at Oude, and at Mithila, under two dynasties, which are distinguished as the solar and lunar races. It is to this period that the memorable events celebrated in the Muhabharut and the Ramayun belong. The Aryan conquerors were of the military caste of kshetriyus, and the brahmins served them as sacrificial priests. It has been conjectured that this age of conquest and progression was favourable to the growth of brahminism, and that to it belongs the large pantheon of gods which came into vogue, the institution of caste, and the introduction of animal sacrifices. The brahmins gradually advanced their pretensions to a divine origin, and to divine authority, and at length brought the kshetriyus under their yoke, and assumed not only supremacy over rajas and princes, like Pope Hildebrand, but represented even the deities of the Vedic Aryans as subordinate to them.

The Muhabharut.

Of the events of the heroic age, only two have been rescued from oblivion, in the immortal epics of the Muhabharut and the Ramayun. These are, the great war of the two branches of the lunar race, and the expedition of Ramu, a sovereign of the solar race to

the Deccan and Ceylon. The scene of warfare in the Muhabharut lies in the neighbourhood of Delhi, while the kingdom of Ramu lay farther south, and it is natural to conclude that the one preceded the other in point of time.
B.C. The story of the Muhabharut runs thus: The city of
1400 Hustinapore, about sixty miles distant from Delhi, was governed by the king Pandoo, who in a hunting excursion wounded two deer with his arrows, on which they assumed their natural shape, and sprang up as a brahmin and his wife. The brahmin inflicted a curse on him, of which he died soon after, leaving five sons, who were designated the Pandoos. The blind brother of Pandoo, Dhriturastu, was then placed on the throne, and his wife gave birth to a progeny of sons, who are called the Kooroos. The cousins were educated together in the royal palace, but a feeling of jealousy arose between Yoodisteer, the eldest of the Pandoos, and Dooryudhun, the eldest of the Kooroos, which resulted in the banishment of the former to a city, usually identified with Allahabad. There the Kooroos still plotted the destruction of their relatives, and they were fain to escape to the jungle. At this period the raja of Punchalu, which cannot, however, be identified, allowed his daughter Drupudee to perform the *swuyumburu*, that is, to make choice of a husband for herself; and he proclaimed a great tournament, not differing greatly from the tournaments of the middle ages in Europe. A pole was fixed in the ground, on the top of which was placed a golden fish, and beneath it a revolving wheel, and it was proclaimed that whoever succeeded in directing the arrow through the wheel and piercing the eye of the fish, should win the queen of beauty. The plain was covered with the pavilions of noble and princely suitors and their splendid equipages and retinue; and, among them appeared the five Pandoos, in the humble guise of brahmins. One of them, Urjoon, with his bow of 'celestial virtue,' pierced the eye of the fish, and Drupudee threw the garland round his neck and led him away. Her father, however, considered himself disgraced by an ignoble alliance with a brahmin, but was overjoyed when he discovered that the victor was of the noble race of the kshetriyus. In accordance with the practice of polyandry which appears to have been prevalent at the time, she became the wife at once of the five brothers.

The Pandoos returned to Hustinapore in triumph, and the blind old king offered to divide his kingdom between them and his own family, and they proceeded to the site of the present Delhi, and having overcome the aboriginal inhabitants erected the city of Indruprustha. They were successful in extending their territory and popular in governing it, and Yoodistheer, in the pride of his heart, determined to offer a royal sacrifice, as an assertion of his supremacy. Dooryudhun, the eldest son of the king, envious of the glory acquired by his cousin, invited him to a gambling match, the ruling passion and the vice of the kshetriyus. In an evil hour Yoodistheer accepted the challenge, and staked in succession, his kingdom, his brothers, himself, and his wife, and lost them all. The condition of the game was that the losing party should go into exile in the country for twelve years and for one year in the city. The Pandoos submitted to this injunction, and having wandered the prescribed period in the forest, visiting the hermitages of the holy sages, determined to demand the restoration of their share of the kingdom. Dooryudhun haughtily refused their request, and they resolved to assert their right by arms. The contest was one between cousins for the possession of a quantity of land, which, since their capitals lay within sixty miles of each, must have been of very limited extent, but the poet has given loose to his imagination, and princes from the remotest parts of India, from regions then unknown to the Aryans, are brought upon the field, and the number said to have been engaged exceeds in number all the present inhabitants of the globe; the chariots and elephants are reckoned by millions; the plain overflows with rivers of blood, and whole armies are destroyed by a single talismanic weapon. The battle doubtless formed one of the most memorable events of that early period of society, and it was preserved in tradition and commemorated in ballads, and, a thousand years after, elaborated into an epic poem of a hundred thousand couplets, by the illustrious Vyasu. The conflict, which is said to have raged for eighteen days, ended in the triumph of the Pandoos. Yoodistheer was installed raja at Hustinapore, and celebrated his victory by the proud sacrifice of the horse, the emblem of universal sovereignty. He and his brothers and their common wife eventually assumed the character of devotees, and disappeared in the Himalaya. The real hero of the Muhabharut was Krishnu, the son of a cowherd, who established his kingdom at Dwarka, on the western coast, married 16,000 wives, and was slain at the fountain of the

The battle of Kooroo Kshetru.

lotus by the irrepressible Bheels. He was deified after his death, and placed second in the Hindoo triad of the brahminical theogony, which was not completely organised till centuries after the events of the Muhabharut. The object of the epic was to identify him, when his worship was introduced, with those transactions which were among the most cherished recollections of the Aryan race, as an incarnation of the deity.

Between the events commemorated in the Muhabharut and the Ramayun the Aryans would appear to have burst

The Ramayun.

the boundary of their original settlement and extended their conquests to the south and the east,

B.C. 1200

and to have established two kingdoms, the one at Uyodhyu, or Oude, and the other at Mithila, both designated by way of distinction the solar race. The order of events in the Ramayun may be thus epitomized:—Ramu, the hero of the poem and an incarnation of the deity, was the eldest of the four sons of Dushuruthu, the king of Oude. Junuka, the sovereign of the neighbouring kingdom of Mithila, had a beautiful daughter, Seeta, whom he promised to bestow on the prince who could bend the bow with which the god Seeva had destroyed the other gods, and which was preserved as an heirloom in the royal armoury. Ramu broke the bow in the midst and won the princess. The marriage ceremony was performed by the raja himself, and not by the priests. Ramu returned to Oude, and was appointed heir apparent; but the raja's second wife, who had gained his affection by her beauty, was anxious to obtain the throne for her own son, Bharutu, and persuaded her uxorious husband to consent to the banishment of Ramu. On the morning fixed for his installation he was constrained to quit the royal palace with his wife and his brother Lukshmunu, and he proceeded into the forest, from hermitage to hermitage, and terminated his wanderings at Nassik on the Godavery, where he erected a hut. The sister of Ravunu, the king of Lunka, or Ceylon, called also Taprobane, or the island of Ravunu, passing by the bower, was struck with the beauty of Ramu, and endeavoured to prevail on him to desert Seeta, and marry her. Her offers were rejected with scorn, when she rushed upon Seeta and threatened to devour her, on which Lukshmunu, at the request of Ramu, cut off her ears and nose. She returned to Ceylon, and in revenge for the injury she had sustained, persuaded her brother to carry off the lovely Seeta. Ravunu, described as a monster with ten heads and twenty arms, assumed the form of a mendicant and appeared before the hermitage, and having caused his brother to take the form of a deer, and decoy the two brothers after him, seized upon Seeta and carried her off through the air in his chariot to Ceylon. Ramu having discovered the place of her concealment, assembled an army of the wild inhabitants of the south, probably the aborigines, poetically described as bears and monkeys, under their sovereign Soogreevu, and his general Hunooman, subsequently deified as the great baboon, and proceeded to the island. He spanned the straits between it and the continent with a bridge, and after many severe conflicts recovered Seeta and slew Ravunu. But as she had resided in the palace of Ravunu she was required to submit to the ordeal of fire to testify her purity, and the poet affirms that after she had ascended the pile, the three hundred and thirty millions of gods assembled in the heavens to behold the scene, and the god of fire arose from the flames, and bearing Seeta on his knees presented her to her husband. They returned in triumph to Oude, and Ramu was installed raja. The epic is so intermingled at every turn with the grotesque fancies of mythology, and the agency is so constantly described as supernatural, that it is difficult to extract from it the germs of historical truth on which it was based. But it appears clear that it indicates the first expedition of the Aryans to the Deccan, that the southern division of it was still peopled with the aborigines, and that the island of Ceylon was the seat of a higher civilisation, probably wafted from Egypt. It led to no permanent conquest, as the army of monkeys and bears which aided Ramu, after accompanying him in triumph to his capital, returned to their forests, and we hear no more of them on the page of history till they had been transformed into orthodox Hindoos. It must not be forgotten that the poem was composed ten centuries after the events it celebrates, when brahminism was consolidated into a dominant system, which it was intended to support.

Next to the Vedus, the Code of Munoo is the most important of the Hindoo shasters. It embodies the ancient religious traditions, to which additions were made from century to century, and which were collected, as it is said, by Vyasu. It gives us the constitution of a Hindoo commonwealth when the brahmins had completely superseded the ancient authority of the kshetriyus

B.C. 900

Munoo.

and established religious depotism in the state such as no priesthood has ever enjoyed. The ancient and simple worship of the Vedus was supplanted by an elaborate system of ceremonies and by animal sacrifices. Ramu, Krishnu, and other gods, who subsequently became popular, are not mentioned with reverence or with disapprobation. There is no intimation of regular orders, or of the immolation of widows. Brahmins eat beef and flesh of all kinds, and intermarry with women of inferior castes, and various other practices are permitted which would at the present day entail excommunication. The style is less rugged than that of the Vedus, but not so polished as that of the epics; and the date of its compilation is generally fixed at 900 B.C.

SECTION II.

FROM THE AGE OF BOODDHU TO THE MAHOMEDAN INVASION.

THE next event of importance in the ancient history of India is the appearance of Booddhu, or Sakhya Moonee, as the great reformer of religion and morals. He was born of a princely Aryan family of kshetriyu parents in the year 598 B.C. He resided with his own family till his twenty-eighth year, when, disgusted with the decay of religion and the spread of superstition, he retired from society and passed many years in constructing his system of religion and philosophy. He repudiated the entire system of caste, and thus rendered his doctrines acceptable to those who had suffered from it, while it made the brahmins his irreconcilable enemies. He rejected the whole pantheon of the Hindoos, and endeavoured to bring back his countrymen to the simplicity of the Vedus. The priesthood, instead of being an hereditary caste, was recruited from the various ranks of society, and bound by a vow of celibacy, and required to relinquish the pleasures of sense. He obtained many disciples before his death, which is fixed at 543 B.C., but it was not till two centuries later that boodhism became the religion of the state. The preservation and worship of relics was one of the distinguishing features of his creed. Eight cities are said to have contended for his remains, and the dispute was at length settled by distributing them in various provinces.

Booddhu.

The most sacred of these relics was the tooth, which was at length assigned to Orissa, and magnificently enshrined on the spot where subsequently arose the Hindoo temple of Jugernath, and it remained there, with some interruptions, for nearly a thousand years.

B.C. 521

Invasion of Darius.

The first authentic record we possess of any invasion of India is that of Darius, king of Persia, who was seated on the throne 521 B.C., and extended his conquests from the Grecian Sea to the Indus. Upon a report of the wealth of the country from his admiral, Scylax, who constructed a fleet on the higher portion of that river and sailed down to the sea, he despatched an expedition to India and annexed several of its provinces to his great empire. The extent of his conquests it is impossible to trace, but his Indian possessions must have been of no small magnitude since they were considered more valuable than any other satrapy, and are said to have furnished one-third of the revenues of the empire, and were paid in gold.

Invasion of Alexander the Great.

Two centuries after, Alexander the Great, the greatest military and political genius of antiquity, if not of any age, subverted the Persian empire, and sweeping through its provinces in Central Asia, took possession of Afghanistan. He advanced through its terrific defiles, and encountered the same stern resistance from its wild highlanders which, for more than twenty centuries they have opposed to every intruder. 327
He crossed the Indus, as generally supposed, at Attock, and entered the Punjab, where he received the submission of one of its princes, and was hospitably entertained by another. But Porus, whose dominions stretched eastward to the Jhelum, offered a more determined resistance to his arms than he had experienced since he left Macedonia; and, by a singular coincidence, it was in the same region that the English, twenty-two centuries later, met with a more formidable opposition than they had encountered throughout the conquest of India for a century. The chivalry of Porus fought with the same gallantry as the troops of the Khalsa, but they could not withstand the veterans of Alexander, and, after an engagement as obstinate as Ferozeshuhur or Sobraon, that high-minded prince gracefully submitted to the superiority of his conqueror, and was treated by him with his habitual generosity. Alexander now heard of the great Gangetic kingdom of Mugudu, the king of which, it was reported, could bring 30,000 cavalry, and 600,000 infantry, and 9,000 elephants

into the field, and he became impatient to plant his ensigns on the battlements of its splendid capital, Palibothra. But on reaching the banks of the Beyas, his troops, worn out with the fatigues and wounds of eight campaigns, refused to advance any farther. He employed menace and flattery by turns, but nothing could shake their resolution, and he was obliged to make that river the term of his conquests. He caused a flotilla to be constructed on the Indus, and transported his army down to the sea-coast, not, however, without serious opposition from the Malli, the inhabitants of Mooltan. He had fully resolved to return to India with a body of fresh troops, but he died of fever caught in the
B.C. marshes of Babylon at the early age of thirty-two. His
324 name does not appear in any Hindoo record, which only shows their imperfect character, but it is a household word in Central Asia, and his fame was widely diffused through India by the Mahomedans, among whom he is esteemed one of the first of heroes, and it was carried far and wide with the stream of their conquests, and the distant islander of Sumatra and Java may be found extolling the exploits of the mighty Secunder.

The most important kingdom at this period in Hindostan was that of Mugudu, designated by the Greek historians that of the Prasii, the capital of which was Pali-

The kingdom of Mugudu.

bothra, supposed to be the modern Patna. It was probably founded about the sixth century before our era, by a colony of Tartars, or Scythians, denominated the Takshuk or Nagas, the serpent dynasty, so called from the worship of snakes which they introduced, and which has never been eradicated. About the time of the Macedonian invasion, the throne was occupied by Nundu. He was assassinated by his minister, Chundra-
325 gooptu—called by the Greek historians, Sandracottus—a man of ignoble birth but of extraordinary genius, who had measured swords with Alexander the Great under Porus, and who now seized the throne and established the Mauryan dynasty. The empire of Alexander after his death was partitioned among his marshals, and the province of Babylon, in which was included his eastern possessions, fell to the lot of Seleucus, one of the ablest and most enterprising of them. He determined to carry out the ambitious projects of his master, and advanced with a large army into the Gangetic provinces, where he was opposed by Chundra-gooptu with the whole strength of Mugudu. According to the Greek historians he was vic-

torious, but it is difficult to reconcile this assertion with the fact recorded by themselves, that Seleucus concluded a treaty with him and ceded all his conquests east of the Indus for an annual tribute of fifty elephants. Megasthenes, an eminent philosopher, was appointed his representative at the court of Palibothra, and it is from the fragments of his writings which have come down to us that we gather any knowledge of the state of northern India at that period. It is said to have been divided into a hundred and twenty principalities. Chundra-gooptu was succeeded by his son Mitra-gooptu, a man of the same large and liberal views as his father, and it was under their enlightened administration that the country attained its B.C.
highest prosperity. Highways were constructed from the 300
capital to the Indus, in one direction, and in the other to Broach, then the great emporium on the western coast, with caravanseras at convenient intervals. Their dominion extended to the sea-coast at Ganjam on the west, around the bay to Aracan on the east. They gave especial encouragement to commerce, and their subjects embarked in maritime enterprises, crossed the bay of Bengal, and founded colonies in Java and the other islands of the Archipelago, into which they introduced the Hindoo religion and the Pali language, the classical variety of the Sanscrit.

Asoka, the grandson of Chundra-gooptu, who ascended the throne 260 B.C., stands forth as the most distinguished prince of this period, the glory of the Mauryan Asoka.
dynasty. His dominions extended from Orissa
to the Indus, and included provinces both in the Deccan 260
and in Afghanistan. The boundaries of this great kingdom were marked by stone columns, many of which are still extant. His edicts were engraved on the face of rocks, and on *lats*, or pillars, in various localities from the bay of Bengal to the Himalaya and Peshawur; and a permanent record has thus been preserved of the great events of his reign. He established courts of justice, and abolished the punishment of death. He promoted the progress of civilisation, and gave a new impulse to commerce. Breaking through the isolation of the brahminical system—which still continues after the lapse of more than twenty centuries to fetter the native mind—he established a friendly intercourse with Greece and Egypt, and it is to this connection that we trace the introduction of stone architecture and of sculpture into India, which was totally unknown before his time. Some of the temples were

excavated in the rock, and others erected on the plain. Of these, the most magnificent is the shrine at Sanchi, commenced in 225 B.C. Asoka embraced the booddhist creed, and made it the religion of the state. A great booddhist synod was held soon after, and religious missions were despatched to Tibet, China, Cambodia, Siam and Ceylon, and the creed was extensively diffused beyond the limits of India. He died in 226 B.C., after a reign of thirty-seven years, and with him sank the grandeur of the dynasty, which has the peculiar merit of having produced three illustrious princes in succession. It was succeeded in 188 B.C. by the dynasty of the Sungas, which, though of limited duration, was distinguished by the erection of another series of booddhist temples and monasteries.

The establishment of booddhism as the religion of the state, deprived the brahminical hierarchy of their ascendancy. The Hindoo annalists assert that ignorance and infidelity had overspread the land; the sacred books were trampled under foot, and mankind had no refuge from the monstrous brood—of booddhists. The holy sages, dwelling on Mount Aboo, carried their complaints to the father of creation, who was floating on a hydra in the sea of curds. He commanded them to return to the sacred mount and recreate the race of the kshetriyus, whom their own champion Pooroosram had formerly annihilated. The fountain of fire was purified by water from the Ganges, and each of the four gods who accompanied them formed an image, and cast it into the fire, upon which there sprang up the four men who afterwards became the founders of Rajpoot greatness. They were sent forth to combat the monsters, who were slain in great numbers; but as they fell on the ground, fresh demons arose, when the gods stopped the renewal of the race by drinking up the blood. This allegory, independent of the flattery it is intended to convey to the royal houses of Rajpootana, evidently points to some political revolution, which checked the progress of booddhism and restored to a certain degree the power of the brahmins. But booddhism continued for more than ten centuries to divide the allegiance of princes and people at different eras and in different provinces, with the creed of Munoo, and from time to time we have notices of booddhist sovereigns who brought all the resources of the state to the support of their creed.

The Ugni Kools.

About the year 629 A.D., Huen-tsang, a Chinese booddhist,

travelled through the continent of India, in order to visit its various shrines. In his travels, which have been preserved in the Chinese language, he states that while he found the creed in a state of decay in some provinces, he found it flourishing and dominant in Cunouge, in Mugudu, in Malwa and in Surat. About the eighth century of our era, the booddhists appear to have been subjected to a more implacable proscription than they had experienced for many centuries by Shunkur Acharjyu, a brahmin reformer; and from that time they decayed rapidly, and they entirely disappear from India soon after the invasion of the Mahomedans, while they increased and multiplied in the Indo-Chinese nations and in China, and the creed is at the present time professed by a larger number than the votaries of Hindooism.

Prevalence of Booddhism.

About the year 56 B.C. the Andhra dynasty obtained possession of the throne of Mugudu, and flourished till 436 A.D. Their dominion extended into the Deccan, with Warungul for their capital, and Oojein as the great metropolis of their power in the north. The founder of the dynasty, Vikrum-aditya, was the most illustrious and powerful monarch of the age; his memory continues to be cherished with profound veneration, and the era he established is still current. He was a munificent patron of literature, and encouraged the resort of the learned to his court from all parts of India by princely donations. The classic writers of that Augustan age have exhausted the resources of flattery in his praise; indeed, the extravagance of their panegyrics has induced some Indian antiquarians to regard him as a myth. Some of the most exquisite productions in the Sanscrit language were compiled under his auspices. It was about this period, a century or so before the Christian era, that India appears to have attained its greatest literary eminence, and the highest stage of civilisation it has ever reached. At a time when the western colony from the cradle of the Aryan race, which is supposed to have migrated to Europe and formed the aborigines of Great Britain and Gaul, of Germany and Scandinavia, was sunk in barbarism, the eastern stream of colonists, in India, had cultivated the science of law, of grammar, of astronomy, and of algebra, and had dived into the subtleties of philosophy and metaphysics. They had made their classic language, the Sanscrit, the most perfect and refined medium for the communication of thought, and

The Andra dynasty.

B.C. 57

Augustan age of Sanscrit literature.

enriched it with poetry, which has enchanted every succeeding generation. But with all this high cultivation, they neglected one of the most important branches of human knowledge, that of history. The Pooranus, of which the earliest is placed in 800 A.D., are the only treatises which pretend to anything like an historical character; but they furnish us with little beyond a barren record of royal races and rulers, none of which, however, can be implicitly depended upon. The most laborious researches of antiquarians have only resulted in deducing from half-defaced coins and servile inscriptions a chronological series of dynasties and princes, with here and there a fact, of little interest, and of no practical utility to the student of history. It is idle for him to fancy that he has gained much, if any, valuable knowledge when he has simply loaded his memory with an empty catalogue of genealogies. Yet the ten centuries preceding the arrival of the Mahomedans present little else, and a cursory glance at the date and locality of successive dynasties is all that the student can desire.

Neglect of history.

Eastward of the Andhra dominions lay the great kingdom of Bengal, containing the estuary of the Gangetic valley, with the ancient and magnificent city of Gour, or Lucknoutee for its capital. It was governed, first by the boodhist dynasty of Pal, and then by the Hindoo dynasty of Sen. While boodhism was the religion of the state, Hindooism fell into decay, and Adisoor, the founder of the Sen family, sent to Cunouge, the sanctuary of the Hindoo creed, for five sound and pure brahmins, who became the ancestors of the present brahminical communities of Bengal. They were accompanied by five attendants, from whom the kayusts, or writer caste, the second in dignity, are descended. The Sen dynasty was on the throne when the Mahomedans in 1192 A.D. conquered the country. Shortly before the Christian era Cashmere was invaded by a tribe of Tartars, which was displaced by a dynasty of Gundurvus. They were boodhists, and under a long succession of kings, contributed the most celebrated structures to the architecture of India. They appear to have enjoyed extensive dominion, as some of their grandest edifices were erected on the Kistna in the Deccan. They are said to have invaded Ceylon, but their succession cannot be traced beyond 622 A.D.

Ten centuries of annals—Bengal.

Cashmere: the Gundurvus.

In the first century before the Christian era, Nahapan

established the dynasty of the Shahs in Surat, on the western coast. They are supposed either to have been a Parthian tribe, who invaded India through Sinde, or Persians of the Sassanian race. They adopted the creed of Booddhu, and to the founder is attributed the excavation and the construction of the wonderful cave temple of Karlee between Bombay and Poona. They were conquered about 318 by the Bullabhis, who are likewise designated the Gooptus, and who would appear to have extended their power over a large portion of northern India. The second monarch of the line is said to have overrun Ceylon, but no traces of them are to be found after 525.

The Shahs of Surat.

During this period of ten centuries, northern India was parcelled out among various dynasties, of whom Mr. Elphinstone, in his valuable history, enumerates no fewer than eleven: Mugudu, Cunouge, Mithila, Benares, Delhi, Ajmere, Mewar, Jeypore, Jessulmere, Sinde and Cashmere. Of the princes of these kingdoms some claimed the dignity of *Muharaj-adheeraj*, or emperor of India; but however extensive may have been their conquests, it is much to be doubted whether any of them ever succeeded in 'bringing all India under one umbrella,' as the Moguls and the English have since done. Regal vanity doubtless induced some of them to assume the appellation of 'Lords Paramount' on their coins and inscriptions, but on examining the most accurate list of the claimants to that lofty title, that of Mr. Fergusson, we find that in the brief space of two hundred and forty-three years no fewer than ten monarchs arrogated it to themselves in Malwa, in Cunouge, in Surat, and even in the obscure state of Kulyan in the Deccan; and in some cases there is only a period of twenty years given for the acquisition of this universal sovereignty.

Various kingdoms of northern India.

The early history of the Deccan is involved in even greater obscurity than that of Hindostan. At the period of the expedition of Ramu the inhabitants in the lower Deccan are described as bears and monkeys; but at the extreme south of the peninsula, as he approached Ceylon, he entered the continental possessions of its king, Ravunu, and came in contact with a higher civilisation than that of the Aryans. At a subsequent period—some suppose nine or ten centuries before the Christian era—we find even the land of the bears and the monkeys peopled with a civilised race, which is commonly

The Deccan.

supposed to have entered India through Sinde and spread over the Deccan. To distinguish them from the Aryan colonists of Hindostan they are generally designated Dravidian, and their language, the Tamul, attained a high state of culture, and was enriched with a noble literature—and that by some of the servile class—long before the Sanscrit, with which it has no affinity, had attained perfection. Surrounded on all sides, except the north, by the sea, a constant intercourse was maintained with Greece and Egypt, and this may have contributed to the early civilisation of the peninsula. The most ancient and authentic history of the Deccan records the existence of two dynasties, that of the Pandyas, which was first in point of time, and that of the Cholas, which was the most powerful. The capital of the Pandyas, after two removals, was fixed at Madura, and its dominion lay along the Malabar coast. The kingdom of the Cholas, which some identify with Coromandel, was founded by an emigrant from Hindostan who established his capital at Canchi, or Conjeveram, and eventually removed it to Tanjore. Of the history of Telingana, no reliable records are extant, but about the eleventh century the Bellal dynasty obtained paramount power in this division of the country. Another dynasty also rose to distinction in the north of the Deccan, denominated the Chalukyas, and their capital was eventually established at Kulyan, in the territory now belonging to the Nizam. In their inscriptions they claim to have brought under subjection the Cholas and Pandyas in the south, and the Andhras of Warungul in the north, and there is reason to believe that for some time they may have been without a rival in the Deccan. The dynasty subsisted till 1182 A.D., when it was subverted by the Jadows of Deoghur, the modern Dowlutabad. Of the Mahrattas on the western coast only two facts can be traced, the existence of Tagara, a great emporium in the time of the Romans, and of Salivahun, the king of some unknown province, who was a bitter persecutor of the booddhists, and who is remembered only by his era, which prevails throughout the Deccan. Of Orissa nothing is known before the introduction of booddhism, except that the country was a marsh, and the people 'barbarous and as black as crows.' The tooth of Booddhu, the most sacred of his relics, was, in the distribution of his remains, allotted to this kingdom, and his creed appears

Its superior literature.

Pandyas and Cholas.

Telingana and Chalukyas.

The Mahrattas and the Ooriyas.

to have predominated in it for ten centuries, during which the rocks were studded with shrines and monasteries. It was subjected to various invasions by sea and land, and on one occasion the precious tooth was conveyed for safety to Ceylon, of which it has ever since been, in one sense, the palladium. The Kesari dynasty superseded the booddhist
monarchs in 473, and established the supremacy of Hin- A.D.
dooism, of which they were the ardent devotees. They en- 473
joyed power for more than six centuries, which seem to have been passed in little else but in building temples and founding religious communities. The country was covered with settlements of brahmins, of whom ten thousand were introduced from Cunouge. Bhoobaneshur became the ecclesiastical metropolis of Orissa, and was crowded with seven thousand temples, in honour of Seeva, less than a tenth of which remain, but they are sufficient to attest the zeal and the taste of that religious dynasty.

CHAPTER II.

SECTION I.

INTRODUCTION OF MAHOMEDANISM—THE GHUZNI DYNASTY.

A.D. 569 MAHOMED was born at Mecca, in Arabia, A.D. 569, and at the age of forty announced himself as a prophet commissioned by the Almighty to convert the human race to the 'true faith' by the agency of the sword. He obtained many proselytes in his native land by his genius and eloquence, and, having raised an army of Arabs to subjugate the surrounding nations to his creed and his power, commenced that career of conquest which was pursued by his successors with unexampled vigour and rapidity. Province after province and kingdom after kingdom succumbed to them, and before the close of a century they had conquered Egypt, Syria, Northern Africa, and a part of Spain. Persia was prostrate before them, and they were advancing towards Cabul. A few years after the death of Mahomed, the Caliph Omar founded Bussora, at the estuary of the Tigris, and his generals were enabled to make descents upon Sinde and Beloochistan by sea. 705 to 715 Under the Caliph Walid, between 705 and 715 A.D., that province was entirely subjugated, and the banner of the crescent was planted on the turrets of Mooltan. About the same period the Mahomedans advanced into Central Asia, and overran the country north of the Oxus. The general of the Caliph, Mahomed ben Cossim, likewise con- 711 quered the kingdom of Guzerat, and eventually advanced to Chittore, the capital of Rajpootana, when the gallant young Bappa placed himself at the head of the Rajpoot forces, and expelled the invader. On his return from the field he was raised to the throne, and founded the present royal family of Oodypore. The Rajpoot annals record that in the days of Khoman, the grandson of Bappa,

Rise of Mahomedan power.

Chittore was again invaded by Mahomed, the governor of Khorasan, when the other princes in the north hastened to his assistance; and a very patriotic description is given of the different tribes which composed the northern chivalry on this occasion. With their aid Khoman was enabled to defeat the invader, with whom he is said to have fought twenty-four battles. The Mahomedans were thus expelled from all the territory they had been endeavouring to acquire for a century and a half, and it was not till three centuries after their first invasion that they succeeded in making a permanent lodgment in India. A.D. 750

The dynasty of Ghuzni.

The opulent regions of Khorasan and Transoxania, which had been conquered by the Caliphs in the first century of the Hejira—the Mahomedan era, which dates from the flight of Mahomed from Mecca to Medina—continued under their government for about a hundred and eighty years; but after the death of the renowned Haroun-al-rashid, the contemporary and friend of Charlemagne, the central authority began to decay, and the governors of provinces to assume independence. Ismael Samani, a Tartar, seized upon Khorasan, Transoxania, and Afghanistan, in 872, and fixed his capital at Bokhara, where his dynasty—usually designated that of the Samanides—continued to reign for about a hundred and twenty years. The fifth prince in descent had a Turkish slave, Aluptugeen, a man of courage and good sense, who rose to be governor of Khorasan. On the death of his patron he was consulted about the choice of a successor, and having voted against the son of the deceased king—who was, however, raised to the throne by the other chiefs—he was deprived of his post and retreated with a band of trusty followers to Ghuzni, in the heart of the Soliman mountains, where he succeeded in establishing his independence. He had purchased a slave of the name of Subuktugeen in Tartary, in whom he discovered great powers of mind, and whom he raised to the highest offices. He stepped into the throne on the death of his sovereign, A.D. 976. 976

Hindoos attack Subuktugeen.

The establishment of a powerful kingdom under a vigorous monarch in the vicinity of the Indus created no little alarm in the mind of Jeypal, the Hindoo sovereign of the Punjab, and he led a large army across the river, and attacked Subuktugeen at Lughman in the Cabul passes. On the eve of the engagement a violent storm of wind, rain, and thunder swept down the valley, which alarmed the superstitious soldiers of Jeypal to such a degree that he was constrained to sue for an accommodation, which was not granted without the promise of a heavy payment; but on hearing that his opponent had been obliged to march to the westward to repel an invasion, he refused to fulfil his engagement, and imprisoned the king's messengers. Subuktugeen, having disposed of his enemies, marched down to the Indus to avenge this perfidy. Jeypal succeeded in enlisting the aid of the rajas of Delhi, Ajmere, Callinger, and Cunouge, and advanced across the Indus with an immense force, but was again defeated, and the authority of Ghuzni was established up to the banks of the Indus.

A.D. Subuktugeen died in 997, and was succeeded at first by
997 his son Ismael, and a few months after by his second son, the renowned Mahmood of Ghuzni. From his early youth he had accompanied his father on his various expeditions, and acquired a passion for war and great military experience. He ascended the throne at the age of thirty, and became impatient to enlarge his dominions, and contemplated with delight the glory of extending the triumphs of his creed in the untrodden plains of India. He began his crusade against

Mahmood of Ghuzni. His expeditions.

1001 the Hindoos in 1001, and conducted no fewer than twelve expeditions, of more or less importance, against them. He left Ghuzni in August. Jeypal crossed the Indus a third time, and in the neighbourhood of Peshawur was again defeated and captured. He was generously released, but resigned the throne to his son Anungpal, and sought death on a funeral pyre to which he had himself set fire. Passing over several minor expeditions, we come to the fourth, which was directed against Anungpal, who had instigated a revolt against Mahmood in Mooltan, in conjunction with six of the most powerful rajas of the north. The Hindoos again took the fatal resolution of crossing the Indus, and were a fourth time defeated with the loss of 20,000 men. The next expedition was a mere plundering excursion to Nagarcote, a place of peculiar sanctity, and so strongly fortified as to have been made the depository of the wealth of the neighbouring princes. The stronghold was easily captured, and despoiled—according to the Mahomedan historians—of 700 maunds of gold and silver plate, 200 maunds of pure gold ingots, 2,000 maunds of unwrought silver, and twenty maunds of jewels. The sixth expedition was directed against Thanesur, one of the most ancient and wealthy shrines in India. Anungpal implored Mahmood to spare it, but he made the characteristic reply that the extermination of idolatry was his mission, and that his reward in paradise would be measured by his success in accomplishing it. All the costly images and shrines, the accumulation of centuries, together with 200,000 captives, were transported to Ghuzni, which began to wear the appearance of a Hindoo colony.

After several minor expeditions Mahmood determined to A.D.
penetrate to the heart of Hindostan, and to plant his 1017
standard on the banks of the Ganges. With an army, it is said, of 20,000 foot and 100,000 horse, attracted chiefly from Central Asia by the love of adventure and the lure of plunder, he burst suddenly on the city of Cunouge, which had been for centuries the citadel of Hindooism. The descriptions given of the magnificence of the city and the splendour of the court, both by Hindoo and Mahomedan writers, stagger our belief, more especially when we consider the limited extent of the kingdom. The army of the state is said to have consisted of 80,000 men in armour, 30,000 horsemen, and 500,000 infantry; yet the raja made his submission after a short and feeble resistance. Mahmood left it uninjured, and turned his footsteps to the great ecclesiastical city of Muttra, the birthplace and sanctuary of the deified hero Krishnu, filled with shrines, blazing with jewelry. For twenty days the city and the temples were given up to plunder, and the idols were melted down or demolished. Some of the temples were spared for their great solidity or their surpassing beauty. "Here are a thousand edifices," wrote the conqueror, "as firm as the creed of the faithful, most of them "of marble, besides innumerable temples. Such another "city could not be constructed under two centuries."

Expedition to Cunouge and Multra.

Passing over two expeditions of lesser moment, we come 1024
to the last and most celebrated, the capture of the shrine of Somnath, the most wealthy and the most renowned on the continent of India. At the period of an eclipse, it is said to have been resorted to by 200,000 pilgrims. The image was daily bathed with water brought from the Ganges, 1,000 miles distant. The establishment consisted of 2,000 brahmins, 300 barbers to shave the devotees, 200 musicians, and 300 courtezans. To reach the temple Mahmood had a painful march of 350 miles across the desert. The raja retreated to the fortified temple, and the defenders on the first attack withdrew to the inner sanctuary, and prostrated themselves before the idol to implore its help. The neighbouring chiefs hastened

Expedition to Somnath.

with large forces to the defence of the shrine, and Mahmood was so severely pressed by them that he, in his turn, prostrated himself on the ground to invoke divine assistance; and then, springing into the saddle, cheered on his troops to victory. After 5,000 Hindoos had fallen under their sabres, Mahmood entered the temple and was struck with astonishment at its grandeur. The lofty roof was supported by fifty-six columns, elaborately carved, and studded with jewels. The shrine was illuminated by a single lamp, suspended by a golden chain, the lustre of which was reflected from the numerous precious stones embossed in the walls. The image, five yards in height, one half of which was buried in the earth, faced the entrance, and Mahmood ordered it to be demolished, when the priests threw themselves at his feet and offered an immense ransom for it, but he replied that he had rather be known as the destroyer than the seller of idols. Then, lifting up his mace, he aimed a blow at it, and the figure, which was hollow, burst asunder, and poured a larger treasure at his feet than the brahmins had offered for its ransom. The wealth obtained on this occasion exceeded any he had acquired in his previous expeditions, and the mind is bewildered with the enumeration of the treasures and jewels which he carried back. The sandal-wood gates were sent as a trophy to his capital where they remained for eight centuries, till they were brought back in a triumphal procession to India by a Christian ruler.

He retired to Ghuzni after a toilsome and perilous march through the desert, and died in the sixtieth year of his age.

A.D. 1030 Death and character of Mahmood.

Two days before his death he caused the most costly of his treasures to be displayed before his eyes, and is said to have shed tears at the thought of leaving them. Mahmood was not only the greatest conqueror, but the grandest sovereign of the age. He extended his dominions from the sea of Aral to the Persian Gulf, and from the mountains of Kurdestan to the banks of the Sutlege, and the order which reigned through these vast territories gave abundant proof of his genius for civil administration. His court was the most magnificent in Asia, and few princes have ever surpassed him in the munificent encouragement of letters. He founded and richly endowed a university at his capital, which was adorned with a greater assemblage of literary genius than any other monarch in Asia has ever been able to collect. His taste for architecture was developed after he had seen the grand edifices of Cunouge and of Muttra, of Thanesur and Somnath, and his capital, which at the beginning of his reign was a collection of hovels, was ornamented with mosques, porches, fountains, aqueducts, and palaces.

The dynasty of Ghuzni may be said to have reigned, though it did not flourish, for a hundred and fifty-six years after the death of Mahmood, inasmuch as it was not dispossessed of its last territories before 1186. During this period, the attention of its princes was so incessantly distracted by the political and military movements of Central Asia, and more especially by the aggressions of the Seljuks, as to leave them little leisure for the affairs of India. It would be idle to encumber the attention of the reader with the revolutions beyond the Indus, which have no bearing upon the interests of India, or with the catalogue of the sovereigns engaged in them. The provinces of Lahore and Mooltan were permanently annexed to the throne of Ghuzni, though more than one effort was made by the Hindoo princes to drive the Mahomedans across the Indus.

Progress and close of the Ghuzni dynasty. A.D. 1186

SECTION II.

FROM THE EXTINCTION OF THE HOUSE OF GHUZNI TO THE ACCESSION OF THE HOUSE OF TOGHLUK.

THE dynasty of Ghore, which succeeded that of Ghuzni, was founded by Eis-ood-deen, a native of Afghanistan, who entered the service of Musaood, the king of Ghuzni, and obtained the hand of his daughter together with the principality of Ghore. His son was married to Byram, the last sultan of Ghuzni, who put him to death on the occasion of some family quarrel. The brother of the deceased prince, Seif-ood-deen, took up arms to revenge his death, and Byram was obliged to fly, but he returned soon after with a larger force, and conquered his opponent, whom he butchered with studied ignominy. Alla-ood-deen, his brother, vowed a bitter revenge, and a battle was fought under the walls of Ghuzni, when Byram was defeated and fled to Lahore, but perished on the route. Alla-ood-deen then proceeded to wreak his vengeance on the city of Ghuzni, which had become the grandest in Asia, and gave it up for three,

Origin of the House of Ghore.

and, according to some authors, for seven days, to indiscriminate slaughter, flame, and devastation. The superb monuments of the kings of Ghuzni were levelled with the ground, and the palaces of the nobles sacked and demolished. This savage vengeance has fixed an indelible stigma on his memory, and he is branded by Mahomedan historians as 'the incendiary of the world.' He was succeeded in 1156 by an amiable and imbecile youth, who was murdered within a twelvemonth, when Gheias-ood-deen was raised to the throne, and associated his brother Shahab-ood-deen, the renowned Mahomed Ghory, with him in the government, the most important functions of which were left in his hands. The harmony which subsisted between the two brothers for forty-five years, and the exemplary loyalty which Mahomed, though in possession of the real power of the state, continued to manifest towards his brother in an age of universal violence, deserve especial commemoration.

Gheias-ood-deen. A.D. 1156

Mahomed Ghory was the real founder of Mahomedan power in India, and it may be serviceable to glance at the condition of the Hindoo thrones north of the Nerbudda on the eve of their extinction. The kingdom of Cunouge had passed under the authority of the Rathore tribe of Rajpoots. The kings of Benares who professed the booddhist creed had become extinct, and the principality had been divided between the rulers of Cunouge and Bengal. Bengal was independent under the dynasty of the Sens. Guzerat was governed by the Bhagilas, and the powerful kingdom of Ajmere by the Chohans. The last King of Delhi, Prithee raj, was of the Tomara tribe, and he had adopted his grandson, the raja of Ajmere, and bestowed his daughter on him. With the chief of Guzerat for his ally, the king of Cunouge was engaged in mortal conflict with the king of Delhi, with whom were associated the rajas of Chittore and Ajmere. The arrogant raja of Cunouge had, moreover, determined to celebrate the sacrifice of the horse, the emblem of universal sovereignty, and this vainglorious assumption was resented by half the powers of Hindostan, which was thus divided into two hostile camps, with its rulers engaged in deadly hostilities, when the Mahomedan invader was thundering at its gates. On the threshold of this great revolution we pause for a moment to notice the virtues of Bhoje-raj, the last of the great Hindoo sovereigns of India. He was of the ancient and

State of the Hindoo kingdoms.

Bhoje-raj.

time-honoured tribe of the Prumuras, who still continued to rule, but with diminished splendour, the kingdom of Oojein. Seated on the throne of Vikrum-aditya, he resolved to emulate him in the encouragement of literature. His memory is consecrated by the gratitude of posterity, and his reign has been immortalised by the genius of poetry.

Mahomed Ghory turned his attention to India with all A.D.
the vigour of a young dynasty. In 1176 he took the 1176
province of Ooch, at the junction of the rivers of the Punjab and the Indus. Two years later he was defeated in his attempt on Guzerat. He subsequently overran Sinde, and took possession of the two provinces of Mooltan and the Punjab, which alone had remained to the house of Ghuzni, which thus became extinct. Having no longer any Mahomedan rival within the Indus, his entire force was brought to bear on the great Hindoo monarchies. At this period there was little trace of the invasion of Mahmood; the prosperity of the country was renewed, and it teemed with wealth and
abounded in temples; but the year 1193 brought a tem- 1193
pest of desolation which completely overwhelmed the Hindoo power in the north. Prithee raj, the gallant but thoughtless king of Delhi, though he had wasted his strength in his struggle with the raja of Cunouge and his associates, was still able to bring a force of 200,000 horse into the field with a proportionate number of foot. The two armies joined battle at Tirauri, not far from Thanesur, the battle-field of Hindostan, when the king of Ghore was completely defeated, and was happy to escape with the wreck of his army across the Indus.

Mahomed Ghory.

Having recruited his army with Turks, Tartars, and Afghans, he recrossed the Indus to wipe out his disgrace. The Hindoos met him on their old and, as they considered it, fortunate ground, with an augmented force of infantry and cavalry; 150 chiefs rallied round the standard of Delhi, and the king sent an arrogant message to Mahomed, granting him permission to retire without molestation. He replied, with apparent humility, that he was merely his brother's lieutenant, to whom he would refer their message, and the moderation of this reply was interpreted as a symptom of weakness. The Caggar flowed between the two armies, and Mahomed, after having in vain endeavoured to surprise the Hindoos by crossing it during the night, feigned a retreat, which drew the enemy in confusion after him, when he charged

Defeat of the Hindoos.

them with 12,000 chosen horse, and, as the historian relates, "this prodigious army, once shaken, like a great "building, tottered to its fall, and was lost in its own ruins." The raja of Chittore fell, gallantly fighting at the head of his Rajpoot cavalry. The king of Delhi was taken prisoner, and butchered in cold blood. Mahomed then proceeded to Ajmere, where he stained his reputation by the massacre of several thousands of his captives. Mahomed returned to Ghuzni laden with plunder, leaving one of his slaves, Kootub-ood-deen, who had risen to eminence
A.D. by his talent, to continue his conquests. He captured
1193 Meerut and Coel, and eventually Delhi, which now became the seat of Mahomedan power in India. The kings of Cunouge and Guzerat, who had looked on with malicious delight while the Mahomedans smote down their Hindoo opponents, had no long respite themselves. Mahomed
1194 returned to India the next year with a powerful force, and defeated Jey-chunder, the Rathore raja of Cunouge, on the banks of the Jumna, and captured Benares, where he demolished a thousand temples. Upon this reverse, the whole tribe of Rathores emigrated in a body to Rajpootana, and established the kingdom of Marwar, and the ancient city of Cunouge, which had seen the days of Ramu sank to insignificance. Kootub-ood-deen lost no

Bengal and Behar.

time in despatching one of his slaves, Bukhtyar Ghiljie, to conquer Behar, which offered no resistance. That officer then advanced to Bengal, which was under the rule of Lukshmunu Sen, eighty years of age, who usually held his court at Nuddea. He appears to have made no preparations for the defence of the country, and was surprised at a meal, and fled for refuge to Jugernath. It is particularly worthy of note, that while the heroic Rajpoots, the kings of Delhi and Cunouge, and other princes in the north-west, offered a noble resistance to the Mahomedans, Bengal fell, without the slightest effort for its independence. It remained under Mahomedan rule for five centuries and a half, till it was transferred to a European government by the issue of a single battle, which cost the conquerors only seventy men. Bukhtyar delivered up Nuddea to plunder, and then seized on Gour, the ancient capital. He subsequently invaded Bootan and Assam, but was gallantly repulsed by the highlanders, and died of chagrin on his return to Bengal.

During these transactions Mahomed marched against the king of Kharizm, the modern Khiva, and, though at

first victorious, experienced so crushing a defeat that it was A.D.
with difficulty he made his way back to Ghuzni, 1203
the gates of which were shut against him by the

Death of Mahomed.

governor. Revolts at the same time broke out in India on the news of his reverses. He succeeded eventually in restoring his authority, and was returning to his capital, when he was murdered on the banks of the Indus by a
band of Gukkers, who stole unperceived into his tent and 1206
revenged the loss of a relative in the late war. He governed the kingdom forty-nine years, forty-five in conjunction with his brother, and four after his death. His military operations in India were on a larger scale, and their result was more permanent than those of Mahmood of Ghuzni. Mahmood attacked the most opulent towns and temples and carried their wealth to Ghuzni. It was a sudden tornado of spoliation, and when it had passed over, the sovereigns recovered their power, and the country resumed its prosperity. But Mahomed of Ghore in the course of ten years completely demolished the Hindoo power, and at the period of his death northern India, from the Himalaya to the Nerbudda, with the exception of Malwa, had come under a permanent Mahomedan government. The treasure left by Mahomed is stated at a sum which exceeds belief, more particularly the five maunds of jewels. He had no children, and his nephew was proclaimed throughout his dominions, and ruled them for six years. On his death there was a general scramble for power between the
governors of the different provinces, and in 1215 Ghuzni 1215
was taken by the king of Kharizm, and the dynasty of Ghore disappears from the page of history.

The Slave dynasty. Kootub-ood-deen,

Kootub-ood-deen, to whose management Mahomed had confided his Indian conquests, was invested with the full sovereignty of them by his successor, and assumed the insignia of royalty at Lahore in 1206, from which year the real foundation of Mahomedan power in India is usually dated.
The dynasty which he founded is known in history as that 1206
of the slave kings. He made one expedition across the Indus and overcame Eldoze, another of the slaves of Mahomed, who had caused himself to be crowned at Ghuzni, and claimed the submission of Kootub. Kootub himself was soon after defeated and returned to India, and from that time forward contented himself with the dominions he possessed there. To commemorate the capture of Delhi, he commenced the magnificent Kootub-

Minar in that city, which was completed by his successor.
A.D. He died in 1210, after an independent reign of five years.
1210 While Central Asia was the scene of convulsion created by the ambition of its different rulers, and more especially

Jenghiz Khan.

1219 by the violence of Mahomed the turbulent king of Kharizm, its polity was entirely subverted by the memorable irruption of Jenghiz Khan. He was the petty chief of the Moguls, a tribe of nomadic Tartars, roaming with their flocks and herds on the north of the great wall of China. By the age of forty he had established his authority over all the tribes, and burst with resistless force on China, and, after sacking ninety cities, obliged the emperor to cede the provinces north of the Yellow River. With an army of 700,000 men he then poured down on the Mahomedan principalities of Central Asia, and defeated Mahomed of Kharizm, who is said to have left 160,000 dead on the field. From the Caspian sea to the banks of the Indus, the whole region for more than a thousand miles was laid waste with fire and sword. This tide of desolation which swept over the country was the greatest calamity which has ever befallen the family of man. Although Jenghiz Khan did not invade India, he gave a predominant influence to the Moguls, who, after the lapse of three centuries, were led across the Indus by Baber, and placed on the throne of India.

Transactions during the Slave dynasty.

Kootub was succeeded by his son Aram, who was dethroned within a year, and Altumsh, his slave and son-in-law, was raised to supreme authority, which he enjoyed for twenty-five years. He was occupied in reducing to subjection the few districts which
1226 to 1236 still remained in the hands of the Hindoos, in curbing his subordinate governors, and consolidating the new empire. He reduced the strong fortresses of Rinthimbore in Rajpootana, of Gwalior, and of Mandoo. He captured Oojein, the venerable capital of Vikrum-adityu, and destroyed his magnificent temple of Muhakal, and sent the images to Delhi to be mutilated and placed as steps of his great mosque. He was succeeded by his son, who was deposed within six months for his vices, and his sister Rezia was raised to the throne. "She was," says the historian, "endowed with every princely virtue, and those
1236 "who scrutinised her actions most severely could find in her "no fault but that she was a woman." She managed the affairs of the empire with singular talent, revised the laws, appeared

daily on the throne in the habit of a Sultan, and gave audience to all comers. But an Abyssinian slave had gained her favour and was appointed to the command of the army; the nobility were aggrieved, insurrections broke out, and she took the field against the rebels, but was taken prisoner and put to death after a reign of three years and a half. The two succeeding reigns were without events, and occupied only six years, when Nazir-ood-deen,
a grandson of Altumsh, mounted the throne. The reign of A.D.
this quiet and studious monarch extended to twenty years. 1246
He was remarkable for the simplicity of his habits, his frugality, and continence, and for the royal Mahomedan virtue of transcribing the Koran. The merit of all the important events of his reign belongs to his great minister, Bulbun, the Turkish slave and son-in-law of Altumsh. Throughout this reign the provinces contiguous to the Indus were constantly subjected to the ravages of the Moguls whom Jenghiz Khan had established in Central Asia, and twenty-five of the princes whom they had expelled were hospitably entertained at the court of Delhi. He died without issue, and was succeeded by his minister, Bulbun, the greatest statesman in the annals of the slave
dynasty. He was a prince of great energy and ability, but 1266
is represented by some historians as a monster of cruelty, by others as a model of perfection. During an insurrection in Merut he is said to have put 100,000 to death, and the rebellion in Bengal was punished with such extreme severity as to constrain the ministers of religion to interpose their influence to stay the savage execution of women and children. On the other hand, he set an example of the most rigid abstemiousness, and punished immorality with great rigour. His court was maintained on a scale of great magnificence, and adorned with the presence of men of literary genius, whom he attracted by his munificence; but he made it a rule to employ no Hindoos in the public service. His accomplished son, Prince Mahomed, the idol of the age, was sent to repel a
renewed invasion of the Moguls. They were defeated, 1279
but the illustrious youth fell in the field, and with him perished the hopes of the dynasty. Bulbun was succeeded by one of his grandsons, who was speedily superseded by another, and on his falling a victim to his debaucheries, a struggle for power arose between the Tartar mercenaries and the Afghan Ghiljies. The Tartars were cut to pieces, and the dynasty, which began in 1205 with the slave

Kutub, terminated in 1288, within three years of the death of the slave Bulbun.

The victorious Ghiljie, Feroze, then in his seventieth year, mounted the throne, and assumed the title of Jellal-

A.D. 1288 Dynasty of the Ghiljies. ood-deen. The dynasty, which lasted only thirty years, was rendered memorable by the extension of Mahomedan power over the Deccan. The reign of Jellal-ood-deen was marked, except in one instance, by an injudicious lenity, which relaxed the whole frame of government; the governors withheld their tribute, and the roads were infested with banditti. In the fifth year of his reign, his nephew, Alla-ood-deen, a man of great energy, violent ambition, and no scruples of conscience, projected a marauding expedition to the south. Avoiding all communication with his uncle, he swept down across the Nerbudda with a body of 8,000 chosen horse, and suddenly presented himself before the fortress of Dowlutabad. Neither the king nor any of the neighbouring Hindoo princes were prepared for resistance, and the town with all

1294 its treasures fell a prey to the invader. The audacity of this adventure struck terror into the chiefs on the line, and before they were prepared to encounter him he was enabled to return, on the twenty-fifth day, without any interruption. This expedition revealed the wealth and the weakness of the Deccan to the Mahomedans, and paved the way for its subjugation. The aged emperor, then in his seventy-seventh year, was delighted to find his nephew return in safety, laden with plunder and covered with glory. His ministers endeavoured to put him on his

1295 guard against the ambitious designs of his nephew, but the over-confident monarch was induced to cross the Ganges to welcome him, and at the first interview was treacherously assassinated by men placed in ambush in the tent.

Alla-ood-deen hastened to Delhi, and put the two sons of his uncle to death and imprisoned their mother; but he

Alla-ood-deen. endeavoured to efface the memory of these atrocities by the just exercise of the power he had so nefariously acquired, and by the exhibition of games and festivities; he was never able, however, to suppress his arbitrary temper, and his reign, though long and glorious, was always disturbed by conspiracies. He was ignorant of letters when he ascended the throne, but he applied successfully to study, and surrounded himself with learned men, in whose society he took great pleasure. His government

was stern and inflexible, but not unsuited to the exigencies of the time. The military operations of his reign, which extended to twenty-seven years, were divided between the north and south of India. Early in his reign he finally A.D.
conquered Guzerat, which had assumed independence, and 1297
two years after obtained possession of the fortress of Rinthimbore and then of Chittore, which brought the Rajpoots "under the yoke of obedience." His territories to the north-west of Delhi were constantly disturbed by the inroads of the Moguls from Central Asia, and in 1298 Kutlugh Khan marched down from the Indus with an army of 200,000 men upon Delhi, which was crowded with fugitives till famine began to stare them in the face, when 1298
Alla-ood-deen marched out and dispersed this vast host. The invasion was twice repeated, and as often repelled, and the emperor, to deter these inveterate enemies by a severe example, caused the heads of all his male prisoners to be struck off and erected into a pillar at Delhi.

Expeditions to the Deccan.

His first expedition to the Deccan, when seated on the throne, was directed against Warungul, the ancient capital of Telingana, but it was not successful. Three years later, a larger army was sent under the command of Malik Kafoor, a eunuch, once the slave, but now the favourite general of the emperor, and the object of envy to the nobles of the court. He overran the Mahratta country and recovered Dowlutabad, which had revolted. In the previous expedition against 1306
Guzerat, the wife of the raja had fallen into the hands of the victors and was placed in the imperial harem, where her singular beauty and her talents excited the admiration of the emperor. She had borne a daughter to her former husband, whose attractions were said to be equal to her own, and the generals were ordered diligently to seek her out. She was unexpectedly discovered and conveyed to Delhi, where she made such an impression on the king's son that he married her;—at so early a period do we find inter-marriages between the Mahomedans and the Hindoos in 1309
vogue. In 1309, Kafoor ravaged the north of Telingana, and conquered Warungul. The next year he was sent with a large army down to the Carnatic, and reached the capital after a march of three months. The raja was defeated and made prisoner, and with him ended the Bellal dynasty of the Deccan. Kafoor then ravaged the eastern provinces along the Coromandel coast down to the extreme limit of the peninsula, and, as a memorial of his 1310

victories erected a mosque on the island of Ramisseram, between the continent and the island of Ceylon, contiguous to the magnificent temple erected ages before in honour of Seeta, the wife of the hero of the Ramayun. The value of the plunder he acquired in these expeditions was calculated by historians deemed sober, at a hundred crores of rupees.

Extinction of the Ghilzie dynasty.

In the decline of life Alla-ood-deen exhibited an in-
1312 fatuated attachment to Kafoor, whose depravity equalled his talents, and a spirit of discontent spread throughout the provinces. His strength, both of body and mind, was impaired by constant indulgence, and the empire, which had been sustained by his energy, fell into a state of anarchy. Guzerat, Chittore, and Deoghur deserted their allegiance, and he sank
1316 into the grave under a cloud of misfortunes. His conquests were greater than had ever been achieved before in India; his internal administration was eminently successful, and the wealth and prosperity of the country were increased. His death became the signal for revolutions The infamous Kafoor seized upon the regency and put out the eyes of the two sons of his benefactor. The nobles of the court, however, caused him to be put to death, and placed the deceased emperor's third son upon the throne, who lost no time in putting the instruments of his elevation to death, and extinguishing the sight of his youngest brother. He reconquered some of the provinces which had revolted, but on his return to the capital gave himself up to the most degrading vices, while his favourite, Khosroo, a converted Hindoo, undertook an expedition to the Deccan and ravaged the maritime province of Malabar, which Kafoor had spared. Khosroo returned to Delhi laden with booty, assassinated his master, and usurped the throne, and then proceeded to massacre the royal family; but Ghazee Toghluk, the governor of the Punjab, marched on Delhi with the veteran troops of the marches, disciplined
1321 by constant conflicts with the Moguls, and put an end to the reign and life of the monster.

SECTION III.

THE DYNASTY OF TOGHLUK TO THE MOGUL DYNASTY.

GHAZEE TOGHLUK was desirous of placing some scion of the royal house upon the throne, but the family had been exterminated during the recent convulsions, and he yielded to the wishes of the nobles and people to accept it himself. His father was originally a slave of the emperor Bulbun, but raised himself to high honour by his abilities. His reign, which lasted only four years, was as commendable as his accession had been blameless. Bengal had prospered for forty years under the viceroyalty of Kurrah, the son of the emperor Bulbun, and as charges had been brought against him, Ghazee Toghluk investigated them in person, and, finding them groundless, confirmed him in the government; and the native historian illustrates the mutations of fortune at this period by the remark that it was the son of the father's slave who granted the royal umbrella to his son. An expedition was sent into Telingana; the capital, Warungul, was captured, and the Hindoo dynasty which had flourished there for two centuries and a half became extinct. Jona Khan, the son of the emperor, on his return from this campaign, gave an entertainment to his father in a magnificent pavilion which fell unexpectedly, but not accidentally, and crushed him to death.

A.D. 1321

Ghazee Toghluk.

Jona Khan, who ascended the throne and assumed the title of Mahomed Toghluk, is one of the most extraordinary characters in the Mahomedan history of India—a singular compound of opposite qualities. He was the most accomplished sovereign of the age, skilled in every science, and versed even in Greek philosophy; the liberal patron of learning, temperate to the verge of asceticism, and distinguished in the field by his gallantry and military skill. But all these virtues were neutralised by such perversity of disposition and such paroxysms of tyranny as to render him the object of general execration. It was the intoxication of absolute power which led him to acts bordering on insanity. He began his reign by completing the reduction of the Deccan; he extended the limits of the empire beyond any of his predecessors, and brought the remotest districts into as good order as those

1325

Mahomed Toghluk; his caprices.

around Delhi; yet, before his death the whole of the Deccan was lost to the crown by his follies. He assembled a large army for the conquest of

Expedition to Persia.

A.D. Persia, but, after exhausting his resources, the troops de-
1325 serted for want of pay, and became the terror of his own subjects. To replenish his treasury he resolved to march into China and levy contributions in that remote region, but the army of 100,000 men which he sent across the snowy range, after encountering incredible hardships, was all but exterminated by the Chinese and the exasperated highlanders, and the few who escaped to tell the tale were butchered by his own orders. Hearing that the Chinese had a paper currency in use, he determined to introduce it into his dominions, to the ruin of thousands and the general derangement of commerce. His exactions drove the husbandmen into the woods, and filled the country with banditti. By way of revenge he surrounded a large tract of territory with his troops, and driving the wretched inhabitants into the centre, slaughtered them with all the

Change of capital.

1338 brutality of a battue. In 1338 he took the field against his nephew, who had been driven into revolt, and the young prince was captured and flayed alive. On reaching Deoghur, he was so enchanted with the beauty of the situation and the mildness of the climate, that he resolved to make it the capital of the empire, and changed its name to Dowlutabad. He then ordered the inhabitants of Delhi to migrate to it, and thousands of men, women, and children were constrained to travel a distance of eight hundred miles; but he planted the road with full-grown trees. The project of transplanting the metropolis failed, but not till it had inflicted incalculable misery on the people. At the same time, as if to mock the calamities of his subjects, he erected a splendid mausoleum over the grave of a decayed tooth.

These caprices and oppressions produced the usual harvest of insurrections. The Afghans crossed the Indus and ravaged the Punjab, and when they retired the Gukkers completed the desolation of the pro-

Dismemberment of the empire.

1340 vince. Bengal revolted, and remained independent for two centuries. Two fugitives from Telingana established a Hindoo kingdom near the Toombudra, with Beejanuger for its capital. About the same time a descendant of the royal house of Telingana founded an independent principality at Golconda; and these two Hindoo
1344 powers maintained a vigorous struggle for many years with the Mahomedan kingdoms which arose in the Deccan.

A still more important revolution wrested the remaining provinces south of the Nerbudda from the sceptre of Delhi. A large body of Moguls who had settled in Guzerat raised the standard of revolt. The emperor proceeded against them with his usual vigour, gave up the cities of Surat and Cambay to plunder, and desolated the province as if it had been the possession of an enemy. The Moguls fled to the Deccan, and being joined by those whom the emperor's oppressions had exasperated, took possession of Dowlutabad, where they proclaimed Ishmael Khan, an Afghan, king, and, after one reverse, established a new monarchy, known in history as the Bahminee kingdom. Mahomed Toghluk died in Sinde after a reign of twenty-one A.D.
years, leaving the throne of Delhi dispossessed of the whole 1351
of the Deccan and of the province of Bengal.

Feroze Toghluk and his successors.

Mahomed Toghluk was succeeded by his son Feroze, whose reign extended to thirty-seven years, and though mild and beneficent, was by no means brilliant. He discouraged luxury by his own example, repealed vexatious taxes, and abolished torture and mutilation. His ruling passion was architecture; and the Mahomedan historian records with pride the erection of forty mosques, thirty colleges, twenty palaces, a hundred hospitals, a hundred public baths, a hundred and fifty bridges, and two hundred towns. But the noblest memorial of his reign was the canal he constructed between the source of the Ganges and the Sutlege, which bears his name, and keeps it fragrant in the recollection of posterity. After a reign of thirty-four years he abdicated the throne in favour of his son Mahomed Toghluk the second; who
gave himself up to indulgence, and constrained his father 1388
to resume his power, but at the age of ninety, he resigned the sceptre to his grandson. During the next ten years the throne was occupied by four princes, two of whom held authority in the capital at the same time and for three years waged incessant war with each other. Hindostan
fell a prey to anarchy; four independent kingdoms were 1394
carved out of the imperial dominions, and nothing remained to the crown of Delhi but the districts immediately around the capital.

Four independent kingdoms.

These kingdoms were all founded by the Mahomedan viceroys; no effort was made by the Hindoos to take advantage of the confusion of the times, and regain their supremacy, and the ancient chiefs of Rajpootana were the only depository of Hindoo

power in Hindostan. Of these kingdoms two, Malwa and Guzerat, rose to great power and eminence; while the two others, Candesh and Jounpore, were of minor weight and more limited duration. Dilawur Khan of Ghore, the
A.D. viceroy of Malwa, who assumed independence, established
1401 his capital at Mandoo, fifteen miles north of the Nerbudda. Mozuffer Khan, a Rajpoot converted to Mahomedanism, and like all converts, more especially in India, a virulent persecutor of his former creed, was sent by one of the feeble successors of Feroze Toghluk to supersede the suspected governor of Guzerat, and, seeing no power at Delhi
1396 to enforce obedience, threw off the yoke of allegiance. The viceroy of Candesh, which consists of the lower valley of the Taptee, followed his example, and formed a matrimonial alliance with the new king of Guzerat. Still nearer the capital, Khoja Jehan the vizier of Mahomed Toghluk the third, availed himself of the weakness of the throne, and "assumed the royal umbrella," in Jounpore. The empire
1394 of Delhi, distracted by these revolts, and shorn of its fairest provinces, fell an easy prey to the ruthless invader who was now advancing to despoil it of its wealth.

Timur.

The Ameer Timur, or Tamerlane, was born in the neighbourhood of Samarcand, of a Turki family which had
1398 been in the service of Jenghiz Khan. His lot was cast at a period when the decay of vigour in the governments in the east offered the fairest opportunity of conquest to any daring adventurer. He was raised to the throne of Samarcand at the age of thirty-four, and in a few years prostrated every throne which stood in the way of his ambition, and became at once the scourge of Asia and the terror of Europe. He led the hordes of Tartary to the conquest of Persia, Khorasan and Transoxiana, of Mesopotamia and Georgia, and brought a portion of Russia and Siberia under subjection. Having mastered the whole of Central Asia, he sent his grandson to invade India, but as he met with more opposition than was expected, Timur himself crossed the Indus at Attock, September 12, 1398, with ninety-two squadrons of horse, and advanced to Bhutnere, which was surrendered by the inhabitants on terms; but, by one of those mistakes which seemed always to occur in his capitulations, they were put to the sword and the town burnt to the ground. Villages and towns were abandoned as he advanced, but on his arrival at Delhi, he found himself encumbered with prisoners, and, according to the statement of the historians, which were doubtless ex-

aggerated, he caused 100,000 men to be massacred in cold blood. A battle was fought under the walls of the capital, between the veterans of Timur and the effeminate soldiers of the empire. The emperor Mahomed Toghluk the third was defeated and fled to Guzerat, and Timur entered the city and caused himself to be proclaimed emperor. Disputes, as might have been expected, arose between the citizens and his ferocious soldiers, and the whole of the Mogul army was let loose on the devoted city. The inhabitants sold their lives dearly, but their valour was quenched in their blood. The scenes of horror defy all description; entire streets were choked up with the dying and the dead. For five days Timur remained a tranquil spectator of the plunder and conflagration of the city, while he celebrated his victory by a magnificent feast. Having glutted his revenge and satiated his cupidity he proceeded "to offer "up to the divine Majesty his humble tribute of grateful "praise for his success, in the noble mosque of polished "marble, erected by Feroze on the banks of the Jumna." This whirlwind of desolation lasted six months, and Timur A.D.
recrossed the Indus in March 1399. Mahomed Toghluk re- 1399
turned to Delhi after the departure of Timur, and continued to exercise a precarious authority for twelve years, when Khizir Khan, the governor of the Punjab, marched to Delhi, and extinguished the dynasty of the Toghluks, after it had subsisted ninety-one years.

The dynasty established by Khizir Khan which lasted 1414
only thirty-six years, is designated in Indian history the dynasty of the Syuds, as they claimed descent Dynasty of
from the Prophet. The founder professed to be the Syuds.
only the lieutenant of Timur, who had bestowed the government of the Punjab on him, and caused money to be coined and prayers to be read in his name. His administration, which was extended to nine years, was beneficial to the distracted provinces, but, with the exception of his own province, he recovered none of the revolted districts. 1421
His son, Mobarik, was assassinated after a reign of thirteen years, in which no event of importance requires to be noted. Synd Mahomed who succeeded him left the throne to his son Alla-ood-deen, during whose feeble reign the territory annexed to the crown was still farther reduced till at length it extended twelve miles from Delhi on one side and only one in another. In 1450 Beloli Lodi 1450
marched down to Delhi, and the emperor resigned the empty honours of royalty to him without a sigh, and re-

tired on a pension to Budaon where he passed the remaining twenty-eight years of his life in cultivating his garden.

The grandfather of Beloli Lodi, the founder of this dynasty, was an Afghan, of the tribe of Lodi, or Lohance, engaged in the transport of merchandize, in which he had amassed a fortune. He repaired to the court of Feroze Toghluk, and gradually rose to the government of Mooltan. He was not content with the narrow limits to which the imperial domains had been reduced, but his chief object was the conquest of Jounpore, which had become independent in 1394 by the revolt of Khoja Jehan. The Jounpore dynasty flourished for eighty-two years, under six sovereigns, the most illustrious of whom, Ibrahim, occupied the throne for one half that period. Under his beneficent rule the country reached the summit of prosperity. Learned men from all parts of Asia were invited to his court, which was esteemed the most polished and illustrious in India. His capital was adorned with superb and massive edifices, the remains of which still excite our admiration. Not merely was it the rival of Delhi in magnificence, but the strength of the kingdom was so pre-eminent that the struggle between the emperor and the king was prolonged with varied success for twenty-eight years, during which Delhi was twice besieged by the arms of Jounpore. Hostilities were occasionally suspended by a hollow truce,

The dynasty of Lodi. *A.D. 1391* *The kingdom of Jounpore.*

1478 but they came to a final issue in 1478, when the last of the "kings of the east," as the dynasty was termed, fled to Bengal, and the kingdom was reannexed to the dominions of Delhi. Beloli Lodi succeeded in extending the territories of the crown from the Jumna to the Himalaya, and from the Indus to Benares; and after a reign of thirty-eight years bequeathed the throne to his son Secunder, who added Baber to his conquests. But his administration, though otherwise just and equitable, was marked by the oppression of the Hindoos, whose pilgrimages he prohibited, and whose temples he demolished in every direc-

1517 tion, erecting mosques with the materials. In 1517, Ibrahim, the third and the last of the line, succeeded to the crown, and alienated his nobles by his arrogance and hauteur to such a degree that his reign of nine years was a constant succession of revolts, which broke out in Behar, in Jounpore and in the Punjab, where the governor opened negotiations with Behar for the invasion of India. The emperor's own brother joined him at Cabul. The success which attended the expedition of the Mogul will be narrated in a subsequent chapter. Having thus reached the threshold of the period when the imperial throne was transferred to the last Mahomedan dynasty, under which it was gradually restored to its integrity, we turn back to the progress of events in Hindostan and in the Deccan when it was first dismembered.

Candesh became independent about the year 1399, and A.D.
was not reannexed to the empire till the reign of Akbar, 1399
two centuries after. It was a small principality, **Candesh.** of no note in history, remarkable only for the fertility of its soil, and the prosperity of its people; it was, moreover, always considered subordinate to its more powerful neighbour Guzerat. The independence **Guzerat.**
of Guzerat was established in 1396 by Mozuffer 1396
Shah, and a succession of thirteen princes governed it for 165 years, till it expired in 1561. At the period of the revolt the province was of limited extent, consisting of the land lying between the mountains and the sea, but it was enlarged by successive acquisitions. The great figure it makes in history is owing to the energy and ability of its princes, the first of whom Mozuffer, the son of a Rajpoot convert, was constantly at war with the king of Malwa, or with the raja of Edur, the most powerful Hindoo principality in the north. His son Ahmed Shah reigned thirty- 1411
eight years, and was likewise incessantly engaged in hostilities with his neighbours, but he brought the country into good order, and built the town of Ahmedabad, which he made his capital, and adorned with such a profusion of magnificent mosques, caravanseras, and palaces, as to lead the Mahomedan historians to pronounce it the handsomest city in the world. The next two reigns, which extended to sixteen years, were occupied chiefly with struggles with Koombho, who was then building up a great Hindoo power in Rajpootana. Mahomed Shah, who ascended the throne at the age of fourteen, shed a lustre on it for a 1459
period of more than half a century. The European travellers who visited his court formed the most extravagant conceptions of his power, and asserted that a portion of his daily food consisted of mortal poisons with which his system became so impregnated that if a fly sat on him it fell down dead. He was the original of the picture drawn by the British poet of the prince of Cambay, 'whose food was asp, and basilisk, and toad.' But even without

the power of digesting poisons he was a most puissant prince. He captured Gernar, a Hindoo fortress renowned for its antiquity and its strength. He overran Cutch, defeated an army of Belooches, and annexed Sinde to his dominions. But the distinguishing feature of his reign was the navy he constructed, and the numerous naval expeditions which he undertook. He cleared the coast of pirates, who are said to have fought twenty battles before they were subdued. His memorable conflict with the
A.D. Portuguese will be narrated in a future chapter. He was
1511 succeeded by his son, Mozuffer the second, whose reign of fourteen years consisted of constant campaigns against Malwa, and the renowned Rana Sanga of Rajpootana.

The rapid disappearance of two of his sons, in a single
1526 year, opened the throne to his third son, Bahadoor Shah,

Bahadoor Shah.

who subdued the hereditary foe of his dynasty, the Hindoo prince of Edur, and compelled the kings of Berar, Ahmednugur and Candesh to do him homage. His next exploit led to a more splendid result. The king of Malwa having provoked his hostility, he marched against him in conjunction with his ally, Rana Sanga, captured both his capital and his person, and annexed the
1534 kingdom to his own territories. Soon after, the brother of the last emperor of Delhi of the Lodi family, which had been dispossessed by the Mogul Baber, sought an asylum at the court of Guzerat, and Bahadoor Shah supplied him with the means of raising an army, which was however defeated. Humayoon, then emperor of Delhi, incensed at this proceeding, marched down to Guzerat, expelled Bahadoor, and took possession of the kingdom. But he was soon after recalled to defend his own throne against Shere Khan; dissensions broke out among his generals, and Bahadoor was enabled to recover his throne. After a reign of ten years he was drowned in the harbour of Diu,
1535 as he left the vessel of the Portuguese admiral. The next sovereign was distracted for sixteen years by the factions of his chiefs. Two pageants were set up in succession by the courtiers, but they eventually partitioned the kingdom among themselves. At length, after nearly twenty years of convulsions, Akbar put an end to this state of anarchy by annexing the kingdom to the throne of Delhi, after it
1572 had been alienated a hundred and seventy-six years

Malwa became independent in 1401, under Dilawur Ghore, who bequeathed the throne four years

Malwa.

1401 after to his son Hoosein Ghore. His reign of

twenty-five years was passed in incessant wars with his neighbours. His son was assassinated by his minister, A.D.
Mahomed Khan Ghiljie, who mounted the throne, and 1435
during a period of forty-seven years proved himself the ablest of the kings of Malwa. He appears to have had the unobstructed range of northern India, as we find him besieging Delhi, and establishing his son as governor of Ajmere. It was recorded of him that 'the tent was his house, and the battle-field his resting place.' His son,
Gheias-ood-deen, mounted the throne in 1482, and, having 1482
invited his courtiers to a splendid entertainment, informed them that he had passed thirty-four years of his life in the field, fighting by the side of his gallant father, and that he was resolved to spend the remainder of his days in peace and enjoyment; while therefore he retained the royal dignity, he should leave the management of public affairs to his son. The youth was proclaimed vizier, and the king retired to his seraglio, which he had stocked with 15,000 of the most beautiful women he could procure. In this female court the pomp and parade of royalty was strictly maintained. The royal body-guard consisted of 500 Turki maidens, arrayed in male attire, and of 500 Abyssinian maidens. Strange to say, he was allowed to retain this pageantry for eighteen years, without any attempt at rebellion. His son succeeded him in 1500 and his reign of twelve years was marked only by cruelty and sensuality. Mahmood, the last king, was assailed by the Rajpoots, and rescued by Bahadoor Shah, king of Guzerat; but he was incapable of gratitude, and attacked his benefactor,
who marched down to his capital in conjunction with the 1531
Rajpoots, and extinguished the kingdom after a hundred and thirty years of independence.

Rajpootana.

At the period of the first invasion of the Mahomedans in 1001, the Rajpoots appear to have been in possession of all the governments in northern India; but, although they succumbed to the conquerors, they continued to maintain a spirit of independence under their respective chieftains in the table-land of Rajpootana, in the centre of Hindostan. The most important of these chiefs was the rana of Oodypore, in his capital of Chittore. At the beginning of the sixteenth century the throne was filled by Rana Sanga, whose genius and valour raised it to the height of power. His army consisted of 80,000 horse and 500 war elephants; and seven rajas of superior rank and more than a hundred of inferior note attended his stirrup into the field. The chiefs next in importance, the rajas of Jeypore and Joudpore, or Marwar, served under his banner, and he was the acknowledged head of the Rajpoot tribes. The national historian dwells with pride on the eighteen battles he fought with Guzerat and Malwa. His genius consolidated the power of that gallant and chivalrous race, and prepared it for the resistance which it was soon to offer to the Moguls, which, if it had been successful, would doubtless have restored the sovereignty of Hindostan to the Hindoos.

It has been stated that the oppressions of Mahomed Toghluk led to the establishment of an independent Mahomedan government in the Deccan, by Hussun

A.D. 1347 The Bahminee dynasty.

Gunga, an Afghan, in 1347. Out of gratitude to his Hindoo patron, he took the additional title of Bahminee, by which the dynasty is known in history, and extended his authority over all the territories belonging to the crown of Delhi south of the Nerbudda, with the exception of those included in the two Hindoo kingdoms of Beejanuger and Telingana. His son, who

1358 succeeded him in 1358, commenced his reign by attacking the king of Telingana, from whom he obtained the surrender of a throne, which, with the jewels he added to it, was valued at four crores. In a drunken revel he offered an insult to the king of Beejanuger, who attacked the town of Moodgul, and put the inhabitants to the sword. Mahomed, the king, swore that food and sleep should be unlawful to him till he had propitiated the martyrs of Moodgul by the slaughter of 100,000 infidels. He entered the raja's territories, and ravaged them without mercy; and having, as he supposed, completed his vow, granted him honourable terms, and on his return devoted his attention to the improvement of his country. After a reign of seventeen years he left the crown to his son, but he was murdered by his uncle. Feroze, the son of the

1397 assassin, mounted the throne in 1397, and his reign, together with that of his brother, which extended over thirty-seven years, are considered the palmy days of the dynasty. He made twenty-four campaigns, and carried fire and sword through the length and breadth of the Carnatic. At the same time, he was an eminent patron of literature. He likewise established a mercantile marine, and instructed his commanders to bring the most learned men and the handsomest women from every port they visited. His seraglio is said to have contained beauties

from thirteen different countries, and the historians affirm that he was able to converse with each one in her own tongue. He likewise made a point of copying sixteen pages of the Koran daily. Towards the close of his reign he attacked the raja of Beejanuger, and was totally defeated, when the triumphant Hindoos retaliated on him for the destruction of their temples, by the demolition of his mosques. His brother, Ahmed Shah, in his turn defeated the Hindoos, and pursued them with unrelenting severity from day to day, not pausing till the number of the slain was reported to have reached 20,000. We pass on to the last monarch of the dynasty. Mahomed Shah, who was placed on the throne at the age of nine, was affectionately nurtured by his minister Mahomed Gawan, A.D.
the most eminent general and statesman of the age, through 1463
whose energetic efforts the kingdom reached its greatest limits, and was extended from the Malabar to the Coromandel coast, and from the Nerbudda to the Kistna. His internal administration was equally successful, and the prosperity of the country rose to its highest measure. The envious courtiers succeeded, however, in alienating the king from the man to whom he was under these obligations, and in a fit of drunken revelry, he ordered him to be put to death. Gawan was then in his seventy-eighth year, and he knelt down with his face towards Mecca, and received the fatal blow. Though he had held high office under five kings, he died in graceful poverty. The king himself became a prey to remorse, and died within a twelve month. It is unnecessary to pursue the history of this dynasty; Mahomed Shah, his son, ascended the throne
in 1482, and lived on, though he cannot be said to have 1482
reigned, for thirty-seven years. The kingdom crumbled away as governor after governor revolted, and was at length resolved into five independent sovereignties.

1. Adil Shah, the adopted son of Mahomed Gawan, 1489
founded the kingdom of Beejapore and the Adil Shahee dynasty in 1489, which retained its independence for one hundred and ninety-seven years, until it was absorbed by Aurungzebe in 1686.

Five independent kingdoms.

2. Hussun Bheiry, who instigated the murder of Ma- 1490
homed Gawan, was executed by order of his master, and his son Ahmed Nizam raised the standard of revolt in 1487, at Ahmednugur, where he established the Nizam Shahee dynasty, which continued for one hundred and fifty years, till it was subverted by Shah Jehan in 1637.

A.D. 3. Imad-ool-moolk made himself independent at Berar
1484 in 1484, and commenced the Imad Shahee dynasty, which was extinguished at the end of ninety years by the king of Ahmednugur in 1574.

4. Koolee Kootub, a Turkoman, who rose to be governor
1512 of Golconda, established his independence there in 1512, under the name of the Kootub Shahee dynasty, which subsisted for a hundred and seventy five years, and was extinguished by Aurungzebe in 1687.

5. Ahmed Bereed, who was appointed minister on the
1498 murder of Mahomed Gawan, gradually absorbed all the power of the state, and erected what remained of its domains into an independent state at Beder. It was of limited extent, and the period of its extinction is uncertain.

This partition of the Deccan among five independent sovereigns who were constantly at war with each other, or with the Hindoo monarchs, subjected the wretched country to perpetual desolation; but there can be little advantage to the reader in wading through a long succession of sieges and battles, and encumbering the memory with a string of names and dates of no interest. The salient events of this long period of anarchy will come up in the history of the Mogul empire, in which they were eventually absorbed after more than a century and a half of conflict.

SECTION IV.

THE MOGUL DYNASTY—BABER—HUMAYOON—AKBAR.

1526 In the month of April 1526 Sultan Baber captured Delhi, and established the Mogul dynasty, which continued to flourish with only one interruption, and with increasing lustre, for a hundred and eighty years, under a succession, unprecedented in Indian history, of six sovereigns, distinguished by their gallantry in the field, and, with one exception, by their ability in the cabinet.

The Mogul dynasty.

Baber, the sixth in descent from Timur, was the son of Sheikh Mirza, the ruler of Ferghana on the upper Jaxartes. His mother was a descendant of Jenghiz Khan, and he inherited the spirit of enterprize which distinguished both his renowned ancestors, and at the early age of fifteen commenced that adventurous career which he pursued without intermission for thirty-

Baber's early career.

five years. His first campaign was directed against the city of Samarcand, the capital of Timur and the metropolis of Transoxiana, but though he captured it three times, he was as often expelled from it. For eight years he was engaged in a series of perilous and romantic enterprizes, and experienced vicissitudes of fortune which would have crushed an ordinary mortal, but which only seemed to give fresh vigour to his buoyant spirit. In the year 1504, seeing little prospect of success in his native province, he seized the city of Cabul, of which he retained possession for twenty-two years, incessantly employed in defending or enlarging his dominions. His greatest peril arose from the progress of the Uzbeks, a tribe of ferocious Turks and Tartars, then swarming from their native hive, whose leader, Sharbek, had swept the posterity of Timur from Khorasan and Transoxiana. In his march towards the Indus the Uzbek captured Candahar, and threatened Cabul, and would probably have extinguished the hopes and the ambition of Baber had he not been recalled to resist the hostility of Ishmael Shah, who had recently founded the dynasty of the Sophis in Persia. The Uzbek chief was routed and slain, but the footing which his tribe obtained in Transoxiana they retain with vigour to this day. Baber, who had again occupied Samarcand, and had been again expelled from it, now turned his attention to India, where the imbecility and the unpopularity of the emperor, Ibrahim Lodi, offered an allurement too strong for a descendant of Timur to resist. He was invited to invade it by men of influence who had been alienated from the emperor by his oppressions, and more particularly by his own brother, who sought refuge at Cabul. In the course of five years, commencing with 1519 he made five irruptions across the Indus, with alternate success and disappointment. In 1526 he undertook his last and crowning expedition, with an army not exceeding 12,000 men, but, though a heterogeneous mixture of mercenaries, they were all veterans, disciplined in many fields. The destiny of India was decided on the field of Paniput, where the emperor Ibrahim encountered him with, it is said, 100,000 troops and 1000 elephants, and was totally discomfited and fell. Delhi opened her gates to the conqueror, and in May 1526 he vaulted into the vacant throne. But Delhi had long ceased to be the capital and the mistress of India. The great Mahomedan empire which, in the early days of Mahomed Toghluk, embraced the whole continent, had been broken up a century and a half before

Baber in India.

May 1526

State of India.

by his extravagances, and the victory of Baber only gave him possession of the districts to the north-west of the capital, and a strip of territory extending along the banks of the Jumna down to Agra. The various provinces were in the hands of independent rulers. In the southern extremity of India the great Hindoo monarchy of Beejanuger was lord of the ascendant. Farther north lay another Hindoo principality, and the territories of the five kingdoms recently formed on the dissolution of the Bahminee monarchy. Guzerat was governed by a wild youth who had recently absorbed Malwa. Bengal, including Behar, was ruled by an Afghan king. Orissa was still in possession of its ancient Hindoo dynasty, and in northern India Rana Sanga had consolidated Hindoo sovereignty in Rajpootana, and was at this time the most powerful ruler north of the Nerbudda.

Baber's victory over the Rajpoots.

Rana Sanga, elated by the success he had recently obtained over the king of Malwa in conjunction with the king of Guzerat, espoused the cause of the dethroned family of Lodi. All the Rajpoot princes ranged themselves under his banner, and he advanced with 100,000 men, the flower of the
A.D. Rajpoot chivalry, to drive Baber back across the Indus. In
1527 the first engagement at Biana, Baber experienced a very disastrous defeat: some of his officers and men deserted their colours, others went over to the enemy, and all were disheartened, but he did not allow himself to despair. He states, in his interesting memoirs, that he repented of his sins, and determined to reform his life, that he forswore the use of wine, melted down his silver and gold goblets, and determined to live like a true Moosulman and cultivate his beard. His enthusiasm reanimated his troops, and in the engagement to which he led them, he obtained a splendid victory which completely crippled and humbled
1528 the Rajpoot power. The next year he attacked and mastered Chanderee, a Rajpoot fortress hitherto deemed impregnable; and in the succeeding year recovered Oude and northern Behar, and chastised the king of Bengal. But his constitution, which had been impaired by early indulgences, was worn out by these exertions in an uncon-
1530 genial climate, and he died at Agra in 1530, at the age of fifty, and was interred at Cabul, in a beautiful spot he had selected for his grave, the simple and chaste monument erected over which has continued to attract the admiration of three centuries. No

His death and character.

Mahomedan prince in India is held in higher estimation than Baber. His career exhibited all that romantic spirit of adventure of which nations are always proud. His personal courage bordered on rashness; his activity appears fabulous; for thirty-eight years, as he records, he had never kept the feast of Ramzan twice in the same place. But he was rather a valorous soldier than a great general, and lost almost as many battles as he won, but he never lost heart, and was as buoyant after a defeat as after a victory. Amidst all the bustle of war he found leisure for the cultivation of literature, and his poetry has been not a little admired. There is no Indian prince with whose individual character and tastes and feelings we are so familiar; and this is owing to his interesting autobiography, in which he records his transgressions with so much candour, and his repentance with so much sincerity, and his friendships with such warmth, that the reader is led involuntarily to regard him as a personal friend. A.D.

Humayoon succeeded his father in 1530, at the age of 1530
twenty-six, and the first act of his reign displayed the weakness of his character. His brother Camran, the governor of Cabul and Candahar, refused to acknowledge his authority, but he resigned those provinces to him—adding thereto the Punjab—and thus deprived himself of the means of recruiting his army with the hardy mountaineers of Afghanistan, and, as Baber's veterans died out, was obliged to depend on those whom he could enlist from his half-subdued subjects in India. In the third year of his reign he was involved in hostilities with Bahadoor Shah, the wild king of Guzerat, who had furnished the dethroned family of Lodi with the means of 1534
assailing him. Bahadoor was defeated, and obliged to take refuge at the land's-end of Diu, and the whole province was occupied by the Mogul troops. Humayoon then proceeded against Chumpanere, a fortress likewise considered impregnable, but with 300 troops he climbed a perpendicular rock by means of spikes driven into it, and captured it at once. He was immediately after recalled to Agra to arrest the progress of Shere Khan, but was defeated and expelled from India after a reign of ten years, and a new dynasty mounted the throne.

Humayoon.

Shere Khan was an Afghan of noble parentage, born at Sasseram, in Behar, where his father held a jageer under the governor. He enlisted as a private soldier under the revolted viceroy of

Dynasty of Shere Shah.

Jounpore, but cultivated his mind with great assiduity and educated himself for a future career of ambition. A long series of adventures, ended in his obtaining posses-
A.D. sion of Behar, and invading Bengal, and it was to oppose
1535 his alarming progress that Humayoon was recalled from Guzerat. He marched down upon him, but wasted six months in the siege of Chunar, which was at length captured by the powerful artillery of Humayoon manned by Portuguese gunners and directed by Roomy Khan, a Turk of Constantinople, whom he had brought with him from Guzerat. Meanwhile Shere Khan had defeated the king of Bengal and captured Gour, but not deeming himself sufficiently strong to resist the imperial troops he retired to the mountain region of Behar and deposited his family and his treasures in the stronger fortress of Rhotas.
1538 The emperor took possession of Gour, but when the rains set in, the delta of the Ganges became a sheet of water, and his army was isolated and decimated by sickness and desertion. Shere Khan then issued from his fastnesses, took possession of Behar and Benares, recovered Chunar, and pushed his detachments up to Cunouge. Humayoon was obliged to retreat towards his capital, but was intercepted and defeated, and Shere Khan assumed the imperial title.

Defeat of Humayoon.

Humayoon at length reached Agra after his defeat, and employed eight months in recruiting his force, while his rival was employed in organising the provinces he had conquered. The two armies met at Cunouge, where the emperor experienced a second and more fatal defeat, and fled first to Delhi, and
1540 then to Lahore; thus at the end of fourteen years, the power which the energy and perseverance of Baber had established was subverted, and scarcely a vestige of Mogul sovereignty remained in India, while the throne of Delhi reverted to the Afghans. Humayoon fled to Sinde and was engaged for eighteen months in fruitless negotiations with its chiefs. He then threw himself on the kindness of the Rajpoot prince of Marwar, but was rudely repulsed from his court and pursued with an armed force by his son. The wretched emperor, after suffering incredible hardships in crossing the desert, at length succeeded in reaching Amercote with only seven mounted attendants; and there his queen, who had nobly shared with him the torments of the journey, gave birth to a son, afterwards the illustrious
1542 Akbar. After another series of reverses, he quitted India and repaired to Candahar.

Leaving Humayoon across the Indus, we turn to the A.D.
career of Shere Shah, who mounted the throne and esta- 1540
blished a new dynasty, which however did not
last more than sixteen years. In 1542 he con- Shere Shah.
quered the province of Malwa, and reduced the great
fortress of Raiseen, of boundless antiquity. Here his repu-
tation was tarnished by the only stain ever attached to it.
The garrison capitulated on terms, but the Mahomedan
doctors assured him that, according to the doctrines of the
Koran, no faith was to be kept with unbelievers, and they
were slain to a man. In 1544 he invaded Marwar, which was 1544
defended by 50,000 Rajpoots, and he was exposed to such
peril, that, in allusion to the barrenness of the country, he
exclaimed that "he had nearly lost the empire for a
"handful of millet." Soon after, the capture of Chittore
placed Rajpootana at his feet, and he then proceeded to
attack Callinger, an ancient and strong fort in Bundlecund,
but was killed by the explosion of a magazine. The five
years of his reign form the most brilliant period in native 1545
history. He was equally qualified for the duties of war
and of peace—a consummate general, and a liberal and
enlightened statesman. Though incessantly engaged in the
field, he reformed every branch of the civil administration;
and of his institutions it is sufficient to say that they
became the model of those of Akbar. He constructed a
grand trunk road, lined with trees, from Bengal to the
banks of the Indus, erected caravanseries, and excavated
wells for the convenience of travellers; he was, moreover,
the first prince to establish a mounted post. His second
son Selim, after quelling a dangerous rebellion, was enabled
to enjoy the throne in peace for nine years, indulging his
hereditary taste for architecture. It was the profligacy of
his brother and successor, known in history as Adili, which
at length extinguished this short-lived dynasty. Having
exhausted the treasury, he began to resume the estates of
his Patan nobles, who went one by one into rebellion, and
established five independent authorities, and nothing was 1544
at length left to the crown but the districts immediately
around Delhi.

To turn to the career of Humayoon. He proceeded from
India to Candahar, but was driven from it by the hostility of
his brother, and constrained to seek refuge at the Restoration
court of Persia, where he was subject to all the mor- of Huma-
tifications a capricious despot could inflict. He was yoon.
even constrained to undergo the indignity of putting on the

A.D. Kuzzilbash, or red cap of the Persians, and it was "proclaimed
1544 "by a triumphal flourish from the king's band." After repeated importunity, he was furnished with 14,000 horse for the conquest of Afghanistan, but only on condition of ceding the frontier provinces to the king. Candahar was captured after a siege of five months, and made over to the Persian prince who had accompanied him to receive possession of it. On his death Humayoon put a large portion of the Persian garrison to the sword—an act of perfidy which has left an indelible blot on his memory. He then marched to Cabul, and after various severe struggles succeeded in
1553 wresting it from his brothers, one of whom he deprived of sight, with excruciating torture. The increasing confusion in India led him to make a bold stroke to recover his throne. He crossed the Indus and encountered the formidable army of Secunder Soor, who had seized the Punjab on the dissolution of the imperial authority, and gained a complete victory. It was in this battle that the young Akbar earned his spurs. Humayoon hastened to Delhi, and remounted the throne which he had lost fifteen
1555 years before, but was not destined to enjoy it long. Six months afterwards, while descending the steps of his library, he heard the muezzin's call to prayer, and, as usual, stopped to repeat the creed, and then sat down; but on endeavouring to rise, the staff on which he leaned slipped over the polished steps, and he fell headlong over
1556 the parapet, and expired within four days, in the forty-ninth year of his age, and, including the period of his exile, the twenty-sixth year of his reign.

Akbar, the pride and ornament of the Mogul dynasty, was only thirteen years and three months of age when he

Akbar's early years.

was called to the throne, which he adorned by his genius for fifty years. He was contemporary with Queen Elizabeth, his reign having begun two years before, and ended two years after hers. The administration was managed during his minority by Byram Khan, a Turkoman, the companion of Humayoon in all the vicissitudes of his career, and an eminent statesman and general, but austere, arrogant, and exceptionally bigoted. Hemu, one of the greatest commanders of the age, and, though a Hindoo, most loyal to the deposed emperor Adili, on hearing of the death of Humayoon, deposited his master at Chunar, and moved up to the capital with 100,000 men. Agra and Delhi opened their gates to him, and the ministers of Akbar entreated him to abandon India, and retire to

Afghanistan; but Byram advised an immediate and vigorous attack, and Akbar supported his opinion. The two armies met at Paniput, and the destiny of India was again A.D.
decided on that memorable field. Hemu was completely 1556
defeated, and conducted bleeding into the presence of the young monarch. Byram urged him to secure the religious merit of slaying an infidel, but he refused to imbrue his hands in the blood of a gallant and now helpless foe, and Byram struck off the head of the captive with one stroke of his scimitar. It was the military talent and the energy of Byram which had seated the Moguls again on the throne, and maintained Akbar's power; but the minister had grown too big for a subject, and for four years after his accession Akbar felt himself to be a cipher in his own court. Such bondage was intolerable to a high-spirited prince, and, at the age of eighteen, he resolved to emancipate himself from it. While out, therefore, on a hunting party, he suddenly returned to Delhi without his minister, and issued a proclamation, announcing that he had taken the government into his own hands, and that no orders were to be obeyed which did not issue from himself. Byram felt that his power was waning, and retired to Nagore, giving out that he was going on pilgrimage to Mecca, not without the hope of being reinstated, but Akbar sent him a message dismissing him from all his offices. He immediately went into revolt, and having raised an army, attempted an invasion of the Punjab, but was defeated and captured. As he entered the royal presence with his turban humbly cast around his neck, and threw himself at the feet of the prince he had cherished from the cradle, Akbar hastened to raise him, seated him on his right hand, and, after investing him with a robe of honour, offered him his choice of any post in the empire. He preferred a retreat to Mecca, but was assassinated on the route by an Afghan, whose father he had put to death.

Akbar was now his own master at the age of eighteen. 1560
Born amidst hardships, and trained up in adversity, he was beset with difficulties which would have broken a spirit of less energy. Of all the Mahomedan dynasties which had ruled India, that of the Moguls was the weakest. It was not connected with any large and powerful tribe beyond the Indus, ready to advance and support the ascendency of its fellow-countrymen in India. His army was a collection of mercenaries drawn to his

Akbar's difficulties.

A.D. standard from the various countries of Central Asia by the
1560 hope of plunder. His officers were a band of adventurers
to
1567 bound to him by no ties of hereditary loyalty, and more disposed to carve out principalities for themselves than to build up a Mogul empire. Before he could attempt to recover the dominions of the crown, it was necessary for him to establish his authority over his own chiefs, and for seven years he was engaged in crushing their revolts. In the first year of his reign, his territories were confined to the Punjab and the districts around Agra and Delhi, but he gradually recovered Ajmere, Gwalior and Oude. The son of the late emperor Adili made an attempt to recover his throne; he was defeated by Zeman Shah, but the general, despising the youth of his sovereign, withheld the royal share of the booty, and Akbar was obliged to take the field against him. Adam Khan, another general, was sent to expel the Afghans from Malwa; but, after defeating them, kept the fruits of the victory to himself. Akbar marched against him, but consented to accept his submission, and he requited this lenity by stabbing the vizier while at prayer in a chamber adjoining that occupied by the emperor, who thereupon ordered him to be thrown headlong into the Jumna. Soon after, Abdoolla Khan, a haughty Uzbek, who had been received with a host of his countrymen into the Mogul service, "withdrew his neck from the yoke of "obedience," but Akbar came down upon him with promptitude, and constrained him to fly to Guzerat. Great dissatisfaction was thereby created among the Uzbek officers, and a treasonable confederacy was organised in the army. One of their number, Asof Jah, was sent to subjugate the little Hindoo principality of Gurra, on the Nerbudda, near Jubbulpore, then governed by the Princess Doorgawutee, who was no less renowned for her valour than for her beauty. She commanded her army in person, and maintained the conflict with a noble heroism, till she
1564 received a wound in her eye. The troops, missing her presence, began to give way, when, to avoid falling into the hands of the enemy, she seized the stiletto of the elephant driver, and plunged it into her bosom. Her martial exploits are still a favourite theme with the bards of the Deccan. The principality was conquered by Asof Jah, but he appropriated the largest share of the rich booty to his own use, and then joined the confederacy, which now embraced the most considerable of Akbar's generals. His danger was extreme; it was no less than a

struggle for the throne, and the question at issue was, whether the empire should be Uzbek or Mogul. His detachments were repeatedly defeated, but he maintained the conflict with unflinching resolution for two years. At this critical juncture he was obliged to quit the pursuit of the Uzbeks, in consequence of the revolt of his brother, to whom he had entrusted the government of the Punjab. It was at once crushed, but on his return to the south he found that the revolted generals had taken possession of Allahabad and Oude, and were preparing to march on the capital. Though the rains had set in, when military operations are usually suspended in India, he did not hesitate to take the field against them, and, by his promptitude and vigour, succeeded at length in breaking up the confederacy. He had now subdued all his adversaries by his valour, or his clemency, and, at the age of twenty-five, he had the happiness of seeing his authority completely established over all the revolted provinces.

General Uzbek conspiracy.

With a spirit of liberality foreign to preceding conquerors, Baber determined to strengthen his throne by matrimonial alliances with the Hindoos. Humayoon had espoused the daughter of the raja of Jeypore. Akbar had likewise married two Rajpoot princesses, and his son had followed his example. Offices of great dignity and responsibility were conferred on these Hindoo princes, and they took a pride in these imperial alliances. But the orthodox house of Chittore, wrapped up in its religious exclusiveness and hauteur, disdained every such connection, and excommunicated those who had adopted them. The raja had given encouragement to the king of Malwa, and Akbar was determined to chastise him. The throne was at the time occupied by Oody Sing, the degenerate son of the illustrious Rana Sunga. He took refuge in the hills on the approach of the Mogul troops, and left the defence of his capital to Jeymul, the Rajpoot chief of Bednore, esteemed by his countrymen the bravest of the brave. The siege was protracted by his skill and valour, but he was killed by a bolt from the bow of Akbar. His death deprived the garrison of all confidence, and they devoted themselves to death with the accustomed solemnities. The women threw themselves on the funeral pyre of the chief, and the men rushed recklessly on the weapons of the Moguls, and perished to the number of 8,000.

Matrimonial alliances with the Rajpoots.

Attack of Chittore.

A.D. 1568

Akbar's next enterprise was of greater magnitude. The kingdom of Guzerat, enlarged by the conquests of Bahadoor Shah, had been a prey to faction since his death in 1537, and four weak and profligate princes had occupied the throne in thirty-five years. Etimad Khan, once a Hindoo slave, who managed the government for Mozuffer the third, seeing no other mode of terminating the distractions of the country, invited Akbar to take possession of it, and he proceeded to Patun, where that feeble monarch resigned the sceptre to
A.D. 1572 him, and Guzerat was again annexed to the crown of Delhi, after two centuries and a half of independence. But no sooner had he returned to his capital with the bulk of his army, than a turbulent chief of the name of Mirza raised a new revolt, and the imperial general was reduced to extremities. The rains had set in, but Akbar was ready for action at all seasons. He immediately despatched 2,000 cavalry, and followed them with 300 of his own guards, marching 450 miles in nine days. The promptitude of his
1573 movements confounded the rebels, and the subjugation of the province was rendered complete.

Conquest of Guzerat.

The attention of Akbar had been directed to Bengal while he was engaged in Guzerat. Under the successor of Shere Shah, the Afghan governor of the province assumed independence, and four kings of his line reigned in Bengal during a period of thirty years, The last was assassinated soon after he ascended the throne, which was then seized by Soliman, an illustrious Afghan, who determined on the conquest of Orissa, which was effected by his general, Kala-pahar. Soliman died in 1573, and was succeeded by Daood Khan, a debauchee and a coward, who, considering himself a match for Akbar, ventured to attack a fort above Ghazeepore. Akbar ordered an army down for the conquest of the kingdom, and the king retired to Orissa, where he encountered the Mogul army, and was defeated, but was allowed to retain the kingdom as a feudatory. The next year, on the withdrawal of the imperial troops, he revolted, and was defeated. He fell in the action, and with him terminated the last line of
1576 the Afghan kings of Bengal, which they had held for a period of two hundred and thirty-six years. The Mogul officers seized the jageers of the discomfited Afghans, but on being summoned to account for the revenues, and to produce the roll of the troops they were bound to maintain, they rose in a body, and 30,000 of Akbar's finest cavalry

Akbar invades Bengal.

appeared in arms against him. The new conquest was lost A.D. 1577 for a time, and the spirit of disaffection was spreading through Oude. In this emergency the emperor, finding it impossible to trust the fidelity of his Mogul officers, sent an army of Rajpoots under the celebrated raja, Toder Mull, to reduce the province. He succeeded in giving a severe blow to the insurgents, but the war was protracted and the Afghans of Orissa took advantage of the confusion, and recovered their footing in the southern districts of Bengal. The great Rajpoot, raja Man Sing, was then despatched to quell this formidable insurrection, but it was not before the year 1592, after a dozen engagements and sixteen years 1592 of conflict, that the authority of the emperor was fully established in this province.

Conquest of Orissa.

Two years after the conquest of Bengal, the kingdom of Orissa was added to the Mogul empire. Orissa had for 1578 twenty centuries been considered the Holy Land of India, and the region of pilgrimage under three successive creeds. For more than seven centuries it was the depository of the sacred tooth of Booddha, until that relic was removed to Ceylon. Then came the Hindoo dynasty of the Kesaris, who covered it with thousands of temples in honour of Seeva. This was succeeded by the dynasty of the Gunga-bungsas, who are believed to have come from the Gangetic province, and who assumed the title of Lords of the Elephant. Their dominions covered 40,000 square miles, and extended from the banks of the Hooghly to the banks of the Godavery. They gave the ascendency to the worship of Vishnoo, and although Jugernath, a form of that god, makes his first appearance in that land of religious merit early in the fourth century, it was under the auspices of this dynasty that the 'Lord of the World' attained that supreme homage throughout the continent which he still maintains. The first sovereign of the line was fourteen years in erecting the magnificent temple at Pooree, and the resources of the state were exhausted by a succession of princes, in ecclesiastical endowments and the support of brahmins. Inroads were occasionally made by the Mahomedan rulers of Bengal, but the Hindoo princes of Orissa continued to maintain their independence with great vigour till the death, in 1532, of the last able monarch of the Gangetic dynasty, which was followed by a period of anarchy for twenty-four years, when Soliman, the king of Bengal, sent his general, Kala-pahar, to invade it. He was a brahmin by birth, but had embraced the religion of the Prophet to obtain the hand of a princess of Gour, and became the unrelenting oppressor of his former creed. He defeated the raja, and with him ended the independence of this ancient and renowned kingdom. Kala-pahar persecuted the brahmins and confiscated the religious endowments which had accumulated during twenty generations of devout monarchs. He destroyed the idols and pulled down the temples to erect mosques with the materials, and he dug up the image of Jugernath from the Chilka lake, into which it had been thrown for safety, and conveying it to the banks of the Hooghly, committed it to the flames. According to popular rumour, the arms and legs of the idols dropped off at the sound of his kettledrums. Upon the conquest of Bengal, the king Daood took refuge in Orissa, and was pursued by the generals of Akbar, and after more than one revolt, was slain, and Orissa became a province of the Mogul empire.

A.D. A short time previous to this invasion of Bengal by
1560 Akbar, the ancient city of Gour, the metropolis of Bengal, was depopulated and abandoned. It was admirably situated on the confines of Bengal and Behar for the government of both provinces. It had been the capital of a hundred kings, who adorned it, more especially those of the Mahomedan creed, with massive and superb edifices. It extended along the banks of the river, and was defended from its encroachments by a stone embankment, said to have been fifteen miles in length. This magnificent city, the abode of wealth and luxury, was suddenly prostrated by some pestilence which has never been explained, and has since been the abode of wild hogs and tigers.

The city of Gour.

The next event of importance in the reign of Akbar was
1586 the conquest of Cashmere, by his brother-in-law, the raja of Jeypore. The king, on his submission, was enrolled among the nobles of the court, and this noble valley, considered the paradise of Asia, which enjoys "a delicious climate, and exhibits in the midst of snowy "summits a scene of continual verdure," became the summer residence of Akbar and his successors. The effort to curb the highlanders between the Indus and the passes into Afghanistan, which was next undertaken, proved a more arduous task. These wild mountaineers had been for ages the plague of every ruler of the province. They regarded it as their hereditary vocation to plunder travellers passing through the defiles, and to levy black mail on the industry of

Conquest of Cashmere.

the valleys. Akbar sent a strong army under the raja of Jeypore to subjugate them, but it was assailed in the passes and annihilated; and the Mahomedan historian records that of 40,000 horse and foot, scarcely a man returned. Such wholesale destruction would appear incredible, if we had not witnessed a repetition of it, in the same scenes, under the British Government in 1841. The rajas Toder Mull and Man-sing imposed some restraint on their violence by the establishment of military posts which cut off their supplies from the plains; but they were as troublesome as ever a century after in the reign of Aurungzebe. Soon after, Akbar proceeded to the conquest of Sinde, and reannexed Candahar to the crown; and thus, after a series of conflicts which extended over twenty-five years, he found himself at length undisputed master of his hereditary dominions across the Indus, and of all the territories north of the Nerbudda which had ever belonged to the imperial throne, and it only remained for him to extend his authority over the Deccan. A brief notice of the progress of events in that division of India during the sixteenth century will be a suitable introduction to the expedition which the emperor now undertook.

The Khyberees. A.D. 1586

1591

Sinde and Candahar. 1594

SECTION V.

AKBAR. INVASION OF THE DECCAN. HIS DEATH.

It has been stated in a previous chapter that five independent kingdoms—Beejapore, Ahmednugur, Golconda, Beder, and Berar—arose on the ruins of the Bahminee kingdom. Beder rarely appears on the page of history, and Berar which was never of much weight in the politics of the Deccan, was absorbed by Ahmednugur in 1572. The attention of the kings of Golconda was chiefly directed to the subjugation of the various Hindoo principalities which lay on its eastern frontier, and stretched along the Coromandel coast from Orissa southward. It appears also to have gradually absorbed the Hindoo state of Telingana, with its capital at Warungul, which had assumed independence on the fall of the Bahminee kingdom. Beejapore and Ahmednugur,

The Deccan in the sixteenth century.

which bordered on each other, were engaged in constant hostility. Within the circle of their territories was included the region inhabited by the Mahrattas, which had formerly belonged to the Hindoo kingdom of Deoghur, conquered by Alla-ood-deen in 1295; and the origin and growth of their importance is to be attributed primarily to the training they received in the constant warfare of these princes. During the sixteenth century the armies of these two Mahomedan states were constantly recruited by Mahratta soldiers, sometimes to the extent of 20,000. There was not as yet any bond of national unity among them, and they sold their mercenary swords to the highest bidder, without caring whether their own countrymen might not be fighting in the opposite ranks.

But the great event of that century was the extinction of Hindoo power in the Deccan. To the south of the Kistna lay the great Hindoo monarchy of Beejanuger, established in 1336, which had maintained a perpetual conflict with the Bahminee dynasty, and subsequently with the kingdoms which arose on its decay. In the early period of the sixteenth century Beejanuger had attained its greatest extent and power. It was enriched by maritime commerce; and all the Hindoo chiefs south of the Kistna—below which the Mahomedans had no footing—were completely under its control, even where they were not under its government. No single state was able to cope with it. The reigning raja, Ram-raj, had recently wrested several districts from Beejapore; he had overrun Golconda, laid siege to the capital, and exacted large concessions from the king. The four Mahomedan kings—Beder still existed—felt the necessity of restraining the growth of his power, and, suspending their mutual jealousies, formed a quadruple alliance against him. It was nothing less than a conflict between the Hindoos and the Mahomedans for the supremacy of the Deccan. Although Ram-raja called up all the strength of his Hindoo feudatories from the south down to its extreme limits, the enumeration of his host by Ferishta appears fabulous. His younger brother is said to have commanded a wing of the army consisting of 20,000 cavalry, 100,000 foot, and 500 elephants. His second brother had another wing of equal strength, while the raja himself led the flower of the army. The confederate force was likewise prodigious, and included 20,000 elephants and 600 pieces of artillery of all calibre. This important battle, known in history as that of Talli-

Beejanuger.

kotta, which lies at a short distance from the Kistna, was A.D.
fought on the 25th January, 1565, and it resulted in the 1565
total defeat of the raja, and the slaughter, as the Mahomedan historians boast, of 100,000 infidels. The raja, seventy years of age, was beheaded in cold blood, and his head was preserved as a trophy at Beejapore, and annually exhibited on the anniversary of his death. The Hindoo power in the south was irretrievably broken, but dissensions among the victors enabled the brother of the raja to retain a fraction of his territory, and to establish his court eventually at Chundergiree, which has been rendered memorable in the history of British India as the town, where, seventy years after the battle of Tallikotta, the descendant of the raja granted the East India Company the first foot of land they ever possessed in India, and on which they erected the factory of Madras.

Akbar's views on the Deccan.

At the period of Akbar's invasion of the Deccan, the three Mahomedan princes were those of Beejapore, Golconda, and Ahmednugur. This expedition was, doubtless, dictated by the "lust of territorial "aggrandisement;" but, if it had been completely successful, it would have been an unquestionable blessing to the country. Nothing could be more deplorable than the condition of the Deccan at this period. Its various kings had no occupation but war, aggressive war without even the excuse of provocation. Scarcely a year passed in which villages were not desolated, and the fair fruits of industry blasted by their mutual hostilities; and the substitution of a single authority, even though despotic, was a real godsend. On the death of Boorhan Nizam Shah, the king of Ahmednugur, four factions arose in the state, the most powerful of which sent an invitation to Akbar, which he accepted at once; but, before the force which he despatched could reach the capital, another revolution placed the government in the hands of Chand

Chand Sultana of Ahmednugur.

Sultana, the aunt of the minor raja. This cele-
brated woman, the favourite heroine of the 1595
Deccan, and the subject of a hundred ballads, determined to defend the city to the last extremity. The Moguls had constructed three mines, two of which she countermined; the third blew up, leaving a large opening in the wall, and her officers prepared to desert the defence. The sultana flew to the spot fully armed, with a drawn sword in her hand, and a veil over her face. Combustibles of every description were thrown into the breach, and so

heavy a fire was directed upon it, that the assailants were constrained to retire. It is a popular and cherished tradition that, when the shot was exhausted, she charged the guns with copper, then with silver, and lastly with gold. Her allies were now approaching, and the Mogul camp was straitened for provisions. Morad, the son of

The sultana cedes Berar.

A.D. Akbar, offered to retire upon the cession of Berar,
1596 and the sultana, who placed little confidence in her own troops, reluctantly accepted these terms. Within a year the kings of Ahmednugur, Golconda, and Beejapore formed a league to drive the Moguls out of the Deccan, and brought 60,000 troops into the field. An action was fought at Soniput, which lasted two days without any decisive result. Discord broke out among the Mogul officers, and Akbar,
1599 who had resided for fourteen years near the Indus, felt the necessity of proceeding to the Deccan in person. He advanced to the Nerbudda, and sent his son Morad to lay siege to Ahmednugur. The government of Chand Sultana was in a more disturbed state than ever, and, seeing defence hopeless, she felt the necessity of negotiating a peace with the Moguls, when the soldiery, instigated by her enemies, burst into her chamber, and put her to death.

Her tragic death.

The city was stormed and plundered, and the
1600 young king and the royal family were sent prisoners to Gwalior; but the kingdom was not incorporated with the Mogul territories till thirty-seven years later.

This was the last political event of any importance in the
1601 reign of Akbar, who returned to the capital in 1601. The last four years of his life were embittered by the misconduct of his eldest son Selim, a violent and vindictive prince, and the slave of wine.

Last four years of Akbar's life.

He took up arms against his father, but was conciliated by a grant of the provinces of Bengal and Orissa. He had contracted an inveterate dislike of Abul Fazil, one of the most illustrious and esteemed of the emperor's officers, equally eminent as a general, a statesman, and a historian, to whose classic pen his reign is indebted, in no small degree, for its lasting renown. Selim caused him to be assassinated by a zemindar of Bundlecund. In September 1605, Akbar began to feel the approach of death. The profligacy of Selim had induced an influential body of courtiers to contemplate the elevation of a younger son to the throne, but Akbar assembled them around his dying couch, and in their presence ordered Selim to gird his own scimitar to his side, as a token of the bequest of the empire. Then, addressing the assembled omrahs, he asked forgiveness for whatever offence he might have given them, and, after repeating the Moslem confession of faith, expired in the odour of sanctity, though he had lived the life of a heretic. He died at the age of sixty-three, after a reign of forty-nine years.

Death of Akbar.

A.D. 1605

Akbar is described as "a strongly built and handsome "man, with an agreeable expression of countenance, and "very captivating manners." He was not only the pride of the Mogul dynasty, but incomparably the greatest of all the Mahomedan rulers of India. Few of these princes have ever exhibited greater military talent or personal courage. He never fought a battle which he did not win, or besiege a town which he did not take. Yet he had no passion for war; and he had no sooner turned the tide of victory by his skill and energy, than he left his commanders to complete the work, and hastened back to the more congenial labours of the cabinet. The glory of his reign rests not so much on the extent of his conquests, as on the admirable institutions by which they were consolidated and improved. In the early part of his career he was a devout follower of the Prophet, and, at one time, contemplated a pilgrimage to his tomb, the earnest longing of every Mahomedan. But, about the twenty-fifth year of his reign, he began to entertain latitudinarian views. Rejecting all prophets, priests, and ceremonies, he professed to take simple reason as his guide. The formula of his creed seems to have been: "There is no god but God, and "Akbar is his Caliph." Yet with all his scepticism, he was not without a touch of superstition, of which he afforded an instance by the awe and veneration with which he adored the image of Jesus Christ and the Virgin, when shown to him by the Roman Catholic missionaries. The tendency of his measures was to discourage Mahomedanism. He changed the era of the Hegira; he restrained the study of Arabic, and of Mahomedan theology, and wounded the dearest prejudices of the faithful by prohibiting the beard, though it was enjoined by the Koran. Nothing but the ascendency of his character, and his brilliant success in war and in peace, could have preserved his throne amidst the discontents occasioned by these heterodox proceedings. Amidst a people with whom the persecution of infidels was regarded as a sacred duty, he adopted the principle, not only of religious toleration, but of religious equality, and determined to rest the strength of his throne upon the attach-

Character of Akbar.

ment of all his subjects. He secured the loyalty of the Hindoos by inviting them to share the highest civil offices and military commands with those of his own creed. He abolished the jezzia, the odious capitation tax inflicted on unbelievers, rescinded the pilgrim tax, sanctioned the marriage of Hindoo widows, and positively prohibited suttees.

Under the supervision of the Hindoo raja, Toder Mull, the great financier of the age, he remodelled the whole revenue system of the empire, and thus brought to maturity the great plans which Shere Shah in his brief reign of five years had inaugurated. The lands were measured according to a uniform standard, and divided into three classes according to their character and fertility. The demand of the state was fixed, generally, at one-third the produce, and then commuted into money. The settlement was made with the ryots, to the exclusion of all middle-men, and all arbitrary cesses were abolished. The whole empire was divided into fifteen provinces or soobahs, each of which was placed under the authority of a soobadar. He was entrusted with full powers, civil, military and financial, and assisted by a military commander and finance minister, who were accountable to him, though nominated by the crown. Akbar's military system was the least perfect of the departments of the state, and was enfeebled by paying the commanders for their men by the head, which created an irresistible temptation to present false musters, and to fill the ranks with vagabonds. The same organisation which pervaded the state establishments was introduced into every division of the court, and the whole was regulated, to the minutest detail, by the emperor himself. Every department was maintained upon a scale of imperial magnificence, of which there had been no example since the establishment of the Mahomedan power in India. During his progress through the country his camp was a moving city, and the eye was dazzled by the splendid tents of his ministers and officers, and more especially by the royal tents, blazing with ornaments and surmounted with gilt cupolas. A taste for literature was diffused through his court. Translations were made under his directions from the Hindoo classics, and his accomplished courtier, Fiezi, was directed to make a correct version of the Evangelists.

His revenue settlement.

Splendour of his court.

CHAPTER III.

SECTION I.

REIGN OF JEHANGEER.

On the death of Akbar, Selim stepped into the throne and A.D.
assumed the title of Jehangeer, the Conqueror of the World. 1605
The great empire to which he succeeded was in a state of profound tranquillity, not disturbed by any insubordination among the public officers nor by foreign aggression. His first measures were judicious and benevolent. He confirmed most of his father's ministers in their posts, remitted some vexatious taxes which had survived his father's reforms, and made arrangements for giving easy access to the complaints of his subjects. He likewise replaced the Mahomedan creed on the coin, and manifested a superstitious obedience to the precepts of the Koran. But the quiet of the realm was speedily interrupted by the rebellion of his son, Khosroo, to whom he had always ex- 1606
hibited a feeling of strong antipathy. The unhappy youth fled to the Punjab, and collected a force of 10,000 men, but was pursued and captured, when the emperor exhibited the brutality of his disposition by causing 700 of his adherents to be impaled alive, while Khosroo was deliberately carried along the line to witness their agonies.

Accession of Jehangeer.

The event which exercised the greatest influence on the reign of Jehangeer was his marriage with Noor Jehan, contracted in the sixth year of his reign. This celebrated princess was the daughter of a Persian noble, who had been reduced to poverty, and, following the current stream of emigration, proceeded to India to repair his fortunes. During the journey his wife gave birth to a daughter, under very distressing circumstances. A merchant, who happened to be travelling on the same route, offered them timely assistance, and conveyed them in his own train to the capital. He took the father into his service, and eventually introduced him to the Court of

Noor Jehan.

Akbar, where he rose to considerable eminence. As the daughter grew up, she received all the accomplishments which the metropolis of the empire could provide, and attracted admiration by her exquisite beauty and elegance. In the harem of Akbar, which she visited with her mother, she excited the passion of prince Selim; but as she had been already betrothed to a young and gallant Persian noble, who had acquired the title of Shere Afghan, from having killed a tiger in single combat, the marriage was completed by the orders of the emperor, and a jageer in the distant province of Burdwan was bestowed on him, to withdraw his wife from the capital. But Jehangeer had no sooner mounted the throne than he determined to remove every obstacle to the gratification of his wishes, and the noble Persian perished in an affray which was not believed to be accidental. His lovely widow was conveyed to the capital, and the emperor offered to share his throne with her; but she rejected his advances with such disdain as to disgust Jehangeer, and she was consigned to neglect in the harem. Reflection served to convince her of her folly,
A.D. and she contrived to throw herself in his way and to re-
1611 kindle his passion. The nuptials were celebrated with extraordinary pomp, and she was clothed with honours such as no princess had ever enjoyed before in India. Her name was associated with the emperor's on the coin, and announced in these graceful terms: "By order of Jehangeer, gold acquired a hundred-"fold value by the name of Noor Jehan." Her talents for business were not inferior to her personal charms, and her influence was beneficial in softening the emperor's disposition, and producing that reformation in his habits which marked the early years of his reign. Her taste imparted grace to the splendour of the court, while, at the same time, she curtailed its extravagance. Her brother was raised to high office, and her father placed at the head of the administration, which he managed with great ability.

Her marriage with the emperor.

The capture of Ahmednugur and the murder of Chand Sultana did not ensure the conquest of the kingdom. A kinsman of the late king was placed on the throne by Malik Amber, the chief of the Abyssinian nobles of the court. He holds the foremost rank in the history of the
1610 Deccan monarchies as a statesman and general of surpassing ability. He took entire charge of the administration, and maintained the sinking fortunes of the state for many years with singular energy. Planting himself on the

borders of the Deccan, he repeatedly drove the Moguls across the Nerbudda. Two powerful armies were sent by Jehangeer into the Deccan; one was completely baffled by Malik's peculiar mode of warfare, and obliged to retreat, and the other was too disheartened by this event to advance A.D. far. His artillery, which was obtained from the Portuguese 1612 in his ports, was greatly superior to that of the imperial army. He availed himself, moreover, of the contingents of the Mahratta chieftains, which served to foster and to mature their military power, and it was under his banner that Shahjee, the father of Sevajee, laid the foundation of the greatness of his family. Malik Amber had no natural passion for military enterprises, though his success in the field has seldom been surpassed. It was his attention to the duties of peace on which his renown rests, and his revenue settlements rival those of the raja Toder Mull.

Subjugation of Oodypore.

Jehangeer's failure in the Deccan was counterbalanced by his success in Rajpootana. Pertab Sing, the rana of Oodypore, who is still idolized by his countrymen for the heroism with which he repelled the Moguls and eventually regained the provinces they had conquered, was succeeded by his son Omrah, who, though equally valliant, was not equally fortunate. He was attacked by Shah Jehan, the favourite and the gallant son of Jehangeer, and obliged to acknowledge his fealty to the empire. The independence of Oodypore, which had been maintained for eight centuries, was virtually extinguished, 1614 for although Shah Jehan, himself of Rajpoot blood on the mother's side, generously restored the territories he had conquered to the fallen rana, it was only as the vassal of the emperor of Delhi.

Sir Thomas Roe.

The tenth year of the reign of Jehangeer was rendered memorable by the arrival of Sir Thomas Roe, as the ambassador of James I., to solicit privileges 1615 for the East India Company. The result of his embassy will be stated in its place hereafter. Here it may be sufficient to remark that he was fascinated with the oriental magnificence of the court, which completely eclipsed the tinsel pomp of his own master; but he saw little comfort among the people, who were ground down by extortion. The emperor dispensed justice daily in person, but retired in the evening to his cups, which he seldom quitted before his reason was obscured. The different governments were farmed out; the courtiers were universally corrupt, and military discipline was relaxed. There

was a large influx of Europeans at the court; one of the emperor's nephews had embraced Christianity, and the emperor himself had an image of Christ in his rosary.
A.D. Shah Jehan, the emperor's gallant son, who was married
1615 to the niece of Noor Jehan was now declared heir apparent, and sent in the following year to invade the Deccan. The prosperity of Malik Amber had created a feeling of envy at the court, and he was still farther weakened by the desertion of the king of Beejapore. He was constrained, therefore, to cede to Shah Jehan the fortress of Ahmednugur, as well as all the conquests he had made from the Moguls. Within four years he renewed the war, and drove the imperial troops across the Taptee. Shah Jehan was again selected to
1620 command the army, and the usual success attended his arms. Malik Amber was deserted by his own officers, and obliged to purchase peace by a large sacrifice of territory and treasure.

Shah Jehan, heir apparent.

Just at this juncture Khosroo, the brother of Shah Jehan,
1621 died, and his own misfortunes began. Noor Jehan had bestowed her daughter by Shere Afghan on Shahriar, the youngest son of the emperor, and, in the hope of retaining her power under his weak administration, determined to secure the reversion of the throne for him To remove Shah Jehan out of the way, she persuaded Jehangeer to employ his great military talents in recovering Candahar from the Persians, who had recently conquered it. Shah Jehan was fully aware of the danger of quitting India, and began to stipulate for securities. His request was pronounced treasonable; all his jageers were confiscated,
1622 and he was driven into revolt, and Mohabet, the most eminent of the imperial commanders, was directed to proceed against him. After a partial and indecisive action in Rajpootana, Shah Jehan injudiciously retreated to the Deccan, where he arrived with the loss of his prestige. Malik Amber and the kings of Beejapore and Golconda refused him any assistance; his own troops began to desert his standard, and he retired to Telingana. On reaching
1624 Masulipatam, he marched along the coast up to Bengal, and, having taken possession of that province as well as of Behar, advanced towards Allahabad. Mohabet, who had lost sight of him, on hearing of his progress, hastened from the south to the banks of the Ganges, and Shah Jehan was obliged a second time to fly to the Deccan, but was pursued with such vigour that, seeing his fortunes desperate, he

Intrigues of Noor Jehan.

sought reconciliation with his father, for which he was obliged to give his two sons as hostages.

A new scene now opens in this drama. Mohabet, the greatest subject in the empire, and the prime favourite of the emperor, manifested no disposition to second the wishes of Noor Jehan, and raise her son-in-law, a prince devoid of energy or ability, to the throne, and she resolved on his destruction. A charge of embezzlement during his last expedition was trumped up against him, and he was summoned to the court to answer it. He came, but with a body of 5,000 Rajpoots. He had recently betrothed his daughter to a young nobleman, without having first obtained the usual consent of the emperor. Jehangeer summoned the youth into his presence, and, in a fit of brutal rage, ordered him to be stripped naked and scourged with thorns before the courtiers. Mohabet perceived that his ruin was determined on, and resolved to strike the first blow. The emperor was then on his way to Cabul, and was encamped on the Hydaspes, which the army crossed in the morning on a bridge. The emperor had not recovered from the debauch of the previous night, and remained behind with a slender guard, when Mohabet proceeded to his tent, and seized his person. Seeing himself helpless, he submitted to mount an elephant, together with his cupbearer and his goblet, and to proceed to Mohabet's tent.

A.D. 1625

Noor Jehan's persecution of Mohabet.

Mohabet seizes the emperor.

Noor Jehan crossed the river in disguise the next morning, and joined the army which she led to the rescue of the emperor; but the Rajpoots had broken down the bridge, and she advanced at the head of her troops to a ford which had been discovered, mounted on a large elephant, and fully armed. The struggle was long and deadly. In spite of all her efforts, her troops were precipitated into the stream by the shower of balls, rockets, and arrows which Mohabet's Rajpoots discharged from their vantage ground. Her elephant was assailed with particular violence, and of the numerous missiles aimed at her, one at length struck the infant son of her daughter, whom she carried in her lap. The ford became a scene of universal confusion. The elephant driver was killed, and the elephant was wounded and borne down the stream back to the opposite bank. Her female attendants hastened to the spot, and found the howda, or seat, covered with blood, and the empress employed in binding up the wound of the infant. Noor Jehan yielded to necessity, and joined the emperor

Noor Jehan rescues him.

in his captivity, and affected to be reconciled to Mohabet, who had assumed the command of the army, and marched on to Cabul. There the fertile genius of the empress was employed in cajoling Mohabet and throwing him off his
A.D. guard, while, by a series of skilful manœuvres, she gradually,
1626 and without observation, assembled a body of troops. Seeing his position becoming daily less secure, Mohabet was led to make her offers of submission. She agreed to condone his revolt on condition that he should proceed in pursuit of Shah Jehan, who had fled to Sinde. Mohabet dreaded a reign of weakness under Shahriar, and resolved to join Shah Jehan; and Noor Jehan, on hearing of this defection, ordered him to be hunted through the empire, and set a price on his head. But all her plans of ambition were at once extinguished by the death of the emperor. After his liberation, he proceeded from Cabul to Cashmere, but his constitution was exhausted by a life of indulgence; he was seized with a violent fit of asthma, and died on his way to Lahore, on the 28th October, 1627,
1627 in the sixtieth year of his age, and the twenty-second of his reign. He was contemporary with James the First of England. Not only were their reigns of the same duration, but there was a remarkable similarity in their characters. They were both equally weak and contemptible, both the slaves of favourites and drink; and by a singular coincidence, they both launched a royal decree against the use of tobacco, then recently introduced into England and India, and in both cases with equal success.

Death of Jehangeer.

SECTION II.

SHAH JEHAN AND AURUNGZEBE.

1627 On the death of Jehangeer, Asof Khan, one of the chief ministers of the cabinet, the brother of Noor Jehan, though he owed his position to her influence, determined, from a patriotic motive, to support Shah Jehan, and invited him to the capital, while at the same time he placed the empress under restraint. Her power expired with the death of her husband, and she retired from the world upon an annuity of twenty lacs a year, and passed the remaining twenty years of her life in cherishing his

Accession of Shah Jehan.

memory. Shah Jehan was proclaimed emperor at Agra, and rewarded the instruments of his elevation—Asof Khan and Mohabet—with offices of the highest dignity. His reign was distinguished by a passion for magnificence, A.D.
which was developed on the very first anniversary of his 1627
accession, when he was weighed against silver and gold and precious substances; vessels filled with jewels were waved over his head—from the superstitious notion of averting misfortune—and then scattered on the floor for a general scramble. The expense of this festival was computed at a crore and a half of rupees.

Wars in the Deccan.

The first ten years of his reign were occupied with military operations in the Deccan. The genius of Malik Amber had restored much of its former splendour to the kingdom of Ahmednugur, but he had recently died at the age of eighty, and the country was distracted by factions. The king of Beejapore, Ibrahim Adil Shah, renowned for the grandeur of his buildings, had died about the same time, bequeathing to his successor a flourishing country and an army, reported, not without exaggeration, at 80,000 horse and upwards of 200,000 infantry, sufficiently powerful to cope for years with the whole strength of the Mogul empire. The king of Golconda was employed in extending his authority over his Hindoo neighbours to the east and the south. These three Deccan monarchies had recovered their former limits, and of all the conquests made by Akbar nothing remained to the crown of Delhi but the eastern portion of Candesh and Berar. The war in the Deccan on which Shah Jehan entered in the second year of his reign, was occasioned by
the revolt of Jehan Lodi, an Afghan adventurer of low birth, 1628
but great courage and enterprise, who had commanded the imperial troops in the Deccan, but was disliked and mistrusted by the emperor. Suspecting some sinister designs on his part, he marched out of his palace at Agra at the head of 2,000 of his veteran Afghans, with his kettledrums beating a note of defiance, and fought his way to the Deccan, where he was joined by many adherents, and supported by the king of Ahmednugur. The revolt became so serious that Shah Jehan ordered three armies into the field and proceeded in person to the Deccan. The king of Ahmednugur was defeated. Jehan Lodi sought aid of the king of Beejapore and was refused, and he then endeavoured to make his way to Afghanistan, but was brought to bay in Bundlecund, where he fell pierced with

wounds, after having performed prodigies of valour at the head of 400 men who adhered to his fortunes to the last.

Moorteza Nizam, of Ahmednugur, after his defeat, had fallen out with his minister Futteh Khan, the son and successor of Malik Amber, and imprisoned him, but, when threatened with disorder and ruin on all sides, restored him to power. The ungrateful

Extinction of Ahmednugur.

A.D. 1630 Abyssinian rewarded his kindness by putting him and his chief adherents to death, and then, after placing an infant on the throne, offered his submission to the emperor. But Shahjee, the Mahratta chief, who had risen to great importance under Malik Amber, found himself strong enough to set up a new pretender to the throne, and obtained possession of the greater portion of the country. The Deccan was thus as far from being subjugated as ever, and Shah Jehan deemed it necessary to undertake another expedition

1637 in person. Shahjee was driven from Ahmednugur, and the whole force of the empire was brought to bear on Beejapore, the king of which had made common cause with Ahmednugur, and now maintained a struggle of five years with the imperial generals. To baffle their efforts, he created a desert for more than twenty miles round his capital, destroying every particle of food and every vestige of forage. Both parties became at length weary of this war, and listened to terms of accommodation. The result of this conflict of eight years may be thus briefly summed up: the kingdom of Ahmednugur was extinguished, after a century and a half of independence; a portion of it was ceded to Beejapore for a tribute of twenty lacs a year, and the remainder absorbed in the Mogul dominions, while the king of Golconda consented to pay an annual subsidy.

1637 Shah Jehan was soon after gladdened by the recovery of Candahar. Ali Merdan, the governor under the Persians, was driven into revolt by the tyranny of his sovereign, and made over the town and territory to the Moguls. He was taken into the service of Shah Jehan, and employed in many military expeditions beyond the Indus, but his fame rests on the public works he constructed in India, and more especially, on the noble canal near Delhi, which still preserves the grateful remembrance of his name. After several years of repose, the emperor determined to prosecute the dormant claims of his family on the distant regions of Balkh and

Candahar and Ali Merdan.

Budukshan, and he proceeded to Cabul. Ali Merdan and Morad, the emperor's son, reduced Balkh, but it was immediately after overrun by the Uzbeks. Raja Juggut Sing was then sent with 14,000 Rajpoots, and they manifested their loyalty to a just and tolerant government by crossing the Indus, in spite of their Hindoo prejudices, traversing the lofty passes of the Hindoo Coosh, constructing redoubts by their own labour—the raja himself taking an axe like the rest—and encountering the fiery valour of the Uzbeks in that snowy region. Aurungzebe, the emperor's third son, was subsequently sent there, but, after gaining a great victory was obliged to retreat in the depth of winter, and with the loss of the greater part of his army; after which the emperor had the moral courage to relinquish this ill-advised enterprise.

Two years after, the king of Persia, marched down on A.D.
Candahar, and recaptured it, and Aurungzebe was directed 1647
to recover it, but was obliged to retire after having in vain besieged it four months; a second expedition led by him, and a third by his brother Dara, were equally unsuccessful. These failures were followed by two years of tranquillity, 1653 to 1655
during which Shah Jehan completed the revenue settlement of the possessions he had acquired in the Deccan.

Renewal of the war in the Deccan.

The year 1655 marks an important era in the history of Mahomedan India;—the renewal of the war in the Deccan, which continued for fifty years to exhaust the resources of the Mogul empire, and hastened its downfall. During the eighteen years of peace which followed the treaty made with Ibrahim Adil Shah, the king of Beejapore, he had devoted his attention to the construction of those splendid palaces, mausoleums, and mosques by which his reign was distinguished, and to the conquest of the petty Hindoo chiefs in the south. The king of Golconda had punctually paid his subsidy, and manifested every disposition to cultivate the favour of the emperor. The Deccan was tranquil, but in an evil hour Aurungzebe was appointed viceroy, and resolved to efface the disgrace of his repulse from Candahar by the subjugation of its two remaining kingdoms. An unexpected event gave him the desired pretext. Meer Joomla, born of indigent parents at Ispahan, had repaired to Golconda, and amassed prodigious wealth in commerce and maritime enterprises. He was taken into the service of the king, and, having risen to the office of vizier by his extraordinary talents, led the armies to the southern provinces of the

Deccan, and established the royal authority over many of the Hindoo chieftains. While absent on one of these expeditions his son incurred the displeasure of the king, and Meer Joomla, unable to obtain any consideration from him, determined to throw himself on the protection of the Moguls.

Aurungzebe was but too happy to take up the quarrel; and, with the permission of his father, sent a haughty mandate to the king to grant redress to the youth, to which the king replied by placing him in confinement and confiscating all the estates of the family. Shah Jehan ordered his son to enforce compliance with his command by the sword, and he advanced to Hyderabad, now become the capital of the kingdom, with the most friendly assurances. The king was preparing a magnificent entertainment for his reception, when he was treacherously attacked and obliged to seek refuge in the hill fort of Golconda. Hyderabad was plundered and half burnt, and the king was constrained to submit to the humiliating terms imposed on him of bestowing his daughter on one of Aurungzebe's sons with a rich

Aurungzebe's proceedings in the Deccan.

A.D. dowry, and paying a crore of rupees as the first instalment
1656 of an annual tribute; but the emperor, who had a conscience, remitted a considerable portion of it. Aurungzebe now prepared for a wanton attack on Beejapore. A pretext was found in the assertion that the youth who had recently succeeded to the throne was not the real issue of the late king, and that to the emperor belonged the right of deciding the succession. Aurungzebe suddenly burst upon the territory while the bulk of the army was absent in the Carnatic; two important forts were captured, and the capital was invested. The king was obliged to sue for peace on reasonable terms, which were peremptorily refused, and the extinction of the dynasty appeared inevitable, when an event occurred in the north which gave it a respite of thirty years. News came posting down to the Deccan that Shah Jehan was at the point of death, and that the contest for the empire had begun; and
1657 Aurungzebe was obliged to hasten to the capital to look after his own interests.

His attack on Beejapore.

Shah Jehan had four sons. Dara, the eldest, had been declared his heir and entrusted with a share of the government. He possessed great talents for government, and an air of regal dignity; he was brave and frank, but haughty and rash. Soojah, the second,

Shah Jehan's sons.

though addicted to pleasure, had been accustomed to civil and military command from his youth, and was at this time viceroy of Bengal, which he had governed with no little ability and success for twenty years. Aurungzebe, the third, was the ablest and most ambitious, as well as the most subtle of the family. Morad, the youngest, though bold and generous, was little better than a sot. Dara was a freethinker of Akbar's school. Aurungzebe was a fierce bigot, and courted the suffrage of the orthodox by reprobating the infidelity of Dara. The claims of primogeniture had always been vague and feeble in the Mogul dynasty, and were, moreover, always subordinate to the power of the sword. When therefore four brothers, each with an army at his command, aspired to the throne, a conflict was inevitable.

A.D. 1657

Soojah takes the field.

Soojah was the first in the field, and advanced from Bengal towards Delhi. Morad, the viceroy of Guzerat, seized the public treasury and assumed the title of emperor. Aurungzebe extorted a large sum from the king of Beejapore, and moved northward to unite his fortunes with Morad, whom, with his usual craft, he succeeded in cozening. He saluted him as emperor, and congratulated him on his new dynasty, declaring that, as for himself, he was anxious to renounce the vanities of the world, and proceed on pilgrimage to Mecca, as soon as he had succeeded in releasing his father from the thraldom of the godless Dara. Morad was so simple as to give credit to these professions, and their united armies advanced to the capital. Dara prepared to meet both attacks, and sent raja Jey Sing, of Jeypore, and his own son, to oppose Soojah, and raja Jeswunt Sing to encounter Aurungzebe. The selection of two Hindoo generals to command the armies which were to decide the fortunes of the Mogul throne affords the strongest evidence of the principle of fidelity which the generous policy of Akbar and his two successors had inspired in the Hindoo mind. At this juncture, Shah Jehan recovered his health, and endeavoured to resume his authority; but it was too late. Soojah was defeated and obliged to fly to Bengal, and, the year after, was pursued by Meer Joomla, and obliged to seek refuge in Aracan, where he was basely murdered, together with the whole of his family. Aurungzebe defeated the Rajpoot raja at Oojein, and then advanced to Agra, where Dara met him with a superior army, but, contrary to the wise advice of his father, hazarded an

Dara defeats Soojah.

Shah Jehan's recovery.

A.D. 1658 engagement in which he was completely overpowered, and fled. Three days after, Aurungzebe entered the capital in triumph, deposed his father, and mounted the throne.

Shah Jehan deposed.

The character of Shah Jehan is thus described by his native biographer :—"Akbar was pre-eminent as a warrior "and a lawgiver; Shah Jehan for the incomparable "order and arrangement of his finances, and the "internal administration of the empire. But although the "pomp of his court and his state establishments were such "as had never been seen before in India, there was no in-"crease of taxation, and no embarrassment to the treasury." By the general consent of historians, the country enjoyed greater prosperity during his reign than under any previous reign, and it has therefore been characterised as the golden era of the Mogul dynasty. This is to be attributed to that respite from the ravages of war which afforded scope for the pursuits of industry; for though engaged in foreign wars, his own dominions enjoyed uninterrupted repose. He was the most magnificent prince of the house of Baber; but in nothing was the splendour of his tastes more visible than in the buildings he erected. He contributed to the grandeur of many of the cities of India by the construction of noble palaces. It was he who founded the new city of Delhi, in which his castellated palace, with its spacious courts, and marble halls, and gilded domes, was the object of universal eulogy. Of that palace, the noblest ornament was the far-famed peacock throne, blazing with emeralds, rubies, and diamonds, the value of which was estimated by one of the European jewellers of his court at six crores of rupees. To him also the country was indebted for the immaculate Taj Mehal, the mausoleum of his queen, the gem of India, and the admiration of the world. But all his establishments were managed with such vigilance and care, that after defraying the cost of his numerous expeditions, he left in his treasury, according to his native biographer, a sum not short of twenty-four crores of rupees, though the annual income of the empire did not exceed thirty.

Character of Shah Jehan.

Aurungzebe having thus obtained possession of the capital and the treasury, threw off the mask. He no longer talked of renouncing the world and becoming a pilgrim, but assumed all the powers of government, and took the title of Alumgeer, the Lord of the World. His father was placed in

Aurungzebe disposes of his brothers.

honourable captivity in his own palace, where he was
treated with the greatest respect, and survived his depo-
sition seven years; but Aurungzebe did not consider his
throne secure while there remained any member of his A.D.
family to disturb it. Morad was invited to an entertain- 1658
ment, and allowed to drink himself into a state of helpless-
ness, when he was taken up and conveyed to the fort of
Agra. Soojah was chased by Meer Joomla out of India.
Dara fled to Lahore, but was driven from thence to
Guzerat, where he obtained aid from the governor, and was 1660
enabled to advance against the emperor, but was defeated,
and sought refuge with the raja of Jun, whom he had
formerly laid under great obligations. That ungrateful
chief, however, betrayed him to his vindictive brother, who
paraded him on a sorry elephant through the streets of
Delhi, where he had recently been beloved as a master.
A conclave of Mahomedan doctors was convened, who
gratified the emperor's wishes by condemning him to death
as an apostate from the creed of the Prophet. His body
was exhibited to the populace on an elephant, and his head
was cut off and carried to Aurungzebe. His son, Soliman,
was betrayed by the raja of Cashmere, and, like his
father, was paraded through the streets of the capital, but
with his hands bound in gilded fetters; and his noble bearing
and his deep calamity are said to have moved the spectators
to tears. He and his younger brother, together with a son
of Morad, were consigned to death in the dungeons of
Gwalior. Morad himself, after a mock trial for some exe-
cution he was said to have ordered when viceroy of
Guzerat, was likewise put to death.

Aurungzebe had thus in the space of three years secured,
to all appearance, the stability of his power by the con-
finement of his father, and the destruction of his brothers
and their families, when his own life was threatened by a
dangerous attack of illness, and his court was filled with
intrigues while he lay helpless on his couch. One
party espoused the cause of his eldest son, Muazzim,
and another that of Akbar, his brother, while the rajah
Jeswunt Rao advanced from Rajpootana and Mohabet
from Cabul, to liberate and reinstate Shah Jehan. But
Aurungzebe, having passed the crisis of the disease,
summoned the officers of his court to renew their alle-
giance to him, and his recovery dissolved all these disloyal 1662
projects.

A short time previous to the illness of the emperor,

Meer Joomla, who had been appointed governor of Bengal, assembled a large army and proceeded up the Brumhapooter, for the conquest of Assam, and eventually of China. The capital was reduced without difficulty, but the rains set in with extraordinary violence; the river rose beyond its usual limits, and the whole country was flooded. The supplies of the army were cut off, and a pestilence completed its disasters, while Meer Joomla was obliged to retreat, and was pursued by the exasperated Assamese. He returned to Dacca in disgrace, and died there at a very advanced age, leaving behind him the reputation of the ablest statesman and general of that age of action. In the letter of condolence which the emperor sent to his son, on whom he conferred all his father's honours, he said, "You have lost a father, and I, the greatest and most dangerous of my friends." After the recovery of Aurungzebe, it became necessary for him to send an army to check the devastations of the Mahrattas; and the reader's attention must now be called to the origin and progress of this nation, which rose to dominion on the ruins of the Mogul empire, and for more than a century swayed the destinies of India.

Meer Joomla in Assam.

A.D. 1663

SECTION III.

RISE AND PROGRESS OF THE MAHRATTAS.

THE country inhabited by the Mahrattas, designated in the Hindoo shasters, Muharastra, is generally considered to extend from the Wurda on the east to the sea coast on the west, and from the Satpoora range on the north down to a line drawn due east from Goa. The salient feature of the country is the Syhadree mountains, called the ghauts, which traverse it from north to south at a distance of from thirty to fifty miles from the sea, and which rise to the height of 4,000 or 5,000 feet above its level. The strip of land along the sea coast is called the Concan. The inhabitants are of diminutive stature, and present a strong contrast to the noble figure of the Rajpoot, but they are sturdy, laborious, and persevering, and distinguished for cunning. "The Rajpoot is the most worthy antagonist, "the Mahratta the most formidable enemy." This mountain region was difficult of access, and its salient points were

Rise of the Mahrattas.

strengthened by fortifications. For centuries the Mahrattas had been known as plodding accountants and managers of villages and districts, and it was not till the sixteenth century that they came to be noticed as soldiers. Their country was comprised within the territories of Beejapore and Ahmednugur, and the two kings, who were incessantly at war with each other, or with their neighbours, were happy to employ the Mahratta chiefs in raising levies of their hardy countrymen, each one commanding his own body of free lances. It was the wars which raged for a century in the Deccan which cradled their military prowess, and no small portion of the national aristocracy trace their origin to the distinction gained in these conflicts and the lands they acquired; but it was chiefly under Malik Amber that they made the most rapid strides to military and political importance. A community of village clerks and husbandmen was transformed into a nation of warriors, and it only required a master spirit to raise them to empire. Such a spirit appeared in Sevajee.

Origin of Shahjee.

Mallojee Bhonslay was a man of ignoble rank, but a valiant captain of horse in the service of the king of Ahmednugur at the beginning of the seventeenth century, and obtained from the venal court the jageers of Poona, Sopa and some other districts. His son Shahjee inherited the jageers on his death in 1620, and A.D.
augmented his military force and his importance by a close 1620
alliance with Malik Amber. Nine years after he joined the revolt of Jehan Lodi, already mentioned, but deserted his cause when it began to wane, and went over to the Moguls, by whom he was rewarded with the title of a commander of 5,000, and the confirmation of his jageer. Soon after he again changed sides, and on the capture of the young king was sufficiently strong to set up a pretender and obtain possession of all the districts of the kingdom, from the sea to the capital. After a warfare of three years with the imperial troops, he was driven out of the country, and having obtained an asylum at the court of Beejapore, was entrusted with an expedition to the Carnatic. His success was rewarded with the extensive jageers in the vicinity of Bangalore, which he had conquered, and he formed the design of establishing an independent Hindoo kingdom in the extreme south of the peninsula, resigning his Poona jageer to his son Sevajee.

Sevajee, the founder of the Mahratta empire, was born 1627
in 1627, and—his father having taken a second wife—was

placed under the tutelage of Dadajee Punt, a Brahmin, who, in conformity with the national usage in a community in which all the chiefs were illiterate, managed the affairs of the estate. Sevajee, who was never able to read or write, became expert in the use of the weapons required in the hills, and in all manly exercises, and an accomplished horseman. He likewise grew up a devout and rigid Hindoo, with a profound veneration for brahmins and a cordial hatred of mahomedans. His young imagination was kindled by the recital of the

Birth and early life of Sevajee.

A.D. national epics, and he longed to emulate the exploits cele-
1643 brated in them. At the age of sixteen, he formed an association of youths of wild and lawless habits, with whom he engaged in hunting or marauding expeditions, and thus became familiar with every path and defile in the hills. Having trained the inhabitants of his native glens, the Mawulees, to arms and discipline, he commenced his career
1646 of ambition at the age of nineteen by capturing the hill fortress of Torna, and the next year erected the fort of Rajgurh, which became his headquarters. These proceedings roused the attention of the king of Beejapore, and Shahjee, to whom the jageer belonged, was called to account for them. He remonstrated with Dadajee Punt, the guardian of his son, who entreated Sevajee to desist from a course which must inevitably bring destruction on the family; but the old man perceived that the purpose of his pupil was not to be shaken, and, worn out with age, disease, and anxiety, sunk into the grave; but just before his death is said to have sent to Sevajee, and advised him to prosecute his schemes of independence, to protect brahmins, kine, and husbandmen, and to preserve the Hindoo temples from violation.

Captures the fort of Torna

Sevajee immediately took possession of the jageer, and
1648 with the treasure which had been accumulated by his guardian, augmented his force, and within two years extended his authority over thirty miles of territory, attacked a convoy of royal treasure and carried off three lacs of pagodas to his eyrie in the mountains. The audacity of these and similar proceedings roused the indignation of the Beejapore monarch, who seized the father Shahjee, and threatened him with death. Sevajee, then twenty-two, entered into a negotiation with the emperor Shah
1649 Jehan on his father's behalf, which is believed to have saved him from a cruel death, though he was detained for four years at Beejapore, till the increasing disorders in the Carnatic

Sevajee's acquisitions.

induced the king to release him and send him back to his government. During the period of his father's detention, Sevajee discreetly abstained from further encroachments, but renewed them on his release, and by an act of base treachery, which has inflicted a deep stain on his memory, caused two chieftains of Jowlee to be assassinated.

While Aurungzebe was engaged in hostilities with Beejapore, Sevajee professed himself a devoted servant of the throne of Delhi, and obtained a confirmation of his title to the lands he had wrested from the empire. But no sooner had the prince set his face towards Delhi to secure the crown, than the Mahratta chief began to ravage the Mogul territories. To extend his operations to a more distant sphere, he likewise organised that corps of light horse which afterwards became the scourge of India. At the same time, he took a body of mahomedans into his service, but placed them under Mahratta officers. The success of Aurungzebe's efforts to obtain the throne gave just alarm to Sevajee, and he sent an envoy to Delhi to excuse his incursions and to conciliate the emperor, and offered to protect the Mogul interests in the Concan if they were intrusted to his charge. Aurungzebe considered that the security of these possessions in the Deccan was likely to be promoted by encouraging the Mahratta adventurer, and consented to his occupation of that maritime province; but in his attempt to take possession of it, Sevajee experienced the first reverse he had ever sustained.

His intercourse with Aurungzebe.

A.D. 1657

The court of Beejapore was at length roused to the danger of these incessant encroachments, which had been increasing in audacity for fourteen years, and sent Afzool Khan with a body of 12,000 horse and foot and a powerful artillery to suppress them. He was a vain and conceited nobleman, and Sevajee determined to destroy him by treachery. He professed a humble submission to the king, and offered to surrender all the territories he had usurped if he were allowed to hope for forgiveness. Afzool Khan was thrown off his guard by this flattery, and agreed to give a meeting to Sevajee with only a single attendant. Sevajee performed his religious devotions with great fervour, and advanced with all humility to the interview, and while in the act of embracing Afzool, plunged a concealed weapon into his bowels, and despatched him with his dagger. The troops of the murdered general were suddenly surrounded by a body of

1659

Afzool Khan assassinated.

Mahrattas placed in ambush, and routed with the loss of all their equipments. The success of this stratagem, notwithstanding the atrocity of the deed, obtained the admiration of his countrymen beyond many of his other exploits, and the weapon was carefully preserved as an heirloom in the family. Sevajee followed up his victory by plundering the country to the very gates of the capital. The king then took the field in person, and recovered many of the forts and much of the territory he had lost. The war was protracted for two years with varied success, but generally in favour of the Mahrattas. A reconciliation was at length effected, and a treaty concluded through the mediation of Shahjee, who paid a visit to his son after an absence of twenty years. He congratulated him on the progress he had made towards the establishment of a Hindoo power,
A.D. and encouraged him to persevere in the course he had
1662 begun. At this period, Sevajee, then in his thirty-fifth year, was in possession of the whole coast of the Concan, extending four degrees of latitude, and of the ghauts from the Beema to the Wurda. His army, consisting of 50,000 foot and 7,000 horse, was out of all proportion to his territories and his resources, but he was incessantly engaged in war, and made war support itself by his exactions.

Sevajee being now at peace with Beejapore, let loose his
1663 predatory bands on the Mogul possessions, and swept the country to the suburbs of Aurungabad. The emperor appointed his own maternal uncle, Shaista Khan, to the viceroyalty of the Deccan, with orders to reduce Sevajee to submission. He captured Poona, and took up his residence in the house in which Sevajee had passed his childhood, and the Mahratta chief conceived the design of assassinating the Mogul general in his bed. He got up a marriage procession, and entered the town in disguise with thirty followers, and proceeding unperceived to the palace, suddenly attacked its inmates. The viceroy escaped the assault with the loss of two fingers, but his guards were cut down. Sevajee, baffled in his project, returned to his encampment amidst a blaze of torches. This daring exploit was so completely in harmony with the national character as to be viewed with greater exultation than some of his most famous victories.

Shaista Khan attacks Sevajee.

1664 The operations of Sevajee were now extended to a bolder enterprise. A hundred and fifty miles from Poona lay the city of Surat, the greatest emporium of commerce on the western coast, and two of the firms in the

Attack of Surat.

town were considered the most wealthy merchants in the world at the time. It was, moreover, the chief port to which devout Mahomedans resorted from all parts of India to embark on pilgrimage to Mecca. Sevajee suddenly appeared before it with 4,000 of his newly raised cavalry, and after plundering it leisurely for six days, returned to A.D.
his capital. He met with no resistance except from the 1664
European factories. Sir George Oxenden, the English chief, defended the property of the East India Company, and likewise of the natives under his protection, with such valour and success as to extort the applause of Aurungzebe. It is worthy of note that this was the first occasion on which European soldiers came into collision with native troops, and that the result filled both Hindoos and Mahomedans with astonishment.

Sevajee creates a fleet.

On his return from this expedition, Sevajee heard of the death of his father at the age of seventy, and immediately assumed the title of raja, and struck the coin in his own name. Finding that his power would not be complete unless he could obtain the command of the sea, he had been employed for some time in constructing a navy, and while his troops were employed in ravaging the Mogul territories on land, his fleet was engaged in capturing the Mogul vessels bound to the Red Sea and exacting heavy ransom from the opulent pilgrims. In February, 1665, he secretly drew together a fleet consisting of eighty-eight vessels and embarked with 4,000 troops to Barcelore, then a great trade mart on the Malabar coast, where he obtained large booty, and returned to his capital before it was known that he had left it. On his return, he found that a large Mogul army commanded by the renowned Rajpoot raja Jeysing, and the general Dilere Khan, had entered his territories. Aurungzebe, an intense bigot, had felt greater indignation against Sevajee for obstructing the progress of the devout pilgrims than for any of his audacious assumptions of power, and the largest force yet sent against him now entered his territories, and reduced him to such straits that he was constrained to have recourse to negotiations.

He is attacked by Jeysing and Dilere Khan.

They resulted in the memorable "Convention of Poorundur," 1665
in which it was stipulated that he should restore all the forts and districts he had taken from the Moguls with the exception of twelve, which he was to retain as a jageer, and that his son Sambajee should hold rank as a noble in the command of 5,000 men. But he dexterously inserted a

clause in the treaty granting him, in lieu of certain pretended claims on the old Nizam Shahee state, assignments of a fourth and a tenth of the revenue,—termed by him the *Chout* and *Surdeshmookee*,—of certain districts above the ghauts, the charge of collecting which he took on himself. So eager was he to obtain the imperial authority for this grant, that he offered a sum of forty lacs of pagodas for it, and intimated his intention of visiting the emperor at Delhi, and "his desire to kiss the "royal threshold." This is the first mention of the celebrated claim of *chout*, which the Mahrattas marched throughout India to enforce. In the communication which Aurungzebe addressed him on this occasion, no allusion was made to this claim, the insidious tendency, or even the import, of which the imperial cabinet could not comprehend, and Sevajee assumed that the principle was tacitly conceded.

Origin of the Chout.

Sevajee had now entered the service of the Moguls and lost no time in marching with 10,000 horse and foot against
A.D. 1665 Beejapore, though his half-brother commanded the Mahratta contingent in its services. Aurungzebe was gratified with his success and invited him to court, to which he repaired with an escort of 1,500 troops. But he found himself regarded by the emperor in the light of a troublesome captain of banditti, whom it was politic to humour, and he was presented at the durbar with nobles of the third rank. He left the "presence" with ill-concealed indignation, and is said to have wept and fainted away. It became the object of the emperor to prevent his leaving Delhi, and his residence was beleagured, but he contrived to elude the vigilance of his guards and made his escape in a hamper, and reached Rajgurh in the disguise of a
1666 pilgrim, with his face smeared with ashes. The Rajpoot commander in the Deccan was not insensible to the influence of money, and Sevajee was thus enabled through him to make his peace with Aurungzebe, who acknowledged his title of raja and even made some addition to his jageer. Having now a season of greater leisure than he had yet enjoyed, he spent the years 1668 and 1669 in revising and completing the internal arrangements of his government, and nothing gives us a higher idea
1668 and 1669 of his genius than to find a rough soldier, who was unable to read or write, and who had for twenty years been employed in predatory warfare, establishing a form of government and a system of civil polity so well suited to the consolidation of a great kingdom. His military

Sevajee at Delhi

Revision of his institutions.

organisation, which was equally distinguished for its rigid discipline and its strict economy, was admirably adapted to the creation of a new and predominant power in India.

Tranquillity of Hindostan.

A.D. 1666 to 1670

This was also the most prosperous period of Aurungzebe's long reign. The empire was at peace; the emperor was held in the highest esteem throughout the Mahomedan world, and received complimentary missions from the Scheriff of Mecca, the Khan of the Uzbeks, the king of Abyssinia, and the Shah of Persia. But his restless ambition again kindled the flames of war, which continued to rage, without the intermission of a single year, during the remaining thirty-seven years of his reign, and consumed the vitals of the empire. Finding it impossible to inveigle Sevajee into his power, he issued the most peremptory orders to pursue him to the death. Sevajee prepared for the conflict with unflinching resolution. He opened the campaign by the capture of two important fortresses, and, with an army of 14,000 men, again plundered Surat, where the Company's factors once more covered themselves with renown by their military energy. He overran the province of Candesh, and for the first time levied the *chout* on a Mogul province: in this instance it was simply black mail. Aurungzebe was dissatisfied with the inactivity of his general, and sent Mohabet with an army of 40,000 against Sevajee, who met his opponents for the first time in the open field and gained a complete victory, which elevated the crest of the Mahrattas, and not a little disheartened the Mogul generals.

War with Sevajee.

1672

Aurungzebe's conflict with the Khyberees and Sutnaramees

The turbulent Khyberees and Eusufzies in Afghanistan, the hereditary enemies of order and peace, had again broken out and defeated the Mogul general in the passes subsequently rendered memorable by the annihilation of a British army. The emperor determined to undertake the subjugation of these incorrigible highlanders in person, and led his army as far as Hussun Abdal, where he left the expedition to his son, who was obliged to content himself with the nominal submission of the tribes, after a bootless warfare of two years. On his return to Delhi Aurungzebe found himself involved in an unexpected and formidable difficulty. Such is the nature of the natives of India, that the peace of the country is liable to be broken any day by the most insignificant cause: the shape of a turban, or the make of a cartridge. On this occasion it was the violence of a single police officer, who insulted a sect of Hindoo fanatics called

1673

A.D. Sutnaramees. Their excitement created an émeute, and the
1676 émeute grew into a revolt. The devotees assembled in thousands, and being joined by some disaffected zemindars, defeated the troops sent against them, and obtained possession of the two provinces of Agra and Ajmere; a general revolt, therefore, appeared imminent. They gave out that they possessed the magic power of resisting bullets, and the imperial troops naturally shrank from an encounter with them, till Aurungzebe wrote out texts of the Koran with his own hand, and attached them to his standards, when the confidence of his troops was revived and the rebellion quelled.

Revival of persecution.

Akbar and his two successors had adopted the wise and generous policy of granting the Hindoos religious liberty and equality, and they served the state as zealously and faithfully as the Mahomedans, even when employed against their own countrymen. The same principle appears to have prevailed in some degree during the early period of Aurungzebe's reign, and he had formed two family alliances with Rajpoot princes; but his defeat in the Khyber, and the revolt of the fanatics, appear to have embittered his temper, and roused a feeling of bigoted animosity. No pains or penalties were inflicted on the Hindoos for the profession of their creed, but they were made to feel that they lay under the ban of the ruling power of the empire. Aurungzebe ordered that no Hindoos should in future be employed in the public service, and
1677 he reimposed the odious poll-tax, the jezzia, on infidels. His measures, however disguised, breathed the spirit of intolerance. The Hindoo temples in Bengal, and even in the holy city of Benares, were demolished, and mosques erected on the sites, and the images used as steps. These bigoted proceedings produced a feeling of disaffection in every province, but it was only in Rajpootana that they created political disturbance. Jeswunt Sing, the faithful Rajpoot general of the emperor, had died in Cabul, and as his widow and family passed through
1677 Delhi, Aurungzebe surrounded their encampment with troops, intending to detain them as hostages. They were rescued by the contrivance of Jeswunt Sing's minister, and conveyed to Joudpore; but this ungenerous treatment of the family of a devoted servant roused the indignation of the high-spirited Rajpoots, and the country was speedily in a blaze. Aurungzebe lost no time in marching into it,
1679 and obliged the rana of Oodypore to make his submission;

Revolt of the Rajpoots.

but on a second revolt, he summoned troops from every direction, and let them loose on the unhappy country. The Joudpore territory was laid waste, villages were de- A.D.
stroyed, families carried into slavery, and the inhabitants 1679
made to feel the extremities of war. The Rajpoots retaliated by plundering the mosques and burning the Koran in Malwa. The alienation of the various tribes was complete. After this period they were often at peace with the empire, and furnished their contingents of troops, whom Aurungzebe was happy to employ as a counterpoise to his Mahomedan soldiers; but that cordial loyalty to the Mogul throne which had for a century made them its most reliable champions, was extinct. It was during these disturbances that the emperor's son Akbar went over to the Rajpoots, and was encouraged by them to assume the title and functions of royalty, and to march with an army of 70,000 men against his father; but he was defeated, and fled to the Mahrattas.

Sevajee assumes royalty.

To return to Sevajee. He took advantage of the absence of Aurungzebe in the Khyber, and the death of the king of Beejapore, to annex the whole of the Concan, and likewise of a considerable tract above the ghauts. He had long struck the coin in his own name, and he now determined to proclaim his independence, and to assume all the ensigns of royalty and the pomp of a Mahomedan potentate. After many religious solemnities, 1674
on the 6th June, 1674, he was enthroned at his capital, Rajgurh, and announced himself as the "ornament of the "Kshetriyu race, and lord of the royal umbrella." He was weighed against gold, which was distributed amongst the brahmins, who found to their chagrin that he only weighed ten stone. Two years after he undertook one of the most extraordinary expeditions on Mahratta record, with the object of recovering his father's jageer in the distant south from his brother. Having concluded an armistice with the Mogul general who had charge of the operations against him, by a large douceur,

His expedition to the Deccan.

he marched to Golconda with an army of 30,000 foot and 1676
40,000 horse, and extorted a large supply of money and artillery from the king, together with an engagement to cover his territories during his absence, on condition of receiving half his acquisitions in land and money. He then proceeded to pay his devotions at the shrine of Purwuttum. Naked, and covered with ashes, he assumed the character of a devotee, and after having,

His fanaticism.

for nine days, committed various acts of superstitious folly, which at one time led his officers to doubt his sanity, he resumed the command of his army, which he had sent forward in advance. He swept past Madras, then an unnoticed factory, and captured fort after fort, not excepting even the redoubted fortress of Gingee (pronounced Jinjee) "tenable "by ten men against an army," and at Trivadey, 600 miles from his own territory, met his brother Vencajee. He held possession of Tanjore, and the other jageers bequeathed to him by his father, and refused to share them with his brother, who thereupon occupied them by force, and sent
A.D. his horse to ravage the Carnatic. The dispute between the
1678 brothers terminated in a compromise, by which Vencajee
was to retain the jageer, paying half the revenues to Sevajee, while he was to keep possession of all the conquests he had made from Beejapore. He reached Rajgurh after an absence of eighteen months, but no portion of his conquests or of his plunder did he think of surrendering to the king of Golconda.

Aurungzebe attacks Beejapore.

The next year Aurungzebe sent a formidable army to
1679 besiege Beejapore, and the regent, during the minority
of the king, invoked the aid of Sevajee, who laid waste the Mogul territories between the Beema and the Godavery, and subjected the town of Aurungabad to plunder for three days. Meanwhile, his son Sambajee, who had been placed in durance by his father for an attempt to violate the wife of a brahmin, made his escape, and went over to the Mogul general, and was received with open arms; but Aurungzebe ordered him to be sent as a prisoner to his father's camp. Sevajee renewed his exertions for the relief of Beejapore upon a fresh concession of territory; but in the midst of these events, all his plans of ambition were demolished by his death, which happened at Rajgurh, on the 5th April, 1680, in the fifty-third year of his age. Aurungzebe did not conceal his

Death and character of Sevajee.

1680 satisfaction at the death of his formidable oppo-
nent, but he did full justice to his genius. "He was," he said, "a great captain, and the only one who has had "the magnanimity to raise a new kingdom, while I have "been endeavouring to destroy the ancient sovereignties of "India; my armies have been employed against him for "nineteen years, and, nevertheless, his state has been always "increasing." That state, at his death, comprised a territory 400 miles in length and 120 in breadth. It was created by his own genius, and consolidated by a com-

munion of habits, language, and religion among his countrymen. He is one of the greatest characters in the native history of India, greater even than Hyder Ali and Runjeet Sing, who subsequently trod the same path of ambition and conquest. He did more than simply found a kingdom; he laid the foundation of a power which survived the decay of his own family, and he kindled a national spirit of enthusiasm which in a few years made the Mahrattas the arbiters of the destiny of India.

SECTION IV.

AURUNGZEBE TO MAHOMED SHAH.

AURUNGZEBE having now in a great measure subdued the opposition of the Rajpoot tribes, determined to bring the whole strength of the empire to bear on the subjugation of the Deccan. It was a wanton and iniquitous aggression, and, by a righteous retribution, recoiled on himself, and led to the downfall of his dynasty. In the year 1683 he quitted Delhi, which he was destined never to see again, with an army of unexampled magnitude. The finest cavalry was assembled from the countries beyond and within the Indus, supported by a large and well-equipped body of infantry, and several hundred pieces of artillery, under European officers. A long train of elephants, intended both for war and equipage, and a superb stud of horses accompanied the camp. There was, moreover, a large menagerie of tigers and leopards, of hawks and hounds without number. The camp, which resembled a large moving city, was supplied with every luxury the age and country could provide. The canvas walls which surrounded the emperor's personal tents were twelve hundred yards in circumference, and they contained halls of audience, courts, cabinets, mosques, oratories, and baths, all adorned with the richest silks and velvet and cloth of gold. There is no record of such extravagant luxuriousness in any modern encampment. Yet, amidst all this grandeur, the personal habits and expenditure of the emperor exhibited the frugality of a hermit. With this unwieldy army Aurungzebe advanced to Aurungabad, and, by a strange infatuation, signalised

Aurungzebe proceeds to the Deccan.

A.D. 1683

Invasion of the Concan.

his arrival in the Deccan by ordering the hateful jezzia to
A.D. be imposed on the whole Hindoo population. His first
1684 expedition was disastrous. His son Muazzim was sent to lay waste the Concan with 40,000 cavalry; the little forage that was to be found in the rocks and thickets of that wild region was speedily destroyed; the Mahratta cruisers intercepted the supplies sent from the Mogul ports; the Mahratta light horse blocked up the passes, and prevented the approach of provisions; and the wreck of this noble army, exhausted by hunger and pestilence, was happy to find shelter under the walls of Ahmednugur.

Invasion of Beejapore and Golconda.

1685 Aurungzebe then sent his son to attack Beejapore, and in this the last year of its national existence, the king and his troops defended their independence with exemplary courage. They cut off the supplies of the Mogul army, intercepted its communications, and obliged it to retire. On the failure of this expedition the emperor turned his force against Golconda, the king of which had formed an alliance with the Mahrattas. His chief minister was a Hindoo of singular ability, and had equipped an army of 70,000 men for the defence of the country; but the employment of an infidel gave offence to the bigoted Mahomedan courtiers. The minister was murdered, and Ibrahim Khan, the general, treacherously went over to the enemy with a large portion of the army. The helpless king sought refuge in the fort of Golconda; the capital, Hyderabad, was plundered for three days by the Mogul soldiers, whom their commander was unable to restrain, and the treasure which Aurungzebe had destined for his own coffers was, to his great chagrin, partitioned among them. The king was obliged to sue for
1685 peace, which was not granted him without the promise of two crores of rupees.

Conquest of Beejapore and Golconda.

1686 Aurungzebe now brought his whole strength to bear upon Beejapore. The lofty walls of the city were of hewn stone six miles in circumference, with a deep moat and a double rampart. The artillery was, as it had always been, superior to that of the Moguls, and the emperor was constrained to turn the siege into a blockade. The garrison was reduced to a state of starvation and obliged to capitulate; and on the 15th October Beejapore was blotted out of the roll of Indian kingdoms, after an independent career of a hundred and fifty years. This Adil Shahee dynasty employed its resources in works of utility or magnificence which were without a rival in

India. The majestic ruins of the palaces in the citadel, and of the mosques and tombs in the city, after two centuries of decay in an Indian climate, still attract the admiration of the traveller. "The chief feature in the scene is the "mausoleum of Mahomed Adil Shah, the dome of which, "like the dome of St. Peter's, fills the eye from every point "of view, and though entirely devoid of ornament, its "enormous dimensions and austere simplicity invest it with "an air of melancholy grandeur, which harmonises with the "wreck and desolation around it. One is at a loss in seeing "these ruins, to conjecture how so small a state could have "maintained such a capital." The fate of Golconda was not long delayed. Aurungzebe, with his usual craft, advanced into the country on pretence of a pilgrimage to the tomb of a saint, and extracted from the fears of the monarch all his treasure, even to the jewels of the seraglio, and then charged him with the crime of having employed a brahmin for his minister and formed an alliance with the infidel Mahrattas. The prince, though addicted to pleasure, defended his capital with a heroism worthy his ancestors, but it was at length taken, though only by an act of treachery, and the royal house of Kootub Shah became extinct, A.D.
after a brilliant career of a hundred and seventy years. 1687

Confusion in the Deccan.

The ambition of Aurungzebe was now consummated. His power was extended over regions which had never submitted to the sovereignty of the Mahomedans, and after seven centuries, the whole of India did unequivocally acknowledge the supremacy of a Lord Paramount. The year 1688 was the culminating point of Moslem grandeur, and likewise of its decay. The misfortunes of
Aurungzebe commenced with the fall of Golconda. The 1688
governments which had maintained public order in the Deccan had disappeared, and no system of equal vigour was established in their stead. The public authority had been maintained in the extinct states by a force of 200,000 men; the Mogul force on their subjugation did not exceed 34,000. The disbanded soldiery either joined the predatory bands of the Mahrattas, or enlisted under disaffected chiefs. There was no vital energy at the head-quarters of the emperor. Oppressions were multiplied, and no redress could be obtained. The Deccan became a scene of general confusion, and presented a constant succession of conspiracies and revolts which consumed the spirit of the Mogul army, and the strength of the empire.

Sevajee's son Sambajee, succeeded to the throne after much 1680 intrigue and opposition, and at first exhibited considerable vigour and method, but it was not long before he gave way to the ferocity of his natural disposition. He had none of his father's qualifications except his ardent bravery. He put his widow to death, and imprisoned his brother Raja Ram; he threw the ministers into irons, and beheaded those who opposed his wishes, and proceeded so far as to execute a brahmin. These atrocities alienated the great men who had contributed to build up

Sambajee's reign and cruel death.

A.D. the Mahratta power. Sambajee rendered himself still
1681 farther an object of general contempt by his infatuated attachment to a favourite, Kuloosha, a Cunouge brahmin, a man totally unfitted for the conduct of public affairs, which was entrusted to him. In the early period of his reign he
1684 took an active share in driving Prince Muazzim out of the Concan. He was engaged for several years in endeavouring to reduce the power of the Portuguese, but without success, and was incessantly in conflict with the forces of Aurungzebe. He formed an alliance with the king of Golconda, and, to create a diversion in his favour, plundered the cities of Boorhanpore and Broach, and likewise despatched bodies of Mahratta horse to the relief of the capital, but they acted without vigour. In fact, under his inefficient rule, the discipline introduced by Sevajee had been relaxed and the morale of the army deteriorated. On the extinction of the two Mahomedan powers of Beejapore and Golconda, Aurungzebe directed his whole attention to the reduction of his remaining opponent, and fort after fort was captured, while Sambajee abandoned public business, and resigned
1688 himself to sloth and pleasure. One of the emperor's generals, at length, succeeded in surprising him after a night's revel, and he was conveyed on a camel to the imperial presence. The emperor at first deemed it politic to spare his life to secure the surrender of the Mahratta
1688 fortresses, and asked him to turn Mahomedan. "Not if "you would give me your daughter in marriage," was his reply, pouring at the same time a torrent of abuse on the Prophet. Aurungzebe ordered his tongue to be cut out, deprived him of his sight, and consigned him to death with excruciating torture. He had occupied the throne for nine years, amidst the contempt of his subjects, but
1689 his tragic death excited emotions of pity amongst them, and gave a keener edge to their detestation of the Mahomedans.

The Mahrattas were now exposed to the whole power of

the Mogul empire under the immediate eye of the emperor, whose personal reputation, together with the grandeur of his establishments, and the prestige of the imperial throne, filled them with a feeling of awe, and they bent to the storm. The cabinet elected Shao, the infant son of Sambajee, to succeed him, and appointed his uncle, Raja Ram, regent. Of the great kingdom founded by Sevajee, there was only a mere vestige left in the north, and it was resolved to preserve the embers of Mahratta power by emigrating to the south. Raja Ram and twenty-five chiefs made their way in disguise to the Mahratta jageers in Tanjore with many romantic adventures carefully preserved in the ballads of the nation, and established the Mahratta court at Gingee. The regent soon after despatched two of his ablest generals with a large force, which was increased in its progress, to desolate the Mogul territories in the north, and they extended their ravages up to Satara, where Ram-chundur was left in charge of the Mahratta interests. He devised a new plan for molesting the Moguls. Among the Mahrattas the thirst for plunder was always the strongest national passion; indeed, the only word for "victory" was "the plunder of the enemy." To this predatory spirit he gave an extraordinary impulse, as well as a systematic direction, by conferring the right to levy the "*chout*" and the "*tenth*" for the state treasury on any Mahratta chieftain who could bring his followers into the field, and allowing them to appropriate the new exaction he invented of *ghaus dana*, or food and forage money, to their own use. Under this new impetus, every mountain glen and valley poured forth its tenants, and Aurungzebe, instead of having the army of a single responsible chief to deal with, had a hundred-headed hydra on his hands.

The Mahratta Court retires to Gingee.

A.D. 1689

1690

New exactions of the Mahrattas.

1692

The imperial army was ill-fitted to contend with this new swarm of assailants. Its silken commanders were not the iron generals of Akbar, and they vied with each other only in the display of extravagance. The spread of effeminate luxury had eaten up the spirit of enterprise, and there was nothing they desired so little as the sight of an enemy. There was a total relaxation of discipline. The stipend of the commanders was regulated by the number of their men, and not only was it never honestly maintained, but the ranks were filled up with miserable recruits, totally unable to cope with the Mahratta soldiers, accustomed to hard fare

Comparison of the Mogul and Mahratta armies.

A.D. and harder work. "The horse without a saddle," as the army
1692 was aptly described, "was rode by a man without clothes; "footmen inured to the same travail, and bearing all kinds "of arms, trooped with the horse; spare horses accompanied "them to bring off the booty and relieve the wounded or "weary. All gathered their daily provision as they passed. "No pursuit could reach their march. In conflict their "onset fell wherever they chose, and was relinquished even "in the instant of charge. Whole districts were in flames "before their approach was known, as a terror to others to "redeem the ravage."

Siege of Gingee.

The rallying point of the Mahrattas at this time was the fort of Gingee, the siege of which lasted as long as the siege of Troy. Zoolfikar Khan, the ablest of the Mogul generals, was sent against it, but he was too often in collusion with the Mahratta chiefs. It was during the languor of the siege that Suntajee, the Mahratta general, having defeated the imperial forces in the
1697 north, and augmented his army, appeared before it with 20,000 horse. The besieging army was besieged in its turn, and Cam-buksh, the son of the emperor, the nominal commander-in-chief at the time, was driven to conclude a humiliating convention. It was disallowed by Aurungzebe, who recalled his son and sent Zoolfikar Khan, a third time to command the army, but as he was again in communication with the garrison, the siege was protracted till the emperor threatened him with degradation if it was not successful. The fort was then assailed in earnest, and fell, but Zoolfikar connived at the escape of Raja Ram, who
1698 made his way to his native mountains, and selected Satara as the capital of the Mahratta power. He was able in time to collect a larger army than Sevajee had commanded, and he proceeded to collect what he termed the "Mahratta dues" with vigour, and the settlement of the Deccan was as distant as ever.

To meet the increasing boldness of the Mahrattas,
1699 Aurungzebe separated his army into two divisions, one to be employed in protecting the open country, the other in capturing forts. The first he entrusted to Zoolfikar, who repeatedly defeated the Mahrattas, but was unable to reduce their strength, and they always appeared more buoyant after a defeat than his own troops after a victory. Aurungzebe reserved to himself the siege of the forts, in which he was incessantly employed
1701 for five years. It is impossible to withhold our admira-

Plans of Aurungzebe.

tion of the spirit of perseverance exhibited by this octogenarian prince during these campaigns in which he was subjected to every variety of privations. Amidst all these harassing operations his vigour was never impaired. All the military movements in every part of the Deccan, in Afghanistan, in Mooltan, and at Agra were directed by the instructions he issued while in the field. With indefatigable industry he superintended all the details of administration throughout the empire, and not even a petty officer was appointed at Cabul without his sanction. But all his energy was unable to cope with the difficulties which were accumulating around him. The Rajpoots were again in open hostility, and other tribes, emboldened by his continued absence, began to manifest a spirit of insubordination. The treasury was exhausted by a war of twenty-five years' A.D.
duration, and the emperor was tormented with incessant 1705
demands for money, which he was unable to meet. The Mahrattas became more aggressive than ever, and in every direction around his camp, north and south, east and west, nothing was seen but the devastation of the country and the sack of villages. In these deplorable circumstances he made overtures to the Mahrattas, and offered them a legal title to the *chout* and the *tenth* of the revenues of the Deccan, but they rose in their demands, as might have been expected, and the negotiations were thus broken off.

He treats with the Mahrattas.

The imperial camp began to retire to Ahmednugur closely followed by the Mahrattas, who 1706
plundered up to its very precincts, and converted the retreat into an ignominious flight. Twenty years before Aurungzebe had marched from his capital in all the pride and pomp of war; he was now returning to it in a state of humiliation, with the wreck of a broken army, pursued by a victorious foe, and he expired at Ahmednugur on the 27th February, 1707.

His death. 1707

Remarks on his reign.

Of all the princes of the house of Baber, Aurungzebe is the greatest object of admiration to the native historians, and his name is invested even among Europeans with an indefinite idea of grandeur, but the illusion vanishes on a close inspection of his biography. Few characters in Indian history, whether amongst its Mahomedan or English rulers, have been more overrated. The merit of his personal bravery, his civil administration, and of his attention to business will be fully admitted, but for twenty-five years he persisted in a war of intolerance and aggression, though he must have been aware that it was sapping the foundations of the empire. He had no heart and no friend; he was crafty and suspicious, and often cruel; he mistrusted all his officers, and they repaid him by precarious loyalty. Notwithstanding his manifest abilities, the rapid decay of the empire dates from his reign, and may in some measure be traced to his personal character.

On the death of Aurungzebe, his son, prince Azim, came in to the encampment, caused himself to be proclaimed emperor, and marched towards the capital. At the same time, the eldest son, Prince Muazzim, who had

Bahadoor Shah

A.D.
1707 been nominated heir to the empire, was hastening to Delhi. The armies met in the neighbourhood of Agra, and Prince Azim was defeated and fell in action. Prince Akbar was a fugitive in Persia, and the remaining son of Aurungzebe, Cam-buksh, who was assembling troops in the Deccan, was defeated by Zoolfikar Khan, with the aid of a Mahratta contingent, and there ceased to be any rival to the throne which Prince Muazzim ascended at the age of sixty-seven, with the title of Bahadoor Shah.

The Mahrattas were unable to take advantage of these distractions by their internal dissensions. Raja Ram, the

Discord among the Mahrattas.

1700 regent, died soon after his return to Satara, and the government was administered for seven years by his widow Tara Bye, in the name of her own son. The lineal heir, Shao, the son of Sambajee, was a captive in the Mogul encampment, but treated with great kindness. Prince Azim, when starting for the capital, had released him, and afforded him the means of asserting his rights, on condition of his doing homage to the Mogul throne. Tara Bye proclaimed him an impostor, and collected an army to resist his claims, but he obtained possession of Satara and in 1708 assumed the functions of royalty. In this family contest, the Mahratta sirdars espoused opposite sides, and drew their swords on each other. In the course of five years the son of Tara Bye died; her minister superseded her authority and placed another son of Raja Ram on the throne of Kolapore, which became the capital of the junior branch of Sevajee's family, and the rival of Satara. Bahadoor conferred the viceroyalty

Rival house of Kolapore.

1708 of the Deccan on Zoolfikar, the chief instrument of his elevation, and as his presence was required at court, the administration was left in the hands of Daood Khan, a noble Patan, famous throughout the Deccan for his matchless daring and his love of strong drink, of whom

it is recorded that when he visited Madras, Mr. Pitt, the father of the first Lord Chatham, the governor, gave him a grand entertainment in the council chamber, and that the A.D.
Patan "pledged the chief largely in cordial waters and 1708
"French brandy, amidst a discharge of cannon." By the desire of his master, he granted to the Mahratta the concession of the *chout* on the six soobahs of the Deccan, which Aurungzebe in his extremity had offered them, and this arrangement, though made by a subordinate authority, kept them quiet to the end of the reign. The tranquillity of Rajpootana was secured by the same spirit of conciliation and concession to its three principal chiefs of Oodypore, Jeypore, and Joudpore.

The Sikhs.

The emperor was now called to encounter a new enemy in the north—the Sikhs. About the end of the fifteenth century, Nanuk, the founder of their religious community, taught that devotion was due to God alone, that all forms were immaterial, and that the worship of the Hindoo and the Moslem was equally acceptable to the Deity. The sect increased in numbers, but was fiercely persecuted by the bigoted Mahomedan rulers, who massacred their pontiff the year after the death
of Akbar. In 1675, Gooroo Govind, the tenth spiritual 1675
successor of Nanuk, conceived the idea of forming the Sikhs into a military as well as a religious commonwealth. He abolished all distinction of caste, but required every member of the society to be pledged as a soldier from his birth or his initiation, and to wear a peculiar dress and to cultivate his beard. He inculcated reverence for brahmins and prohibited the slaughter of cows. This union of martial and religious enthusiasm rendered the Sikhs a formidable body, and they had to maintain an arduous struggle with the Mahomedans, who captured the strongholds of the Gooroo, murdered his mother and sisters, and mutilated, slaughtered, or dispersed his followers. Still the sect grew and multiplied, and towards the close of Aurungzebe's reign, under a formidable chief of the name of Bandoo,
extended its depredations to the vicinity of Delhi. 1710
Bahadoor Shah took the field against them and drove them back to the hills.

Death of Bahadoor Shah and Jehander Shah.

On his return from this expedition he died at Lahore,
after a brief reign of five years, at the age of 1712
seventy-two. His death was followed by the usual scramble for power among his four sons, three of whom were defeated and killed. The survivor

mounted the throne with the title of Jehander Shah, and put all the members of the royal family within his reach to death; he resigned himself to the influence of a dancing girl, and indulged in the most degrading vices. His career
A.D. was cut short by his nephew, Ferokshere, the viceroy of
1713 Bengal, who marched up to Delhi, and deposed and murdered the wretched emperor, as well as the noble but crafty Zoolfikar.

Ferokshere.

Ferokshere, the most contemptible, as yet, of the princes of his line, mounted the throne, and for six years disgraced it by his vices, his weakness, and his cowardice. He owed his elevation to two brothers descended from the Prophet, and thence denominated the Syuds. Abdoolla, the eldest, was appointed vizier, and his brother, Hoosen Ali, commander-in-chief, but the emperor held them in detestation, and his reign was little else than a series of machinations to destroy them. Hoosen Ali was sent against the Rajpoot raja of Joudpore in the hope that the expedition would prove fatal to him; but he concluded an honourable peace with the prince and induced him to give the hand of one of his daughters to the emperor. The nuptials, which were celebrated with great splendour, were rendered memorable by an incident which will be noticed in a subsequent chapter.

Nizam-ool-moolk.

The office of viceroy of the Deccan had been bestowed
1714 on Ghazee-ood-deen. The family had emigrated from Tartary to seek its fortunes in India, and he had risen to distinction in the service of Aurungzebe, who granted him the title of Cheen Killich Khan, to which was now added that of Nizam-ool-moolk. He was a statesman of great ability and experience, but of still greater subtilty. During the seventeen months in which he held the office of viceroy he fomented the dissensions between the houses of Kolapore and Satara. Shao had been brought up in all the luxury of a Mahomedan seraglio, and was fonder of hunting, hawking, and fishing than of the business of the state. The Mahratta commonwealth was falling into a state of anarchy, when the genius of Ballajee Wishwanath placed the party of Shao in the ascendant, and rekindled the smouldering energies of the nation. Ballajee, a brahmin, was originally a simple village accountant, but rose through various gradations of office till he became a power in the state, and was appointed Peshwa, or prime minister. It was to his energy that the rapid expansion of the Mahratta power is to be

Ballajee Wishwanath.

attributed, and he may justly be regarded as the second founder of its greatness.

With the view of separating the two brothers, the Syuds, from each other, Ferokshere displaced Nizam-ool-moolk, and appointed Hoosen Ali viceroy of the Deccan. At the same time he sent secret instructions to the renowned Daood Khan to offer him the most strenuous opposition, and he rushed at once into the field, and attacked him with such impetuosity as to disperse his army like a flock of sheep; but in the moment of victory he was killed by a cannon ball, and the fortune of the day was changed. His devoted wife, a Hindoo princess, stabbed herself on hearing of his death. Hoosen Ali, flushed with his success, took the field against the Mahrattas, whose depredations had never ceased, but was completely defeated. In these circumstances, distracted by Mahratta encroachments on the one hand, and on the other by the hostility and intrigues of the emperor, he entered into negotiations with Ballajee Wishwanath which resulted in a convention as disgraceful to the Mogul throne, as it was fortunate for the Mahratta state. Shao was acknowledged as an independent sovereign over all the dominions which had belonged to Sevajee. The *chout* and the *tenth* of the revenues of the six soobahs in the Deccan, which were valued at eighteen crores—their assumed product in their most palmy state—were conferred on him, together with the tributary provinces of Tanjore, Mysore, and Trichinopoly, on condition that he should furnish a contingent of 15,000 troops, and be responsible for the peace of the Deccan. This was the largest stride to power the Mahrattas had yet achieved. They were furnished with a large and permanent income by these assignments on districts stretching from the Nerbudda to Cape Comorin, and from the Malabar to the Coromandel coast, the collection of which gave them a right of constant and vexatious interference with the internal adminstration of every province. An army of Mahratta officers, chiefly brahmins, was planted throughout the country with indefinite powers of exaction for the state, which they did not fail to turn also to their own profit.

Hoosen Ali.

A.D. 1716

His concessions to the Mahrattas.

1717

Ferokshere was advised to disallow the convention, and the breach between him and the Syuds became wider. Abdoolla called up his brother, who hastened to the capital, accompanied by 10,000 Mahrattas under Ballajee, and entered it without opposition. The emperor made the most abject submission, but was dragged

Death of Ferokshere.

from the interior of the zenana, where he had taken refuge, and assassinated. Two puppets were then placed on the throne, but they disappeared in a few months by disease or poison, and a grandson of Bahadoor Shah was raised to

A.D. 1719 Accession of Mahomed Shah.

the imperial dignity, and assumed the title of Mahomed Shah, the last who deserved the name of emperor of India. Weak and despicable as Ferokshere had been, his tragic death created a feeling of compassion throughout the country. The popular indignation against the Syuds was increased, and they found themselves the mark of universal execration; but the great object of their alarm was Nizam-ool-moolk, who, though he had been united with them in opposition to Ferokshere, was now alienated from their cause. He marched across the Nerbudda with a large force into the Deccan, where he had many adherents both among the Mahrattas and the Mahomedans, defeated two armies sent against him, and remained master of his position. Meanwhile, Mahomed Shah was fretting under the yoke of the Syuds, and, under the discreet guidance of his mother, formed a confederacy among his nobles to relieve himself from it. Distracted by the difficulties which accumulated around them, they resolved that Hoosen Ali should march against Nizam-ool-moolk, taking the emperor with him, while Abdoolla remained at

1720 Delhi to look after their common interests. Five days after the march commenced, a savage Calmuk, instigated by the

Hussun Ali assassinated.

confederacy, approached the palankeen of Hussun Ali, under the pretence of presenting a petition, and stabbed him to the heart. In the conflict which ensued the partizans of the emperor were victorious, and he returned to Delhi. Abdoolla, whose energy rose with his danger, set up a new emperor and marched against Bahadoor Shah, but was defeated and captured, though his life was spared in consideration of his sacred lineage.

SECTION V.

MAHOMED SHAH TO NADIR SHAH'S INVASION.

MAHOMED SHAH entered Delhi with great pomp, a free

1720 monarch a twelvemonth after he had ascended the

Proceedings of Mahomed Shah.

throne; but his reign, though long, was marked by the tokens of rapid decay. The canker worm was at the root of the august Mogul throne, and every year disclosed its ravages. He abolished the odious jezzia, and bestowed high appointments on the rajas of Jeypore and Joudpore; but the rana of Oodypore, wrapped up in his orthodox dignity, refused all intercourse with the court and sank into obscurity. Saadut Ali, a Khorasan merchant, who had taken an active share in the recent proceedings, was appointed soobadar of Oude, and laid the foundation of the royal dignity, which was extinguished in 1856. A.D. 1720

Origin of Saadut Ali, Soobadar of Oude.

The office of vizier was reserved for Nizam-ool-moolk, who repaired to the capital, but found the emperor immersed in pleasure, and so indifferent to the interests of the state as to have given the custody of the imperial signet to a favourite mistress. He endeavoured to rouse him to a sense of his responsibilities at a time when the empire was crumbling around him, but the emperor rejected all advice, and joined his dissolute companions in turning to ridicule the antiquated habits and solemn demeanour of the venerable statesman, then in his seventy- 1723
fifth year. Disgusted with the profligacy of the court, and despairing of any reform, he threw up his office and returned to his government in the Deccan. The emperor loaded him with honours on his departure, but instigated the local governor at Hyderabad to resist his authority; but he was defeated and slain, and the Nizam fixed on that city, the capital of the Kootub Sahee dynasty, as the seat of his 1724
government, and from this period may be dated the origin of the kingdom of the Nizam.

Nizam-ool-moolk.

Ballajee had accompanied Hoosen Ali with his troops to Delhi, but made his submission to Mahomed Shah, and obtained from him a confirmation of the grants which had been made by the Syud Hoosen, and returned to Satara with these precious muniments, fourteen in number, and died soon after. The political arrangements he made before his death established 1720
the predominant authority of the eight brahmins who formed the cabinet, and it was likewise extended throughout the interior, by means of the brahmin agents employed to collect "Mahratta dues." He was succeeded by his son Bajee Rao, who had been bred a soldier and a statesman, and "united the enterprise, vigour, and "hardihood of a Mahratta chief with the polished "manners and address of a Concan brahmin." The interest of the succeeding twenty years in the history of India centres in the intrigues, the alliances, and the conflicts of

Ballajee Wiswanath's acquisitions and death.

Bajee Rao and his movements.

the Mahratta statesman at Satara, and the crafty old Tartar, Nizam-ool-moolk, at Hyderabad, who made peace and war without any reference to the authority of the emperor at Delhi. Bajee Rao felt that unless employment could be found abroad for the large body of predatory horse who formed the sinews of the Mahratta power, they would be employed in hatching mischief at home. Fully aware of the weakness of the empire, he urged on his master, Shao, "to strike the trunk of the withering tree; the branches
A.D. "must fall off of themselves. Now is our time to drive
1724 "strangers from the land of the Hindoos. By directing our "efforts to Hindostan the Mahratta flag shall float, in "your reign, from the Kistna to the Attock." But Shao had been bred in the luxuriance of a Mogul seraglio, and Bajee Rao, finding his ardour ill-seconded by his effeminate sovereign, was constrained to act for himself; and thus the house of the Peshwa waxed stronger, and the house of Sevajee weaker.

Affairs of Guzerat.

Nizam-ool moolk, while vizier, had appointed his uncle, Hamed Khan, governor of Guzerat, in opposition to the court, and Sur-booland Khan was sent to expel him. Hamed defeated him with the aid of two Mahratta commanders, whom he had rewarded with a grant of the *chout* and the *tenth* of the revenues of the province. Bajee Rao took advantage of this discord to send Sindia, Holkar, and Puar, of Dhar, to levy contributions in Malwa, while he himself proceeded on the same errand to Seringapatam in the south. Alarmed by the increasing audacity of the Mahrattas, Nizam-ool-moolk endeavoured to renew the dissensions of the rival houses of Kolapore and Satara.

Dissensions between Kolapore and Satara.

They were at issue for their respective shares of the assignments granted to the Peshwa on the revenues of the six soobahs of the Deccan; and the Nizam, as the representative of the emperor, called on them to substantiate their claims before him. Bajee Rao, indignant at this attempt to interfere in the domestic affairs of the Mahratta commonwealth, assembled an army and marched against him, and though the Nizam was supported by a large body of
1727 Mahrattas, he was driven into a position which constrained him to enter upon negotiations. The Peshwa, having his eye upon the course of proceedings in Guzerat, granted him favourable terms. Sur-booland had succeeded in establishing his authority in that province, and the Peshwa was negotiating with him to obtain for himself the grant of the

chout and the *tenth* which Hamed Khan had granted to the two Mahratta generals. To expedite the bargain he sent his brother to ravage the country, and the Mogul governor was obliged to purchase peace by conceding his demands. While Bajee Rao was thus engaged, Sambajee, the ruler of Kolapore, crossed the Wurda and laid waste the territories of Shao. He was defeated, and obliged to sign an acknowledgment of his cousin's right to the whole of the Mahratta dominions, with the exception of a small A.D.
tract of country around Kolapore, to which this branch of 1730
Sevajee's family was to be confined. The principality still exists, while the kingdom of the elder branch has been absorbed in the British Empire. The Nizam now found a new instrument of mischief in Dhabaray, the Mahratta commander-in-chief, who was mortified to find that the prize of the *chout* and other dues he had obtained from Hamed in Guzerat, had been carried off by the Peshwa. Under the instigation of the Nizam, he proceeded with an army of 33,000 men towards Satara, on the pretence of re-
leasing his master, Shao, from the tyranny of Bajee Rao, but 1731
he was defeated, and fell in action. The Mahratta interests in Guzerat were then entrusted to Peelajee Gaikwar, whose immediate ancestor was a cowherd, and whose descendants still occupy the throne of Baroda.

Rise of Sindia and Holkar.

To this period also belongs the rise of the families of Holkar and Sindia, destined to play an important part in the subsequent politics of India, and whose descendants continue to wear the crowns they acquired. Mulhar Rao Holkar was the son of a herdsman who exchanged the crook for the sword, and by his daring courage recommended himself to Bajee Rao, by whom he was entrusted with the very agreeable charge of levying contributions in eighty-four villages in Malwa. Ranojee Sindia was of the caste of husbandmen, and entered the service of Ballajee as a menial, but was introduced into his body-guard, and became one of the foremost of the Mahratta chieftains in that age of enterprise. Like Holkar, he was sent to establish the Mahratta authority in Malwa, and these assignments became the nucleus of their future dominions.

Bajee Rao's incursions in Hindostan.

After the defeat of Dhabaray, the Nizam was, to a certain extent, at the mercy of Bajee Rao, but they both perceived that it would be for their common interest to come to an understanding, and they entered into a secret compact, which stipulated that the

A.D. Nizam's territories should not be molested, while Bajee Rao
1731 should be at liberty to plunder the Mogul territories in the north. He accordingly crossed the Nerbudda, and laid waste the province of Malwa. The imperial governor was at the time employed in coercing a refractory chief in Bundlecund, who called in the aid of Bajee Rao, and rewarded his services by the cession of a third of the province of
1732 Jhansi, and thus the Mahratta standard was for the first time planted on the banks of the Jumna. The government of Malwa was then bestowed on the Rajpoot raja Jeysing, whose reign was rendered illustrious by the patronage of science, the erection of the beautiful city of Jeypore, with its palaces, halls, and temples, and its noble observatory. The profession of a common faith promoted a friendly
1734 intercourse between him and Bajee Rao, the result of which was the surrender of the province to the Mahratta, with the tacit concurrence of the helpless emperor.

His increased demands.

These multiplied concessions only served, as might have been expected, to inflame the ambition and to increase the demands of the Peshwa. Great as were the resources of the Mahratta commonwealth, the larger portion of the revenues was absorbed by the different feudatories, and only a fraction reached the treasury at Satara. The magnitude of Bajee Rao's operations had involved him in debt; his troops were clamorous for pay, and the discipline of the army necessarily suffered by these arrears. He demanded of the imperial court a confirmation of the assignments granted by Sur-booland Khan on the revenues of Guzerat, of the rights he had acquired
1736 in Bundlecund, and the absolute cession of the rich province of Malwa. The feeble cabinet at Delhi endeavoured to pacify him by minor grants, which only led him to increase his claims, and he proceeded to demand the cession of all the country south of the Chumbul, together with the holy cities of Muttra, Benares, and Allahabad. To quicken the apprehensions of the emperor, he sent Holkar to plunder the Dooab, the province lying between the Jumna and the Ganges, but he was driven back by Saadut Ali, the soobadar of Oude. This was magnified into a great victory, and it was reported that the Mahrattas had been obliged to retire. "I was compelled," said Bajee Rao, "to
1737 "tell the emperor the truth, and to prove to him that I was "still in Hindostan, and to show him flames and the Mah-"rattas at the gates of his capital." He therefore took the field in person, and marching at the rate of forty miles a

day, suddenly presented himself before the gates of Delhi. The consternation in the capital may be readily conceived; A.D. but the object of Bajee Rao was not to sack the city, but 1737 to intimidate the emperor into concessions, and circumstances rendered it advisable for him to retreat to Satara.

The Mahrattas now appeared to be paramount in India, and the Nizam was considered the only man who could save the empire from extinction. He listened to the overtures of the emperor and proceeded to Delhi, where he was invested with full powers to call out all the resources of the state; but they were reduced to so low a point that the army under his personal command could only be completed to 30,000 men, with which he returned to the south. Bajee Rao crossed the Nerbudda with 80,000 men. Owing, perhaps to his great age—ninety-three—perhaps to over confidence in the great superiority of his artillery, the Nizam entrenched himself near Bhopal. Bajee Rao adopted the national system of warfare, laid waste the country, intercepted all supplies, attacked every detachment which ventured beyond the lines, and on the twenty-fifth day of the siege obliged the Nizam to sign a humiliating treaty, granting him the sove- 1738 reignty of Malwa and the territories up to the Chumbul, and engaging to use his influence to obtain from the imperial treasury the sum of half a crore of rupees, which he had not ceased to demand; but that treasure was to find a very different destination.

Defeat of the Nizam by Bajee Roa.

It was in the midst of these distractions that Nadir Shah appeared on the banks of the Indus, and India was visited with another of those tempests of desolation to which it had been repeatedly subject for some centuries. The Persian dynasty of the Sofis, which had occupied the throne for nearly two centuries, was subverted in 1720 by the Ghiljies, the most powerful tribe in Afghanistan. Shah Hossen, the last of that royal line, was besieged by them in his capital, Ispahan, then in the height of its prosperity, and after enduring for six months the extremities of misery and starvation, went out with his court in deep mourning to the Afghan camp, and surrendered his crown to Mahmood, the Afghan chief. He died at the end of two years, and was succeeded by his son Asruf. Nadir Shah, the greatest general Persia has produced, was the son of a shepherd of Khorasan, and commenced his career by collecting a band of freebooters. Finding himself, at length, at the head of a

Nadir Shah.

powerful army, he freed his native province from the
Afghans, and then constrained the Ghiljie monarch to
A.D. resign all his father's conquests in Persia. He raised
1729 Thamasp, the son of the dethroned Sofi king, to the throne;
but after expelling the Turks and the Russians from the
provinces they had conquered, deposed Thamasp and be-
1731 stowed the nominal sovereignty on his infant son, while he
himself assumed the title of king, upon the importunity, as
it was affirmed, of 100,000 nobles, soldiers, and peasants
1736 whom he had assembled on a vast plain To find employ-
ment for his troops and to gratify his own ambition and
avarice, he carried his arms into Afghanistan, and resolved
to re-annex Candahar to the Persian throne. While engaged
in the siege of that town he sent a messenger to Delhi to
demand the surrender of some of his fugitive subjects,
but, owing to the distraction of the times, the claim was
1738 neglected. A second messenger was murdered at Jellala-
bad. The Government of India had from time immemorial
paid an annual subsidy to the wild highlanders who oc-
cupied the passes between Cabul and Peshawur, and the
imperial cabinet doubtless trusted to their power to arrest
the progress of Nadir. The payment of this black mail
had, however, been for some time withheld, and they
opened the gates of India to the Persian monarch, who
crossed the Indus with 65,000 of his veteran troops and
overran the Punjab before the court of Delhi was aware
of his approach.

Capture of Delhi, and massacre.

The emperor Mahomed Shah marched to Kurnal to
meet this invasion, but experienced a fatal defeat, and pro-
ceeding to the Persian camp, threw himself on
the compassion of the conqueror. The object of
Nadir Shah was treasure and not conquest, and it is
affirmed that he was prepared to retire on the payment of
two crores of rupees; but Saadut Ali, the soobadar of Oude,
having some cause of offence with the emperor, represented
to the Persian that this was a very inadequate ransom for
so rich an empire, and that his own province alone could
afford this sum. Nadir resolved, therefore, to levy exactions
under his own eye. He entered Delhi in March, and on the
1739 succeeding day a thousand of his soldiers were massacred
upon a report of his death. He went out to restore order,
but was assailed with missiles, and one of his chiefs was
killed by his side, upon which he issued orders for a general
massacre. For many hours the metropolis presented a
scene of rapine, lust, and carnage, and 8,000 are said to

have fallen victims to his infuriated soldiery. Yet so complete was the discipline he had established that every sword was sheathed as soon as he issued the order. He took possession of all the imperial treasures, including the peacock throne; plundered the nobles, and caused every house to be sacked, sparing no cruelty to extort confessions of wealth. From the disloyal Saadut Ali he exacted the full tale of two crores, and the traitor terminated his existence by poison. The governors of other provinces were not A.D.
spared; and Nadir Shah, after having thus subjected the 1739
capital and the country for fifty-eight days to spoliation, and feeling satisfied that he had exhausted the wealth of the empire, prepared to retire with an accumulation of thirty-two crores of rupees. He restored Mahomed Shah to the throne, but annexed all the provinces west of the Indus to the crown of Persia. On his departure he issued a proclamation to the princes of India, stating that he was now proceeding to the conquest of other regions, but that if any report of their having revolted from "his dear "brother, Mahomed Shah," reached his ears, he would return and blot their names out of the book of creation.

State of India.

The Mogul power, which had been in a state of rapid decay since the death of Aurungzebe, received its death blow from the invasion of Nadir Shah, and the sack of the capital. The empire was breaking up into fragments, and the authority and the prestige of the throne was irrecoverably gone. The various provinces yielded only a nominal homage to the crown. All its possessions beyond the Indus were permanently alienated. In the extreme south of the peninsula the Mogul sovereignty was a matter of history. The Nabob of the Carnatic acknowledged no superior. The rest of the Deccan was shared between the Nizam and the Mahrattas. In the provinces of Guzerat and Malwa, the power of the Peshwa was already predominant. The allegiance of the princes of Rajpootana was very vacillating. The viceroys of Oude and Bengal, the richest provinces of India, acknowledged the emperor as their suzerain, but yielded him no obedience. Even in the vicinity of the capital, new chiefs were, as the native historian remarks, "beating the "drum of independence." The house of Baber had accomplished the usual cycle of Indian dynasties, which seldom exceeded two centuries, and its sceptre was now to pass into the hands of a company of European merchants, with the sea, and not Central Asia, for the base of its enterprise.

Having thus reached the period when the Mogul throne ceased to exercise any influence on the politics of India, we turn to the progress of the European settlements on the continent, and to the history of the East India Company, which began its career with a factory, and closed it by transferring the Empire of India to the Crown of England.

CHAPTER IV.

SECTION I.

RISE AND PROGRESS OF THE PORTUGUESE.

For five centuries the tide of Mahomedan invasion had rolled across the Indus from Central Asia, and spread from north to south. A new era now dawns upon us, ushered in by the appearance of a European fleet, and the progress is, henceforth, from south to north. The Mahomedans entered India in the spirit of conquest; the Europeans came in search of trade. The productions of the East had, from time immemorial, been a great object of desire to the inhabitants of the West, who had been accustomed to obtain them through many circuitous channels. In the middle ages the trade had enriched the republics of Venice and Genoa, and a general anxiety was created to obtain direct access to India. During the fifteenth century the spirit of maritime adventure was strongly developed in Europe, and more especially in the small but spirited kingdom of Portugal, in which great progress had been made in the science of naval architecture. This spirit was warmly encouraged by its sovereigns, who fitted out a succession of expeditions, and gradually advanced along the coast of Africa, making fresh discoveries in each voyage. At length, John II. sent three vessels, under the command of Bartholomew Dias, to discover the southern limit of the African continent. He was the first navigator to double the Cape, where the tempestuous weather he encountered led him to
A.D. 1486 Discovery of the Cape. designate it "The Cape of Storms"; but his delighted sovereign, hoping to reach India by

this route, more appropriately called it the Cape of Good Hope. Soon after, Christopher Columbus, the enterprising Genoese sailor, convinced that India was to be discovered by sailing west, offered his services to king John, but they were not accepted, and he proceeded on his adventurous expedition under the auspices of the king of Spain, and the continent of America was discovered in 1492.

Eleven years elapsed after Dias had rounded the Cape before any attempt was made to improve the discovery. King John was succeeded by Emanuel, who entered on the field of enterprise with great ardour, and in 1497 fitted out three vessels in the hope of finding a way to India from the Cape. The little fleet, consisting of vessels of small tonnage, was entrusted to Vasco de Gama, who A.D.
quitted Lisbon, after the performance of religious solem- 1497
nities, on the 8th July, 1497, amidst the acclamations of the king, the court, and the people. Having reached the Cape in safety, he launched out boldly into the unexplored Indian Ocean, where, while traversing three thousand miles, nothing but the sea and the sky was visible for twenty-three days. He sighted the Malabar coast in May, Discovery
1498, and brought his enterprise to a glorious of India.
issue as he cast anchor off the town of Calicut. It lay 1498
in that portion of the Deccan which the Mahomedan arms had not reached, and belonged to a Hindoo prince styled the Zamorin, who gave the Portuguese commander an honourable reception, and at once granted him the privilege of trade in his dominions. But the commerce of the Malabar coast, with its fifty harbours, had hitherto been monopolised by the traders from Egypt and Arabia, who felt no little jealousy at the arrival of these interlopers, and having gained over his minister, persuaded the Zamorin that the Portuguese were not the merchants they represented themselves to be, but pirates who had escaped from their own country, and had now come to infest the eastern seas. The feelings of the prince were at once changed to hostility, and Vasco, after a residence of several months on the coast, seeing little hope of an amicable intercourse, set sail on his return. He entered the Tagus, after an absence of twenty-six months, on the 29th of 1499
August, 1499, in regal pomp, and received the homage of the court and the people, who crowded to the beach to admire the vessels which had performed this wonderful voyage. It was six years and a half after Columbus had astounded the nations of Europe by the discovery of the New World,

that Vasco increased their amazement by announcing the discovery by sea of the way to India, the region of fabulous wealth.

Second expedition—Cabral.

The king of Portugal lost no time in following up the enterprise, and immediately fitted out an expedition, which consisted of thirteen ships and 1,200 men, the command of which was given, not to Vasco, but to Cabral, who was, however, well qualified for the undertaking. He was accompanied by eight friars, and directed to carry fire and sword into every province
A.D. which would not receive their teaching. After launching
1500 into the Atlantic, his fleet was driven, in 1500, by the violence of the wind, to the coast of South America, where he discovered, and took possession of, Brazil, which has ever since remained an appanage of Portugal. On the 13th of September he anchored off Calicut, and having restored the hostages who had been taken away by Vasco, was graciously received by the Zamorin, and obtained permission to erect a factory. But the Mahomedan traders effectually prevented his obtaining any cargoes, and he seized one of their richest vessels, and having transferred its contents to his own ships, set it on fire. An attack was immediately made on his factory, and fifty men were killed. Cabral resented it by capturing and burning ten other vessels, after he had taken possession of their cargoes. He then cannonaded the town from his fleet, and sailed to the neighbouring port of Cochin, where he formed an alliance with the chief, a dependent of the Zamorin, and returned to Lisbon.

Second voyage of Vasco.

The disasters which Cabral had encountered induced the officers of state to advise the abandonment of these enterprises, but the king was ambitious of founding an oriental empire, and having obtained a bull from the Pope conferring on him the sovereignty of all the countries visited by his fleets in the East, he assumed the title of "Lord of the navigation, conquest, and commerce "of Ethiopia, Persia, Arabia, and India." A third expedition, consisting of fifteen vessels, was fitted out and entrusted to Vasco de Gama, who, on his arrival at Calicut, de-
1502 manded reparation for the insult offered to Cabral, which was peremptorily refused, and he set the town on fire. He then proceeded to the friendly port of Cochin, where he left Pacheco with a handful of men to protect the Portuguese factory, and unaccountably set sail for Europe. The Zamorin of Calicut marched to the attack of Cochin for

having harboured the Portuguese, and invested the factory, but though his troops exceeded those of Pacheco by fifty to one, they were ignominiously defeated, and the superiority of European to Asiatic soldiers, which has ever since been maintained, was now for the first time exhibited, and the foundation was laid for European ascendancy in India. A.D.

In 1505, the king of Portugal sent out Almeyda with 1505
the grand title of viceroy of India, though he did not possess a foot of land in it. Almeyda had to encounter a new and more formidable opponent. Almeyda.
The Venetians, who had hitherto monopolised the lucrative trade of India, regarded with a jealous eye the attempts of the Portuguese to divert it into a new channel round the Cape. The bulk of the commerce which had made their island the queen of the Adriatic and the envy of Europe, was conveyed through Egypt, where they enjoyed a paramount influence, and they prevailed on the Sultan to send a fleet down the Red Sea to sweep the interlopers from the coast of India, and assisted him with naval materials from their forests in Dalmatia. The king of the maritime province of Guzerat was equally alarmed at the growing power of the Portuguese on the sea, and sent his ships to co-operate with the Egyptian fleet. They came up with a portion of the Portuguese fleet in the harbour of Choul, and defeated it. Young Almeyda was killed in the action; his father determined to avenge his death, and, finding that Dabul, one of the greatest commercial marts on the coast, had taken part with the Egyptian fleet, reduced it to ashes, with great slaughter. He then proceeded in search of the combined fleets, and found them Naval actions.
anchored in the harbour of Diu, and obtained a splendid 1508
victory over them; but he stained his reputation by the massacre of his prisoners to avenge the death of his son.

He had been previously superseded by Albuquerque, sent out by the court of Lisbon to take charge of the Portuguese interests in India. He was a man of great enterprise and boundless ambition. He attacked Albuquerque.
the town of Calicut, but lost a fourth of his force in the assault. He came to the conclusion that, instead of these desultory attacks in which the Portuguese had hitherto been engaged, it would be more advisable to make a permanent establishment on that coast, in some port and town which would afford a safe harbour for their ships, and become the citadel of their power. He fixed on Goa, on

the coast of Canara, situated on an island twenty-three miles in circumference, and one of the most valuable ports on that coast. It thus became the metropolis of the Portuguese dominions in India, and every effort made from time to time to capture it by the native princes proved unavailing. He now assumed the position of an eastern prince, and received embassies with oriental pomp. He proceeded to the remote provinces in the Malay archipelago, where he established his authority, and carried his commercial enterprises to Siam, Java, and Sumatra. His efforts were next directed to the west, and he obtained possession of Ormuz, the great emporium of the Persian Gulf. The genius of Albuquerque had thus in the course of nine years built up a great European power in the East. He appeared rather to eschew than to court territorial possessions, but his power throughout the eastern seas was irresistible, and his authority was supreme along 12,000 miles of coast, on which he had planted thirty factories, many of which were fortified. But his last days were clouded by the ingratitude of his country. In the midst of his triumphs he was superseded by the intrigues
A.D. of the court; the reverse broke his heart, and he died
1515 as he entered the harbour of Goa. He was interred in the great settlement which he had established, amidst the regrets of Europeans and natives, by whom he was equally beloved.

The Portuguese sixteenth century.

During the whole of the sixteenth century the maritime power of the Portuguese continued to be the most formidable in the eastern hemisphere, and the terror of every state on the sea-board. They took possession
1517 of the Island of Ceylon, and in 1517 proceeded to China, and established the first European factory,
1531 at Macao, in the Celestial Empire. In 1531 they equipped an armament of 400 vessels, with an army of 22,000 men, of whom 3,600 were Europeans, and captured Diu, which,
1537 though lost for a time, was regained. In 1537 the king of Guzerat implored the Grand Seigneur to assist him in freeing India from the presence of the infidels, and a large fleet, with 7,000 Turkish soldiers on board, was fitted out at Suez, and being joined by the Guzerat army, 20,000 strong, laid close siege to Diu. Sylviera, the commander, had only 600 men for its defence, but he sustained the siege, amidst the deepest privations, with European gallantry, for eight months. The assailants, driven to despair, were obliged to withdraw, and the fame of the foreigners who had baffled the united forces of the Sultan of Turkey and the king of

Guzerat was diffused through India. The most memorable event in the annals of Portuguese India was the combination formed for their expulsion by the kings of Ahmed- A.D.
nugur and Beejapore and the Zamorin of Calicut. The 1570
siege of Goa, which they undertook, lasted ten months, but was at length abandoned after the confederates had lost 12,000 men. The king of Bengal, pressed by Shere Sing,
in 1538 sent an embassy to Goa to implore the aid of the 1538
Portuguese Governor-General, who despatched nine armed vessels with troops to his assistance. This was the first introduction of Europeans into the valley of the Ganges. The Portuguese established a factory at a place called the Gola, or granary,—subsequently designated Hooghly,—and completely drew off the trade of the province from the neighbouring town of Satgang, which had been the great mercantile emporium of Bengal for fifteen centuries. The factory grew to be a flourishing town, adorned with numerous churches, and so strongly fortified, that when the Moguls subsequently attacked it with three armies, they were unable to carry it by storm, but were constrained to have recourse to mines.

Rise of the Dutch and decay of the Portuguese.

At the beginning of the seventeenth century, when the greatness of the Portuguese had reached its zenith, they were encountered, and eventually supplanted by a European rival. The Dutch, having thrown off the yoke of Spain, entered upon a career of maritime enterprise with extraordinary ardour. In 1596
they sent an expedition round the Cape to the eastern islands, 1596
which returned laden with spices and other valuable commodities, and gave so great a stimulus to the spirit of commerce that, within five years, forty vessels, of from four to six hundred tons burden, were embarked in the trade. They gradually wrested the spice islands and Malacca and the island of Ceylon from the Portuguese, but not without many a sanguinary conflict. An expedition, undertaken jointly by the king of Persia and the East India Company, deprived the Portuguese of Ormuz, and within a century and a half of the arrival of Vasco de Gama there remained nothing to the crown of Portugal of its eastern possessions but Goa, Mozambique, and Macao in China. The commerce of the Dutch lay chiefly with the eastern archipelago; on the continent of India they never possessed more than a few factories.

SECTION II.

PROGRESS OF THE FRENCH TO THE PEACE OF AIX-LA-CHAPELLE.

THE great advantages which the trade of India had conferred on the Portuguese and Dutch inspired the French with a desire to participate in it, and several attempts were made to acquire a commercial footing in the East during the first half of the seventeenth century, but without success. At length, the great minister, Colbert, who had created the French navy and harbours, took up the matter, and established the French East India Company. Its first enterprise was directed to the island of Madagascar, but it was abandoned, owing to the unhealthiness of the climate and the hostility of the natives, and the Company took possession of the uninhabited island of Bourbon and of the larger island of the Mauritius in its vicinity. In April, 1674, Martin, the earliest of the French colonists, and a man of remarkable energy, having obtained a grant of land on the Coromandel coast from the native prince, laid the foundation of the town of Pondicherry, which he was permitted to fortify. Three years later it was threatened by Sevajee in his southern expedition, which has been noticed in a previous chapter, but was saved by the tact of Martin. War broke out at length between Holland and France, and the Dutch, envious of the prosperity of Pondicherry, sent a fleet of nineteen vessels against it. Martin was obliged to capitulate, and all hope of establishing French power on that coast appeared to wither away. The Dutch improved the fortifications and rendered it one of the strongest fortresses in India, but four years after were obliged to restore it by the treaty of Ryswick. Martin, with his usual energy, strengthened the works, and attracted native settlers by his honest dealings and his conciliatory manners; and on the spot which he had occupied thirty-two years before with six European settlers, there had grown up at the period of his death a noble town with 40,000 inhabitants. The charter of the Company was cancelled in 1719, and it was absorbed in the schemes of Law, of Mississippi notoriety. On the collapse of his project, the Company was re-organised as a commercial association; the town gradually recovered its prosperity, which had been affected by the extinction of the Company, and was

The French East India Company.

A.D. 1674

Erection of Pondicherry.

1676

1719

embellished by the taste of its governors, who also rivalled the native princes in the state they now assumed. A.D.

M. Dumas was appointed governor of Pondicherry in 1735 1735. He united great energy of character with, what is so rarely found among Europeans in India, a genial disposition, which in an eminent degree conciliated both the native princes and the people. Rughoojee Bhonslay, the raja of Berar, poured down with 50,000 Mahratta troops, and Dost Ali, who had become nabob of the Carnatic amidst the confusion of the times, endeavoured to arrest his progress, but was signally defeated and fell in battle. His son, Sufder Jung, and his son-in-law, Chunda Sahib, prevailed on M. Dumas to grant them and their families and property an asylum at Pondicherry, the strongest fortress on the coast. He received them in princely state, surrounded by his horse and foot guards, and they and their cortege entered the gates of the town under a royal salute. Soon after Sufder Ali made his peace with the Mahrattas, upon an engagement to pay a crore of rupees, and was installed nabob of the Carnatic without any reference to the emperor, or even to his representative in the Deccan, Nizam-ool-moolk. His family was withdrawn from Pondicherry, but the family and the wealth of Chunda Sahib remained under the protection of the French ramparts. Rughoojee Bhonslay, disappointed of this treasure, sent a force of 16,000 men to demand the payment of sixty lacs of rupees and the surrender of Chunda Sahib's family. Dumas had organised a body of 1,200 Europeans and 4,000 or 5,000 native troops—the germ of a sepoy army—and he received the envoy with courtesy, and after showing him over his military stores and equipments, and drawing up his force, desired him to assure his master that so long as a single Frenchman was left there would be no surrender. The resolute character of Dumas, and the resources of the garrison, made a deep 1740 impression on the Mahratta prince, but it was French cordials rather than French bayonets that carried the day. M. Dumas sent by the envoy a present of French liqueurs to Rughoojee, who gave them to his wife, and she was so delighted with them as to insist on a further supply. The desire to gratify her, combined, doubtless, with a reluctance to risk an assault on a fortress of European strength, led to a negotiation which ended in the retreat of the Mahrattas. M. Dumas was congratulated by the native princes of India on his successful resistance

Dumas, governor of Pondicherry.

Rughoojee Bhonslay.

of the redoubted Mahrattas, and the emperor conferred on him and his successors the title of nabob, and the rank of a commander of 4,500 horse.

Dumas was succeeded by Dupleix, a man of extraordinary genius, and one of the most illustrious statesmen in the annals of French India. He had acquired a large fortune in trade before he was appointed Intendant of Chandernagore, on the banks of the Hooghly, where a French factory had been established in 1676. It had never flourished, while the English factory at Calcutta had been rising in wealth and importance, but the creative genius of Dupleix in the course of ten years made it one of the most opulent European factories in Bengal. At the period of his assuming the charge of the town not more than half-a-dozen small coasting craft were to be seen at the landing-place; before his departure seventy vessels were engaged in trade to Yeddo, to Mocha, to Bussorah, and to China. He established agencies in the great marts in the interior, and his transactions were extended to Thibet. He surrounded the town with fortifications, and assisted in the erection of two thousand houses. He was appointed to the government of Pondicherry in October, 1741, and well knowing that in the East the pomp of state is always an element of political strength, made such a display of magnificence, and exacted such deference as an officer of the Mogul Empire, as to dazzle the princes and people of the Deccan, and to augment the reputation of French power. His first attention was given to the improvement of the fortifications, but before they were completed he was informed by the Directors of his company that war between France and England was imminent; and, moreover, that they would be unable to supply him with money, ships, or soldiers. At the same time he learned that a large naval squadron was ready to sail from England, while he could only muster 436 European troops, and had only a single vessel of war at his disposal. In this emergency he determined to invoke the aid of the native princes whose friendship his predecessors had assiduously cultivated, and to solicit Anwar-ood-deen, who had been appointed nabob of the Carnatic by Nizam-ool-moolk, to lay an injunction on the governor of Madras to abstain from any aggression on the French settlement. The governor considered it prudent to obey the order. The anxieties of Dupleix were likewise relieved by the arrival of Labourdonnais with a powerful

Energy of Dupleix.

A.D. 1741

1746

War between France and England.

1745

French fleet. This officer, a man of singular enterprise, A.D. 1746
had been for several years governor of the Mauritius and Bourbon, and had raised the islands by his energy and ability to a state of the greatest prosperity. He found the greater part of the Mauritius on his arrival covered with an almost impenetrable jungle, and inhabited by a sparse and indolent population. He created magazines and arsenals, barracks and fortifications; he erected mills, quays, and aqueducts, and gave the settlement that importance in the operations of his nation, which it maintained for nearly seventy years; but the value of all his noble qualities was impaired by his pride and arrogance. The two fleets were not long before they came to an engagement.

The conflict between the French and the English in India, which began with this naval battle in 1746, forms an important era in its modern history. Hitherto, the European settlements dotted around the Malabar and Coromandel coasts, content with the peaceful pursuits of commerce, had taken no share and little interest in the revolutions of power in the interior, and in the rise and fall of states. Down to the present time, moreover, while the French and English nations were often at war in Europe, during seventy years their Indian settlements lay peaceably side by side. But the scene was now changed. The governors of the two Companies embarked in a struggle for supremacy, embodied native troops and imported regiments from Europe, directing their attention more to the operations of war than of commerce, and, in more than one instance, fighting to the death in India after peace had been restored in Europe. They formed alliances and were drawn into conflicts with the native princes, which served to demonstrate the vast superiority of European soldiers over native troops, and this led to the rapid acquisition of political influence in the country, and, by an inevitable consequence, to the possession of territory. Within the brief period of eleven years after the two European powers had fired the first shot at each other, the French had acquired the undisputed authority of a territory in the south, containing a population of thirty-five millions, and in the north the English had the supreme command of provinces exceeding in area and population the whole of Great Britain.

Result of the conflict.

The two fleets met in July, 1746. The action was inde- 1746
cisive, but the English admiral, on the plea that one of his ships stood in need of repairs, sailed away to the south

and left Madras, which he had been sent out to protect, at the mercy of the French. The little hamlet on which the British ensign was planted in 1639, had in the course of a century expanded into a town with a native population of between one and two hundred thousand. The fortifications of Madras, which had never been very substantial, were now dilapidated, and of the small garrison of two hundred Europeans few had ever seen a shot fired. Against this defenceless town Labourdonnais advanced with a large fleet, 1,100 European troops, and 800 native sepoys and Africans. The President, after a decent resistance, surrendered it, and Labourdonnais held it at ransom for a sum of about sixty lacs of rupees; but Dupleix asserted that as long as the English held possession of the settlement, Pondicherry could not be expected to flourish, and he was determined to extinguish all English interests on the coast. The violent altercations which arose between these two able but inflexible men may be readily imagined. Meanwhile, the monsoon set in with exceptional violence, and the French fleet suffered to such an extent as to oblige Labourdonnais to return to the islands to refit. Dupleix immediately annulled the convention he had made with the president of Madras, and conveyed all the European officers prisoners to Pondicherry. Labourdonnais retired to France, where he was followed by the accusations of Dupleix and of the enemies he had made, and was thrown into the Bastile, where he lingered for three years, and, though released when the charges against him were disproved, died of a broken heart.

Capture of Madras.

Sept 21st, 1746

1753

On the approach of the French armament, the president of Madras, in his turn, had appealed to the nabob of the Carnatic, as Dupleix had done, and prevailed on him to prohibit any attack on the town. Dupleix, however, found little difficulty in persuading him to withdraw the injunction by promising to make over the settlement to him when it was captured, but after he had obtained possession of it it appeared too valuable a prize to be relinquished. The nabob was irritated beyond measure, and asked who were these foreigners that they should thus set him at defiance, with a handful of European and native troops not equal to a twentieth of his own army? His son was sent with 10,000 men to drive the French from Madras, but half a dozen rapid discharges of cannon bewildered them, and they retired more quickly than they had advanced. Dupleix, on hearing of the investment of the town, despatched a reinforcement consisting of 230 Euro-

Battle of St. Thomé.

peans and 700 sepoys. The son of the nabob marched to meet the detachment, and came up with it at St. Thomé, about four miles from Madras. The commander, Paradis, though without guns, assaulted the enemy with such vigour that the young nabob, who was mounted on a lofty elephant, and carried the royal ensign, was the first to fly from the field. He was followed precipitately by the whole body of 10,000 men, who never paused till they were almost in sight of Arcot. This engagement, although small in comparison with others, may be considered one of the most important and decisive battles in India. For the first time it gave the European settlers confidence in their own strength, and took all conceit of fighting out of the native princes. It taught the Europeans to disregard the disparity of numbers, however great, and dissolved the spell which had hitherto held them in abject subjection to the native powers. Nov. 4th, 1746

Siege of Pondicherry.

The success of the French induced the nabob at once to change sides. The only possession left to the English on the coast was Fort St. David, and Dupleix sent an expedition against it; but it was defended by the earliest of our Indian heroes, Major Stringer Lawrence, and the French were obliged to retire, after four unsuccessful assaults. Soon after, admiral Boscawen arrived off the coast with a large fleet and a large reinforcement of troops, and it was determined to retaliate on the French by the capture of Pondicherry. The admiral unhappily determined to take the conduct of the siege on himself, but being altogether ignorant of military science and impatient of advice, he was subject to an ignominious failure. After having invested it for fifty days with the largest European force, little short of 4,000 men, which had ever yet been assembled in India, he was obliged to raise the siege, but not before he had lost one-fourth of his troops. Dupleix lost no time in trumpeting his success throughout India, and he received congratulations from the nabob at Arcot, from the Nizam at Hyderabad, and even from the emperor at Delhi. Immediately after this event, the peace of Aix la Chapelle restored Madras to the English, and Dupleix had the mortification of seeing his hated rivals reinstated in all their possessions. 1746 1748 1748 1749

SECTION III.

FROM THE PEACE OF AIX LA CHAPELLE TO THE YEAR 1756.

It might have been expected that the English and the French would now sheathe their swords and return to the pursuits of commerce; but, as the great historian, Orme, remarks, "The two nations having a "large body of troops at their disposal, and being "no longer authorised to fight with each other, took the "resolution of employing their armies in the contests of "native princes, the English with great indiscretion, the "French with the utmost ambition." The English were the first to set the example; they were anxious to obtain an accession of territory on the coast, and they accepted the offer of Sahoojee, who had been deposed from the government of Tanjore, to cede the town and district of Devicotta, at the mouth of the Coleroon, if they would restore him to the throne. A force of about 1,500 men was accordingly sent under Major Lawrence, who obtained possession of the town, after a long and clumsy siege—the first the English were engaged in. But he found the cause of Sahoojee hopelessly unpopular, and returned to Madras, and persuaded the president to come to an accommodation with Pertab Sing, the prince then on the throne.

English invade Tanjore.

A.D. 1749

Dupleix, however, aimed at a higher object than the acquisition of an insignificant town and a few miles of territory on the coast. He had seen a single battalion, consisting only in part of Europeans, disperse a native army, of ten times its number, like a flock of sheep. The rise of this new military power filled the minds of the native princes with awe; and Dupleix determined to avail himself of their rivalries, and the fermentation of the times, to erect a French empire in India. Chunda Sahib, the most enterprising prince in the Deccan, had been deprived of the important town of Trichinopoly by the Mahrattas, and carried away prisoner to Satara, where he languished for seven years. He was exceedingly popular throughout the Carnatic, and Dupleix conceived that his ambitious plans would be promoted by making him the nabob, in the room of Anwar-ood-deen, whose government was greatly disliked. He therefore obtained his liberation by the payment of a ransom of seven lacs of rupees; and Chunda Sahib speedily collected a body of 6,000 men, and advanced

Ambition of Dupleix.

towards the borders of the Carnatic. Just at this period, Nizam-ool-moolk, the soobadar of the Deccan, and the founder of the kingdom of Hyderabad, died at a patriarchal age, and the affairs of the Deccan were thrown into a state of confusion which greatly facilitated the ambitious projects of the French governor. Of the five sons of the Nizam, Nazir Jung, though often in revolt against his father, happened to be with him at the hour of death, and having obtained possession of the treasury and bought over the chiefs in the army and the state, proclaimed himself soobadar. But there was a grandson of the Nizam, Mozuffer Jung, the son of his daughter, whom he had destined for the succession, and in whose favour he had obtained a *firman* from the emperor of Delhi. He lost no time in collecting an army to assert his claim to the throne, and was joined by Chunda Sahib, to whom he promised the nabobship of the Carnatic. The French at once embarked in the cause, and a force was despatched to his aid under the command of Bussy, the ablest officer in the French service. The confederates encountered the army of Anwar-ood-deen at Amboor; he was completely defeated, and fell in action, and his son, Mahomed Ali, fled to Trichinopoly, where the treasures of the state were deposited. Mozuffer marched the next day to Arcot, and assumed the state and title of soobadar of the Deccan, and conferred the government of the Carnatic on Chunda Sahib. They then proceeded to Pondicherry, where Dupleix received them with an ostentatious display of oriental pomp, and was rewarded by the grant of eighty-one villages.

Death of Nizam-ool-moolk.

Death of Anwar-ood-deen.

JULY 1749

Mahomed Ali, finding that he could not hold Trichinopoly against the victors, sought the aid of the president of Madras, who sent a small detachment of 120 men to support him. It was a feeble movement, but it had the important effect of engaging the English in the cause of Mahomed Ali, which from that time forward they considered themselves bound in honour to support, under every vicissitude, as a counterpoise to French influence. Meanwhile, Nazir Jung assembled an army of 300,000 men, of whom one-half were cavalry, with 800 pieces of cannon, and marched in search of the confederates. At Valdaur, about fifteen miles from Pondicherry, he was joined by Major Lawrence with 600 Europeans, while Dupleix augmented the contingent with Mozuffer to 2,000 bayonets. But on the

English and Mahomed Ali.

1750

Nazir Jung in the Carnatic.

eve of the engagement, thirteen of the French officers refused to fight; the force became demoralised, and nothing could stop its precipitate flight to Pondicherry. Chunda Sahib joined in the retreat, but Mozuffer determined to throw himself on the mercy of his uncle, who took an oath to protect him, and then loaded him with irons. Nazir Jung, now undisputed master of the Deccan, appointed Mahomed Ali nabob of the Carnatic. All Dupleix's plans were apparently demolished by this blow, but never did the fertility of his genius appear more conspicuous than on this occasion. He sent envoys to treat with Nazir Jung, and they discovered that his three Patan feudatories of Kurnool, Cuddapa, and Savanoor, were displeased at his proceeding, and prepared to revolt. Dupleix opened a correspondence with them, and, at the same time, to intimidate the soobadar into a compliance with his terms, sent an expedition to Masulipatam, and occupied the town and district. He attacked and defeated the force of Mahomed Ali, the remnant of which sought refuge in the renowned fort of Gingee. It was immediately besieged by Bussy, and within twenty-four hours of his appearance before it, the French colours were

Capture of Gingee by Bussy.

1750 flying on its ramparts, though the armies of Aurungzebe had besieged it for nine years. It was the first instance in which a European force had attacked a fortress considered impregnable, and its success spread a feeling of dismay through the Deccan, and created the conviction that nothing could withstand European valour.

Nazir Jung, astounded by these proceedings, hastened to concede all Dupleix's demands—that the town and district of Masulipatam should be made over to him, Mozuffer Jung released, and Chunda Sahib installed nabob of the Carnatic. The soobadar concluded a treaty on these terms with Dupleix, but Dupleix had previously come to an understanding with the three mutinous Patan nabobs, and had directed Bussy to attack the army of the soobadar as soon as he received a requisition from them. Bussy was ignorant of the settlement which Dupleix had made with Nazir Jung when he was called upon to assail him by the Patan chiefs. He accordingly marched with 800 Europeans and 3,000 sepoys, and ten guns, against the soobadar's army, which he found stretched over eighteen miles of ground, and obtained a complete victory. "Never," remarks the historian of these events, "since the "days of Cortes and Pizarro did so small a force

Bussy defeats Nazir Jung.

"decide the fate of so great a sovereignty." As the nabobs were moving off to join the French, Nazir Jung rode up to them with burning indignation, and engaged in a hand to hand struggle with the nabob of Cuddapa, whom he upbraided with his treachery. The nabob lodged two balls in the heart of his unfortunate master, and having cut off his head, presented it to Mozuffer Jung.

Mozuffer Jung soobadar.

Mozuffer Jung, then confined in the camp, whom Nazir Jung had ordered to be decapitated if the day went against him, was proclaimed soobadar of the Deccan, and proceeded in company with Chunda Sahib to Pondicherry to express his obligations to Dupleix, and to make a suitable return for his aid. Dupleix, arrayed in the gorgeous robes of an imperial noble, received him with oriental magnificence. A splendid tent was erected, and in the presence of the native chivalry of the Deccan, Dupleix invested him with the office of soobadar, and, having paid homage to him, received the title of governor of all the country lying between the Kistna and Cape Comorin. Dupleix then presented Chunda Sahib to the soobadar, and requested that the real sovereignty and emoluments of the Carnatic might be granted to him. Mozuffer Jung was extremely anxious to return to the capital, and requested Dupleix to allow a French force to accompany him, and Bussy was sent with 300 Europeans and 3,000 disciplined sepoys. The encampment broke up from Pondicherry on the 7th of January, but within three weeks the turbulent Patan nabobs who had conspired against Nazir Jung, entered into a conspiracy against his successor. Their troops were speedily dispersed by Bussy; but Mozuffer Jung, rejecting all advice, insisted on pursuing them and was struck dead by the javelin of the nabob of Kurnool. The camp was thrown into wild confusion, but Bussy's presence of mind never forsook him. He immediately assembled the officers and ministers, and, with the ascendancy he had gained, prevailed on them to assent to his proposal of raising Salabut Jung, the brother of Nazir Jung, to the vacant dignity, and he was drawn from confinement to rule over thirty-five millions of subjects. The camp then moved forward, and in due course reached Aurungabad, then the capital of the Nizam. Dupleix had now attained the summit of his ambition, and the power of the French had reached its zenith. The soobadar reigned over the northern division of the Deccan, but it was virtually ruled by a French general, whose authority was supreme.

1751

Salabut Jung soobadar.

A.D. In the south, all the country south of the Kistna was under
1751 the sway of Dupleix and all its resources were entirely subservient to his interests.

We turn to the proceedings in the Carnatic, where the French and English were employed for four years in attempts to obtain possession of Trichinopoly, which they both considered essential to the control of the country. It was held by Mahomed Ali, with the aid of a small body of English troops, and Dupleix, in conjunction with Chunda Sahib, sent a strong detachment under Law, the nephew of the famous South Sea financier, to expel them. It was on this occasion that the military genius of Clive, the founder of the British empire in India, was first developed. The son of a private country gentle-

Career of Clive.

1744 man, he came out to India in 1744, in the civil service of the East India Company. Two years after, he was in Madras when it surrendered to Labourdonnais, and made his escape to Fort St. David, where he exchanged the pen for the sword and took part in the defence of the fort. He was present at the abortive siege of Pondicherry by admiral Boscawen,
1748 and in the assault on Devicotta, where he attracted the admiration of Major Lawrence. He was attached to the force which the president of Madras, Mr. Saunders,
1749 despatched to the relief of the besieged garrison of Trichinopoly, and he perceived, by the instinct of his military genius, that it must fall unless some diversion could be
1751 created in its favour. He returned to Madras, and advised Mr. Saunders to sanction an expedition against Arcot, the capital of the Carnatic, which he was convinced would have the effect of drawing off a considerable portion of Chunda Sahib's army for its defence. The president, who, happily, appreciated his merits, entrusted the enterprise to his direction, and he marched with 200 Europeans and 300 sepoys, and eight officers, of whom one half were in the mercantile service and six had never been in action. They were allowed to enter the town, and, as Clive had calculated, Chunda Sahib withdrew 10,000 men to recover it. The fort was a mile in circumference, defended by a low and lightly built parapet and by towers, of which several were in a state of decay, and the ditch was dry and choked up. From the day of its occupation, Clive had been incessantly occupied in repairing the fortifications.

Clive's defence of Arcot.

1751 During the siege, one of his officers had been killed and two wounded, and another had returned to Madras. The troops fit for duty were reduced to 120 Europeans and 200 sepoys, but with this handful of men he sustained for seven weeks the incessant assault of Chunda Sahib's force, aided by 150 French soldiers. The last assault lasted eighteen hours, after which Clive had the unspeakable gratification of seeing the enemy strike their tents and retire in despair. "Thus," says Orme, "ended this memorable siege, maintained for "fifty days under every disadvantage of situation and force "by a handful of men in their first campaign, with a spirit "worthy of the most veteran troops, and conducted by the "young commander with indefatigable activity, unshaken "confidence, and undaunted courage, and notwithstanding "he had at this time neither read books nor conversed "with men capable of giving him much instruction in the "military art, all the resources he employed in the defence "of Arcot were such as were indicated by the greatest "masters of the art." Truly did the great statesman, William Pitt, designate him the heaven-born general.

Operations at Trichinopoly.

On his return from Arcot, Clive was employed in a variety of enterprises, in which he distinguished himself by the same energy and talent. After the French had besieged Trichinopoly in vain for a twelvemonth, they were driven into a position which obliged the A.D.
commander, Law, to surrender at discretion with all his 1752
troops, stores, and ammunition. In the early part of the siege, Mahomed Ali had called in the aid of the great Mahratta general, Morari Rao, of the regent of Mysore, and of the troops of the raja of Tanjore. Chunda Sahib, reduced to extremity by the surrender of his French allies, sought an asylum with the Tanjore general, who caused him to be assassinated at the instigation of Mahomed Ali; and that prince, as barbarous as he was cowardly and perfidious, after feasting his eyes with the sight of his
murdered rival, caused his head to be cut off and bound 1752
to the neck of a camel and paraded five times round the walls of the city. Unknown to Major Lawrence, he had promised to make over the fortress of Trichinopoly, which it was important for the English to hold, to the Tanjore general. Disgusted with this baseness, Major Lawrence withdrew to Madras, leaving a body of European troops to hold the citadel. Mahomed Ali refused to fulfil the bargain, and the Tanjore troops joined the French in the siege, which Dupleix lost no time in renewing. The operations in and around it continued with little interruption for two years; but even the fascinating pages of Orme are not

sufficient to induce the reader to wade through the narrative of the marches and counter-marches, the successes and the discomfiture, which marked these dreary campaigns. Suffice it to state that the French were three times worsted by the superior tactics of Major Lawrence, and that on one occasion the English sustained a memorable defeat, and that their native allies consequently deserted them. Dupleix at length, proposed the appointment of commissioners to treat of an accommodation, but the English agents, Mr. Vansittart and Mr. Palk—who had divested himself of his holy orders to enter the Civil Service—defeated the object by insisting, as an indispensable preliminary, that Mahomed Ali should be acknowledged nabob of the Carnatic. To these terms, Dupleix, to whom the soobadar had granted the control of the Carnatic affairs, could not be expected to agree, and the operations
A.D. of war were resumed, and continued with varied success
1754 till the 1st of August, 1754, when Dupleix was suddenly superseded by the arrival of his successor, and all his schemes of ambition were at once subverted.

Fall of Dupleix.

The French and English had been tearing each other to pieces in India, while the mother countries were at peace in Europe. The two Companies had been straining their energies and wasting their resources in the cause of native princes whose fidelity was always doubtful. Their attention had been withdrawn from the counting-house to the field. They were both anxious, especially the English East India Company, to terminate this anomalous state of things, which the president at Madras attributed primarily, and not without justice, to the ambition of Dupleix. There was an influential minority at the French Board hostile to him, and they were strengthened by the disasters of the campaign of 1753. The cabinet of St. James, moreover, sent over a strong remonstrance to the French ministry, and supported it by the despatch of an entire regiment and four ships of war, under Admiral Watson, and the Directory in Paris was thus induced to take up the question in earnest, and they sent out Godeheu, a member of their own body, with absolute authority over all the French settlements in the East Indies. He had already been in their service in India, and had always lived on the most friendly terms with Dupleix, but being a man of base and treacherous disposition, solicited permission to send him home in irons at the time when he was making fulsome protestations of cordiality. On his arrival at Pondicherry he spared no pains to degrade and ruin him. The public accounts showed that twenty-five lacs of rupees were due to him for sums he had advanced to carry on the Government, from the fortune he had acquired before he assumed office, but Godeheu refused to allow these accounts to be audited. Dupleix had been in the habit of assisting the native allies with advances from his own purse on the security of certain districts, but Godeheu seized the districts, and farmed them out for the benefit of the Company. Dupleix, dishonoured and beggared, quitted the scene of his glory on the 14th October, 1754. On his arrival in Paris he was A.D. 1754 at first received with some show of distinction, but as soon as the Directors were assured that all differences had been adjusted in India, they treated him with hostility, and for ten years, to the day of his death, refused even to look into his accounts. He was pursued by creditors who had advanced money to Government on his security, and during the last three months of his life his house was in the hands of bailiffs. Three days before his death he wrote in his diary,—"I "have sacrificed my youth and my fortune to enrich my "country. I am treated as the vilest of mankind." Thus perished the second victim of the ingratitude of the French East India Company. Of those illustrious men who have 1764 established European supremacy in India, Dupleix stands among the foremost. He was the pioneer of European conquest. It was he who taught the way to govern native states by a handful of civil functionaries and a small body of European troops, and it was he who created a sepoy army. No Indian statesman has ever exhibited a more fertile political genius, and it is not improbable that, if he had remained in power in India for two or three years, with the two thousand European troops brought out by Godeheu, he would, in conjunction with Bussy, have made the French as complete masters of the Deccan as the English became of Bengal and Behar two years after.

Convention between France and England.

Godeheu and Mr. Saunders, the commissioner on the part of the East India Company, agreed upon an immediate suspension of arms, and concluded a convention which provided that the territories of the two Companies should eventually be of equal value when the convention was ratified in Europe. Mahomed Ali was confirmed as nabob of the Carnatic. The treaty was most disastrous to the French. It gave up all they had been contending for;—the nabobship of the Carnatic, the Northern Sircars, their allies, their influence, and their

honour. Both parties bound themselves for ever "to "renounce all Moorish government and dignity," and never to interfere in the affairs of the native princes. The ink, however, was scarcely dry before the treaty was given to the winds. The English despatched a force to subdue the districts of Madura and Tinnevelly for their nabob, and the French sent a detachment to seize Terriore.
A.D. But the prospects of peace were at once dissipated by the
1756 proclamation of war between France and England in 1756, and hostilities were prosecuted with greater fury than ever for five years.

SECTION IV.

CAREER OF BUSSY—WRECK OF THE FRENCH POWER—NATIVE STATES, TO PANIPUT.

To turn to the brilliant career of Bussy in the north of the Deccan: In military genius he stands on a level with Clive, but was greatly his superior in the art of political organisation. For several years he had been in association with natives of distinction, and had obtained a thorough knowledge of the native character. He also acquired the tact of managing them by the exercise of that wise accommodation to their feelings and habits, in which the French have always been more successful than the English. Having elevated Salabut Jung to the throne, he

Bussy at the capital.

JUNE 29TH, 1751 conducted him in triumph to his capital; but his elder brother, Ghazee-ood-deen, who held a high position in the court of Delhi, had obtained a patent of appointment to the soobadaree of the Deccan, and, having gained over the Mahrattas by the promise of a large section of territory, commenced his march to the south. His ally, the Peshwa, with 40,000 horse, advanced to encounter Salabut Jung, laying the country waste on his march. Bussy, with his handful of Europeans and 2,000 sepoys, and eight or ten field pieces, received the shock of the Mahratta cavalry, who came thundering down upon him in full speed with shouts of triumph. He awaited their approach with perfect coolness, and then poured volleys of grape with great
1751 rapidity into their ranks, and in a few moments they turned round and fled in disorder. This was the first time the Mahratta horse, the terror of the Deccan, had encountered a European force in the field, and

He defeats the Peshwa.

the result of the conflict increased the power and influence of Bussy in no ordinary degree. He followed up his success with great spirit, and vigorously pursued the Peshwa within twenty miles of Poona, and constrained him to A.D.
sue for an accommodation. Meanwhile, Ghazee-ood- 1752
deen was advancing from the north with 150,000 men. The army of Salabut Jung was mutinous for want of pay, and Bussy wisely advised him to conciliate the Peshwa by ceding the territory west of Berar from the Taptee to Godavery, which had been promised by Ghazee-ood-deen, and which, being in a remote corner of his dominions, it would not be easy to protect. There was living at the time at Aurungabad, where Ghazee-ood-deen's army was encamped, one of the widows of Nizam-ool-moolk, to whom she had borne one son, Nizam Ali, and it was her earnest desire to seat him on the throne of the Deccan. To remove Ghazee-ood-deen out of the way, she invited him to a feast and urged him to partake of a particular dish, which she had prepared, she said, with her own hands. It was poisoned, and he died the same night, and his troops immediately dispersed.

Murder of Ghazee-ood-deen.

The ascendancy which Bussy had acquired at the court of the soobadar had raised him many enemies, and the minister, though under great obligations to him, began to plot his destruction. At the beginning
of 1753 he was obliged to resort to the sea-coast for the 1753
restoration of his health, and the treacherous minister, having dispersed his European forces in small bodies over the country, and withheld their pay, entered into a hostile correspondence with the president of Madras. One of his letters fell into the hands of Bussy, who felt that his cause was lost unless he could regain his influence, and though still labouring under disease, determined to make an immediate effort to baffle his enemies. He directed the detachments which had been scattered to assemble near Hyderabad, and, marching 500 miles to Aurungabad, unexpectedly presented himself at the court with 4,500 men, Europeans and natives. Not only was his ascendancy restored, but he was enabled to obtain from the fears of the soobadar and his ministers a grant of the four Northern Sircars for the maintenance of his force. They lay on the Coromandel coast, protected by a chain of hills running parallel with the sea, stretching about 450 miles along the coast, and from 30 to 100 miles inland. They contained many important towns, admirably adapted by the bounty of Providence and the

The Northern Sircars.

industry of the inhabitants to sustain a lucrative commerce, and already yielded a revenue of half a crore of rupees. "These territories," remarked the great historian, "rendered the French master of the greatest dominion, "both in extent and value, that had ever been possessed in "Hindostan by Europeans, not excepting the Portuguese "when at the height of their prosperity."

On his return from the coast, Bussy found the soobadar resolved on an expedition to Mysore, in conjunction with

A.D. 1754 Bussy's trials.

the Mahrattas, to extort whatever sums, under the pretence of tribute, could be obtained, and Bussy was informed that he "must attend the stirrup of "his sovereign." But the regent of Mysore was in alliance with the French authorities at Pondicherry, and had sent the flower of his army to co-operate with them in the siege of Trichinopoly. Bussy was placed in a serious dilemma, from which he was relieved only by his extraordinary tact. He accompanied the soobadar's army with 500 European troops, and assumed the command of the expedition. He moved forward with such rapidity as to astound the Mysore regent and dispose him to agree to terms, and, assuming the character of a mediator, prevailed on the soobadar to accept of fifty-six lacs of rupees, to realise which he was obliged to despoil the females of their jewels and the temples of their wealth. Soon after, Bussy, joined by a Mahratta
1756 force and the army of the Nizam, was sent against the rebellious nabob of Savanoor, and was enabled to bring him to acknowledge the sovereignty of the Nizam; but his ever vigilant enemies misrepresented his proceedings to the Nizam, and induced that silly prince to dismiss him summarily, while he was yet in the south-west several hundred miles distant from the capital, and from his own resources. Bussy received the order of dismissal with his

Dismissal of Bussy.

usual imperturbability. After crossing the Kistna, finding his ammunition running short, he turned out of his way to Hyderabad, and took up a position at Charmal, which he fortified. His ungrateful master, whom he had raised from a prison to a throne, summoned every tributary and dependent to his standard, and for two months assailed the encampment of his benefactor, who defended himself with his usual skill—his sepoys had deserted him—and was at length released from danger by the fortunate arrival of reinforcements from the coast. Salabut Jung was in a fever of alarm, and sued humbly for a reconciliation, and within three months of his dismissal

the authority of Bussy was more firmly established than ever. The zemindars in the Northern Sircars took advantage of this season of embarrassment to revolt, and Bussy was obliged to give five months of un- A.D. 1756
remitting attention to the settlement of the province. The incidental effect of these events on the fortunes of the English in India deserves particular notice. It was during this period that Clive re-captured Calcutta, as will be hereafter related, and defeated the nabob, who sent an urgent request to Bussy to advance to his aid in Bengal. But he was detained by the necessity of regaining his power in his own province, and when the pacification of the province was complete, and he was prepared to move up through Orissa with a powerful body of troops, he heard to his mortification that Chandernagore had already surrendered. His presence in Bengal before that event might have given a different turn to the battle of Plassy.

Bussy's triumph.

During the absence of Bussy on the coast, the impotent 1756
Salabut Jung was threatened with ruin by his profligate minister, who had seized the fortress of Dowlutabad, and placed the authority of the state in the hands of one of the Nizam's brothers. The crown was falling from his head, and the country was threatened with convulsions, when Bussy started from the coast with his army, and, traversing a region never yet trodden by Europeans, reached Aurungabad, a distance of four hundred miles, in twenty-one days. His presence extinguished these conspiracies as if by the wand of a magician. The minister was killed in a tumult created by his own devices; Nizam Ali fled, and Dowlutabad was recovered by a *coup de main*, and the French head-quarters were fixed in an impregnable position. Bussy had now been for seven years the arbiter of the Deccan. He had placed the interests of France on a foundation not to be shaken by any ordinary contingency, and they were as substantially established in the 1756
south of India as those of England were in the north by the victory of Plassy; and it seemed as if the empire of India would be divided between these two European nations. But it was otherwise ordained; the power of the one was destined to become permanent and expansive, that of the other was extinguished by the folly of one man. Lally arrived in India in 1758 as governor of the French 1758
possessions, and partly from caprice and partly from envy, ordered Bussy to quit the scene of his triumphs and return to Pondicherry with all his force.

Bussy relieves Salabut Jung.

Recall of Bussy.

Bussy considered obedience the first duty of a soldier, and, to the inconceivable surprise of the native princes, both Hindoo and Mahomedan, who trembled at the sound of his name, at once retired from the Deccan at the period of his greatest strength, and the sun of French prosperity in India set not to rise again.

Lally—Siege of Madras.

Lally, a member of an Irish Roman Catholic family, which retired to France on the flight of James II., had from his early youth, and for forty years, been trained in arms. His military reputation stood so high that when war broke out between France and England in 1756, he was considered the fittest man to command the large armament the French ministry was sending to India to establish French power. He was
A.D. accompanied by the scions of the most illustrious families
1758 in France. He landed at Pondicherry in April, 1758, and marched at once against the English factory at St. David's, which was surrendered within a month. The time was peculiarly favourable for the expulsion of the English from the Deccan. Madras was unfortified, its European force and its fleet were in Bengal, and the French commanded the sea and were paramount on land. Lally was bent on attacking Madras without delay, but he was basely thwarted by the admiral, who refused the aid of his ships, and by the council of Pondicherry, who would not afford him any pecuniary assistance. Seven years before this time the rajah of Tanjore, pressed by the demands of Mozuffer Jung and Chunda Sahib, had given them a bond for fifty-six lacs of rupees, which was considered valueless, and made over to Dupleix. As a last resource, Lally resolved to supply his military chest by demanding payment of this bond. With the largest European and native force which had ever till then taken the field, he hurried on to Tanjore; on his route he levied forced contributions, and blew six brahmins from the guns. The town was besieged for a fortnight, and a practical breach had been made when an English fleet appeared on the coast, and threatened Carical, the French depôt; Lally, who had only twenty cartridges left for each man and two days' provisions, raised the siege and retired. On his return to Pondicherry, he prevailed on the council to grant him some aid towards the siege of Madras, which
1758 was the object nearest his heart, and in November advanced to it with an army of 2,000 European foot and 300 European cavalry, the first ever seen in India, besides a large force of sepoys. The garrison of the fort

Siege of Madras.

consisted of 1,758 Europeans and 2,200 natives, but they were under the command of the veteran Lawrence, who was supported by thirteen officers trained under his own eye. The siege was prosecuted for two months with great vigour, and a breach was at length effected, but, at the last moment, the refusal of his officers to second him defeated Lally's plans, and the appearance of an English fleet in the roads obliged him to raise the siege and retire. Misfortunes thickened upon him. The Northern Sircars were occupied by a force despatched from Calcutta by Clive, under the gallant Colonel Forde, and Salabut Jung, having no longer anything to hope or fear from the French, threw himself into the arms of the English, and bound himself by treaty never to allow a French force to enter his service.

Siege raised. A.D. 1759

Lally returned to Pondicherry, with his army, officers as well as men, in a state of insubordination. But his hopes were raised by the arrival of a powerful fleet consisting of eleven vessels, the smallest of which carried fifty guns; the English squadron was scarcely less powerful. In the engagement which ensued both parties were crippled, but neither of them beaten. The French admiral, however, disregarding the entreaties and even the menaces of the authorities at Pondicherry, sailed away with his whole fleet to the Isle of France, leaving the command of the sea with the English. The French troops mutinied for their pay, which was ten months in arrear, and marched out of Pondicherry towards Madras, but were induced to return by the discharge of a portion of it. Lally, determined to bring on an engagement, marched on Wandewash, and captured the town and laid siege to the fort. The English force under Colonel Coote, an officer second in ability only to Clive, came up for its relief. The result was a pitched battle, known as the battle of Wandewash, one of the most severely contested and most decisive which had as yet been fought in India, in which the French, after prodigies of valour, sustained a signal defeat. It was the last struggle for empire between the French and English on the plains of India, and it demolished the hopes of establishing a French power. Lally fell back on Pondicherry, where he encountered nothing but intrigue and sedition from those who ought to have been unanimous in sustaining the national honour at this crisis. "From this time," he said, "without money, without ships, without even provisions,

Naval engagement. 1759

French defeated at Wandewash. 1760

"Pondicherry might be given up for lost." Coote, in the
A.D. meantime, drove the French from all the towns and posi-
1760 tions they held in the Carnatic, and prepared for the siege of Pondicherry, when the folly of the Court of Directors had well-nigh marred it, by sending out orders to supersede him by the Honourable Colonel Monson, the second in command. In the first independent enterprise of Colonel Monson, his success was so equivocal as to present an ill-omen of his efforts, but he was disabled by a severe wound, and Colonel Coote was prevailed on by the council of Madras to resume the command. The town was subject to a strict blockade during the rains, and vigorously besieged as soon as they ceased. Lally was thwarted at every turn by the civil functionaries who detested him, and in whom every spark of honesty and loyalty was extinct; but he maintained a long and energetic defence with a spirit and courage which elicited the applause of his English opponents, and he did not surrender the town until he was reduced to two days' provisions. As the victors
1761 marched into it, their feelings were deeply excited by the skeleton figures to which the noble forms of the two gallant regiments Lally had brought out with him were reduced by months of fatigue and famine. The French Court of Directors had sent instructions to Lally to erase the English settlements from the land. The despatch had fallen into the hands of the English Directors, and, by their orders, Pondicherry was levelled with the ground, and not a roof left of that noble colony. The war which, with a brief interval, the two nations had waged for fifteen years, terminated in the extinction of the French power. The ambitious hope of establishing a French empire in India, which had equally animated Labourdonnais and Dupleix, Bussy and Lally, was extinguished. Their settlements were, indeed, restored at the peace of Paris in 1763, but they never recovered their political position in India. Lally returned to Paris and was thrown into the Bastile, where he lingered for three years. He was then brought to trial, denied the assistance of counsel, and condemned to death for having betrayed the interests of the king and the company. He was drawn on a dung cart to the scaffold and beheaded, the third illustrious victim of the ingratitude of his country in fifteen years.

Siege of Pondicherry.

Capture of Pondicherry.

Fate of Lally.

SECTION V.

NATIVE STATES, FROM THE SACK OF DELHI, 1739, TO THE BATTLE OF PANIPUT, 1761.

To return to the events in the native states, from the invasion of Nadir Shah in 1739, to the battle of Paniput in 1761. The atrocities perpetrated by Nadir Shah on his return to Persia, for eight years, were at length terminated by his assassination. But a new and more formidable foe to India arose on his death in the person of Ahmed Shah, the chief of the tribe of Abdalee Afghans, who was proclaimed king at Candahar before the close of the year, and became supreme in the regions beyond the Indus. Encouraged by the success of Nadir Shah, whom he had accompanied in his expedition, he turned his attention to India and occupied the province of Lahore, and advanced to Sirhind, where he was defeated by prince Ahmed, the son of the emperor of Delhi, who obliged him to recross the Indus. Mahomed Shah, the emperor, after a reign of more than thirty years, during which the imperial throne had been steadily becoming weaker, died in 1748, and was succeeded by his son Ahmed, who appointed the nabob of Oude his vizier. Alarmed by the growing power of the Rohillas, who had taken advantage of the invasion and of the confusion of the times to enlarge their power in Rohilcund, the Vizier attacked them and was defeated, and his province overrun, when he had recourse to the humiliating and dangerous expedient of calling in the Mahratta chiefs Holkar and Sindia, by whose aid he chased the Rohillas back to their hills. To gratify their avarice, he authorised them to plunder the conquered territory, which did not recover from the effect of their ravages for many years.

Ahmed Shah Abdalee.

A.D. 1747

His first invasion.

Ahmed Shah, having recruited his force, again occupied the Punjab and Mooltan, and sent an envoy to Delhi to demand the formal cession of them. The emperor, under the influence of a profligate eunuch, complied with the request. The Vizier, then absent in the pursuit of the Rohillas, hastened to Delhi, but being too late to prevent the surrender of the provinces, invited the eunuch to a banquet and caused him to be assassinated. The emperor was exasperated by this outrage, and enlisted the services of Ghazee-ood-deen, the grandson of Nizam-

1751

His second and third invasion.

ool-moolk and the son of the prince who was poisoned by
his mother-in-law. This brought on a civil war between the
emperor and the Vizier, and for six months the capital
was deluged with blood. Ghazee-ood-deen then called to
his assistance Holkar's mercenaries, and the Vizier, unable
to cope with them, consented to an accommodation, and
was allowed to retain possession of Oude and Allahabad,
which were now finally alienated from the empire. The
emperor, unable to bear the arrogance of Ghazee-ood-deen,
marched out of his capital to oppose him while he was
engaged in the siege of Bhurtpore, but was defeated and
made prisoner, when the monster deprived him and his
A.D. mother of sight, and raised one of the princes of the blood
1754 to the throne, with the title of Alumgeer the second.
He then proceeded to the Punjab and expelled the
Alumgeer II. Emperor. lieutenants of Ahmed Shah, who no sooner
heard of the insult than he hastened to avenge
it, and having recovered the Punjab, advanced to Delhi.
Ghazee-ood-deen made the most abject submissions, and
was forgiven, but the Abdalee was determined to obtain a
pecuniary indemnity, and gave the city up to plunder. For
many days the atrocities of Nadir Shah's time were
repeated, and the wretched inhabitants were a second time
1756 subject to the insolence and rapacity of a brutal soldiery.
Soon after, several thousand unoffending devotees were
sacrificed in the holy city of Muttra at the time of a
religious festival. A pestilence which presently broke out
in his camp obliged him to recross the Indus. He left
his son Timur in charge of the Punjab, and at the particular
request of the emperor, placed the Rohilla chief
1757 Nujeeb-ood-dowlah in command of the imperial army to
protect him from the designs of Ghazee-ood-deen.

That abandoned minister immediately called the Mahrattas
to his aid, and Rughoonath Rao, more commonly
Mahratta grandeur. known in history as Raghoba, advanced and captured
Delhi after a siege of a month, and then
proceeding to the Punjab, drove the force of Timur back
1758 into Afghanistan and planted the Mahratta standard for
the first time on the banks of the Indus. He returned to
Poona, after having conferred the government of the
province on a Mahratta officer. The Peshwa had, meanwhile,
been intriguing for the possession of Ahmednugur,
the most important city south of the Nerbudda, and at
length obtained it by treachery. This aggression brought
on hostilities with Salabut Jung and his brother Nazir

Jung, who had been reconciled. They had no longer the support of Bussy's genius or his troops, and even Ibrahim Khan, the ablest of Bussy's native generals, had been dismissed, and gone over with a powerful and well-served artillery to A.D.
the Peshwa. The Nizam was reduced to such straits as to 1758
be obliged to agree to whatever terms the Peshwa might dictate, and obliged to surrender four of the most important fortresses in the Deccan, to confirm the possession of Ahmednugur, and to make over districts yielding fifty-six lacs of rupees, which reduced the Mogul possessions in the Deccan to a very narrow circle. The power of the Mahrattas was now at its zenith; it was acknowledged equally on the banks of the Indus and of the Coleroon, and it was predominant both in Hindostan and in the Deccan. The vast
resources of the commonwealth were wielded by one chief 1759
and directed to one object, and they began to talk proudly of establishing Hindoo sovereignty throughout the continent of India.

The Abdalee's fourth invasion.

Raghoba had left Holkar and Sindia to support the Mahratta interests in the north, and to despoil Rohilcund, of which Sindia had laid waste thirteen hundred villages in the course of a month, but he was soon after driven across the Jumna by the nabob
Vizier. Just at this juncture the north of India was 1759
astounded by the report that Ahmed Shah Abdalee had crossed the Indus a fourth time in September, with a large army, to recover and extend his possessions. During his advance, Ghazee-ood-deen, dreading an interview between the Abdalee and the emperor Ahmed Shah, whom he had blinded, put him to death, and placed an unknown youth on the throne, who was, however, never acknowledged. Holkar and Sindia were in command of 30,000 horse, but they were widely separated from each other, and the Abdalee determined to attack them before they could form a junction. Sindia was overpowered, and lost two-thirds of his army. Holkar was routed with great carnage. The news of these reverses only

Defeat of Sindia and Holkar.

served to inflame the ardour of the Peshwa and his cabinet, 1759
and it was resolved at Poona to make one grand and decisive effort to complete the conquest of India. The command of the force destined to this object was entrusted to Sudaseo Rao Bhow, commonly known as the Bhow, the cousin of the Peshwa, a general who had seen much service and was not wanting in courage and energy, but rash and impetuous, and filled with an overweening conceit of his own abilities.

A.D. 1760 The army which now moved up to encounter Ahmed Shah was the largest with which the Mahrattas had ever taken the field. Its gorgeous equipments formed a strong contrast with that of the humble and hardy mountaineers of Sevajee. The Mahrattas had already begun to assume the pomp of Mahomedan princes The spacious and lofty tents of the chiefs were lined with silks and brocades, and surmounted with glittering ornaments. The finest horses richly caparisoned, and a train of elephants with gaudy housings, accompanied the army. The wealth which had been accumulated during half a century of plunder was ostentatiously displayed; and cloth of gold was the dress of the officers. The military chest was furnished with two crores of rupees. Every Mahratta commander throughout the country was summoned to attend the stirrup of the Bhow, and the whole of the Mahratta cavalry marched under the national standard. It was considered the cause of the Hindoos as opposed to that of the Mahomedans, and the army was therefore joined in its progress by numerous auxiliaries, more especially from Rajpootana. Sooruj Mull, the Jaut chieftain, brought up a contingent of 30,000 men. The army was, however, encumbered with two hundred pieces of cannon, and Sooruj Mull wisely advised the Bhow to leave them at Gwalior or at Jhansi, and resort to the national system of warfare, cutting off the supplies, and harassing the detachments of the enemy; but this sage counsel was haughtily rejected, and the Jaut withdrew from the camp in disgust, together with some of the Rajpoot chieftains. The Bhow entered Delhi and defaced the palaces, tombs, and shrines which had been spared by the Persian and Afghan invader. The

The battle of Paniput.

1761 two armies met on the field of Paniput, where for the third time the fate of India was to be decided. That of the Mahrattas consisted of 55,000 cavalry in regular pay, 15,000 predatory horse, and 15,000 infantry, who had been trained under Bussy, and were now commanded by his ablest native general. The Mahomedan force numbered about 80,000 chosen troops, besides irregulars almost as numerous, with seventy pieces of cannon. After a succession of desultory engagements, some of them, however, of considerable magnitude, the Mahrattas formed an entrenched camp, in which, including camp followers, a body little short of 300,000 was collected. Within a short time this vast multitude began to be straitened for provisions. Cooped up in a blockaded encampment, amidst dead and dying animals, and surrounded by famishing soldiers, the officers demanded to be led out against the enemy. The battle began before daybreak on the 7th of January, and the Mahratta chiefs nobly sustained their national reputation; but about two hours after noon Wiswas Rao, the son of the Peshwa, was mortally wounded, and Sudaseo Rao Bhow fled from the field, and the army became irretrievably disorganised. No quarter was asked or given, and the slaughter was prodigious. Not one-fourth of the troops escaped with their lives, and it was calculated that from the opening of the campaign to its close the number of casualties, including camp followers, fell little short of 200,000. Seldom has a defeat been more complete or disastrous. There were few families throughout the Mahratta empire which had not to mourn the loss of some relative. The Peshwa died of a broken heart, and his government never recovered its vigour and integrity. All the Mahratta conquests north of the Nerbudda were lost, and though they were subsequently recovered, it was under separate chieftains, with individual interests, which weakened their allegiance to the central authority. The Abdalee having thus shivered the Hindoo power, turned his back on India, and never interfered again in its affairs. The Mogul throne may be said to have expired with the battle of Paniput. Its territory was broken up into separate and independent principalities; the claimant to the throne was wandering about Behar with a band of mercenaries; and the nation which was destined to establish a new empire, and, in oriental phrase, to "bring the various "tribes of India under one umbrella," had already laid the foundation of its power in the valley of the Ganges. To the rise and progress of the English Government we now turn.

Prodigious slaughter.

Effect on the Mogul empire.

A.D. 1761

SECTION VI.

THE EAST INDIA COMPANY IN BENGAL.

THE wealth which Portugal had acquired in the sixteenth century by the trade to the east raised an earnest desire in England to obtain a share of it; and Drake, Cavendish, and other navigators were impelled by the spirit of maritime enterprise, which Queen Elizabeth fostered, to undertake voyages of discovery in

The East India Company.

A.D. the eastern seas. In 1583 Fitch and three other adven-
1583 turers traversed the length and breadth of the unknown continent of India, and the accounts they brought home of the opulence of its various kingdoms, and the grandeur of the cities, opened up the vision of a lucrative commerce to the English nation. The ardour of enterprise was, however, damped by the unsuccessful issue of a voyage of three years undertaken by Captain Lancaster, but it was revived by the report of the first mercantile expedition of the Dutch, which had resulted in a rich return. An association was accordingly formed in London, consisting
1600 of "merchants, ironmongers, clothiers, and other men of "substance," who subscribed the sum of £30,133, for the purpose of opening a trade to the East. The next year Queen Elizabeth granted them a charter of incorporation, under the title of the "East India Company," which for a hundred and fifty years confined itself to commercial pursuits, and then took up arms in defence of its factories, and impelled by the normal law of progression, became master of the continent of India.

The first attention of the Company was drawn to the spice islands in the eastern archipelago, in which the Dutch were endeavouring to supersede the Portuguese. The chief object of the India trade at that period was to obtain spices, pepper, cloves, and nutmegs, in return for the exports from England of iron, tin, lead, cloth, cutlery, glass, quicksilver, and Muscovy hides.

Its first enterprises.

1601 The first expedition sailed from Torbay in April, 1601. Eight voyages were undertaken in the next ten years, which yielded a profit of more than a hundred and fifty per cent. A portion of this return was obtained by piracy on their European rivals, which all the maritime nations at that period considered a legitimate source of gain. In 1611 the Company despatched vessels to Surat, then the great emporium of trade on the western coast of India; but the Portuguese were determined to repel the interlopers, and planted a squadron of armed vessels at the mouth of the Taptee. In the several encounters which ensued, the Portuguese were invariably discomfited, and as they were universally dreaded by the natives for their oppressions, the reputation of the English rose high, and they obtained
1613 permission to establish factories at Surat, Ahmedabad, and other towns. These privileges were confirmed by the emperor Jehangeer.

Soon after, the Company prevailed on James I. to send

Sir Thomas Roe as his ambassador to the court of Delhi, A.D. 1615
where he met with a distinguished reception *Sir T. Roe's embassy.*
and obtained further privileges for the Company.
The Company also succeeded in wresting Ormus from the
Portuguese, and obtained a commercial footing in the
Persian Gulf, but it never proved to be of any value. In
1620 the Company's agents for the first time visited the 1620
valley of the Ganges, and set up a factory at Patna; but
it was through the patriotism of Mr. Boughton, *Mr. Boughton's disinterestedness.*
one of their surgeons, that they obtained permission
to settle in Bengal. The emperor was
at the time in the Deccan, and his daughter being taken
seriously ill, he sent to the Company's factory at Surat to
request the services of an able physician. Mr. Boughton
was despatched to the camp, and effected a cure; and being
requested to name his own reward, asked permission to
establish factories in Bengal, which was at once granted.
Two years after, the emperor's second son, who had been
appointed viceroy of Bengal, established his court at
Rajmahal. One of the ladies of the seraglio was attacked
with disease, and the services of Mr. Boughton were again
solicited, and he again declined any personal remuneration,
but obtained permission for his masters to plant factories
at Hooghly and Balasore.

The first factory of the Company on the Coromandel
coast was opened at Masulipatam and then transferred to
Armegaum; but as the trade did not flourish, the *Madras.*
superintendent accepted the invitation of the raja
of Chundergiree, the last representative of the Hindoo
kingdom of Beejanuger, to settle in his territories, and a
plot of ground was accepted at Madraspatam, one of the
most inconvenient places for trade on the Coromandel
coast, on which the Company erected a fort, called, after the 1639
patron saint of England, Fort St. George, around which
arose the city of Madras. Surat continued to be the port of
the Company on the western coast till 1662, when, on the
marriage of Charles II. to the Infanta Catherine, *Bombay.*
the daughter of the king of Portugal, he
bestowed the port of Bombay as her dowry, and the 1662
Crown, finding it more expensive than profitable, made
it over to the Company, who removed their chief establishments
to it. The annals of the Company for a period of
forty years in Bengal are barren of events. They enjoyed
great prosperity, and their trade flourished to such an
extent that it was erected into a separate Presidency, but

the simple men of the counter in Dowgate were at length seized with a fit of political ambition, which brought them to the verge of ruin.

The Court of Directors had obtained admiralty jurisdiction from the Crown, with liberty to seize all interlopers.

The Company's ambition.

The profits of the Company had, as usual, led to the establishment of a new and rival Company in London, which it was deemed advisable to root out. The agent of the old Company, with the view of excluding them from Bengal, had sought permission of the Mogul viceroy to erect a fortification at the mouth of the river, but he resented their application by increasing the duty on their exports, in violation of the firman granted by the emperor. Such impositions which had frequently been made before, had been eluded by a discreet distribution of presents, but on the present occasion the Company assumed a high tone, and determined to seek redress by engaging in hostilities with the Mogul empire, then in the

A.D. 1685 zenith of its power. With the permission of the Crown, they sent out admiral Nicholson with twelve ships of war, carrying 200 guns and 1,000 soldiers, to seize and fortify Chittagong, to demand the cession of the neighbouring territory, and to establish a mint. But these ambitious prospects were destined to a severe disappointment. The fleet was dispersed in a storm, and a portion of it sailed to Hooghly where the advanced-guard of 400 men had already arrived from Madras. The appearance of this formidable armament induced the nabob to seek an accommodation, when three intoxicated sailors reeled into the bazaar, and fell out with the police. Both parties were

Battle at Hooghly.

reinforced, and a regular engagement ensued, which resulted in the defeat of the Moguls. The admiral set the town on fire, and burnt down five hundred houses. Job Charnock, the chief of the Company's factory, dreading an attack from the nabob's troops, moved down with all his establishment to the village of Chuttanutty, and then to the island of Ingelee, a swamp in the Soonderbun, where half his people perished of jungle fever. He was relieved from this embarassing position by the appearance of an envoy from the nabob with proposals of peace. The Court of Directors, who were determined to carry their views by force, had directed their chief at Bombay to blockade Surat, which was the pilgrim port on the western coast, and the departure of devout Mahomedans to the shrine of the Prophet was at once stopped. Aurungzebe's fanaticism over- came his pride, and, in order to open the road to Mecca, he condescended to seek accommodation with the infidels who had blocked it up. A treaty was accordingly concluded, and Charnock returned to Chuttanutty, but not to remain there. The Court of Directors, hearing of the proceedings at Hooghly, determined to prosecute the war with increased vigour, and despatched Captain Heath with several vessels of war to Bengal. On his arrival, he disallowed the treaty and commenced warlike operations, and embarking the whole of the Company's property and officers on fifteen vessels, proceeded to Balasore, which he burnt, and then crossed over to Chittagong. Its fortifications were stronger than he had expected, and he sailed to Madras, where he landed all the Company's establishments. Aurungzebe, incensed at these renewed aggressions, ordered all the English factories in every part of India to be confiscated, and nothing remained of the Company's possessions except the fortified towns of Madras and Bombay. Sir John Child, the governor of Bombay, sent two gentlemen to the emperor's encampment at Beejapore to treat for a reconciliation. Aurungzebe by the recent conquest of Beejapore had extended his power over the whole of India; but though it was irresistible on the land, the English were masters of the sea, and they blockaded the Mogul ports, and both obstructed the pilgrimage, and destroyed the trade of the Moguls. Nor was he insensible to the loss his subjects sustained by the suspension of the English trade, which was calculated at a crore of rupees a year, and he agreed "to overlook their "offences," and restore their factories. The nabob of Bengal, who was favourable to them, lost no time in acquainting Mr. Charnock at Madras with the emperor's wishes, and beseeching him to return to Bengal. He landed at Chuttanutty on the 24th of August, 1690, and in the neighbouring village of Calcutta laid the foundation of the future metropolis of British India. This spasm of ambition did not last more than five years, and for half a century afterwards the servants of the Company were instructed to consider themselves "the representatives of a body of merchants, and to live "and act accordingly."

Stoppage of pilgrimage.

A.D. 1688

Bengal abandoned.

1690

Foundation of Calcutta.

The Company having now a settlement of their own in

A.D. 1695 Bengal, were anxious to place it, like Madras and Bombay, in a state of defence; but it was contrary to the policy of the Mogul empire to permit the multiplication of such fortifications. The forts at the two other Presidencies had been erected before the authority of the Moguls was extended over the territory in which they were situated. The nabob of Bengal refused the permission which the governor had sought, but in 1695 the zemindar of Burdwan revolted, and in conjunction with Rehim Khan, the chief of the Orissa Afghans, plundered Hooghly, and threatened the foreign settlements. The danger to which they were exposed was strongly represented to the nabob, who was bewildered by the rebellion, and he desired the agents of the Companies, in general terms, to provide for their own security. Immediately every hand was set to work, night and day, to raise the fortifications, by the Dutch at Chinsurah, the French at Chandernagore, and the English at Calcutta. In compliment to the reigning monarch the fortress was designated Fort William.

Erection of Fort William.

The Company was now threatened by a more formidable opponent in London. The dazzling profits of the India trade had drawn forth a multitude of competitors, but they succeeded in obtaining a renewal

Rival companies.

1693 of their charter from the Crown in 1693. A few months after, however, the House of Commons passed a resolution to the effect, "that it is the right of all Englishmen to trade "to the East Indies unless prohibited by Act of Parlia-"ment." This gave fresh animation to those who were eager to share in the trade, and they petitioned Parliament for a charter, backed by the tempting offer of a loan of two millions to the treasury at eight per cent., and it was accepted. The old Company had not been able to offer more than a third of the sum, and they were ordered to wind up their affairs in three years. But the rivalry of the two Companies was found, even in the first year, to be fatal to the public interests. Their competition enhanced the price of produce in every market in India, and created a scarcity. The native officers, courted by two parties, fleeced them in turn, and oppressed both, and the money which should have been laid out in investments was squandered in bribes, to the extent of seven lacs of rupees. At Surat, the agents of the old Company were seized by the agents of their rivals, dragged through the streets and delivered to the Mogul authorities of the town

Disastrous results.

as disturbers of the public peace. The nation became at length sensible of the disastrous results of this contention, and in 1702 the two Companies were amalgamated under the title of the "United Company of Merchants "trading to the East." Their former privileges were granted by the Crown; the new charter was sanctioned likewise by Parliament, and the strength of union inspired them with greater animation in the prosecution of their commerce. The fortifications of Calcutta were silently but diligently improved, and gave confidence to the native merchants, who came there in large numbers, and it became one of the most flourishing settlements in the province. But the history of it from this time to the battle of Plassy, for more than fifty years, and more especially during the viceroyalty of Moorshed Kooly Khan and his successor, is only a register of the extortions of the Mogul government, and the contrivances of the president to evade them. It is an unvaried tale of insolence and plunder on the one part, and humiliating submission on the other, which was at length avenged by the battle of Plassy.

A.D. 1702

Their union.

1702

In the year in which the Companies were united, Moorshed Kooly Khan was appointed dewan, or financial administrator, of Bengal. He was the son of a poor brahmin in the Deccan, and was purchased and circumcised by an Ispahan merchant. On the death of his master, he obtained service with the dewan of Berar, and by his financial ability attracted the notice of Aurungzebe, who appointed him dewan of Bengal in 1702. He was soon after invested with the soobadaree, or viceroyalty of the three provinces of Bengal, Behar, and Orissa, and removed the capital to the new city of Moorshedabad, which he founded and called after his own name. He was aware that the prosperity of Bengal was greatly promoted by its maritime trade, and gave every encouragement to the Mogul and Arab merchants, but regarded the fortified factories of the foreign companies, and more especially that of the English, with great jealousy, and when firmly seated in power, trampled under foot the privileges obtained from the emperor by the English Company. He imposed heavy taxes on the trade of the Company, which they had no means of evading except by the offer of exorbitant bribes.

Moorshed-Kooly-Khan.

The president in Calcutta determined, therefore, to appeal to the emperor, and despatched an embassy to 1715

Delhi with presents so costly as to make the Court of Directors wince. Moorshed Kooly used all his influence at court to defeat an application directed against his own interest and authority, and would doubtless have succeeded in baffling it but for an unexpected event. The emperor Ferokshere was betrothed to a Rajpoot princess, but the nuptials were postponed in consequence of a sharp attack of disease, which the royal physicians were unable to subdue. On the advice of one of the ministers, who was favourable to the English, Mr. Hamilton, the surgeon of the mission, was called in, and effected a cure. He was required by the grateful emperor to name his own recompense, and, imitating the noble patriotism of Mr. Boughton, only asked that the emperor would grant the privileges the embassy had been sent to solicit, the chief of which was permission to purchase thirty-eight villages adjacent to Calcutta. Many objections were raised to this concession by the representatives of the Bengal viceroy, but it was at length conceded. The possession of these villages, extending ten miles on each side of the river, would have given the Company the complete control of the maritime trade of the province, and Moorshed Kooly threatened the zemindars with his vengeance if they parted with a single inch of land. The firman became a mere piece of waste paper.

Embassy to Delhi.

A.D. 1717

Moorshed Kooly Khan is one of the greatest names in the Mahomedan history of India. He was as eminent a financier as Toder Mull. He caused an accurate survey to be made of the lands, and revised the assessment; he divided the province into chuklas, or districts, and appointed officers over each to collect the rents, who became rich and powerful zemindars, and as the office, as usual, became hereditary, assumed the title and the state of rajas. Of these rajas, only one—in Burdwan—retains his zemindaree unimpaired at the present time. The Mahomedan officers were regarded as sieves, which retained nothing; the Hindoo officers as sponges, which could be squeezed when saturated with plunder, and they were accordingly employed in the collections, to the entire exclusion, except in one instance, of the professors of the creed of the Prophet. The revenues of Bengal were a little in excess of a crore and a quarter of rupees, of which one-third was reserved for the expenses of the Government, and a crore regularly transmitted to the imperial treasury, the viceroy invariably accompanying

1702 to 1725

Administration of Moorshed.

the procession which conveyed the tribute in person, the first march out of Moorshedabad. Though severe in the exaction of revenue, he was eminently just in his administration, constant to one wife, frugal in his domestic habits, and exemplary in his charities. Under his administration the prosperity of the country was abundantly increased. A.D.
He died in 1725, and was succeeded by his son-in-law, 1725
Soojah-ood-deen, a Turkoman noble from Khorasan, who retained his post in spite of the intrigues at the imperial court, chiefly through the punctual transmission of the tribute. He was succeeded in 1739 by his son, Serefraz 1739
Khan, at the time when Nadir Shah was plundering Delhi, and as the dictate of prudence, the nabob ordered the coin to be struck and prayers to be read in his name.

SECTION VII.

SACK OF CALCUTTA AND CONQUEST OF BENGAL.

WITHIN a twelvemonth Aliverdy Khan, a native of Turkistan who had been entrusted with the government of Behar, succeeded, by large bribes and larger promises to the venal ministers of the emperor Mahomed Shah in obtaining the office of viceroy, and marched against Serefraz, who was defeated and slain. 1741
Aliverdy had been employed for twenty years in public affairs, and was eminently fitted by his talents to adorn the position he had clandestinely obtained, and it was through his energy that Bengal was saved from becoming a Mahratta province. While Rughoojee Bhonslay was employed in the Carnatic, as narrated in the last chapter, one of his generals, Bhaskur Punt, entered Bengal and laid waste the whole country west of the Bhagruttee, from Cuttack to Rajmahal. A division of his army 1742
suddenly appeared before Moorshedabad and plundered the suburbs and extorted two crores and a half of rupees from the Setts, the most opulent bankers in Hindostan. The Mahratta commander then moved down upon Hooghly, which he plundered, and the wretched inhabitants crowded for shelter into the foreign settlements. The president at Calcutta sought permission of the viceroy to surround the settlement with an entrenchment, which was readily granted, and the work was prosecuted with vigour, but sus-

Aliverdy Khan.

Mahratta Invasion.

pended on the retirement of the enemy and never com-
A.D. Mahratta pleted. This was the celebrated Mahratta Ditch,
1742 Ditch. which, though it has disappeared like the old
wall of London, long continued to mark the municipal boundaries of the town, and to give its citizens the soubriquet of the "inhabitants of the Ditch."

The Mahrattas, though invariably defeated, renewed their ravages from year to year. The recollection of these
Orissa ceded to the Mahrattas. devastations was not effaced for several generations from the memory of the inhabitants in the western districts, and the invasion of the Burgees—the name by which the Mahrattas were called—continued, even in the present century, to be an object of horror. Wearied out with the conflict of ten years, which ruined the country and exhausted the revenue, Aliverdy, then in his seventy-fifth year, agreed to pay the raja of Berar the *chout* on the revenues of Bengal, and to cede the province of Orissa to him. The nabobs of Bengal con-
1751 tinued, however, to retain the name of Orissa as one of the three soobahs under their rule, though nothing was left of it to them but a small territory north of the Subunreka. Aliverdy devoted the remaining five years of his viceroyalty to repairing the ravages of this harassing warfare,
1756 and died in April, 1756, at the age of eighty. The very next year the sovereignty of the three provinces passed from the Turkoman Mahomedans to the English, and became the basis of the British empire in India.

Aliverdy Khan bequeathed the government to his favourite grandson Suraj-ood-dowlah, a youth of twenty, who had
1756 Suraj-ood-dowlah. already become the object of universal dread and abhorrence for his caprices and cruelty. He had long evinced particular animosity towards the English, and the Court of Directors had specially enjoined the president to place Calcutta in a state of defence. The factory was reported to be very rich, and the young tyrant had marked it out for early spoliation, but an unexpected event hastened his movements. Before he came to power he had despoiled the Hindoo governor of Dacca, and placed him in confinement. His son Kissendas, anxious to place his family and treasures in a state of security, under pretence of a pilgrimage to Jugernath, proceeded with a large retinue to Calcutta, where he received a cordial welcome from the president, Mr. Drake. Immediately on the death of the old nabob, Suraj-ood-dowlah peremptorily demanded the surrender of Kissendas

with all his wealth. It was followed by a second communication, ordering him to demolish the fortifications which it was reported he had erected at Calcutta. Mr. Drake replied that he had only put the ramparts facing the river in repair, in the prospect of a war with France, but he refused to give up the refugee to whom he had given protection. The young soobadar was at this time marching into Purneah to coerce the refractory governor, his cousin; but enraged at this opposition to his wishes, he ordered his army to turn back and march directly down to Calcutta.

The town was ill-prepared for such an assault. During A.D.
fifty years of peace the defences had been neglected, and 1756
warehouses had been built up to the ramparts.

Capture of Calcutta.

The attention which the French had always paid to the fortification of their settlements formed a singular contrast to the indifference manifested by the English; and Chandernagore was at this time so thoroughly defensible that it would have baffled all the attacks of any native army. After the capture of Madras by Labourdonnais, the Court of Directors had sent out orders to strengthen the works, and these orders were repeated with increased importunity as the health of the old viceroy declined. But their servants in Calcutta were too busily intent on amassing fortunes to heed these injunctions, and their infatuation down to the latest moment was exceeded only by their cowardice when the crisis came. The militia was not embodied, and the powder furnished by a fraudulent contractor was deficient both in quality and in quantity. There were only 174 men in garrison, not ten of whom had ever seen a shot fired, and the besiegers were 50,000 in number. Yet, against these odds, Clive would have made as noble and successful a defence as he did at Arcot; but the governor was Drake, and the commandant Minchin.
The nabob's army sat down before it on the 17th June; 1756
the town was occupied the next day, and the day after, it was determined to send the women and children on board the vessels anchored off the fort. As soon, however, as the watergate was opened, there was an indiscriminate rush to the boats, many of which were capsized. The enemy sent some "fire arrows" at the ships, which did no damage at all, but the commanders immediately weighed anchor and dropped down the river two miles. Two boats alone remained at the stairs, and Mr. Drake, without leaving any instructions, quietly slipped into one of them; he was followed by the military commander, and they rowed down

A.D. 1756 to the ships. As soon as this base desertion of their posts became known, and calmness had been restored, Mr. Holwell was unanimously placed in command, and it was resolved to defend the fort to the last extremity. It held out for forty-eight hours, during which signals were made day and night to the vessels anchored below, and they might have come up with perfect ease and safety and have rescued the whole of the gallant garrison, but not a vessel moved. On the 21st the enemy renewed the attack with redoubled vigour: more than half the force was killed or wounded, and the European soldiers broke into the liquor stores and became unfit for duty. Mr. Holwell was obliged to agree to a parley, during which the nabob's soldiers treacherously rushed into the fort and obtained possession of it. Search was immediately made for treasure, but only five lacs of rupees were found in the vaults, and the nabob's indignation knew no bounds.

The Black Hole.

The nabob retired about dusk to his encampment. The European prisoners were collected together in a veranda, while the native officers went in search of some building in which they might be lodged for the night, but none could be found, and they were desired to move into an adjoining chamber, which had been used as the lock-up room of the garrison. It was not twenty feet square, with only a single window, and, however suitable for the confinement of a few refractory soldiers, was death to the hundred and forty-six persons now thrust into it, in one of the hottest months of the most sultry season of the year. The wretched prisoners soon became frantic with suffocating heat and intolerable thirst, and called upon the sentries to fire upon them and put them out of their misery. They sank one by one in the arms of death, and when the door was opened in the morning, only twenty-three were dragged out alive, the most ghastly of forms. This is the tragedy of the Black Hole, which has fixed an indelible mark of infamy on the name of Suraj-ood-dowlah. Yet so little did it appear an extraordinary occurrence that it excited no attention in the native community, and is not even mentioned by the great Mahomedan historian of the period. The nabob returned to Moorshedabad and confiscated all the property of the Company at the out factories, and they were as completely expelled from Bengal as they had been seventy years before in the reign of Aurungzebe.

Extinction of the Company.

1757 But the time of retribution was not distant. The Court

of Directors had regarded the progress of Bussy in the Deccan with a feeling of great jealousy, and determined to contract an alliance with the Peshwa to arrest it. Clive, who had been received with distinguished honour by the Company and the ministry, was sent for this purpose to Bombay with a considerable force, but on his arrival found the president and his council inflexibly averse to embark in so perilous an enterprise. Admiral Watson happening to arrive at the same time with his fleet from Madras, it was determined to employ the powerful armament thus assembled in rooting out the piratical chief Angria on that coast. His power had become so formidable, and his audacity had increased to such an extent, that in the previous year his corsairs had overpowered three Dutch ships of war, respectively, of fifty, thirty-six, and eighteen guns, the two largest of which they burnt. The English fleet and army proceeded against Geriah, his capital, and within an hour after the attack began, the whole pirate fleet was in a blaze. In the arsenal were found two hundred pieces of cannon, with a very large store of ammunition, and twelve lacs of rupees, which the captors, with very commendable wisdom, distributed among themselves without ceremony. The admiral and Clive then returned to Madras, where information had just been received of the sack of Calcutta; and although a strong party in the council was still bent on a conflict with Bussy, the majority came to the conclusion that it was their first duty to retrieve the affairs of their masters in Bengal. An expedition was accordingly fitted out and entrusted to the genius of Clive, who sailed from Madras with admiral Watson's fleet, on which were embarked 900 Europeans and 1,500 sepoys.

Clive's movements —Geriah.

A.D. 1755

They entered the Hooghly, and on the 15th December reached Fulta, where they found the dastardly Drake and his fellow fugitives in the ships on which they had taken refuge in June. A little higher up the river there was a small fortification at Budge Budge, held by the Hindoo general of the nabob, who had been left in charge of the army. It was attacked by Clive, and a ball happening to pass too close to the commander's turban, he hastened back to Calcutta. Not deeming himself, however, safe there, he fled to Moorshedabad, leaving 500 men to defend the fort, which was delivered up to Clive on the 2nd January, when the Company's standard was again hoisted on its ramparts. The nabob had persuaded himself that the

1756

Capture of Calcutta.

1757

English would never again enter his dominions, and he was filled with indignation when he heard of their audacity. He refused to listen to any overture from Clive, and thus marched down in haste with an army of 40,000 men. Finding a contest inevitable, Clive determined to take the initiative, and long before dawn on the 5th February marched out with his entire force, augmented by 600 marines, and assaulted the nabob's encampment. Towards sunrise a February fog bewildered the troops and weakened the strength of the attack, but the Nabob, who had never been under fire before, and had moreover seen many of his officers fall around him, hastened to make overtures of peace, and a treaty was concluded on the 9th February. All the former privileges of the Company were restored, and permission was given to establish a mint and to fortify Calcutta. Information had soon after been received of the declaration of war between England and France. The French settlement of Chandernagore, twenty miles above Calcutta, was garrisoned with 700 Europeans, besides a large body of native troops, and Bussy was encamped with a victorious army at a distance of only four hundred miles in the Northern Sircars. The nabob had no sooner signed the treaty than he importuned Bussy to march up to Bengal and expel the English. Clive felt that the junction of the two French forces would compromise the position of the Company, and he determined to attack Chandernagore before it could be effected. He attacked it by land while admiral Watson bombarded it with his fleet, and the town was surrendered upon honourable terms after a very gallant resistance of nine days. When the capture had been effected, Clive remarked, "We cannot stop here," and his prediction has been verified by a century of progress which has carried us beyond the Indus.

Battle at Dumdum.

Capture of Chandernagore.

Meanwhile, the violence and the atrocities of the nabob
1757 continued to augment the disgust of his ministers and officers. Every day produced some new act of oppression, and in May, Meer Jaffier, the military paymaster and general, and the brother-in-law of Aliverdy Khan, entered into a combination with other officers of state, and the all-powerful bankers, the Setts, to supersede him. There was at Moorshedabad at the time one Omichund, who had settled in Calcutta about forty years before, and amassed immense wealth by contracts with the Company, and who maintained the state of a prince. He ac-

Confederacy at the capital.

companied the nabob to the capital after the battle of the 9th February, constantly attended the durbar, and obtained such influence in the public councils as to render it advisable for the confederates to take him into their confidence. A.D.
Clive was invited to join the league with magnificent offers 1757
for the Company; and as he was convinced that "there could "be neither peace nor security while such a monster as the "nabob reigned," he entered readily into their plans. A secret treaty was concluded, stipulating that the English should instal Meer Jaffier, and that he should pay a crore and three-quarters of rupees to make good their losses. Omichund got scent of the treaty and threatened to disclose the transaction to the nabob—which would have led to the immediate massacre of the whole party—unless an additional article was inserted guaranteeing to him a donation of thirty lacs, and a commission of five per cent. on all the payments. Clive on hearing of this outrageous demand came to the conclusion that "art and policy were "warrantable to defeat the plans of such a villain," and he drew up a fictitious treaty on red paper, in which his demand was provided for, while the real treaty, authenticated by the seals of the confederates, contained no such stipulation. He is said to have died within a year raving mad, but this statement is utterly unfounded. This is the only act in the bold and arduous career of Clive which does not admit of vindication, though he himself always defended it, and declared that he was ready to do it a hundred times over.

Battle of Plassy.

Clive marched from Chandernagore on the 13th June with 900 Europeans, consisting partly of the 39th Regiment of foot, who still carry on their colours "Primus in Indis," 2,100 natives, and ten pieces of cannon. He marched up to Cutwa, where he called a council of war, which voted against any farther advance; but immediately after he resolved to carry out the enterprise, and on the night of the 22nd moved on to the grove of Plassy. The nabob's army, consisting of 50,000 horse and foot, was encamped in its immediate vicinity. Meer Jaffier had taken an oath to join Clive before or during the engagement, but he did not make his appearance, and was evidently waiting
the result of events. On the memorable 23rd of June the 1757
nabob's troops moved down on the small band of English troops, and Clive advanced to the attack. The enemy withdrew their artillery; Meer Mudun, the general-in-chief, was mortally wounded and expired in the presence of the nabob,

who was unable to control his terror, but mounted a swift camel and fled at the top of his speed with 2,000 horse, and did not pause till he reached Moorshedabad. His army immediately dispersed, and this battle, which decided the fate of Bengal and Behar, and eventually of India, was gained with the loss of only seventy-two killed and wounded. As soon as the victory declared in favour of Clive, Meer Jaffier advanced with his troops to congratulate him, and to obtain the fruits of it. Suraj-ood-dowlah on reaching the capital found himself deserted by all his courtiers, and after a day of gloomy reflections, descended in disguise from a window in the palace with a favourite eunuch and a concubine, and embarked in a boat in the hope of overtaking M. Law, a French officer, whom Bussy had sent up with a small force. He proceeded up the river and landing at Rajmahal to prepare a meal, entered the hut of a religious mendicant, whose ears he had ordered to be cut off the preceding year. He was recognised and made over to those who were in pursuit of him, and conveyed back to Moorshedabad, eight days after he had quitted it. Meerun, the son of Meer Jaffier, immediately caused him to be put to death, and his mangled remains were paraded the next day through the city and buried in the tomb of his grandfather.

A.D. 1757

Clive at Moorshedabad.

Clive entered Moorshedabad on the 29th of June, and proceeded to the palace, where the great officers of state were assembled, and having conducted Meer Jaffier to the throne, saluted him as soobadar of Bengal, Behar, and Orissa. The change in the position of the English in the course of a twelvemonth appears more like a scene in a fairy tale than in sober history. In June, 1756, Calcutta had been sacked and burnt, and the Company extirpated. In June, 1757, they had not only recovered the seat of their commerce and extinguished their European rivals, but defeated and dethroned the nabob, and disposed of the sovereignty of a country larger and more populous than England. Of the treasures at Moorshedabad more than two crores were made over to the conquerors, and the first instalment of eighty lacs was conveyed in a triumphant procession to Calcutta, along the road where, a twelvemonth before, Suraj-ood-dowlah had marched back to his capital with the plunder of Calcutta. For the Company Clive reserved only the fee simple of 600 yards of land around the Mahratta Ditch, and the zemindaree rights of the districts south of Calcutta. For himself, he rejected the magnificent offers of the opulent nobles who were anxious to secure his favour, and contented himself with a gift of sixteen lacs from Meer Jaffier. When his services were afterwards forgotten, and he was upbraided in the House of Commons with his rapacity, he replied indignantly—" When I recollect entering the treasury of " Moorshedabad, with heaps of gold and silver to the right " hand and to the left, and these crowned with jewels, I " stand astonished at my own moderation." Intelligence of the loss of Calcutta was eleven months in reaching England, and seven weeks after the Directors heard of its recovery and of the brilliant results of the battle of Plassy. Seventy years before they had sent admiral Nicholson with a powerful armament to establish them as a political power in Bengal, but so completely had they dismissed all the dreams of ambition, that with the richest provinces of India at their feet, the only satisfaction they expressed was that their factors would now be able to provide investments for two years without drawing upon them.

CHAPTER V.

SECTION I.

PROCEEDINGS IN BENGAL FROM THE BATTLE OF PLASSY TO HASTINGS' ADMINISTRATION.

A.D.

THE emperor of Delhi was at this time a puppet in the hands 1757
of his unprincipled minister, Ghazee-ood-deen, and his eldest son and heir, Ali Gohur, had succeeded in making his escape from the capital, and raising the imperial standard. India was swarming with military adventurers ready to take service under any chief, and the prince found no difficulty in collecting an army of 40,000 men, and, being joined by the nabob Vizier of Oude, invaded Behar, and appeared before the city of Patna. Clive lost no time in advancing to its defence, and the prince retired in all haste on his approach. During his flight he was reduced to such distress as to throw himself on the con-
sideration of Clive, and the heir and descendant of Ak- 1758
bar and Aurungzebe was happy to receive a donation of eight thousand rupees to relieve his necessities.

Invasion of Ali Gohur.

The influence which Clive necessarily exercised in the

A.D. government of Bengal from his character and position
1759 Battle at Chinsurah. tended to lessen the importance of Meer Jaffier, and his court and family could not fail to remember with chagrin that the foreigners who now overshadowed the throne had only three years before approached it as suppliants. The nabob, looking about for the means of counterbalancing Clive's ascendancy, began to intrigue with the Dutch at Chinsurah. The governor of Java, moreover, viewed with no friendly eye the superior advantages which the English had acquired in Bengal, and in the hope of fishing up some prize in the troubled waters of the province, fell in with the projects of the nabob, and despatched a fleet of seven vessels with 700 Europeans and 800 well-trained Malay sepoys to Chinsurah. Clive was resolved not to tolerate any rival European influence in Bengal, and, although the two nations were at peace, seized the vessels, and directed Colonel Forde to intercept the progress of the troops. That officer shrank from the responsibility of attacking the soldiers of a friendly power, and requested a written authority from his chief. Clive was sitting at cards when the Colonel's letter was placed in his hands, and sent a reply in pencil on the back of one of them—"Fight them immediately. I will send you the "order in council to-morrow." The Dutch force was attacked and defeated as it approached Chinsurah. Immediately after the action, the nabob's son appeared in sight with an army of 7,000 men who were to have joined the Dutch if the fortune of the day had gone against the English. Clive exacted from the Dutch the expense of the expedition sent to defeat their plans, and having sent a haughty and defiant despatch to the Court of Directors, from whom he had long been estranged, embarked for England on the 25th of February, 1760.

1760 At the period of Clive's departure, the prince Ali Gohur was advancing a second time to the invasion of Behar. Second invasion of Ali Gohur. On his route, he heard of the assassination of the emperor, his father, by Ghazee-ood-deen, and assumed the imperial dignity under the title of Shah Alum. The nabob Vizier joined his force in the hope of adding Behar to his possessions, and they moved down upon Patna. Colonel Calliaud, one of the great soldiers trained under Lawrence and Clive, marched up to the defence of the town, together with 15,000 of the nabob's troops under his son Meerun, and the imperial force was completely routed. The emperor, having received

a promise of assistance from the Mahrattas, marched down through the hills in the hope of surprising Moorshedabad. 1760
Colonel Calliaud followed him without loss of time, and the two armies confronted each other about thirty miles from the city; but the emperor hearing no tidings of his Mahratta auxiliaries, broke up his encampment and marched back to Patna, to which he laid close siege for nine days. All hope of prolonging the defence was fading away when Captain Knox, who had been despatched in haste by Colonel Calliaud, was seen approaching the walls with a handful of troops. He had performed the march from Moorshedabad to Patna, under the burning heat of a Bengal sun, in the extraordinary space of thirteen days, marching himself on foot to encourage his men. The next day he attacked the emperor's camp, and completely defeated him and dispersed his entire force. The nabob of Purneah, who had been intriguing with him, now threw off the mask and immediately advanced to his aid with 12,000 men and thirty pieces of cannon. To the utter amazement of the natives, Captain Knox marched out with a battalion of sepoys, 200 Europeans, a squadron of cavalry, and five field pieces, and, after a conflict of six hours, completely routed the nabob. The native historian dwells with admiration upon the conflict, and describes the breathless anxiety with which the inhabitants of Patna crowded on the walls watching the exit of this gallant little band, and the delight with which they were welcomed back, covered with dust and sweat. This was another of those daring exploits which in our early career established the prestige of our arms and contributed to give us the empire of India. Colonel Calliaud and Meerun arrived after the engagement; Meerun was struck dead by a thunderbolt as he lay in his tent, and the country was rid of a monster, in whose cabinet was found a list of three hundred men of note whom he had destined to destruction.

Gallantry of Captain Knox.

Clive had become so completely identified with the existence of British power in Bengal that it seemed to the public officers as if the soul had departed from the Government on his retirement. He was succeeded by Mr. Vansittart, a man of great probity, but without any strength of character. He belonged to the Madras service, and the appointment was resented by the members of the Bengal council, who set themselves to thwart him on every occasion. To increase the confusion

Mr. Vansittart governor.

which bewildered his weak mind, three of the elder members of council who had signed the contumacious letter of Clive to the Court of Directors were peremptorily dismissed by them, and their places were filled, on the rule of rotation, by men of violent passions, who regarded Mr. Vansittart with a feeling of hatred, and he was constantly outvoted in council. The death of Meerun increased the complication. Notwithstanding his profligacy, his vigour had been the main stay of his father's government, and on his death the administration fell into a state of complete anarchy. The troops besieged the palace for their arrears, and Meer Jaffier sent his son-in-law, Meer Cossim, to Calcutta to obtain pecuniary assistance from the council, but the treasure obtained at Moorshedabad had been dissipated, and there was scarcely a rupee in the treasury. It was vain to expect any further supplies from the nabob, and the council determined to depose him and to elevate Meer Cossim to the throne, on his promising to reward his
A.D. benefactors with twenty lacs of rupees, to make good all
1760 arrears, and to transfer three rich districts in lower Bengal

Meer Cossim nabob.

to the Company. Mr. Vansittart proceeded to Moorshedabad with a military force to persuade the nabob to resign the Government, and the old man was obliged, though not without the greatest reluctance, to yield, and retire to Calcutta. Meer Cossim met the difficulties of his position with great skill and energy. He curtailed the extravagance of the court establishments; he obliged the public officers to disgorge their plunder; he revised the land assessments, and added a crore of rupees a year to his rent-roll. He faithfully discharged all his obligations to the Company and to the members of the council, but the great object he set before himself was to emancipate himself from their control, and to become the soobadar in reality, and not in name only. He removed the seat of government from Moorshedabad to Monghyr, three hundred miles from Calcutta, and strengthened the works of that important fortress. In the course of three years he created a force of 15,000 cavalry and 25,000 infantry; he established a large arsenal, he manufactured firelocks, and cast cannon, and had made great progress in consolidating his power, when a storm was raised by the unprincipled conduct of the council board in Calcutta, which in a few months swept him from the throne.

From time immemorial a large proportion of the public
1762 revenue had been derived from the duties levied on the

transport of goods through the country. Under the firman A.D. 1762
of the emperor, the merchandise of the Company
intended for export by sea was allowed to pass
free, under a *dustuk*, or pass, signed by the president. The battle of Plassy transferred all power to the Company, and their servants immediately embarked on the inland trade of the country, and claimed a similar exemption for their private investments. The native merchants, in order to pass their own cargoes duty free, adopted the plan of purchasing passes from the civilians, and the boys in the service were thus enabled to realise two or three thousand rupees a month. The country traders, moreover, frequently hoisted the English flag; and as it was deemed indispensable to maintain its immunity, Company's sepoys were sent to release their boats whenever they were seized by the nabob's officers. The trade of the country was paralysed, and its peace destroyed, and the two ruling powers were brought into a state of perilous antagonism. These encroachments, which were rare during Clive's administration, increased to an alarming extent on his departure. In order to remedy these disorders Mr. Vansittart proceeded to Monghyr, and concluded a convention with the nabob, which provided that the trade of the Company's servants should pay nine per cent., though that of his own subjects was often weighted with twenty-five per cent. On his return to Calcutta he found the members of council indignant at this unauthorised concession, and resolved not to pay more than two and a half per cent., and that only on
the article of salt. The nabob then determined to put all 1763
parties on an equality, and abolished all transit duties throughout the provinces. The council voted this measure a crime, and demanded, as a matter of right from one whom they had raised to authority, that the native traders should be subject to the usual duties, while their own flag was exempt. This flagitious demand was indignantly resisted by the only two honest men in the council, Mr. Vansittart and Mr. Hastings.

The transit duties.

The Company's factory at Patna was unfortunately at this time under the charge of Mr. Ellis, the most inveterate of Meer Cossim's opponents, and the most violent and unscrupulous of the civilians. He was resolved to bring about a change in the government, and, in a time of peace, suddenly seized on the city of Patna with a handful of European troops. The native commandant, on hearing that the soldiers were rendered

War with Meer Cossim.

incapable by drink, returned to the town and recaptured it, and Mr. Ellis and his officers, who had proceeded up the river, were overtaken and brought back prisoners. Meer Cossim was no sooner informed of this wanton aggression than he ordered every Englishman in the province to be seized. Both parties now prepared for war. The nabob augmented his army, and invited the fugitive emperor and the Vizier of Oude, who was hankering after Berar, to join his forces. The English army, consisting of 650 Europeans, 1,200 sepoys, and a troop of native cavalry, opened the campaign on the 2nd July, although the rains, the season of military inaction, had just set in. The nabob's advanced guard at Cutwa was defeated. With the army stationed at Geriah to dispute the advance of the British force, there was a long and arduous battle of four hours, and never had native troops fought with greater resolution and valour than the newly-raised battalions of the nabob; but nothing could withstand the spirit of the English soldiers. The nabob's army abandoned its guns and encampment and fled. Early in November the English commandant carried the fortified entrenchment at Oodwa-nulla, and the nabob fled to Patna, after having ordered all his European prisoners to be put to death. His own native officers indignantly refused to imbrue their hands in the blood of brave and unarmed men; they were soldiers, they said, and not executioners. But Raymond, subsequently known as Sumroo, a name of infamy, who had been a sergeant in the French army, and was now in the employ of the nabob, offered his services, and, proceeding to the house where the prisoners were confined, poured in volley on volley through the venetian windows, till forty-eight English gentlemen, and a hundred English soldiers, lay lifeless on the floor. The campaign was completed in four months by the capture of Patna and the flight of Meer Cossim to Oude, where the nabob Vizier did not scruple to despoil him of his property.

A.D. 1763

Massacre of Europeans.

On the breaking out of the war with Meer Cossim, the Council determined to place Meer Jaffier again on the throne, but the old man, seventy-two years of age, and scarcely able to move for the leprosy, was previously required to confirm the grant of the three districts already mentioned to the Company, to concede the flagrant exemption from the transit duties in which the war had originated, and to make further donations to the civil and military officers. But in a few months, the govern-

Meer Jaffier again nabob.

ment having a large army to maintain in the field, found itself on the verge of bankruptcy, which was not to be wondered at, considering that peculation was universal, from the highest to the lowest official. Meer Jaffier was therefore brought down to Calcutta to concert the means of replenishing the treasury. The members of council demanded a payment of five lacs of rupees a month for the public service as long as the war lasted, and they insisted on a donation at first of ten lacs, and eventually of fifty lacs, for themselves, for what they had the effrontery to term "compensation for losses." These harassing importunities, A.D.
combined with age and disease, served to hasten his end, 1765
and on his return to Moorshedabad he expired in January, 1765.

Death of Meer Jaffier.

The making of nabobs had for the last eight years been the most lucrative occupation of the senior civil and military officers of the Company, and the fourth occasion which now arose was not to be neglected.

His son nabob.

The Court of Directors, exasperated by the iniquities of their servants, had peremptorily ordered them to execute covenants to abstain from the receipt of presents from the natives of the country. But these injunctions were given to the winds, and, with the covenants on the council table, the son of Meer Jaffier was obliged to become responsible for the payment of twenty lacs of rupees to the members of the council board before he was allowed to succeed him. The conduct of these men for five years after the retirement of Clive was marked by a degree of profligacy of which it would not be easy to find a parallel in any age or country. Fortunes of vast amount were acquired by the most nefarious means in the shortest period; every idea of common morality was treated with sovereign contempt, while luxury, corruption, and debauchery pervaded every rank, and threatened the dissolution of government.

Six months after the close of the war with Meer Cossim, the nabob Vizier determined to take advantage of the confusion of the times to acquire possession of the province of Behar, and marched down upon Patna with a large but ill-trained force, accompanied by the fugitive emperor and the disinherited nabob of Bengal. The attack was unsuccessful, and he withdrew his encampment to Buxar. Meanwhile Major Munro, who had assumed the command of the army, found the sepoys in a state of flagrant
mutiny, and demanding increased pay and large 1764
gratuities. With undaunted resolution the Major resolved

Mutiny of the Sepoys.

to subdue this spirit of revolt at once, and twenty-four of the ringleaders were arraigned before a court martial, consisting of native officers, and condemned to death. Twenty of them were blown away from the guns, and the discipline of the army was restored. This was the first of that series of mutinies which have broken out from time to time among the sepoys, and which in less than a century culminated in the dissolution of the whole army of the Bengal Presidency. At the close of the rains, the Major did not hesitate to lead this army, so recently in a state of in-
OCT. 23RD, 1764 subordination, to Buxar, where the nabob Vizier had been encamped for several months. His army, consisting of

Battle of Buxar.

50,000 troops, was completely routed, with the loss of his entire camp and a hundred and thirty guns. The victory of Buxar was an important supplement to the victory of Plassy. It demolished the only independent power in the north of India, and it left the Company masters of the entire valley of the Ganges from the Himalaya to the sea. The Vizier fled to Bareilly, and offered to redeem his forfeited kingdom by the payment of half a crore of rupees to the Company and the army, and a large douceur to the commandant, but the negotiation came to nothing. Immediately after the victory, the emperor joined the English camp, and began to negotiate for a share of the territories of his late ally, the nabob Vizier, and the council was contemplating a division of them between him and the Company, when Clive made his appearance in Bengal.

On his return to England in 1760, Clive was received
1760 with great distinction by the king and his great minister,

Clive's second appointment.

Mr. Pitt, who pronounced him "a heaven-"born general," and he was honoured with an Irish peerage. But the Court of Directors, in which his enemies were predominant, treated him not only with malevolence, but with injustice, and he was obliged to file a bill in equity to recover an annuity which Meer Jaffier had settled upon him, and which they had ungratefully sequestered. The war with Meer Cossim, the massacre of the Europeans, and the total disorganisation of the government, had dissipated the golden dreams of prosperity in which the Company had been indulging. The Proprietors began to tremble for their dividends, and they constrained the Directors, to their infinite reluctance,
1765 to send Clive out to retrieve their affairs. He landed at Calcutta on the 3rd of May, 1765, and found the whole

service steeped in corruption, and felt himself justified in asserting that "there were not five men of principle to be found "in it." His first duty was to enforce the signature of the covenants the India House had prescribed to abolish the receipt of presents. The corrupt officials questioned his right to make such a demand, but he reduced them to silence by declaring that he would dismiss every one who refused to sign them, and send him back to England; and they found it prudent to submit to his iron will. Having thus, in the course of seven weeks fully established his authority in the Government, Clive proceeded to the upper provinces to dispose of the imperial questions

Arrangement with the nabob. A.D. 1765

which awaited his decision. To prevent another rising like that of Meer Cossim, he took away the power of the sword from the nabob of Moorshedabad, and assigned him out of the revenues of the province the sum of fifty-three lacs for the expenses of his court and the administration of justice. The young nabob exclaimed with delight, "Thank God, I shall now have as many dancing-"girls as I like." The Vizier of Oude had forfeited

With the Vizier of Oude. 1765

his kingdom by the result of the war he had wantonly waged against the Company; but Clive, who was indisposed to the enlargement of the Company's territories, determined to restore it to him, with the exception of the two districts of Corah and Allahabad, which he reserved for the emperor, who was now a dependant on the bounty of the English. Clive treated the vagrant

With the emperor. 1765

prince with much consideration, and assigned him an annual payment of twenty-five lacs of rupees from the revenues of the country, in addition to the product of the districts. Looking back on the cession of Oude with the light of a century of experience, we are enabled to perceive that it was anything but judicious; and that if Clive had at that period annexed it, and given it the benefit of a British administration, as in the case of Bengal and Behar, he would have conferred a boon on the population, and benefited the Company's government.

The emperor had repeatedly offered the Company the *Dewanee*, that is, the revenues of the three provinces, and Clive now took occasion to solicit the official

The Dewanee.

grant of it. Orissa was still considered one of them, although all but one district in the north belonged to the Mahrattas. This act was completed on the 12th of August, 1765, a memorable day in the political and constitutional history of British India. As a substitute for a throne two dining-tables were put together in Clive's tent, with a chair on them, and covered with embroidery. The emperor took his seat, and transferred the government of twenty-five millions of people and a revenue of three crores to Lord Clive, as the representative of the East India Company. The Mahomedan historian of this period, scandalized by the simplicity of this great transaction, exclaims with indignation that "a business of so much "importance, which at other times would have required "the sending of wise ministers and able envoys, was done "and finished in less time than would have been taken up "in the sale of a jackass." What will appear scarcely less remarkable is the expansion of Clive's sentiments.

A.D. 1765 Extension of Clive's views.

On taking leave of the Court of Directors in 1764, he assured them that nothing but extreme necessity ought to induce them to extend their views of territorial acquisition beyond the three districts ceded to them by Meer Cossim. Before sixteen months had elapsed, he congratulated them on having become the sovereigns of three kingdoms; yet, with this demonstration of the vanity of all such resolutions, he again ventured to circumscribe the British empire in India, and after acquiring the Dewanee, declared that "to extend our "possessions beyond the Curumnassa,"—the north-west boundary of the three soobahs,—"would be a scheme so "extravagantly ambitious that no Government in its senses "would dream of it." Not more than eighty-four years after this solemn denunciation, our boundary had crossed the Indus and was extended to the Khyber Pass.

This transaction was scarcely completed when the new empire, which Clive assured the Directors that "all the "princes of Hindostan could not deprive us of "for many years," was shaken to its foundation by the mutiny of the European officers.

1766 Mutiny of the European officers.

They had been accustomed to an extra allowance, called *batta*, when in the field, which the gratitude of Meer Jaffier had doubled when he was first raised to the throne, and, as it was not withdrawn when they were in cantonments, they considered it a permanent right. When the Court of Directors became responsible for the finances of the country, they found that the military expenses swallowed up its resources, and they ordered this extravagant allowance to cease; but the timid Council was deterred by the imperiousness of the officers from executing their orders. The duty of reduction was imposed on Clive as he left England, and on his arrival he announced that the double batta was to cease on the 1st of January, 1766. The officers immediately formed a confederacy to resist the order, and it was agreed that two hundred of them should resign their commissions on the same day, and, as an army of 50,000 Mahrattas was advancing to invade Behar, they felt confident that the Government would be obliged to retain their services on their own terms.

But they had to deal with a man of inflexible resolution, who declared that he must see the bayonets levelled at his throat before he would yield to their demands. [Clive's inflexibility. A.D. 1766] He directed the commandants to accept the resignation of every officer, and to send him under arrest to Calcutta. He ordered up officers and cadets from Madras; he engaged the services of others in the settlement, and proceeded with those who remained faithful, to the head-quarters of the army, arrested the ringleaders, and ordered them to be tried by court-martial. In the course of a fortnight this formidable conspiracy was quashed by his undaunted firmness. He was fully aware, however, that all the officers of Government had a real grievance in the preposterous policy of the Court of Directors, who limited their allowances to a pittance on which it was not possible to live, and forbad all engagement in trade, while they were surrounded with wealth, which their official position enabled them to grasp with ease. He therefore established a Society for conducting a traffic in salt, on the principle of a monopoly, the profits of which, after a large reservation for their masters in Leadenhall Street, were to be proportionately divided among their servants, civil, military, medical, and ecclesiastical. But it was speedily suppressed by the Directors, who substituted for it a commission of two and a half per cent. on the gross revenue of the province.

After a residence of twenty-two months in India, Clive was driven home by an acute attack of disease. It has fallen to the lot of few men to exercise so important and so permanent an influence on the [Clive in England. 1767] course of human affairs. He not only made the Company sovereigns of a country larger than England, with a revenue of imperial magnitude, but he laid the foundation of an empire in the east with an irrepressible element of expansion. Still more, he established the supremacy of Europe in Asia, which has ever since been growing more complete, and is never likely to be shaken. His reception

in England corresponded, at first, with his eminent merits, but the tables were soon turned against him. His greatness excited envy and censure. He had made many enemies in India by his stern probity and resolution, and they purchased India stock that they might wreak their vengeance on him. One Sullivan, a Director, who possessed great power at the India House, pursued him with inveterate malignity, and the Court of Directors, who had always been hostile to him, now manifested their feelings by restoring to the service those whom he had cashiered for peculation or mutiny. The king's ministers joined the hue
A.D. and cry. The Attorney-General proposed to confiscate all
1773 the donations he had received from native princes. In Parliament his conduct was stigmatised as a "mass of the "most unheard of villanies and corruption." But the feeling of the House revolted from the proposal which was made to fix a brand of infamy on him, and substituted for it a resolution that he had rendered great and meritorious services to his country. But his lofty spirit
1774 could ill brook the treatment to which he had been subject, and, under the pressure of physical and mental suffering, he put a period to his existence.

Death of Clive.

The next five years of administration were a disgrace to
1767 to 1772 the national character. No sooner was the strong arm of Clive removed, than the whole system of Government was paralysed by the rapacity of the Company's servants. The covenants they had signed were treated as waste paper, and they plunged into the inland trade of the country, and prosecuted it with the strength of their official authority. The Council had not the power and still less the inclination to restrain these abuses. The nefarious charges of commissaries, contractors and engineers drained the treasury. Every man who was permitted to make out a bill against the state made a fortune. These evils were indefinitely aggravated by the memorable famine of 1770, which swept away one-third of the population of the lower provinces.

Five years of anarchy in Bengal.

SECTION II.

PROGRESS OF EVENTS AT MADRAS AND BOMBAY, 1761—1772.

HAVING thus narrated the progress of events in the Gangetic valley, we turn to the transactions in the Deccan during this period, and to the intrigues, perfidy, and hostilities in which the Mahrattas, the Nizam,

Affairs at Madras.

and Hyder Ali, were incessantly involved. The extinction of the French power in 1761 placed the protégé of the English, Mahomed Ali, in the position of nabob of the Carnatic. Among the native princes of the time he was distinguished by his imbecility and his unscrupulousness. His army was a mere rabble, and the Company's Government found itself encumbered with the expense of defending a territory of 50,000 square miles without the command of its revenues. The country had been without any settled government for twenty years; it had been despoiled by successive invasions, and it was now administered by a court profligate and wasteful, supported by loans raised at
Madras on usurious interest, which impaired the Conduct of A.D.
strength of those who borrowed them, and the Mahomed Ali. 1762
morals of those who provided them. The governor of Madras was constrained to make a demand of fifty lacs from the nabob to discharge the obligations incurred in seating him on the throne; but his treasury was empty, and he proposed to him to obtain funds from the
spoliation of several chiefs, and more particularly Spoliation of Tanjore. 1763
of the raja of Tanjore, from whom a contribution of twenty-four lacs in four instalments was extorted. The peace of Paris restored to the French all the possessions they had held in India, and provided, moreover, that Mahomed Ali should be acknowledged by both parties
nabob of the Carnatic, and Salabut Jung Peace of Paris.
soobadar of the Deccan. He had been deposed 1763
eighteen months before by his brother Nizam Ali, who, on hearing that his right to the throne had been acknowledged by these two great powers, caused him to be assassinated.

On the memorable 12th of August, 1765, Clive obtained from the emperor, at the same time with the Dewanee, a firman releasing the nabob of the Carnatic from all
dependence on the Nizam, and a grant of the The Northern Sircars. 1765
northern Sircars to the Company. These districts on the Coromandel coast had furnished Bussy with the sinews of war, but, on his departure, had been wrested from the French by Colonel Forde. Nizam Ali was not disposed to submit to the alienation of this province, and on hearing that an English force was marching down to occupy it, threatened to send his army and exterminate it. The government of Madras was at this time in the hands of Mr. Palk, who had gone to India as one of the Company's chaplains but renounced his orders, went into the civil service, in which he amassed a noble fortune, and on his return to

England obtained a baronetcy. The feeble Council of the Presidency directed the commander to suspend all military operations and proceed to Hyderabad to negotiate a treaty;
A.D. and on the 12th November, 1766, he concluded the humili-
1766 ating convention which provided that the Company should hold the northern Sircars, which had been conferred on them by the supreme authority in India, as vassals of the contemptible soobadar of the Deccan, paying a tribute of seven lacs of rupees a year. But the Madras Presidency went further, and involved the Company in the intricate web of Deccan politics, by agreeing to furnish the Nizam with two battalions of infantry and six pieces of cannon, "to settle everything right and "proper in the affairs of his highness' government," well knowing that his immediate object was to employ them in attacking Hyder Ali.

Disgraceful conduct of Madras.

The rise and progress of this extraordinary chief, one of the three men who during the last two centuries have risen from obscurity to be the founders of great kingdoms in India, will now demand the reader's attention. Mysore was one of the provinces of the Hindoo empire of Beejanugger, extinguished in 1564, and fell to the lot of a family of Hindoo princes, who gradually enlarged their territories, and, though repeatedly invaded by the Mahrattas, maintained their independence for two centuries, till they were dethroned by Hyder Ali. His family emigrated from the Punjab, and his father raised himself to the post of head-constable and obtained the command of a
1702 small body of troops. Hyder was born about the year 1702, and remained without distinction for forty-seven years. It was not before 1749, during the struggles of the French and English for power in the Deccan, that he attracted the attention of the regent of Mysore at the siege of Deonhully, and was pro-
1749 moted to an important command. This brief epitome affords no space for narrating the progress of his career; and it is sufficient to notice that he augmented his resources by false musters, and by his incomparable tact and duplicity gradually absorbed the chief authority in the state. Having at length acquired the absolute command of the army, he constrained the feeble raja to resign the sceptre to him and to retire into private life on an annuity, which
1761 was soon after curtailed. He was a brave soldier, a bold and skilful general, and a brilliant administrator. Like Sevajee and Runjeet Sing, he was unable to read or write, and it may

Rise and progress of Hyder.

His birth.

His first distinction.

be questioned whether either of them could have passed the modern test of talent in a competitive examination, but they could all three create empires and govern them. Hyder became master of Mysore at the age of sixty, and devoted himself for twenty years to the aggrandisement of his power at the expense of his neighbours. Within two years he extended his authority up to the Kistna, and A.D.
overran the territory of Bednore on the summit 1763
of the western ghauts, which overlooks the maritime province of Canara. The capital, then esteemed the most wealthy city in the Deccan, fell without a struggle, and Hyder always attributed his subsequent prosperity to the treasure he obtained in it. He had previously cast off the title of Hyder Naik, or constable, and assumed the dignity of Hyder Ali Khan Bahadoor, and he now introduced a style of greater splendour and etiquette into his court.

Acquires Bednore.

The Peshwa, Ballajee Rao, died of a broken heart on hearing of the fatal battle of Paniput, and was succeeded by his son Mahdoo Rao, then eighteen years of age. The Nizam determined to take advantage 1761
of the weakness of the Mahrattas, to recover the districts his predecessor had been obliged to cede to them in their palmy days, and having formed an alliance with Bhonslay, raja of Nagpore, marched upon Poona, which 1763
he plundered and partially burnt. Raghoba, the uncle of the Peshwa, retaliated by laying Hyderabad under contributions, and the two armies met on the banks of the Godavery. Before the battle, Raghoba had managed to buy off the raja of Nagpore by the promise of lands valued at thirty-two lacs a year, and on the eve of the battle he accordingly deserted the Nizam, who was defeated with great slaughter. But as the Mahrattas were incensed at the raja for joining the Nizam, and the Nizam was annoyed by his desertion at a cri- 1766
tical moment, they united their forces, invaded his kingdom, and stripped him of the greater portion of the territory he had acquired by his perfidy.

War between the Mahrattas, the Nizam and Hyder.

Mysore had hitherto been regarded by the Mahrattas as a reserve field for plunder when there happened to be no other marauding expedition on hand, but the rapid rise of a new power under Hyder Ali, with an army of 20,000 horse and 40,000 foot, one half of which consisted of well-disciplined battalions, aroused the alarm and the indignation of the Poona cabinet, and it was determined to chastise his audacity. An army was accordingly despatched into the country, and Hyder was

Mahrattas attack Hyder.

A.D. 1765 brought for the first time into contact with the Mahrattas, and suffered a signal defeat. The next year the Peshwa again took the field, and the Mysore army was a second time defeated, with the loss of 10,000 men, and Hyder considered himself fortunate in being relieved from the Mahrattas by restoring the greater portion of the districts he had usurped, and paying an indemnity of thirty-two lacs of rupees. To compensate for these losses he invaded the maritime province of Malabar, which had never been subjugated by the Mahomedan arms. The gallant Nairs, or military chieftains, offered a noble resistance, but the whole province was nevertheless occupied, and the Mysore flag was planted on the towers of Calicut, the chief of which was still designated the Zamorin, as in the days of Albuquerque, two centuries and a half before. From these schemes of conquest Hyder was recalled to defend his own dominions and to resist a confederacy of the Mahrattas and the Nizam, into which

1765 Repeated defeat of Hyder.

1766 the Company was unwillingly drawn by the fatal article in the treaty of the 12th November, 1766, which bound the Madras Government to assist the Nizam with an auxiliary force. He now claimed the fulfilment of this engagement, and, in an evil hour, Colonel Smith was sent with an army to co-operate with him and the Mahrattas in coercing

1767 Hyder. The Mahrattas forestalled the Nizam, and crossing the Kistna in January, let loose their predatory horse on Hyder's northern dominions, and constrained him to purchase their retreat by the payment of thirty lacs of rupees.

Colonel Smith, on his arrival in the Nizam's camp, found that he was basely negotiating with Hyder for a joint attack on the English army, and he withdrew with the bulk of his force to defend the frontier of the Carnatic. The bargain with Hyder was completed by an engagement on the part of the Nizam to fall on the British force on receiving an immediate payment of twenty lacs of rupees and a promise of six lacs of annual tribute. The confederate armies numbered 42,000 cavalry and 28,000 infantry, with a hundred guns, while the British force did not exceed 1,030 sabres and 5,800 bayonets, with sixteen guns. With this disproportionate force Colonel Smith twice defeated the allies and captured sixty-four pieces of cannon. During these operations Hyder's eldest son Tippoo, then seventeen years of age, suddenly advanced to Madras with

Operations of the British force.

1767 Col. Smith defeats the confederates.

a body of 5,000 horse, and plundered the country houses of the Madras gentry, and the members of Government only escaped being captured by the eagerness of the Mysore troops for plunder. In the meantime, the Government of Bengal sent an expedition by sea under Colonel Peach, to create a diversion in the Nizam's territories. He landed on the coast, carried everything before him, and advanced to Warungul, within eighty miles of Hyderabad, and the Nizam deserted Hyder, and hastened to make his peace with the English.

The Nizam's territories attacked.

The affairs of the Nizam were now in a desperate condition. He had been defeated in two engagements; his northern territories were occupied and his capital was threatened; and the Madras President, Mr. Palk, might have dictated his own terms. It might have been expected that he would, at least, have declared the former treaty annulled by the monstrous perfidy of the Nizam; but, after several weeks of negotiation, he concluded another treaty, the most disgraceful which had ever sullied the annals of the Company. It confirmed the dishonourable engagement to pay tribute for the northern Sircars, which had been granted by the imperial firman "to the Company, their heirs and descendants for ever and "ever, free, exempt and safe from all demands of the "imperial dewanee office and the imperial court," and it postponed the possession of the Guntoor Sircar till the death of the Nizam's brother, Basalut Jung, to whom he had illegally assigned it. Hyder Ali, who had been a sovereign prince for seven years, was contemptuously described in the treaty as Hyder Naik, or constable, a rebel and a usurper, and it was stipulated that the English Government should wrest the Carnatic Balaghaut, the table-land of Mysore, from him, and hold it as a fief of the Nizam on the payment of seven lacs a year, and likewise pay *chout* for it to the Mahrattas, who were no parties to the treaty. To crown their folly the Madras Council again involved their masters in all the intrigues and dangers of Deccan politics, by engaging to assist the Nizam, the most treacherous prince in that age of perfidy, with two battalions of sepoys and six pieces of artillery whenever he should require them. The treaty was reprobated by the Court of Directors, who remarked, "We cannot take a view of your conduct "from the commencement of your negotiations for the "Sircars, without the strongest disapprobation, and when "we see the opulent fortunes acquired by our servants since

Disgraceful treaty with the Nizam.

A.D. 1768

"that period, it gives but too much weight to the public "opinion that this rage for negotiations, treaties and "alliances, has private advantage for its object more than "the public good." A truer verdict was never pronounced in Leadenhall Street. During this disgraceful decade the Madras Presidency was sunk in peculation and profligacy as deeply as that of Bengal, with the additional vice of official poltroonery.

Hyder, who was fully cognizant of this treaty which
A.D. treated him as an usurper, and bound the English Govern-
1768 War with Hyder. ment to dismember his dominions, saw that he had now to maintain a struggle for his political existence, and he prepared for the conflict. An expedition from the Bombay Presidency had destroyed a portion of his fleet and captured some of his towns on the Malabar coast; but he speedily recovered them, and returned to prosecute the war in his eastern districts. In the management of the war into which the Madras Council had so wantonly plunged, they exhibited the same spirit of infatuation as in their negotiations. Two "field deputies" were sent to control the movements of the force, and the supply of the commissariat was entrusted to the imbecile nabob of the Carnatic, who disappointed the Government, as a matter of course. But notwithstanding every disadvantage, Colonel Smith overran half Hyder's territories and captured some of his principal fortresses. Under the dread of a simultaneous invasion of the Mahrattas, Hyder deemed it prudent to bend to circumstances, and offered to cede the Baramahal and to pay down ten lacs of rupees; but the President,
1768 Col. Smith's success. inflated by recent successes, advanced the most extravagant and inadmissible demands, and Hyder prepared for a mortal struggle. Colonel Smith, who had remonstrated with the Council on the folly of their proposals, was recalled to Madras, and the tide now began to turn against the Company. The siege of Bangalore was raised, and Hyder, with his usual energy and rapidity, recovered all the forts he had lost; descended into the Baramahal, and turned south to Tanjore, and having exacted four lacs of rupees from the raja, moved up northwards towards Madras. The consternation of the community may be readily conceived. It was now the turn of the bewildered
1769 Hyder dictates peace. Council to sue for an accommodation, but after a fruitless negotiation, they obtained an armistice of only twelve days when they had asked for forty. Hyder resumed his course of desolation. He drew Colonel

Smith, who had been reinstated in his command, to a distance of one hundred and forty miles from Madras, and determined to bring the war to a termination by dictating peace under its walls. Placing himself at the head of 6,000 of his best cavalry he marched a hundred and thirty miles in three days and a half, and suddenly making his appearance at St. Thomé, about four miles from Madras, demanded that an order should be sent to stop the pursuit of Colonel Smith, who was following him with the greatest rapidity, and that the President, Mr. Du Pré, who had succeeded Mr. Palk, might be sent to his camp to treat with him. Hyder was master of the situation and dictated A.D.
his own terms. A treaty was concluded on the 3rd April, 1769
the salient points of which were a mutual restitution of conquests, and an alliance offensive and defensive. Hyder was to be assisted by a British contingent if he was attacked by any of the powers in the Deccan, and for the third time did the Madras Council involve the Company in the ever shifting and perilous politics of the Deccan. Thus ended the second Mysore war, with the loss of all the acquisitions which had been made and all the treasure which had been expended, and above all, of the prestige of the English arms.

Hyder Ali, having settled his dispute with the Madras 1770
Government, and obtained the promise of its support, withheld the payments due to the Mahrattas and invaded their territories. The Peshwa assembled a large army with the determination to subjugate Mysore. Hyder's forts were rapidly reduced and his districts laid waste, and he was induced to make overtures of peace; but as the Peshwa demanded a crore of rupees the negotiation was broken off. Hyder then advanced with 35,000 men and forty guns to Milgota, where he found himself entrapped into a false position.

Hyder and the Mahrattas at war.

After sustaining an incessant cannonade for eight days he 1771
commenced a stealthy retreat by night to Seringapatam, twenty-two miles distant. It was, however, discovered, and the Mahrattas assaulted the fugitive army with great vigour, and it was saved from annihilation only by their eagerness for plunder. Hyder's capital was besieged for five weeks, and he importuned the President of Madras for that assistance which he was bound to afford by the recent treaty. The President and Council considered it of vital consequence for the honour and the interests of the Company to support him, but they were overruled by the

interference of Sir John Lindsay, whom the prime minister, deluded by the representation of the nabob of the Carnatic, had, by an act of incredible folly, sent out as the king's representative to his court. The authority of the Company's Government was at once superseded by that of the Crown, and the profligate nabob not only set the Madras Council at defiance, but induced Sir John to insist on an alliance with the Mahrattas. Hyder Ali, deprived of British support, was reduced to extremities, and obliged to purchase peace by the payment of thirty-six lacs of rupees and submitting to an annual tribute of fourteen lacs, and making a

A.D. 1772 *Hyder's loss of territory.* cession of territory which reduced the kingdom of Mysore to smaller limits than it comprised at the beginning of the century. He never forgave or forgot this desertion, and ten years later exacted a fearful penalty.

Eight years after the Mahrattas had been expelled from Hindostan by the battle of Paniput, the Peshwa equipped an army of 50,000 horse and a large body of

1769 *Mahratta expedition to Hindostan.* infantry, with a numerous artillery, to recover their footing, and renew their spoliations. The first operations of this force were directed against the Rajpoots, from whom they exacted ten lacs of rupees; and then against the Jauts, who agreed to pay them sixty-five lacs; after which they overran the districts of the

1770 Rohillas, and ravaged the whole of the Dooab, or country lying between the Jumna and the Ganges, and returned to Delhi before the rains. The emperor, after the arrangement made with Lord Clive in 1765, had continued to reside at Allahabad, in the tranquil enjoyment of the annuity settled on him, and of the revenues of Corah and Allahabad, while the districts around Delhi still attached to the Crown were administered by Nujeeb-ood-dowlah, and, on his death, by his son Zabita Khan. The emperor was naturally desirous of mounting the throne of his ancestors and establishing his court in the ancient capital. The Mahrattas were equally desirous of seating him on it, and obtaining the important influence of his name. In spite of the advice of the Council in Calcutta, who warned him of the danger of such a movement, he threw himself into their arms, and was by them installed on the 25th December.

The next year the Mahrattas again overran Rohilcund, and the Rohilla chiefs were driven to solicit the aid of the Vizier of Oude. There are few transactions involved in greater obscurity than the negotiations between the Mahrattas, the Rohillas, and the Vizier, on this memorable occasion. It would appear that the Mahrattas offered to retire on receiving forty lacs of rupees, or a bond for that amount from the Rohilla chiefs, but guaranteed by the Vizier himself. The Vizier endorsed the bond, and received an instalment of five lacs from Hafiz Ruhmut, the Rohilla chief, but neglected to pay any portion of it to the Mahrattas. Meanwhile, the Mahrattas offered to cancel the demand on the Rohillas if they would join in an attack on Oude, receiving half the conquered territories; but they refused to listen to the proposal, and cast in their lot with the nabob Vizier. Several detachments of Mahrattas laid waste a portion of Rohilcund, but they were held in check by the combined force of the Rohillas, of the Vizier, and of the English brigade sent to protect the country. The Peshwa Mahdoo Rao, meanwhile, died at Poona, and his successor planned an expedition to the Carnatic, and recalled the whole of the Mahratta force from Hindostan, and they quitted it laden with the booty of three campaigns. At the close of the previous year the emperor, unable any longer to support the arrogance and rapacity of the Mahrattas, met them in the field, but his army was completely defeated, and he was obliged to open the gates of Delhi to their hostile battalions, and submit to all their demands.

A.D. 1772

Negotiations with the Rohillas.

1773

The British Government in India at this period presented a singular anomaly. The agents of a London trading Company had acquired the sovereignty of provinces larger and more populous than England. They were making war and peace, putting up and pulling down thrones, and disposing of princely revenues. Their servants in India, with salaries of three and four hundred rupees a month, were coming home, year after year, with colossal fortunes, and setting up establishments which cast the ancient aristocracy into the shade. The Indian nabobs, as they were called, were exposed on the stage and avoided in society, from the impression that their sudden and enormous wealth had been acquired by injustice and oppression. The machinery of the Government at home had been constructed for the management of commerce, and was ill suited for the administration of an empire. The posts in India which afforded the means of amassing these ambitious fortunes were at the disposal of the Directors, who were elected by the votes of the Proprietors. A vote was consequently considered so valuable

Reform of the Government.

that in 1771 the ship's husbands, then a wealthy and powerful body, bought fifteen lacs of rupees of stock to create three hundred votes. The India House became a scene of jobbery and corruption never seen in England before. The
A.D. Indian Government was equally fetid in London and in
1771 Calcutta. A general cry was raised for Parliamentary investigation, which was redoubled by the financial embarrassments of the Company. The frauds of their servants in India had exhausted their treasury. With an annual revenue of two crores and a half of rupees, they owed more than a crore and a quarter in England, and a crore in Calcutta. It was in these circumstances of impending bankruptcy that the Court of Proprietors voted themselves a dividend at the rate of twelve and a half per cent. The Court of Directors borrowed of the bank of England as long as the bank would lend, and then solicited a loan of a million from the English exchequer, to prevent the doors of the India House from being closed. The ministers referred them to Parliament, which was consequently convened
1772 earlier than usual. A select Committee was appointed to collect evidence, when the scenes of violence and iniquity by which the British name had been disgraced in India were, for the first time, laid bare to the nation, and Parliament determined at once to take the regulation of Indian affairs into its own hands. The Company protested against this invasion of their chartered rights, but the universal odium they had incurred throughout the country placed them at the mercy of the ministry. The vicious constitution of their corporation was reformed. The Directors were to be chosen for four years instead of one; the votes of the Proprietors were to be limited to four, whatever amount of
1773 Regulating Act. stock they might hold; and twelve hundred of the proprietors were disfranchised at a stroke. The governor of Bengal was appointed Governor-General upon two lacs and a half a year, with a Council consisting of four, on one lac each, and a Supreme Court was to be established in Calcutta on the model of the courts of Westminster, with a Chief Justice and three puisne judges. The Act, which was designated the "Regulating Act," purified the home administration, but it shook the British power in India to its foundation.

CHAPTER VI.

SECTION I.

MR. HASTINGS'S ADMINISTRATION TO THE DEPARTURE OF MR. FRANCIS.

WARREN HASTINGS was appointed in the Act the first Governor-General of India. He had landed in Calcutta as a writer on the Company's establishment in 1750, and was employed for the first seven years in appraising silks and muslins and copying invoices. *Warren Hastings's early career.* A.D. 1750 The great events which followed the battle of Plassy afforded the first opportunity of developing his talents, and he was selected by Colonel Clive to represent the Government at the durbar of Moorshedabad, then the most 1760 important of subordinate offices in the service. Three years after he came by rotation into the Council board, and offered a strenuous resistance to those profligate measures of his colleagues which brought on the war with Meer Cossim. He returned to England after fifteen years' 1765 service comparatively poor, while Mr. Vansittart, who sailed in the same ship with him, was reported to have taken home little short of fifty lacs. After a residence of several years in England the Court of Directors restored him to their service, and appointed him second member of Council at Madras, where he exhibited such zeal and ability as to be selected to take charge of the Government of Bengal. Hastings found the administration in a state of complete anarchy. *Governor of Bengal.* 1772 The double Government established by Clive, which was considered a masterpiece of policy, had turned out to be the curse of the country. The management of the revenue, which embraced the most important functions of Government, was in the hands of natives, acting under the venal court of the nabob, though nominally under the control of the English Resident, and they were practically without any control whatever. The people were oppressed by the native functionaries and zemindars, who enriched themselves at the expense of the state. Supervisors were appointed in 1769 to check these abuses, but they knew nothing of the language or of the people, or of the value of the lands, and became mere tools in the hands of their rapacious banians, or head officials. The Court of Directors determined therefore "to stand forth as Duan," as they termed it, and

to take on themselves the collection and management of the revenues through the agency of their own European servants. To Hastings was committed the arduous duty of carrying out this difficult policy, and he entered upon it with his accustomed resolution. A new revenue settlement was formed under the immediate direction of members of the Council. The charge of civil and criminal jurisprudence was committed to the covenanted servants of the Company,
A.D. 1773 His vigorous reforms. and the treasury was removed from Moorshedabad to Calcutta, which became from that time forward the capital of Bengal. Without the aid of a lawyer, he drew up a simple code of regulations for the courts he had established, which exhibited in a remarkable degree the versatility of his talents. All these organic changes were completed in the brief space of six months.

The first military operations of Hastings's administration exercised unhappily a very inauspicious influence on his reputation. The Vizier had long eagerly coveted the
The Rohilla war. possession of Rohilcund, and the Mahrattas had no sooner returned to their own country, as already stated, than he importuned Hastings to assist him in seizing it, with the offer of forty lacs of rupees, as well as a subsidy of more than two lacs of rupees a month for the pay of the troops employed in the service. He represented that the Rohillas had offered to pay him forty lacs to deliver them from the Mahrattas, that they had been expelled by his army, aided by a brigade of Company's troops, and that the Rohilla chiefs now repudiated the obligation. The Vizier's tempting offer was made at a time when the Court of Directors, overwhelmed with debt and disgrace, were importuning the Council by every vessel for remittances. The treasury at Calcutta was not only empty, but more than a crore of rupees in debt. The nabob wanted territory and Hastings wanted money, and he persuaded his conscience that the statements of the Vizier were true, and that the ingratitude of the Rohillas merited punishment, more especially as this act of retributive justice would likewise promote the interests of the Company.

Hastings proceeded to Benares and concluded a treaty with the nabob to that effect, and at the same time restored
1773 Treaty with nabob. to him the two districts of Corah and Allahabad, which Clive had taken from him and made over to the emperor, and which the emperor had transferred under compulsion to the Mahrattas. For this grant the treasury was enriched by a further payment of fifty lacs. The nabob

Vizier, having secured the aid of an English force, demanded of the Rohilla chief the balance of the bond, of which only five lacs had been paid. Hafiz Ruhmut offered to make good whatever the Vizier had actually paid to the Mahrattas, though they had left the country by orders from Poona and not through any exertions on his part; but as nothing had been paid them, the offer was treated with contempt. The Rohilla chief, seeing the storm ready to burst, offered to compromise the claim, but the perfidious Vizier raised his demand to two crores. The Rohillas determined, therefore, to defend themselves to the last extremity, and brought 40,000 troops into the field, but they were defeated and dispersed, and the brave Hafiz Ruhmut fell with three of his sons. The Vizier remained beyond the reach of fire, but as soon as the battle was decided let his troops loose to plunder. "We have the "honour of the day," exclaimed the English commandant, "and these banditti the profit of it." This transaction is one of the few stains on the bright and honourable career of Hastings. It is doubtless true that the Rohillas, who had recently occupied the country, were, like all other Afghan tribes in Hindostan and the Deccan, dangerous and formidable neighbours, and might at any time have joined the Mahrattas and overrun Oude, which the Company's Government was bound to defend, but the war unquestionably originated in the rapacity of the Vizier and also in the necessities of the treasury in Calcutta. The assertion that half a million of people were driven across the Ganges, and that "the country became a howling wilderness," was an oriental figure of speech.

A.D. 1774 — Rohillas defeated.

Six months after the conquest of the Rohillas, the four judges of the Supreme Court, and the three new councillors, landed in Calcutta, and the new Government was proclaimed on the 20th November. Of the councillors, Colonel Monson was a scion of nobility and had served on the Coast; General Clavering was the personal favourite of the king, and all powerful with the prime minister; and Mr. Francis, the reputed author of *Junius*, was equally distinguished by his talents and his malignity. They came out with the impression that the Government was a compound of tyranny and corruption, and that Hastings was a monster of iniquity whom it was the duty of virtuous men to oppose in every mode. At the first meeting of Council in which Hastings presided as Governor-General, they outvoted him, and at once divested

1774 — New Government in Calcutta.

him of all power in the Government. They proceeded to recall Mr. Middleton, whom Hastings had placed as the Company's representative at Lucknow, and sent Mr. Bristow one of their friends to occupy the post, thereby proclaiming the extinction of Hastings's authority throughout Hindostan. They ordered the officer in command in Oude peremptorily to withdraw the brigade, and to demand the payment of all arrears from the Vizier within a fortnight, and thus compromised the safety of Oude, and the faith of the British Government.

During these transactions the Vizier died, upon which Mr. Francis declared that every engagement between the Company's Government and that of Oude was thereby cancelled, except that which referred to the payment of arrears. Mr. Francis accordingly constrained his son to enter into a new treaty, and though he had denounced Hastings for "letting out "British troops for hire to the Vizier," not only repeated the bargain, but increased the hire of the troops. He likewise obliged the Vizier to cede to the Company the province of Benares, valued at twenty-two lacs a year. The deceased Vizier had accumulated two crores of treasure, which were buried in the vaults of the zenana. His widow and his mother, historically known as the "begums," claimed the whole of this property under the terms of a will, which, however, was never produced. The Vizier was under heavy obligations to the Company, and the troops, 100,000 in number, were twelve months in arrear. The treasure was state property and answerable in the first instance for its debts, but Mr. Bristow constrained the Vizier to affix his seal to a deed assigning three-fourths of it to the princesses, under the guarantee of the Government in Calcutta. The troops mutinied for pay, and it was reported that 20,000 were slaughtered, but the state was preserved from a revolution by the presence of the Company's brigade.

A.D. 1775 Violent conduct towards Oude.

As soon as it became known that Hastings's authority was extinct, and that the surest mode of obtaining the favour of those who were now in the seat of power was to bring accusations against him, a swarm of informers hastened to Calcutta and filled the antechambers of his opponents. Charges of every variety were rapidly manufactured and eagerly welcomed, and the triumvirate placed it on the minutes of Council "that there "appeared to be no species of peculation from which the

1775 Accusations against Hastings.

"Honourable the Governor-General had thought it reasonable to abstain, and by which he had amassed a fortune "of forty lacs of rupees in two years." The most important and memorable of these charges was that brought forward by Nunkoomar. He was by birth a brahmin, who had taken an active part in public affairs at Moorshedabad and Calcutta, and had accumulated a crore of rupees by intrigue and treachery. He had been repeatedly denounced to the Council by the Court of Directors for his knavery. On this occasion he came forward and offered to impeach Hastings of having received a bribe of three lacs and a half from Munee begum, who had been appointed by him to superintend the nabob's household.

The hostile councillors proposed to confront him with the Governor-General in the Council chamber, but Hastings asserted that he knew what was due to the character and dignity of the head of the Government, and would not preside at the board to be criminated by the dregs of society. He dissolved the sitting and retired, when his opponents placed General Clavering in the chair, and called in Nunkoomar, who descanted on the venality of Hastings, and produced a letter from Munee begum, which testified to the payment of the douceur. The Council immediately voted that the Governor-General had clandestinely and illegally received the sum of three lacs and a half, and should be called upon to refund it to the treasury. The begum denied all knowledge of the letter; the best Persian experts pronounced the signature a forgery, but the seal appeared to be genuine, and the mystery was not cleared up till, after Nunkoomar's death, facsimiles of the seals of every eminent character in the state were found in his cabinet. For the vindication of his own character Hastings now brought an action for conspiracy in the Supreme Court against Nunkoomar and several others. The judges admitted the charge, and held him to bail.

Hastings's dignified conduct. A.D. 1775

Eight weeks after the commencement of this suit, a native merchant in Calcutta brought an action for forgery against Nunkoomar. It had been instituted originally in the old mayor's court, and Nunkoomar was committed to prison, but released through the intervention of Hastings. On the establishment of the Supreme Court this suit, together with all others then pending, was transferred to its files. The forgery was established by the clearest evidence, before a jury consisting

Trial and execution of Nunkoomar. 1775

of the most respectable European residents in Calcutta, and he was found guilty and hung in the most conspicuous portion of the town. This transaction was long considered the culminating crime of Hastings's administration. It was asserted in high quarters that the brahmin was murdered by Hastings through the forms of law, and that the execution was designed to stifle all further accusations. But time, the vindicator of truth, has dispelled the clouds of prejudice. The coincidence of the charge of Hastings against Nunkoomar and of the native against Nunkoomar was purely accidental. There has never been a particle of evidence to connect Hastings with the forgery suit, and his own assertion that he had neither prompted nor encouraged it must be considered conclusive. The sentence, however conformable to the sanguinary laws of England at the time, was essentially iniquitous. The crime was not capital by the law of India, nor in the opinion of the native community, and it was committed before the Supreme Court brought the weight of English law to press on India. The odium of the deed is divided between the judges of the Supreme Court and the triumvirate who, possessed of supreme power, declined to suspend the execution of the sentence pending a reference to England, which they must have known would have saved his life.

The Court of Directors, to whom both parties had appealed against each other, passed a vote of censure on Hastings, but it was overruled by the Court of Proprietors, who entertained an exalted opinion of his merits. During

Hastings tenders his resignation.

A.D. 1776

the height of the conflict in Calcutta, Hastings, worried by the opposition and insults of his opponents, had instructed his agent in London to tender his resignation, but two or three months later, having recovered the tone of his mind, revoked the authority. The agent, however, seeing the strength of the current against Hastings both in Leadenhall Street and Downing Street, took upon himself to intimate to the Court of Directors that he was authorised to offer his patron's retirement from office. Then ensued several months of violent disputes in the Court between Hastings's friends and enemies, which resulted in a resolution by the majority that he had positively resigned his post, although his letters revoking his first instructions were before them, and they proceeded to fill up the vacancy. The intelligence of these transactions created a serious convulsion in Calcutta. General Clavering, the senior member of council, determined to take possession of the Government, and was sworn in by his colleagues as Governor-General; but Hastings, who repudiated the fact of his resignation, refused to give up the keys of the fort or of the treasury, and issued his commands to all civil and military officers to obey no orders but his own. The dispute was drifting into hostilities, which must have been fatal to the public interests, when Hastings brought it to a safe issue by offering to refer the question to the arbitrament of the judges of the Supreme Court, who, after long and anxious deliberation, continued till four in the morning, decided that any assumption of authority by Sir John Clavering would be illegal. He died shortly after, and Hastings recovered his authority for a time by his own casting vote; but he was systematically opposed by Mr. Francis upon every question, political, military, and administrative. The contest ended, according to the barbarous practice of the period, in a duel, in which Mr. Francis was wounded, and soon after returned to England.

Violence and death of Gen. Clavering. A.D. 1777

Duel between Hastings and Francis. 1780

SECTION II.

WAR WITH THE MAHRATTAS.

To resume the thread of affairs in the Mahratta commonwealth, the constitution of which was passing through great and important changes. The four chiefs—Sindia and Holkar, the Gaikwar and the raja of Nagpore—originally the generals of the Peshwa, were outgrowing his authority, and developing into independent princes, and enjoyed two-thirds of the Mahratta revenues. The military force of the state, consisting of 100,000 splendid cavalry, with a proportionate strength of foot and artillery, was no longer under the single control of the Peshwa; a large portion of it acted under the command of these princes, each one of whom had his own individual interests to pursue. The young Peshwa, Mahdoo Rao, little inferior to any of his race in the cabinet or in the field, died in November, and was succeeded by his younger 1772
brother, Narrain Rao, who recalled the troops from the banks of the Ganges, as already stated. After a brief reign of nine months he was assassinated, as the Mahrattas universally believed, by the orders of his uncle Raghoba, a

Progress of Mahratta affairs.

brave soldier, but an inveterate intriguer, always imprudent

Raghoba assassinates the Peshwa.

A.D. and never fortunate. He took possession of the
1773 vacant throne, and at once plunged into hostilities with the Nizam, and constrained him to make a large cession of territory, which, however, by an act of infatuation, he restored to him. He then proceeded against Hyder, from whom he obtained nothing but empty promises. From these southern expeditions he was recalled to the seat of government by a formidable confederacy raised against him by the leading ministers at Poona. They had received intimation that the widow of the deceased Peshwa was about to become a mother, and they conveyed her for security to a hill fortress, taking the precaution of sending with her a number of brahmin females in the same condition, to meet the contingency of her giving birth to a daughter. The widow was confined of a son, who was
1774 installed as the Peshwa Mahdoo Rao the second, and a regency was formed to conduct the Government. Raghoba

Raghoba's movements.

hastened towards Poona, and with the aid of Morari Rao of Gooty, the greatest Mahratta general of the age, who had measured swords with Lawrence and Clive, inflicted a crushing defeat on the army of the regency; but, instead of following up his victory by advancing at once upon the capital, and taking advantage of the consternation which prevailed, he turned off to Boorhanpore, and moved across the Nerbudda. There he was joined by Sindia and Holkar, as they returned from Rohilcund, and advanced into Guzerat to secure the aid of the Gaikwar's troops.

Raghoba negotiates with Bombay.

Raghoba now opened negotiations with the President of Bombay, and made an offer of money and territory, in return for military support, which was eagerly embraced. The Company, whose possessions had
1775 been confined for a century to Bombay, had always coveted the acquisition of the harbour of Bassein, and the island of Salsette, separated from it by a narrow channel. The President offered to assist Raghoba with a body of troops, on his providing funds for their maintenance, and ceding these coveted possessions in perpetuity to the Company; but he could not bring himself to alienate the island and the harbour, which the Mahrattas prized the more highly as they had been wrested from a
1739 European power, the Portuguese, about thirty years before. An engagement was nevertheless concluded with him, and a British force of 1,500 men sent to his aid. While the

negotiation was pending, the Bombay authorities received information that a large armament was about to be sent from Goa to recover Bassein and Salsette, and as they considered that the Portuguese were likely to be more troublesome neighbours than the Mahrattas, proceeded to take A.D.
summary possession of them. Meanwhile, the regency at 1774
Poona having succeeded, by large offers, in detaching Sindia and Holkar from the cause of Raghoba, sent a large force to attack him. He was routed at Wassud, and fled with 1,000 horse to the encampment of Colonel Keating, who had by this time reached Surat with the Bombay detachment.

A treaty was then presented for his acceptance, which 1775
stipulated that the Bombay Government should furnish him with a body of 3,000 troops to reinstate him as Peshwa, on condition of his ceding territory of the annual value of nineteen lacs of rupees, making an immediate payment of eighteen lacs, and irrevocably ceding Salsette and Bassein; and he could no longer continue to refuse this demand. It was this treaty, called the treaty of Surat, which involved the Company in the first Mahratta war, and it was concluded without the knowledge of Hastings and the Supreme Council.

Treaty of Surat.

The Bombay authorities having thus embarked in a war with the regency, ordered Colonel Keating to march down on Poona. 1775

Battle of Arras.

He found the Mahratta army strongly posted at Arras, and it was on this field that the English and Mahratta forces met for the first time since the gentlemen of the factory of Surat had gallantly repulsed Sevajee in 1669. The disproportion of the armies was as ten to one, but the Mahratta generals sustained a signal defeat and fled precipitately across the Nerbudda, after having thrown their guns into it. The Gaikwar, who had hitherto held aloof, now hastened to join Raghoba, and promised to furnish him with a large supply of money and to secure to the Company a share of the revenues of Broach. The Mahratta fleet was simultaneously crippled by the English commodore. The campaign had been prosperous beyond the highest expectation, and the insignificant Presidency of Bombay had obtained territory of the value of twenty-four lacs a year. The Poona regency was tottering, and the Nizam had been emboldened by their weakness to exact a considerable cession of territory.

These brilliant prospects were marred by the folly and perversity of Mr. Francis and his associates. They

pronounced the treaty impolitic, dangerous, and unjust, and
A.D. 1775 Folly of the Supreme Council. above all unauthorised by the Supreme Council, which had been invested with the control of the minor Presidencies, and they sent peremptory orders to annul the treaty and recall the army from the field. Hastings equally disapproved of the treaty, but took a statesman's view of their position, and affirmed that as the Company's Government was actually involved in war, it should be prosecuted with vigour, and concluded as speedily as possible. At the same time the majority in Council deputed Colonel Upton to Poona to disavow the proceedings of the Bombay Government, and to open negotiations with the regency. It was in vain the Bombay authorities remonstrated on the imprudence of destroying their influence, and withdrawing the victorious troops from the field, and the disgrace of violating a solemn engagement.

Colonel Upton, on his arrival at Poona, found the astute ministers determined to take advantage of these divided
1776 Col. Upton at Poona. councils. They extolled to the skies "the wisdom "of the great governor of Calcutta, who had "ordered peace to be concluded;" but when the Colonel proposed that Salsette and Bassein should be guaranteed to the Company, they assumed an arrogant tone, and demanded the immediate surrender of Raghoba, and the restoration of all the territory the Company had recently acquired. The insolent demands of the regency roused the indignation of Mr. Francis and his colleagues, and they determined to support Raghoba; the troops were again ordered to take the field, and a supply of treasure was despatched to Bombay. But the regency, after a little more bluster, came to terms with
1776 Treaty of Poorundur. Colonel Upton, and the treaty of Poorundur was concluded, which stipulated that Raghoba should disband his army, and retire to the banks of the Godavery, that all the territorial acquisitions of the Company should be relinquished with the exception of Salsette, which "might be retained if the Governor-General desired it," and that twelve lacs of rupees should be paid for the expenses of the war "by way of favour." Considering that all the advantages of the late campaign had been on the side of the English, the Bombay President was justified in pronouncing the treaty "highly injurious to the interests and "reputation of the Company." It was a flagrant breach of faith with Raghoba; it shook the confidence of the native princes in the engagements of our Government, and it

inflated the regency with an undue sense of its power, which led to future difficulties.

Four months after the signature of the treaty, a despatch was received from the Court of Directors approving of the treaty of Surat, directing that the territories A.D.
ceded by Raghoba should be retained, and that 1776
the other Presidencies should assist in supporting

Decision of the Court of Directors.

him. The Bombay Council, smarting under the indignity which had been inflicted on them, gave the treaty of Poorundur to the winds, invited Raghoba to Bombay, and settled a monthly allowance on him. The Poona regency raved at this violation of the treaty, but their strength was weakened by discord between the aged premier Succaram Bapoo and his younger associate Nana Furnavese. To increase the complication of affairs at Poona, a French adventurer, of the name of St. Lubin, arrived 1777
there in March, and announced himself as the

St. Lubin.

envoy of the king of France, then on the eve of a war with England. He was authorised, he said, to offer the regency the support of 2,500 Europeans, and equipments for 10,000 sepoys, as well as officers to discipline and command them. Nana Furnavese affected to believe in his mission, and made over to him the harbour of Choul, only twenty-three miles from Bombay, for the reception of the troops.

Second despatch from Directors.

Soon after another despatch was received from the Court, regretting the sacrifices made by the treaty of Poorundur, and stating that while the Directors were determined to adhere to it, if any attempt were made to evade any of its provisions, the Bombay Government should be at liberty to renew the alliance with Raghoba. The President found little difficulty in discovering infractions of a treaty which the Mahrattas never intended to respect, and prepared to espouse the cause of Raghoba. These movements were quickened by a revolution in the cabinet at Poona which placed the 1778
partisans of Raghoba in the ascendant, and an envoy was sent to Bombay to request the President to conduct him to the capital with a military force. Within a few months a counter-revolution placed Nana Furnavese in power, and extinguished the party of Raghoba, but the Bombay Council were determined not to abandon him. Their passions were enlisted in his cause, which they identified with their own honour; and, without adequate preparation, without alliances, without even a commander in whom they had any confidence, they determined to launch a handful of men against

the whole strength of the Mahratta empire. Nana Furnavese prepared to meet the coming storm, increased his army, provisioned his forts, and refitted his fleet.

A new treaty was now made with Raghoba, which differed little from that of Surat. An army of 4,000 men,
A.D. 1778 Expedition to Poona. of whom 600 were Europeans, was sent to capture the Mahratta capital, under Colonel Egerton, an officer utterly unfit for the charge. Encumbered with 19,000 bullocks, besides other cattle, the army moved at the rate of two miles a day, while the forces of the enemy were accumulating around it. Colonel Egerton resigned the command to Colonel Cockburn, but the responsibility of all movements lay with Colonel Carnac, who had been sent as civil commissioner with the force. On reaching Tullygaum, which had been burnt, a report was spread that the Mahrattas intended also to burn Chinchore, and even the capital itself. Colonel Carnac was seized with a panic, and though only eighteen miles from Poona, with eighteen days' provisions in the camp, determined, in the first instance, to open a negotiation with the regency, and then to retreat. Without waiting for the result of the negotiation, he threw his heavy guns into a pond, and commenced his retreat, hotly pursued by the enemy. On the evening
1779 Convention of Wurgaum. of the 12th January the army encamped at Wurgaum. The Mahrattas brought up their guns during the night, and assailed the camp with great vigour in the morning. The bewildered Carnac declared that even a retreat was now impossible and made overtures to Nana Furnavese, who demanded the surrender of Raghoba before he would listen to terms. The commissioner would have complied with the demand had he not saved them from this infamy by delivering himself up to Sindia, and, under the auspices of that chief, the British army was rescued from destruction by a convention which sacrificed all the acquisitions obtained since 1773, and for the first time obliged the British Government to give hostages to a victorious enemy. The Court of Directors lost no time in dismissing Colonels Egerton, Cockburn, and Carnac from their service. Bombay was now at the mercy of the Mahrattas, and its preservation depended on the arrival of General Goddard's expedition from Hindostan.

Hastings, who had recovered his ascendancy in Council, gave his sanction to the proposal of the Bombay Council to support Raghoba, and resolved likewise to send an expedition from Bengal across the continent, to frustrate the intrigues of the French at Poona, and to strengthen the Bombay Presidency. The force consisted of between 4,000 and 5,000 men, and was destined to march from the banks of the Jumna to Bombay, through 1,000 miles of unknown country occupied by chiefs who were far more likely to be hostile than friendly. It was pronounced by Mr. Dundas, the India minister, one of "the frantic military exploits of Hastings," but it was through such frantic exploits that British power and prestige had been established in India by a handful of foreigners. It was conducted by General Goddard, one of the most illustrious names in the history of British India. So strict was the discipline which he maintained, so punctual his payments, and so conciliatory his intercourse with the chiefs and people on the route, that they cheerfully supplied him with all his requisitions. The raja of Bhopal particularly distinguished himself by his generous hospitality, though threatened with the vengeance of the Mahratta regency. On reaching Boorhanpore the general heard of the misfortunes of the Bombay force, and turned out of his route to Surat, by which he avoided an encounter with a body of 20,000 horse sent from Poona to intercept him.

General Goddard's expedition. A.D. 1778

The timely arrival of General Goddard on the western coast, and the *éclat* of this celebrated expedition, proved the salvation of the Bombay Presidency, and restored the reputation of the British arms. The convention of Wurgaum was equally repudiated by the Bombay Government and by Hastings, who directed General Goddard to open a fresh negotiation with the regency on the basis of the treaty of Poorundur. In the mean time Sindia connived at the escape of Raghoba, who repaired to Surat, where he was honourably entertained by General Goddard, and received an allowance of half a lac of rupees a month. The reception granted to him gave mortal offence to the regency, who determined to join the confederacy which had just been formed against the Company, and in reply to the General's categorical demand of a reply to his proposal, informed him that the surrender of Raghoba, and the restoration of Salsette, were the indispensable preliminaries of any treaty; he therefore dismissed their vakeels and prepared for war. At the same time he concluded a treaty, offensive and defensive, with the Gaikwar, which provided that he should join the English camp with 3,000 horse, and receive possession of all the Peshwa's territories north of the Myhee, and make

General Goddard's continued success. 1779

over certain districts south of it to the Company. On the
A.D. 10th February General Goddard captured the noble city of
1779 Ahmedabad, the modern capital of Guzerat, and, having dispersed an army of 20,000 horse with which Sindia and Holkar were advancing to attack him, encamped for the season on the banks of the Nerbudda.

The success which meanwhile attended our arms in the north-west of Hindostan was equally brilliant. Hastings

Capture of Gwalior.

sent a force of 2,400 infantry, with cavalry and artillery, under the command of Major Popham, one of the most enterprising officers in the service, to protect the little principality of Gohud, sixty miles south-east of Agra, from the encroachments of Sindia. He marched in February, and after having captured Lahar,
1780 without a battering-train, by the sheer gallantry of his men, proceeded to the celebrated fortress of Gwalior, on the summit of a stupendous rock scarped almost entirely round, and deemed throughout India impregnable. Sir Eyre Coote, the veteran hero of the Carnatic, then General in chief in Bengal, pronounced the attempt to capture it an act of madness, but Popham had set his heart on the "glorious "object," as he called it, and lay about the fort for two months silently maturing his plans. On the night of the 3rd of August, under the guidance of Captain Bruce, twenty European soldiers and two companies of sepoys, led by four officers, applied their scaling ladders to the successive stages of rock and battlements; the bewildered garrison made a feeble resistance; and at daybreak, without the loss of a single man, the British ensign was waving over the ramparts. The report of this achievement resounded through India, and served to wipe out the disgrace of the "infamous convention" of Wurgaum, as Hastings always designated it, and which he said it was worth millions to obliterate. Major Camac, who succeeded Major Popham, brought up an additional force, and not only invaded Sindia's possessions in Malwa, but threatened his capital,

1781 Defeat of Sindia.

and he was obliged to quit Poona to attend to the defence of his own dominions. Major Camac, who was no soldier, allowed himself to be surrounded by the more numerous army of Sindia. His camp was reduced to a state of starvation, and he would have been obliged to surrender had not Captain Bruce, who had distinguished himself at Gwalior, made a vigorous attack on Sindia's camp during the night. The surprise was complete, and he lost elephants, horses, baggage, and men, but, above all, his reputation, while the crest of his rival, Holkar, was elevated by a successful attack on General Goddard.

Towards the close of 1779 Hastings received intimation of a general confederacy organised by the Nizam to extinguish the power of the Company, which embraced all the princes of India with the exception of the Gaikwar. A simultaneous attack was to be made on all the Presidencies. Hyder was to invade Madras; the attack of Bombay was assigned to Sindia, Holkar, and the regency; while the raja of Nagpore was to enter Bengal through his province of Cuttack. England was at the same time at war with the French, and they were intriguing at Poona. Never had the Company been menaced with such peril, and it required the extraordinary genius of Hastings to avert it. Hyder was the first in the field, and burst upon the Carnatic, as will be hereafter narrated. Bombay was left to its own resources, and the governor, Mr. Hornby, proved equal to the emergency. The gallant Colonel Hartley had cleared the Concan of the Mahrattas, but it was again invaded by Nana Furnavese, and he had to sustain for two days the assault of 20,000 Mahratta horse with only 2,000 exhausted troops, and 600 sick in his camp. On the third day the Mahratta general was killed, and the army became dispirited and retired. General Goddard ascended the ghauts with a large force, in the hope of capturing Poona, but he was incessantly assailed by the Mahrattas, and, being vigorously attacked by Holkar with 25,000 troops, was obliged to retreat to Bombay with the loss of 450 of his troops—the only reverse he experienced in his victorious career.

Confederacy against the English. A.D. 1779

1781

The raja of Nagpore, in accordance with the compact, sent his son Chimnajee with 30,000 troops to Cuttack, but he was lukewarm in the cause of the allies, and loitered seven months on the road. On reaching the province he found himself straitened for funds, and he accepted the offer of sixteen lacs of rupees which Hastings made him on condition of his withdrawing from the confederacy. Hastings was thus enabled to buy off the most formidable member of the league, and to save Bengal from the horrors of predatory warfare. To relieve Madras from the pressure of Hyder's army, Hastings resolved to send a detachment of Bengal troops; but as the sepoys had recently broken into revolt, and murdered their officers, to avoid a sea voyage, he adopted the bold plan of sending them by land seven hundred miles along the coast,

Nagpore detached from the league. 1780

A.D. through unknown and probably hostile provinces. This 1781 was another of the "frantic military exploits of Hastings," but it effectually overawed the native chiefs and augmented our prestige. The raja of Nagpore, on the receipt of the money, agreed to send 2,000 horse to co-operate with this expedition, which Colonel Pearce conveyed to Madras in safety.

After his defeat by Major Camac, Sindia perceived that with a victorious enemy in the heart of his dominions he had everything to lose by continuing a conflict which might end in driving him across the Nerbudda and destroying his influence in the Mahratta commonwealth. He accordingly made overtures to the British commandant which Hastings was but too happy to accept. They resulted in a treaty, signed on the 13th October, by which all the territories of Sindia west of the Jumna were restored to him, and he agreed to negotiate a peace between the Company and the regency at Poona; and, at all events, to remain neuter. Hastings's anxiety for peace with the Mahrattas was quickened by the arrival of a French armament on the Coast, which he feared might result in the extirpation of our nation from the Carnatic. To bring the war with the Mahrattas to a close, he was ready to sacrifice every foot of ground which had been gained from them, not excepting even the harbour of Bassein.

Peace with Sindia. 1781

After a succession of disappointments the treaty of Salbye was at length completed on the 17th May through the mediation of Sindia, who undertook to guarantee the settlement, and thus acquired additional consequence among the Mahratta chiefs. All the territory acquired by the Company since the treaty of Poorundur was relinquished, and it was stipulated that Hyder Ali should be required to restore all his conquests in the Carnatic and to release his prisoners within three months, on pain of being treated as an enemy by the regency. Nana Furnavese, after having accepted the treaty, delayed the ratification of it for six months, while he endeavoured to make advantageous terms with Hyder for repudiating it. Hastings's impatience for the completion of this pacification was raised to fever heat by the receipt on the 5th December of a copy of the resolution of the House of Commons, to the effect that he had acted contrary to the honour and policy of the nation, and that it was the duty of the Court of Directors to remove him from the head of affairs. The promulgation of this vote throughout

Treaty of Salbye. 1782

India would not only have prevented the ratification of the treaty, but paralysed the authority of Government in every court; but on the 7th the death of Hyder dispersed the cloud of anxiety, and Nana Furnavese immediately affixed the Peshwa's seal to the treaty. The peace thus concluded with the Mahratta powers continued unbroken for twenty years.

A.D. 1782

SECTION III.

PROCEEDINGS AT MADRAS, 1771—1780.

WE revert now to the progress of events at the Madras Presidency and in the south of India. The little Hindoo kingdom of Tanjore had been in a great measure exempt from the ravages of war during the hostilities with Hyder, which terminated in the peace dictated by him under the walls of Madras. Mahomed Ali, the nabob of the Carnatic, now came forward and importuned the Madras Council to assist him in plundering the raja, as former nabobs had done. The demands of the nabob were exorbitant, but, after a little virtuous reluctance, the President sent an army into the country. The Tanjorines offered a spirited defence, but a breach was at length effected in the fortifications, when the nabob's second son, without consulting the English commander, who had been dragged into this unholy crusade, signed a treaty with the raja after having extorted an engagement to pay fifty lacs of rupees. In less than two years he again demanded the assistance of the Madras Council to exterminate the raja, on the plea that a fifth of the payment was still due, and that he had been in communication with Hyder Ali and the Mahrattas. The President was fully aware that to meet the extortion he had been under the necessity of pledging his crown jewels and even his principality—to the Dutch at Negapatam, instead of to the English at Madras—but was base enough to resolve on his ruin. An army was despatched in September; the raja was deposed and the principality made over to the unprincipled nabob. The Court of Directors, indignant at this infamous proceeding, expelled the President, Mr. Wynch, from the service and peremptorily ordered the country to be restored to the raja. Lord Pigot, who had been in the Madras civil service forty years and amassed a fortune of forty lacs of rupees, obtained an Irish

Proceedings at Tanjore. 1771

1773

Directors restore the raja. 1774

peerage on his return to England, and was now sent out as governor of Madras; and, though offered a bribe of sixty lacs of rupees by the nabob to prevent the execution of the Court's orders, proceeded in person to Tanjore and seated the raja on his ancestral throne.

The restoration was no sooner proclaimed than Paul Benfield, a Madras civilian, came forward and advanced a claim on the revenues. Nothing can more clearly demonstrate the total demoralisation of the Company's service at Madras at that period than the fact that this man, who came to India without a farthing, and whose salary had never exceeded three hundred rupees a month, should not consider it preposterous to assert that for money lent to the nabob he had assignments on the revenues of Tanjore of sixteen lacs, and for money lent to individuals he had assignments on the present crop of more than seven lacs. After long deliberation, the Council rejected his claim; but as they and other members of the civil service were creditors, real or fictitious, of the nabob to the extent of a crore and a half of rupees, they perceived that they were thereby impairing their own claims and the question was reconsidered. Lord Pigot and his friends strenuously resisted these nefarious proceedings, but a majority of seven to five voted that the assignments made to Benfield were valid. The breach in the council became wider. Lord Pigot suspended two of the members, and placed Sir Robert Fletcher, the Commander-in-Chief, under arrest, and the majority retaliated by placing the governor himself in confinement and seizing the Government. The Court of Directors ordered that he should be restored to his position and then resign the service. Seven of the members of Council were dismissed, and Sir Thomas Rumbold, who had been in the public service in Bengal, was placed at the head of the Government, but neither was his administration smooth, and it ended in his recall.

A.D. 1774 Paul Benfield.

1776 Lord Pigot confined.

Basalut Jung, who held the Guntoor Sircar as a fief of his brother the Nizam, had taken a small French force into his service, but had acceded to the request of the Madras Government to receive a British detachment in its stead, and to make over the Sircar for its support. The treaty was no sooner signed than it was leased for ten years to the nabob Mahomed Ali, that is, to his creditors, and a key was thus furnished to the transaction. Mr. Holland was deputed to Hyderabad to explain it to the Nizam, who expressed no little resentment at this inde-

1779 Guntoor Sircar.

pendent negotiation with one of his feudatories, and this
interference with the affairs of his family. But when
Mr. Holland proceeded farther to request, on the part of the
Madras Government, that the sum of seven lacs which was
paid as tribute for the Northern Sircars should be remitted,
his indignation knew no bounds, and he charged the
Madras authorities with a flagrant breach of faith. It was
under the influence of this feeling of irritation that he set A.D.
himself to organize the general league for the expulsion of 1779
the English previously alluded to. Hastings on hearing
of these proceedings immediately superseded the authority
of the Madras Government at the Nizam's Court, and
assured him that the intentions of the British Government
were honourable and pacific; that the Sircar should not be
occupied, and that the annual tribute should be paid up as
soon as possible. By these assurances Hastings was enabled
to neutralize the Nizam in the contest for existence which
was now impending.

The second war with Hyder Ali commenced in 1780, but
before entering on the narrative of it, a review of his pre-
vious progress for eight years appears necessary.
It has been stated that the crushing defeat he
experienced at Milgota reduced his possessions
within a very narrow compass, but the confusion created at
Poona by the murder of the Peshwa enabled him to recover
his position. In November he subjugated the principality 1773
of Coorg, which offered a noble resistance and was subjected
to extraordinary barbarity. He promised the sum of five
rupees for each head, and distributed the reward in person,
and seven hundred heads were piled up before he ordered
the carnage to cease. The next year he reconquered the
districts of which the Mahrattas had dispossessed him, and 1774
strengthened his authority in Malabar. Alarmed by these
incessant encroachments, and by the support he afforded to
Raghoba, the regency at Poona formed an alliance against
him with the Nizam, and the combined armies took the field
in 1776; but the generals were corrupted by the gold of 1776
Hyder, the expedition proved abortive, and his power was
extended up to the banks of the Kistna. Notwithstanding
the refusal of the Madras Government to afford him aid, in
accordance with the treaty, under the sinister influence of
Mahomed Ali and Sir John Lindsay, he renewed the appli-
cation, to enable him to meet the continued hostility of the
Mahrattas. He asked only for a supply of stores and arms,
and a small body of troops, for which he was prepared to

Progress of Hyder Ali, 1773-1780.

make a suitable return in money, but the Madras Council, who were still controlled by the nabob, resisted every overture and turned him into an irreconcilable enemy.

Information was soon after received of the commencement of war between France and England, and Pondicherry,

A.D. 1779 War with France. which had been completely rebuilt, was captured after a gallant resistance of ten days. In announcing this success to Hyder, the governor of Madras intimated that it was his intention to send an expedition against the French settlement at Mahé, a small port on the

Capture of Mahé. Malabar coast, through which Hyder had been in the habit for three years of receiving supplies and recruits from Europe. He replied that he should support the French garrison with all his strength, and retaliate any attack by invading the Carnatic; the place was nevertheless attacked and taken, though his colours were hoisted side by side with those of his French allies. While Hyder's feelings were in this state of irritation, an envoy arrived from Poona to request that, as he had the same reason as the regency to complain of the perfidy of the English, he would join the general confederacy which had been formed to expel them from India. The regency promised an amicable adjustment of all differences, the relinquishment of the *chout*, and a confirmation of his right to all the territories he had acquired up to the Kistna. Their proposal was accepted with avidity.

Preparations were now made on the largest scale. Hyder, in his seventy-eighth year, superintended every arrange-

1780 Hyder bursts on the Carnatic. ment in person, and by the end of June had equipped the most efficient force ever collected under the banner of a native prince. It consisted of 90,000 horse and foot, a large proportion of which had been trained under European officers. His artillery consisted of a hundred guns, directed also by European skill and science, and his commissariat had been admirably organised by the Hindoo Poornea, one of the ablest of his officers. While this portentous cloud was advancing towards Madras, the Government was buried in a fatal security, and the Commander-in-Chief declared that there was not the slightest cause for apprehension, but this illusion was speedily dispelled. Hyder, having completed his preparations, and proclaimed a *jehad*, or holy crusade, in every mosque and temple in Mysore, burst on the Carnatic on the 20th of July, and his progress was marked by the blaze of villages and towns, and the desolation of the country. He appeared determined to exhaust all the resources of cruelty which his ferocious nature could suggest. The wretched inhabitants were driven with their flocks and families to Mysore, and those who lingered were mutilated. All the forts, except four, held by English lieutenants, were surrendered by the venal or dastardly officers of the nabob.

The Madras army did not exceed 8,000, of which number 2,500 were under Colonel Baillie in Guntoor, and it was not till clouds of smoke were seen in every direction from St. Thomas's Mount, nine miles from Madras, that orders were issued to take the field. Sir Hector Munro moved out to Conjeveram to relieve Arcot, which contained the few military stores the nabob possessed, and which Hyder had besieged. Colonel Baillie was ordered to join Sir Hector with expedition, but he halted on the banks of the Cortilla when it was fordable, and the next day it was swelled by the rains, and continued impassable for ten days. Hyder Ali sent Tippoo with the flower of his army to prevent the junction, and an action was fought on the 6th September, in which Tippoo was so severely handled that he informed his father that no impression could be made on the English force without reinforcements, while Colonel Baillie informed the general that it was no longer in his power to join him at Conjeveram. Instead of proceeding at once with his whole force, Sir Hector simply detached Colonel Fletcher with 1,100 men to reinforce Colonel Baillie. So great was the dread which Hyder entertained of British prowess, that he had determined, in case of a junction of the two forces, to raise the siege of Arcot and retire. Colonel Fletcher and Colonel Baillie moved forward till the evening of the 9th, and a short march would have completed their union with the main body, but by an act of incredible fatuity Colonel Baillie ordered his men to lie on their arms for the night. Hyder Ali, seeing no preparation for any movement on the part of Sir Hector, brought his whole force up against Colonel Baillie. He planted his guns during the night with great skill, and on the morning of the 10th September the encampment was enveloped by the whole Mysore army. The troops fought like heroes, and the European force, when reduced to 300, still demanded to be led against the enemy; but Colonel Baillie refused to sacrifice the lives of these brave men, and held out a flag of truce, when Hyder's soldiers rushed on them and would have butchered the whole body but for the interference of

March of Madras army. A.D. 1780

Defeat of Baillie. 1780

the French officers. Of eighty-six officers, seventy were killed or wounded, and the whole army, with all its stores, baggage, and equipments, was irretrievably lost. Had the Commander-in-Chief moved up when the cannonade was first heard, Hyder, attacked on both sides, must have suffered a severe defeat; but the dastardly Munro threw his heavy guns into the great tank or pond at Conjeveram, destroyed his stores, and retreated in haste and disorder to Madras, hotly pursued by the enemy.

A vessel was immediately despatched to Calcutta with information of the disaster. To the embarrassment of a war with the Mahrattas was now added that of a war with Hyder, which had opened with the greatest disgrace the English arms had as yet suffered in India; but never did the genius and resolution of Hastings appear more conspicuous than on this occasion. "All my "hopes," he wrote, "of aggrandizing the British name and "enlarging the interests of the Company have given instant "place to the more urgent call to support the existence of "both in the Carnatic; nor did I hesitate one minute to "abandon my own views for such an object." He suspended Whitehill, the officiating governor of Madras who had refused to restore the Guntoor Sircar; he despatched every soldier that could be spared, together with fifteen lacs of rupees, for the exclusive use of the army, not to be fingered by the civilians; and the whole expedition was equipped and embarked within three weeks. The veteran Sir Eyre Coote, who had extinguished the French power on the Coast twenty years before, consented to take the command, and retrieve the honour of the Company amidst the scenes of his early triumphs. Hastings also adopted the hazardous expedient of stopping the Company's investment and devoting the funds to the expedition; but even this resource was found insufficient, and he was obliged, for the first time in his administration, to have recourse to a loan.

Energy of Hastings.

Coote proceeds to Madras.

A.D. 1780

SECTION IV.

PROCEEDINGS AT MADRAS, FROM THE DEFEAT OF COLONEL BAILLIE TO THE PEACE WITH TIPPOO, 1780–1784.

SIR EYRE COOTE arrived at Madras, eight weeks after the A.D. 1781 disaster of Colonel Baillie, but found the equipment of the army so wretched, and the difficulty of obtaining supplies in a country swept by hostile cavalry so great, that it was ten weeks before he could make any movement. But his arrival raised the drooping spirits of Madras, and checked the career of Hyder, who, instead of driving the English, as he had hoped, into the sea, found himself confronted by his old opponent. Hyder had obtained possession of Arcot through the treachery of the nabob's brahmin commandant, and was engaged in besieging Wandewash, which was defended by Lieutenant Flint with the same gallantry which had been displayed by Clive at Arcot. The hostile armies remained inactive for four months; the English for want of provisions, and Hyder from a dread of encountering them. Coote then attacked the fortified temple of Chillumbrum, but was repulsed, and Hyder was emboldened to risk a general engagement, and marching a hundred miles in two days and a half, attacked the English on the 1st of July at Porto Novo; but after an engagement of six hours' duration, was totally defeated, with the loss of 10,000 men, while the casualties on the side of Coote did not exceed 300. The Bengal brigade was conducted along the coast by Colonel Pearce with admirable skill, and without a single accident, and he reached Pulicat in July. Hyder detached Tippoo to intercept it, and Coote marched 150 miles to form a junction with it, which he effected on the 2nd of August. Hyder had brought up the whole of his army to oppose his return, and taken up his position on the field where, exactly a twelvemonth before, Colonel Baillie's army had been exterminated, which the astrologers assured him was a lucky spot and a lucky day. The result of the battle was doubtful, and both parties claimed the victory by firing a salute. In the month of September there was a third engagement at Solingur, in which Hyder was completely defeated, with the loss of 5,000 men, while only 100 fell on the side of the English.

Difficulties of Coote.

Battle of Porto Novo. 1781

Of Pollilore.

Of Solingur.

Soon after the army retired into cantonments for the season at Madras, after a campaign in which all Hyder's plans were baffled by the superior strategy of Coote, and Coote's movements were crippled for want of supplies and equipments.

In the brief period of seven years, two governors of Madras had been dismissed by the Court of Directors; one had been suspended by Hastings, and a fourth deposed by his own Council. The Presidency was demoralized to the core by corrupt transactions with the nabob, and the Court of Directors resolved to place the government in the hands of one who was free from all local associations, and untainted by the general corruption. Their choice fell on Lord Macartney, an Irish peer of great political experience and dignified character. He reached Madras in June, with the first intelligence of the war between Holland and England. Hyder lost no time in forming an alliance with the Dutch on the basis of mutual co-operation against the English. Their principal settlement on the Coromandel coast was Negapatam, 160 miles south of Madras, garrisoned by an army of 6,500 men. Contrary to the advice of Sir Eyre Coote, Lord Macartney equipped an expedition from Tanjore and Madras, which was confided to Sir Hector Munro, and greatly strengthened by the marines and seamen. The settlement was captured in November, and found to contain a large quantity of military stores besides two valuable investments. Two months after, Trincomalee, the noblest harbour in Ceylon, was also captured from the Dutch. But, notwithstanding the successes of the year, the pressure of the war was severely felt on the finances of Madras. All the revenues of the Carnatic, which ought to have been available for its defence, were absorbed by the nabob and his rapacious creditors, and the Government was at length constrained to assume the entire control of the province, reserving one-sixth for the nabob.

A.D. 1781 Lord Macartney governor of Madras.

1781 Capture of Negapatam.

Colonel Braithwaite had been despatched to protect Tanjore from the ravages of Tippoo, with a detachment of 2,000 men, almost all sepoys. The treachery of his guides betrayed him into a position where he came unexpectedly on Tippoo's army of 20,000 horse and 20,000 infantry and twenty guns; for twenty-eight hours his force maintained the unequal contest without flinching, but was at length overpowered. "The annals of war,"

1782 Colonel Braithwaite.

says the historian Mill, "can seldom exhibit a parallel to "the firmness and perseverance of this little army." This disaster was counterbalanced on the opposite coast by a sortie under Major Abingdon from Tellicherry, where he had been besieged for eighteen months, and the capture of 1,200 prisoners with sixty pieces of cannon. Hyder's despondency. A.D. 1782
Hyder began now to give way to despondency; his French allies had not made their appearance; Hastings had succeeded in detaching Sindia, the Nizam, and the raja of Nagpore from the grand confederacy, and the Peshwa now threatened to combine with the English, and wrest from him all the territories he had gained between the Kistna and the Toombudra. He lamented to his minister his folly in having plunged into a war with the Company. "The defeat of many Braithwaites and many "Baillies," he said, "will not crush them. I may ruin "their resources by land, but I cannot dry up the sea, and "I must be exhausted by a war in which I gain nothing "by fighting." The western coast he considered the weakest part of his dominions, and he determined to concentrate his efforts in that direction. He had issued orders to blow up the fortifications of Arcot, and to lay waste the Carnatic, without leaving a vestige of human habitation, when these gloomy forebodings were dissipated by the arrival of the French armament.

The French fleet was commanded by Suffrein, one of the greatest admirals France has produced. He met Admiral Hughes returning from the capture of Trincomalee, and an engagement ensued which proved indecisive. Naval actions. 1782
Suffrein then proceeded to Porto Novo, and landed 2,000 French soldiers and 1,000 disciplined Africans. In June, Sir Eyre Coote attempted the capture of Arnee, Hyder's chief depôt in the south, but after an indecisive action under its walls, Hyder succeeded in rescuing his treasure and his stores. Two other actions were in the meantime fought between the fleets without any practical result, and Suffrein having refitted his ships, sailed to the south. Lord Macartney had received intelligence that a second French force had arrived at Galle, and he began to tremble for Trincomalee and Negapatam. He entreated Admiral Hughes to hasten to the defence of Trincomalee; but he was jealous of interference, and sluggish in his movements, and on entering the harbour found that the place had capitulated four days before. The fleets now came again in contact, but the result was again indecisive.

A.D. 1782 This was the fourth naval action of the year, which was distinguished as much by the activity of the fleets as by the inefficient operations of the army.

Admiral Hughes goes to Bombay.

Admiral Hughes on his return to Madras announced his intention of proceeding to Bombay to refit his vessels after four severe actions. The governor represented the desperate condition to which the affairs of the Company would be reduced on his departure, with Hyder master of the Carnatic, Bussy daily expected with large reinforcements, and the French masters of the sea and intercepting the supplies of grain on which Madras depended
1782 for its subsistence. But he was deaf to every remonstrance, and set sail on the 15th of October. That same night the monsoon set in with a terrific gale; the shore was strewed for miles with wrecks; the largest vessels went down at their anchors, and a hundred coasting craft laden with rice were irrecoverably lost. Four days after Admiral Bickerton arrived in the roads from England, with a considerable fleet; and having landed 4,000 troops, resisted all the importunity of the Government to remain for the protection of the coast, and insisted on putting to sea to join his commander. Madras was now subject to all the horrors of famine. The ravages of Hyder had driven the wretched inhabitants into the town for shelter and subsistence, and for some time the deaths amounted to 1,500 a week. Sir Eyre Coote's shattered constitution required him to retire to Bengal, and the monsoon suspended all military operations.

Death of Hyder.

Soon after the defeat of the Mysore army at Tellicherry in February, Colonel Humberstone, who succeeded to the com-
1782 mand, marched into the heart of Mysore, and sat down before Palghaut, one of the strongest fortresses Hyder possessed, but the Bombay Council ordered him peremptorily to retire. Hyder lost no time in sending Tippoo with a contingent of French troops to repel this invasion, which might have penetrated to his capital. He came up with the retiring force at Paniani, and assaulted it in four columns, but was driven back with great loss, when he determined to turn the attack into a blockade, while waiting for his heavy guns. But on the 12th of December the whole of his army was seen to strike its tents, and march off to the eastern coast. A dromedary express had arrived the preceding evening with despatches announcing that "the ever-victorious spirit of Hyder," to use the language of his native biographer, "had taken its flight to Paradise." Worn out by the fatigues of war, and suffering from a

cancer in his back, he sunk on the 7th of December, at the age of eighty, leaving behind him the reputation of one of the ablest, most enterprising, and most successful princes in the modern history of India. A.D. 1782

An Asiatic army deprived of its head always becomes a scene of confusion and intrigue. On this occasion the danger was increased by the absence of Hyder's successor, four hundred miles away; but it was averted by the consummate prudence of Poornea, the ablest of his ministers. The death of Hyder was carefully concealed; his body was embalmed and sent to Seringapatam, like a chest of valuable plunder. All orders continued to be issued in his name, and his closed palankeen with the usual retinue moved out at the usual hour from the canvas enclosure of his tent. Tippoo, on his arrival in the camp, gratified the troops by a liberal donation, and entered upon the possession of a kingdom with a treasure of three crores of rupees and jewels of countless value, and an army of 100,000 men in a high state of efficiency. But the fatality which had blighted the Madras Presidency for fifteen years still seemed to pursue it. The departure of Sir Eyre Coote placed the army under the command of General Stuart, who was perverse, insubordinate, and incapable. Lord Macartney urged him to take advantage of the consternation in Hyder's camp when his death was known, but he affected to disbelieve the report, and the golden opportunity of striking a decisive blow was lost. With a nobler army and a more ample commissariat than Sir Eyre Coote had ever possessed, he allowed sixty days to pass without any effort. The anxiety which this inactivity created was happily relieved by the sudden departure of Tippoo for the opposite coast. The alarming intelligence he received of the progress made by the British force there induced him, without waiting for the arrival of Bussy, then hourly expected, to break up his encampment and proceed in person to avert the danger.

Concealment of his death.

Obstinacy of General Stuart. 1783

Bussy landed at Cuddalore on the 10th April, and found himself at the head of 2,300 Europeans and 5,000 sepoys; but he found also to his mortification that Tippoo had left only 3,500 troops to co-operate with him. General Stuart, having no longer any excuse for delay, began his march towards Cuddalore with a fine park of artillery, and an army of 14,500 men, of whom 3,000 were Europeans. Nothing was wanting to the efficiency of this army—the largest ever yet assembled at

Bussy and Stuart at Cuddalore.

the Madras Presidency—but a commander; and the troops were looking with intense eagerness for their beloved old chief to lead them again to victory; but Sir Eyre Coote, who had been persuaded by Hastings to return to Madras, died three days after he had landed. The expedition now moved on to Cuddalore at the rate of three miles a day,
A.D. 1783 and the town was invested on the 7th June. On the 13th Bussy made a sally, which resulted in a general action, and he was defeated, with the loss of thirteen guns; but the victory was dearly purchased with the loss on the side of the English of 68 officers and 920 European soldiers. On the same day Suffrein made his appearance in the offing, and the two fleets came to an engagement, which was as indecisive as the former which had preceded it. Admiral Hughes proceeded to Madras to refit, and Suffrein reinforced Bussy with 2,400 marines and soldiers. On the 25th June, Bussy made a sortie, and was repulsed with heavy loss. But General Stuart, who had been peddling about Cuddalore for three weeks, had made no progress in the siege, while his force was daily wasting away from sickness, fatigue, and wounds; and Bussy was waiting for the maturity of his errors to strike a decisive blow, which would have resulted, there can be little doubt, in the disgrace and retreat of the English army, and possibly also in the investment and capture of Madras. From this danger the Company was happily saved by the arrival of
1783 intelligence that peace had been concluded between France and England. Hostilities at once ceased, and Tippoo was deprived of all the aid of the French troops. General Stuart on his arrival at Madras was placed under arrest by Lord Macartney and sent to England. It was he who had arrested Lord Pigot with great treachery; and the facetious remark of the nabob's second son on this occasion is not unworthy of record:—"General Stuart catch one lord, and "one lord catch General Stuart!

Expedition from Bombay.

The abrupt departure of Tippoo to the Western coast was occasioned by the success of an expedition sent by the Bombay Government against his possessions in that quarter. On hearing of the death of Hyder, General Matthews was despatched, contrary to his own better judgment, to seize Bednore on the tableland of Mysore. The ascent of the ghauts, which had been fortified at every point, presented the most formidable obstacles, but they were surmounted by the gallantry of the 42nd Highlanders. When, however, the army arrived in front of the fortress, it was unexpectedly and unconditionally surrendered. The Mysore commander, who was a favourite with Hyder, but hated by his son, had obtained the sight of a letter from him to one of the officers at Bednore, containing an order to deprive him of his command, and, if necessary, to put him to death; and he made over the fortress to the general. After obtaining possession of it, he relaxed his vigilance, and allowed his men to disperse over the country in search of plunder. Tippoo hastened to recover it, and it was surrendered only when it had become a heap of ruins. Tippoo then descended to the siege of Mangalore, which forms one of the most memorable events of the war. The garrison, commanded by the valorous Colonel Campbell of the 42nd Highlanders, consisted of 700 Europeans and about 2,000 native sepoys, while the investing force numbered 100,000 men with 100 guns. The privations sustained by the garrison have seldom been exceeded. The place was defended for nine months with unsurpassed fortitude, and did not capitulate till the defenders were reduced to 850 mere skeletons.

A.D. 1783

Fall of Mangalore.

While Tippoo was wasting his strength and his reputation on this siege, which cost him half his army, the Madras Government sent a force of 13,500 men across the Peninsula into the heart of the Mysore territory, under the command of another of the Company's great soldiers, Colonel Fullarton, who would in all probability have brought the war to a speedy and successful issue, if he had not been thwarted by the folly of the Madras authorities. After having captured the renowned fort of Palghaut and the important city of Coimbatoor, he was on the point of marching on the capital, while the Mysore army was employed at Mangalore, when he received orders to suspend all operations, and to restore the districts he had occupied. Lord Macartney, contrary to the express orders of Hastings, had opened negotiations with Tippoo, at the very time when the Peshwa, in accordance with the stipulations of the treaty of Salbye, was threatening him with hostilities if he did not come to an accommodation with the English. The governor of Madras had even offered of his own accord a suspension of arms till the reply was received, and the progress of Colonel Fullarton was according arrested. Lord Macartney was so ignorant of the native character as not to be aware

Colonel Fullarton's success. 1783

that a proposal of negotiation is more likely to render it abortive than successful.

Tippoo treated the proposal with silent contempt for three months, and then sent one of his most astute officers to cozen the Madras authorities, and they were actually persuaded to despatch two commissioners to his camp at Mangalore. Tippoo was thus enabled to represent in every durbar that the British Government had sent two officers of rank from Madras to sue for peace. Disputes arose between the envoy of Tippoo and the commissioners which were referred to Madras; and the Council, after reviewing their position, ordered Colonel Fullarton to relinquish all his conquests and retire, instead of directing him to push on to Seringapatam with his victorious army, and bring the war to a successful issue. Hastings, with his profound knowledge of the native character, reprobated the negotiation through these commissioners, and maintained that it ought to have been committed to Colonel Fullarton, and dictated under the walls of the capital; but he was now powerless. The Court of Directors had recently renewed the condemnation of his proceedings, and the members of his Council had consequently deserted him; the conduct of the negotiations was therefore left to the Madras authorities, who fully maintained on this occasion their traditionary characteristic of imbecility.

Folly of the Madras Government.

The commissioners were marched leisurely through the country, detained at every stage, and subjected to constant indignity. On the fall of Mangalore they were admitted into the Mysore camp and insulted by the erection of gibbets in front of their tents. The treaty, based on a mutual restitution of conquests, was at length signed. All that could be said of it was that it was not more disgraceful than those which the governor and Council of Madras had been invariably making for fifteen years. It was equally injurious to the reputation of the Company and inimical to the interests of peace, and it entailed the necessity of another conflict to correct the arrogance with which it inspired Tippoo, and to which he gave expression in the following announcement:—"The English commissioners stood with "their heads uncovered and the treaty in their hands for "two hours, using every form of flattery and supplication "to induce compliance. The vakeels of Poona and Hyder-"abad united in the most abject entreaties, and his majesty, "the shadow of God, was at length softened into assent."

Treatment of the commissioners.

A.D. 1784 Treaty of Mangalore.

SECTION V.

THE SUPREME COURT—CHEYT SING—THE BEGUMS—CLOSE OF HASTINGS'S ADMINISTRATION—PROCEEDINGS IN ENGLAND.

TO RESUME the thread of events in Bengal. The Supreme Court, established in Calcutta in 1774, was intended to protect the natives from the oppression of Europeans, and to give the Europeans the blessing of their own laws. The judges were commissioned to administer every branch of English law, and were invested with all the prerogatives of the King's Bench. Parliament had thus, in its wisdom or ignorance, established two independent powers in this new conquest, without deeming it necessary to define the limits of their respective authority, and a collision between them became inevitable. The first stroke fell upon the zemindars. They had been accustomed to use coercion in the collection of their rents from the ryots, who had seldom paid them without it. The Supreme Court was no sooner established than it began to issue writs against them at the suit of any ryot who was persuaded to sue them under the instigation of the attorneys who spread themselves over the country. They were dragged down to the Court in Calcutta, and sent to gaol if they were unwilling or unable to furnish bail. Even when the arrest was pronounced to have been illegal, they received no compensation for the expense and indignity to which they had been subject.

A.D. 1774

The Supreme Court.

Its encroachments

A feeling of dismay spread over the country, such as had not been felt for thirty years, since the invasion of the Mahrattas. The arrest and humiliation of the zemindars destroyed their credit and authority, and enabled the ryots to evade the payment of their rent with impunity. If the defaulters were subjected to confinement, the attorneys advised them to apply to the court for a writ of *habeas corpus*, when they were brought down to Calcutta and discharged. The zemindars pleaded these proceedings as an excuse for withholding payment of their dues to government, and its resources, which were then dependent solely on the land revenue, were placed in extreme peril.

In revenue matters,

The criminal judicature of the country, which embraced

A.D. the police of thirty millions of people, had been entrusted to
1775 *In criminal judicature.* the nabob of Moorshedabad and to his judicial and executive officers; but the judges of the Supreme Court declared that he was a phantom, a mere man of straw, without any right to the exercise of any authority whatever, and in one instance they issued a process of contempt against his Highness. They affirmed that the orders of the Provincial Courts established by Government, were of no more value than if they had been issued by the king of the fairies. They denied that the East India Company itself had any authority in India, beyond that of an ordinary commercial association, and affirmed that the Governor-General in Council was subject to their jurisdiction, and that it would be penal for him or any public officer to disobey any process they might issue. The judges doubtless acted conscientiously, but the whole fabric of Government was, nevertheless, shaken to its foundation, and the country was threatened with universal anarchy.

1779 The aggression of the Court reached its climax in the Cossijurah case. A native brought an action against the *The Cossijurah case.* raja, living at a distance from Calcutta, and not subject to the Court, and two sheriff's officers were sent with a body of eighty men armed with muskets and swords to execute the writ of the Court, and bring him up to Calcutta. They invaded his zenana and packed up his idols, but he escaped their vigilance. Hastings considered that it was time to vindicate the authority of Government, and afford protection to its subjects; and ordered the party to be intercepted on their return, and liberated on their arrival in Calcutta. To prevent the recurrence of such visitations, he issued a proclamation to landholders of every degree to consider themselves exempt from the jurisdiction of the Supreme Court unless they had especially bound themselves to submit to it. The Court then issued a process against the Governor-General and the Council, which they treated with the contempt it deserved.

Petitions were addressed to Parliament both by the native and the European community, praying for redress, *Appointment of Sir E. Impey.* but three years elapsed before it was granted. In
1780 the meantime Hastings provided a more immediate remedy by offering the post of chief judge in the Sudder Court, the Company's court of final appeal, to the Chief Justice, upon a salary of 7,000 rupees a month. He accepted the office, but declined any remuneration. All

the encroachments of the Crown Court ceased at once. The appointment was severely censured in Leadenhall Street and in Parliament, and Sir Elijah Impey was recalled and impeached, but honourably acquitted. The arrangement proved to be in a high degree beneficial to the interests of the country. Hastings had recently remodelled the judicial system, and though he placed over the civil courts the best men the service could furnish, they were necessarily without any judicial experience; and the Chief Justice, a lawyer of great eminence, was thus enabled to give form and consistency to their proceedings. With this object he drew up a code of regulations, clear and concise, and adapted to the simplicity of native habits, and it has formed the basis of subsequent legislation.

Cheyt Sing.

The pecuniary difficulties of this period were greater than had been felt for seven years. There was war with Hyder Ali then ravaging the Carnatic, war with the Mahrattas, and war with the French and with the Dutch. The entire expense of all military operations fell on the treasury of Bengal—the only Presidency which paid. Heavy loans had been contracted; the credit of Government was low, and Hastings was obliged to cast about him for some exceptional source of relief. By the political constitution of India, a feudatory was always liable to a demand for extraordinary aid to meet the exigencies of his superior lord. The grandfather of Cheyt Sing, the raja of Benares, had, in the confusion of the times, succeeded in carving out a little principality for himself, which he held of the Vizier of Oude, and which Mr. Francis had constrained the Vizier to transfer to the Company, giving the raja a *sunnud*, or deed, which fixed his annual payment at twenty-two lacs of rupees. Hastings now made a demand on Cheyt Sing of five lacs of rupees and a body of 2,000 horse to assist in protecting Behar. The requisition was strictly constitutional, and the raja paid it for some time, but at length endeavoured to evade farther payment on the plea of poverty. Hastings was assured that he had amassed a crore and a half, which was to a great extent true, and he construed his reluctance into a crime, and determined, as he said, "to make "him pay largely for his pardon, to exact a severe vengeance "for his delinquency, and to draw from his guilt the "means of relief to the Company's distresses." Hastings had occasion to visit Benares, and the raja, anxious to avert his displeasure, met him on the way, and offered

Hastings's requisition.

A.D. 1780

A.D. 1781 him twenty lacs, but he raised his demand to fifty lacs. On reaching the city, Hastings transmitted him a statement of his offences, and placed him under arrest by sending the two companies of sepoys he had brought with him to mount guard on his palace. The populace rose on them, and, as they had brought no ammunition, massacred them all, as well as their officers.

During this *émeute* the raja escaped across the river, but the situation of the Governor-General was perilous in the extreme. His native force was annihilated. He was in a city renowned for its turbulence, and in the midst of an infuriated mob; and he and the thirty gentlemen with him had only their own swords to trust to. Happily, the multitude, instead of attacking Hastings in his defenceless state, hastened across the river to join the raja. The whole province was soon in a state of revolt, but Hastings never lost his self-possession; and it was at this critical period that he continued and completed the negotiations with Sindia which issued in the treaty of Salbye, with as much calmness as if he had been residing in his own garden-house in Calcutta. Equally remarkable was the confidence manifested by Sindia in the destinies of the Company, by affixing his seal to it under such circumstances. Troops arrived rapidly from various quarters; but Hastings, not considering his position tenable, made his escape by night through a window, and rowed down to Chunar.

Escape of the raja.

The raja collected an army of 20,000 men, but it was repeatedly defeated, and his last fortress, Bidgegurh, in which his treasure was deposited, was surrendered by his begums. Major Popham, the commander, took advantage of an incautious expression in one of Hastings's letters, and divided the whole of the prize money, forty lacs of rupees, at once, among the officers and men, to the infinite annoyance of Hastings, who had been calculating on the receipt of it to relieve his pecuniary embarrassments. This is one of those transactions in the career of Hastings for which it would be difficult to offer any palliation. Cheyt Sing was contumacious in having hesitated to afford the necessary aid to his suzerain in a great public emergency; but the imposition of a fine of fifty lacs for demurring to the payment of a tenth of that sum was a vindictive proceeding, and has always been considered a blot on his administration.

The raja subdued.

1781

The loss of the raja's treasure was a source of deep

anxiety to Hastings. There were 60,000 troops in the field, and the treasury was empty. The arrears which were due from the Vizier, however, amounted to a crore and a half of rupees, and Hastings looked to this source for relief, when the Vizier waited on him at Chunar, and informed him that his own funds were exhausted, and that it was no longer possible for him to maintain the English troops employed in protecting his territories. He then alluded to the treasures of the begums, and requested permission of the Governor-General to take possession of them and thus discharge his obligations to the Company. At the same time it was asserted, but on the worthless testimony of Colonel Hannay, that the begums had abetted the rebellion, as it was officially termed, of Cheyt Sing, and supplied him with troops and money. Hastings, under the severe pressure of circumstances, persuaded himself that "the begums had made war on the Company," and he yielded to the earnest solicitations of the Vizier, and authorised the spoliation of the princesses. Seventy-five lacs of rupees were extracted from their vaults, and transmitted to Calcutta, but not before the two eunuchs, their ministers, had been subject to torture. For this act of atrocity, Hastings is no farther responsible than as it might be considered the result of his own injustice. To this treasure the begums had no legitimate title; it was the property of the state and answerable for its obligations, but six years before, their right to it had been acknowledged under the seal of the Government in Calcutta, which ought to have been considered sacred. Hastings was so little conscious of the turpitude of this transaction that he ridiculed the censure which "men of virtue" might cast on it. But posterity has vindicated the principles of public morality, and although Hastings had no personal interest in the transaction, but was led into it by a mistaken loyalty to the interests of the Company, it has been the subject of general censure.

Plunder of the Begums.

A.D. 1782

These proceedings were severely condemned by the Court of Directors, and the members of his Council thereupon united in opposition to him, and he justly complained that while he was held personally responsible for the safety of India, his degradation had been proclaimed in every native court, and in the Council he had only a single vote. In a letter of the 20th March to the Directors, after alluding to the patience and temper with which he had submitted to the indignities heaped

1783.

Close of Hastings' administration.

A.D. on him during his long service, he announced his determina-
784 tion to retire from the Government. He proceeded to Lucknow, and in compliance with the injunctions of the Court of Directors restored the jageers which had been sequestered to the begums, adjusted all accounts with the Vizier, and then withdrew the Resident. On his return to Calcutta he addressed valedictory letters to the princes and chiefs of India, by all of whom he was held in the highest esteem,
1785 and embarked for England in February.

Impeachment of Hastings.

From the king and queen Hastings met with a gracious reception, and even the Court of Directors greeted him with a courteous address. With one exception, the ministry likewise evinced a very friendly disposition towards him, and Mr. Dundas, who had moved the vote of censure upon him in the House of Commons, in terms exceptionally virulent, now pronounced him the "Saviour of India." But Mr. Pitt, the prime minister, was strongly biassed against him, and while applauding his genius and his success refused to advise the king to confer any mark of distinction upon him. Burke, who had made Indian politics his especial study for many years, had contracted a feeling akin to personal animosity towards him, and aided by the local knowledge and the unmatched rancour of Mr. Francis, who had obtained a seat in Parliament, denounced his conduct in the House of
1786 Commons. The House was induced to vote his impeachment at the bar of the House of Lords on twenty-two charges. Of these only three were of any serious import; the Rohilla war, the treatment of Cheyt Sing, and the spoliation of the begums; the rest were the mere litter of Mr. Francis's malignity. The trial commenced on
1788 the 13th February, 1788, and presented the most august spectacle which had been witnessed in England since the trial of the bishops, a century before. The queen, the princesses, the Prince of Wales and his royal brothers, and the peers in their ermine proceeded in state to Westminster Hall to witness the opening of the proceedings. But the most memorable scene in this great drama was the galaxy of genius in the seats appropriated to the managers of the House, Fox and Burke, and Sheridan and Grey, and Windham, names of imperishable renown in the annals of the country. In the presence of this illustrious assembly Warren Hastings, who had given law to the princes and people throughout the continent of India, was arraigned as a culprit. The management of the trial was left with

the Whigs, who conducted it with ability which has never been surpassed, and in a spirit of animosity which has seldom been equalled. They applied to him the epithets of thief, tyrant, robber, cheat, swindler, sharper, captain general of iniquity and spider of hell; and then expressed their regret that the English language did not afford terms more adequate to the enormity of his offences. The trial dragged on for seven years, and ended in his complete and honourable acquittal, but it cost him ten lacs of rupees, A.D.
and reduced him to poverty. 1795

The most severe censor of his administration, the philosophic historian Mill, admits that "he was beyond all "question the most eminent of the chief rulers "whom the Company ever employed, nor is "there any one of them who would not have succumbed under the difficulties he had to encounter." Censurable as some of his acts undoubtedly were, the grandeur of his career is by many considered as casting his offences into the shade, and one of the most eminent statesman of the day asserted that "though he was not blameless, if "there was a bald place on his head, it ought to be covered "with laurel." While the king and his ministers were losing an empire in the west, he was building up another in the east. The authority of the Company was limited to the valley of the Ganges when he assumed the government. He was anxious to avoid territorial acquisitions—and, indeed, he made none—but it was the object of his ambition to extend the influence of the Company to every court in India, and to render it the paramount power on the continent; and this object he fully accomplished, in the midst of unexampled difficulties. At the time of his retirement the Company was recognised as the most substantial and important power in India, whose favour was courted and whose hostility was dreaded equally by Tippoo, the Nizam, and the five Mahratta princes. No British ruler, moreover, has ever secured to an equal extent, not merely the homage but the warm attachment of the people under his government, by whom, after the lapse of a century, the name of "Hustin Sahib" is still pronounced with a feeling of veneration.

Character of Hastings.

In February 1781, the petitions of the inhabitants of Calcutta against the encroachments of the Supreme Court were presented to the House and referred to a select committee, of which Mr. 1781
Burke was the life and soul, and which presented

Reports of Committees.

twelve able reports. On the receipt of intelligence of
A.D. 1782 Hyder Ali's irruption into the Carnatic, a secret committee was appointed, of which Mr. Dundas was chairman. On the presentation of the report, he denounced the conduct of Hastings and the governors of Madras and Bombay, and moved the recall of Hastings from Bengal, and Hornby from Bombay, for having acted in a manner repugnant to the honour and policy of the nation, and brought calamities on India, and enormous expenses on the Company. The House voted the recall of Hastings, and the Court of Directors responded to it; but the Court of Proprietors, which, at this time, comprised men of higher standing and of greater eminence than the superior Court, passed a vote of thanks to Hastings for his eminent services. The pecuniary embarrassment occasioned by the expensive wars waged in India constrained the Company to apply to Parliament for the loan of a crore of rupees, which was not refused, but it weakened still farther their position, which had been seriously damaged by the unfavourable reports of the two committees, and there was a general outcry for remodelling the Government of India.

Mr. Fox, then at the head of the coalition ministry, accordingly introduced his famous India bill, which had
1783 Fox's India Bill. been drafted by his colleague Mr. Burke. It provided that all the powers of Government should be transferred for four years from the Company to a Board consisting of seven Commissioners, to be nominated in the first instance by Parliament, and subsequently by the Crown, while the trade was to be managed by nine assistant Directors. The patronage of the India House was at the time estimated at two crores of rupees a year, and it was maintained that the transfer of it to the ministry would be fatal to the constitution. The Court of Directors, threatened with extinction, filled the town with complaints of the violation of chartered rights, and inflamed the public mind by a caricature representing Mr. Fox as Carlo Khan, mounted on an elephant and assailing the India House; but the bill passed the House of Commons by a majority of two to one. The king had been persuaded that it would take the crown from his head and place it on the brows of Mr. Fox, and by the exercise of an unconstitutional influence, he induced the House of Lords to throw it out, and he lost no time in dismissing the ministry.

Mr. Pitt, then in his twenty-fourth year, was placed at

A.D. 1784

the head of the new administration, and brought in another India bill, which provided for the appointment of a Board of Commissioners by the Crown, with power "to check, superintend, and control all the "acts, operations and concerns," connected with the civil and military government and revenues of India. A secret committee, consisting of the chairman, deputy chairman, and the senior member of the Court of Directors was to act in subordination to the Commissioners, and control all correspondence of any importance; and twenty-one of the Directors were thus excluded from all influence in the administration of India. Mr. Fox's bill annihilated the Company, but, under Mr. Pitt's bill they retained their golden patronage and their social position and the trappings of dignity, but the substantial power of Government was transferred to the Crown. The Proprietors, who had recently set the House of Commons at defiance in the matter of Hastings' recall, were restricted from interfering with any of the decisions of the Board of Commissioners, usually denominated the Board of Control, and, though they retained the empty privilege of debate, were reduced to a state of political insignificance. It was, moreover, resolved that "to pursue schemes of conquest and acqui- "sition of territory was contrary to the wish, the honour, "and the policy of the British nation;" but this renewed attempt to stop the growth of the British empire in India only afforded another exemplification of the vanity of human wishes.

Pitt's India Bill.

1785

Mr. Dundas was appointed President of the Board of Control, and one of the first questions which came before him related to the debts of the nabob of Arcot. For many years he had been living on loans obtained at an exorbitant premium and usurious interest, for which he gave assignments on the districts of the Carnatic. When his court was removed from Arcot to Madras, the town became the focus of intrigue and fraud. All classes, both in and out of the service, not excepting the members of Council, embarked in the traffic of loans, which became the shortest road to fortune. Everyone was eager to obtain access to the pagoda-tree, as it was called, then in full bloom. Hastings, on taking over the revenues of the Carnatic to support the war with Hyder, was anxious to deal summarily with this incubus on its resources, and proposed to deduct a fourth from the principal, to consolidate it with the interest to a fixed date,

The Nabob of Arcot's debts.

and pay off the amount by instalments. But the creditors would not listen to any proposal to cut the tree down.

Mr. Pitt's India bill made provision for the investigation of these claims preparatory to their liquidation, and the Court of Directors entered on the duty with great alacrity, but Mr. Dundas removed the case out of their hands, and determined to pay off the debts without enquiry. The princes of India had already discovered that the most effectual mode of counteracting the Government of India, both in England and abroad, was to subsidize members of Parliament. The nabob of Arcot adopted this expedient on a magnificent scale. Paul Benfield was sent to London with large funds, established an office in Westminster for the purchase of boroughs, and in the general election of 1783, made no fewer than eight members of Parliament, whose votes were placed at the disposal of the ministry. It was to this Parliamentary influence that the anomalous proceedings of Mr. Dundas were generally attributed, by which Paul Benfield secured the undisturbed enjoyment of a sum little short of sixty lacs of rupees. The heaviest class of the loans was fixed, with interest, at two crores and a quarter, but it cost the Company five crores before it was paid off.

Mr. Dundas's extraordinary proceedings. A.D. 1784

Mr. Fox's Indian Bill made it penal for any servant of the Company, civil or military, to engage in money transactions with any native prince, but no such clause was inserted in Mr. Pitt's bill, and the nabob and his friends embarked in the fabrication of fresh loans while the liquidation of the old loans was in progress, and on the payment of the last pagoda brought forward new
1805 demands, to the incredible amount of thirty crores of rupees. Parliament was now resolved that they should be subject to a severe scrutiny, and a board of Commissioners was appointed at Madras to investigate them, and another board in London to receive appeals. Their labours extended over fifty years, and cost India a crore of rupees, but they reduced the claims from thirty-two crores of rupees to about two and a half. Mr. Dundas's proceedings regarding the revenues of the Carnatic were
1785 equally disastrous. The nabob had received a larger income from them while they were under the management of the Company than when administered by his own officers, but those officers and his creditors lost the opportunity of plunder, and induced him to become importunate for the restoration of the country.

Fabrication of new loans.

Revenues of the Carnatic.

Contrary to the advice of the Court of Directors, Mr. Dundas ordered the districts to be given back to the nabob, that is, to his creditors, who began again to reap a rich harvest, while the Madras Presidency, with an army seven months in arrears, was reduced to a state bordering on bankruptcy.

CHAPTER VII.

SECTION I.

ADMINISTRATION OF LORD CORNWALLIS—MYSORE WAR.

ON the departure of Hastings, Mr. Macpherson, the senior member of Council succeeded temporarily to the Government. He had originally gone out to India as purser of one of the Company's vessels, but attached himself to the nabob of the Carnatic and returned to England as his agent, and through the influence of the Duke of Grafton, who highly appreciated his abilities, was appointed to the Madras civil service, from which he was subsequently promoted to the Bengal Council. The great merit of his brief administration, which lasted only twenty-two months, lay in his economical reforms which resulted in the laudable reduction of a crore and a half of annual expenditure. A.D. 1785

Mr. Macpherson officiating Governor-General.

The Government of the Company's possessions since the battle of Plassy had hitherto been given to one of the officers on their own establishment in India, but it was found that whatever advantage might be derived from his local knowledge and experience was counterbalanced by the trammels of local associations, and the difficulty of exercising a due control over those who had once been his equals. The ministry determined, therefore, to select for the office of Governor-General a nobleman of high character, unfettered by any Indian ties of friendship or relationship. Lord Macartney, the governor of Madras, was chosen for the appointment, but he disgusted Mr. Dundas by endeavouring to make terms with the ministry, and Lord Cornwallis was 1786

Lord Cornwallis Governor-General.

A.D. 1786 nominated in his stead, and he assumed charge of the Government in September, 1786. And thus, by the singular caprice of events, the man who had surrendered a British army to Washington at York Town, which entailed the loss of America, was appointed to govern India, while the man who had saved India under the most arduous circumstances was subjected to a prosecution for high crimes and misdemeanours.

The Government of Lord Cornwallis commenced under the most auspicious circumstances. Hastings's administration had been crippled by the chronic opposition of the home authorities at the India House and Downing Street. Lord Cornwallis enjoyed the entire confidence of Mr. Pitt, and of the Board of Control, to which the Directors were subordinate, and of which his friend Mr. Dundas was President. The office of Commander-in-Chief was likewise united with that of Governor-General, and Lord Cornwallis was thus enabled to control all the military arrangements and expenditure. Hastings had only a single voice in the Council, while his successor was invested with the power of overruling the votes of his colleagues whenever he deemed it necessary. The Court of Directors had been in the habit of nominating their friends and relatives to the most lucrative appointments in India, and the influence of this independent connection greatly fettered the authority of government, and fostered and protected abuses. Hastings had protested against it, but he had not sufficient official strength to secure success; Lord Cornwallis, on the other hand, was strong in the support of Mr. Pitt and Mr. Dundas, and threatened to resign the Government unless it was discontinued; It is not, therefore, a matter of surprise that the arrival of Lord Cornwallis should have quenched the spirit of faction and intrigue, and given a higher tone to the Government.

Advantages of Cornwallis's position.

The first three years of his administration were occupied

1786 to 1789 in the reform of abuses, which were to be traced mainly to the vicious and traditional policy of the Court of Directors of giving small salaries, and allowing indefinite perquisites. The salaries came from their own treasury, but the perquisites from the pockets of the people. Every man, as Lord Cornwallis remarked, who returned to England rich was deemed a rogue, and every man who went home poor a fool. He found the system of peculation in full vigour. The treasurer was lending the public funds at twelve per cent.

Lord Cornwallis's economical reforms.

The Commander-in-Chief had given two of his favourites the lucrative commission of raising two regiments, but while they drew full allowances for the men, the regiments existed only on paper. The collectors of the land revenue, who were also armed with the power of magistrates, monopolised the trade of the district under fictitious names, and amassed fortunes. The post of political Resident at the court of the raja of Benares was considered worth four lacs of rupees a year, while the salary attached to it did not exceed a thousand rupees a month.

A.D. 1786 to 1789

Lord Cornwallis's stern vigour.

Lord Cornwallis set himself to the task of reforming these abuses with unflinching vigour. He hunted out frauds in every corner, put a period to jobbing agencies, and exorbitant contracts. He refused to allow men of power and influence at home to quarter their friends and kindred, and sometimes their victims at the gambling-table, on Indian appointments, and he had the courage to decline the recommendations of the Prince of Wales, "who," he wrote, "was always pressing "some infamous and unjustifiable job upon him;" but it was not till he had convinced the Court of Directors of the truth which Clive and Hastings had in vain pressed on them, that "it was not good economy to put men into "places of the greatest confidence, where they have it in "their power to make fortunes in a few months, without "giving them adequate salaries," that the purification of the public service became practicable. It has continued to improve ever since, notwithstanding the growth of the empire, and the Indian service now presents an example of administrative integrity which has seldom, if ever, been equalled.

The affairs of Oude.

The Vizier lost no time in renewing the request he 1786 had not ceased for years to make, to be relieved from the expense of the Company's troops stationed in his dominions for their protection, but the rapid increase of Sindia's encroachments in Hindostan, and the growing power of the Sikhs, convinced Lord Cornwallis that the troops could not be withdrawn without great risk, but he reduced the charge by one third. The Vizier was likewise delivered from the pressure of the European harpies, who, under the predominance of British influence, had long been preying on him, one of whom, Colonel Hannay, had amassed a fortune of thirty lacs in a few years. He likewise conferred an inestimable boon on him by peremptorily refusing to recognise the claims of any of his private creditors, whether European or native, and thus saved him from the fate of the nabob of Arcot. But he did not fail to remonstrate with him, though in vain, on the abuses of his administration. The only concern of the Vizier was to obtain the means of personal gratification, and hence the zemindar was allowed to squeeze the ryot and the ministers to squeeze the zemindar, and he squeezed the ministers and public officers when they were sufficiently gorged with plunder, and squandered the money in boundless dissipation.

By the treaty with the Nizam, the Guntoor Sircar was assigned to the Company after the death of his brother Basalut

The Guntoor Sircar.

Jung. He died in 1782, but the Nizam steadily evaded the surrender of it, and Lord Cornwallis,
A.D. when taking leave of the Directors, was directed peremptorily
1788 to demand it. In 1788, he drew a body of troops to the frontier, and instructed the Resident to claim the full execution of the treaty. To his great surprise, the Nizam at once acceded to his wishes, but he also expressed his confidence that the Company's Government would with equal alacrity fulfil the obligations to which they were bound by the other articles of the treaty; which were, to assist him with two battalions of troops, and six pieces of artillery whenever he should require their services, and to reduce and transfer to him the province of the Carnatic Balaghaut, then usurped by Hyder Naik. With his usual duplicity he despatched an envoy simultaneously to Tippoo to propose an alliance for the extirpation of the English. Tippoo readily embraced the proposal, and demanded the hand of one of the Hyderabad princesses, but the Tartar blood of the son of Cheen Killich boiled at the idea of a matrimonial alliance with the son of a naik, or head constable, and the negotiation was broken off.

Lord Cornwallis was disconcerted by this manœuvre. Since the unfortunate treaty of 1768, the Company's

Lord Cornwallis's imprudent letter.

Government had twice acknowledged Hyder and Tippoo as the lawful sovereigns of this province, and to furnish the Nizam with the English brigade he desired would lead to dangerous complications; on the other hand, it was important to prevent his throwing himself into the arms of Tippoo. To meet the diffi-
1789 culty, Lord Cornwallis addressed an official letter to him, engaging to transfer the province if it should come into the possession of the Company with the aid of his troops, and likewise to furnish him with the brigade on condition

that it should not be employed against any of the allies of the Company, a list of whom, which did not include the name A.D.
of Tippoo, was subjoined. Tippoo was naturally irritated 1789
to find that the dismemberment of his dominions was within the contemplation of the Governor-General, and that he was prepared to place a British force at the disposal of the Nizam, with liberty to employ it against him. That this communication was highly injudicious will not be questioned; but it is idle to attribute the war with Tippoo six months after to its influence, inasmuch as he had fitted out an expedition against the raja of Travancore six months before the date of it.

Travancore and the Madras Government.

The little principality of Travancore, at the southern extremity of the Malabar coast, had been placed under British protection by the treaty of Mangalore. Tippoo, who had long coveted the possession of it, had been for some time assembling an army to invade it, and the raja, to strengthen his defences, had purchased two towns in the neighbourhood of the Dutch. Tippoo demanded the surrender of them on the plea that they belonged to his vassal, the raja of Cochin. The raja appealed to Lord Cornwallis, who directed the authorities at Madras to inform both him and Tippoo that if the Dutch had really held independent and unreserved possession of these places, the raja was to be supported in retaining them. Mr. Holland, the governor of Madras, more unprincipled than any of his predecessors, not only withheld this communication from Tippoo, but endeavoured to extort a lac of pagodas for himself from the raja as the condition of supporting him. The army on the Coast was likewise kept in an inefficient state, and the pay of the troops was allowed to fall into arrears, while, in direct violation of the orders of Lord Cornwallis, the public revenues were appropriated to the payment of the creditors of the nabob, of whom he was one of the principal. Tippoo suddenly
attacked the "lines of Travancore," as they were termed, 1789
—the defensive wall the raja had erected—and was repulsed with the loss of 2,000 men, upon which he ordered up a battering train from Seringapatam, and reinforcements from every quarter. This wanton attack of an ally was an unequivocal declaration of war against the Company, but Holland proposed a pacific adjustment of the question to Tippoo, and soon after deserted his post and embarked for England.

Lord Cornwallis considered it essential to our honour to

defend an ally, and to take up the gauntlet which Tippoo had thrown down. It was not a time for pottering over Acts of Parliament, and he proceeded at once to offer alliances, offensive and defensive, to the two native powers in the Deccan, the Nizam and the Peshwa, which their hatred and dread of Tippoo led them to accept with great alacrity. A tripartite treaty was concluded which provided that they should simultaneously attack Tippoo's dominions, and join the British army with 10,000 horse, if required, for whose services they were to be reimbursed, and that the Mysore territories and forts conquered by their united arms should be equally divided among them.

Lord Cornwallis's alliances.

A.D. 1790

General Medows, an officer of acknowledged ability, had arrived at Madras as governor and Commander in Chief, and Lord Cornwallis entrusted the conduct of the campaign to him. The deficiency of the commissariat, owing to the profligate neglect of Holland, retarded the departure of the army for several months, but the General was enabled to march from Trichinopoly on the 26th of May, at the head of a force of 15,000 men. Coimbatoor was captured in July, and Palghat
1790 and Dindigul, both deemed impregnable, in September, but the force was injudiciously separated, and Tippoo, by a masterly movement, interposed between the divisions, one of which suffered heavy loss both in men and guns. When the war became inevitable Lord Cornwallis adopted the bold plan of Hastings, and despatched a large expedition to Madras along the coast where we had no allies; and, notwithstanding the able dispositions of Tippoo to prevent its junction with the Madras army, it was effected without a conflict. Tippoo then proceeded southward, closely followed by General Medows, but these marches and countermarches, which were without result, subjected the troops to severe fatigue, and weakened their confidence in the General. The campaign proved abortive, and Lord Cornwallis determined to take the command of the army into his own hands.

General Medows's abortive campaign.

He arrived at Madras on the 12th December and made the most vigorous preparations to take the field. Meanwhile, Tippoo proceeded to the north, and having ravaged the Carnatic, marched south to Pondicherry, and despatched a mission to Paris, to Louis XVI., soliciting the aid of 6,000 troops, for whom he would make suitable provision. The unhappy king was then in the vortex of the Revolution, and replied: "This resembles the affair of

Second campaign.

"America, of which I never think without regret. My "youth was taken advantage of at that time, and we are "suffering for it now; the lesson is too severe to be for- "gotten." The army was assembled at Vellore, on the 11th February, and marched without any opposition to Bangalore, which capitulated on the 21st, but not before Tippoo had succeeded, by forced marches, in removing his seraglio and his treasure. The Nizam's contingent of 10,000 horse was assembled at Hyderabad in the preceding year, but did not enter Tippoo's dominions till it was certain that he had marched southward, and that there was no risk of encountering him. In 1791, they hastened to join Lord Cornwallis's camp as soon as they heard that Bangalore had capitulated; but there was neither discipline nor valour in their ranks, and the flaunting cavaliers were unable to protect their own foraging parties, and soon ceased to move beyond the English pickets. Lord Cornwallis was now in full march on Seringapatam, and Tippoo determined to try the result of a battle. It was fought at Arikera, and he sustained a total defeat. From the summit of the hill, where the last shot was fired, the eastern face of the capital greeted the eyes of the victors; but here, to their deep chagrin, the campaign terminated. For several weeks the army had been suffering the extremity of want. The stores, scanty when the army began its march, were rapidly exhausted; Tippoo's light horse intercepted all supplies, and created a desert round the camp. On the 20th May the artillery officers reported that the bullocks were reduced to such a state that they could no longer drag the heavy guns, and Lord Cornwallis was convinced that the safety of the army depended on an immediate retreat. General Abercromby, who had been sent with a force from Bombay to cooperate with Lord Cornwallis from the western coast, had arrived within forty miles of the capital, but was directed on the 21st May to destroy a portion of his siege guns and bury the rest and retire to the coast. The next day Lord Cornwallis destroyed his own battering train and began his melancholy return to Madras.

A.D. 1791

Battle of Arikera.

By the coalition treaty, signed on the 1st June, the regency at Poona engaged to furnish 10,000 troops to operate against Tippoo, but the minister, Nana Furnavese, still allowed his envoys to remain at the court, in the hope—which he did not conceal—that, at the eleventh hour, Tippoo might be induced to purchase his neutrality by

The Mahratta army.

a concession of territory. When this expectation vanished and the Mahratta force took the field, it became evident that the primary object of the Nana was to use the British artillery in recovering the fortresses which Tippoo had wrested from the Mahrattas, and six months were occupied in the siege of Dharwar. Hence, in the first campaign of 1790, the Peshwa's force rendered no assistance whatever. In the campaign of 1791 it joined the army of Lord Cornwallis only on the first day of the retreat. If he had received any intimation of its approach, the result of the campaign might have been different; but his intelligence department was deplorable, while Tippoo's admirable establishment of scouts intercepted all communication. The bazaar of the Mahratta army, rich with the spoils of India, presented a singular contrast to the poverty of the English camp, and the provisions they brought, though sold at an exorbitant price, proved a seasonable relief to the famishing English soldiers. The Mahratta sirdars, who had been enriching themselves by pillage from the day they took the field, set up a plea of poverty, and demanded an advance of fourteen lacs of rupees, which Lord Cornwallis was constrained to make to prevent the transfer of their alliance to Tippoo. It was on this occasion that he followed the example of Hastings, and took the funds provided for the Company's investment out of the holds of their ships.

Preparations for the third campaign.

On his return to Madras Lord Cornwallis employed the
A.D. 1791 army in the conquest of the Baramahal and the capture of the fortresses with which the country was studded. Nothing filled the native princes with such awe of the military power of the Company, as the ease and rapidity with which such forts as Kistnaghery, Nundidroog, Savandroog, and others that were deemed impregnable, were captured, while they considered themselves fortunate if forts of inferior strength were
1792 taken after a siege of six months. Early in January Lord Cornwallis took the field with a convoy surpassing in magnitude anything which had been seen before, and which led Tippoo to exclaim: "It is not what I see of the "resources of the English that I dread, as what I do not "see." The army consisted of 22,000 men and eighty-six field pieces and siege guns. It was augmented, but by no means strengthened, by about 8,000 of the Nizam's troops, more showy than serviceable, and a small contingent of Mahratta horse. On the 5th February the whole force reached a position which commanded a view of Seringapatam,

A.D. 1792

situated on an island of the Cauvery, protected by three lines of defence mounting three hundred guns, and surrounded by a hedge of thorny plants absolutely impervious to man or beast. Tippoo's army was encamped on the northern bank of the stream, in a strongly fortified position, which Lord Cornwallis reconnoitred on the 6th, and determined to storm the same night. The generals of the allies were lost in astonishment when they heard that the English commander had gone out "like an ordinary "captain," in a dark night without guns, to assail these formidable lines. The conflict, which was carried on throughout the night, terminated in the capture of all Tippoo's redoubts, and the establishment of the British force in the island itself. Soon after Lord Cornwallis was strengthened by the junction of General Abercromby's force of 6,000 men from Bombay, and the operations were pushed on with such vigour that Tippoo was assured by his principal officers that no dependence could any longer be placed on his troops, and that he had nothing left but submission. Threatened as he was with the loss of his kingdom he accepted the severe terms dictated by Lord Cornwallis:—that he should surrender half his dominions, pay a war indemnity of three crores, and give up two of his sons as hostages. The generals of the Peshwa and the Nizam left the negotiations entirely with the English plenipotentiary; but after they had been completed, the Mahratta commander put in a demand of sixty lacs for himself and the Nizam's general, as a "reasonable remuneration for their labours in the negotiations," but consented to its reduction by one half. From documents found at Seringapatam when it was captured six years later, it appears that the generals of both the allies were all the time engaged in a clandestine correspondence with Tippoo, the perfidious object of which was happily defeated by the prompt movements of Lord Cornwallis and the early completion of the treaty. The coalition treaty provided that the territories and fortresses conquered by their united exertions should be equally divided among the three signataries. The Mahrattas had given no assistance in the war; indeed, their main body did not join the English camp until a fortnight after the treaty had been signed. The Nizam's force had done nothing but consume food and forage; but Lord Cornwallis determined to adhere with scrupulous fidelity to the original compact, and made over a third of the indemnity, as well as of the territory, to each of his

A.D. 1792 confederates, annexing only one third, of the annual value of forty lacs of rupees, to the Company's territories.

Remarks on the growth of the empire.

This was the first acquisition of territory after it had been resolved to prevent it by Act of Parliament. Mr. Pitt, when introducing his Bill in 1784, stated that his first and principal object was to prevent the governor of Bengal from being ambitious, and bent on conquest; but, though the dread of territorial expansion was the bugbear of the day, and continued to haunt the India House and Downing Street till we had absorbed all India, the tendency of our policy for twenty years had lain in an opposite direction. Clive had given back the kingdom of Oude in 1765, when it was forfeited by the issue of the war, and he denounced any attempt to extend our dominions beyond the Curumnussa. Hastings was at one time prepared to relinquish the Northern Sircars; Lord Cornwallis, soon after he assumed the Government expressed his wish to withdraw from the Malabar coast, and reduce Bombay to the position of a factory; and Lord Shelburn, when prime minister in 1782, proposed to abandon Madras, and give up everything but Bengal and Bombay. If the size of the Indian empire had depended on the wishes or the policy of the public authorities of the day, it would have been comprised within very narrow limits.

Cause of the growth.

The increase of the Company's dominions in India, which was reprobated by the Court of Directors, by Parliament and by the ministry, arose from the progress of circumstances over which none of those authorities had any control. From time immemorial, aggression had been the vital principle of all native states. Twenty-five centuries before, the father of Hindoo legislation had placed conquest among the foremost of royal virtues. "What the king has not got," said Munoo, "let him "strive to gain by military strength;" and it was a precept never disregarded. The Mahomedans adopted this standing rule, not only in reference to infidel princes, but to those of their own creed. Every new dynasty proceeded to attack and appropriate the dominions of its neighbours. During the eighteenth century, the political cauldron in India had been seething with more than ordinary violence. The four chief powers of the period, Tippoo, the Nizam, the Peshwa and Sindia, who, had been established within the previous sixty years, were maintained in vigour by the impulse of aggressiveness. Scarcely a year had passed without an invasion of the rights of some prince in Hindostan or the Deccan. It was in this state of things that the Company appeared on the scene, and took up arms for the defence of their factories, and by the superior discipline and valour of their troops became a first-rate military power, and consequently an object of jealousy and dread to the belligerent princes of India. It was the restlessness and encroachment of the native princes, and not the ambition of English rulers, that gave rise to nearly all the wars in which they were engaged. The slightest symptom of weakness, and too frequently the appearance of moderation, became the signal for hostility; and when the aggression was subdued it appeared the dictate of prudence to prevent the repetition of it by reducing the resources of the aggressor, and depriving him of some portion of his territory. And thus has the British empire in India been gradually extended by a mysterious and inexorable necessity, which has overpowered not only the opposition of the India House and the ministry, and the denunciations of English patriots, but the omnipotence of Parliament. The House of Commons ratified all the proceedings of Lord Cornwallis, not excepting even the acquisition of territory, and the king conferred on him the dignity of a marquis. The precedent has been scrupulously followed ever since, and every Governor-General who has enlarged the British dominions in India has received the thanks of Parliament and been decorated with honours by the Crown.

A.D. 1792

SECTION II.

LORD CORNWALLIS'S ADMINISTRATION—REVENUE AND JUDICIAL REFORMS—PROGRESS OF SINDIA.

THE brilliant success of the Mysore war reflected great credit on Lord Cornwallis; but the permanent reputation of his administration rests on his revenue and judicial reforms. The changes which had been so repeatedly made in the revenue arrangements during the thirty years of our rule were found to have been equally detrimental to the welfare of the ryots and the interests of the state, and Lord Cornwallis, soon after his arrival, affirmed that agriculture and internal commerce were in a state of rapid decay, and that no class appeared to flourish

Revenue reforms.

but the money-lenders. The Court of Directors felt the necessity of adopting some decisive policy to arrest the progress of ruin, and accordingly framed their memorable letter
A.D. of the 12th April, the salient points of which were, that the
1786 settlement should be made with the old zemindars, and not with farmers or with temporary renters,—on the ground of fiscal expediency, and not as a matter of right,—and for a period of ten years, and eventually, if it was found to work well, in perpetuity. Lord Cornwallis employed three years in endeavouring to acquire information on the subject to serve as the basis of a settlement. The fee simple of the land had always been considered as belonging to the sovereign, but the Court of Directors, acting on a generous and enlightened policy, determined to confer it on the zemindars, and thus give them a permanent interest in the soil. The land thus became real property, and a large and opulent class of landholders was thereby created. The relationship between the zemindar and the ryot was an important question, and involved in great perplexity, which has not yet been removed. The zemindar had always squeezed out of the ryot every farthing that could be realised, leaving him little beyond a rag and a hovel. Mr. Shore, who superintended the settlement, the ablest revenue officer in India, was of opinion that some decisive provision should be made to ensure an equitable adjustment of the demands of the zemindar, but, unfortunately, the regulations passed to protect the ryot from extortion were indefinite and inadequate. He was, indeed, permitted to resort to law, but to expect that a poor cultivator could appeal to the courts against a rich and powerful landlord was an absurdity. This defect was unquestionably a blot in the settlement, which, in other respects, was benevolent, if not beneficent.

After the settlement had been completed, the important question arose whether it should be decennial or permanent.

1792

The permanent settlement.

Lord Cornwallis maintained that a fixed and unalterable settlement was the only panacea for the evils which afflicted the country, and the only protection from the still greater ruin which threatened it, and that the grant of this boon would give the zemindars an irresistible inducement to promote the cultivation of the land and the welfare of the ryots. On the other hand, Mr. Shore, who was far better acquainted with the subject than the Governor-General, opposed with equal tenacity the proposal to make the settlement irrevocable. He argued that the Government had only the roughest estimate of the capabilities of the land and of the collections, that the land revenue formed the bone and muscle of the public resources, and that it was preposterous to fix the revenue for ever without any definition of the boundaries of estates, and when a third of Bengal was a jungle. As to the public spirit of the zemindars which a permanent settlement was expected to foster, he justly remarked that the whole zemindary system was a mere conflict of extortion on the one part and resistance on the other, and that it was vain to hope for any improvement. The question was referred to Leadenhall Street, and some of the Directors, influenced partly by their own local experience in India and partly by Mr. Shore's opinion, proposed to make it decennial. It was then placed before the Board of Control, and Mr. Pitt, who had studied Indian subjects as no prime minister has ever studied them since, closely investigated it for a week in conjunction with Mr. Dundas and Mr. Charles Grant, and came to the determination to make the settlement permanent, and it was promulgated at Calcutta on the 22nd March, 1793. It was the boldest and most important administrative measure the Company had ever ventured upon. Under its operation cultivation has been extended, and the opulence of the provinces has been augmented; the zemindars, and those who have acquired interests in the land under them, have grown wealthy, and the comfort of the cultivators has, perhaps, been promoted. But it is now universally felt that the permanent character given to it was an egregious blunder, and that a term of fifty years, if not of a shorter period, would have equally promoted the object in view. No margin was allowed to meet the inevitable increase of expenditure which would be required for the defence of the country, or for the improvement of it by the institutions of civilisation. The Government has, however, continued for a period of eighty years to maintain the settlement to the very letter with scrupulous fidelity under every emergency, and has thus exhibited an example of good faith heretofore unknown in India.

A.D. 1793

The administration of Lord Cornwallis was likewise distinguished by a radical change in the fiscal and judicial branches. The control of the revenue was concentrated in a board in Calcutta. A civil court was established in each district and in the principal cities, presided over by a covenanted servant of the Company. Four courts of appeal were erected at Calcutta,

Civil and criminal courts.

A.D. 1793 Dacca, Moorshedabad, and Patna, from whose decisions an appeal lay to the sudder or chief court at the Presidency, composed of the Governor-General and the members of Council. The judges of the four courts of appeal were to proceed on circuit twice a year to administer criminal justice and to hold jail deliveries. The district judges were likewise invested with magisterial powers, and authorised to pass sentence in trivial matters, and to commit delinquents for trial before the judges of circuit. Within circles of about twenty miles a native officer, called a daroga, was appointed to arrest offenders on written charges, and to take security, not only for his appearance, but also for that of the witnesses, before the magistrate. For more than ten years the simple rules for the administration of justice drawn up by Sir Elijah Impey had been the manual of the courts. Lord Cornwallis determined that all the regulations affecting the rights, the property, and the persons of the subjects of Government should be embodied in a code, and translated into Bengalee and Persian. Mr. George Barlow, a civilian of mark, but without any legal education, was entrusted with the charge of drawing up the new code, and he expanded the ordinances of Sir Elijah into a bulky folio of regulations, but without improving them. This volume of laws, however valuable as a monument of British philanthropy, was little suited to the habits or wants of a people accustomed to prompt and simple justice. The course of procedure was loaded with formalities, and, combined with the multiplication of technical rules, tended to defeat the object in view. Every suit became a game of chess; "justice," as the natives observed, "was made sour by delay," and equity was smothered by legal processes. To crown the grievance, the business of the courts was transacted in a language—the Persian—equally foreign to the judges, the suitors, and the witnesses.

The code.

The wisdom and judgment manifested in Lord Cornwallis's various institutions have always been freely acknowledged, but they were deformed by one great and radical blemish. From the days of Akbar all civil and military offices, even those of the highest grade, had, with occasional exceptions, been open to all the natives of the country; and, in the early days of Hastings, some of the most important offices in the state had been enjoyed by natives of merit or influence. Lord Cornwallis pronounced the natives unworthy of trust, and considered that the administration in every department

1793 Exclusion of natives.

ought to be conducted by the Company's covenanted servants, some three hundred in number, to the entire exclusion of native agency, with the exception of the daroga on twenty-five rupees a month, and a moonsiff to try petty civil suits, to be paid by a commission on them; in other words, by the encouragement of litigation. Every prospect of honourable ambition was thus closed at once against the natives of the country, and the fatal effects of this ostracism were speedily visible in the inefficiency of the whole system of government.

The only other event of any note in the year 1793 was the capture of Pondicherry on the declaration of war between France and England at the outbreak of the Revolution. Lord Cornwallis embarked for England in October, after a memorable reign of seven years, during which period he had contributed to the purity and vigour of the power created by the daring of Clive, and consolidated by the genius of Hastings. The dignity of his character, and his firmness and integrity, combined with his calmness and moderation, conciliated and swayed the native princes, and commanded the cheerful obedience of the European servants.

Capture of Pondicherry. A.D. 1793

The treaty of Salbye, which Sindia had concluded with Hastings in 1782 on the part of the Peshwa, gave him an elevated position in the Mahratta commonwealth. He was no longer the mere feudatory of Poona, but an independent chief, and an ally of the British Government, and he determined to push his schemes of ambition in Hindostan, for which circumstances were peculiarly favourable. The imbecile emperor was a mere puppet in the hands of his minister, Afrasiab Khan, who invited Sindia, in his master's name, to assist in demolish-
ing the power of his rival, Mahomed Beg, and he accord- 1784
ingly advanced with a large army to Agra, where he had an interview with the emperor. Soon after Afrasiab was assassinated, and Sindia became master of the situation, and was appointed the executive minister of the empire, with the command of the imperial troops. The districts of Agra and Delhi were assigned for their support, and he was thus put in possession of the Doab, the province lying between the Jumna and the Ganges, and its great resources. Intoxicated with this success, he preferred a demand for the *chout* of Bengal, which was indignantly
rejected by Mr. Macpherson, the officiating Governor- 1785
General. He then proceeded to demand the arrears of

Progress of Sindia.

tribute, which he stated at sixty lacs of rupees, from the Rajpoots at the gates of Jeypore. The greater portion of the amount was paid, but, on his demanding the balance, the Rajpoots made common cause to resist him. In the battle which ensued, he was deserted by Mahomed Beg, and by the whole of the imperial troops, who took over
A.D. eighty pieces of cannon to the enemy. He was discomfited
1787 and fled from the field, and in his extremity entreated Nana Furnavese, the head of the regency at Poona, to aid him in supporting the Mahratta authority in Hindostan. The Nana was jealous of his growing power, but despatched troops under Holkar, although rather with the object of watching his movements than of supporting them.

Ishmael Beg. Mahomed Beg fell in the battle, but his place was supplied by his nephew, Ishmael Beg, who laid siege to Agra, on the part of the Rajpoots, and was joined by Gholam Khadir, a Rohilcund jageerdar, and his free lances. Sindia advanced to raise the siege, but was again completely defeated in a battle fought on the 24th April. Gholam Khadir was recalled to defend his own jageer from the encroachments of the Sikhs, now rising into power, and Sindia took advantage of his absence to attack Ishmael Beg,
1788 who was defeated, and escaped from the field by the swiftness of his horse. He joined Gholam, and the united chiefs advanced to Delhi, of which Gholam obtained possession, and his licentious soldiery were let loose on the imperial city, which was subjected for two months to such scenes of violence, rapine and barbarity, as were said to be "almost without example in the annals of the world." The ladies of the seraglio were exposed and dishonoured,
1788 and some of them starved to death, and the unhappy monarch, plundered and dethroned, was deprived of sight by this monster of cruelty. Ishmael Beg turned with horror from these atrocities, and accepted service with Sindia, who proceeded to Delhi, reseated the emperor with great pomp on his throne, and made every effort to alleviate his sorrows. Gholam Khadir fled on his approach, but was captured, and deliberately hacked to pieces. The turbulent Ishmael Beg did not long remain faithful to Sindia, but again joined the Rajpoots, whom Sindia de-
1790 feated at Patun in 1790, and the next year at Mairta. The success of both these engagements was due chiefly to
1791 the disciplined battalions of the Count de Boigne, a native of Savoy, an officer of distinguished ability and great military experience, who had come out to India in search of

employment, and entered the service of Sindia, and induced him to create a sepoy corps on the model of the Company's army. De Boigne raised and organised a large force, disciplined by European officers, the majority of whom were natives of France. It was eventually augmented to 18,000 regular infantry, 6,000 irregulars, 2,000 irregular horse and 600 Persian cavalry, with 200 pieces of artillery. This formidable force rendered Sindia the paramount native power in Hindostan, and the most important member of the Mahratta body.

Sindia offered to join the alliance against Tippoo, promoted by Lord Cornwallis, on condition that the Company's Government should guarantee all the possessions he had acquired in Hindostan, and furnish him with two battalions of troops, similar to those granted to the Nizam. These proposals were considered inadmissible, and he declined to become a party to the treaty of Poona. That he might, however, be in a position to take advantage of circumstances in the war in which the princes of the Deccan were about to be engaged with Tippoo, he proceeded with an army to the Mahratta capital, greatly to the annoyance of Nana Furnavese, who dreaded his ambitious designs. He had obtained from the impotent emperor the title of Vakeel-i-Mootluk, or regent of the Mogul empire, for the Peshwa, and for himself the office of hereditary deputy, and he gave out as the pretext for the journey that he was proceeding to the Mahratta capital to invest the Peshwa with this dignity. The Nana and the ministers could not view without disgust the acceptance of honours by the head of the Mahratta power from the puppet of an emperor, but their opposition was unavailing. Sindia had gained a complete ascendency over the young Peshwa by his cheerful and genial demeanour, which formed a strong contrast to the stern and morose bearing of the prime minister, Nana Furnavese. Sindia had, moreover, brought a variety of rarities for him from Hindostan, and studied to make arrangements for his amusement. The ceremony was imposing beyond anything which had been seen at Poona. A grand suite of tents was pitched in the vicinity of the city, a throne was placed to represent that of the Great Mogul, on which the patent and the insignia were deposited. The Peshwa, surrounded by his whole court and the representatives of foreign powers, approached the throne and made his obeisance, and then retiring to another tent was invested

Sindia at Poona.

A.D. 1792

Investiture of the Peshwa.

1792

with the gorgeous robes of the office, and returned to Poona with such pomp and grandeur as the inhabitants had never before witnessed. Sindia and Nana Furnavese, though plotting each others' destruction, maintained an outward appearance of civility, but their armies could not be restrained from hostility in Hindostan. The forces of Holkar and Sindia were jointly engaged in levying tribute from the Rajpoots, but they quarrelled about the division of the spoil. Sindia's commander, De Boigne, with 20,000 horse and 9,000 infantry, attacked Holkar's army, consisting of 30,000 men, including four battalions disciplined by his French general. Holkar was completely
A.D. defeated, and the four regiments were all but annihilated,
1792 only one European officer escaping the carnage. This victory rendered Sindia the first power among the Mahrattas, and deepened the apprehensions of his rival Nana Furnavese, but he was relieved from all anxiety by the
1794 Death of Mahdajee Sindia. unexpected death of Sindia, on the 12th February. For thirty-five years he may be said to have passed his life in his camp, devoting his time and energies to the improvement of his army and the increase of his possessions. From his father he received a small principality, and he bequeathed to his son a kingdom, extending from the Sutlege to Allahabad, and including two-thirds of Malwa, and some of the fairest provinces in the Deccan, and the most efficient military force in India.

The period for which their exclusive privileges had been granted to the Company expired in 1793, and the Court of
1793 The new Charter. Directors applied to Parliament for the renewal of them. But new commercial and manufacturing interests had been springing up in England with great vigour, and petitions poured into the House from Liverpool, Glasgow, Bristol, Manchester, and other seats of industry and enterprise, protesting against the exclusion of the country from any share in the trade of India. The India House met these representations by the bold assertion that it was essential to the national interests that the Company should be the sole agents for conducting the commerce and the government of India. The ministry found the existing state of things exceedingly comfortable, inasmuch as Indian affairs were, on all essential questions, under their control. Lord Cornwallis had placed the finances of India in a flourishing condition, and Mr. Dundas, the India minister, asked the House with an air of triumph, whether they were prepared to interrupt this tide of

prosperity and the growing commerce of India for a mere theory. His arguments were received with blind confidence in a House in which free trade was considered the inevitable road to ruin; and the monopoly of the Company was renewed for twenty years, although, to meet the clamours of the merchants, the Company were directed to allot 3,000 tons a year for their private trade. An effort was made by Mr. Wilberforce to obtain permission for missionaries and schoolmasters to proceed to India and give instruction, religious and secular, to the natives who might desire it, but it was resisted by the ministry, the Court of Directors, and the old Indians. The charter of 1793 was a faithful mirror of the views of an age in which it was considered that the introduction of free trade and European settlers, of schoolmasters and missionaries, would be fatal to the British power in India.

SECTION III.

SIR JOHN SHORE'S ADMINISTRATION.

LORD CORNWALLIS was succeeded by Sir John Shore, one of the ablest of the Company's servants, and the author of the permanent settlement. In a letter to Mr. Dundas on the subject of appointing his successor, Lord Cornwallis had said that "nobody but a "person who had never been in the service, and who was "essentially unconnected with its members, who was of a "rank far surpassing his associates in the government, "and who had the full support of the ministry at home, "was competent for the office of Governor-General." This letter, however, did not reach England till after the selection of Sir John Shore had been made, at the instance of Mr. Pitt, who was favourably impressed with the industry, the candour, and the ability exhibited by him in reference to the revenue settlement. He entered on his duties on the 28th October, 1793.

Sir John Shore's antecedents.

A.D. 1793

The first question which arose to try the mettle of the new Governor-General was connected with the politics of the Deccan. After the termination of the war with Tippoo, Lord Cornwallis, anxious to secure permanent peace to the Deccan, submitted to the two native princes who were parties to the tripartite treaty of

The guarantee treaty.

1793

1790 the draft of a "treaty of mutual guarantee," which would have established a balance of power in the Deccan, and guarded the rights of the princes from mutual aggression. The Nizam, as being the weakest, agreed to it with alacrity; but the Mahrattas had a long account against him which it was not their policy to close, and which they intended to settle by the sword, and they therefore, declined any engagement which would interfere with the designs they formed against him. After twelve months of fruitless discussion, Lord Cornwallis was obliged to abandon all hope of securing the concurrence of the Poona regency. Sindia had been the most strenuous opponent of the guarantee treaty, and his death seemed to present a favourable opportunity for renewing the negotiation, and making a vigorous effort to preserve the tranquillity of the Deccan, then menaced by the Mahrattas. They fully anticipated some decisive interference on the part of the Company's Government, such as they knew Lord Cornwallis would have undertaken. But they soon perceived that the sceptre was now in feeble hands, and they hastened their preparations when they found that Sir John Shore had resolved to limit his intervention to "good "offices." The Nizam, who advanced counter claims of even greater amount than those of the Mahrattas, immediately claimed the fulfilment of the treaty of 1790; but Sir John lacked the spirit of his predecessor. He had a morbid dread of offending the Mahratta powers, and he paid a servile homage to the Act of Parliament which discountenanced native alliances, though Lord Cornwallis had driven his coach through it, and he resolved to remain neuter in the impending struggle. It is, however, due to his memory to state that this decision was evidently influenced, to a considerable extent, by the incompetency of the Commanders-in-Chief at all the Presidencies, with none of whom could he venture to undertake hostilities.

Rejected by the Mahrattas. A.D. 1793; 1794

To assemble a Mahratta army when there was any hope of plunder had never presented any difficulty. On this occasion the young Peshwa, having determined to take the field in person, summoned his feudatories of every degree, and it proved to be the last time they were ever assembled together under the national standard. Sindia, Holkar, the raja of Nagpore, the Gaikwar, and the southern jageerdars, each furnished a quota, and the whole force numbered 130,000 horse and foot, with 150 guns, while the army of the Nizam amounted to about

1795 Expedition against the Nizam.

110,000. The Nizam had engaged a French officer of the name of Raymond to discipline two battalions, which were increased to twenty-three when the struggle with the Mahrattas appeared inevitable. In the ranks of Sindia were likewise 10,000 men commanded by Perron, and 2,000 with Holkar, under Dudrenec; and the most efficient soldiers on each side were under the command of natives of France.

The two armies met on the 12th March, a little in advance of the village of Kurdla, which has given its name to this decisive battle. The advanced guard of the Nizam Battle of Kurdla. A.D.
put to flight one large division of the Mahratta 1795
infantry, but the whole of the Nizam's cavalry broke and fled when it was assailed by the French force. Raymond's infantry had, however, obtained considerable advantage over Perron's, and there was some prospect of his ultimate success, when he was peremptorily ordered by his master to withdraw from the field. The Nizam had taken his zenana with him, and his favourite sultana, terrified by the roar of the cannon, insisted upon his retiring beyond its reach. The dotard yielded to her importunities, and the whole army retreated in wild confusion, although scarcely two hundred men had fallen in both armies. The Nizam took refuge in Kurdla, and within two days was obliged to sign a humiliating treaty, making cessions of territory of the value of thirty-five lacs a year, paying the sum of three crores of rupees, and delivering up his minister, the only able man at his court, to the Peshwa. The two battalions of Company's troops in his service were not permitted by Sir John Shore to assist him during the battle; and on his return to Hyderabad he dismissed them in disgust, and ordered Raymond to use every exertion to augment and discipline his sepoys, and assigned districts for their support. The power and influence in the Nizam's councils which Lord Cornwallis had secured for the Company, were thus transferred to the French.

The battle of Kurdla completely prostrated the Nizam, and the Mahrattas would doubtless have returned to complete his humiliation, but for the unexpected death of the Peshwa, and the confusion which it occasioned. Death of the Peshwa. Nana Furnavese had, with occasional intermissions, enjoyed the chief control in Mahratta affairs during his minority; but though the Peshwa was now of age, he was still kept in a state of galling tutelage, which at
length became insupportable, and on the 25th October he 1795

threw himself from a terrace in his palace, and expired two days after, bequeathing the crown to his cousin Bajee Rao, the son of the once famous Raghoba, who was then held in durance by Nana Furnavese. Then ensued a scene of intrigue and anarchy, which lasted more than three years, and which has scarcely a parallel in the native history of India. After a variety of convulsions, the fortunes of the Nana were reduced to the lowest ebb, but retrieved by his extraordinary genius. "The vigour of his judgment," observes the historian of the Mahrattas, "the fertility of "his resources, the extent of his influence, and the com- "bination of instruments he called into action, surprised "all India, and from his European contemporaries pro- "cured him the title of the Mahratta Machiavelli." He proposed to restore to the Nizam the territory which had been wrested from him, and to remit the balance remaining due, and having thus gained his assistance, as well as that
A.D. of Sindia and Holkar, marched in triumph to Poona,
1796 where he seated Bajee Rao on the throne, and regained his own power as prime minister. But Bajee Rao, the most perfidious of native princes, incited Sindia to destroy him, and he was treacherously seized at a banquet and
1797 sent prisoner to Ahmednugur. The Peshwa then made arrangements for the assassination of Sindia, but his courage failed him at the last moment, and he exhibited for the first time that indecision of character which marked all his future career.

Mutiny of European officers.

Mr. Dundas had announced his opinion that India could only be retained by a large European army, that the proportion of European to native troops should be as one to three, and that the whole force should be placed under the Crown, and "act in concert "with the general strength of the empire." The scheme of amalgamation which Lord Cornwallis had drawn up
1794 was not altogether approved by the Board of Control, or the Court of Directors, and Mr. Dundas undertook to draw up a second. But the European officers of the Company, who were opposed to any amalgamation, were already in a state of mutiny, and Sir John Shore found, on assuming the Government, that he had to deal with the insubordination of a whole army. The officers repressed their resentment while they awaited the arrival of Mr. Dundas's regulations, but their patience was exhausted by delay. On Christ-
1795 mas day Sir John convened the Council, and informed them that delegates had been elected from each regiment

to form an executive board, and that every regiment had bound itself to protect their persons and make good their losses. The terms which this board was to demand from the Government were, that the native regiments should not be reduced, or the European regiments increased, beyond a certain limit, and that all allowances which had been granted to the army at any time should be restored. If these conditions were not accepted, they were prepared to seize the Governor-General and Commander-in-Chief, and to take possession of the Government.

Submission of the government.

The Council was thunderstruck by this announcement. It was a crisis similar to that which the undaunted spirit of Clive had quelled in two months, thirty years before; but there was no Clive at Calcutta. Orders were sent to Madras and the Cape for troops, and the admiral was desired to bring up his fleet, and even De Boigne was asked for a regiment of Sindia's cavalry. The Commander-in-Chief went to Cawnpore, and by his courteous manners soothed the feelings of the officers, but it was the firmness of the artillery that stemmed the tide of mutiny. The long-expected regulations of Mr. Dundas arrived in May 1796, and disgusted all parties. The Governor-General himself described them as a mass of confusion. The flame of revolt blazed forth afresh in the army, and remonstrances poured in upon the bewildered Government. Sir John Shore, in writing to the Court of Directors, stated that the pressure was so severe that he had been obliged to give way. The regulations were modified and concessions made which exceeded even the expectations of the army. The intelligence of this submission filled the ministry with such alarm that it was resolved to supersede Sir John Shore forthwith, and Lord Cornwallis was importuned to proceed to India, if only for twelve months, and restore order. He was accordingly sworn in as Governor-General on the 1st February, and the appointment was duly notified at all the Presidencies. But the mutineers had a representative body of officers sitting in London, and, incredible as it may appear, the Court of Directors and the Board of Control, after having recalled Sir John Shore for his weakness, entered into negotiations with them and made concession after concession, and silenced one of the ringleaders by a lucrative post at the India House. An order was passed in reference to the mutiny which Lord Cornwallis described as "milk and water," and he threw up the appointment in disgust.

A.D. 1796

1797

The last act of Sir John Shore's administration was marked by as much vigour as those preceding it had been signalised by feebleness. The Vizier of Oude was a man of good disposition, but spoiled by the enjoyment of absolute power, and vitiated by the fools, knaves and sycophants who composed his court. The Government was completely effete, and but for the protection of British bayonets, the country would have been absorbed by the Mahrattas or the Sikhs. Before his departure from India, Sir John Shore visited Lucknow and endeavoured to impress on the Vizier the necessity of reforming the abuses of the administration; but whatever favourable impression he might have produced in the morning was effaced in the evening when the prince was surrounded by buffoons and parasites, or stupefied with opium. Six weeks after Sir John's return to Calcutta, he sank into the grave, exhausted by indulgence, and the succession of Vizier Ali, whom he had acknowledged as his son, was sanctioned by the Government of India.

Oude.

Death of the nabob.

Information was received soon after that his birth was spurious and his character atrocious, and Sir John returned to Lucknow to ascertain the truth, when he obtained evidence that he was not even the illegitimate son of the late Vizier, but the offspring of a man of the lowest caste, and likewise that his profligacy had created a feeling of universal disgust. Sir John was convinced that he had been accessory to an act of injustice, and as the late ruler had left no legitimate issue, he conferred the throne on his brother, then residing at Benares. He was required on being installed, to sign a new treaty, by which the defence of the country was entrusted to a body of 10,000 British troops, for whom an annual subsidy of seventy-five lacs of rupees was allotted, that the native army of the state should not exceed 35,000 troops, that the fortress of Allahabad, the key of the north-west provinces, should be made over to the Company, and the Vizier eschew all foreign negotiations. During these arrangements, Sir John Shore was encamped with a small force near the town of Lucknow, and exposed to eminent danger from the violence of Vizier Ali, and the bands of desperate men in his pay, under the command of a reckless adventurer, who had 300 pieces of cannon, and openly talked of assassinating the Governor-General. The fearlessness which he exhibited in this perilous position, as

A.D. 1797 Vizier Ali.

1798 Saadut Ali Nabob.

well as the resolution and justice of his proceedings, created general admiration in India, and the Court of Directors applauded the "great temper, ability and firmness he "had displayed on this occasion." The arrival of the Vizier with a large force from Benares rescued him from danger, and on his return to Calcutta he embarked for England, A.D. and was raised to the peerage as Lord Teignmouth. 1798

CHAPTER VIII.

SECTION I.

LORD WELLESLEY—LAST MYSORE WAR.

SIR JOHN SHORE was succeeded by Lord Mornington, subsequently created Marquis Wellesley, then in his thirty-eighth year, under whose vigorous rule the power of the Company was rendered paramount throughout India. At the Board of Control, where he had occupied a seat for four years, he had acquired a comprehensive knowledge of Indian affairs, and he moreover enjoyed the advantage of Mr. Pitt's personal friendship and the confidence of Mr. Dundas. He called at the Cape on his way to India, and had the good fortune to meet there Lord Macartney and Lord Hobart, both of whom had been governors of Madras, as well as Major Kirkpatrick, formerly resident at Sindia's court, and more recently at Hyderabad, and obtained from their communications the most important information regarding the views and the position of the various princes in India. 1798

Lord Wellesley.

At the commencement of this important epoch, it may be useful to glance at the state of India. After the humiliation of Tippoo Sultan, Lord Cornwallis endeavoured to establish a balance of power in the Deccan. But there never had been any real balance of power in India, and aggression and rapine had been the only principle of action among its princes. Wars were commenced and prosecuted without any semblance of justice, and restrained only by the power of resistance. Eighteen months after the departure of Lord Cornwallis, the battle

State of India.

of Kurdla prostrated the power of the Nizam; the Peshwa was reduced to extremity by the encroachments of Sindia; and even the appearance of a balance of power in the Deccan was irretrievably lost. The Government of Calcutta had become an object of derision in all the native courts, and a prolongation of Sir John Shore's nerveless administration would have entailed very serious calamities. In the south, Tippoo was brooding over his misfortunes, and husbanding his resources to retrieve them. Though deprived of half his dominions, he was still able to maintain a powerful army in full efficiency. The Nizam had augmented the battalions under Raymond to 14,000, men and the French, who were animated by the national hatred of England which then prevailed in France, exercised a paramount authority in the state. Sindia was supreme at Poona and at Delhi, and enjoyed all the influence and authority still attached to the imperial throne. His territories in the Deccan extended to the Toombudra, and skirted the frontiers of the Nizam and the Peshwa, while in Hindostan it extended to the Sutlege, and abutted on the dominions of the Vizier and of the Company. The French battalions, raised and disciplined by De Boigne, had been augmented to 40,000 men, in no way inferior to the Company's sepoy army, with 450 guns, and fortresses, arsenals, foundries, depôts, and all the appliances of war. Lord Cornwallis had bequeathed to his successor a surplus revenue of a crore and eighty lacs of rupees a year, but it had dwindled into a deficit, and the Company's credit was so low that the treasury could not raise a loan under 12 per cent.

Lord Wellesley landed in Calcutta on the 17th May, and within three weeks was startled by the receipt of a proclamation issued by the governor of the Mauritius, stating that envoys had arrived from Tippoo Sultan with despatches for the Government in Paris, proposing an alliance offensive and defensive, and requesting the aid of a body of troops to assist him in expelling the English from India. Soon after it was announced that a French frigate had landed 150 men, including officers, from the Mauritius at Mangalore, on the Malabar coast, who had proceeded to Seringapatam and entered the Mysore service. Lord Wellesley determined to anticipate the hostile movements of Tippoo, and directed General Harris, the officiating governor of Madras, to assemble the Coast army for an immediate

A.D. 1798. The Mauritius proclamation.

march on Seringapatam, and called on the Nizam and the Peshwa, the signataries of the treaty of 1790, to furnish their quota of troops in accordance with its twelfth article.

The Presidency of Madras was thunderstruck with this venturous project. They had a morbid dread of the Mysore power, which had dictated peace under the walls of Madras, and annihilated Baillie's force, and ravaged the Carnatic; and they conjured up the memory of all the disasters which had for twenty years attended their wars with Hyder and Tippoo. The entire disposable force of the Presidency did not exceed 8,000 men, and they were destitute both of draft cattle and commissariat stores; and far, they said, from being in a condition to march on Tippoo's capital, the force was not equal to the defence of the Company's territories, if he should invade them. On the other hand, the Mysore ruler could muster 60,000 troops, a large portion of whom consisted of the celebrated Mysore horse; his infantry was in part disciplined by French officers; he possessed a hundred and forty-four field-pieces, a rocket brigade, a long train of elephants, an ample supply of draft and carriage cattle, and a splendid commissariat. In these circumstances Lord Wellesley found it impossible to strike an immediate blow, but he issued peremptory orders for the speedy equipment of the army, and he met the remonstrances addressed to him in his own imperious style, by threatening with his severest displeasure "those who presumed to "thwart him, and arrogated to themselves the power of "governing the empire committed to his charge."

Dismay at Madras.

A.D. 1798

The state of affairs at Hyderabad demanded Lord Wellesley's earliest attention. The troops, to the number of 14,000, disciplined and commanded by French officers, presented a serious difficulty. They could not be taken into the field as a portion of the Nizam's contingent, without the risk of their joining the Sultan, with whose French officers they were in constant correspondence; while to leave them behind without an adequate force to watch them, was equally perilous. At this critical juncture, moreover, Lord Wellesley received a communication from Zeman Shah, announcing his intention to cross the Indus and enter Hindostan, and asking the British Government to assist him in driving the Mahrattas back into the Deccan. He was the grandson of Ahmed Shah Abdalee, who had astounded India by his

Lord Wellesley's embarrassments.

victory at Paniput forty years before; and the prospect of another Abdalee invasion created a universal feeling of excitement, if not of alarm. Thus beset with embarrassments in the north and in the south, Lord Wellesley resolved boldly to carry out his policy of alliances with the native princes on his own responsibility, without waiting for the sanction of the Court of Directors or the ministry. He found that the Company had not augmented their security by curtailing their influence, but had drifted into a position in which it was less perilous to advance than to stand still. He determined to break up that policy of isolation which had been erroneously considered the safeguard of British power, and within three months after he had taken the chair at the Council board, negotiations were opened throughout the continent, and every durbar was electrified by the revival of that energy which recalled the days of Hastings and Cornwallis.

A.D. 1798

Negotiations at Hyderabad.

Lord Wellesley found it necessary to dispose of the French force at Hyderabad before he took the field against Tippoo. The great minister of the Nizam, Meer Alum — otherwise called Musheer-ool-Moolk — on being released from Poona and resuming his office, was alarmed at the power which the French officers had obtained in the state, and was disgusted with their arrogance. He lost no time in proposing to Sir John Shore to substitute an English subsidiary force for the French battalions; but Sir John had not the nerve for so bold a proceeding. Lord Wellesley eagerly embraced the proposal, and made an offer to protect the state from all unjust claims in every quarter with a body of 6,000 troops, to be subsidised by the Nizam, on condition that the French corps should be dismissed, and the settlement of all disputes with the Mahrattas referred to the British Government. The Nizam manifested great reluctance to contract an alliance which he could never shake off, with so irresistible a power as the Company, but his minister persuaded him that it was better to repose under the protection of a power governed by the principles of honour, than to be perpetually exposed to the avarice of the Mahrattas and the ambition of Tippoo.

Proposed alliance with the Peshwa.

In the preceding year the Peshwa solicited the aid of a British force to protect him from the encroachments of Sindia, but it was declined by Sir John Shore. He then concluded an alliance with the Nizam, and ceded territory of the annual value of eight lacs of rupees as the price of his assistance.

Sindia revenged himself by releasing Nana Furnavese, whom he held in confinement, and inviting Tippoo to join him in an attack on the Nizam. These manœuvres led to a temporary reconciliation between Sindia and the Peshwa, and it was at this juncture that the proposal of a subsidiary alliance, which included the reference of all claims on the Nizam to the arbitrament of the British Government, was renewed. The Peshwa was too astute not to perceive that such an alliance involved the extinction of his political importance, and it is not to be wondered at that he, in common with the other princes of India, with whom independence had a charm, the value of which was enhanced by its risks, should have been indisposed to resign it. But the Peshwa assured the Resident that he would faithfully observe the conditions of the tripartite treaty in the approaching war with Tippoo, and a large Mahratta force was ostensibly ordered into the field.

A.D. 1798

Extinction of the French force.

To give effect to the treaty with the Nizam, troops were despatched to Hyderabad; but at the last moment he evinced an invincible reluctance to place himself in a state of helpless and irretrievable dependence on a superior power, and he fled to the fortress of Golconda. The Resident was obliged to assume a high tone and to assure the minister that his master would be held responsible for this breach of faith. He was at length convinced that there was more danger in endeavouring to evade the engagement than in fulfilling it, and a proclamation was issued dismissing the French officers, and releasing the sepoys from the obligation of obedience to them. Officers and men were thrown into a state of confusion and dismay by this unexpected order—Raymond was no longer at Hyderabad—but the British force was moved into a position which completely commanded the French encampment and placed their magazines at its mercy. In this helpless state, the officers sent to inform the Resident that they were ready to place themselves under his protection; but the men, to whom large arrears were due, rose in a body and placed the officers in confinement, and it was not without great difficulty they found refuge in the English camp. Captain Malcolm, a young and ambitious officer, then rising into notice, succeeded in quelling the excitement by the payment of their arrears; and before the evening this large body of disciplined troops, possessed of a powerful train of artillery and well-stored arsenals, was disarmed without the loss of a single life. This great achievement, the first act of the new Government, filled the native princes, who were calculating on the decay of the Company's power, with amazement, while the ability with which it was planned, and the promptitude with which it was executed, diffused a spirit of confidence throughout the civil and military services which contributed in no small degree to the success of Lord Wellesley's plans.

A.D. 1798 On the 8th October, Lord Wellesley received information that Bonaparte had landed in Egypt, on his way to the East and he reiterated his orders to press forward the organisation of the Madras army, which he promised to strengthen by the addition of 3,000 volunteer sepoys from Bengal, and with the 33rd Foot, under the command of Colonel Wellesley, afterwards the Duke of Wellington. On hearing that the disbandment of the French force at Hyderabad had been completed, he addressed his first letter to Tippoo, upbraiding him with his embassy to the Mauritius, and the connection he had formed with the inveterate enemies of the British nation, "which "must subvert the foundations of friendship subsisting "between him and the Company." He proposed to depute Major Doveton to his court, to propound a plan calculated to remove all doubt and suspicion. To infuse vigour into these arrangements he resolved to proceed in person to Madras, where he landed on the last day of the year, and assumed the control of all political and military movements, leaving the local administration in the hands of the governor.

Communication with Tippoo.

Tippoo's reply was altogether evasive. He asserted that the vessel which had gone to the Mauritius was sent by a mercantile tribe, and that "the "French, who were full of vice and deceit, had put about "sinister reports to ruffle the minds of the two Sircars." He declined the proposed conference with Major Doveton as superfluous, "inasmuch as his friendship and regard "for the English were perfectly apparent." At this very time, however, he was despatching one of his French officers to the Directory in Paris, to solicit 10,000 troops, to be employed at his expense in expelling the English; and he was likewise inviting Zeman Shah to join him in prosecuting a holy war against the infidels and polytheists. "Please God," he wrote, "the English shall become "food for the unrelenting sword of the pious warriors." Lord Wellesley addressed another letter to him on the 9th

1799 *Tippoo's replies.*

January, demanding a reply in twenty-four hours, to which Tippoo, after a considerable delay, replied that he was going on a hunting excursion, as was his wont, and that Major Doveton might be despatched after him.

A.D. 1799

Every moment now became precious. The capital, Seringapatam, was the heart of Tippoo's power, his principal granary, and his only arsenal. Owing to the rise of the Cauvery around the island on which it was built, it was impregnable from June to November, and it was necessary to reduce it before the rains set in. After waiting in vain for a definite reply, Lord Wellesley ordered the army to take the field. It was the largest and the most complete in point of equipment and discipline which had ever yet assembled under the Company's colours. It consisted of 20,802 men, of whom 6,000 were Europeans, with a battering train of forty guns, and sixty-four field-pieces and howitzers, and 10,000 of the Nizam's cavalry, as well as the Hyderabad subsidiary force, which, under the command of Colonel Wellesley and Captain Malcolm, had become a most efficient auxiliary. The entire army was commanded by General Harris, whose personal knowledge of the route was of great value. Tippoo, leaving his generals to watch the movements of the general at Madras, proceeded with the flower of his army to the Malabar Coast to oppose the Bombay force marching on his capital.

Progress of the army.

Tippoo on the Malabar Coast.

On the 5th March, Tippoo unexpectedly appeared before its advanced guard. General Stuart, the commandant, with the main body, was ten miles in the rear, and it fell to the gallant General Hartley—a name of high renown on that coast—to meet the shock. His little force, and more especially the battalions under Colonel Montresor, bore the assault of the whole of Tippoo's force for six hours with the most determined resolution, but as they were reduced to their last cartridge the general happily came up and decided the fate of the day. Tippoo retreated through the wood with the loss of 2,000 men, and six days after marched off in an opposite direction to resist the advance of General Harris, whose army stood on the table land of Bangalore on the 15th March. Contrary to the advice of his most experienced officers and his French commander, Tippoo fixed on Malavelly as the field for disputing the progress of the British army, and the battle ended in his complete discomfiture on the 27th March. 1799

Battle of Malavelly.

He felt certain that General Harris would pursue the

northern route to the capital as Lord Cornwallis had done, and he had taken the precaution to lay it waste, not leaving a particle of food or forage. But the general moved down in an opposite direction, and crossed the Cauvery at the hitherto unknown ford of Sosilla, without any interruption. Nothing could exceed the rage and dismay of Tippoo when he discovered that all his plans were frustrated by this strategy, and he called a meeting of his officers, and asked their advice with tears in his eyes; they declared that they would make one last and desperate effort for the defence of the capital and the kingdom, and, if unsuccessful, die with him.

The siege.

Seringapatam was invested on the 6th April, and the siege was pushed on with such vigour that Tippoo was induced to propose a conference. General Harris informed him that the only terms on which he was authorised to treat were the cession of half his territories, the payment of a war indemnity of two crores, and the delivery of four of his sons and four of his chief officers as hostages. These terms were rejected by the Sultan. On the 4th May
A.D. 1799 the breach was reported practicable, and the troops were led to the storm by General Baird, a distinguished officer, who had been immured in the dungeons of the fort for four years, in irons, by Hyder and Tippoo. He ascended the parapet at one in the afternoon, and exhibited his noble figure in the view of both forces, and then, drawing his sword, desired his men to follow him, and show themselves worthy the name of British soldiers. A small and select band of Tippoo's soldiers met the forlorn hope in the breach, the greater portion of whom on either side fell in the desperate struggle. The works were defended with great valour, more especially in the gateway where Tippoo had taken his station, and where he fell covered with wounds. The fortress was captured, and, as his remains were conveyed through the city, the inhabitants prostrated themselves before his bier, and accompanied it to the superb monument of Hyder, where he was interred with the imposing rites of Mahomedan burial, and the honours of a European military funeral.

Remarks.

Thus fell the capital of Mysore, though garrisoned by 20,000 troops, and defended by 287 pieces of cannon, and abundantly supplied with provisions and military stores. It was the opinion of Lord Wellesley, and of the best military authorities in the camp, that, considering the strength of its fortifications, and the difficulty of approaching it, a thousand French troops under an able commander might have rendered it impregnable. A.D. 1799 But throughout the siege, and indeed throughout the campaign, Tippoo had failed to exhibit either wisdom or energy. He rejected the advice of his most experienced officers, and listened only to the flatteries of youths and parasites, and the predictions of astrologers. During the line of march General Harris was so heavily encumbered with his ponderous siege train and endless impediments, that his progress was restricted to five miles a day, and it was a miracle that he was not constrained, like Lord Cornwallis, to turn back for want of provisions. There were numerous occasions on which an active and skilful enemy might have impeded his march till the rains set in, and rendered the campaign abortive; but all these opportunities were neglected by Tippoo in a spirit of infatuation. The success of the army was owing to a combination of boldness and courage, and good fortune. Tippoo was forty-six years of age at the time of his death. He possessed none of his father's abilities for peace or war. He was a compound of tyranny and caprice, of superstition and bigotry, and likewise an atrocious persecutor. In the opinion of his own subjects, Hyder was born to create an empire, and Tippoo to lose it.

Security of the Deccan.

For half a century the Deccan had been the scene of convulsions, and the great source of anxiety and expense to the Court of Directors, whose possessions, even in the intervals of peace, had always been insecure. Lord Wellesley terminated this state of jeopardy. Within a twelvemonth after he landed in Calcutta, he had extinguished the French force and influence at Hyderabad, and obtained the command of all the resources of the Nizam. He had subverted the kingdom of Mysore, and established the authority of the Company, without a rival, in the Deccan, on so solid a basis that it has never since been menaced. The capture of Seringapatam in less than a month resounded through the continent of India, and the extinction of one of its substantial powers struck terror into the hearts of its princes, and exalted the prestige of the Company's Government. These advantages were not, however, obtained without a violation of those solemn injunctions which the wisdom of Parliament, of the ministry, and of the India House had periodically repeated to restrain the growth of British power in India, and hence, in writing to Mr. Pitt, Lord Wellesley said, "I suppose

A.D. 1799 "you will either hang me, or magnificently honour me for "my deeds. In either case, I shall be gratified, for an "English gallows is better than an Indian throne." He was magnificently honoured—by the king with a step in the peerage, and by Parliament with its thanks.

New Mysore kingdom.

The issue of the war had placed the whole of the Mysore dominions at the disposal of the Governor-General, and he exercised the rights of conquest with great wisdom and moderation. He resolved to make over a portion of it to the family of its ancient and disinherited princes, though they had passed out of all recollection, and were living in abject poverty and humiliation. A child five years of age was drawn from a cottage and seated on a throne, with a revenue of fifty lacs of rupees a year. The kingdom was bestowed on him as a free gift, and it was emphatically declared to be personal and not dynastic. Every allusion to heirs and successors was therefore distinctly eliminated. Indeed, Lord Wellesley did not hesitate to affirm that the territories placed under the nominal sovereignty of the raja whom he created, constituted an integral portion of our own dominions, and they were treated in this light for more than sixty years.

The remaining territories.

The remaining territories were thus partitioned. Districts of the annual value of about thirty lacs, were allotted to the Company, but charged with the payment of about eight lacs a year to the families of Hyder and Tippoo, and territory valued at about twenty-four lacs was transferred to the Nizam. The Peshwa was not overlooked. He had not only violated his engagement by taking no part in the campaign, but, with his usual duplicity, had received envoys from Tippoo, and accepted a gratuity of thirteen lacs of rupees from him, and concerted a scheme for attacking the dominions of the Nizam while his army was employed in the siege of Seringapatam. But Lord Wellesley overlooked this duplicity, and offered him out of the spoils of Mysore districts yielding ten lacs of rupees, on condition of his excluding the French from his dominions, and admitting the mediation of the British Government in the questions still in dispute with the Nizam. The offer was rejected, and the reserved territory was divided between the Company and the Nizam.

Prize money.

The personal property captured at Seringapatam rather exceeded a crore of rupees and Lord Wellesley took on himself the responsibility of anticipating, as he said, the assent of the Crown, and the sanction

of the Directors, and directed the immediate distribution of it among the troops—the third instance in which prize money had been, not unwisely, divided in India, without waiting for dilatory orders from England. The Court of Directors manifested their sense of Lord Wellesley's merits by offering him ten lacs from the proceeds of the captured stores; but his high sense of honour induced him to decline it, upon which they settled an annuity of half a lac of rupees a year on him. To complete this narrative of the last Mysore war, it only remains to be stated that a daring adventurer, Dhondia Waug, collected together a body of Tippoo's disbanded cavalry and proceeded northward, plundering towns and villages. Success brought A.D.
crowds to his standard, and the peace of the Deccan was 1800
seriously menaced. At length, Colonel Wellesley set out in pursuit of him with four regiments of cavalry, and after chasing him for four months without any relaxation, at length brought him to bay, and he was killed, and his army broken up.

SECTION II.

LORD WELLESLEY—THE CARNATIC—OUDE—FORT WILLIAM COLLEGE—WAR WITH SINDIA AND NAGPORE.

Cession of territory by the Nizam.

THE refusal of the Peshwa to refer the settlement of his demands on the Nizam to the arbitration of the British Government, pointed out to his able minister the treatment he might expect from Mahratta rapacity, and he was anxious to secure his master against it. He proposed, therefore, to Lord Wellesley that the subsidiary force should be augmented and territory allotted for its support in lieu of the monthly payment then made in money. The proposition was, on a variety of considerations, welcome to the Governor-General, and the arrangement was speedily completed. The force was increased to eight battalions, and districts yielding sixty-three lacs a year were made over in perpetual sovereignty
to the Company, under the stipulation that the British 1800
Government should guarantee all the remaining territories of the Nizam from every attack. The districts thus transferred consisted simply of those which had been assigned to him from the Mysore territory in the wars of 1792 and 1798. The transaction was mutually advantageous. It

extended the Company's territories to the Kistna, and it relieved the Nizam of all further apprehension from his hereditary and insatiable enemies—and that without the alienation of any portion of his patrimonial kingdom. It is true, that by resigning the defence of his dominions and the royal prerogative of conducting negotiations with foreign princes, he lost his political independence; but, on the other hand, he secured the continuance of his royal dynasty. Every other throne in the Deccan has been swept away, while the descendant of the Tartar, Cheen Killich Khan, still continues to hold his regal court at Hyderabad. About the same time the raja of the little principality of

Tanjore mediatised.

Tanjore was mediatised. His debts to the Company were cancelled on the resignation of his

A.D. 1800 territory, out of the revenues of which he received four lacs a year, and a fifth of its improved resources.

By the treaty concluded with the nabob, Mahomed Ali, by Lord Cornwallis in 1792, certain districts were hypothe-

State of the Carnatic.

cated for the support of the Company's troops who defended the country. That prince, who had been placed on the throne by the Madras Government in the days of Clive and Coote and had occupied it for fifty years, died

1795 in 1795. His son Oomdut-ool-omrah was surrounded, as his father had been, by a legion of rapacious Europeans, many of them in the public service, who fed his extravagance by advances at exorbitant interest, and, contrary to the stipulations of the treaty, received assignments on the districts pledged for the support of the troops. The loans thus furnished the nabob with the means of paying his instalments to the Government of Madras with punctuality, but they served also to increase his embarrassments, though the crisis was for a time postponed. At the particular request of the Court of Directors, Lord Hobart, the governor of Madras, proposed to the nabob to transfer the districts to the Company in lieu of the pecuniary payment, and offered him as an inducement, to relinquish debts due to the Government, to the extent of a crore of rupees. But though the arrangement would have been highly beneficial to the nabob, it was not to the interest of his creditors, who held him at their mercy, to resign the lands which they subjected to rack rent, and the proposal was rejected. Lord Hobart then proposed to resort to force, on the ground that as the nabob had violated the treaty of 1792 by granting these assignments, it was no longer binding on the Company; but Sir John Shore peremptorily refused his concurrence. The correspondence thereupon became acrimonious, and the matter was referred to Leadenhall Street, and Lord Hobart was recalled. The Court, however, requested Lord Wellesley to call at Madras on his way to Calcutta, and make another effort to obtain the sanction of the nabob to the surrender of the districts, which were in a state of rapid decay, as a substitute for the payment he was bound to make; but, under the sinister influence of the harpies around him, the proposal was again spurned.

Lord Hobart's recall. A.D. 1798

The nabob was bound by treaty "not to enter into any "negotiation or political correspondence with any European or native power without the consent of "the Company." But on the capture of Seringapatam, it was discovered that both the late and the present nabob had been engaged in a clandestine correspondence with Tippoo by means of a cypher, which was found; and that they had made important communications to him, inimical to the interests of the Company. The fact of this intrigue was established by the clearest oral and documental evidence, to the satisfaction of the Governor-General, the governor of Madras, the Court of Directors, and the Board of Control; and Lord Wellesley came to the conclusion that "they had not only violated "the treaty, but placed themselves in the position of "enemies of the Company, by endeavouring to establish a "unity of interests with their most inveterate foe." The obligations of the treaty were considered to be extinct, and it was resolved to deprive the family of the government of the Carnatic, reserving a suitable portion of the revenue for its support. But when the period for action arrived, the nabob was on his death-bed. On his death his reputed son, whom he had nominated his successor, was made acquainted with the evidence of his father's and his grandfather's treacherous correspondence with Tippoo, and informed that all claim on the consideration of Government was forfeited. His succession to the throne was no longer a matter of right, but of favour, and would be conceded only on condition of his making over the Carnatic to the Company, with the reservation of a suitable provision for the maintenance of his court and family. He refused to accept the title on these terms, and it was granted to a cousin, of whose legitimate birth there was no question. The nabob was mediatised, and the Carnatic became a British province. The territories obtained from

Clandestine correspondence. 1799

The nabob mediatised. 1801

Mysore and the Nizam, from the nabobs of the Carnatic and Tanjore, may be said to have created the Madras Presidency. Of the population, which, according to the latest census, amounted to twenty-two millions, eighteen are inhabiting the districts which Lord Wellesley annexed to it.

While Zeman Shah was advancing into Hindostan, Lord Wellesley despatched a native envoy to the king of

A.D. 1800 *Embassy to Persia.*

Persia to induce him to threaten his hereditary dominions in Central Asia, and constrain him to retire from India. The agent urged that the Shah was a Soonee, and had grievously oppressed the Sheahs, the ruling sect in Persia, and that it would be an acceptable service to God and man to arrest the progress of so heterodox a prince. The pious monarch swallowed the bait, and instigated Mahomed Shah to invade the territories of his brother Zeman Shah, who was obliged to recross the Indus in haste. But Lord Wellesley farther deemed it advisable to send a more imposing embassy to the court of Ispahan "to establish British influence in Central Asia, "and prevent the periodical disquietude of an invasion by "Zeman Shah, with his horde of Turks and Tartars, "Usbecks and Afghans." The officer selected for this duty was Captain Malcolm, who was eminently qualified for it by his thorough knowledge of the oriental character and weaknesses, and his acquaintance with eastern languages, as well as his admirable tact and invariable good humour. The embassy was equipped in a style of magnificence intended to dazzle the oriental imagination, and to inspire the Persian court with a due sense of the power and majesty of the British empire in the east. The result, which had been in a great measure anticipated by the native agent, was not commensurate with its cost, which made the Court of Directors wince; but it secured the object of establishing British influence in Persia, at least for a time.

Lord Wellesley could not consider India safe while a French army held possession of Egypt; and he proposed

Expedition to the Red Sea.

to the ministry to send a force from India to support the army which he felt confident they would despatch, to co-operate with the Turkish

1800 Government in expelling it. After long delay the necessary orders were received from Downing Street, and an army consisting of 4,000 European troops and 5,000 volunteer sepoys, was sent up the Red Sea under General Baird, with the animating remark of the Governor-General, "that "a more worthy sequel to the storm of Seringapatam "could not be presented to his genius and valour." The troops landed at Cosseir, in the Red Sea, and after traversing 120 miles of arid and pathless desert to the Nile, encamped, on the 27th August, on the shores of the Mediterranean; but the report of its approach, combined with the energy of the commander from England, had induced the French general to capitulate before General Baird's arrival. The history of India abounds with romantic achievements, but no incident can be more impressive than the appearance of sepoys from the banks of the Ganges, in the land of the Pharaohs, marching in the footsteps of Cæsar to encounter the veterans of his modern prototype. A.D. 1800

Within a month of the surrender of the French army in Egypt, the preliminaries of peace between France and England were signed by the former Governor-General, Lord Cornwallis, at Amiens. The Court of Directors immediately issued orders for their military establishments to be reduced, but Lord Wellesley, with great forethought, wisely suspended the execution of them. The treaty of Amiens was no sooner ratified than Bonaparte despatched a large armament to Pondicherry, which the treaty had restored, consisting of six vessels of war, a large military staff, and 1,400 European troops, under the command of M. Leger, who was designated, in his patent, "Captain-General of the French establishments east of "the Cape." It was to be followed by a second squadron of equal magnitude. For three years it had been the great aim of Lord Wellesley to eradicate French influence from India, and as he had now succeeded in excluding it from the Deccan, he could not regard the re-establishment of a powerful French settlement on the Coromandel coast without a feeling of anxiety. He felt that all the relations of Government with the native states would be at once deranged, and the seeds of a more arduous conflict than the last planted in the soil of India, ever fruitful in revolutions. The order to restore Pondicherry was reiterated from Downing Street, but, by an act of unexampled audacity, Lord Wellesley directed Lord Clive, the governor of Madras, to inform the French admiral on his arrival that he had resolved to postpone the restitution of the French settlements till he could communicate with the ministry in England. The French fleet returned to the Mauritius, and the recommencement of hostilities in

Peace of Amiens. 1802

Europe saved India from the danger to which it would have been exposed if the continuance of peace had enabled Bonaparte to give full scope to his designs.

Demand on the nabob of Oude.

On the approach of Zeman Shah to the Indus, Lord Wellesley, well-knowing that the kingdom of Oude would be one of the early objects of spoliation, requested Sir James Craig, the commandant, to communicate his views on the defence of it. He replied that the rabble of troops maintained by the Vizier was not simply useless, but actually dangerous; and that if he were required to take the field against the Shah, he could not leave them behind with safety. The Court of Directors had stated that the British force, 13,000 in number, was too weak for the protection of the country, more especially since Sindia had planted an army of more than 30,000 disciplined troops, commanded by European officers, on its frontier, watching an opportunity of springing on its opulent districts. The existing treaty had allotted a subsidy of seventy-six lacs of rupees a year for the payment of this force, and also provided for its augmentation, if necessary.
A.D. 1800 Lord Wellesley now pressed on the Vizier the absolute necessity of disbanding his disorderly soldiers, and devoting the fifty lacs of rupees thereby saved to the support of a larger British force.

Discussions with the nabob.

This reform would have placed the military power of the kingdom absolutely in the hands of the Company; to this the nabob manifested an invincible repugnance, and he proposed to abdicate in favour of his son, and to retire into private life with the treasure he had accumulated. Lord Wellesley stated that he was prepared to sanction his retirement provided he took up his residence in the British dominions, and vested the government of the kingdom permanently in the hands of the Company, but could not permit him to withdraw the treasure which belonged to the state. The nabob immediately withdrew his abdication, and Lord Wellesley expressed great indignation at his insincerity and duplicity, as he termed it, and charged him with having made a proposal, which was from the first illusory, in order to defeat the reform of his military establishment, which was imperatively required. Several regiments were ordered to march into the Oude territory, and the nabob was directed to provide for their maintenance. He remonstrated in earnest language, but Lord Wellesley returned his communication, which he said was deficient in the respect due to the first British authority in India. The proceedings began to assume a very vexatious appearance. The Vizier continued to exhibit a spirit of passive resistance, and Lord Wellesley's correspondence was marked by increasing hauteur; but he was desirous, if possible, to avoid the appearance of a compulsory cession of the districts, and despatched his own brother and private secretary, Mr. Henry Wellesley, afterwards Lord Cowley, to overcome his repugnance; but the nabob continued inflexible, and persisted in asserting that it would inflict an indelible stain on his reputation throughout India to deprive one of its royal houses of such a dominion.

Deputation of Mr. H. Wellesley. A.D. 1801

The Resident at length brought the discussion to an issue by ordering the intendants of the districts selected for the support of the British force to transfer their collections and their allegiance to the Company. The nabob deemed it vain any longer to contend with such negotiators, and on the 12th November, signed a treaty which made over to the Company in perpetual sovereignty districts yielding one crore and thirty-five lacs of rupees. The security which this transfer of military power gave to the possessions of the nabob as well as of the Company will admit of no question. A British army, fully adequate to the defence of the country, was substituted for the wretched troops of the nabob, always an object of more dread to their masters than to their enemies; a valuable addition was made to the strength and resources of the Company, and a large population was rescued from oppression. But of all the transactions of Lord Wellesley's administration, this acquisition of territory by the process of compulsion has been the most censured. For any justification of it we must look to the position of the country. The throne of Oude was upheld by British bayonets alone, and the dynasty would have ceased to exist in a twelvemonth, if they had been withdrawn. Under the perpetual menace of a Mahratta invasion, it was necessary that a large and efficient force should be maintained there; but it was not possible for the Company to support such a force with only one-third of the revenues. The settlement of the provinces thus ceded by the Vizier was entrusted to a commission, consisting of members of the civil service, with Mr. Henry Wellesley as president, but he received no additional allowance. Their labours were completed within a year; the Court of Directors, however, lost no time in denouncing this appointment, though temporary, as "a virtual super-

New treaty with the nabob. 1801

"cession of the just rights of the civil service," and drafted a despatch, peremptorily ordering Mr. Wellesley to be dismissed; but the President of the Board of Control drew his fatal pen across it. At the same time they expressed their cordial approbation of the terms of the treaty, which, among other merits, created thirty new appointments for their favourite service.

Lord Wellesley unhappily approved and maintained the erroneous policy initiated by Lord Cornwallis of excluding natives from any share in the government of the country, and working it exclusively by the European agency of the covenanted servants; but he determined to qualify them for their important duties by a suitable education. The civil service was originally a mercantile staff, and India continued to be treated more in the light of a factory than of an empire. The public servants rose, as they had done a century before, through the grades of writer, factor, and junior and senior merchants, and though they were required to perform the functions of magistrates and judges, of secretaries of state and ambassadors, it was deemed sufficient, if, before they left England, they were initiated into the mysteries of the counting-house, and understood book-keeping by double-entry. Of the laws and institutions, and even the language of the people, they were not required to know anything. Lord Wellesley was resolved to remove this glaring anomaly by founding a college in Calcutta, in which their European education should be completed, and they should acquire a knowledge of the laws, literature, and language of the natives.

The College of Fort William.

A.D. 1800

Like all Lord Wellesley's plans, the institution was projected upon a scale of imperial magnificence; and it was, moreover, erected without so much as consulting the Court of Directors, and they passed a peremptory order for its immediate abolition. Lord Wellesley was mortified beyond measure by this subversion of one of his most cherished schemes, which exposed him to the contempt of India, and he gave vent to his feelings in a passionate appeal to his friends in the ministry, and entreated them to save from extinction an institution he deemed invaluable —which indeed, he regarded with greater pride than the conquest of Mysore. On receiving the orders from Leadenhall Street, he passed a resolution abolishing the college, with the sullen remark that it was done "as an act of "necessary submission to the controlling authority of the "Court;" but in a second resolution he allowed eighteen

Its grandeur.

1802

months for the gradual abolition of it; and in the meantime the Court of Directors, under the pressure of the Board of Control, consented to the continuance of it on a reduced scale.

and reduction.

At the renewal of the charter in 1793 the ministry endeavoured to silence the clamours of the merchants and manufacturers of England, as already stated, by obliging the Court of Directors to allot them 3,000 tons of freight annually, but this concession was found inadequate to the demand. The commerce of India was, in fact, bursting the bonds of the monopoly, which, however serviceable it might have been during the infancy of our connection with India, was altogether unsuited to an age of development. The trade of Calcutta had been rapidly expanding, and was forcing itself into the continental markets, in foreign vessels provided with cargoes by English capital. In 1798 the exports in vessels under the flags of America, of Portugal, and of Denmark, had exceeded a crore and a half of rupees.

A.D. 1793

Private trade.

Shipbuilding had likewise made great progress in Calcutta during the previous ten years, and Lord Wellesley, finding 10,000 tons of India-built shipping in the port on his arrival, chartered a large portion of it for the use of the private merchants. In his letter to the Court of Directors on the subject, he said that it would be equally unjust and impolitic to extend any facilities to British merchants which would sacrifice or hazard the Company's rights and privileges, and that the commercial indulgence he had granted extended only to such articles of Indian produce and manufacture as were necessarily excluded from the Company's investments. Mr. Dundas, who entertained the same liberal views as Lord Wellesley, was anxious to authorise the Government of India to license India-built shipping "to bring home "that which the means and capital of the Company were "unable to embrace." But at the India House the dread of interlopers was still in undiminished vigour. Though the cream of the India trade was still to be assured to the Company, the Directors would not permit others to obtain the dregs. The proceedings of Lord Wellesley were emphatically reprobated; he lost caste irretrievably in Leadenhall Street, and the treatment he experienced from the Directors during the last three years of his Indian career was scarcely less rancorous than that which had embittered the life of Warren Hastings. Notwithstanding the remon-

1799 to 1801

Disapproval of Lord Wellesley's conduct.

strance of the minister, they passed a direct vote of censure on the commercial policy he had patronised.

A.D. 1802 As soon as the arrangements in Oude were completed, Lord Wellesley tendered his resignation, assigning to "his "Honourable Masters," as he termed them, no other reason than the full accomplishment of his plans for the security and prosperity of the empire. To the prime minister, however, he unburdened his mind, and informed him that the real cause of his retirement was the invariable hostility of the Court and the withdrawal of their confidence. They had peremptorily ordered the reduction of the military establishments, while he considered it, in the existing circumstances of the empire, essential to its security to maintain them in full vigour. They had cut down the stipends he considered advisable at the close of the war, and had selected for especial censure and retrenchment, the allowances granted by the Madras Government to his brother General Wellesley to meet the cost of his important and expensive command in Mysore; this he considered "the most direct, "marked, and disgusting indignity which could be devised." They had abrogated the power vested in the Governor-General in Council by Parliament of enforcing his orders on the minor Presidencies, though they might happen to supersede the injunctions of the Court, and they had destroyed the authority of the Supreme Government over them by reversing this regulation. They had wantonly displaced officers of the highest ability and experience who enjoyed the full confidence of the Governor-General, and, contrary to law, had forced their own nominees into offices of emolument, for which, moreover, they were totally unfit.

Resignation of Lord Wellesley.

Lord Wellesley vigorously remonstrated against this practice. "If the Government of India," he said, "was thus "to be thwarted in every subordinate department, deprived of all local influence, and "counteracted in every local detail by a remote authority "interfering in the nomination of every public servant, it "would be impossible to conduct the government under "such disgraceful chains." Lord Castlereagh, the President of the Board of Control, was anxious to retain the services of Lord Wellesley, and placed his letter to the premier in the hands of the chairman at the India House. He did not disguise from him the great dissatisfaction and jealousy felt by the Company with regard to certain of Lord Wellesley's measures, and, more especially to the employment of

The causes of it.

Mr. Henry Wellesley. He had, in fact, wounded them on A.D.
the two points on which they were most sensitive—their 1802
monopoly and their patronage. But Lord Castlereagh was assured that the Court were not unmindful of his eminent services, and would request him to postpone his departure to the 1st January 1804; little dreaming of the momentous consequences of this resolution. Before that date, the Mahratta power was prostrate, and the map of India reconstructed.

SECTION III.

LORD WELLESLEY—MAHRATTA AFFAIRS—TREATY OF BASSEIN—WAR WITH SINDIA AND NAGPORE.

Death of Nana Furnavese.

THE extinction of the kingdom of Mysore, and the complete control established over the Nizam, left the British Government without any antagonist but the Mahrattas, and the two rival powers now confronted each other. The offer of a subsidiary alliance to the Peshwa, made by Lord Wellesley in 1799, which would have introduced the thin end of the wedge of British ascendancy was rejected under the advice of Nana Furnavese. That
great statesman closed his chequered career in March, 1800. 1800
For more than a quarter of a century he had been the mainspring of every movement in the Mahratta commonwealth, which he had regulated by the strength of his character and the wisdom of his measures, not less than by his humanity, veracity and honesty of purpose, virtues which were not usually found among his own countrymen. "With him," wrote the Resident at Poona, "departed all "the wisdom and moderation of the Mahratta Government." His death left Sindia without a competitor at Poona, where he exercised supreme authority, and it was not without delight that the Peshwa contemplated the rising power of his rival, Jeswunt Rao Holkar.

The Holkar family.

Mulhar Rao Holkar, who raised himself from the condition of a shepherd to the dignity of a prince, and established one of the five Mahratta powers, died at the age of seventy-six, after a brilliant career of forty years. His only son died soon after, leaving a widow,
Aylah bye, and a son and daughter. The son died in 1766, 1766
and his mother, a woman of extraordinary talent and energy, resisted the importunity of the chieftains to adopt

a son and retire into private life. She resolved to undertake the government of the state herself, and selected Tokajee Holkar, one of the same tribe, though not of her kindred, to command the army. Through his singular moderation and the commanding genius of the bye, this perilous arrangement, which placed the military power in the hands of a distinguished soldier, while the civil government was administered by a female, was perpetuated without jealousy for thirty years. She sat daily in durbar and gave audiences without a veil, and dispensed justice in person. She laid herself out to promote the welfare of the country by the encouragement of trade and agriculture, and raised Indore from the obscurity of a village to the rank of a capital. She acquired the respect of foreign princes by the weight and dignity of her character, and in an age of universal violence was enabled to maintain the security of her dominions. She was the purest and most exemplary of rulers, and she added one more name to the roll of those illustrious females who have adorned the native history of India by their talents and virtues.

A.D. 1795

She died in 1795, and Tokajee two years later, and the reign of anarchy began, and continued without abatement, for twenty years. Mulhar Rao, the son of Tokajee, assumed the command of the army and the government of the state, but he was attacked and killed by Sindia, who was thus enabled to reduce the rival house of Holkar to a state of complete subordination. Jeswunt Rao, the illegitimate son of Tokajee, fled from the field to Nagpore, but the raja, anxious to conciliate Sindia, placed him in confinement, but he contrived at length to make his escape, and took refuge at Dhar, which, under the same hostile influence, he was obliged to quit, with seven mounted followers and about a hundred and twenty ragged half-armed infantry. He determined now to trust his fortunes to his sword, and giving himself out as the champion of his nephew, the young son of his brother Mulhar, called upon all the adherents of the house of Holkar to rally round him and resist the encroachments of Sindia; and the freebooters who swarmed in Central India flocked to his standard.

Early movements of Jeswunt Rao.

Jeswunt Rao was soon after joined by Ameer Khan, a Rohilla adventurer, about twenty-five years of age, together with a large body of free lances, and for eighteen months they spread desolation through the districts lying on the Nerbudda, but were at length

Ameer Khan.

obliged to separate when the field of plunder was exhausted. Ameer Khan proceeded eastward to the opulent town of Saugor, where he subjected the inhabitants to every species of outrage, and acquired immense booty. Nothing gives us a clearer view of the anarchy and wretchedness of Hindostan at this period than the ease with which Jeswunt Rao was able, in the space of two years, to collect under his standard, by the hope of plunder, a force of 70,000 Pindarees and Bheels, Afghans and Mahrattas. With this force Holkar entered Malwa, and the country was half ruined before Sindia could come to its rescue from Poona. To expel Holkar he despatched two bodies of his troops, one of which, though commanded by Europeans, was obliged to lay down its arms, and the other was attacked with such vigour that of its eleven European officers seven fell in action and three were wounded. The city of Oojein, Sindia's capital, was saved from indiscriminate plunder, by submitting to a contribution of fifteen lacs. At Poona, Bajee Rao, relieved from the presence of Sindia, subjected his feudatories to extortion and his people to oppression, which led to the appearance of numerous bodies of brigands, one of which, Wittojee, the brother of Jeswunt Rao, was constrained to join. He was captured and sentenced to be trampled to death by an infuriated elephant, while Bajee Rao sat in the balcony of the palace to enjoy the yells of the expiring youth. Jeswunt vowed sharp vengeance, and it was not long before he found an opportunity of executing it.

A.D. 1800

A.D. 1801

Sindia, having ordered Shirjee Rao, his father-in-law, and the greatest miscreant of Central India, to join his camp, proceeded in pursuit of Holkar, who was totally defeated on the 14th October. The wretch entered the capital, Indore, and gave it up to plunder. The noblest edifices in the city, which had been erected and adorned by Aylah bye, were reduced to ashes. Those who were possessed of property were tortured to reveal it, and the wells were choked up with the bodies of females who destroyed themselves to escape dishonour. Holkar was not long in recovering the blow. His daring spirit was exactly suited to the temper of the age, and his standard was speedily crowded with recruits, with whom he proceeded to the north, plundering every town and village in his progress, and to the horror of his lawless, but superstitious soldiery, not sparing even the shrines of the gods. He then laid waste the province of Candesh, and

1801

Sindia defeats Holkar.

moved down on Poona, and the Peshwa began to tremble for his safety. Lord Wellesley had not ceased to renew the offer of the subsidiary alliance when there appeared any prospect of success. The negotiation fluctuated with the Peshwa's hopes and fears, and when Sindia, who had earnestly dissuaded him from accepting it, sent ten battalions of infantry and a large body of cavalry to protect him from the assault of Holkar, it came to an abrupt termination.

Holkar continued to advance to Poona, and the dismayed Peshwa made him the most abject offers, but they were haughtily rejected. The combined army of Sindia and the Peshwa encamped in the vicinity of the capital, consisted of 84,000 horse and foot. Sindia's force comprised ten battalions under the command of Col. Dawes, while Holkar had fourteen battalions, disciplined and commanded by European officers. The battle of Poona, which was long and obstinately contested, ended in the complete victory of Holkar, who captured the whole of the baggage, stores and encampment of the allies. The Peshwa, who had kept out of the reach of fire, fled precipitately to the sea coast, where he obtained the accommodation of a British vessel from the governor of Bombay and embarked for Bassein, which he reached on the 6th December. Holkar entered the capital and placed the Peshwa's illegitimate brother, Amrut Rao, on the throne, after exacting the promise of an immediate payment of two crores, and territory yielding another crore, as well as the command of the army and the control of the state. After two months of singular moderation he gave up the capital to pillage. Bajee Rao, now became eager for the alliance as affording him the only chance of regaining his crown, and on the last day of December, he signed the memorable treaty of Bassein, by which he agreed to entertain a body of 6,000 English troops, and a suitable complement of artillery, and to assign districts yielding twenty-six lacs for their support, to entertain no Europeans in his service, and to refer all his claims upon the Nizam and the Gaikwar to the arbitration of the Governor-General. The treaty likewise guaranteed the southern jageerdars in the enjoyment of their ancient rights.

Battle of Poona. — A.D. 1802

The treaty of Bassein. — 1802

The treaty of Bassein, viewed in connection with its consequences, forms one of the most important events in the history of British India. Although the authority of the Peshwa had long ceased to

Remarks on the treaty.

possess its former importance in the Mahratta counsels, he was still regarded by the other chiefs as the centre of their national unity, and the recognised chief of the Mahratta commonwealth, and the extinction of his independence essentially weakened its power. It has been the subject of warm controversy, but the sound judgment of the Duke of Wellington, then General Wellesley, based upon his extensive Indian experience, may be considered conclusive. "The treaty of Bassein," he asserted, "and the measures adopted in consequence of it, afforded "the best prospect of preserving the peace of India, and "to have adopted any other measure would have rendered "war with Holkar nearly certain, and war with the whole "Mahratta nation more than probable." This opinion has been fully confirmed by posterity. War with the Mahratta powers was inevitable; the treaty may have hastened it, but it must not be forgotten that it likewise deprived them of all the resources of the Peshwa's Government.

A.D. 1803

Umbrage of Sindia and the Nagpore raja.

The establishment of the Company's paramount authority at the Mahratta capital gave great umbrage to Sindia and to the raja of Nagpore. The former found all his ambitious projects in the Deccan defeated, and exclaimed: "The treaty takes the "turban from my head." The Nagpore raja was at once deprived of the hopes he and his ancestors had cherished of some day obtaining the office of Peshwa. The two chiefs immediately entered into a confederacy to obstruct the objects of the treaty, and Bajee Rao himself had no sooner signed it, than he despatched an envoy to solicit their aid to frustrate it. Holkar, whose plans were thwarted by this masterly stroke of policy, agreed to join the coalition on condition that the domains of his family should be restored to him; but, although he was reinstated in them, he no sooner perceived Sindia involved in hostilities with the British Government, than he let loose his own famishing hordes on his possessions in Malwa.

Lord Wellesley's military movements.

Lord Wellesley, who had early information of this coalition, informed Sindia and the raja of Nagpore that he was desirous of maintaining friendly relations with them unimpaired, but would resist to the full extent of his power any attempt to interfere with the treaty. To be prepared for every contingency, he ordered the whole of the Hyderabad subsidiary force, and 6,000 of the Nizam's own infantry, and 9,000 horse, under Colonel Stephenson, up to the frontier. General

Wellesley likewise marched up 600 miles in the same direction with the Mysore contingent, 8,000 infantry, 1,700 cavalry, and 2,000 of the celebrated Mysore horse, under an able native commander. The southern jageerdars were induced by the influence which General Wellesley had obtained over them, to join him with 10,000 troops. Amrut Rao, whom Holkar had left in command at Poona, had declared his determination to reduce it to ashes when he could no longer hold it; but the city was saved by the energy of General Wellesley, who made a forced march of sixty miles in thirty-two hours to rescue it. Soon after

A.D. 1803

Bajee Rao quitted Bassein, and on the 13th May, the day which had been selected by his astrologers, entered Poona, accompanied by British bayonets, and ascended the throne under a British salute.

Development of Sindia's designs.

The designs of Sindia became daily more evident. He marched down with a large force from Oojein to form a junction with the raja of Nagpore, who moved up to meet him with a large force on the 17th April. Both princes informed the Resident that it was their intention to proceed to Poona "to adjust the "government of the Peshwa." He assured them that any such movement would be considered an act of hostility, and involve the most serious consequences. Various communications were intercepted in different directions, which placed their warlike designs beyond doubt; and, on the 23rd May, therefore, Colonel Close, the Resident at Sindia's court, was instructed to demand a categorical explanation of his intentions, when he replied that, with regard to the negotiations on foot, he could give no decisive answer till he had seen the raja of Nagpore, then encamped about forty miles distant, "when you shall be informed whether "there is to be war or peace." Lord Wellesley considered this announcement not merely an insult to the British Government, but an unequivocal menace of hostility on the part of both princes, who had planted their armies on the frontiers of the two allies, the Nizam and the Peshwa, whom the Government were bound to defend. The complication of affairs at this juncture was increased by the arrival of the French armament, already mentioned, at Pondicherry, which Sindia announced to all the Mahratta princes as the reinforcement of an ally. The confederates continued to prolong the discussions for two months, while they were employed in pressing Holkar to join them. During this period of suspense, the perfidious Peshwa continued to importune Sindia to avoid any concession, but advance at once to Poona "to settle affairs." He obstructed the progress of supplies, and lost no opportunity of embarrassing the Government.

Time was now invaluable, but no reply could be received to any reference to Calcutta under six weeks, and Lord Wellesley, therefore, ventured to take upon himself the responsibility, for which he was afterwards captiously censured, of vesting full powers, civil, military, and diplomatic, in reference to the conduct of Mahratta affairs in the Deccan, in General Wellesley, and at the same time furnished him with a clear exposition of his views of policy. The general received this commission on the 18th July, and lost no time in calling on the allied chiefs to demonstrate the sincerity of the pacific declarations they were making, by withdrawing their forces from a position, not necessary for the security of their own territories, but menacing equally to the Nizam, the Company, and the Peshwa. A week of frivolous and fruitless discussion then ensued, during which Sindia had the simplicity to say that they were not prepared to determine on any movement, as the negotiation with Holkar was not yet complete. Wearied with these studied delays, General Wellesley gave them twenty-four hours for their ultimatum, when they proposed that the British armies should retire to their cantonments at Bombay, Madras, and Seringapatam, while their forces fell back forty miles to Boorhanpore. To this General Wellesley replied: "I offered you peace on terms of equality, and "honourable to all parties: you have chosen war, and are "answerable for all consequences." On the 3rd August the British Resident withdrew from Sindia's camp, and the Mahratta war of 1803 commenced.

Delegation of powers to General Wellesley.

A.D. 1803

SECTION IV.

LORD WELLESLEY—WAR WITH SINDIA AND NAGPORE.

LORD WELLESLEY, finding a war with Sindia and the raja of Nagpore inevitable, determined to strike a decisive blow at their power, simultaneously, in every quarter of India. In the grand combinations of this campaign he was his own war minister, and never under

Preparations for war.

the Company's rule had the resources of Government been drawn forth upon a scale of such magnitude and applied with such promptitude and effect. In the Deccan the advanced force under General Wellesley of about 9,000 men, and of Colonel Stephenson, consisting of about 8,000, was appointed to operate against the main armies of the confederates. In the north 10,500 troops were assembled under General Lake, to attack Sindia's possessions in Hindostan, which were defended by his French battalions; and a force of 3,500 was allotted for the invasion of Bundlecund. On the western coast an army of 7,300 men was organised to dispossess Sindia of his possessions in Guzerat, while 5,200 men were to occupy the province of Cuttack, belonging to the raja of Nagpore, on the eastern coast. The whole force of about 43,500 men was animated by that traditionary spirit of enterprise and enthusiasm which had created the British empire in India, and which, on this occasion, was heightened by unbounded confidence in the statesman at the head of the Government. The armies of the confederates were computed at 100,000, of whom one half consisted of cavalry, with a superb train of artillery of many hundred pieces.

As soon as the Resident had quitted Sindia's camp, General Wellesley opened the campaign by the capture of

Capture of Ahmednugur.

A.D. 1803

the strong fortress of Ahmednugur, Sindia's great arsenal and depôt in the Deccan, and by taking possession of all his districts south of the Godavery. Meanwhile the confederates spent three weeks in marching and countermarching, apparently without any definite object. General Wellesley, misled by his guides, was unexpectedly brought, after a march of twenty-six miles, to a position from which he could behold Sindia's encampment, consisting of 50,000 men and 100 guns, stretched out before him, and he resolved to bring on an immediate action without waiting for the junction of

Battle of Assye.

Colonel Stephenson's force. The handful of British troops which had to encounter this formidable array at Assye, did not exceed 4,500. The Mahratta infantry was entrenched behind formidable batteries, which the General had particularly enjoined the officer commanding the advance not to assail in front, but he charged up to the muzzle of the guns; the carnage was appalling, but the indomitable courage and energy of the troops, more especially the 74th, bore down all opposition, and Sindia's splendid infantry, standing by the guns to the last, was at length overpowered and dispersed. The victory was the most complete which had ever crowned the Company's arms in India, but it was dearly purchased by the loss of one-third of its numbers. Sindia lost 12,000 men and all his guns, ammunition, and camp equipage. His army was a complete wreck, and he retreated with a small body of horse to the Taptee. Colonel Stephenson was sent in pursuit of him, and captured the flourishing town of Boorhanpore and the strong fortress of Aseergurh. Meanwhile all Sindia's districts in Guzerat were occupied, and nothing remained to him but his possessions in Hindostan.

A.D. 1803

Sindia's possessions in Hindostan.

This valuable territory had been enlarged and consolidated by the indefatigable exertions of the late Mahdajee Sindia, and chiefly through the army raised and disciplined by the Count de Boigne, on whose retirement to France the command devolved on General Perron. Dowlut Rao, since his accession to his uncle's throne in 1794, had continued to reside at Poona that he might maintain a paramount influence in the Mahratta councils, and the administration of these provinces in the north devolved on the general, who conducted it with great ability and moderation. He had succeeded in extending the control of Sindia over the Rajpoots, and was rapidly stretching it over the Sikhs up to the banks of the Sutlej. His advanced posts approached the Indus in one direction and Allahabad in the other, and the territory under his control yielded a revenue of two crores of rupees. His army consisted of 28,000 foot, not inferior in any respect to the Company's sepoy army, with 5,000 cavalry and 140 guns. The jeopardy to which the interests of the Company were continually exposed by the presence of this powerful force, entirely under French influence, along the whole of the north-west frontier was but too apparent, and Lord Wellesley considered it an object of the highest importance to extinguish it. Happily for the accomplishment of his wishes Sindia's Mahratta officers entertained such jealousy of the extraordinary power granted to a foreigner that he considered his position no longer tenable, and was contemplating his retirement when the war broke out.

Capture of Allygurh.

General Lake had been entrusted with the same plenary powers in Hindostan which had been confided to General Wellesley in the Deccan. He opened the campaign by advancing against General Perron's

encampment, but he withdrew his army 15,000 strong without firing a shot, upon which General Lake laid siege to Allygurh, the great arsenal and depôt of Sindia in Hindostan. It had been fortified with extraordinary skill by
A.D. French officers, but it was captured by a *coup de main*,
1803 through the irresistible gallantry of the 76th Highlanders. The number of guns captured amounted to 281. Shortly after, Perron having learnt that his enemies at Sindia's court had procured an order for his dismissal, obtained permission to pass through the British camp on his way to Lucknow, and was received with the distinction due to his rank and his talents. General Lake then advanced from Allygurh towards Delhi, and within sight of its minarets encountered the French force under General Bourquin, 19,000 in number. The battle was severely contested, but the British infantry, led again by the 76th Highlanders, and by the Commander-in-Chief in person, advanced calmly amidst a storm of grape and chain shot, and charged with the bayonet; the ranks of the enemy reeled, and then broke up in confusion.

Three days after the engagement, General Bourquin and three of his officers delivered up their swords to
The troops enter Delhi. General Lake. The city of Delhi was immediately evacuated by Sindia's troops, and the British standard was hoisted upon its battlements. The emperor, though a prisoner and sightless, was still considered the fountain of honour by Hindoos and Mahomedans, and a patent of nobility under the imperial seal was as highly prized in the remotest provinces of the Deccan as it had been in the days of Aurungzebe. "General
1803 "Lake," in the magniloquent proclamation of Lord
15th Wellesley, "was ushered into the royal presence, and
Sept. "found the unfortunate and venerable emperor, oppressed "by the accumulated calamities of old age and degraded "authority, extreme poverty and loss of sight, seated "under a small tattered canopy, the remnant of his royal "state, with every external appearance of the misery of "his condition." Lord Wellesley made a noble provision for his support, and then formed the judicious resolution of removing him and the royal family from the dangerous associations of Delhi, and proposed Monghyr for his future residence; but the emperor clung with such tenacity to the spot which had been for six centuries the capital of Mahomedan power that the Governor-General was reluctantly constrained to relinquish the design. For this

generous but imprudent act the Government was required to pay a fearful penalty half a century later. A.D. 1803

Leaving Colonel Ochterlony in command at Delhi, General Lake marched down to Agra, which capitulated after a protracted siege, when the treasure found in it, about twenty-eight lacs of rupees, was promptly and prudently distributed among the officers and men, "in anticipation of the approval of the home authorities." On the outbreak of the war Sindia had sent fifteen of his French battalions across the Nerbudda to protect his possessions in Hindostan. They were considered the flower of his army, and were usually called the "Deccan Invincibles," and nobly did they sustain the reputation they had gained. Including the fugitives from Delhi they formed a body of 13,000 horse and foot, with 72 pieces of cannon, under native commanders. General Lake came up with their encampment at Laswaree on the 1st November, and they fought as native soldiers had never fought before when they had no European officers to animate them. They were at length overpowered, but not till one-half of their number, as reported, lay on the field killed or wounded. The general himself conducted all the movements, and impetuously led the charge in person, more to the credit of his gallantry than of his military talent. Though a dashing soldier and adored by his men, he was a very indifferent general, but the flagrant errors of the day were covered—as they have since been on more than one occasion—by the chivalrous valour of the men at the sacrifice of their lives.

Battle of Laswaree.

Alarmed by the reverses he had sustained, Sindia made overtures which resulted in an armistice, and General Wellesley was now enabled to turn his whole attention to the raja of Nagpore, whom he had been closely following. On the 28th November he came up with his whole army at Argaum, and obtained a complete victory. The fortress of Gawilgurh surrendered in the middle of December, and General Wellesley prepared to march upon Nagpore, which must have at once capitulated. The province of Cuttack had also been occupied by a British army without a single casualty. The raja, reduced to extremities by these rapid reverses, and trembling for his capital and his throne, hastened to sue for peace, and the treaty of Deogaum was negotiated and concluded in two days by Mr. Mount-Stuart Elphinstone on the 18th December. Cuttack was

Battle of Argaum. Submission of Nagpore. 1803

A.D. 1803

annexed to the Company's territories, and the uninterrupted communication between Calcutta and Madras, which the Court of Directors had coveted for many years, and for which they were at one time prepared to pay a large sum, was established. The opulent province of Berar was made over to our ally the Nizam, though during the campaign his officers had behaved with more than ordinary perfidy. The raja likewise engaged to refer all his differences with the Nizam and the Peshwa to the arbitrament of the British Government. These cessions of territory, which comprised some of his most valuable districts, reduced him to the position of a secondary power in India.

Sindia could no longer hesitate to accept the severe terms dictated by the Governor-General. His French battalions, the bulwark of his power, were annihilated. His territories in the Deccan, in Guzerat and in Hindostan, the rich patrimony bequeathed to him by his uncle, had been wrested from him, and nothing lay before him but the extinction of his power. He yielded to necessity within a fortnight after the raja of Nagpore had agreed to the treaty of Deogaum, and signed the treaty of Sirjee Anjengaum. He was obliged to cede all his territories lying between the Ganges and the Dooab, and those north of the principalities of Jeypore and Joudpore, the fortress and territory of Ahmednugur in the Deccan, and Broach and its dependencies in Guzerat. He relinquished all claims on the Peshwa, the Nizam, and the Gaikwar, and acknowledged the independence of the rajas and feudatories in Hindostan with whom Lord Wellesley had recently concluded treaties. The war which produced these great results was scarcely of five months duration, and it was concluded before it was known in Leadenhall Street that it had commenced. Ahmednugur with its territory was made over to the Peshwa, and the wealthy districts in Hindostan were united with those which had been acquired from the Vizier of Oude, to form a separate province now known as the North West Presidency. Having thus reduced the Mahratta power in Hindostan, Lord Wellesley was anxious to prevent the renewal of it by establishing a barrier between the possessions of Sindia, north of the Nerbudda and those of the Company, and General Lake was instructed to conclude treaties of alliance with the Jaut prince of Bhurtpore, and the princes of Jeypore, Joudpore, Machery, Boondee and Gohud, who were thereby absolved

Submission of Sindia.

Treaties of alliance in the north.

from all allegiance to the Mahratta powers, and relieved A.D. 1803
from all dread of their encroachments.

The genius of Lord Wellesley had thus, in the course of five years, reorganized the political condition of India, and placed his masters on the pinnacle of power. The Company had now become the absolute sovereigns of the most valuable portion of the continent, the protector of the states not included within its possessions, and the umpire in the disputes of all. Its authority was established on a more solid basis than that of Akbar or Aurungzebe. The reputation and splendour of Lord Wellesley's administration had now reached its culmination, and the disasters which clouded the remainder of his Indian career were owing entirely to the blunders of the Commander-in-Chief, though his Government was necessarily saddled with the obloquy of them.

SECTION V.

LORD WELLESLEY—WAR WITH HOLKAR—COLONEL MONSON'S RETREAT.

DURING the war with Sindia and the raja of Nagpore, Hol- 1804
kar, instead of uniting his forces with theirs, sought more profitable employment for them in predatory excursions into Hindostan. On the conclusion of the peace he marched upon the wealthy town of Muhesur, where he was reported to have obtained a crore of rupees, by which he was enabled to take into his pay the soldiers whom Sindia and the raja of Nagpore had disbanded. His army was thus augmented to 60,000 horse, and 15,000 foot, a force far exceeding his requirements or his resources, and which could only be maintained by plunder. He was assured by the Governor-General and General Wellesley that, as long as he abstained from invading the dominions of the Company or of their allies, no attempt should be made to interfere with his movements. But repose was incompatible with his condition; his fortune was in his saddle, and his reckless disposition led him to throw himself on the British buckler. In March he demanded of General Wellesley the cession of certain districts in the Deccan which he affirmed had once belonged to his family, and he sent to General Lake to demand the *chout* as the inalienable right of the Mahrattas, and threatened "if his "demands were not complied with, that countries many

Holkar's proceedings.

A.D. 1804 "hundred miles in extent should be plundered, and calamities fall on many hundred thousand human beings by a "continued war, in which his armies would overwhelm "them like waves of the sea." These insolent menaces were followed up by an inroad into the territories of the British ally, the raja of Jeypore.

War with Holkar.

Lord Wellesley felt that there could be no prosperity or even peace in Central India while this large predatory horde continued to roam through it under this rampant chief, and that an army of observation would be found to be far more costly than an army of action; and on the 16th April directed Generals Wellesley and Lake to take the field against him. General Lake moved into the Jeypore territory, and chased him out of it. General Wellesley then in the Deccan urged him to continue the pursuit without pause, and assured him that if it was prosecuted with vigour, the war would be over in a fortnight. By an act of incomprehensive fatuity, General Lake rejected this advice, withdrew his army into cantonments, and sent Colonel Monson with a weak force to follow Holkar. Lord Wellesley strenuously urged him either to recall the brigade or to strengthen it, but General Lake did neither. Colonel Monson was as remarkable for his personal bravery as for his professional incompetence. With a detachment feeble in numbers, and not supported by a single European soldier, with only about 2,500 worthless irregular horse, he advanced into the heart of Holkar's territory to encounter a force ten times its number, and commanded by the most daring soldier of the day; and he neglected to make any provision for supplies, or for crossing the various streams which would become unfordable in two or three weeks.

Colonel Monson's retreat.

1804 On the 7th July Colonel Monson received the alarming intelligence that Holkar had called up his whole force and was marching upon him, and that Colonel Murray, whom General Wellesley had ordered up from Guzerat to support him, had fallen back. The provisions in his camp were only equal to two days' consumption, and he deemed it necessary to make an immediate retreat. Whenever the troops stood at bay, Holkar, notwithstanding the immense superiority of his force, sustained a repulse. At Rampoora Colonel Monson was reinforced by two battalions sent to his aid by General Lake, and was well supplied with provisions; but he unaccountably lingered there twenty-four days, during which time Holkar never once ventured to attack him. He then recommenced his retreat, which soon became a disgraceful rout, and the last sepoy straggled into Agra fifty days after he had begun to retire. Twenty-three years before Colonel Camac had, with equal indiscretion, marched into the heart of Sindia's territories, and found himself in the same predicament as Colonel Monson; yet, by the unfailing expedient of a bold and aggressive movement, Sindia was completely defeated, and lost guns, ammunition, encampment, and reputation. But for the imbecility of the commander, the same triumph would have crowned the valour of the troops under Colonel Monson, and Lord Wellesley would not have had to lament the loss of five battalions of infantry and six companies of artillery. This was the most signal disgrace the Company's arms had sustained since the destruction of Colonel Baillie's detachment by Hyder, and it was commemorated in ribald songs in the bazaars throughout the continent. The raja of Bhurtpore, who was the first to seek the alliance of the Government in the flood-tide of success in 1803, was the first to desert them when the tide appeared to be ebbing.

A.D. 1804

Flushed with success, Holkar advanced to Muttra with an army estimated at 90,000 men, and General Lake, with his usual energy, rapidly assembled his regiments to meet this unexpected inroad. Meanwhile, Holkar planned the daring project of seizing the city of Delhi and obtaining possession of the person of the emperor, and of the influence still attached to his name. Leaving his cavalry to engage the attention of General Lake, he suddenly appeared before the gates of the city on the 7th October. It was ten miles in circumference, 1804
defended only by dilapidated walls and ruined ramparts, and filled with a mixed and unruly population. The garrison was too weak to admit of reliefs, and provisions were served to the troops on the battlements; but Colonel Ochterlony, with a spirit worthy of Clive, defended it for nine days against the utmost efforts of the enemy, 20,000 strong, with 100 pieces of artillery. Holkar at length drew off his force in despair, and sending back his infantry and guns into the territory of his new ally, the raja of Bhurtpore, set out with his cavalry to lay waste the Company's districts in the Doab.

Holkar besieges Delhi.

General Lake left his infantry under General Fraser, to

watch Holkar's battalions, and started in pursuit of him with six regiments of cavalry, European and native, and his horse artillery, giving him no rest night or day. Holkar generally contrived to keep twenty or thirty miles ahead of him, ravaging the defenceless villages as he swept along; but, after a forced march of fifty miles in twenty-four hours, the general succeeded in overtaking him at dawn, at Futtygurh, on the 17th November. The enemy's horses were at picket, and the men asleep beside them in apparent security, when several rounds of grape announced the arrival of their pursuers. Holkar sprang on his horse, and galloped off with a few troopers, leaving the rest of the troops to shift for themselves, and they were dispersed and cut up in all directions. He hastened back to rejoin his infantry, but found on recrossing the Jumna, that they had suffered an irreparable defeat. General Frazer with a force of 6,000 men had attacked his army consisting of fourteen battalions of foot, a large body of horse and 160 guns, and obtained a decisive victory, capturing more than half his artillery; but the victory was dearly purchased by the loss of the general. During the engagement, a destructive fire was opened on the British force from the fortress of Deeg, belonging to the raja of Bhurtpore, which was immediately invested and captured.

Pursuit of Holkar.

A.D. 1804

Battle of Deeg.

The fortunes of Holkar were now at the lowest ebb. General Jones, who had succeeded the incompetent Colonel Murray, had captured all his forts in Malwa, and marched up, unmolested, to General Lake's encampment. The large host with which he had proudly appeared on the banks of the Jumna only four months before had disappeared, and the annihilation of his power appeared inevitable, when every advantage was thrown away by the fatal resolution of General Lake to invest Bhurtpore. The town was eight miles in circumference, surrounded by the invulnerable bulwark of a mud wall of great height and thickness, protected by numerous bastions and by a broad and deep ditch, filled with water, and defended by 8,000 of the raja's troops and the remnant of Holkar's infantry. General Lake turned a deaf ear to all advice, and without a sufficient siege train, or an engineer officer of any experience, without even making a reconnaissance, commenced the siege with breathless impetuosity. Four consecutive attacks were made upon it during fifteen weeks, which entailed the unprecedented

Siege of Bhurtpore.

loss of 3,200 in killed and wounded, of whom 103 were officers. The siege was abandoned on the 21st April; but the raja, who had severely felt the loss of all the revenues of his districts and the exactions of Holkar, sought an accommodation with the Government, and a treaty was soon after concluded on condition of his contributing twenty lacs of rupees in four instalments towards the expenses of the war. But this issue of the campaign did not cover the disgrace of our failure, the remembrance of which was perpetuated even in the remote districts of the Deccan by rude delineations of British soldiers hurled from the battlements of Bhurtpore.

A.D. 1805

Hostile attitude of Sindia.

This pacification was hastened by the hostile attitude of Sindia. By the treaty of Sirjee Anjengaum, he had agreed to relinquish all claim on the rajas with whom Lord Wellesley had concluded treaties. But, when the list was presented to him four months after, he was exasperated to find the name of the rana of Gohud included in it, and also the fort of Gwalior. He scouted the idea of considering the rana, whose territories he had absorbed twenty years before, as an independent prince, or of making over to him the fortress of Gwalior, which he valued not merely for its strength, but as a personal gift from the emperor. General Wellesley affirmed that Sindia had subscribed the treaty with the distinct understanding that the fort and territory should remain with him, and it was in ignorance of this agreement that Lord Wellesley had resolved to consider Gohud as an independent principality. General Wellesley said, "that he would sacrifice "it, and every other frontier town ten times over, to "preserve our credit for good faith." Major Malcolm, the envoy at Sindia's court, was equally urgent, but Lord Wellesley, who was entirely in the wrong, imperiously persisted in his resolution, and Sindia was obliged to submit, but the loss continued to rankle in his bosom.

Confederacy against Government.

The disastrous retreat of Colonel Monson and the failure of the siege of Bhurtpore, produced a profound sensation throughout Hindostan. The victors of Assye had been chased by Holkar up to the walls of Agra. The captors of Gwalior had been baffled before a mud fort in the plains, and an impression was created that the Company's good fortune was on the wane. A hostile confederacy was secretly formed, which included Sindia, Holkar, Ameer Khan, and the raja of Bhurtpore; and Sindia ventured to attack our allies

A.D. 1805 and to invade Saugor. At the instance of his minister, Sirjee Rao, the encampment of Mr. Jenkins, the Resident, was plundered, and he was placed under restraint. Sindia moreover assembled an army of 40,000 men, and moved on towards Bhurtpore, with the intention, he said, of negotiating a peace between the raja and the British Government. Lord Wellesley could not fail to feel acutely the insult which such a proposal implied, but he and his brother were anxious to avoid a rupture with Sindia at this time. The *morale* of the army was low, and the north-west frontier was defenceless. The Resident dissuaded Sindia from crossing the Chumbul towards Bhurtpore, assuring him that it would inevitably result in a war, and advised him to return to his own capital; but he said his funds were exhausted, and General Wellesley assured Lord Wellesley that he was really impoverished by his late losses, and under the advice of the General an advance of money was made to him from the treasury, on which he retraced his steps to Subulgurh.

Movements of the confederates.

He was joined soon after by Ameer Khan and Holkar, with about 3,000 of the cavalry which yet adhered to his standard. The confederates pressed Sindia for money, but his exchequer was exhausted, and he gave them permission to despoil his general, Ambajee Anglia, who had amassed two crores in his service, and Shirjee Rao, Sindia's father-in-law, extorted fifty lacs of rupees from him by torture. The atrocities of this miscreant constrained Sindia to discard him, and Ambajee having been appointed in his stead, broke up the alliance between his master and Holkar and Ameer Khan, and the path was thus opened for an accommodation with the British Government. Sindia had nothing to expect, but everything to lose, by a struggle with the Company, and he was sincerely desirous of the restoration of concord. Lord Wellesley was equally anxious for the re-establishment of a good understanding, that he might reduce the burdens of the state. He had determined to restore Gohud and Gwalior, as a matter of policy, and another month or six weeks would have brought about an amicable adjustment of all differences, and placed the tranquillity of India on a solid basis; but,

Supersedure of Lord Wellesley.

1805 on the 30th July he was superseded by the arrival of Lord Cornwallis, and his whole scheme of policy was at once subverted.

The administration of Lord Wellesley is the most

memorable in the annals of the Company. He found the empire beset with perils in every quarter; he bequeathed it to his successor in a state of complete security, with the prestige of our power higher than it had ever stood. He annihilated the French force at Hyderabad, demolished the kingdom of Mysore, and became master of the Deccan. He extinguished the more formidable battalions of French troops in the employ of Sindia, and turned his possessions in Hindostan into a British province. He paralysed beyond redemption the great Mahratta sovereigns; he doubled the territories and resources of the Company; he exhibited a special genius for creating and consolidating an empire, and he would rank as the greatest of the Governors-General if he had not been preceded by Warren Hastings and followed by Lord Dalhousie. He was resolved to quench those internecine contests among the princes of India which, for a century since the death of Aurungzebe, had turned its fairest provinces into a desert. He felt as his brother the Duke of Wellington, then General Wellesley, happily expressed it, "that no permanent system of policy could be adopted to "protect the weak against the strong, and to keep the "princes for any length of time in their relative positions, "and the whole body in peace, without the establishment "of one power which, by the superiority of its strength "and its military system and resources, should obtain a "preponderating influence for the protection of all." The Company was to be this preponderating power, but the Company was still a commercial body, with an instinctive dread of military operations, which interrupted its investments and disturbed its balance-sheet. The mercantile spirit was still in the ascendant in Leadenhall-street, whereas Lord Wellesley maintained that "as long as the "Company represented the sovereign executive authority "in this vast empire, its duties of sovereignty must be "paramount to mercantile interests." These antagonistic views created a strong feeling of antipathy towards him at the India House. Parliament, moreover, had thought fit to interdict all increase of territory and all alliances with native princes without the sanction of the Court of Directors, and they hoped under the shadow of this injunction to continue at peace with the native princes, and to pursue their mercantile enterprises without any impediment. But, in defiance of this rule, Lord Wellesley had been engaged in wars from Cape Comorin to the Sutlej, had broken the power

A.D. 1805

Remarks on his administration.

A.D. 1805

of prince after prince, and loaded the Company with the responsibility of governing one half and controlling the other half of India. The vastness of his schemes, and the audacity of his aspirations, confounded them; and even his friend Lord Castlereagh, the President of the Board of Control, regarded with a feeling of anxiety the vast extent of our dominion and our responsibilities. The announcement of the war with Holkar, however inevitable, filled up the measure of his delinquencies, and completed the dismay of the India authorities in Leadenhall-street and at the Board of Control; and it was resolved to supersede him, and "to bring back things to the state the legislature "had prescribed in 1792;" in other words, to put the political clock back a dozen years.

Attempt at impeachment.

On the return of Lord Wellesley to England, an attempt was made to subject him to an impeachment. A Mr. Paull, originally a tailor, had gone out to India as an adventurer, and having amassed a fortune in the hot-house of corruption at Lucknow, obtained a seat in Parliament, and brought articles of charge against Lord Wellesley of high crimes and misdemeanours which were dropped on the dissolution; and Paull having failed to obtain a seat at the election, put a period to his life. Lord Folkstone subsequently renewed the charge, but the resolution of censure which he proposed was negatived by 182 to 31. On the other hand, the vindictive Court of Proprietors passed a vote of condemnation by 928 to 195. But thirty years later, when truth had triumphed over passion and prejudice, the Court of Directors took occasion, on the publication of his despatches, to assure him by a unanimous resolution, "that "in their judgment he had been animated throughout his "administration by an ardent zeal to promote the well-"being of India, and to uphold the interest and "honour of the British empire; and that they "looked back to the eventful and brilliant period "of his administration with feelings common to their "countrymen." They voted him a grant of 20,000*l.* and ordered his statue to be placed in the India House as a recognition of his services.

Applause of the Court of Directors.

CHAPTER IX.

SECTION I.

LORD CORNWALLIS AND SIR G. BARLOW.

Lord Cornwallis's brief rule and death.

Lord Cornwallis was Mr. Pitt's invariable refuge in every Indian difficulty. When the Company's possessions were considered to be in danger from the proceedings of Warren Hastings, Lord Cornwallis was sent out to restore their security. When again, in 1797, Sir John Shore's weakness had brought on the mutiny of the officers which threatened the dissolution of Government, he was entreated to go out, if only for a year; and now he was importuned a third time in 1805 to undertake the office of Governor-General, and save the empire from the ruin with which it was supposed to be threatened through Lord Wellesley's ambition. His constitution was exhausted by thirty years of labour in America, in India and in Ireland, but he would not refuse what he considered the call of duty, and he landed at Calcutta on the 30th June, with the finger of death visibly upon him. (A.D. 1805) Within twenty-four hours Lord Wellesley had the mortification to learn that his whole system of policy was to be immediately demolished. Lord Cornwallis lost no time in announcing that it was his object to restore the native princes to a condition of "vigour, efficiency, and "independent interest," and to remove the impression of our design to establish British control over every Indian power. He was resolved, in fact, to steer the vessel of the state in 1805 by the ephemeris of 1793.

Lord Cornwallis's policy.

He immediately proceeded up the country by water, and on the 19th September sent a despatch to Lord Lake defining the policy he intended to pursue. He proposed to restore all Holkar's family domains when he manifested a reasonable disposition; to give up Gohud and Gwalior to Sindia, and even to waive the demand which had been made by Lord Wellesley of the release of the Resident, Mr. Jenkins, whom Sindia detained in honourable bondage, if it was found to be an obstacle to a reconciliation with that chief; to abrogate the treaty with Jeypore; to remove the emperor and his family to some town near Calcutta, and to restore Delhi to the Mahrattas; to dissolve all the alliances concluded with the princes north of the Chumbul, and to compensate them for the loss of our protection from the territories we had acquired beyond the Jumna, which was to be our future boundary. Before this letter could reach Lord Lake, Lord Cornwallis was in his grave. It was dictated to his secretary at a time when he was in such a state of mental and physical debility, that it may be questioned whether he fully comprehended the scope and consequences of this abrupt and fundamental change of policy. He was put on shore at Ghazeepore, where he expired on the 5th October. He had not the genius of Hastings or of Lord Wellesley, and his merits as a Governor-General have been over-rated, but none of the rulers of British India have ever more richly earned the esteem and confidence of Europeans and natives by his sterling integrity, his straightforward and manly character, and the spirit of justice and moderation which regulated all his actions.

His death.

A.D. 1805

Sir George Barlow, the senior member of Council, succeeded temporarily to the office of Governor-General. He had presided for many years over some of the most important offices in the state, in which he had acquired a rich fund of experience. He had been extolled for his official aptitude and ability by three successive Governors-General, and though the ministry had wisely resolved never again to place any local officer at the head of the Government, they had yielded to the recommendation of Lord Wellesley, and given him the reversion of the highest office. But Sir George was simply a first-rate civilian, eminently qualified for every subordinate department, but destitute of that patrician dignity and that elevation of mind which the management of the empire required. While he continued under the influence of Lord Wellesley's master spirit, he cordially adopted his large and comprehensive policy, and became so closely identified with it that he lost the prospect of succeeding him when that policy was discarded at the India House. This fact was communicated to him by Lord Cornwallis, and may not have been without its influence in converting him to the opposite line of policy, of which he now became

Sir G. Barlow and his policy.

the unflinching advocate. He hastened to inform Lord A.D. Lake that it was his intention to dissolve all our alliances 1805 with the native princes, to relinquish all right to interfere in their affairs, and to withdraw from all connection with any state beyond the Jumna. Lord Wellesley proposed to rest the security of our dominion on the establishment of general tranquillity under our supremacy. Sir George considered that our position would be equally secure if the native states were allowed to tear one another to pieces, and were thus deprived of all leisure to attack us. This despicable policy was aptly described by Mr. Metcalfe, subsequently Governor-General *ad interim*, as "disgrace without compensation, treaties without security, and peace without tranquillity."

Sindia was as anxious to avoid a second collision with the Government of Calcutta as the Governor-General himself, and an envoy was sent to the head-quarters of Lord Lake, then about to start in pursuit of Holkar. A treaty was concluded on the 25th December, 1805 by which Gohud and Gwalior were restored to him, and it was stipulated that the Chumbul should be the boundary of the two states, and that the British Government should enter into no treaties with the rajas of Oodypore, Joudpore, and other chiefs whom he claimed as his feudatories. Northern India swarmed with military adventurers, consisting of the fragments of the armies disbanded by Sindia and the raja of Nagpore, and of the irregulars whom our Government had dismissed; hence Holkar, notwithstanding his reverses, was able to collect a body of 12,000 horse and 3,000 foot, whom it was important to disperse. Lord Lake set off in pursuit of him at the head of his cavalry and light infantry, and a British army was, for the first time, conducted to the banks of the Sutlej by the general who had been the first to camp on the Jumna. On crossing the Sutlej Lord Lake was brought into communication with Runjeet Sing, the young chieftain of twenty-four, then employed in laying the foundation of a new kingdom in the Punjab; and on the banks of the Beyas (the ancient Hydaspes) concluded a treaty with him by which he engaged to afford no further assistance to Holkar, and to oblige him to evacuate the Punjab forthwith. Holkar, now a helpless fugitive, was pursued to the holy city of Umritsir, and sent an envoy humbly to sue for peace, which he was ready to accept on any terms.

Peace with Sindia.

Under the positive instructions of Sir George Barlow,

A.D. 1805

Disgraceful treaty with Holkar.

the draft of a treaty was presented to him which provided for his complete reinstatement in power, the restoration of all the territories which had belonged to his family, and the relinquishment of all interference with the chiefs whom he claimed as his dependents. He was required to relinquish all right to Rampoora, and all claim on Boondee, to entertain no Europeans in his service, to return to Hindostan by a prescribed route, and to abstain from injuring the territories of the Company or their allies. To Holkar, whose fortunes were now desperate, these proposals appeared like a godsend, but their incredible leniency convinced him that they could only be dictated by fear, and his envoy returned with a demand for eighteen additional districts in Hindostan, and liberty to levy contributions on Jeypore, both of which were peremptorily refused. Fresh difficulties were started by his envoys, till Lord Lake threatened to recommence the pursuit, when the ratified treaty was at once produced. But Sir George Barlow was displeased with the terms of the treaty both with Sindia and Holkar. He considered that to fix the Mahratta boundary on the banks of the Chumbul, might imply a pledge to protect the princes beyond it from their rapacity; and he therefore added declaratory articles withdrawing British protection from every state to the west of the Jumna. Rampoora was voluntarily surrendered to him, and he fired a royal salute on the occasion, declaring at the same time that "the English were great rascals, and never to be "trusted." The raja of Boondee had the strongest claims on the gratitude of the Company as a constant and faithful ally, and as having two years before afforded shelter and aid to Colonel Monson in his retreat, in spite of the menaces of Holkar. Lord Lake made a strenuous effort to save him, but Sir George was deaf to every remonstrance, and cancelled the article in the treaty which protected him from the rapacity and revenge of Holkar.

The raja of Jeypore.

The course pursued toward Jeypore was yet more disgraceful. The raja was the first to accede to Lord Wellesley's system of subsidiary alliances, but he wavered in his fidelity when Colonel Monson was flying before Holkar, and Lord Wellesley informed Lord Cornwallis that this defection had cancelled his claim to our alliance. In the following year Holkar entered his territories and claimed his assistance against the Company, but Lord Lake assured him that the boon of our protection would be restored to him if he resisted the advances of that chief, and in this hope he afforded cordial and efficient aid to our detachments proceeding in pursuit of him. Lord Cornwallis, who was the soul of honour, said that any promise Lord Lake had given to the raja should be held sacred. Sir George Barlow, however, refused to acknowledge any such obligation, and as Holkar entered the Jeypore territory, bent on plunder and revenge, informed him that the protection of Government was withdrawn for the breach of his engagement during Colonel Monson's retreat. Lord Lake, indignant at the contempt with which his expostulations were treated and the degradation of the national character, threw up all his political functions.

A.D. 1806

Holkar was bound by the treaty to return to Hindostan by a prescribed route, and to abstain from all aggression on the territories of the Company or their allies. But to save the field allowances Sir George Barlow directed Lord Lake to hasten out of the Punjab; and Holkar no sooner found him across the Sutlej than he let loose his predatory bands on the districts of the Punjab; nor was there any article of the treaty which he did not violate with audacity. He halted for a month in the Jeypore territory, and, seeing the British support withdrawn from the raja, extorted eighteen lacs of rupees from him, and then marched down to wreak his vengeance on Boondee. This disastrous termination of the Mahratta war sowed the seeds of a more momentous contest. The wisdom of Lord Wellesley's policy was amply vindicated by the twelve years of anarchy which followed the subversion of it; while the adoption of a neutral policy and of a system of isolation fostered the growth of a new predatory power, which it eventually required an army of 100,000 men to extinguish.

Aggression of Holkar.

It was not long before the evils of this policy of non-interference became visible. The rana of Oodypore was regarded as the "sun of Hindoo glory," and an alliance with his family as the summit of social distinction. The beautiful daughter of the reigning prince had been betrothed to the raja of Joudpore, and on his premature death was claimed by his successor; but her hand was given to the raja of Jeypore. The rivals appealed to arms, and 100,000 men, consisting not only of Rajpoots, but of Sindia's Mahrattas and Ameer Khan's Patans, were brought into the field. In February 1807 the raja of Joudpore sustained a crushing defeat, but soon

Desolation of Rajpootana.

A.D. after succeeded in detaching Ameer Khan from his ally,
1807 the raja of Jeypore, by the promise of half a crore of rupees, and the plains of Jeypore were laid waste by him. The rana of Oodypore, who had taken no part in the war of which his daughter was the innocent cause, was notwithstanding subjected to plunder by Sindia and Ameer Khan, and in his extremity supplicated the Governor-General for protection, offering to make over half his territories for the defence of the remainder. Rajpootana was bleeding at every pore, and its princes, the rajas of Joudpore and Jeypore, the rana of Oodypore as well as Zalim Sing, the renowned regent of Kotah, invoked the aid of British authority, and represented that there had always been in
1807 India some supreme power to which the weak looked for protection from the ambition and rapacity of the powerful. The Company, they said, had now succeeded to this position, and were bound to fulfil the responsibilities attached to it. The Mahrattas and the Patans, who were now spreading desolation through the country, could offer no resistance to the British arms, and the Governor-General had only to speak the word, and peace and tranquillity would be restored. But any such interference was contrary to the prevailing policy of the India House; the request of the rana of Oodypore was refused, and he was obliged to come to a compromise with Ameer Khan and assign him a fourth of his dominions to preserve the rest from rapine, and likewise to submit to the indignity of exchanging turbans with the Patan freebooter.

The great blot in Sir George Barlow's administration was the abandonment of Rajpootana, but he earned no little credit for the resolution with which he maintained the peace of the Deccan. Meer Alum, the able minister of the Nizam, had become obnoxious to his master by his steady support of the British alliance, and was obliged to take refuge at the Residency to escape assassination. The Nizam then proceeded to open negotiations with Sindia and Ameer Khan, and to assemble troops with the undisguised intention of dissolving all connection with the Company's Government. Sir George
1806 Barlow "felt that the dissolution of the alliance would "subvert the very foundation of British power and ascend-"ency in the political scale in India. The position we "abandoned at Hyderabad would be immediately occupied "by our enemies, and the result would be universal "turbulence and distrust." On this occasion therefore he

Hyderabad.

did not hesitate to discard the principle of neutrality, A.D. and to order the Nizam to restore Meer Alum to his post, 1806 and submit to a more direct interference of the Resident in the management of his affairs. Equally meritorious were his proceedings at Poona. The Court of Directors considered the treaty of Bassein the source of multiplied embarrassments, and were desirous of withdrawing from Mahratta politics, and allowing the Peshwa to resume his position as the head of the Mahratta commonwealth. Sir George resisted with energy every effort to modify the treaty, and had the courage to state to his masters that, while he desired to manifest every attention to their wishes, there was a higher obligation imposed on him, that of maintaining the supremacy of British rule, which would be compromised by any deviation from the policy established by Lord Wellesley at Poona.

The Peshwa.

The state of the finances demanded the early attention of Sir George. The pecuniary difficulties of the Company had always arisen from the wars in which they had been involved. There was no elasticity in a revenue derived almost exclusively from the land, and any extraordinary demand on the treasury could only be met by having recourse to loans. With the return of peace and the alleviation of the military pressure, the finances, with one exception, had recovered their spring. The extensive military operations of Lord Wellesley had augmented the public debt and brought on one of the intermittent fevers of alarm at the India House. It was overlooked that our wars in India had generally terminated in an accession of territory and revenue which speedily overbalanced the encumbrance they had entailed. Thus, in Lord Wellesley's administration the increase of the debt amounted to about eight crores and a half of rupees, and the permanent increase of revenue to about seven crores. By the cessation of war and the reduction of the regiments of irregulars, the deficit which had appalled Leadenhall-street was converted into a surplus, which, with little fluctuation, remained steady for twenty years.

The finances.

In the month of July the Government was astounded 1806 by the massacre of European officers and soldiers by the native sepoys in the fort of Vellore. It was situated eighty-eight miles west of Madras, and only forty from the frontier of Mysore, had been selected, contrary to the wise judgment of the Court of Directors, for the residence of Tippoo's family, and it was speedily filled

The Vellore mutiny.

A.D. 1806 with 1,800 of their adherents and 3,000 emigrants from Mysore. The European troops in the garrison consisted of about 370 men, and the sepoys numbered about 1,500, many of whom were Mahomedans who had been in the service of Tippoo. At 3 o'clock in the morning of the 10th July the sepoys suddenly assaulted the European barracks, and poured in volley after volley through the venetian blinds, till eighty of the soldiers had been killed and ninety-one wounded. They then proceeded to the residence of the officers, of whom thirteen fell victims to their treachery. During the massacre an active communication was kept up between the mutineers and the palace of the Mysore princes, many of whose followers were conspicuous in the scene. Provisions were also sent out to the sepoys, and the royal ensign of Mysore was hoisted amidst the shouts of the crowd. The remaining Europeans held their position till they were rescued by the gallantry of Colonel Gillespie, who was in garrison at Arcot, eight miles distant, and who, on hearing of the outbreak, started without a moment's delay with a portion of the 19th Dragoons and his galloper guns, and arrived in time to rescue the survivors.

Cause of the mutiny.

The searching investigation which was made revealed the cause of the mutiny. The new Commander-in-Chief, Sir John Cradock, soon after his arrival obtained permission of the governor, Lord William Bentinck, to codify the military regulations, but upon the express condition that no rules should be added without the permission of Government. Unknown to the governor, the adjutant-general took on himself to introduce several innovations which interfered with the religious prejudices of the sepoys. But that which gave them peculiar offence was the new form prescribed for the turban, which bore some resemblance to a European hat, an object of general antipathy to the natives. A report was industriously spread through their ranks by the Mahomedans, who led the hostile movement, that the new turban was the precursor of an attempt to force them to become Christians; and the panic-stricken and exasperated sepoys were thus stirred up to mutiny and massacre. The Court of Directors were overwhelmed by the news of this catastrophe, and in that wild and vindictive spirit which terror inspires, instantly recalled the governor and the Commander-in-Chief before a single line of explanation had been received from either. Lord William Bentinck remonstrated against the gross injustice of punishing him as an accomplice in measures with which he had no farther connection than to obviate their evil consequences. The Court, in their reply, bore testimony to his uprightness, disinterestedness, zeal and respect for the system of the Company, but also remarked that, "as the misfortune which happened under "his administration placed his fate under the government "of public events and opinions which the Court could not "control, so it was not in their power to alter the effect of "them." A.D. 1806

Of the panic created by the mutiny at the Council board in Calcutta, the unoffending missionaries were made the victims. In 1793, Mr. Carey had proceeded to Bengal to establish a Christian Mission, and laboured with much zeal but little success for seven years in the Malda district. In 1799, Mr. Marshman and Mr. Ward proceeded to join him, and, being without a licence, were ordered to quit the country the day after their arrival, but obtained an asylum at the Danish settlement of Serampore and were taken under the protection of the Danish crown. There they were joined by Mr. Carey, and established a fraternity which, under the designation of the "Serampore Missionaries," has attained historical distinction as that of the pioneers of Christian civilisation in Hindostan. They opened the first schools for the gratuitous instruction of native children; they set up printing-presses and prepared founts of type in the various Indian characters; they compiled grammars of the Bengalee, Sanscrit and other languages, into which they translated the Sacred Scriptures. They gave their chief attention to the cultivation and improvement of the Bengalee language, and published the first prose works which had appeared in it, and laid the foundation of that vernacular literature which has since obtained a large development. They, and the converts who had joined them, were tacitly permitted to itinerate in the districts of Bengal, and met with considerable success in the propagation of Christianity. But missionary efforts had always been viewed with mistrust by the Court of Directors and by their servants in India, on the ground that they might disturb the prejudices of the natives and create disaffection. The mutiny at Vellore was hastily ascribed to an interference with the religious prejudices of the Madras sepoys, and Sir George Barlow, under the influence of alarm, considered it necessary peremptorily to interdict the

The propagation of Christianity.

A.D. 1800 to 1806

A.D. 1806 labours of the Serampore Missionaries. The Vellore panic gradually died out, and the restrictions imposed on them were allowed to fall into abeyance.

Supersession of Sir George Barlow.

The Court of Directors had always been anxious to have the highest office in India left open to their own servants, and the great zeal which Sir George Barlow had manifested in carrying out their non-intervention policy recommended him to them as the permanent successor of Lord Cornwallis. The death of Mr. Pitt and the dissolution of his ministry introduced the Whigs to Downing-street, and within twenty-four hours of their accession to power they were called upon to make provision for the Governor-Generalship. The President of the Board of Control, new to office, agreed as a temporary measure to the nomination of the Court, and Sir George Barlow's commission was made out and signed; but ten days after the ministry announced that they had selected Lord Lauderdale for the office. The Court of Directors strenuously resisted the appointment, not only as an abrupt and contemptuous rejection of their nominee, but likewise on personal grounds. His ostentatious admiration of the French revolution, which led him to drop his aristocratic title, might have been forgiven; but he had rendered himself obnoxious to them by his advocacy of Fox's India Bill, and, more recently, by his support of Lord Wellesley's free-trade policy. The Directors refused to sanction the appointment, and the ministry retaliated by cancelling the nomination of Sir George Barlow. The controversy between them was carried on for many weeks with great acrimony, but was at length terminated by the nomination of Lord Minto, the President of the Board of Control.

SECTION II.

LORD MINTO'S ADMINISTRATION—FOREIGN EMBASSIES.

A.D. 1807 Lord Minto had been engaged for many years in the administration of public affairs. As Sir Gilbert Elliot he was one of the managers nominated by the House of Commons to conduct the impeachment of Warren Hastings, and the prosecution of Sir Elijah Impey was committed to his especial charge. He

Lord Minto governor-general.

A.D. 1807

was subsequently minister plenipotentiary at Vienna, and had been for twelve months President of the Board of Control, where he obtained an insight into the machinery and character of the Indian Government. He was an accomplished scholar, a statesman of clear perceptions and sound judgment; mild and moderate in his views, yet without any deficiency of firmness, and distinguished above his predecessors for his singular urbanity. He was accepted by the Directors with the understanding that he should eschew the policy of Lord Wellesley, and tread in the footsteps of Lord Cornwallis and Sir George Barlow. His first act in India was an act of clemency. On his arrival at Madras he found 600 of the Vellore mutineers awaiting their sentence. The Supreme Government had sentenced them to transportation beyond sea, a punishment equivalent to death, but Lord Minto adopted the more lenient course of expelling them from the service, and declaring them incapable of re-enlistment.

Anarchy in Bundlecund.

On reaching Calcutta, his attention was immediately called to the state of anarchy into which the feeble policy of his predecessor had plunged the province of Bundlecund. The country was overrun by military adventurers who lived only by plunder, and 150 castles were held by as many chieftains who were perpetually at feud with each other. The inhabitants, a bold and independent race, were, moreover, disgusted with the stringency of the judicial and revenue systems we had introduced, and deserted their villages, and too often joined the banditti with which the country swarmed. The two strongest forts in the province, Callinger and Ajygurh, were held by chiefs who bid defiance to the British Government. Lord Lake considered the possession of these fortresses essential to the tranquillity of the country, and urged Sir George Barlow to reduce them, but he considered that "a certain extent of dominion, power and "revenue would be cheaply sacrificed for security and "tranquillity in a more contracted circle." The sacrifice was made, but the security was farther off than ever. The two chiefs who had seized the forts, together with some of the most notorious leaders of banditti, received a legal title to the lands they had usurped, with permission to settle their quarrels among themselves by the sword.

Within five weeks after Lord Minto had assumed the Government he recorded his opinion that "it was essential "not only to the preservation of political influence over

A.D. 1807 "the chiefs of Bundlecund, but to the dignity and reputation of the British Government, to interfere "for the suppression of intestine disorder."

Vigorous policy of Lord Minto.

The simple announcement that the British Government was determined to enforce its full authority through the province was found sufficient to induce the numerous chiefs to make their submission, and to engage to refer every dispute to its decision. The renowned fortress of Callinger, which had baffled all the efforts of Mahmood of Ghuzni eight centuries before, and which the Peshwa's general had recently besieged two years without success, was surrendered after an arduous struggle. The fortress of Ajygurh was likewise mastered, and peace and prosperity were restored to Bundlecund.

Career of Runjeet Sing.

The difficulty of maintaining the principle of non-interference was again demonstrated before Lord Minto had been a year in India, in reference to the proceedings of Runjeet Sing, whose career now claims attention. On the retirement of the Abdalee after the battle of Paniput, the Punjab became the scene of confusion, and the semi-military, semi-religious community of the Sikhs was enabled to enlarge and consolidate its power. It was divided into fraternities or *misils*, the chief of each of which was the leader in the field and the umpire in time of peace. Churrut Sing, the head of one of them, commenced a series of encroachments on his neighbours, and his son Maha Sing pursued the
1792 same course of ambition. He died in 1792, leaving an only son, Runjeet Sing, who at the early age of seventeen commenced that career of conquest which resulted eventually in the establishment of a power as great as that of Sevajee or Hyder Ali.

His encroachments in Sirhind.

Runjeet obtained possession of the city of Lahore, the ancient seat of authority in the Punjab, and succeeded in absorbing the various Sikh *misils*. By the year
1806 1806 his dominions were extended to the banks of the Sutlej, and he cast a wishful eye on the province of Sirhind, lying beyond that river, and occupied by about twenty independent Sikh chieftains. They had been obliged to bend to the authority of Sindia when General Perron established his power over the province, and on the extinction of Mahratta rule in that region transferred their allegiance to the British Government, and considered themselves subject to the sovereignty of the Company, and entitled to its protection. Runject

Sing proceeded with his usual caution, and by inducing one or two of the chiefs to invite his intervention for the settlement of their differences, obtained a pretext for entering Sirhind with an army. On his return from one of these expeditions in 1807, he levied contributions indiscriminately in every direction, seized upon forts and lands and carried off all the cannon which he could lay his hands upon. A.D. 1807

These repeated inroads filled the Sikh chieftains with alarm, and in March, 1808, a deputation proceeded to Delhi to implore the protection of the British Government, whose vassals the envoys stated they had always considered themselves since the downfall of Sindia's power. Runjeet was anxious to discover the views of the Governor-General in reference to this appeal, and addressed a letter to him expressing his wish to cultivate friendly relations with the Company, and adding, "the country on this side the Jumna—except the "stations occupied by you—is mine; let it remain so." This bold demand of the province of Sirhind brought up the important question whether an energetic and ambitious chieftain, who had in ten years erected a large kingdom upon the ruin of a dozen princes, should be allowed to plant his army, composed of the finest soldiers in India, within a few miles of our frontier, and Lord Minto boldly assumed the responsibility of taking the Sikh states of Sirhind under British protection, and shutting up Runjeet Sing in the Punjab. 1808

Appeal of the Sikh chiefs to Government.

The treaty of Tilsit, concluded in 1807 between the emperor of Russia and Napoleon, was supposed to include certain secret articles intended to afford facilities for the invasion of India by the French. It was determined, therefore, by the ministry to anticipate the designs of the French emperor, and to block up his path by forming defensive alliances with the rulers of the intermediate kingdoms of Persia, Afghanistan, and the Punjab. The most difficult of these negotiations, that with Runjeet Sing, was entrusted by Lord Minto to Mr. Metcalfe, a young civilian of high promise, who had been trained up in the school, and, indeed, under the eye of Lord Wellesley. He was sent to Lahore to accomplish two objects which appeared mutually irreconcilable—to frustrate Runjeet Sing's passionate desire of annexing the province of Sirhind, and to obtain his co-operation to prevent the entrance of a French army into our territories. Mr.

Mission to Lahore.

A.D. 1808 Metcalfe was treated with feelings of suspicion and hostility, and when he was at length permitted to propound the object of his mission was given to understand that, although Runjeet Sing did not object to the proposed treaty, in which, however, he had less interest than the Company, it must recognise his sovereignty over all the Sikh states beyond the Sutlej. Mr. Metcalfe replied that he had no instructions to make this concession; but while the negotiation was in progress, Runjeet Sing broke up his camp at Kussoor, crossed the Sutlej a third time, and for three months swept through the province, plundering the various chiefs, and compelling them to acknowledge his authority.

Runjeet ordered to retire.

Lord Minto resolved to lose no time in arresting his progress, and, if necessary, to have recourse to arms. Napoleon, moreover, had begun to be entangled in the affairs of Spain, and all idea of invading India, even if it had ever been seriously entertained, was abandoned. Having, therefore, no longer anything to ask of Runjeet Sing, Lord Minto was enabled to assume a bolder tone, and to resolve on making a military demonstration. The Commander-in-Chief was directed to hold a force in readiness to advance to the banks of the Sutlej, and a letter was addressed to the Sikh ruler informing him that by the issue of the war with the Mahrattas the Company had succeeded to the power and the rights they had exercised in the north of Hindostan. The Sikh states in Sirhind were now under British protection, and the Maharaja must withdraw from the districts of which he had taken possession in his late raid, and confine his future operations to the right bank of the Sutlej. Runjeet Sing, on his return from the expedition across the river, hastened to Umritsur to exchange the toils of the field for the enjoyments of the harem. Like Hyder Ali, he was the slave of sensual indulgence when not absorbed in the excitement of war. On the evening of his arrival Mr. Metcalfe waited on him to present the Governor-General's letter, but he exclaimed that the evening was to be devoted to mirth and pleasure, and called for the dancing-girls, and then for the strong potations to which he was accustomed, and before midnight was reduced to a state of unconsciousness.

1808 The letter delivered by Mr. Metcalfe remained for several weeks unnoticed, and on the 22nd December he demanded an audience of Runjeet Sing, and announced that a British army was about to take the field, and would sweep his garrisons from Sirhind. He bore the communication for some time with composure, but unable at length to control his feelings, rushed out of the room, vaulted into the saddle, and galloped about the courtyard with frantic vehemence, while his ministers continued the discussion with Mr. Metcalfe. Two months were again wasted in studied delays and constant postponement, but Mr. Metcalfe continued with unflinching firmness to insist on the complete evacuation of Sirhind. Runjeet Sing was constrained to submit, and on the 25th April affixed his seal to a treaty which provided that the British Government should not interfere with his territory or subjects, and that he should abstain from any connection with the states under British protection. The treaty consisted of fifteen lines, and is one of the shortest on record. In the range of our Indian history there are few incidents of more romantic interest than the arrest of this haughty prince in the full career of success by a youth of twenty-four. On the retirement of the British army a garrison was left at Loodiana, which became our frontier station in the north-west, and the British ensign which Lord Wellesley had planted on the Jumna was six years after erected on the Sutlej by Lord Minto.

Runjeet Sing's submission.

A.D. 1809

1808

The embassy to Cabul was fitted out on a scale of magnificence intended to impress the Afghan court with an idea of the power and grandeur of the present rulers of India, and was entrusted to Mr. Mount Stuart Elphinstone, one of Lord Wellesley's school of statesmen. The sovereign of Afghanistan, Shah Soojah, the brother of Zeman Shah who invaded India in the days of Lord Wellesley, gave the mission a cordial reception, but his cabinet did not fail to remark that its object appeared to be more in the interests of the Company than of Afghanistan. They said they had nothing to apprehend from the French, and were desirous of ascertaining what offers they were prepared to make before a definite reply was given. While the negotiation was in progress, the expedition which Shah Soojah had imprudently sent to subjugate Cashmere was completely defeated. His rival brother had obtained possession of Cabul and Candahar, and was advancing on Peshawur. Shah Soojah, whose army was annihilated and whose treasury was empty, earnestly solicited pecuniary aid from the Government of India, and Mr. Elphinstone advised a grant of ten lacs of rupees, which would have enabled him to recruit his force and regain his

Embassy to Cabul.

power; and it might possibly have saved the Government the many crores of rupees spent thirty years after to reseat him on the throne. But the dread of a French invasion had died out, and it was no longer considered necessary to conciliate the ruler who held the gate of India, as Cabul was then deemed. The request was refused; Shah Soojah
A.D. was defeated by his brother and fled to India and became
1810 a pensioner on the Company's bounty.

The third mission to counteract the designs of the French was sent to Persia. The king had wantonly involved himself in a war with Russia and lost some of his most valuable provinces. He applied for aid to the emperor Napoleon, who sent General Gardanne as his representative to Teheran, with a large military staff and a body of engineers to make surveys, and military officers to discipline the Persian troops. A treaty was concluded which provided that a French army marching through Persia should be furnished with supplies and joined by a Persian force; that the island of Karrack, in the Persian gulf, thirty-three miles from Bushire, should be ceded to France, and that all Englishmen should be excluded from the country, if the emperor desired it. The British ministry, who considered the French embassy the precursor of a French army, were determined to counteract these hostile movements by sending an ambassador to the Court, and Lord Minto and General Wellesley united in recommending that Colonel Malcolm, who was eminently qualified for the duty by his skill in oriental diplomacy and languages, and by the popularity he had acquired in his first embassy, should be again sent from Calcutta; but the ministry considered that a representative of the Crown would be likely to carry more weight than an envoy from the Company, and they selected Sir Harford Jones, who had been consul at Bushire, for the office, and
1808 he landed at Bombay in April. But Lord Minto, on his arrival in Calcutta, was resolved to despatch Colonel Malcolm as the representative of the Government of India, and Sir Harford Jones was desired to tarry at Bombay till the result of his mission was known. On reaching Persia Colonel Malcolm, overlooking the paramount influence the French minister had acquired at the Court, assumed a dictatorial tone, and was forbidden to advance farther than Sheraz, where he was desired to place himself in communication with the king's son. Colonel Malcolm took umbrage at this proceeding, abandoned the mission, and,

Affairs of Persia.

English embassy to Teheran.

returning to the coast, embarked with his suite for Calcutta. Sir Harford Jones was then directed by Lord Minto to proceed with his mission.

Ten days after this order had been despatched, Colonel Malcolm arrived in Calcutta, breathing vengeance against the Persian court, and persuaded Lord Minto that the only effectual mode of counteracting the influence of the French was to make a military demonstration, and arrangements were made forthwith to despatch an armament to occupy the island of Karrack. Repeated and peremptory orders were likewise sent to Sir Harford Jones to quit Persia, under the threat of disavowing his mission and dishonouring his bills; but before they could reach him he had accomplished his object and concluded a treaty with the king. The French embassy was dismissed, and the Persian envoy at Paris recalled. Lord Minto felt that Sir Harford had been fully accredited by the Crown, and that the national faith was pledged to his engagements, and he accordingly ratified the treaty. He felt, however, that the rank and estimation of the Government of India had been compromised in the eyes of Asia by the mission from the Crown, and he considered it among the first of his duties "to transmit to "his successor unimpaired the powers, prerogatives and "dignities of the Indian empire in its relations to surrounding nations as entire and unsullied as they were "committed to his hands."

Success of Sir Harford Jones.

A.D. 1808

Another embassy was imprudently fitted out in the most costly style, to eclipse the mission of the Crown, and entrusted to Colonel Malcolm, in order that "he "might lift the Company's Government to its "own height and to the station which belonged "to it." He was welcomed by the king and courtiers with great cordiality, but in the royal presence stood the ambassador of the Crown, "whose face the "Indian Government had spared no pains to blacken in "the eyes of the Persian court." There was every prospect of an unseemly and dangerous collision. The Persian courtiers, finding two rival envoys contending for their favours, were preparing to play off the one against the other, in the hope of a golden shower of presents. But the good sense of Sir Harford and of the colonel smoothed down asperities and defeated the intrigues and cupidity of the court, and the English ministry soon after recalled both envoys, and appointed Sir Gore Ouseley minister from

Colonel Malcolm's second embassy.

1809

the King of England to the Shah of Persia. The cost of Colonel Malcolm's mission was twenty-two lacs, and that of Sir Harford Jones, which was also saddled on the Company, did not fall short of sixteen lacs.

SECTION III.

LORD MINTO'S ADMINISTRATION—AMEER KHAN—MUTINY OF THE MADRAS OFFICERS.

A.D. 1809

WITHIN four months of the signature of the treaty with Runjeet Sing another occasion arose to test the possibility of maintaining the policy of neutrality. The free-booter Ameer Khan, having within ten years created a principality which yielded a revenue of fifteen lacs of rupees a year, was recognised as the head of the Patans in Central India, and aspired to the rank of a prince. His army, however, was too large for his resources, and, after having drained Rajpootana, he was obliged to seek for plunder in a more distant sphere, and selected Nagpore for his next operations. Under pretence of asserting certain fictitious claims of Holkar on the raja, he poured down across the Nerbudda with 40,000 horse and 24,000 Pindarees. The raja was simply an ally of the Company, and had no claim to their protection; but Lord Minto did not hesitate to affirm that "an interfering "and ambitious Mussulman chief at the head of a numerous "army should not be allowed to establish his authority on "the ruins of the raja's dominions over territories con-"tiguous to those of the Nizam—likewise a Mahomedan—"with whom projects might be formed inimical to our "interests."

Ameer Khan and Nagpore.

The raja had not solicited our assistance, but two armies were ordered into the field to protect his territories. The Nagpore general, however, twice succeeded in repulsing Ameer Khan, but he returned a third time and blockaded the raja's army in Chauragurh, while his Pindarees desolated the country. The British divisions were now closing upon him, and Colonel Close took possession of his capital and his territories, and the extinction of his power appeared inevitable, when the troops were unexpectedly recalled, from the apprehension felt by Lord Minto that the further prosecution of hostilities might lead to complications displeasing

Ameer Khan repulsed but not crushed.

to the Court of Directors. He was allowed to recruit his strength, and Central India was left for seven years more at his mercy. But the tide appeared to be turning at the India House against this neutral policy, and the Directors not only questioned the wisdom of the moderation Lord Minto had exercised towards him, but went so far as to advise the conclusion of a subsidiary alliance with the raja of Nagpore.

A.D. 1809

Sir George Barlow was appointed to succeed Lord William Bentinck at Madras. During the twenty months he had filled the office of Governor-General he had alienated society by his cold and repulsive manners, and the absence of all genial feeling in the intercourse of life. He was never able to obtain that personal influence which is essential to the successful administration of public affairs, more particularly in India. The submission he exacted to his will, which in Lord Wellesley was regarded as the natural absolutism of a great mind, was in him resented as the vulgar despotism of power. At Madras he became unpopular by his arbitrary and unjust proceedings, as well as by the lofty assumption of official dignity, and by isolating himself in a small coterie of officials and confidants. But it was the mutiny of the army which fixed a lasting stain on his administration.

Sir George Barlow at Madras.

This was the third time in the course of half a century that the Company's Government had been shaken to its foundation by the insubordination of their European officers. The invidious distinction between the pay of officers in Bengal and Madras, and the monopoly of all posts of command by the officers of the royal army, had created a feeling of discontent among the officers of the Madras army, which was unhappily fomented by the bearing of the Commander-in-Chief, Major-General Macdowall. The Court of Directors had refused him the seat in Council, which, with its liberal allowances, had always been attached to his office, and he did not care to conceal the exasperation of his feelings from the officers under him.

Mutiny of European officers.

Since the conclusion of the war in 1805, the Court of Directors had been importunate for retrenchments, and had threatened "to take the pruning knife into "their own hands" if they found any hesitation on the part of the Madras Government. Among the plans of economy which had been contemplated by Lord William Bentinck and Sir John Cradock was the

Abolition of the tent contract.

A.D. 1809 abolition of the tent contract, which had given the officers commanding regiments a fixed monthly allowance to provide the men with tent equipage, whether in the field or in cantonments. The Quartermaster-General was ordered by the governor in Council to report on the question, and he stated that the nature of the contract was found by experience to place the interests of the commanding officers in opposition to their duty. They took fire at this remark, and called on the Commander-in-Chief to bring him to a court-martial for having aspersed their characters as officers and gentlemen. The Quartermaster-General was placed under arrest, and appealed to the governor, and the Commander-in-Chief was directed to release him. But, while yielding to this authority, he issued a general order of extraordinary virulence, protesting against the interference of Government and denouncing the conduct of the Quartermaster in having resorted to the civil power in defiance of the officer at the head of the army. Sir George Barlow, instead of treating the order with contempt as an ebullition of passion on the part of the general, who was on the eve of quitting the service, issued a counter order equally intemperate, charging him with inflammatory language. Major Bowles, the Deputy Adjutant-General, who had signed the order officially, was suspended; his cause was immediately taken up as that of a martyr; addresses commending his conduct poured in upon him, and subscriptions were raised to compensate the loss of his allowances.

General mutiny.

Three months passed after the departure of the Commander-in-Chief, who was lost at sea, and the ferment had begun to subside, when Sir George Barlow blew the dying embers into a flame. In the height of the excitement a memorial of grievances had been drawn up to the Governor-General, though not transmitted; but on the 1st May Sir George Barlow issued an order suspending four officers of rank and distinguished reputation, and 1809 removing eight others from their commands, on the ground of their having signed the memorial, which had been surreptitiously communicated to him. The whole army was immediately in a blaze. A hundred and fifty-eight officers of the Jaulna and Hyderabad divisions signed a flagitious address to Government, demanding the restoration of the officers, in order "to prevent the horrors of civil war "and the ultimate loss of a large portion of the Company's "possessions in India." The Company's European regiment at Masulipatam placed the commanding officer in arrest, and concerted a plan for joining the Jaulnah and Hyderabad divisions, and marching to Madras and seizing the Government. A.D. 1809

Sir George Barlow had thus by his intemperance and indiscretion goaded the army into revolt, and brought on a portentous crisis; but in dealing with the mutiny he exhibited such undaunted resolution as almost to make amends for having caused it. Colonel Malcolm and other officers of high standing and great experience, advised him to bend to necessity and recall the obnoxious order of the 1st May; but he resolved to vindicate the public authority at all hazards. He called upon all the officers in the army to sign a pledge to obey the orders of Government on pain of removal from their regiments. The sepoys and their native officers generally remained faithful to their salt, and there was no collision except at Seringapatam, where the native regiments under disaffected officers refused to submit, and were fired upon by the royal troops, and a hundred and fifty killed and wounded. The vigorous proceedings of Sir George confounded the officers, and induced them to pause on the brink of a rebellion against their king and their country. Lord Minto, moreover, had announced his intention to proceed at once to Madras, and the general confidence reposed in his justice and moderation promoted the return of the officers to a sense of duty.

Firmness of Sir George Barlow.

1810

The Hyderabad brigade, which had been the first to mutiny, was the foremost to repent. Its example was followed by the other brigades and regiments; the seditious garrison of Seringapatam surrendered that fortress, and a profound calm succeeded the storm which had threatened to overturn the Government. On his arrival at Madras Lord Minto issued a general order reprobating the conduct of the officers, but likewise expressing his anxiety for the welfare and the reputation of the army in kind and conciliatory language. He granted a general amnesty to all but twenty-one officers, who were either cashiered or dismissed; but they were all eventually restored to the service, and in the great Mahratta and Pindaree war, seven years later, had an opportunity of effacing the stain on their character by their gallantry and devotion. The mutiny was the subject of long and acrimonious debates at the India House, which terminated in Sir George Barlow's recall.

The mutiny extinguished.

It was in connection with his administration that Mr. Edmonstone, who had served under two civilian and three noble Governors-General, and who, after filling the highest subordinate office in India, became the Nestor of Leadenhall-street, said, that "he "was averse to selecting Governors from among "those who had belonged to the service, and that a person "of eminence and distinction proceeding from England to "fill that office, if duly qualified by talent and character, "carried with him a greater degree of influence, and "inspired more respect than an individual who had been "known in a subordinate capacity."

Mr. Edmonstone on the Governor-Generalship.

A.D. 1809

The suppression of piracy in the eastern hemisphere is the especial vocation of the English nation; and the attention of Lord Minto was imperatively called, at this time, to this duty. The Arabs, who were the bravest soldiers and the most hardy seamen in the east, were also the most notorious pirates. The chief tribe on the sea coast, the Joasmis, had recently embraced Wahabee tenets, and added the fierceness of fanaticism to their national valour; and the only alternative they offered to their captives was the profession of Mahomedanism or death. Their single-masted vessels, manned with about 150 men, sailed in squadrons, and it was rarely that any native craft was able to escape their pursuit. Hitherto they had prudently abstained from molesting English vessels, but they became emboldened by the inactivity of the Company's cruisers, which were forbidden to interfere with them, and they had recently captured a large merchantman, and cut the throats of all the Europeans on board and thrown them into the sea with the pious ejaculation, "Alla Akbar! great is God!" Lord Minto was determined to root out these buccaneers, and sent a powerful armament against their chief stronghold, Ras-al-Kaima. It was defended with Arab obstinacy and carried by British gallantry. The port, with all the valuable merchandise in it—the accumulation of numerous piratical expeditions—together with a large fleet of pirate vessels, was delivered to the flames, and piracy was for a time suppressed in these waters.

Suppression of piracy.

The possession of the Mauritius and of Bourbon by the French in the bay of Bengal exposed British commerce in the eastern seas to the constant depredation of the privateers fitted out in them. The losses sustained by the merchants of Calcutta from the

Depredations from the Mauritius.

commencement of the war with France in 1793 to the year A.D.
1808 were calculated at between three and four crores of 1810
rupees. By an act of incomprehensible folly, the ministry in England had not only neglected to send an expedition against them, while they were capturing every island in the West Indies, but had positively interdicted any effort on the part of the Indian Government to reduce them. The French cruisers consequently continued to prey on British trade, and to sweep the seas from Madagascar to Java. With six ships of the line and sixteen frigates on the Indian station, six vessels sailing from Calcutta, valued at thirty lacs of rupees, had been captured by French cruisers in as many weeks. A memorial was at length transmitted by the mercantile community to the ministry, complaining of the insecurity of commerce and the supineness of the navy, and the Governor-General and the Admiral were instructed to take decisive measures for the protection of trade. That object, it was supposed, would be attained by blockading the Mauritius; but six of the Company's magnificent Indiamen, valued at more than half a crore of rupees, were captured by French frigates which sailed out of the port, and returned to it in triumph with their prizes, in the teeth of the blockade. An expedition was then sent, in the first instance, to the island of Bourbon, which was captured with a slender effort; but this achievement was overbalanced by a series of unexampled disasters at sea, which were justly attributed to the ignorance and mismanagement of the naval department. Three English frigates were captured, and three set on fire by the French squadron, which maintained its national honour in these seas as nobly as Suffrein in the days of Warren Hastings. Meanwhile, Lord Minto was assembling an armament of overwhelming force, consisting of one 74 gun ship and thirteen frigates, besides sloops and gunboats, and a land force of 11,000 men, which comprised 6,300 European bayonets, and 2,000 seamen and marines, and four volunteer regiments. To oppose this force the French general could only muster 2,000 European soldiers, and a body of half-disciplined African slaves, and, unwilling to sacrifice the
lives of brave men in a hopeless contest, he surrendered 1810
the island on fair and equitable terms.

SECTION IV.

LORD MINTO'S ADMINISTRATION—EXPEDITION TO JAVA—THE PINDAREES—THE NEW CHARTER.

A.D. 1811

Expedition to Java.

THE subjugation of Holland by the emperor Napoleon placed the Dutch settlements in the east at his command, and he spared no pains to complete the defences of the most important of them, the island of Java. He despatched large reinforcements under an officer in whom he had confidence, General Daendels, who repaired the old fortifications and erected new and more formidable works in the vicinity of the capital, Batavia. From some unexplained cause he was superseded by General Jaensens, who had surrendered the Cape to the English squadron four years before. The emperor at his final audience reminded him of this disaster, and said: "Sir, remember that a French general does not allow "himself to be captured a second time." Lord Minto, having obtained the permission of the Court of Directors to proceed against the island, summoned to his counsels Mr.—afterwards Sir Stamford—Raffles, a member of the government of Penang, who had acquired a knowledge of the condition, the policy, and the language of the various tribes in the eastern archipelago superior to that of every other European at the time. The expedition consisted of 90 sail, on which were embarked 6,000 European troops, and about the same number of sepoys, and was the largest European armament which had ever traversed the eastern seas. Lord Minto determined to accompany it as a volunteer, leading the way in the "Modeste" frigate, commanded by his son, and the whole fleet anchored in the bay of Batavia without a single accident on the 4th August. The entire body of troops under the command of General Jaensens amounted to 17,000, of whom 13,000 were concentrated for the defence of Fort Cornelis, which was strong from its natural position, and had been rendered, as was supposed, impregnable by science. It was an entrenched camp between two streams, one of which was not fordable, and the other was defended by strong bastions and ramparts. The entire circumference of the encampment was five miles, and it was protected by 300 pieces of cannon.

Sir Samuel Ahmuty, the General-in-Chief, determined at first to assail it by regular approaches, but the attempt was found to be all but impracticable under a tropical sun, and must have been abandoned when, on the setting in of the rains, the malaria of the Batavian marshes prostrated the army. It was resolved, therefore, to carry it by a *coup de main*, which brought into play the daring spirit of Colonel Gillespie, of Vellore renown, to whom the enterprise was committed. His column marched soon after midnight on the 26th August, and came upon the first redoubt as the day dawned, and carried it at the point of the bayonet. The impetuous valour of his troops mastered the other redoubts in succession, till he found himself in front of the enemy's reserve and of a large body of cavalry posted with powerful artillery in front of the barracks. Having driven them from this position, the Colonel placed himself at the head of the dragoons and horse artillery, and pursued them for ten miles till he had completed the disorganisation of the whole army. Java was won in a single morning, and by the efforts of a single officer. The loss of the French in the field was severe, and 6,000 of their troops, chiefly Europeans, were made prisoners; but the victory cost the invaders 900 in killed and wounded, of whom eighty-five were officers. The Court of Directors had given instructions that on the capture of the island the fortifications should be demolished, and the arms and ammunition distributed among the natives, and the island evacuated. But Lord Minto was not disposed to put weapons into the hands of the natives, and abandon the colonists without arms or fortresses to their vindictive passions, and consign this noble island to the reign of barbarism. He determined to retain it, and committed the government of it to Mr. Raffles, under whose wise and liberal administration it continued to flourish for several years.

A.D. 1811

Capture of Fort Cornelis.

Lord Minto returned to Calcutta in 1812, and immediately after learned that he had been superseded in the Government. The usual term of office was considered to extend to seven years, and Lord Minto had intimated to the Court of Directors his wish to be relieved early in 1814; but the Prince Regent was anxious to bestow this lucrative post on the favourite of the day, the Earl of Moira, who had recently failed in his attempt to form a ministry. Under the dictation of the Board of Control, the Court of Directors were obliged to

1812

Supersession of Lord Minto.

pass a resolution for the immediate termination of Lord Minto's administration. Circumstances detained Lord Moira in England longer than he expected, and Lord Minto did not quit India till within three or four months of the time he had fixed for his departure; but the infliction of this indignity on a Governor-General whose government had been without a failure, and who had given universal satisfaction, reflected equal discredit on the servile ministry and on their royal master.

A.D. 1812

On the return of Lord Minto from Java, it became necessary for the first time to order troops into the field to repel the inroads of the Pindarees. The earliest trace of these freebooters is to be found in the struggles between Aurungzebe and the Mahrattas, whose armies they accompanied into the field. After the Peshwa had delegated the charge of maintaining the Mahratta power in Hindostan to his lieutenants, Sindia and Holkar, the Pindarees nominally ranged themselves under their standards, and were designated Sindia Shahee and Holkar Shahee Pindarees, but they were not allowed to pitch their tents within the Mahratta encampment. Those chiefs found it useful to attach to their armies a body of freebooters who required no pay, and were content with an unlimited license of plunder, and were always ready to complete the work of destruction. The Pindarees found their account in establishing a connection, although indirect, with established governments, to whom they might look for protection in case of emergency. But this relationship did not restrain the Pindarees from plundering the districts of their patrons when it suited their interests, nor did it prevent the Mahratta princes from seizing the Pindaree leaders after their return from a successful foray, and obliging them to give up a portion of their plunder.

The Pindarees.

The withdrawal of British protection from Central India opened a wide field for plunder, and increased the strength and audacity of the Pindarees. Two of the chiefs in the suite of Sindia offered their services to the nabob of Bhopal to plunder the territories of Nagpore; and, when their offer was declined, proceeded to Nagpore, and were readily engaged by the raja to ravage the dominions of Bhopal. On their return the raja did not scruple to break up their encampment and despoil them of the rich booty they had acquired. Of the two leaders, one took refuge with Sindia, and his two sons Dost Mahomed and Wassil Mahomed collected and or-

Pindaree leaders.

ganised his scattered followers. The other died in confinement, when the leadership devolved on Cheetoo, who had been purchased when a child, during a famine, and regularly trained to the Pindaree profession. His superior abilities and daring spirit raised him to the head of the troop, and he was rewarded for his services to Sindia by the title of nabob and a jageer. He fixed his head-quarters at Nimar, amidst the wild fastnesses of the region lying between the Nerbudda and the Vindya range. Kureem Khan another Pindaree leader of note was a Rohilla, who in the progress of events obtained a title and an assignment of lands from Sindia; but, as he continued to encroach upon the Mahratta territories, Sindia determined to crush his rising power, and treacherously seized him at a friendly entertainment. He was placed in confinement for four years, and not liberated without the payment of six lacs of rupees. On obtaining his liberty the Pindarees flocked to his standard in greater numbers than ever. Cheetoo, also was induced to join him, and an alliance was formed with Ameer Khan, then in the spring tide of his career. Their united bands did not fall short of 60,000 horse, and from the palace to the cottage every mind was filled with consternation by this portentous assemblage of banditti in Central Asia. Happily the union was short-lived. Cheetoo, who had always felt the hostility of a rival to Kureem Khan, was prevailed upon to desert him, when his camp was assailed and broken up by Sindia.

A.D. 1812

These were the acknowledged leaders of the Pindarees, to whose encampment the minor chiefs repaired when the season arrived for their annual expeditions. Their ranks were recruited by miscreants expelled from society, and men pursued by their creditors, as well as by men weary of peaceful occupation, and eager for excitement. The Pindaree standard was generally raised at the Dussera, or autumnal festival, towards the end of October, when the rains had subsided, and the rivers became fordable. Leaders of experience and acknowledged courage were selected, who took the command of bodies of 4,000 or 5,000 men, all mounted, and armed with spears of from four to six yards in length. They were not encumbered with either tents or baggage, and they obtained supplies for themselves and their horses from the villages they plundered on the line of march. Neither were they embarrassed with any prejudices of caste, or compunctions of conscience, and the history of their career is not relieved

System of plunder.

by a single generous or chivalrous act. They frequently moved at the rate of forty or fifty miles a day, and as they were unable to remain long in one spot, the greatest despatch was used to complete the plunder of the village; and tortures which almost exceed belief were inflicted on men and women to hasten the discovery of property. Their progress throughout the country was indicated by a stream of desolation, for what they could not carry off they destroyed.

For several years their depredations had been confined to the neighbourhood of the Nerbudda and the frontiers of the Peshwa, the Nizam and the raja of Nagpore; but, as these districts became exhausted, they were obliged to enlarge the sphere of their expeditions, and on one occasion swept through 400 miles of country south of the Nerbudda, and returned without molestation, laden with plunder. The Dussera of 1811 was celebrated by a congregation of 25,000 Pindaree horse, and a detachment of 5,000 plundered up to the gates of Nagpore, and burnt down one of its suburbs. The next year a large body under Dost Mahomed plundered the British district of Mirzapore, and boldly proceeded down towards Gya, within seventy miles of Patna, levying heavy contributions in this new and untrodden field, and then disappeared up the source of the Soane, before a British soldier could overtake them. This was their first invasion of British territory, and, coupled with the periodical devastation of the native states, induced Lord Minto to entreat the Directors to consider whether "it was "expedient to observe a strict neutrality amidst these scenes "of disorder and outrage, or to listen to the voice of "suffering humanity and interfere for the protection of "the weak and defenceless states who implored our assist-"ance against the ravages of the Pindarees and the "Patans." Before he quitted the Government he addressed a second letter to the Directors, pointing out that the augmented numbers, the improved organisation, and the increasing audacity of the Pindarees, rendered the adoption of an extensive system of measures for their suppression, a matter of pressing importance.

Attack on British territories.

A.D. 1812

Lord Minto's administration has never been sufficiently appreciated, perhaps from the circumstance of its intervening between the more active and brilliant careers of Lord Wellesley and Lord Hastings. But it should not be forgotten that his hands were tied by the ruling policy of the India House,

Character of Lord Minto's tion.

which he altogether reprobated. He assured the Court of Directors that "no extent of concession or territorial restitution on our part would have the effect of establishing any real and effective balance of power or forbearance on the part of other states, when the means of aggrandisement should be placed in their hands;" and that "the expectation of augmenting our security by diminishing our power and political ascendancy on the continent of India was utterly vain." He remarked, "that with the native princes, war, rapine, and conquest constituted an avowed principle of action, a just and legitimate pursuit, and the chief source of public glory; sanctioned and even recommended by the ordinances of religion, and prosecuted without the semblance or pretext of justice, and with a savage disregard of every obligation of humanity and public faith, and restrained only by the power of resistance." By these and similar representations he prepared the Court of Directors to abandon the absurd policy of non-intervention, and to assume that supremacy on the continent which was irrevocably established by his successor; but he did not hesitate to vindicate the paramount authority of the British Government on many occasions, in Travancore, in Nagpore, in Bundlecund, and in Sirhind; and to his administration belongs the merit of having swept every hostile and piratical flag from the Indian seas, and established the predominance of British power on the ocean, though he was forbidden to do so on land.

A.D. 1812

Negotiations for a new charter.

The period was now approaching when the question of renewing the Company's commercial monopoly was to come before Parliament. In the preliminary discussions between the ministry and Leadenhall Street, the Court of Directors assumed a lofty tone, and made extravagant demands, which they were obliged gradually to withdraw; but they continued to insist on the renewal of the charter in all its integrity. The President of the Board of Control, however, informed them that the ministry had made up their minds no longer to exclude the merchants of England from the trade of India. The points at issue between the Company and the Cabinet appeared at length to be reduced to the question of opening the outports of England to the enterprise of private merchants, and on this point the Court of Directors determined to take their stand. They affirmed that any diversion of the trade from London to the out-

1809 to 1812

1812

ports would break up large and important establishments, and throw thousands out of bread; would increase smuggling beyond the possibility of control; would entail the ruin of the China trade, and reduce the value of the Company's stock; would paralyse their power in India, and compromise the happiness of its inhabitants; and not only impair the interests of Great Britain in Asia, but imperil the British constitution.

The ministry, however, were not appalled by these terrific spectres, which the genius of monopoly had conjured up, but informed the Directors that if the extension of commercial privileges to the rest of the nation would render it impossible for them to continue the government of India, some other agency might be provided for that object, consistent with the interests of the public and the integrity of the constitution.

Opposition of the Court of Directors.

But the Directors and the Proprietors refused any concession, and expressed their confidence that Parliament would not consent to gratify a few interested speculators by abolishing a commercial system which had existed for two centuries, and was fortified by a score of Acts of Parliament. On the other hand, the claim of the Company to a continuance of their monopoly encountered a strenuous opposition throughout the country. In the twenty years which had elapsed since the previous charter, manufactures and commerce had been developed beyond all former example, and the merchants and millowners demanded the right of an unrestricted trade with India, from their respective ports, and in their own vessels, with such unanimity and vigour, that the ministry felt it impossible to resist the national voice. On the 22nd March the President of the Board of Control brought forward the ministerial propositions, that the Government of India should be continued for twenty years longer in the hands of the Company, with liberty to continue to prosecute their trade, but that the whole nation should be allowed to participate in it; that the Company should enjoy the exclusive trade to China, and that the restrictions on the resort of Europeans to the country should be relaxed so as to amount to a virtual abolition.

A.D. 1813

These propositions were violently opposed by the Directors and Proprietors, and they petitioned Parliament for leave to bring forward witnesses to support their claims. The first witness was the venerable Warren Hastings, then in his eightieth year.

Witnesses of the Directors.

Twenty-six years before he had been arraigned by the House of Commons at the bar of the House of Lords for high crimes and misdemeanours. He had outlived the passions and prejudices of that age, and the whole House rose as he entered and paid a spontaneous homage to his exalted character and his eminent services. But his views of Indian policy belonged to that remote period when he was laying the foundation of the empire; he could not realise the change of circumstances in England and in India, and was opposed to all innovations. The evidence of Lord Teignmouth, of Mr. Charles Grant, of Colonel Malcolm and Colonel Munro, and indeed of all the witnesses marshalled by the India House, ran in the same groove. They maintained that the climate of India and the habits and prejudices of the natives precluded the hope of any increased consumption of British manufactures; that the trade of India had reached its utmost limit, and that it could be conducted to advantage only through the agency of the Company; that the free admission of Europeans would lead to colonisation, and to the oppression of the natives, and the loss of India. But all the authorities and all the evidence the Court of Directors could muster, proved of no avail. The House yielded to the voice of the nation, and opened India to the commercial enterprise of all England. A.D. 1813

The missionary question.

Reference has been made in a previous chapter to the restrictions imposed on the Serampore missionaries by Sir George Barlow during the panic created by the Vellore mutiny, which were removed on his arrival by Lord Minto. But on his return from Java, without the remotest appearance of any political necessity, he was induced to adopt stringent measures against the missionary enterprise, and to order eight missionaries, the majority of whom had recently arrived, peremptorily to quit the country. The hostility of the Court of Directors to missions and to education had all the inveteracy of traditional prejudice, and it became necessary to take advantage of the Charter discussions to apply for the interposition of Parliament. The question was entrusted to Mr. Wilberforce, who, in a speech distinguished for its eloquence, entreated the House to grant permission to place the truths of Christianity before the natives of India for their voluntary acceptance. But the India House and its witnesses, with some exceptions, were as virulently opposed to this concession as to that of free trade, and reprobated the admission of missionary and mercantile agents with equal vehemence. But the voice of the country was raised with more than ordinary unanimity against the monstrous proposition that the only religion to be proscribed in India should be that of its rulers. The House was inundated with petitions from every corner, and from all classes and denominations, and the clause giving missionaries the same access to India as merchants was passed by large majorities.

CHAPTER X.

SECTION I.

LORD HASTINGS'S ADMINISTRATION—THE NEPAUL WAR.

A.D. 1813 THE Earl of Moira, subsequently created Marquis of Hastings, took the oaths and his seat in Council on the 4th October. He was of the mature age of fifty-nine, a nobleman of Norman lineage, with a tall and commanding figure, and distinguished by his patrician bearing. He entered the army at the age of seventeen, and served seven years in the war of independence in America. His life had been subsequently passed in connection with important public affairs, and he brought to his high office a large fund of experience, a clear and sound judgment, and great decision of character, together with the equivocal honour of being the personal friend of the Prince Regent. In his place in Parliament he had denounced Lord Wellesley's wars and his ambitious policy of establishing British supremacy throughout India; but this opinion was reversed as soon as he had taken a survey of the position and prospects of the Indian empire; and before he had been many months in India he recorded his impression that "our object in India ought to be to "render the British Government paramount in effect, if "not declaredly so . . . and to oblige the other states to "perform the two great feudatory duties of supporting "our rule with all their forces, and submitting their "mutual differences to our arbitration."

Lord Hastings Governor-General.

Lord Hastings found his eastern throne no bed of roses. The non-intervention policy—which the authorities in Leadenhall street considered the perfection of political wisdom, and the native princes an obvious token of pusillanimity—had brought on a contempt of our power, and sown the seeds of new wars. The violence of Holkar had ended in insanity; his government lost its strength, and Ameer Khan stepped in and became at once the prop of the throne and the curse of the country. The troops of Sindia had been incessantly employed in aggrandising his power by encroachments on his neighbours. The Peshwa had been husbanding his resources for the first opportunity of shaking off British control. The Pindaree freebooters were spreading desolation through a region 500 miles in length and 400 in breadth; and on the northern frontier of Bengal and Behar a new power had arisen and invaded our districts, and hung like a dark cloud on the mountains of Nepaul. The Company's army, which had been subject to large reductions in a spirit of unwise economy, was found to be inadequate to the defence of our frontier, and the treasury was empty.

A.D. 1813

State of India.

The first and immediate difficulty of Lord Hastings arose out of the encroachments of the Nepaulese or Goorkhas. The valley of Nepaul is embosomed in the Himalaya, and bounded on the north by some of its loftiest and most majestic peaks, and on the south by its first and lowest range. That range is skirted by a magnificent forest, from eight to ten miles in depth, which presents an unbroken series of gigantic trees; no breath of wind reaches the interior, which is littered with rank and decayed vegetation; no animal ventures into it, and no sound of a bird is heard in its recesses. An open plain, called the *teraee*, stretches along the south of the forest, about 500 miles in length and 20 in breadth. The soil is watered by the streams which descend from the mountains, and, when cultivated, produces the most luxuriant crops, but during the greater part of the year is as pestilential as the Pontine marshes.

Description of Nepaul.

About the middle of the fourteenth century, various colonists of Rajpoots entered the country and subdued the aboriginal Newars, and in the course of time were ranged under three tribes. About ten years after the battle of Plassy, Prithee Narrain, the chief of the tribe of Goorkhas, having subdued all the other chiefs, established a new dynasty, with

Rise and progress of the Goorkhas.

A.D. Katmandhoo for its capital. His descendant, an infant, 1805 was placed on the throne in 1805, and Bheem Sen formed a council of regency under his own presidency. The impulse of conquest which the founder had given to the nation continued in undiminished vigour. An expedition was sent to Lassa, and the living type of Booddha was subject to the humiliation of paying tribute to his Hindoo conqueror. But the emperor of China, the secular head of Booddhism, avenged the insult by invading Nepaul and obliging the Nepaulese to send an embassy with tribute to Pekin every three years. The cabinet of Katmandhoo then pushed their conquests eastward to Sikkim, and westward to the mountainous region of the higher Sutlej, where Umur Sing, their renowned general, came in contact with the rising power of Runjeet Sing, but was recalled from the siege of Kote Kangra to the defence of his own country from the assaults of the British Government.

During the twenty-five years preceding the war we treat of, the Goorkhas had come down into the plains and usurped more than 200 British villages, and the subjects of the Company were exposed to continual aggression along the whole line of their frontier. At length they had the presumption to seize upon the districts of Bootwul and Seoraj in Goruckpore, which the Vizier of Oude had transferred to Lord Wellesley in 1802. Lord Minto was anxious, if possible, to avoid a resort to arms, and proposed a conference with the Nepaul ministry, which resulted in demonstrating that they had not the shadow of a right to them. Accordingly,

Their encroachments on British territory.

1813 in June, he demanded the immediate restitution of them, and intimated that, in case of refusal, the Government would be obliged to have recourse to force; but the Nepaul cabinet distinctly refused to evacuate them. Their reply did not reach Calcutta till after the arrival of Lord Hastings, and, upon a careful examination of all the documents, he deemed it indispensable to make a categorical demand that they should be surrendered within twenty-five days. The period expired without any communication from Katmandhoo, and he ordered the magistrate of Goruckpore to expel the Goorkha officers.

1814 Lord Hastings's letter created a profound sensation at Katmandhoo, and convinced the regent that the dispute about these border lands was rapidly merging into a question of peace or war with the British power. A national council was convened to

Goorkhas resolve on war.

discuss the question, when Umur Sing said that his life had been passed amidst the hardships of war, and he was not ignorant of its risks, but he deprecated a war with the British Government, and affirmed that the lands were not worth the hazard. "We have hitherto," he said, "been "hunting deer, but if we engage in this war we shall have "to hunt tigers." But the regent and his party were bent on war, and determined to demand the surrender of the whole of the country north of the Ganges, and, as if to render hostilities inevitable, sent a detachment down to Bootwul, and put the police officer and eighteen of his men to death. The Goorkhas had thrown down the gauntlet, and Lord Hastings had no alternative but to take it up, promptly, without waiting for the result of a reference to Leadenhall Street. This defiance of the British power seemed an act of incredible temerity on the part of the Goorkhas. Their whole army did not exceed 12,000, and it was scattered over a long line of frontier, and their largest gun was only a four-pounder; but uninterrupted success for many years had infused a feeling of confidence into their minds. Their real strength consisted in the impracticable nature of their country, and in our entire ignorance of its localities.

A.D. 1814

Lord Hastings found himself dragged into an arduous conflict with an empty exchequer. On all former occasions the Government had resorted to a loan, but this was difficult, if not altogether impracticable, at a time when their promissory notes were at a discount of nine and ten per cent., and money was worth twelve per cent. in the market. In this dilemma he cast his eye on the hoards of the Vizier, amounting to seven crores of rupees. That prince was anxious to be relieved from the imperious interference of the Resident in the affairs of his government and of his court, and Lord Hastings had expressed a wish to afford him relief from this annoyance; on hearing, therefore, of the embarrassment of the Government, he resolved to evince his gratitude by offering a donation of a crore of rupees. He died while Lord Hastings was on his way to Lucknow, where the offer was renewed by his son and successor. Lord Hastings agreed to accept it as a loan to the Company, bearing interest, though he could not receive it as a gratuity; but he gained little by the aid thus afforded him. Of the old loan at eight per cent., which the Government was endeavouring to convert into a six per cent. stock, about half a crore of rupees was still unredeemed; and

Lucknow loan.

the Vice-President in Council, without any intimation to the Governor-General, employed half the sum obtained at Lucknow in paying it off. This act of folly deprived Lord Hastings of the sinews of war, and would have produced a disastrous effect on the campaign if he had not submitted to the humiliation of soliciting a second crore, which was not, however, given without much reluctance.

A.D. 1814

Plan of the campaign.

With regard to the plan of the campaign, Lord Hastings considered it impolitic to confine his operations to the simple defence of a line of frontier several hundred miles in extent, which it would be found impracticable to guard effectually against an energetic and rapacious enemy. He felt that our military reputation could be sustained only by a bold and successful assault on the strongest of the Goorkha positions. He accordingly planned four expeditions on four points: the western on the Sutlej, the eastern on the capital, and two others on intermediate points. The division under General Gillespie, who had gained a high reputation at Vellore and in Java, was the first in the field, 3,500 strong, and advanced toward the Dhoon valley; during his progress he came upon a small fort at Kalunga, held by 600 Goorkhas. Lord Hastings had warned him against any attempt to storm works which should be reduced by artillery, but, with the reckless daring of his character, he determined to carry it by assault, and as he rushed up to the gate to encourage his men who were staggered by the murderous fire of the Goorkhas, he was shot through the heart. A retreat was immediately sounded, but not before twenty officers and 240 rank and file lay killed or wounded.

1814

Failure of three of the divisions.

A month was lost in waiting for heavy ordnance from Delhi; but after the breach was reported practicable, the assault was repulsed, with another loss of 680 men. Three days of incessant shelling rendered the post untenable, and the brave Goorkha commander made his escape with only seventy survivors. The reputation of the division was not restored by General Martindell, on whom the command devolved, who allowed himself, with an army of 5,000 sepoys and 1,000 Europeans, to be held at bay by 2,300 Goorkhas. The division under General J. S. Wood, which was appointed to penetrate Nepaul through Palpa, was paralysed by similar incapacity, and an army of 4,500 British soldiers, European and native, was not found to be a match for 1,200 of the Nepaul force. The chief reliance of Lord Hastings was placed on the division of General Marley, 8,000 strong, destined to march directly on the capital, only 100 miles from our frontier; but he surpassed the others in imbecility. Two detachments were sent east and west without any precautions, and were fiercely assailed by the enemy. The sepoys fled, but the officers fell fighting with their usual valour, and guns, stores, and ammunition were captured by the enemy. The wretched general made a retrograde movement, and, though reinforced by two European regiments, could not be persuaded to enter the forest; and one morning, at early dawn, mounted his horse, and, without even delegating the command to any officer, galloped back to the cantonments at Dinapore. General George Wood, who succeeded him, was equally devoid of spirit, and the services of the division were lost.

A.D. 1815

This was the first campaign, since the Company took up arms in India, in which their troops outnumbered those of the enemy. Our non-success was owing entirely to the exceptional incompetence of the generals. Lord Hastings regarded his position with extreme anxiety, and, in his diary, stated that if we were to be foiled in this struggle, it would be the first step to the subversion of our power. These reverses were diligently promulgated throughout India, and revived the dormant hopes of the native princes, who began to make military demonstrations. Under the auspices of the Peshwa, who sent envoys to all the courts in India, not omitting even the Pindarees, a secret treaty of mutual support was concluded against the British Government. The army of Sindia was organised on our frontier. Ameer Khan, with 25,000 horse and foot, took up a position within twelve marches of our territories. Runjeet Sing marched 20,000 men to the fords of the Sutlej, and 20,000 Pindarees stood ready for any opportunity of mischief. To meet this emergency, Lord Hastings ordered up the whole of the disposable force of the Madras army to the frontier of the Deccan, and raised additional regiments of infantry, enlisted irregular horse, and increased the strength of the army to 80,000. But the Company's *ikbal*, or good fortune, as the natives observed, was still in the ascendant. Runjeet Sing was recalled by a threatened inroad of the Afghans. Sindia's two commanders, after long discord, attacked each other; the Pindaree leaders quarrelled among themselves; Ameer Khan found more immediate employment in the plunder of Joudpore, and the cloud

Effect of these reverses.

was completely dispelled by the brilliant success of General Ochterlony.

A.D. 1815 The division of this general was appointed to dislodge the Goorkhas from the territories they had acquired on the higher Sutlej, where Umur Sing was in command, and the ablest of the Goorkha generals was pitted against the ablest of the English commanders. The scene of operation was a wild and rugged region, presenting successive ranges of mountains rising one above another to the lofty peaks of the Himalaya, broken by deep glens and covered with thick forests. The general had formed a correct estimate of the bold character of his opponent and of the advantage he enjoyed in his position, and pursued his object by cautious but steady advances. He opened the campaign by the capture of the important fortress of Nalagurh, after a bombardment of thirty hours, with the loss of only one European soldier. During the next five months the valour of the British troops was matched by the gallantry of the Goorkhas, and the skill of British engineers was repeatedly foiled by the tact and resolution of their opponents. The service was the most arduous in which the Company's army had ever been engaged. At an elevation of more than 5,000 feet above the level of the sea, at the most inclement season of the year, amidst falls of snow often of two days continuance, the pioneers were employed in blasting rocks and opening roads for the eighteen-pounders, and day after day the men and the elephants were employed in dragging them up those alpine heights; but the energy of the general, and the exhilarating character of the warfare, diffused a feeling of enthusiasm throughout the army. By a series of bold and skilful manœuvres every height was at length surmounted and every fortress captured but that of Malown. Before General Ochterlony reached it, Lord Hastings had despatched some irregular corps raised by Colonel Gardner, an officer of great merit who had been in the Mahratta service, to occupy the province of Almora. That gallant officer and his new levies speedily cleared it of the Goorkhas, and effectually cut off Umur Sing's communication with the capital, and deprived him of all hope of reinforcements. The Goorkha officers entreated him to make conditions with the general, but the stern old chief spurned their advice, and they passed over to the English camp. He retired into the citadel with 200 men, but when the batteries were about to open upon it he

Operations of General Ochterlony.

hesitated to sacrifice in a forlorn conflict the lives of the brave men who had nobly adhered to him to the last, and accepted the terms offered by his generous foe, who, in consideration of the skill, bravery, and fidelity with which he had defended the country, allowed him to march out with his arms and colours and personal property.

Second Goorkha campaign.

The discomfiture of their ablest general, and the loss of their most valuable acquisition, took away from the regency all confidence in their fastnesses, and induced them to sue for peace. Commissioners came down to Segowlee and signed a treaty on the 2nd December, under an engagement to deliver the A.D.
ratification of it within fifteen days, and a royal salute was 1815
fired in Calcutta in honour of the peace. But the ratification was never sent. Umur Sing and his son had in the meantime arrived at Katmandhoo, and successfully urged the regency to continue the war and to dispute every inch of ground. Another campaign became inevitable, and Lord Hastings had to assemble an army with all speed to strike a blow at the capital before the rains commenced. A force of 20,000 men was collected on the frontier, and placed under the command of General Ochterlony, who advanced with his usual caution and promptitude. Finding the Goorkha works in the first pass unassailable, he determined to turn the flank of the enemy, and on the night of the 14th February marched in dead silence through a 1816
narrow ravine, where twenty men might have arrested a whole army. The force bivouacked for two days and nights without food or shelter, awaiting the arrival of the second detachment, and then advanced to Muckwanpore, within fifty miles of Katmandhoo, where the Goorkha army sustained a signal defeat. The regency lost all conceit of fighting; the treaty duly ratified, was sent down in hot haste, and peace was concluded on the 2nd March on terms singularly moderate. The Goorkhas were not only the most valiant but the most humane foes we had ever encountered in India, and they also proved to be the most faithful to their engagements. Unlike other treaties with Indian princes, this of 1816 has never been infringed; and instead of taking advantage of our embarrassments during the mutiny of 1857, they sent a large force to assist in quelling it.

SECTION II.

LORD HASTINGS'S ADMINISTRATION—TRANSACTIONS WITH NATIVE PRINCES—MAHRATTA AND PINDAREE WAR.

The policy of Lord Wellesley had been steadily repudiated by the Court of Directors, but its wisdom was amply vindicated by the misery which followed its abandonment, and by the desolation of Central India for ten years by the Patans and the Pindarees. Ameer Khan, the Patan, had established a regular government, but the predatory element was always predominant in it. His army was estimated at 10,000 foot and 15,000 horse, with a powerful artillery, and as it was his plan to levy contributions from princes and states, he marched about with all the appliances for the siege of towns. The object of the Pindarees was universal and indiscriminate plunder, and they swept through the country with a degree of rapidity which rendered it impossible to calculate their movements, and baffled all pursuit. On his arrival, Lord Hastings found 50,000 Patans and Pindarees in the heart of India subsisting by plunder, and extending their ravages over an area as large as England.

Patans and Pindarees.

A.D. 1814 One of his earliest acts was to point out to the Court of Directors, in language more emphatic than that of Lord Minto, the increasing danger of this predatory power. He asserted that India could not prosper until the Government "became the head of a "league embracing every power in India, and "was placed in a position to direct its entire strength "against the disturbers of the public peace." But this course of policy was systematically opposed by the two members of his Council. Mr. Edmonstone combined official talent of a high order with long experience, but lacked the endowments of a statesman, and clung to the retrograde policy of Sir George Barlow. Mr. Dowdeswell had all the narrowmindedness of Sir George without a tithe of his ability. In reply to Lord Hastings's representation, the Court, still clinging to the non-intervention policy, forbad him to engage "in plans of general con-"federacy or of offensive operations against the Pindarees, "either with a view to their utter extirpation, or in "anticipation of expected danger." They enjoined him to

Representation to the Court of Directors.

1815

undertake nothing that could embroil them with Sindia, and to make no change in the existing system of political relations; to maintain the course of policy pursued by Sir George Barlow, to reduce the strength of the army, and practise a rigid economy.

Before this communication reached Calcutta, Lord Hastings, in the hope of preventing the Pindarees from crossing the Nerbudda, had entered into negotiations for a subsidiary alliance with the raja of Nagpore, which the Court had sanctioned five or six years before, but the raja persisted in resisting the proposal. Lord Hastings then proposed a similar alliance with Bhopal, with the view of holding the Pindarees in check. Bhopal was a small principality in Malwa, in the valley of the Nerbudda, lying between the British territories and the head-quarters of the Pindarees. The prince was the only chief in Central India who gave any support to the expedition of General Goddard in 1778, and the testimonials granted by him on that occasion are still carefully preserved in the archives of that noble house. In 1813, Sindia and the raja of Nagpore formed a confederacy to absorb its territories, and brought a force of 60,000 men against its renowned minister, Vizier Mahomed, which besieged the capital successively for two years. He implored the interference of the British Government, and Lord Hastings considered that in the existing circumstances of Central India, it was of no little importance to protect a state situated like Bhopal from extinction, and the two Mahratta powers were informed that it was under the protection of the Company. The raja of Nagpore, after some hesitation, withdrew his army, but Sindia assumed a lofty tone—it was at the time of the three failures in the Nepaul war—and declared that Bhopal was one of his dependencies, with which the Government was debarred from interfering by Sir George Barlow's treaty of 1805. But the vigorous preparations made by Lord Hastings to enforce his requisition, and more especially the success of General Ochterlony, staggered him; his two generals attacked each other under the walls of Bhopal, and the siege was raised. But the projected alliance with Bhopal fell to the ground.

A.D. 1814

Proposed native alliances.

1813

Bajee Rao, the Peshwa, was about this time brought into conflict with the Government, which eventually ended in his ruin. He had none of the talents for government which had distinguished his pre-

Affairs at Poona.

decessors, and rested the success of his schemes on intrigue and perfidy. He was the slave of avarice and superstition; he had accumulated five crores of rupees in ten years, but he was lavish in his gifts to temples and brahmins, and his time was passed in constant pilgrimages from shrine to shrine. His efforts to seize on the estates of the great feudatories of the Mahratta empire, denominated the "southern jageerdars," many of them of greater antiquity than his own house, had been defeated by the interposition of the Resident, and increased his disaffection.
A.D. 1813 About the year 1813, one Trimbukjee Danglia, who was originally in the spy department, entered his service, and by his intelligence and energy, and not less by pandering to his vices, obtained a complete ascendancy over his mind. So great was the servile devotion he manifested to his master that he assured Mr. Elphinstone, the Resident, that he was ready to kill a cow at his bidding. Towards the English Government he always manifested an implacable hostility, and was incessantly urging the Peshwa to shake off their alliance and assert his position as the head of the Mahratta power.

Claims on the Gaikwar.

The Peshwa had claims on the Gaikwar extending back for half a century, which, with interest, amounted to little short of three crores. The Gaikwar advanced counter claims of scarcely less amount, and he
1814 deputed his chief minister, Gungadhur Shastree, to Poona, to adjust them; but he would not venture into the city without the guarantee of the Resident. His reception was ungracious, and he was so completely baffled by evasions, that he determined to return to Baroda, upon which Trimbukjee changed his tactics, and spared no pains to gain him over to the interests of his master, who promised to bestow the hand of his sister-in-law on his son. The Shastree was thus induced to compromise the Gaikwar claims, without his concurrence or that of the Resident, for land yielding about seven lacs of rupees a year. An auspicious day was selected by the astrologers for the nuptials, and splendid preparations made for it; but the Shastree, hearing that his master repudiated the treaty, requested that the marriage might be suspended. The Peshwa considered this an unpardonable insult, which could be expiated only with his blood.

The Shastree was accordingly induced to accompany the
1815 Peshwa on his pilgrimage to Punderpore, though warned of his danger, and, soon after his arrival there, yielded

to the importunities of Trimbukjee to pay his devotions at the shrine after dusk. On his return he was waylaid and assassinated. The murder of a brahmin of the highest rank and learned in the shasters, in a holy city, at a period of pilgrimage, and in the immediate precincts of the temple, filled the Mahratta community with horror. But the victim was also the minister of an ally of the Company, and had proceeded to the court at Poona under a safe conduct. The Resident took up the case with promptitude and vigour, and having traced the murder to the agency of Trumbukjee, called on the Peshwa to deliver him up. The demand was resolutely resisted, and the Peshwa began to levy troops and determined to raise his standard, although unable to obtain the promise of assistance he solicited from the other Mahratta powers; but Mr. Elphinstone had taken the precaution of calling up troops to the capital. Bajee Rao's constitutional cowardice mastered every other feeling, and he surrendered his favourite on condition that his life should be spared. He was placed in confinement in the fort of Tanna, when he fully confessed the assassination, but declared that he had not acted without his master's orders.

A.D. 1815

Assassination of the Shastree.

Lord Hastings returned to Calcutta at the close of 1815, and placed on the records of Council an elaborate minute pointing out in stronger language than he had yet used the increasing danger arising from the growth of the Pindaree power, and, in order to suppress it, proposing a general system of alliances under the guarantee of the Company, a revision of our relations with the native powers, and a new settlement of the Mahratta dominions. His two colleagues opposed the proposal and it was sent on to the India House with their dissent. While it was on its way to England, the necessity of some immediate effort was rendered more imperative by their increasing audacity. The *dussera* festival, when the plan of the winter campaign was usually organized, 1815
was celebrated in the autumn of 1815 at Nimar, the head-quarters of Cheetoo, the chief leader, by a larger collection of Pindarees than had been assembled on any previous occasion, and their operations were especially directed against the territories of the Company and of the Nizam. A body of 8,000 crossed the Nerbudda in October, and swept through his provinces as far south as the Kistna, and returned so richly laden with booty that merchants

Lord Hastings' second representation.

were invited from all quarters to purchase it. This extraordinary success attracted fresh crowds to their standard, and a body of 23,000 crossed the Nerbudda in February. One large division poured down on the northern Sircars, A.D. 1816 sacked the civil station of Guntoor on the Coromandel coast, and for ten days plundered the adjacent villages with perfect impunity. Troops were immediately despatched from Calcutta by sea, but the Pindarees had disappeared before their arrival, and it would have been as vain to follow them as to pursue a flight of locusts. It was found on investigation that during this raid 330 villages had been plundered, and many of them burnt; 500 persons had been wounded; 182 put to death, and 3,600 subjected to torture, while the loss of property was estimated at twenty-five lacs of rupees.

This expedition demonstrated the importance of obtaining the co-operation of the raja of Nagpore, through whose 1816 territories the Pindarees had passed, but the raja still continued to resist every proposal of a subsidiary alliance. He died on the 22nd March, and was succeeded by his son Persajee, who was blind, palsied, and a confirmed idiot. His nephew, subsequently known as Appa Sahib, was acknowledged as regent, but was vigorously opposed by the intrigues of the court and the zenana, and threw himself upon the British Government, and offered at once to conclude the proposed alliance. A treaty was accordingly signed on the 29th May, which provided that a body of 6,000 infantry, a regiment of cavalry, and a suitable proportion of artillery, should be subsidized by the Nagpore state, and that the raja should not contract any foreign alliances, and refer all differences with other powers to the arbitration of the Governor-General. Lord Hastings was thus enabled to place on record that in two months he had been able to effect what had been fruitlessly laboured at for twelve years, and he now considered it certain that the Pindarees would not be able again to cross the Nerbudda. A despatch was soon after received from the India House revoking the permission formerly given to contract such an alliance, but it arrived too late to do any mischief.

Subsidiary alliance with Nagpore.

The Court of Directors had in 1813 sanctioned the renewal of the protective treaty with Jeypore which Sir George Barlow had torn up. Ameer Khan and his freebooters having drained Joudpore, fell upon this state, and laid siege to the capital.

Proposed alliance with Jeypore.

The raja despatched an envoy to Mr. Metcalfe, the Resident A.D. 1816
at Delhi, to implore the protection of the Government, and Lord Hastings, having regained his authority in Council by the accession of Mr. Seton who voted with him, resolved to avail himself of the warrant of the Court, and to conclude the alliance. Two divisions of troops, each 9,000 strong, were ordered into the field to expel the Patans from Jeypore, and to meet the hostility of Sindia or Holkar, who, having once subjected the country to plunder, considered that they had established a right over it. The four subsidiary armies of the Peshwa, the Nizam, the Gaikwar, and the raja of Nagpore were ordered forward, but the raja of Jeypore had no intention to fetter himself with any such connection, and, in the true spirit of oriental policy, was negotiating with Ameer Khan, whom he induced eventually to raise the siege by threatening to sign the treaty, and thus bring down the weight of the British armies upon him.

Mr. George Canning, one of the most brilliant of English statesmen, who was appointed President of the Board 1816
of Control in June 1816, was immediately called upon to take into consideration Lord Hastings's proposal to form a general system of alliances with a view to the extirpation of the Pindaree power. New as he was to the Government, it is no matter of surprise that he should have been unwilling to assume the responsibility of so fundamental a change in the policy of the empire, more especially when it was opposed by the councillors in Calcutta, and by those who might be considered his constitutional advisers in Leadenhall Street. Lord Hastings was, therefore, informed that the Court of Directors were unwilling to incur the risk of a general war for the uncertain purpose of rooting out the Pindarees, and that they would not sanction any extended military and political combinations for that purpose. They suggested that the Government might possibly enter into negotiations with some of the Pindaree leaders, or treat with the men to deliver up their chiefs. This advice kindled the indignation of Lord Hastings. The suggestion of the Court to engage one portion of the Pindaree confederation to destroy another, he attributed to the culpable negligence of the Government of India to point out the brutal and atrocious character of these wretches. But immediately after the transmission of this despatch from the India House, Mr. Canning received information of the

Despatches from England.

A.D. 1816 irruption of the Pindarees into the Northern Sircars, and the atrocities they had committed. His views were at once changed, and another despatch was sent under his directions, which stated: "We think it due to your Lordship not to lose an instant in conveying to you an explicit assurance of our approval of any measures you may have authorised or undertaken, not only for repelling invasion but for pursuing and chastising the invaders. We can no longer abstain from a vigorous exertion of military power in vindication of the British name and in defence of subjects who look to us for protection. . . . Any connection of Sindia or Holkar with the Pindarees against us or our allies, known, though not avowed, would place them in a state of direct hostility to us."

Lord Hastings was confident that the Nagpore subsi-
1816–17 diary force planted on the banks of the Nerbudda would effectually prevent the Pindarees from crossing it, but he was painfully disappointed. As the period of the annual swarming approached, Colonel Walker moved up to the Nerbudda with the whole body, numbering 6,000 men, but they were found unequal to the protection of a line a hundred and fifty miles in extent. The Pindaree detachments pushed across between his posts, and a large body dashed down on the British district of Kimedy, and burnt a portion of the town of Ganjam, and but for the accidental arrival of Company's troops to quell an insurrection in Orissa, would have laid the whole province under contribution. Other bodies plundered the territories of Nagpore and Hyderabad. The expeditions of 1816–17 were the boldest they had undertaken, and the success which attended them gave rise to serious considerations. With the Nagpore subsidiary force guarding the Nerbudda, 23,000 Pindarees had crossed it. With 32,000 British troops, besides the Poona brigade and the Nizam's contingent distributed over the country, they had rushed through the peninsula and ravaged both coasts. It was felt that the cost of these defensive measures exceeded the largest calculation of the cost of a campaign to exterminate the freebooters. It was therefore unanimously resolved in Council to abandon the resolution which had been adopted to abstain from any system of offensive operations till the sanction of the home authorities could be received, and to adopt vigorous measures against them without delay.

Pindaree campaign of 1816-17.

1817 Intimation of this determination to extinguish the Pindarees was immediately conveyed to Sindia, and he was requested to cooperate in carrying it into execution, but they had agents at his court, and warm partizans amongst his ministers, who endeavoured to persuade him that his own security would be impaired if he sanctioned the extirpation of these valuable auxiliaries, who were ready at any time to flock to his standard, and who required no pay. The agents of the Pindarees boasted that they would outdo the exploits of Jeswunt Rao Holkar, and that 50,000 of their body would carry fire and sword to Calcutta. But Sindia was not to be misled by this gasconade; he had not forgotten Assye, the Company had recently triumphed in Nepal, they had secured the resources of Nagpore, and the Government in Calcutta was again animated with the spirit of Lord Wellesley, and he promised his co-operation.

Sindia's determination.

During these negotiations at Gwalior events of great importance transpired at Poona. Trimbukjee effected his escape from Tanna, and though the Peshwa manifested unusual cordiality towards the Resident for some time, there was the clearest evidence that he was engaged in correspondence with Holkar, and Sindia, and Ameer Khan, and the Pindarees, for a simultaneous rising against the Government. Under the direction of Trimbukjee, he hastened the enlistment of troops, collected draft cattle, augmented his artillery, provisioned his forts, and deposited his jewels and treasure in the strongest of them. In April, Mr. Elphinstone presented a note to him upbraiding him with the hostile movements he was abetting, and declaring that the good understanding between the Government and him was at an end. At the same time, he peremptorily demanded the surrender of Trimbukjee, and the delivery of three forts as security, and he supported these representations by ordering up troops to Poona. The Peshwa's brave general Gokla urged a bold appeal to arms, but he had not the spirit to adopt this advice. The forts were surrendered, and a reward offered for the apprehension of Trimbukjee.

A.D. 1816

Hostility of Bajee Rao.

1817

On the eve of his comprehensive operations against the Pindarees, Lord Hastings deemed it necessary to exact greater securities from this perfidious prince. Mr. Elphinstone was desired to present him with the draft of a treaty which required him to dismiss the agents of foreign princes accredited to his court, to refer all matters in dispute with them to the arbitrament of the British Government, to renounce all his

Heavy penalty inflicted on him

A.D. 1817 rights in Saugor and Bundlecund, and, in lieu of the contingent of 5,000 horse and 3,000 foot he was bound to furnish, to cede territory yielding twenty-four lacs a year. His ministers endeavoured to mitigate the severity of these penalties, and they affirmed that we appeared to exact a greater degree of fidelity to engagements than any native prince was able to observe. The treaty was nevertheless signed on the 13th June. When the intelligence of these arrangements and of this large addition to the Company's territories reached England, Mr. Canning remarked that this transaction sufficiently proved "the irrepressible "tendency of our Indian power to enlarge its bounds, and "to augment its preponderance, in spite of the most peremptory injunctions of forbearance from home, and the "most scrupulous obedience of them in India. These "measures were considered an unwelcome though justifiable "exception to the general rule of our policy; only the oc-"currence of these exceptions had been unfortunately too "frequent." Before this despatch had left the India House, the Peshwa was a fugitive, and his kingdom a British province.

Holkar's Court.

1811 to 1817 On the death of Holkar in 1811, Toolsee bye, the favourite of his harem—young, beautiful, and fascinating in her address, with great talent for business, but violent and vindictive, resolved to conduct the government as regent. Ameer Khan exercised a preponderating influence in the state, by means of his lieutenant and his battalions when he was absent plundering Rajpootana. He was considered the head of the Patan faction. Tantia joge, a brahmin and a merchant, accepted the office of prime minister, and was the leader of the Mahratta party. The troops of the state were frequently mutinous for pay, when districts were assigned to the commandant, who fleeced the people without mercy, and sacked open villages, and cannonaded walled towns. There was no power in the state stronger than that of the military, and the government was in a state of anarchy. It was at this period, in the autumn of 1817, that the agents of Bajee Rao arrived in the camp to promote the confederacy he was forming against the Government of India.

SECTION III.

LORD HASTINGS'S ADMINISTRATION—WAR WITH THE PESHWA—WITH NAGPORE—WITH HOLKAR—THE PINDAREES.

A.D. 1817

Lord Hastings's new policy.

THE disorganisation of Central India had now reached its climax. The number of armed men who lived by violence fell little short of 100,000, and there was no native potentate with the power, or even the disposition, to restore peace and security. On the 8th July, Lord Hastings proceeded to the upper provinces to reduce this chaos to order. He felt that the only mode of dealing effectually with the Pindarees was to assail them in their haunts, and hunt them through the country till their organisation was completely broken up. He felt, likewise, that, to prevent the revival of such a confederacy, it was necessary to resettle Central India, to define the boundaries of each principality, and to prevent mutual encroachments by the establishment of our paramount power; in short, to restore and complete the system of policy devised by Lord Wellesley twelve years before. But the President of the Board of Control, the Court of Directors, and his own Council, were equally opposed to any such general federation under our supremacy. In his progress up the country, he therefore communicated to the Council his intention to take upon himself the sole responsibility of deviating from the views of the home authorities, and carrying out the general system of alliances he had determined to form.

Treaties of alliance with native princes.

The resolution was executed with promptitude and vigour. The chiefs of Malwa and Rajpootana were informed that the neutral policy had ceased, and that the Government was prepared to admit them to protective alliances. The intelligence was received with exultation throughout those provinces, and the Residency of Delhi was speedily crowded with the agents of nineteen of the princes of Central India. The first to enter into the circle of alliances was the venerable and virtuous Zalim Sing, the regent of Kotah. Then came the youthful and accomplished nabob of Bhopal, who eagerly embraced the alliance his father had refused. The raja of Boondee, ungenerously abandoned to the mercies of Holkar by Sir George Barlow, was now taken again under British protection. The raja of Joudpore, brought to the brink of ruin by the rapacity of the Mahrattas and Patans, eagerly accepted an offer which released him from all further anxiety. Even the proud house of Oodypore, which had never acknowledged the supremacy of Mogul or Mahratta, now submitted to the supremacy of the Company; and lastly, the raja of Jeypore, seeing every other prince bending the knee to the ruling power in India, came into the system of alliances. Within four months, Mr. Metcalfe, the Resident at Delhi, to whom the management of these negotiations was committed, concluded the treaties of alliance with all these princes upon the principle of "subordinate co-operation and ac- "knowledged supremacy."

A.D. 1817

Extent of military preparations.

The military operations on which Lord Hastings entered were upon a larger scale even than those of Lord Wellesley, and embraced the whole extent of country from the Kistna to the Ganges, and from Cawnpore to Guzerat. The armies of the three Presidencies were called out, and, including irregulars and the contingents of native princes, the entire force amounted to 116,000 infantry and cavalry, and 300 guns. The magnitude of this array was out of all proportion to the simple object of exterminating bands of marauders who never stood an attack; but Lord Hastings was not ignorant that the extinction of the Pindarees was opposed to the wishes and the interests of the chief native powers, and that the ever perfidious Peshwa was endeavouring to unite them in a confederacy against the Government; his preparations were, therefore, intended to provide for any adverse movements on their part. Happily, the powers of Governor-General and Commander-in-Chief were united in his person, and all the arrangements, political and military, were regulated by the same undivided authority. The veteran soldier of sixty-five took the field in person. The plan of the campaign provided that four divisions should advance from the Deccan, under the orders of Sir Thomas Hyslop, the Madras Commander-in-Chief, and four from the north-west, and converge on the camps of the Pindarees.

Treaty with Sindia.

In the north it was necessary to place a check on the dubious intentions of Sindia and Ameer Khan. Sindia had at once agreed to the proposal to co-operate in attacking the Pindarees, but rumours had been diffused through his army that Bajee Rao was about

to raise the national standard and assail the Company, and his troops were eager to join in the warfare; he himself also had accepted twenty-five lacs of rupees from the A.D.
Peshwa. On the 10th October, a note was delivered to 1817
him, stating that as he had excited the Pindarees to attack the Company's territories, and had subsequently afforded them an asylum on their return, the Governor-General considered the treaty of 1805 abrogated, and was about to enter into alliances with the chiefs of Malwa and Rajpootana, which that treaty had interdicted. He was now required to manifest his sincerity by placing his troops at the disposal of the British Government, and admitting a garrison into the fortresses of Hindia and Aseergurh. To quicken his decision, Lord Hastings took the field on the 16th October, and having crossed the Jumna marched directly towards Gwalior. By this manœuvre Sindia's communications with the Peshwa and the Pindarees, and even with the bulk of his own army then encamped in his southern districts, was cut off, and he was isolated in his capital with only 8,000 troops. He signed the treaty on the approach of Lord Hastings, and saved his kingdom from the fate which overtook the other Mahratta powers. While the camp lay in the vicinity of Gwalior it was desolated by a visitation of cholera, little, if at all, known previously in India, which reduced the strength of the force, including camp followers, to the extent of nearly 20,000 men. At the height of the disease, Lord Hastings gave instructions to his staff that if he himself should fall a victim to it, his body was to be silently buried in his tent, lest his death should discourage the troops, and embolden Sindia to attack the encampment in its prostrate condition.

Ameer Khan was at this juncture scarcely less important 1817
a chieftain than Sindia. His army consisted of fifty-two battalions with an efficient cavalry, and a hundred and fifty guns. It was as necessary to break up the Patan as the Pindaree force, and Lord Hastings did not hesitate to compass that object by offering to confirm him in the sovereignty of the districts he held belonging to the Holkar state, on the condition of his disbanding his force, and surrendering his guns at a valuation. He wavered at first, but on hearing of the extinction of the power of Bajee Rao and Appa Sahib, he accepted the proposal and became an acknowledged feudatory prince, with a territorial revenue of fifteen lacs a year.

Ameer Khan.

The advance of one division from Hindostan and two from the Deccan towards the head-quarters of the Pinda-

A.D. 1817 Outbreak of the Peshwa. rees, became the signal for the explosion of the plot which the Peshwa had organized among the Mahratta powers against the Company. He himself broke out on the 5th November, the raja of Nagpore on the 26th, and Holkar's army on the 16th December. After the signature of the treaty of the 5th June, he went on pilgrimage to Pundurpore, and soon after received a visit from Sir John Malcolm. The credulous general allowed himself to be so completely cajoled by the craft of the Peshwa into the belief of his cordial attachment to the British Government, that he advised him to increase the strength of his army. Under his advice, moreover, General Smith's army was allowed to quit Poona, and the cautionary fortresses were restored. Bajee Rao now redoubled his preparations for war. From his private hoards he advanced a crore to Gokla his commander, to increase his levies and to provision his forts. He likewise spared no pains to conciliate the southern jageerdars with whom he had always been at issue, and endeavoured to seduce the sepoys from their allegiance by large bribes, but without success. He even laid a plan to assassinate Mr. Elphinstone, but it was discountenanced by Gokla. He returned to Poona in the beginning of October, and it became daily more and more evident throughout the month that a conflict was inevitable. Mr. Elphinstone, therefore, fell back two miles to a more defensible position at Kirkee, and called up a European regiment from Bombay, but, even with this addition, the British force collected for his protection did not exceed 3,000, while the Mahratta army numbered 18,000.

The Peshwa was confident that Sindia and Ameer Khan had already taken the field in accordance with their en-

Battle of Kirkee. gagements, and that their example would be immediately followed by Holkar and the raja of Nagpore; and on the 5th November he plunged into hostilities, but it was on this very day that Sindia signed the treaty which neutralized his power. Towards noon he sent an arrogant message to Mr. Elphinstone, propounding the terms on which he would consent to remain on terms of friendship with the Government. While his messenger was on the way back, the plain was covered with masses of cavalry, and a stream of soldiers issued from every avenue of the city. Mr. Elphinstone wisely advised the commanding officer, Colonel Burr, to take the offensive; and that veteran, though labouring under a disease which soon after proved mortal, boldly charged into that vast host, and obtained a signal victory with the loss of only eighty-six men in killed and wounded. The battle of Kirkee was one of the most brilliant in the annals of British India, and inasmuch as it annihilated the kingdom of the Peshwas was also one of the most decisive. General Smith, hastened back to Poona; but, although the Peshwa had been reinforced by the troops of the southern jageerdars, he declined another engagement; and on the 17th November, leaving his camp standing, decamped southward with his army. Poona surrendered to the General, and thus ingloriously fell the power of the Peshwa one hundred years after it had been established by his great grandfather, Ballajee Wishwanath.

Appa Sahib, the regent of Nagpore, continued on friendly terms with the Resident for several months after the conclusion of the subsidiary alliance, but on the **Affairs at Nagpore.** A.D. 1817
1st February the imbecile raja Persajee was found strangled in his bed, and subsequent enquiries fixed the guilt on Appa Sahib, who immediately mounted the throne. From that time forward there was a marked change in his conduct, and he exhibited an anxiety to relieve himself from the state of dependence in which the alliance had placed him. He entered cordially into the hostile views of the Peshwa, and bestowed a dress of honour on the Pindaree leader, Cheetoo, who visited his court to claim his aid. The Peshwa, then flying before the British troops, conferred on him the title of Commander-in-Chief of the Mahratta empire, and on the 24th November, notwithstanding the remonstrance of the Resident, he proceeded to his camp to be invested with the insignia, and this was immediately followed by an attack on the Residency. It was situated on two hills called the Seetabuldee, the one lower than the other, in the immediate vicinity of the city. The force consisted of about 1,500 men, with four six-pounders. The raja's army mustered 18,000, of whom 4,000 were Arabs, the bravest soldiers in the Deccan, and thirty-six guns. Throughout the night the Mahratta artillery played on the hills, till at length a tumbril exploded, and in the confusion of the moment the Arabs charged up the smaller hill and captured the guns, and turned them upon the larger hill. The whole of the raja's army now began to close upon the encampment in all directions, and to

A.D. 1817 prepare for a general assault. The ammunition at the Residency was running short; one-fourth of the little force, which included fourteen officers, was either killed or wounded, and its total annihilation appeared inevitable, when the fortune of the day was changed by the gallantry of Captain Fitzgerald, commanding the three troops of Bengal cavalry. Contrary to the impassioned protest of his faint-hearted commander, he rushed upon the main body of the enemy's horse with irresistible fury, and captured two guns, which he turned upon them. The sight of this gallant exploit roused the enthusiasm of the jaded troops on the upper hill, who had been eighteen hours incessantly fighting, and officers and men plunged down the hill, fell upon the infantry, and chased it like a flock of sheep.

Deposition of Appa Sahib.

Reinforcements poured into Nagpore from all quarters, and Mr. Jenkins, the Resident, dictated his own terms to the raja. He was required to disband his troops, surrender his guns, and repair to the Residency, and acknowledge the forfeiture of his kingdom; these terms were accepted. Lord Hastings had determined to punish the atrocious perfidy of Appa Sahib by depriving him of the throne; but finding that Mr. Jenkins had engaged to restore his royal dignity, he agreed to uphold the engagement, and the raja resumed his authority on the
1818 8th January. But within a short time he offered the Peshwa, then flying before his pursuers, an asylum in his dominions, and prepared to join his camp himself. He was also detected in exciting the forest tribes to insurrection and impeding the surrender of his forts; and Lord Hastings ordered him to be deposed and sent to the holy city of Benares, with an allowance of two lacs a year; but he saved the Company's exchequer this burden by corrupting his guards on the line of march, and effecting his escape. The next of kin was placed on the throne, and the administration during his minority was placed in the hands of Mr. Jenkins, under whom the country enjoyed twelve years of unexampled prosperity.

Conflict with Holkar.

Lord Hastings had made the offer of a treaty to Toolsee bye, the regent of the Holkar state, and she had responded to it by sending a private communication to the Resident at Delhi, offering to place the young prince and the state under British protection. All the substantial power of the state was, however, in the hands of the military chiefs, and as soon as it was known that the Peshwa had risen in arms they resolved to march

down and join his standard. The regent and the ministers were suspected of a leaning to a British alliance, and the officers placed the chief minister under restraint, and, on the evening of the 20th December, conveyed the bye to the banks of the Sipree and struck off her head, and threw her body into the stream. The army, 20,000 strong, then marched down to join the Peshwa, and in their progress found the British force, which was in pursuit of the Pindaree leader Cheetoo, encamped at Mehidpore, where a decisive engagement was fought on the 21st December. A.D. 1817
The Mahratta army was posted with great skill on the banks of the Sipree, its left defended by an angle of the stream, and its right by a deep morass, and the front protected by a formidable battery of seventy guns. The main feature of the action was the rash step of crossing a difficult river by a single ferry in the face of strong entrenchments, and rushing forward to seize the guns which had silenced the light field pieces of the English army. The sepoys were mowed down by the enemy's cannon, but continued to advance with unshaken steadiness, and at length succeeded in capturing the batteries, though not without the loss of 778 in killed and wounded. The movements of the day were directed by Sir John Malcolm, who was less of a general than of a diplomatist; with better strategy the same result might have been obtained with less slaughter. Holkar's entire camp, with all his guns and military stores, fell to the victors, and the power of the state was irrecoverably broken. A treaty was soon after concluded, and cessions of territory were made to the Company, to Zalim Sing of Kotah, to Ameer Khan, and to his lieutenant, which reduced the kingdom to two-thirds of its former dimensions.

Operations against the Pindarees.

During the rainy season of 1817 the Pindarees were encamped to the number of 23,000 under the three leaders Cheetoo, Kureem Khan, and Wassil Mahomed. They were not ignorant of the measures in progress to extirpate them, and they implored aid of the Mahratta princes, but they had enough to do to protect themselves, and the different bodies of the Pindarees were obliged to disperse as the British detachments advanced upon them. Sindia, indeed, invited Kureem Khan and Wassil Mahomed to Gwalior, but Lord Hastings immediately took up a position which prevented their advance. They then turned off to the west, where they were intercepted by General Donkin, who captured Kureem Khan's elephants, kettle-drums, standards, and family. The two leaders burnt their tents and fled southward with about 4,000 of their best horsemen, and their followers were cut up by the British troops and the exasperated villagers whom they had subjected to plunder. The chiefs were so hotly pursued that they were constrained at length to surrender at discretion, and one of them was settled on a small estate in the province of Ghazepore; the other was placed under surveillance, and put a period to his life by poison. The most renowned of the leaders, Cheetoo, was pursued by Sir John Malcolm; his bivouac was repeatedly beaten up, and he wandered about for a twelvemonth with a handful of followers who gradually deserted him, and being at last separated by hunger from his son and his last companion, plunged into a jungle infested with tigers. After a diligent search his horse was discovered grazing saddled and bridled, and not far off the mangled remains of this renowned freebooter who had recently ridden forth at the head of 20,000 men.

Result of the campaign.

These military and political operations are equally remarkable for the rapidity with which they were executed and for the completeness of their result. In the middle of October 1817, the Mahrattas, Pindarees,
A.D. and Patans, presented an array of more than 150,000 horse
1817 and foot, and 500 cannon, prepared to try conclusions with the British Government. In the course of four months this formidable armament was utterly broken up. The power of Sindia was paralysed; the army of Holkar existed only in name; the Peshwa was a fugitive; the
1818 Patan force of Ameer Khan was disbanded, and the Pindarees had disappeared; the Mahratta commonwealth was irretrievably dissolved, and every military organisation within the Sutlej was extinguished, with the exception of that of Sindia which ceased to be formidable. The effect of the campaign, moreover, was to subjugate not only the native armies but the native mind, and to convince both princes and people that the sceptre of India was now definitely transferred to a foreign power. To the chiefs who lost their independence, and with it that feeling of dignity which was sometimes the parent of royal virtues, the change was a calamity, but to the community at large it was an unquestionable blessing. General tranquillity took the place of universal violence under the guarantee of a power willing and able to maintain it. A feeling of substantial security was diffused through Central India, and its

inhabitants sought the means of subsistence and distinction by cultivating the arts of peace and not by war and rapine. The settlement of India in 1818 was, moreover, built on so sound and solid a foundation that it has required fewer modifications than so great a political structure might have been expected to need. Having thus extinguished all opposition, Lord Hastings proclaimed the universal sovereignty of the Company throughout the continent, and declared that the Indus was to all intents and purposes the boundary of their dominion.

A.D. 1817

Battle of Korygaum.

Bajee Rao began his retreat southward on the 28th November, and on passing Satara caused the raja and his family, the descendants of Sevajee, to be brought into his camp. Finding himself closely pursued by General Smith, he turned northward towards Poona. Colonel Burr, the commandant, immediately called down to his support the detachment left at Seroor, under Captain Stanton, consisting of one battalion of infantry and 300 irregular horse. He commenced his march at eight in the evening, and reached the village of Korygaum, sixteen miles from Poona, at ten the next morning, when, to his surprise, he perceived the whole army of the Peshwa, 25,000 strong, encamped on the opposite bank of the river. The Mahratta troops were immediately sent across against this handful of soldiers exhausted by a fatiguing march through the night, and destitute both of provisions and water, but the officers and men met the shock with invincible resolution. The engagement was kept up throughout the day, and every inch of ground in the village was disputed with desperate valour, but it ended in the discomfiture and retreat of the Mahrattas. The most remarkable feature of this brilliant engagement lay in the fact that the sepoys were without any European support except twenty-four artillery men, of whom twenty were killed and wounded. Of eight officers engaged, three were wounded and two killed; the total loss amounted to 187.

Jan. 1 1818

Pursuit and surrender of the Peshwa.

On leaving Korygaum the Peshwa again marched southward, always keeping ahead of his pursuers, but he was suddenly overtaken at Ashtee, and, after reproaching his general Gokla for allowing him to be surprised, quitted his palankeen and mounted his horse and fled, leaving the general to cover his retreat. Stung with the reproaches of his master, and determined not to survive the day, he placed himself at the head of

300 horse and rushed on the British cavalry, and, after receiving three pistol shots and three sabre cuts, expired on the field of honour, the last and one of the noblest of the great Mahratta commanders. The raja of Satara was rescued at Ashtee. The Peshwa, hunted out of the Deccan, moved again to the north, crossed the Taptee, and advanced to the Nerbudda, but the fords were guarded and the different divisions of the army were closing upon him, when, seeing no chance of escape, he appealed to the weakness of Sir John Malcolm, calling him "his oldest

A.D. 1818 "and best friend." Strange to say, he was admitted to an interview, when he so thoroughly cajoled him by his flatteries, that at a time when his fortunes were desperate and he must have surrendered at discretion, the imprudent general engaged to allow him eight lacs a year, and made other concessions equally unwise and preposterous. Lord Hastings, who had destined him an allowance of only two lacs, was not a little mortified at the prodigality of these terms, but felt himself bound in honour to ratify them. A proclamation had been previously issued announcing that the Peshwa and his family were for ever excluded from the throne. A small portion of the territory, yielding about fifteen lacs of rupees a year, was then erected into a separate principality and bestowed on the descendant of Sevajee, and the remainder was incorporated in the Company's territories. The Peshwa was conducted to Bithoor, near Cawnpore, where he lived long enough to receive two crores and a half of rupees from the treasury in Calcutta.

1818 The country which had been the scene of warfare, was studded with forts which held out for some time after the submission of the princes. They were garrisoned in general by Arab mercenaries, whose services were valued not only for their courage and fidelity, but as a counterpoise to the native soldiery, among whom a spirit of insubordination was traditionary. The capture of the fort of Talneir was marked by the untoward circumstance of the massacre of 300 of the garrison in hot blood, owing to a misunderstanding, and by the unjust execution of the commandant, which tarnished the laurels of Sir Thomas Hislop. At length the only fort which had

Capture of forts.

1819 not submitted was Aseergurh, for the surrender of which Sindia had given an official order on the commandant, but he had private orders not to deliver it, and it was not captured till a battery of more than sixty guns had played on it for a fortnight.

SECTION IV.

LORD HASTINGS'S ADMINISTRATION—HOME PROCEEDINGS—EDUCATION—THE PRESS—PALMER AND CO.

A.D. 1819

Home proceedings.

MR. CANNING moved the usual vote of thanks to Lord Hastings and to the army in the House of Commons; but he qualified his eulogy by stating that the House and the country were in the habit of appreciating the triumphs of our armies in India with great jealousy; that, almost uniformly successful as our military operations had been in that part of the world, they had almost as uniformly been considered questionable in point of justice; that the termination of a war in India, however glorious, was seldom contemplated with unmixed satisfaction, and that the increase of our territories was ascribed by sober reflection and impartial philosophy to a spirit of systematic encroachment and ambition. These considerations, he said, were not necessarily applicable to the Mahratta and Pindaree war, but the House was to understand that the vote was intended merely as a tribute to the military conduct of the campaign, and not in any sense as a sanction of the policy of the war. In the same captious spirit the Court of Directors, while duly appreciating "the "foresight, promptitude, and vigour with which Lord "Hastings had dispersed the gathering elements of a "hostile conspiracy," recorded their deep regret that any circumstances should have led to an increase of territory. Lord Hastings had lost caste at the India House, and its official communications to him were scarcely less acrimonious than those which had been addressed to Clive, to Warren Hastings, and to Lord Wellesley. The despatch written on receiving information of the brilliant termination of the campaign was loaded with petulant and frivolous animadversions, and "not mitigated," as Lord Hastings observed, "by the slightest indication of satis-"faction at the fortunate issue of the military exertions." They censured him for disregarding their orders regarding the reduction of the army, though they had undoubted evidence that, under existing circumstances, on the eve of a great and inevitable conflict, to have carried them out would have been fatal to the interests of the empire. In anticipation of extensive military operations he had remodelled the Quarter-master-General's department, and he was censured by the Court for not having previously obtained their sanction, while they pressed on him the appointment of one of their own nominees to the post, of whom Lord Hastings remarked in his correspondence, that it would be difficult to find in the whole army a field officer more signally unfit for the post. In the same spirit of antagonism, the honours so richly earned by the heroes of Kirkee, and Seetabuldee, and Korygaum, were withheld from them.

Encouragement of education.

The pacification and final settlement of India would have been a sufficient distinction for any administration, but Lord Hastings established a higher claim to public gratitude, by the encouragement which he was the first to give to the intellectual improvement of the natives. The India House had hitherto acted upon the principle that any attempt to enlighten the people would create political aspirations which might endanger their power, and lead to its subversion. Lord Hastings repudiated this policy, and in one of his public addresses stated that "it would be treason against British "sentiment to imagine that it ever could be the principle "of this Government to perpetuate ignorance in order to "secure paltry and dishonest advantages over the blindness "of the multitude." These enlightened views gave an immediate and powerful impulse to the cause of education. Lady Hastings had already set an example by establishing a school at Barrackpore Park, and compiling treatises for the scholars. Schools also sprang up in the districts around Calcutta through the agency of the missionaries, and were fostered by a liberal donation from Government. Some of the most wealthy and influential native gentlemen in the metropolis raised large subscriptions, and established the Hindoo College for the education of their children and relatives in the English language and European science. All the efforts which have since been made with constantly increasing vigour, to impart knowledge to the native community, date from this period.

A.D. 1818

Lord Hastings and the Press.

Emboldened by this liberal policy and the success of Lord Hastings, the Serampore Missionaries, on the 31st May 1818, issued the first native newspaper, entitled the "Sumachar Durpun," or Mirror of Intelligence. This attempt to rouse the native mind from its torpidity, by the stimulus of a public journal, created great alarm among the leading men in the Government, but Lord

Hastings afforded every encouragement to it; he manifested the same spirit of liberality towards the English Press, and, notwithstanding the violent opposition of the members of his Council, removed the censorship which had been imposed by Lord Wellesley during the anarchy of war. In deference, however, to the despotic sensibilities of the governing class, he imposed severe restrictions on the editors regarding the subjects and the personages which were to be exempted from remark, but the exceptions soon fell into abeyance. In vindication of his policy, he A.D.
stated, in reply to an address from Madras, "that he was 1818
"in the habit of considering the freedom of publication "as the natural right of his fellow subjects, to be narrowed "only by special and urgent cause assigned;" and, further, that "it was salutary for supreme authority, even when its "intentions were most pure, to look to the control of "public opinion." This heterodox doctrine gave mortal offence at the India House, and a despatch was immediately drafted, reprobating the abolition of the censorship, and directing that it should be immediately reimposed, but the despatch was suppressed by Mr. Canning.

In the year 1816 the peaceful province of Orissa became 1816
the scene of disturbances. On the acquisition of the country in 1803, a swarm of Bengalee baboos flocked into it, and obtained possession of every official post of influence, and by their knowledge of the mysteries of civil and fiscal legislation were enabled to take advantage of the simplicity of the people, and to deprive them of their lands. The province was also over-assessed, the zemindars were improvident, and half the estates were brought to the hammer, and bought up by the Bengalee officials in the courts, often at a nominal price. To add to the wretchedness of the province, the salt monopoly was introduced, and the cost of this necessary of life was increased sixfold in a country where the sea furnished it spontaneously. Under this accumulation of misery, the people sold all they possessed, and then their wives and children, and finally took to the jungle. The country being thus ripe for revolt, one Jugbundoo, the hereditary commander of the old Hindoo dynasty, raised the standard of rebellion and collected about 3,000 men, with whom he plundered the civil station of Khoorda, and repulsed two detachments of sepoys. This success augmented his force, and he took possession of the town of Pooree, and burnt down the European residences, but the

Disturbances at Cuttack.

Collector escaped with his treasury to Cuttack. The triumph of the insurgents was, however, short, and they were dispersed by the troops which poured into the province. The people were assured that their grievances would be redressed if they were peaceably represented to Government, and they at once submitted to its authority. A special Commissioner was appointed to the charge of the province, the most notorious of the rapacious officials were punished, and the assessment was reduced by 40 per cent. Its tranquillity has never since been interrupted, and another proof has been afforded that, with a moderate assessment and congenial institutions, and an equitable and speedy administration of justice, few countries are more easy to govern than India, even under the sceptre of foreigners.

A.D. 1822 — Financial and territorial increase.

The financial results of Lord Hastings's administration were auspicious. Notwithstanding the war of eighteen months' duration in the mountains of Nepaul, and the employment in the field of eight armies during the Pindaree and Mahratta campaign, the treasury was at no period in so prosperous a condition as at the close of his government. The state bonds, which were at a discount of 12 per cent. on his arrival, were at 14 per cent. premium at his departure. The debt had indeed increased four crores and a half, but the cash balances in the various treasuries exceeded by five crores the amount when he landed. The permanent revenue had increased by six crores, and the permanent expenditure by four, leaving a clear surplus of two crores of rupees; the year 1822 may therefore be considered the palmy period of Indian finance. Lord Hastings entered upon the Pindaree campaign with the confident expectation that the pacification of the continent would be effected without adding a foot to the Company's territories, but "the irre-"pressible tendency of our Indian power to enlarge its "boundary," which Mr. Canning had lamented, was fatal to this hope. The unprovoked aggression and complete overthrow of the Mahratta powers placed their territories at his disposal. He restored the larger portion of their dominions to Holkar and to the raja of Nagpore, but he considered that the annexation of the whole of Bajee Rao's kingdom—the territory of Satara excepted—was forced on him "by the imperious necessity of guarding against the "speedy renewal of a treachery so rooted in its nature as "to admit of no other prevention." It was annexed to the Bombay Presidency, and the management of it entrusted to one of the ablest of the Company's statesmen, Mr. Mount Stuart Elphinstone. The utter indifference manifested by Parliament to Indian affairs throughout Lord Hastings's administration afforded a singular contrast to the active and energetic movements of the Government in India. Mr. Dundas had introduced the practice of an annual budget, that Parliament might be reminded, at least once a year, of the existence of the Indian empire. But so utterly lukewarm had Parliament become to its affairs, that Mr. Canning, the President of the Board, stated to the House that "the Indian budget was always considered a dull "and disagreeable subject, and the practice of making "budget speeches had therefore been discontinued. The "time and attention of the House was quite as much occu-"pied without throwing away a day in the discussion of a "subject which was sure to drive gentlemen away from it." During the five years of his tenure of office, the only occasion on which he touched on the subject of India in the House, except when moving thanks to Lord Hastings, was in reference to a bill for legalizing Scotch marriages there. Yet it was in this period of neglect that the great revolution in Lord Hastings's administration was consummated, that twenty-eight actions were fought, and a hundred and twenty forts captured, and the sovereignty of Great Britain proclaimed throughout the continent of India.

A.D. 1816 to 1821

One of the last acts of Lord Hastings had reference to Hyderabad. Meer Alum, who had managed the affairs of the state with consummate talent for thirty years, died in 1808, when, after an irritating discussion with Lord Minto, Moneer-ool-moolk, whom the Resident described as both a coward and a fool, was appointed minister, while all the substantial power in the state was given to Chundoo Lall, a Hindoo of great ability, experience and energy. The Court of Directors interdicted all interference with the internal administration of Hyderabad, and directed the Resident to confine his attention to the reform of the contingent of 6,000 foot and 9,000 horse, which the Nizam was obliged by the treaty of 1800 to furnish in time of war. These levies, which were a mere rabble, were converted by the strenuous exertions of the Resident into an efficient force, disciplined and commanded by officers drawn from the Company's army, with which it was soon able to vie in military spirit and qualifications. As the force was entirely at the disposal of Chundoo Lall,

Hyderabad and Chundoo Lall.

he was not disposed to check its profuse expenditure. It was not only over-officered, but the officers were overpaid. It became a source of valuable patronage to the Resident, and, however beneficial in time of war, was, in a season of peace, little more than a magnificent job.

A.D. 1809 to 1820

Administration of Chundoo Lall.

The administration of Chundoo Lall was, with some intervals of repose, the scourge of the country for thirty-five years. It was upheld by British power, but not controlled by British honesty; nothing flourished but corruption; judicial decrees could be obtained only for money; the land was farmed out to the highest bidder, and the farmer had the power of life and death; the utmost farthing was wrung from the wretched peasant, hundreds of villages were deserted, and, in the absence of cultivation, food rose to famine prices. The wealth thus obtained was expended by Chundoo Lall in fortifying his position. He erected a noble palace for the Resident and fitted it up with the most costly furniture from Bond street; he bribed the courtiers, and subsidized the zenana, and secured the favour of the Nizam by indulging his royal passion for hoarding. Mr. Metcalfe was appointed Resident in November 1820, and, on surveying the state of the country, resolved on a vigorous reform. Some of his political assistants, and some of the officers of the contingent were placed in charge of districts; a lenient assessment was made, and the current of oppression checked. Security was at once established; villages were repeopled, cultivation was resumed, and rents were collected without a military force.

Palmer and Co.

Mr. Metcalfe had not, however, been long at Hyderabad without perceiving that every prospect of improvement was endangered by the transactions of Palmer and Co. with the state. Mr. William Palmer had established a banking-house at Hyderabad in 1814, and soon after became connected with Chundoo Lall, and began to make advances to the Nizam's treasury. The express sanction of the Government of India to such transactions was required by Act of Parliament; and, with the consent of the Council, and in accordance with the opinion of the Advocate-General, Lord Hastings gave his assent to them, and loans were accordingly made from time to time, but at twenty-five per cent. interest. In 1820, the firm was joined by Sir W. Rumbold, who had married a ward of Lord Hastings, whom he regarded with paternal fondness. In an evil hour, he wrote to Sir William, "The partners "speculate that your being one of the firm will interest me "in the welfare of the house. It is a fair and honest con- "clusion. The amount of advantage which the countenance "of Government may bestow must be uncertain, as I "apprehend it would flow principally from the opinion the "natives would entertain of the respect likely to be paid "by their own Government to an establishment known to "stand well with the supreme Government." This communication was widely circulated by Sir William, and placed the house on a firm footing at Hyderabad, and there was a constant stream of loans, at exorbitant interest, to the Nizam, and fresh assignments of territory as security for them.

A.D. 1820

Mr. Metcalfe's representations.

1821

Mr. Metcalfe could not fail to observe that Palmer and Co. were becoming a dangerous power in the state, that the public revenues were passing into their hands, and that the government of the Nizam was prostrate before them. He ventured at length to communicate his views on the subject to Lord Hastings, but found that his mind had been prepossessed, and his feelings worked on by the correspondence of the Rumbold family; and his representations were resented. Chundoo Lall had been put up by the firm to solicit the sanction of the Governor-General in Council to a loan of sixty lacs, for the professed object of paying up the public establishments, of repaying debts due to native brokers, and making advances to the ryots. Lord Hastings considered these to be legitimate objects, and gave his casting vote to the proposal. But Mr. Metcalfe learnt on his arrival that only a fraction of this loan had found its way to the Nizam's treasury; that the sum of eight lacs was a bonus to the members of the firm, and that the remainder consisted of sums advanced, or said to have been advanced, to the Nizam's minister without the consent of the Government in Calcutta, whose sanction was thus surreptitiously obtained to these loans. This transaction was too gross to admit of any palliation, and it was severely censured both by Lord Hastings and the members of Council. By compound interest at twenty-five per cent., Palmer and Co. swelled their demand on the Nizam to a crore of rupees, and the Government, anxious to put a peremptory stop to these transactions, determined that the whole debt should be at once discharged—with the exception of the clandestine bonus. By the disgraceful treaty of 1768, the Madras Government had engaged to pay the Nizam an annual tribute of seven lacs

A.D. 1822

for the Northern Sircars, and the payment had been punctually made for half a century. It was now capitalized, and the Nizam was released from the grasp of the firm, which became insolvent within twelve months.

Thanks of the India House.

The antipathy of the Court of Directors which was repeatedly manifested towards Lord Hastings by their captious criticisms, their reluctant praise, and their eager censure, became more violent after he had given freedom to the press, and particularly so after Sir W. Rumbold had joined the Hyderabad firm, and they issued peremptory orders to revoke the licence which Government had given to the firm. Their despatch implied a mistrust of his motives in that transaction, and exhibited a determination to identify him with all their obnoxious proceedings. Indignant at these insinuations, and at the offensive tone of their despatches he sent in his resignation, on the ground that he had lost their confidence. They assured him that he was entirely mistaken, and voted him their thanks for "the unremitting "zeal and eminent ability with which, during a period of "nine years, he had administered the government of British "India with such high credit to himself and advantage to "the interests of the Company." The Proprietors eagerly concurred in this opinion, and desired the Directors to convey to him "the expression of their admiration, gratitude, and "applause." He embarked for England on the 1st of January, 1823.

Estimate of his administration.

In the grand work which Lord Hastings accomplished of consolidating the British empire, and, as the natives expressed it, "bringing all India under one "umbrella," he exhibited talent of the highest order, though he may not stand on the same level of political genius with Warren Hastings or Lord Wellesley. His administration was made grateful to the inhabitants of the Mahomedan capital of India by restoring the canal which had been dry for sixty years, and giving them the blessing of pure water without a water cess. The improvement of Calcutta, devised by Lord Wellesley but which he was unable to complete in the last year of his government, was accomplished by Lord Hastings. The ventilation and the health of the town were promoted by opening a street through the centre sixty feet wide, and laying out squares with reservoirs of water; while the foreshore of the river, which was a disgraceful cesspool, was adorned with a noble embankment worthy of the "city of palaces."

No Governor-General ever laboured more assiduously in the performance of his duty. Though approaching the age of seventy, he was at his desk at four in the morning; and in the fervid climate of Bengal, which is now considered insupportable since the means of escaping from it have been multiplied, he worked for seven years at the rate of seven and eight hours a day without a hill station to resort to, or even a sea-going steamer at his command.

A.D. 1824

Debate at the India House.

Within two years of his return to Europe, Mr. Douglas Kinnaird brought forward a proposal in the Court of Proprietors to make him a pecuniary grant befitting the greatness of his services. It served to disclose the strong current of rancour which underlay the crust of official compliment embodied in the tribute of "admiration, gratitude, and applause," which that Court had recently voted. The motion was met by an amendment, calling for all the papers connected with the transactions at Hyderabad. They occupied a thousand foolscap pages, and gave rise to a debate which, having all the relish of personality, was prolonged for six days, at the end of which time, Mr. Astell, the chairman of the Court of Directors, moved as an amendment to the original motion that, "while admitting that there was no ground "for imputing corrupt motives to the late Governor-"General, the Court of Proprietors records its approbation "of all the despatches sent out by the Court of Directors." These despatches, four in number, charged Lord Hastings, among other misdemeanours, with having lent the Company's credit to the transactions at Hyderabad for the sole benefit of Messrs. Palmer and Co., with proceedings which were without a parallel in the history of the East India Company, and with assuming to elude all check and control. The approbation of these despatches was, necessarily, the severest condemnation which could be passed on him, but the vote was carried by a majority of 212. Thus did the East India Company dismiss the man who had raised them to the pinnacle of greatness with the verdict that he was simply "not guilty of having acted "from corrupt motives." But the Company, princely beyond all other rulers in their munificence, were not superior to the influence of vulgar prejudices, and they now added another name to the roll of illustrious men—Clive, and Warren Hastings, and Lord Wellesley—whom they rewarded with ingratitude. Lord Hastings died at Malta on the 24th August, 1827, and in the succeeding year the India House endeavoured to make some atonement for the vote of censure, and placed 20,000*l.* at the disposal of his family.

CHAPTER XI.

SECTION I.

LORD AMHERST—BURMESE WAR—BHURTPORE—BARRACKPORE MUTINY.

ON the receipt of Lord Hastings's resignation, the post of Governor-General was accepted by Mr. Canning, the late President of the Board of Control, but, on the eve of embarkation, the death of Lord Londonderry led to his appointment as foreign Secretary of State. Two candidates then appeared for this splendid office; Lord William Bentinck, who had been unjustly removed from Madras by the Court of Directors in the height of the Vellore panic, and who was pre-eminently qualified for it; and Lord Amherst, whose claim rested on his embassy to Pekin, and the exemplary fortitude with which he had borne the arrogance of the Court. The preference was given to him, and he landed at Calcutta on the 1st August. During the interregnum, the government devolved on Mr. John Adam, the senior member of Council, a meritorious officer of considerable ability and experience, but totally disqualified for the highest post in the empire by the strength of his local partialities and prejudices. His brief administration of seven months is now remembered only by his persecution of the press. Mr. Buckingham had come out to Calcutta in 1818, and established the "Calcutta Journal," the ablest newspaper which had till then appeared in India. He availed himself of the freedom granted to the press by Lord Hastings, and commented on public measures with a degree of freedom which was considered politically dangerous. But the great offence of the journal consisted in the poignancy with which a little knot of wits in the service ridiculed the weaknesses

Mr. Canning Governor-General.

A.D. 1823 Lord Amherst Governor-General.

Mr. Adam.

and follies of some of the leading members of the Government. They had been nursed in the lap of despotism, and resented the sarcasms of the press. Mr. Adam had systematically opposed Lord Hastings's liberality to the press, and only waited for his departure to reverse it. Soon after taking office, therefore, he passed a stringent regulation which completely extinguished all freedom; and as Mr. Buckingham, instead of bending to the storm, which was too violent to last, continued to write with unmitigated severity, he was banished from the country and ruined.

A.D. 1823

Lord Amherst had no sooner assumed the government than he found himself involved in hostile discussions with the Burmese, which, in the course of five months, resulted in a declaration of war. The ultra-Gangetic kingdom of Burmah lies to the east of Bengal, from which it is separated by hills and forests, inhabited by various tribes of barbarians. Four years after the battle of Plassy, Alompra, a man of obscure birth, but cast in the same mould as Hyder Ali and Runjeet Sing, who had began his career with a hundred followers, established a new dynasty at Ava. Aggression and conquest became as usual the element of this new power. The province of Tenasserim was wrested from the Siamese, and the principality of Arracan, which was separated from the Company's territories only by the Teek Naaf, was annexed. More than 30,000 of its inhabitants were driven by the oppression of the Burmese officials to take refuge in the neighbouring districts of Chittagong, where they were settled on waste lands. The Burmese anthorities repeatedly demanded their extradition, but the Governor-General steadily refused to deliver them up to a Government proverbial for its cruelty. The king of Ava, exasperated by our firmness, at length sent a rescript to Lord Hastings, demanding the surrender of the whole of eastern Bengal. "Those districts," he said, "do not belong "to India—they are ours; if you continue to retain them, "we will come and destroy your country." Lord Hastings treated the letter as a forgery, and enclosed it to the king. The course of aggression was continued without cessation, and in 1822, Maha Bundoola, the national hero, reduced the kingdom of Assam, which abutted on the Company's district of Rungpore, and then the principality of Muneepore, at no great distance from our eastern frontier. The dynasty of Alompra had thus, in sixty years, established

Rise of the Burmese.

1761

1822

its authority over territories 800 miles in extent, stretching from the confines of Bengal to those of China. The uniform success of every enterprise had filled the Burmese court with an overweening conceit of its strength, and the evident indisposition of the English Government to engage in war with them inspired the whole nation with a desire to try conclusions with it in the field.

A.D. 1823

Origin of the war.

The immediate cause of the war was an arrogant demand made by the Burmese governor of Arracan for the surrender of the little island of Shahpooree, lying at the estuary of the Teek Naaf, on which a small guard had been posted. The Governor-General proposed a joint commission to investigate the question of right, to which the Burmese replied by sending 1,000 men who put a portion of the feeble detachment to the sword, and hoisted the Burmese flag. Lord Amherst immediately sent a force to dislodge them, and addressed a letter to the king stating that, however desirous he might be of remaining at peace, he must resort to force if such insults were repeated. The court of Ava was now confirmed in the conviction that the English dreaded an encounter with their troops, and Maha Bundoola was despatched with a large army to Arracan, with orders to expel them from Bengal, and to send the Governor-General to Ava bound in the golden fetters which he took with him. Lord Amherst, finding that every effort to maintain peace only served to increase the arrogance of the Burmese, issued a declaration of war in February.

1824

Arrangements of the campaign.

The Burmese were the most contemptible enemy with whom the British arms had come in contact. Their army was a wretched half-armed rabble, without either valour or discipline. Their weapons were simply swords and pikes of an inferior description, with a few muskets, and their chief defence lay in the admirable skill and rapidity with which they were able to construct stockades. At the commencement of the war the Government in Calcutta was profoundly ignorant of the resources, the military force, or even the topography of Burmah, and for the planning of the campaign depended on the advice of Captain Canning, who had acquired some knowledge of the country. He represented that the occupation of Rangoon, the great port of the Irrawaddy, would paralyze the Burmese authorities, and that provisions and draft cattle, as well as the means of building a flotilla to navigate the rivers, might be obtained in abundance. The expedition was assembled in the spacious harbour of Port Cornwallis, in the largest of the Andaman islands, and consisted of about 11,000 troops, European and native, under the command of Sir Archibald Campbell, who had served with distinction under the Duke in Spain. The fleet of transports was convoyed by three vessels of war, and by the *Diana*, a little steamer recently built in Calcutta, the first ever floated in eastern waters. The campaign opened inauspiciously. The defence of the frontier at Chittagong had been left to a small and inadequate force, and a weak detachment of 300 native infantry, under Captain Noton, with some local levies, held a post on the extreme boundary, a hundred miles from the nearest support. Maha Bundoola came down upon this little band with an army estimated at more than 10,000 men. The levies fled at the first onset, the sepoys maintained the conflict gallantly for three days with little food or rest, and were then constrained to retreat, and of the officers five were killed and three wounded.

A.D. 1824

The army at Rangoon.

The expedition arrived off Rangoon on the 12th of May, to the inexpressible surprise of the Burmese, who had never dreamt that the English, whom Bundoola had been sent to expel from Bengal, would venture to attack them in their own territories. The only defence of the town consisted of a teak stockade, with a battery of indifferent guns, which was silenced by the first broadside from the *Liffey*. The troops landed without opposition, but found the town deserted. The Governor had ordered the whole population, men, women, and children, to retire into the jungles with their provisions and cattle, and the order was implicitly obeyed. The British encampment was isolated; all local supplies were cut off, all hope of advancing to the capital, either by land or water, was extinguished, and Sir Archibald was obliged to confine his attention to the shelter of the troops during the rains. Within a week after the occupation of the town, they set in with extreme violence, the country around became a swamp, and malaria brought disease and death into the camp. The want of wholesome food rendered the condition of the troops still more deplorable. There was no lack of cattle around the town, which would have amply supplied their wants, but the Government in Calcutta had forbidden the commander to touch them, in deference to the Boodhist prejudices of the Burmese, and the European soldiers were condemned to starvation, that the cows might live. The army became dependent on supplies from Calcutta, then proverbial for the dishonesty of its contractors; the meat was putrescent, and the maggoty biscuits crumbled under the touch. The troops were left in this state of destitution for five months, owing to the culpable neglect of the commissariat department; and it was only through the prompt and indefatigable exertions of Sir Thomas Munro, the governor of Madras, that the army was preserved from annihilation; but the unhealthiness of the climate and the want of wholesome nourishment filled the hospitals, and of a body of 11,000 scarcely 3,000 remained fit for duty.

A.D. 1825

Conquest of Assam and Aracan.

At the beginning of 1825, General Richards occupied the province of Assam without resistance. Under the advice of the Commander-in-Chief, two expeditions were also organized to enter Burmah by land, the one from the north through Cachar and Muneepore; the other, through Arracan, but both of them proved abortive. The Cachar force under Colonel Shuldham, 7,000 strong, was enabled to advance by the road which the pioneers had opened with infinite labour to a position within ninety miles of Muneepore, but the country beyond it consisted of an unbroken succession of abrupt hills clothed to the summit with impenetrable forests, and dales rendered impassable by quagmires. The rains set in early, and as it was deemed impossible to transport the stores and artillery, and the appliances of civilized warfare through these impediments, the expedition was given up. The Arracan force was still more unfortunate. The commander, Colonel Morrison, was a king's officer of good repute, but he had a contempt for the officers of the Company's service who were acquainted with the nature of the country, and the peculiarities of Indian warfare, and rejected their advice. The army was three months marching 250 miles along the coast, and did not reach the capital of Arracan till it was too late to make any further advance. One-fourth of the force likewise fell victims to the climate, and two-thirds of the remainder were in hospitals. As an organized body, indeed, the army had ceased to exist; and on one occasion, when a wing of a regiment was ordered on parade, only one soldier appeared to answer to his name.

Second campaign.

1824

The king of Ava at length determined to collect the strength of his kingdom for one vigorous effort to expel the invaders, and Maha Bundoola was sent down with 60,000 men to Rangoon, and arrived in front of the British encampment on the 1st December. Within

a few hours, it was enveloped by stockades, which appeared to spring up one after another in rapid succession as if by the wand of an enchanter. But the Burmese, though skilful in fortifying their position, were unable to stand the shock of the British battalions, and, after sustaining two defeats, retired to Donabew, forty miles higher up the river. Sir Archibald Campbell, after having been idly encamped for nine months at Rangoon, and lost two months of the second season of operations, at length moved up towards
A.D.
the capital on the 13th February, in two columns, the one 1825
by land under his personal command; the other by the river under Brigadier Cotton. On coming abreast of Donabew, the Brigadier found that all the resources of the Burmese engineers had been employed in strengthening the fortifications, which stretched a mile along the bank, and were garrisoned by 12,000 men and 150 guns, such as they were. In his assault on the place, he was vigorously repulsed, and, as he had unwisely left one of his regiments in the rear, pronounced his force unequal to the capture of the place. Sir Archibald, who was considerably in advance, felt it necessary to retrace his steps to reinforce Brigadier Cotton, and another month was thus sacrificed. On the 1st April, a shower of shells and rockets was poured down
on the fortified town of Donabew, and the next morning 1825
the whole of the Burmese army was observed to be in full retreat. On the preceding night Bundoola had been killed by the bursting of a shell, and with him expired the courage and spirit of the troops. No further resistance was offered to the expedition, and Prome was occupied without firing a shot; but as the rains were approaching, the campaign, which had lasted only ten weeks, during which the army had advanced 150 miles, was brought to a termination.

Negotiations for peace.

The general proposed to stop at Prome and act on the defensive, though the extraordinary expenses of the war amounted to a lac of rupees a day; but Lord Amherst insisted on an immediate march to the capital as soon as the season permitted. At the same time, he urged the general to welcome any disposition the Burmese might evince for peace, and, the more effectually to secure it, associated the naval commander and Mr. Robertson, a Bengal civilian, in a commission with him, with Mr. Ross Mangles as secretary. The king, on being informed that the general was authorised to treat, sent envoys to ascertain the terms, who were informed that their master would be required to abstain from all inter-

A.D. 1825 ference with Cachar or Assam, to recognise the independence of Munipore, to cede the provinces of Arracan and Tenasserim, to liberate all his prisoners, and pay two crores as a war indemnity. These terms the king rejected with great indignation, and a Burmese army of 40,000 men was sent down to Prome, but it was signally defeated and closely pursued. The negotiations were then resumed by the Burmese envoys, who waived every objection to the cession of territory, but withstood the pecuniary payment, on the score of poverty, with such importunity that the Commissioners were induced to curtail it by one half, and the treaty was signed on this basis on the 3rd January, and the ratification of it promised on the 18th, but it never came. The intermediate period had been employed in the fortification of Melown, opposite the British encampment. It was attacked on the 19th; all the guns, stores, and ammunition were captured, the camp was delivered to the flames, and the army resumed its march to the capital.

The king began now to tremble for his throne, and released two of his European prisoners, whom he sent to reopen the negotiations. They were informed that no severer terms would be exacted in consequence of their perfidious conduct at Melown, but that a fourth of the indemnity must be paid down at once. While the envoys were, however, on their return to Ava, the king determined to make one last effort to avert this humiliation, though he could not muster more than 16,000 troops. Sir Archibald had only 1,300 left under his command, but of these 900 were Europeans. The Burmese force was completely routed, and fled in disorder to the capital with the news of its own disgrace, and the English army advanced to Yandaboo, within forty miles of Ava. The king lost no time in sending the two American missionaries whom he had held for two years in cruel captivity, together with two of his own ministers, to accept whatever terms the Commissioners might dictate. They brought with them the first instalment of the indemnity, as well as the European captives, and the treaty was signed

Final engagement and peace.

1826 on the 24th February on the terms which had been previously proposed, with the addition that a British representative should reside at the court. Thus ended the first war the Company had waged beyond the limits of India, and it was also the most expensive in which they had as yet been engaged, and the least recuperative. It absorbed thirteen crores of rupees, and the return consisted of three thinly inhabited and impoverished provinces.

The Burmese war gave rise to another sepoy mutiny. A.D. 1824
The native regiments from Bengal, owing to religious objections to a voyage by sea were directed to march down to Aracan along the coast. The disaster at Ramoo had diffused through the army a dread of the Burmese soldiers, who were represented as magicians, and the service was regarded with great antipathy. The Bengal sepoys had been accustomed to provide from their own pay for the transport of their baggage, but the public demand for draught cattle had exhausted the supply and doubled the price. The 47th regiment at Barrackpore, one of those warned for service, presented a respectful memorial setting forth the extreme difficulty of procuring the means of conveyance. The military chiefs, instead of investigating this just and reasonable representation, treated it as a token of contumacy, and the men were told that they were to expect no assistance from Government. Discontent ripened into insubordination; excited meetings were held in the cantonments; the sepoys rose in their demands and pledged one another not to march without a supply of cattle, and also an increase of pay. The Commander-in-Chief resolved to crush the spirit of mutiny by force, and two regiments of Europeans, the Governor-General's body guard, and a detachment of horse artillery were marched to Barrackpore and drawn up unperceived in the vicinity of the parade ground. The 47th was paraded and ordered to march forthwith, or to ground arms. The men stood still in a state of mute bewilderment, resolved not to yield, but making no attempt at resistance. A volley was discharged on them by the horse artillery, when they flung down their arms with a piercing shriek, and fled in dismay. The European troops then fired on them, and the body-guard sabred the fugitives. The slaughter on the ground and in the line of pursuit was very severe. The ringleaders were tried by court-martial and executed, and others were sent to work on the roads in irons. A court of enquiry was held which came to the decision that "the mutiny was an ebullition "of despair at being compelled to march without the means "of doing so." When the corps had reached a state of positive mutiny, there was no alternative but military execution, but the Commander-in-Chief incurred a heavy responsibility by treating their legitimate representations with scorn.

Mutiny.

Runjeet Sing, the Jaut chief of Bhurtpore, who had

baffled Lord Lake in 1805, was succeeded by his son in 1823 on whose death without issue the principality devolved on his brother. He applied to Sir David Ochterlony, the Resident at Delhi to recognise his son, a child of six years, as his successor, and he received investiture under the express orders of the Government. About a twelvemonth after, on the death of his father, he was placed on the throne under the guardianship of his maternal uncle. Before a month had elapsed Doorjun Sal, the nephew of the deceased raja, a wild and impetuous youth, put the regent to death, placed his cousin in confinement, and seized on the Government. Sir David, acting on his own responsibility, issued a proclamation calling upon all the Jauts to rally round their lawful sovereign, and ordered a force of 16,000 men and 100 guns into the field to support his rights and vindicate the authority of the Company's Government. Lord Amherst disapproved of this proceeding and considered it imprudent while engaged in a conflict with the Burmese to embark in a new war, and to incur the risk of a second failure before Bhurtpore.

Bhurtpore.

A.D. 1825

A disposition had for some time existed in high quarters in Calcutta to remove the veteran Resident from his post, and in the hope of provoking his voluntary resignation the views of Government commanding him to recall his proclamation and to countermand the troops were communicated to him in a very imperious tone. He replied with great, and perhaps undue, warmth, and having given effect to the orders of Government, tendered his resignation. This ungenerous treatment broke his heart. He felt himself disgraced in the eyes of the native princes and of the public service, and retiring to Meerut died within two months, after an illustrious career of half a century. He was one of the brightest ornaments of the Company's service, equally eminent in the cabinet and in the field, a man born for high command and fitted to strengthen the power and sustain the dignity of Great Britain in India.

Proceedings in Council.

While the army was assembling, Doorjun Sal manifested a spirit of humble submission and professed to be satisfied with the regency, but as soon as the troops were countermanded, he assumed a higher tone and claimed the throne for himself, and prevailed on the chiefs of his tribe to support his pretensions. The little success we had obtained in the Burmese war, had, as on all similar occasions, affected our prestige, and the latent feeling of disaffection to the rule of foreigners

began again to manifest itself in the native community. A.D. 1825
The cause of Doorjun Sal became popular when it was known that he intended to enter the lists with the Company's Government. Rajpoots, Jauts, Mahrattas, Afghans, and not a few of our native subjects crowded to his standard, and an army of 25,000 men was speedily collected for the defence of the place. All the members of Council concurred in opinion that in these circumstances we were bound in honour and policy to support the cause of the youth we had invested with the purple against the usurper, but Lord Amherst still continued to hesitate. Happily Sir Charles Metcalfe arrived at Calcutta at this juncture on his way to Delhi as the successor of Sir David, and in a masterly minute pointed out that as the paramount state in India, we could not be indifferent spectators of anarchy therein without ultimately giving up the country again to the pillage and confusion from which we had rescued it; that a vigorous exercise of our power would be likely to bring back the minds of men to a proper tone, and that the capture of Bhurtpore, if effected in a glorious manner, would do us more honour by removing the hitherto unfaded impression created by our former failure than any other event that could be conceived. Lord Amherst gracefully surrendered his opinion to that of Sir Charles, and it was resolved, if remonstrance with Doorjun failed, to resort to arms.

Capture of Bhurtpore.

To the astonishment of the princes of India who believed that the Burmese war had absorbed all the resources of Government, an army of 20,000 men with 100 heavy ordnance and mortars suddenly sprung up in the midst of them. Throughout India it was remembered that Bhurtpore was the only fortress which the British Government had besieged and failed to capture, and the eyes of all India were fixed upon the second siege, not perhaps, without a latent hope that it might be as unsuccessful as the first. The head-quarters of Lord Combermere, the Commander-in-Chief, were established before it on the 10th December. Thirty-six mortars and forty-eight pieces of heavy ordnance played upon the mud walls for many days without making any impression or creating a practicable breach. A great mine was at length completed, and charged with 10,000 pounds of powder. The explosion took place on the 18th January, and seemed to 1826
shake the foundations of the earth, while enormous masses of hardened earth and blocks of timber, mingled with

A.D. heads, legs and arms, were sent flying into the air, and
1826 the sky was darkened with volumes of smoke and dust. Of the usurper's army, 6,000 were said to have fallen during the siege and the casualties on the side of the English were about 1,000. Doorjun Sal endeavoured to make his escape, but was captured and sent to join the assemblage of disinherited princes at Benares, where he passed twenty-five years on an allowance of 500 rupees a month. The boy raja was then placed on the throne by Sir Charles Metcalfe and Lord Combermere, but the laurels of Bhurtpore were tarnished by the rapacity of the military authorities. The siege was undertaken to expel a usurper, and restore the lawful prince to his rights, but the whole of the state jewels and treasure was seized by the victors to the extent of forty-eight lacs of rupees, and divided among themselves as prize-money, Lord Combermere appropriating six lacs to himself. The proud walls which had bid defiance to the hero of Delhi and Laswaree were levelled with the ground. The capture of the fort produced a profound sensation, as Sir Charles Metcalfe had predicted, throughout India; and, combined with the submission of Burmah, dissolved the sanguine hopes of the disaffected, and restored the prestige of the Company. Lord Amherst was advanced to the dignity of an earl, not of Bhurtpore, his brightest achievement, but of Aracan, the most disastrous of his expeditions.

1823 to 1828 The financial result of his administration was calamitous. The wealth left in the treasury by Lord Hastings was

Finances.

dissipated, the annual surplus turned into a deficit, and an addition of ten crores made to the public debt. On his arrival, and while new to the country and the community, he was led by the superior officers of Government to continue those truculent pro-

The press.

ceedings against the press which they had originated; but it was not long before he adopted a more generous policy, and on his departure was complimented by the journals in Calcutta "on the liberality and "even magnanimity with which he had tolerated the free "expression of public opinion on his own individual "measures, when he had the power to silence them with a "stroke of his pen." He embarked for England in Feb-
1828 ruary, and Mr. Butterworth Bayley, the senior member of Council, assumed charge of the Government.

SECTION II.

LORD WILLIAM BENTINCK'S ADMINISTRATION—MILITARY OPERATIONS—NATIVE STATES—RUNJEET SING.

Lord William Bentinck.

THE stigma unjustly inflicted on Lord William Bentinck's character by his abrupt removal from the Government of Madras in 1806, was at length effaced by his appointment to the office of Governor-General. He was sworn in at the India House in July 1827, while his relative, Mr. Canning, who had promoted
his nomination, was prime minister; but his lamented 1827
death soon after brought into power those who had opposed his elevation, and Lord William Bentinck suspended his departure till he was assured that the new ministry did not object to his appointment; hence he did not reach Calcutta before the 4th July, 1828. With his advent commenced a new and beneficent era in the history of the Company, marked by a bold and energetic improvement in the institutions of the state, although his administration did not open under favourable circumstances. The Burmese war had not only saddled the treasury with an additional debt of ten crores, but created
an annual deficit of a crore of rupees, and Lord William 1828
Bentinck was constrained to enter upon the unpopular duty of retrenchment.

Reduction of allowances.

Two committees were appointed to investigate the increase of expenditure, and to suggest the means of curtailing it. The sweeping reductions which the Court of Directors had already made in the strength of the army, left little for the military committee to suggest, except the diminution of individual allowances, though they were in no case excessive, and, in many cases, inadequate. The civil department afforded a more legitimate field for revision; some offices were abolished, a few were doubled up, and the income of others was curtailed; but the total reductions did not affect the aggregate allowances of the service to a greater extent than six per cent. It was still the best paid service in the world, in the enjoyment of an annual income of ninety lacs, which divided, as it was, among 416 officers, gave each of the members an average allowance of 20,000 rupees a year; but even the moderate contraction of allowances suggested by the committee and adopted by Lord William Bentinck, subjected him to indignities which severely taxed his habitual equanimity.

The half batta order.

Of these economical measures, none excited so much bitterness of feeling as the half batta order. Soon after the beginning of the century the supplementary allowance of full batta was granted to the officers when in cantonments in the lower provinces. The Court of Directors objected to the arrangement, and directed Lord Hastings, and subsequently Lord Amherst, to reduce the amount by one half, but they referred the order back to England for reconsideration, when it was repeated in a more peremptory tone. The latest despatch reached Calcutta soon after the arrival of Lord William, and in obedience to the Court's orders, he issued a notification in November,
A.D. 1828 reducing the allowance one half at all stations within 400 miles of Calcutta. The order raised a flame in the army which at one time created the apprehension of a fourth European mutiny. One officer went so far as to assert that if an enemy were to make his appearance in the field, he did not believe there was a single officer who would give the order to march, or a single regiment which would obey it. The insults inflicted on the Governor-General by the officers of the army rivalled those of the civil service, and were more severe than any of his predecessors had ever experienced. Lord Combermere, the Commander-in-Chief, prevented the organisation of representative committees, as in the mutiny of 1796, but he did not hesitate to pronounce the order unjust; and the Court of Directors declared that they would have superseded him if he had not resigned the service. Lord William Bentinck also considered the order unnecessary, unjust, and impolitic, but he felt that it was beyond his power to suspend the execution of it after the Court of Directors had, for the third time, insisted upon its being carried into effect, without assuming that the Government in Calcutta was the supreme power in the empire. The Court of Directors denounced the tone of the memorials presented to them by the officers as subversive of all military discipline, and, with the full concurrence of the Duke of Wellington, signified their determination to enforce the order at all hazards; indeed, considering the pass at which matters had arrived, they had no other alternative. But the reduction was an egregious blunder; and it appears strange that so astute a body as the Directors should have risked the attachment and confidence of their army for a paltry saving of less than two lacs a year; and it is still more surprising that for the thirty years in which they continued

to administer the Government, they had not the magnanimity to rescind the order, even as a graceful acknowledgment of the services subsequently performed by the army in twenty hard-fought battles.

The native princes had always been in the habit of making grants of land to individuals and to ecclesiastical establishments free from the payment of rent. Some of these religious endowments and grants to charities were held sacred by superstitious chiefs, but in numerous instances they were resumed, both in the Deccan and in Hindostan, on each succession to the throne, and sometimes during the same reign. In the confusion created by the dissolution of the Mogul power, this royal prerogative was usurped by the governors of provinces. On assuming the management of the revenue the Government in Calcutta announced that all grants made previous to 1765 should be deemed valid; but, as there was no register of them, the rajas, zemindars, farmers, and revenue officers, set to work to fabricate and antedate new deeds, and it was subsequently asserted that a tenth of the land revenues had thus been alienated from the state during the infancy of our Government. The revenue settlement of Lord Cornwallis reserved the right of resuming these tenures when their validity had been investigated and disallowed. The overworked collector to whom the duty of the investigation was committed, found himself thwarted at every step by his own mercenary officers, who were in the pay of the occupants; he became lukewarm in the work, and it was necessary either to abandon the pursuit of this lost revenue, or to adopt more effectual measures to recover it. Three weeks before the arrival of Lord William Bentinck, a regulation was passed, appointing commissioners selected from the ablest men in the service, to hear and finally to determine appeals regarding these tenures from the decisions of the collectors, who were thus stimulated into greater activity. These energetic proceedings gave great offence to those affected by them, who pleaded, and not without reason, that the difficulty of substantiating their claims had increased with the lapse of time, that many documents had disappeared by the effects of the climate and the ravages of white ants, and that lands which might have been fraudulently obtained several generations back, had since been bought *bonâ fide* at high prices. Though the holders were in no cases dispossessed, but simply required to pay rent to the state, the assessment of their

Rent free tenures.

A.D. 1828

lands brought great unpopularity on the Government. The legal machinery of investigation cost about eighty lacs of rupees, and the increase of revenue amounted to about thirty lacs a year.

The political and military events of Lord William Bentinck's administration were of minor importance compared with those of previous and subsequent periods, when thrones and dynasties were overthrown, and the map of India was reconstructed. The Cole insurrection however, involved operations of some magnitude. The Coles, Dangars, Santals, and other tribes in the south-west of Bengal who are believed to have been the aborigines of the country, generally retained their independence, except where it had been encroached upon by Rajpoot zemindars, who endeavoured to improve their receipts by substituting a more industrious class of cultivators for these lazy barbarians. The introduction of these men created a strong feeling of discontent, which was augmented by the insolence and rapacity of the Bengal officials who flocked into the province. In 1832, the Coles rose in large numbers, laid waste the fields of the zemindars, burnt down their villages, and put more than a thousand of their men to death, before it was possible to assemble troops. Armed as they were only with bows and arrows and axes, they were easily overcome, and there was much unnecessary slaughter. In the neighbouring district it became necessary to send four regiments into the field before the insurrection was trodden out. The rising was not however without benefit to the people. It induced Lord William Bentinck to relieve them from the incubus of the Company's code and judicial institutions, and to turn the district into a non-regulation province, and place it under the especial control of a commissioner.

The Cole Insurrection.

A.D. 1832

1831 Another insurrection occurred within fifteen miles of Government House in Calcutta. Synd Ahmed, a Mahomedan reformer and fanatic, whose name will come up again hereafter, collected numerous followers in lower Bengal, and more particularly in the suburban district of Baraset. Their bigoted intolerance to those of their own creed, whom they deemed heterodox, and their hostility to Hindoo heretics created a feeling of general animosity, and some of the Hindoo zemindars inflicted heavy penalties on them. They appealed to the magistrates, but the dilatoriness of judicial forms exhausted their patience; and, under the guidance of one Teetoo

Insurrection of Teetoo Meer.

Meer, a Mahomedan mendicant, they proclaimed a *jehad*, or religious war. They defiled a temple with the blood of a cow, and forced its flesh down the throats of the brahmins, and then proceeded to burn down villages and factories, and to erect stockades. In the peaceful province of Bengal, which had not seen the smoke of an enemy's camp for more than seventy years, it was found necessary to call out two regiments of infantry and a body of horse, and some guns. Their stockade, in which they defended themselves for an hour, was captured, and the insurrection was quenched in their blood.

Annexation of Cachar and Coorg.

The administration of the most pacific of Governors-General could not escape the "inevitable tendency" of the empire to enlarge its boundary, but the addition to the Company's dominions during the administration of Lord William Bentinck was so insignificant as to escape observation and censure. The A.D. 1832 chief of the little principality of Cachar in the hills to the north-east of Bengal was murdered in 1832, and amidst the anarchy which ensued the people implored the protectorate of the British Government which Lord William Bentinck did not hesitate to extend to them. This unnoticed nook in the great empire has since acquired a commercial value by the expenditure of a crore of rupees of private capital in tea plantations, for which its position and soil are highly favourable. The principality of Coorg lies on the Malabar coast between Mysore and the sea, and comprises an area of about 1,500 square miles, no portion of which is less than 3,000 feet above the level of the sea. Its chivalrous raja had defended it with so much gallantry against the overwhelming force of Tippoo as to gain the applause of Lord Cornwallis, and also of Lord Wellesley, from whom he received a splendid sword, which was preserved with pride among the heir-looms of the family. But his successor in 1820 exhibited an example of tyranny and cruelty rarely exceeded by the most atrocious of native princes. On coming to the throne he put to death all who had thwarted his views, and to prevent the possibility of being superseded directed all his kinsmen to be taken into the jungles and decapitated. He never scrupled to take the life of any who became obnoxious to him. He likewise manifested a peculiar hatred of the British Government, and as he strictly interdicted the entry of any Englishmen into the province, his atrocities were concealed from observation. In 1832, however, his sister and her husband escaped for their lives, and revealed his barbarities to the Resident in Mysore, who proceeded to his capital and endeavoured, but in vain, to bring him to reason. He addressed letters of extraordinary insolence to the governor of Madras, and even to the Governor-General, while he organized his little force to resist the British authorities. Lord William Bentinck, finding him deaf to every remonstrance, resolved to treat him as a public enemy, and issued a proclamation recounting his cruelties, and announcing that he had ceased to reign.

A.D. 1834

A force of 6,000 men entered the country in four divisions, in different directions, and after penetrating its intricate and perilous defiles, planted the British standard on the ramparts of the capital, Mercara, in April 1832. The country was at once annexed to the Company's territories, and has now been covered with coffee plantations by British enterprise.

Non-intervention policy.

The political policy of Lord William Bentinck was at first regulated by that principle of non-intervention in the internal affairs of native states which was still in favour in Leadenhall Street. In his minute on the Bhurtpore crisis, in 1826, Sir Charles Metcalfe had placed on record that "having become the paramount "power in India we were the supreme guardians of general "law, tranquillity and right." The Court of Directors lost no time in repudiating this doctrine, and laid positive and repeated injunctions on the Government of India to abstain from all interference with the native princes beyond what was necessary to secure the punctual payment of their respective tributes. The Government was thus placed in the invidious position of a strong and inexorable creditor instead of a beneficent guardian of peace. Lord William, however, frequently found it impossible to avoid interposing his imperial authority to frustrate the projects of usurpation, to repress internal anarchy, and to promote harmony between prince and people. His political policy, therefore, presents the appearance of vacillation, and is certainly the least satisfactory portion of his administration.

Mysore raja's misgovernment.

On the construction of the kingdom of Mysore, the administration was placed in the hands of the renowned brahmin Poornea, the great minister of Hyder Ali and Tippoo, and his authority was supported by the invaluable assistance of some of the most experienced of the Company's officers. The country

flourished, and, in the course of ten years, a surplus of two crores was accumulated in the treasury; but the raja, under the influence of his minions and his flatterers proclaimed his majority, when he attained his sixteenth year, dismissed Poornea, and took the administration into his own hands. The Resident reported that he was utterly unfitted for the government by the weakness of his character and his entire subservience to the influence of favourites. The administration steadily deteriorated for twenty years; all the accumulations of Poornea were dissipated; the government became venal and corrupt; the highest offices were put up to sale; crown lands were alienated, and the subjects were crushed by new and grievous taxation. The A.D.
people at length took up arms, and in 1830 one half the 1830
kingdom was in a state of insurrection. Adventurers from all parts joined the insurgents, and the peace of the Deccan, not excepting the Company's territories, was placed in extreme jeopardy. It became necessary to send a large force into the field; but at the same time a friendly proclamation was issued, inviting the people to come in peaceably and represent their grievances to the British officers, with the assurance that they would be redressed if they were found to be real. The natives had full confidence in them, and the insurrection died out.

Management of Mysore taken over.

The Governor-General then informed the raja that, 1832
though tranquillity was for the present restored, he could not allow the name and the influence of the British Government to be identified with these acts of misrule; and that, in order to prevent their recurrence, and to save the Mysore state from ruin, he deemed it necessary to place the entire administration of the country in the hands of British officers, paying over to the raja, in accordance with the terms of the treaty, about four lacs a year and a fifth of the net revenue, which, under more honest management, would be equal to about a lac and a half more. Lord William Bentinck was soon after led to believe from the report of the court of enquiry he had appointed, that the grievances had been somewhat overstated, and he proposed to retain in perpetuity only a sufficient portion of the territory to meet the subsidy, and to restore the remainder to the raja, on the simple condition that the Government should be at liberty to resume this portion if it appeared necessary for the public benefit. The Court of Directors, however, who had entirely approved of all his proceedings, refused to sanction this

proposal, and asserted that the assumption of the whole country was justified by the treaty, and essential to the welfare of the people.

Joudpore.

The non-intervention policy was peculiarly unfortunate for the two Rajpoot states of Joudpore and Jeypore, where the turbulent habits of the feudal nobility rendered the interposition of a paramount power indispensable to the public tranquillity. Man Sing, the raja of Joudpore, had been deposed by his chiefs before the Pindaree war on the ground of his insanity, real or feigned, but had recovered his power if not his reason in 1821, and began to wreak his vengeance on them. They appealed to the Government in Calcutta, but without success, and then brought an army of 7,000 men against the capital. The raja appealed in his turn to Lord William Bentinck, who felt the necessity of interposing his authority to prevent the kindling of war in Rajpootana, and the Resident was ordered to restore concord between the parties, which he effected with a stroke of his pen. But the insane violence of the raja broke out again; he
A.D. not only oppressed his subjects, but gave encouragement
1834 to the robber tribes of the desert, and refused to apprehend Thugs, or to surrender malefactors. A large army was ordered to Joudpore to bring him to reason. The Rahtores, the designation of the tribe, were accustomed to boast in their ballads of "the hundred thousand swords" with which they had supported the throne of Akbar; but the Joudpore envoy now enquired what occasion there could be for an army when a single messenger would have been sufficient to convey the commands of the Governor-General. Every demand was at once conceded.

Jeypore.

During the minority of the raja of Jeypore, his mother acted as regent, and resigned herself to the counsels of one Jotaram, a banker. The haughty barons expelled him from the post of minister, and installed one of their own body, Byree Sal; but the regent ranee obtained the permission of Sir David Ochterlony to recall him. The nobles resented this proceeding, and a civil war appeared inevitable, when Sir C. Metcalfe, who had succeeded Sir David, proceeded to Jeypore, and convened a general meeting of the chiefs, and gathered from their discussions that the majority of them were favourable to the queen mother, when he confirmed her authority, with leave to choose her own minister. Jotaram became again the head of the administration, but the revenues were

misappropriated, the troops unpaid, and the nobles pursued with vindictiveness. An appeal was made to Lord William Bentinck to terminate the disorders of the state by the supreme authority of the Company's Government, but he declined to interfere. Soon after the ranee died, and her death was speedily followed by that of her son, not without suspicion of poison, and the general indignation against Jotaram became so intense that he retired from the capital, and levied an army. Lord William Bentinck had by this time quitted the Government, and his successor accepted the guardianship of the infant heir, A.D.
and despatched a political agent to the capital, who was 1835
just in time to prevent a battle between the party of the exasperated nobles and of the banker. An attempt was made to massacre the agent; he was attacked and wounded as he left the durbar and barely escaped with his life, but his assistant fell under the swords of the assassins. To prevent the recurrence of this anarchy, a more stringent control was established over the affairs of the court.

Affairs of Oude.

In 1818 Lord Hastings assumed the prerogative of conferring the title of an independent king upon the nabob Vizier of Oude, which released him from the necessity of doing homage to any member of the imperial family who happened to reside at Lucknow, even in the most indigent circumstances. The king who was seated on the throne during Lord William Bentinck's administration, had been brought up in the zenana, and his ideas were puerile and effeminate, and his life was devoted to indulgence. The resident, Sir Herbert Maddock, represented the country to be in a state of abject wretchedness; there was no security for life and property, and scarcely a day passed in which an attack was not made on the forts of the zemindars, who seldom paid their rents without compulsion. Lord William himself travelled through the country, and saw nothing but desolation and decay. He considered that, as we protected the king from the indignation of his oppressed people, it was our bounden duty to protect the inhabitants from the abuses of the Government. 1831
In a communication to the king in 1831, he insisted on the adoption of reforms, and distinctly assured him that if he continued to withhold them the entire management of the country would be taken out of his hands, and a sufficient annuity assigned to him for the support of his royal family and court.

In anticipation of this remonstrance, the king recalled

Hakim Menhdy, whom he had dismissed, and reappointed him prime minister. This extraordinary man, the son of a Persian gentleman at Shiraj, had emigrated to India in search of political employment and entered the service of Oude, in which he rapidly rose to distinction. He identified the prosperity of his adopted country with his own happiness, and devoted his splendid talents to the improvement of the administration, though thwarted at every step by the vices of his sovereign. Lord William Bentinck pronounced him one of the ablest men in India, and as a revenue administrator unsurpassed by any officer, European or native. He had gradually amassed a princely fortune, which he expended with more than princely liberality; and there was no portion of Hindostan which had not experienced his generosity. On assuming the Government he introduced important reforms, and had the courage to retrench the profligate expenditure of the zenana, and to curtail the allowances of the parasites of the court. But he was too radical a reformer for the meridian of Oude, and as Lord William Bentinck hesitated to support his authority against the wishes of the king, who was offended, he said, because he had not spoken with sufficient respect of his mother, and

Hakim Menhdy.

A.D. had insulted the portrait of his father, he resigned his
1832 post and retired into the British territories. In reference to the condition of Oude, the Court of Directors had justly remarked that, "it was the British Government "which, by a systematic suppression of all attempts at "resistance, had prolonged the misrule which became "permanent when the short-sightedness and rapacity of a "semi-barbarous Government was armed with the military "strength of a civilised one." In reply to Lord William's representation of the miserable condition of the country, the Court of Directors authorized him at once to assume the government, if circumstances should appear to render it necessary. Lord William, who was on the eve of leaving India, communicated the substance of these instruc-
1834 tions to the king, intimating that the execution of them would be suspended in the hope of his adopting the necessary reforms. But the reforms never came, and the orders were carried into execution twenty years after.

The interview of Lord William Bentinck with Runjeet Sing is one of the most remarkable events in his administration; but, before alluding to it, it is necessary to continue the narrative of his progress after

Progress of Runjeet Sing.

the check he received from Mr. Metcalfe in 1809. Conquest was the one object of his life, and his attention was directed solely to the improvement of his army and the accumulation of treasure, to the comparative neglect of the civil administration. At the close of the rains his army was assembled for some expedition with the regularity of the seasons. This incessant warfare was exactly suited to the martial character of the Sikh population, whom it furnished with congenial occupation and with the means of acquiring distinction and wealth. The prospect of glory and plunder were the two chief elements of their fidelity to their chief. He commenced the formation of battalions on the model of the Company's army, and by incessant attention to their drill, which he superintended in person, converted his raw troops into an efficient force, which he provided with an admirable artillery.

His conquests.

After the subjugation of all the independent Sikh chieftains in the Punjab, he entered into a convention with Futteh Khan, the vizier of Cabul, for a joint expedition to Cashmere; but the vizier anticipated his movements, and, having obtained possession of A.D.
the province by his own unaided efforts, refused to resign 1817
any portion of it to Runjeet, who requited him by the surreptitious seizure of Attock on the Indus, during his absence. This led to a battle, in which Futteh Khan was defeated, and the Sikh authority was permanently extended to the banks of the river. In 1818 Runjeet Sing obtained possession of the province of Mooltan, and taking advantage
of the murder of Futteh Khan, the vizier, whose talents 1818
and energy had alone kept the Afghan monarchy from dissolution, seized upon Peshawur, the capital of eastern Afghanistan, but was speedily driven from it. This disappointment was, however, compensated soon after by the
acquisition of Cashmere, and two years later of the Derajat, 1819
a strip of territory about 300 miles in length, lying on the right bank of the Indus, and stretching down to the confines of Sinde.

Arrival of French officers.

In March 1822, Colonels Allard and Ventura, two 1822
of the French officers of the army of Napoleon who had left Europe on the restoration of the Bourbons and obtained employment in Persia, made their way to Lahore and, after some hesitation, were received into the service of Runjeet Sing. The Sikh soldiery, previously distinguished by their courage, their national enthusiasm, and their religious animation, received

from these officers and from Generals Court and Avitabile, who followed them, the benefit of European tactics and discipline, and became more effective and formidable than the battalions which De Boigne had raised for Sindia, and Raymond for the Nizam.

In March 1823 Runjeet Sing proceeded with an army of 23,000 men to establish his authority in Peshawur, but
A.D. Battle of the Eusufzie highlanders proclaimed a religious
1823 Noushera. war against the infidel Sikhs, and 5,000 of them rushed down from their mountains and completely defeated them. Fresh troops were brought up, and Runjeet eventually remained master of the field, and sacked Peshawur. This battle is memorable from the fact that a body of mountaineers, wild with religious enthusiasm, succeeded in baffling the efforts of four times their number of well trained and disciplined troops. The province was left in the hands of Yar Mahomed, the hostile brother of the ruler of Cabul, on condition of his paying tribute. Four years after, the peace of the country was disturbed by Syud Ahmed, a Mahomedan fanatic, who had been a petty cavalry officer in the service of Ameer Khan, the Patan freebooter, and on the dissolution of his army, turned religious reformer, pretended to have visions from heaven, and succeeded in raising a flame of fanaticism among his co-religionists. Reference has already been made to his visit to Calcutta, from whence he proceeded to Mecca, the fountain of Mahomedan enthusiasm, and returning to India with more excited feelings, entered Afghanistan, where he proclaimed a holy war against the infidels, and raised the green flag of Islam, but was defeated by Runjeet Sing's
1830 disciplined troops, and obliged to fly. He returned in 1830, and obtained possession of the province of Peshawur. Elated with his success, he proclaimed himself Caliph, and struck coin in the name of "Ahmed the first, the Defender "of the Faith," but his assumption and his arbitrary proceedings disgusted his followers, who expelled him from the province, and he was overtaken by the Sikh troops and put to death in May 1831.

In 1827 Lord Amherst took up his residence at the sanitarium of Simla, which lies within 150 miles of Lahore, and Runjeet Sing embraced the opportunity of sending him a complimentary mission, with a magnificent tent of shawls for the king of England which he presented on his return. Runjeet Sing had an extraordinary passion for horses, and Lord Ellen-

Lord Amherst and Runjeet.

borough, then President of the Board of Control, determined to present him in return for the shawl tent with a team of English dray-horses. The Indus was at the time not much better known than in the days of Alexander the Great; and instead of despatching the cattle by the ordinary route through Bengal and Hindostan, Lord Ellenborough resolved that they should be sent up the Indus, with the view of exploring the river, and, if possible, forming friendly relations with the chiefs on its banks. On the arrival of the horses at Bombay, Sir John Malcolm, the governor, selected Lieutenant—afterwards Sir Alexander—Burnes to conduct the mission. At the mouth of the Indus he entered the territory of Sinde, the Ameers of which had always treated the English agents with hostility; and, as they considered his arrival an event of evil omen, subjected him to great indignity, and twice constrained him to retire from the country. They were induced at length to grant him the means of transport, and he reached the confines of the Punjab, through which he was escorted with great pomp, and at the court was received with great courtesy. When the letter from Lord Ellenborough was presented to Runjeet Sing, a royal salute was fired from each of sixty pieces of cannon, and Lieutenant Burnes was treated with distinguished honour as long as he remained at the court. He then proceeded to Simla where Lord William Bentinck was residing, and submitted to him the result of his researches regarding the commerce, politics, and military resources of Sinde and the other states on the Indus. He was directed to return to Bombay through Afghanistan, Balkh, and Bokhara. A.D. 1831

Resources of Runjeet Sing.

The power of Runjeet Sing had been steadily increasing for twenty years. Including the contingents of his jageerdars, his army consisted of 80,000 men, animated with the success of a dozen campaigns, and in part disciplined and commanded by European officers. His artillery consisted of 376 guns and an equal number of swivels. His annual revenue was estimated at two crores and a half, and the vaults of his treasury contained ten crores. Though unable to read or write, he fully comprehended the papers in Persian, Punjabee, and Pushtoo, read to him by his able secretaries, who were in attendance upon him day and night, and to whom he dictated replies. But, though he had reached the summit of power he never arrogated the title of an independent sovereign, but was content to be considered simply as the head of the Khalsa or Sikh commonwealth, a name regarded with a feeling of superstitious devotion by the chiefs and soldiers. He considered it a matter of importance to secure for his throne and dynasty the strength which a close alliance with the British Government could not fail to impart; and Lord William Bentinck, on his side, deemed it politic to demonstrate to the princes of India, who began to regard the progress of a native power under Runjeet Sing with hope, that a feeling of cordiality existed between the two states; and a meeting was accordingly arranged to be held at Roopur, on the banks of the Sutlej.

Meeting at Raopur.

This assembly was the most brilliant in which the representative of the Company had ever taken a part. Lord William Bentinck, like Lord Cornwallis, was distinguished for the simplicity of his habits, and his dislike of the pageantry of power; but he considered it important to give *éclat* to this political meeting in the eyes of India by the grandeur of its display. He descended
A.D. 1831 from Simlah to Roopur on the 22nd October, and Runjeet Sing arrived at the opposite bank of the river three days after with a magnificent court, and 10,000 of his best horse and 6,000 select infantry. The next day he crossed the river on a bridge of boats, preceded and followed by his chiefs mounted on elephants decked in gorgeous housings, while a body of 4,000 horse whom he had brought with him by way of caution, formed the wings of the procession. Presents of every variety and of the most costly description had been collected by the Governor-General from all parts of India, sufficient to efface the memory of the dray-horses. Runjeet Sing scrutinized every article with the curiosity of a child, and saw it carefully packed up and delivered to his master of the jewel office. The following day the Governor-General returned the visit; the scene was one of extraordinary splendour; the Sikh encampment exceeded in magnificence anything which had been seen in India since the days of Aurungzebe, and realised the highest conceptions of oriental grandeur.

The frank manners of Runjeet Sing, his free enquiries and lively conversation, gave an air of ease to ceremonials which were usually stately and stiff. He called up and paraded his favourite horses before Lord William Bentinck, and recounted their names and virtues with much animation. In their company was also brought up one of the dray-horses, as if to contrast his huge and shaggy legs with their elegant limbs. A week was passed in displays, entertainments, and reviews, recalling to mind the days of Mogul magnificence, and the parties separated with a mutual appreciation of each other's power.

Treaty with Sinde.

A.D. 1832

Runjeet Sing had long been eager to add Sinde to his dominions, and to obtain possession of Shikarpore, a commercial mart on the right bank of the Indus, of such magnitude and importance that the bills of its bankers passed current from Calcutta to Astrakhan. During the meeting he sounded the secretaries on the subject of a joint expedition, hinting that, according to Lieutenant Burnes, the treasury contained twenty crores, and that the army was very feeble. But Lord William Bentinck had already deputed Colonel Pottinger to endeavour to conclude a commercial treaty with the Ameers. They were exceedingly reluctant to form any connection at all with the Company, lest the factory should, as elsewhere, grow into a fortress. They yielded at length to the importunity of the Colonel, but in the treaty of commerce they signed caused it to be stipulated "that the contracting parties should never look with an eye of covetousness on the possessions of each other." Within eleven years Sinde was a British province.

SECTION III.

LORD W. BENTINCK'S ADMINISTRATION—ADMINISTRATIVE REFORMS—CHARTER OF 1833—SIR C. METCALF.

Administrative reforms.

THE lustre of Lord William Bentinck's administration is derived from his bold and enlightened reforms, his intrepid philanthropy, and his efforts to promote material progress, in which he far surpassed all his predecessors. For thirty years the local government had been engaged, with no encouragement from England, in establishing British supremacy and consolidating the empire, and it remained to endow it with improved and beneficial institutions. No substantial effort had been made since the days of Lord Cornwallis to improve them, and they had become in a great measure effete. For the work of reformation Lord William Bentinck was particularly qualified, by the clearness of his views, his freedom from traditional prejudices, and his inflexible resolution. His administration therefore forms one of the great landmarks in the history of British India.

The current of civil justice was blocked up by the provincial courts, which Lord William Bentinck described as "resting places for those members of the service "who were deemed fit for no higher responsi- "bilities." With some exceptions, the judicial character of the judges was contemptible, while their discordant judgments in appeal only served to bewilder the judges of the courts subordinate to them. With regard to criminal justice, their agency was a national grievance. The judges went on circuit to hold sessions and gaol delivery twice a year, and the accused were kept in confinement for months before they were brought to trial, while the prosecutors and witnesses were detained throughout this period at their own expense. Under such circumstances, it is of course no matter of surprise that the daroga who came down to institute enquiries was considered by the natives "the messenger of death," and that the concealment of crime became the one object of solicitude throughout the country.

A.D. 1831 The provincial courts.

Lord William earned the gratitude of the country by abolishing a class of tribunals which combined three of the worst vices of law—delay, expense, and uncertainty. The duties of the session were transferred to the judge of the district, who was to hold a gaol delivery every month. A separate Sudder, or chief court, was also established in the North-West provinces, and the natives of Delhi were no longer obliged to travel a thousand miles to Calcutta to prosecute an appeal. A corresponding boon was also conferred on these provinces by the erection of a board of revenue at Allahabad, which placed the control of the revenue of twenty-three millions of people in the midst of them. The value of these improvements was incalculably enhanced by conferring on the natives the great blessing of the use of their own vernacular tongue in all the courts, civil, fiscal, and criminal, to which they were amenable, in lieu of the Persian, which had been adopted from the Mahomedans to whom it was familiar, whereas in the British courts it was foreign equally to the parties, the witnesses, and the judge.

One of the greatest transactions of Lord William Bentinck's administration was the revenue settlement of the North-West provinces. On the acquisition of the latest of these provinces by Lord Wellesley, in 1804, he promised them a permanent settlement at the end of ten years, if it was approved of by

Revenue settlement in the N.-W. P.

the Court of Directors. The Court repudiated the engagement, and ordered it to be limited to five years; but so brief a term was fatal to all agricultural improvement. A landholder considered it an act of folly to lay out money in the improvement of his land when he knew that this would only serve to increase his assessment in two or three years; and as the period of revision approached, wells were filled up, and cultivation was neglected. An effort was made to grapple with this large question in 1822, but the celebrated regulation of that year was too complicated in its details to be worked by the limited agency at the disposal of Government, and at the end of ten years the settlement had scarcely begun. Lord William Bentinck was resolved to remove the opprobrium of this neglect from the administration, and made a tour through the provinces, discussing the question in all its bearings with the revenue officers in each district, and with the revenue board at Allahabad; and on his return to the Presidency issued the regulation for the new settlement in 1833. It possessed the great merit of simplicity, and dispensed with many of the elaborate enquiries required by the former regulation. The lands were minutely surveyed and classified according to their quality, and an accurate measurement of them was placed on record, by which a prolific source of discord and litigation was cut off, and the assessment was then fixed for thirty years by the collector, after a free and friendly communication with the people on the spot. The general management of these large operations was entrusted to Mr. Robert Bird, the ablest financial officer since the days of Sir John Shore. His knowledge of the intricacies of land tenure in the North-West provinces was greater than that of any other man in the service, and he was moreover endowed with that indomitable energy and that sternness of purpose which enabled him to complete the settlement of 72,000 square miles, affecting the vital interests of twenty-three millions of people, in the course of ten years. He was allowed to select his own assistants, and the honour of having served under him was considered as conferring a distinction for life.

A.D. 1833

The measure which above all others has endeared the memory of Lord William Bentinck to the natives of India, was the access he gave them to the public service. Their exclusion from every office except the lowest and worst paid was the cardinal error of Lord Cornwallis's administration. Such ostracism of a whole people, who

Employment of natives.

A.D. 1831 had from time immemorial been accustomed to the management of public affairs in every department, was without a parallel in history. The grandsons of the Gauls who resisted Cæsar became Roman senators; the grandsons of the Rajpoots who opposed Baber, and well-nigh nipped his enterprise in the bud at Biana, were employed by his illustrious grandson in the government of provinces and the command of armies, and shed their blood for him on the shores of the Bay of Bengal and the banks of the Oxus, and rewarded his confidence with unshaken loyalty to his throne, even when it was shaken by the treachery of his Mahomedan satraps. But wherever the Company's sovereignty was extended, every office of the least value was bestowed exclusively on their own European and covenanted servants; and the natives of the country, however capable, were at once excluded from all share in the government of their own country, one of the most honourable aspirations of humanity. Lord William Bentinck was deeply impressed with the viciousness of this policy, and determined "to "throw open the door of distinction to the natives, and to "grant them a full participation in all the honours and "emoluments of the state." This liberal policy was ushered in by the regulations of 1831, which completely reconstructed the legal establishments of the Bengal Presidency, and entrusted the primary jurisdiction of all suits, of whatever character or amount, not excluding those instituted against Government, to native agency. They were subsequently introduced into all other departments, and have manifested such eagerness for state employ as, in some measure, to impair the feeling of personal independence. Another anomaly was likewise removed on this occasion. The Company and their servants, from a morbid dread of offending Hindoo prejudices, had debarred native converts from holding any office, even that of a constable. Lord William Bentinck ordained that in admitting natives to the public service, there should be no distinction of caste, creed, or nation.

The most benignant and memorable act of Lord William Bentinck's administration was the abolition of *suttee*, which had been practised for twenty centuries wherever Hindooism obtained a footing. The

Abolition of suttee.

1805 first effort to interfere with it was made by Mr. George Udny, the member of Council, and Dr. Carey, who presented an address on the subject to Lord Wellesley. He was then on the eve of leaving India, but recorded his opinion in favour of the abolition of it. Some attempts were subsequently made to diminish the number of victims by regulating the procedure, but the Court of Directors justly observed that the practice was thereby rendered more popular, inasmuch as, by prohibiting it in some cases, the Government appeared to sanction it in all others. The question was earnestly discussed for many years by some of the most distinguished servants of the state, but they all shrunk from the proposal of interdicting the practice. In 1823 the Court of Directors sent a despatch to the Government of India, in which all the arguments against abolition were earnestly and honestly combated, and the question was referred to the decision of the local authorities; but Lord Auckland found the opinions of the public officers so discordant, as to be obliged to inform the Court that he was not prepared to recommend the positive prohibition of it; and they placed the question definitively in the hands of Lord William Bentinck on his appointment.

Lord William Bentinck's enquiries.

Lord William Bentinck landed in Calcutta, feeling, as he said, "the dreadful responsibility hanging over his head in "this world and the next, if, as the Governor-"General of India, he was to consent to the "continuance of this practice one moment longer, "not than our security, but than the real happiness and "permanent welfare of the native population rendered "indispensable." He resolved "to come to as early a "determination as a mature consideration would allow; "and having made that determination, to stand by it, yea "or no, and set his conscience at rest." He immediately circulated a confidential communication among more than fifty of the civil and military officers of Government, asking their opinion as to the effect which the abolition would be likely to produce in the country generally, and on the minds of the sepoys in particular. The great majority of the military officers asserted that the immediate and peremptory abolition of the practice would create no alarm among the native troops. Of the civil functionaries three-fourths advocated its positive prohibition. Fortified by these opinions, and secure of the support of the Court of Directors, Lord William Bentinck, on the 4th December, A.D. 1829
1829, promulgated that celebrated regulation which declared "the practice of suttee illegal and punishable by the "criminal courts as culpable homicide." Not the slightest feeling of alarm or resentment was exhibited, except by a few baboos in Calcutta, encouraged by Dr. Horace Hayman

Wilson, the great orientalist, the idol of pundits and brahmins. Within a twelvemonth Lord William Bentinck was enabled to assure the Court of Directors that there never was a greater bugbear than the fear of revolt on this ground. The enlightened natives of the present day regard it in the light of an extinct barbarism, just as we do the human sacrifices of the Druids.

It was during Lord William Bentinck's administration that the first energetic measures were adopted to extirpate

A.D. 1830 Suppression of Thuggee.

the Thugs, a fraternity of hereditary assassins, who subsisted by the plunder of the victims they strangled. There were few districts without some resident thugs, but they generally quitted their homes in small bodies with the appearance of cultivators, leaving their families in the village. As they roamed through the country they attached themselves, as if by accident, to the travellers they met, and entered into free and cheerful conversation with them to obtain the information they required; and, on reaching some sequestered spot, suddenly threw round the neck of the victim a strip of cloth or an unfolded turban, the ends of which were drawn tight till he ceased to breathe. His body was then rifled and thrown into a pit hastily dug with pickaxes which had been consecrated with religious ceremonials. The thugs were bound to secrecy by solemn oaths, and recognised each other by a slang vocabulary. They maintained a special veneration for Doorga, the tutelary goddess of vagabonds, thieves, and murderers, observed her festivals with superstitious punctuality, and presented a portion of their plunder at her most celebrated shrines. They endeavoured to ascertain her wishes by signs and omens, and considered themselves acting under divine authority when they were favourable. They traversed the length and breadth of the country, and their victims were counted by thousands. Lord William Bentinck determined to spare no pains or expense to deliver India from this scourge, and created a special department for its suppression, which he placed under the direction of Major—afterwards Sir William—Sleeman, whose name is inseparably connected in the annals of India with this mission of humanity. He organised a comprehensive scheme of operations which embraced every province, not exempting the native states, and by means of approvers who turned king's evidence, obtained a complete clue to the movements and operations of the gangs. With the aid of an efficient staff of officers whom he had himself selected, he took the field against them in every direction, and within six years 2,000 of these garotters were apprehended and convicted, and sentenced to death or imprisonment, and the fraternity was broken up.

The attention of Lord William Bentinck was directed immediately after his arrival to the establishment of steam communication on the Ganges. Under his direction, two vessels were built in Calcutta and fitted up with engines from England, and they performed the voyage from Calcutta to Allahabad, which had usually employed three months by water, in as many weeks. The enterprise was subsequently transferred to private companies. A still more important object with him was the abridgment of the voyage between India and England. A considerable fund had been raised in Calcutta in 1823 to promote this object, and a premium was offered for any steamer which should perform the voyage in seventy days. The attempt was made in the *Enterprise* by Captain Johnson, round the Cape, but he was 113 days accomplishing it. Lord William determined to try the experiment through the Red Sea, and directed the *Hugh Lindsay*, a small steamer of 400 tons, built at Bombay, to be sent from that port to Suez, which she reached in a month. Three other voyages were performed in succession, and it was demonstrated that, with corresponding arrangements in the Mediterranean, the voyage from Bombay to England might be completed in fifty-five days. The Court of Directors, however, raised an objection to these experiments, and questioned whether the end in view would be worth the expenditure, and at length prohibited any farther employment of the *Hugh Lindsay* in the conveyance of the mails. The subject was then brought before the House of Commons, who passed a resolution that "a regular and "expeditious communication by steam between England "and India was an object of national importance." The *Hugh Lindsay* was again put in requisition, but the Court of Directors were lukewarm, and the enterprise was performed in a perfunctory manner, and fell into abeyance. It was reserved for the Peninsular and Oriental Company to carry to a successful issue the large views of Lord William Bentinck, and, with the aid of the Suez Canal, to bring India within three weeks' distance of England.

A.D. 1830 to 1834

Steam communication.

The course of education received a fresh impulse, as well as a more useful direction, from the efforts of Lord William Bentinck. The Parliamentary

Education—Orientalism.

vote of ten lacs of rupees for "the revival and promotion of literature, and the encouragement of learned natives," was interpreted in Leadenhall Street and in Calcutta to apply to the revival of native literature, to which it was exclusively applied. Mr. Adam distinguished his brief tenure of office by appointing a Committee of
A.D. 1823 public instruction to suggest measures for the better education of the people in useful knowledge, and the arts and sciences of the West. This movement was strengthened by a despatch from the Court of Directors, drawn up by Mr. James Mill, the historian of India, who had obtained an important position at the India House, and exercised a beneficial influence on its counsels. The education department in Calcutta was under the control of Dr. Horace Wilson, the great champion of Oriental literature and institutions, and the Court was requested to sanction the appropriation of funds from the Parliamentary grant to improve the Hindoo college at Benares and the Mahomedan college in Calcutta, and also to establish a Hindoo college at the Presidency. In reply to this request, the Court, at the suggestion of Mr. Mill, stated that, "in proposing to establish seminaries for the purpose of teaching mere Hindoo and mere Mahomedan literature, the Government bound itself to teach a great deal of what was frivolous, not a little of what was purely mischievous, and a small remainder indeed in which utility was in any way concerned. The great end of Government should be, not to teach Hindoo or Mahomedan learning, but useful learning." But Orientalism was still in the ascendent in Calcutta, and with some trifling exceptions to save appearances, the funds continued to be appropriated to the studies which the Court had condemned.

1833 Meanwhile a predilection for an English education was gaining ground in and around the metropolis, and the demand for it was pressed with increased earnestness on the education board. The board was divided into two hostile and irreconcilable parties—the Orientalists and the Anglicists—the one anxious to devote the education funds to the study of the Shastres and the Koran, the other, to the object of unfolding the stores of European science to the natives through the English language; and it became necessary to appeal to the Government. It happened that Mr. Macaulay was not only a member of the Supreme Council, but also president of the board, and he denounced with irresistible force the con-

Predominance of English.

tinued promotion of Orientalism as tending, not to support the cause of truth, but to delay the death of error. "We "are at present," he said, "a board for printing books "which give artificial encouragement to absurd history, "absurd metaphysics, absurd physics, and absurd theo- "logy." The question was brought to an issue on the 7th March, 1835, by the resolution passed by Lord William Bentinck, in which he most cordially concurred, that "the great object of the British Government ought to be "the promotion of European literature and science among "the natives of India; and that the funds appropriated A.D. 1835 "to education would be best employed on English educa- "tion alone." The cause of English education triumphed, and the language and literature of England have become almost as familiar to the upper ten thousand in our Indian empire as the language of Rome was to the same class within the circle of her empire.

The medical college.

The last and crowning act of Lord William Bentinck's 1835 administration was the establishment of the medical college to supersede native quackery, and to give a complete education to native students in every branch of medical science, through the medium of English treatises and English lectures. The most eminent medical officers in the service were placed in the professor's chairs; a library and a museum were created; and every appliance necessary to place it on the same footing of efficiency as a European college was supplied with a liberal hand. Sage men of reputed wisdom predicted the failure of the experiment, inasmuch as contact with a dead body had been considered by the Hindoos a mortal pollution for twenty centuries; but their predictions have proved visionary; the Hindoo students resorted freely to the dissecting-room, and handled the scalpel with European indifference; and the college has proved an incalculable blessing to the country. The students have even crossed the "black water," and visited England to complete their studies, and have successfully competed with their European rivals.

Financial results.

With two trifling exceptions, Lord William Bentinck's administration was a reign of peace, and it produced the usual result on the finances. He found a deficit of a crore, and he left a surplus of a crore and a half, which his successor wasted in the Afghan war, as his predecessor had squandered the surplus left by Lord Hastings on the Burmese war. He embarked for England in March 1835, having held the government for nearly eight

A.D. 1828 to 1835 years. His administration marks the most memorable period in the improvement of India between the days of Lord Cornwallis and Lord Dalhousie. He repudiated the stagnant policy of the Government, and introduced an enlightened and a progressive spirit into every department of the state, the impulse of which still continues in vigorous operation. He infused new blood into the sluggish veins of the public institutions, and imparted life and animation to them. The originality of his plans of improvement was not less remarkable than the boldness with which they were executed. He earned the gratitude of the natives by opening to them an honourable career in the government of their own country, and the applause of Christendom by the moral courage he displayed in putting down suttees. The native and the European community vied with each other in commemorating the blessings of his reign, and in raising a subscription for the erection of his statue in Calcutta. It was enriched by an inscription from the pen of Mr. Macaulay:—"This statue is erected to William Cavendish "Bentinck, who, during seven years, ruled India with "eminent prudence, integrity, and benevolence; who, "placed at the head of a great empire, never laid aside the "simplicity and moderation of a private citizen; who "infused into Oriental despotism the spirit of British free-"dom; who never forgot that the end of government is "the welfare of the governed; who abolished cruel rites; "who effaced humiliating distinctions; who allowed liberty "to the expression of public opinion; whose constant study "it was to elevate the moral and intellectual character of "the Government committed to his charge. This monu-"ment was erected by men who, differing from each other "in race, in manners, in language, and in religion, cherish "with equal veneration and gratitude the memory of his "wise, upright, and paternal administration." On his return to England, Lord William Bentinck was elected member for Glasgow, the only retired Governor-General who ever sat in the House of Commons; and, with the exception of Warren Hastings, he was also the only Governor-General on whom no title of distinction was bestowed by the Crown.

The charter of 1833.

The period for which the commercial and political privileges of the Company had been granted expired in 1833, and it fell to Mr. Charles Grant, the President of the Board of Control, to introduce the question of the new charter to the notice of the House. The two

A.D. 1833

salient points which demanded its attention were those which referred to the continuance of the monopoly of the trade to China and to the government of India. It was found impossible to resist the demands of the merchants and manufacturers for a participation in the commerce of China, and it was thrown open to the country, and the commercial character of the Company ceased altogether, after it had continued for 234 years. The government of India was left in their hands for a further period of twenty years. Several minor, but not unimportant, arrangements were also made in reference to the policy of the Government in India. A fourth Presidency was created to embrace the North-West provinces. The power of legislation was now, for the first time, conferred on the Government, to embrace the whole empire, including all persons—British, foreign, or native—all places, and all things, as well as all courts, whether created by local authority or established by royal charter, but with certain necessary reservations touching the royal prerogative and the privileges of Parliament. A fourth member was also added to the Supreme Council who was to be an English jurist of reputation; and the office was dignified by the genius of Mr. Macaulay. It was moreover enacted that no native of India, nor any native-born subject of his Majesty, should be disabled from holding any place, office, or employment, by reason of his religion, place of birth, descent, or colour. Another clause, which sanctioned the purchase of land by Europeans and their free settlement in India, was opposed to the deep-seated sentiments of the India House, and was not carried without considerable opposition.

Effect of the charter.

In communicating the arrangements of the charter to the Governments in India, the Court of Directors expressed their determination to strain every nerve "to "accomplish the just and benevolent intentions "of their country in delegating to them the legislative as "well as the executive administration of the weightiest, "the most important, and the most interesting of its "transmarine possessions." They invited the full and cordial co-operation of their officers abroad in the discharge of these heavy responsibilities. Released from the management of a large mercantile concern, and the disturbing influences inseparably connected with it, they were enabled to devote their energies exclusively to their great political trust. Their minds acquired a higher tone, and it may be affirmed without the risk of controversy, that, with the exception of an occasional ebullition of traditional prejudice —the old cobwebs of the India House—the principles and measures which they inculcated on their servants in India during the remaining twenty-five years of their rule were marked by a character of wisdom, moderation, and beneficence, of which no other example can be found in the history of conquered dependencies.

A.D. 1835

The Governor-Generalship in dispute.

On the arrival of Lord William Bentinck's resignation, the Court of Directors offered the post to Mr. Mount-Stuart Elphinstone, but the state of his health obliged him to decline it. They then proceeded to pass a resolution that, "adverting to the public "character and services of Sir Charles Metcalfe" —who succeeded temporarily to the office as the senior member of Council—"it would be inexpedient at present "to make any other arrangement for supplying the place "of Governor-General." But the ministry refused to confirm their choice, and took their stand upon the dictum of Mr. Canning, when President of the Board of Control, that "the case could hardly be conceived in which it would "be expedient that the highest office in the Government "of India should be filled otherwise than from England, "and that this main link between the system of the Indian "and the British Government ought, for the advantage "of both, to be invariably maintained." The Court of Directors remonstrated with great warmth against the adoption of a principle which involved the wholesale exclusion of their servants from the highest prize in their service. Soon after, the Whigs gave place to a Tory cabinet, and Lord Ellenborough, the new President of the Board of Control, offered the post a second time to Mr. Elphinstone, who he knew must decline it, and then nominated Lord Heytesbury, a diplomatist of European reputation, to the office. No sooner, however, had he been sworn in at the India House, and received the accustomed allowance for his outfit, and the usual valedictory banquet at the London Tavern, than the Whigs returned to power and immediately cancelled the appointment. The Tory Government which succeeded to power in 1807, had refrained from interfering with the appointment of Lord Minto by their Whig predecessors, though he had not left the shores of England; but the Whig Government of 1837 had not the grace to follow the example. The Court of Directors earnestly protested against a proceeding which made the vital interests of the British empire in India subservient to the claims of political partisanship in England; but Lord Auckland, the Whig First Lord of the Admiralty, was nevertheless sent out to Calcutta.

The Charter Act created a fourth Presidency at Agra, and the eminent services of Sir Charles Metcalfe were rewarded by the grant of the first appointment, and by the still more dignified position of provisional Governor-General. He had not, however, been long at Agra before he was obliged to return to Calcutta, and assume the government on the departure of Lord William Bentinck. He occupied the office for a twelvemonth, and distinguished his administration by the legal establishment of the liberty of the press. The truculent law passed by Mr. Adam in 1823, which still continued on the statute-book, had been enforced on one or two occasions to the ruin of the printers, but the odium of these arbitrary proceedings was found to damage the character of Government. During the latter period of Lord Amherst's government the press was practically free. Lord William Bentinck avowed his invincible aversion to any political restrictions, and, moreover, had a profound contempt for the animadversions of the press; but the freedom it thus enjoyed was only by sufferance. Sir Charles Metcalfe felt that it was no longer possible to stop there. Parliament had recently granted Europeans liberty to purchase land and to make settlements in India, and Government lost the power of deporting those who rendered themselves obnoxious by their pens; Europeans, moreover, expected to enjoy the privilege they possessed in other British possessions of giving expression to their opinions. Sir Charles Metcalfe had always been a warm advocate of the freedom of the press, and, availing himself of the legislative power recently conferred on the Government, he lost no time in passing an Act repealing all the regulations by which it had been gagged, and making it legally free. The Act was received with feelings of enthusiasm by the European community in India, and by the native gentry most distinguished in society, and a subscription was raised to commemorate the event by erecting a noble hall which bears his name.

Sir Charles Metcalfe.

A.D. 1835

In the meantime an important change was made in the position of the Agra Presidency, which had been conferred on Sir Charles. In deference to the earnest wishes of the Court of Directors, it was reduced to the subordinate position of a lieutenant-governorship. Sir Charles naturally felt a re-

Reduction of the Government.

pugnance to descend to the inferior state of a lieutenant of the Governor-General after having himself occupied that supreme post, and he determined to retire from the service; but the chairman of the Court of Directors appealed to his patriotic feelings to retain the office on its reduced scale, and still to give the Company the benefit of his highly valued services. He was decorated with the grand cross of the Bath, and a third time nominated provisional Governor-General. He yielded to these solicitations, and to the importunities of Lord Auckland, and proceeded to Agra, but was not destined to remain there long. Soon after his arrival he heard that the press law had exasperated the India House, and created a complete revulsion of feeling regarding him and his claims. The Court of Directors regarded the freedom of the press with the same antipathy they had formerly felt to freedom of trade, and they took an early opportunity of manifesting their displeasure. The Government of Madras fell vacant, and Sir Charles naturally expected that, after the sacrifice he had made, it would have been conferred on him; but the Court of Directors would not condescend so much as to include his name among the candidates. There was a unanimous acknowledgment at the India House of his pre-eminent qualifications for it, but it was candidly avowed that his late proceeding regarding the press had cancelled every claim on their consideration. To Mr. Melville, the secretary at the India House, he wrote that reports were in circulation of his having incurred the displeasure of the Court of Directors and lost the governorship of Madras in consequence of the press law. If that misfortune had befallen him, it was his earnest entreaty that they would intimate their pleasure that he might retire from their service. After keeping the letter for four months, the Court sent a curt and discourteous reply, on the receipt of
A.D. 1837 which he immediately sent in his resignation, and his connection with the East India Company was brought to a termination by treatment similar to that which had been inflicted on some of the greatest of his predecessors. But the services which the Company thought fit to discard were fully appreciated by the ministry, and he was successively entrusted with the government of two of the most important colonies of the Crown.

CHAPTER XII.

SECTION I.

LORD AUCKLAND—COMMENCEMENT OF THE AFGHAN WAR.

LORD AUCKLAND was sworn in as Governor-General on the 20th March. At the valedictory entertainment given him by the Court of Directors he assured them that "he looked with exultation at the opportunity "now afforded him of doing good to his "fellow-creatures, of promoting education, and "extending the blessings of good government to the "millions in India." Seldom have expectations been so signally disappointed; his melancholy administration is comprised in one disastrous transaction, the Afghan war, the origin of which may be dated in July, 1837, and the catastrophe in which it closed occurred in January, 1841. To form a correct idea of this momentous transaction, it is necessary to trace the convergence of events in Afghanistan and the Punjab, in Persia and Russia, to the period when this ill-starred expedition was undertaken.

A.D. 1836

Lord Auckland Governor-General.

Shah Soojah, the exiled monarch of Cabul and the British pensioner at Loodiana, made a second effort to recover his throne in 1833. He crossed the Indus without the least opposition, and in January defeated the Ameers of Sinde at Shikarpore, and constrained them to make him an immediate payment of five lacs of rupees. On his advance to Candahar he was met by Dost Mahomed and completely routed, when he retraced his steps to his old retreat and pension at Loodiana. While the troops of the Dost were engaged in repelling him, Runjeet Sing made an irruption across the Indus and took possession of the province of Peshawur. At this juncture a wild and predatory tribe on the right bank of the river made repeated inroads into the Hazara district which Runjeet Sing had also subjugated; and as they were traced, whether with or without reason, to the instigation of the Ameers of Sinde, the Punjab army took possession of two of their forts, and both parties stood

Shah Soojah.

1834

Runjeet Sing's designs on Sinde.

ready for a conflict which would doubtless have ended in the discomfiture of the Ameers and the extension of Runjeet Sing's authority throughout the course of the Indus down to the sea, which it was the determination of the Government of India to prevent. It was with difficulty Colonel Pottinger restrained the rulers of Sinde from rushing into war; and Captain Wade, our representative with Runjeet Sing, was obliged to allude forcibly to the risk he must incur if he pursued designs which were opposed by the British Government. On the other hand his gallant and ambitious officers importuned him to resist at all hazards the restrictions thus imperiously placed on the extension of his territories; but he shook his venerable beard, and asked where were now the 200,000 Mahratta swords which had once bade defiance to the Company. He bowed to the majesty of British power, and at once relinquished the expedition to Sinde.

A.D. 1835 — Dost Mahomed at Peshawur.

The loss of Peshawur rankled in the bosom of Dost Mahomed, and he assumed the character of a ghazee, or champion of the faith, and proclaimed a religious war against the infidel Sikhs. The Mahomedan world in Central Asia was immediately in commotion, and from the regions of the Hindoo Coosh, from the wilds of Turkestan, and the farthest recesses of the mountains thousands poured down to join the standard of the Prophet. The spirit of Runjeet Sing appeared to quail before this host of infuriated fanatics; and, while he advanced with his army to the defence of Peshawur, he sent one Harland, an American adventurer, ostensibly on a mission to Dost Mahomed, but in reality to sow dissensions in the Afghan camp; and so successful was he in planting a feeling of jealousy of the growing power of the Dost among his brothers, that one of them abruptly withdrew with 10,000 men. The encampment was thrown into a state of inextricable confusion and dismay. "At break of day," as Harland reported, "not a vestige of the Afghan camp was "to be seen, where, six hours before, 50,000 men and "10,000 horse were rife with the tumult of wild emotion." Dost Mahomed retired with deep chagrin to Cabul.

1836 — Movements of the Dost.

On hearing of Lord Auckland's arrival in Calcutta, the Dost sent him a complimentary letter, and, in allusion to his unhappy relations with Runjeet Sing, asked him "to communicate whatever might suggest "itself to his mind for the settlement of the "affairs of the country." Lord Auckland returned a friendly reply, and stated his intention to send a gentleman to Cabul shortly "to discuss questions of commerce;" but, with regard to the Sikh quarrel, said, "My friend, you are "aware that it is not the practice of the British Government "to interfere with the affairs of other independent states." Despairing of any assistance from the British Government the Dost, at the beginning of 1837, applied to the king of Persia, as to the "King of Islam," to relieve him from the "misery caused by the detestable tribe of Sikhs." Impatient to wipe out the disgrace he had sustained, he sent his son Akbar Khan with a large army into the province of Peshawur, and the Sikhs were completely defeated. Reinforcements were pushed forward from the Punjab with a degree of promptitude and speed which has seldom been exceeded, and the Afghans were in their turn obliged to withdraw to Cabul. It was at this critical juncture that Captain Burnes, Lord Auckland's envoy, made his appearance to discourse of trade and manufactures.

A.D. 1837

Progress of Russia in the East.

The Russians, like the Romans, have systematically devoted their energies to the extension of their power and dominion, and for more than a century have prosecuted schemes of aggrandisement in Europe and Asia without intermission or failure. After having succeeded in bringing the Khirgis Cossacks to subordination, they took up their position on the Jaxartes in 1830, and gradually advanced eastward with a steady pace, fixing their grasp on Central Asia more firmly at every step. On that river they erected a chain of forts extending from its estuary in lake Ural to fort Vernoe, 700 miles eastward. Meanwhile the ambitious diplomatists of Russia had been pushing her influence in Persia, and through Persia up to Afghanistan. On the death of the king Futteh Ali, who had always been favourable to an English alliance, he was succeeded by his grandson Mahomed Shah, who threw himself into the arms of Russia. Since the first mission of Captain Malcolm, the British Government had expended more than a crore of rupees in embassies and subsidies to Persia in order to acquire a predominant influence at the court, which might serve as a bulwark to the empire of India. The ministry had now the mortification of finding this labour and expenditure thrown away, and the British influence at Teheran completely superseded by that of Russia.

The monarchs of Persia had long coveted the possession of Herat, the key of Western Afghanistan, and Mahomed

Shah had resolved on a second expedition to it. The ruler, Shah Kamran, had made repeated inroads into the Persian territory, and, according to official report, had kidnapped 12,000 of the subjects of Persia and sold them into slavery. Mr. M'Neill, the British minister at the court of Teheran, asserted that the expedition to Herat was fully justified by the atrocities of its ruler, but that, in the present state of the relations of Russia with Persia, the entry of a Persian army into Afghanistan would be tantamount to the advance of Russian influence to the threshold of India, which would not fail to disturb the tranquillity of the empire. He used every argument to dissuade the Shah from the expedition, while on the other hand the Russian minister at the court encouraged him to persevere, and offered him every kind of assistance. The ministry in London presented a remonstrance on the subject at St. Petersburg, and the emperor replied that Count Simonich, his envoy, had exceeded his instructions; but he was not recalled, and his proceedings were so completely in accordance with the national feeling that the "Moscow Gazette" threatened that the next treaty with England should be dictated in Calcutta.

Negotiations at Herat.

A.D. 1837

The Shah set out for Herat in the month of July with 50,000 troops and fifty pieces of cannon, exulting in the prospect of overthrowing the Sikhs and following the course of Nadir Shah to Delhi. The expedition was considered as betokening the triumph of Russian over British influence in Persia, and created a profound sensation not only throughout Central Asia, but also in India, where the native princes began to speculate on the humiliation of the Company. The Mahomedans looked for the advent of a countless host of the faithful, backed by 200,000 "Russ." Exaggerated reports of great movements in Central Asia, the cradle of Indian revolutions for eight centuries, were spread far and wide, and in the remote Deccan people began to bury their money and jewels in the ground.

1837

The Herat expedition.

During this commotion Lord Auckland left Calcutta and proceeded to Simla. The north-west provinces were at the time visited with a desolating famine, which was calculated to have swept away 500,000 of its inhabitants, and Lord Auckland, whose camp of 20,000 men served to aggravate the calamity, was entreated to retrace his steps to Calcutta. If he had listened to this advice and returned to the seat of Govern-

Lord Auckland's movements.

ment, and had thus been brought under the wholesome influence of the members of Council, the Company would have been spared the horrors of the Afghan war, but he resolved to continue his progress. At Simla his cabinet council consisted of Mr. Macnaghten, the foreign secretary, Mr. Colvin, his private secretary, and Mr. Torrens, a young civilian of great parts and great impetuosity; but they were all men of much greater strength of character and resolution than Lord Auckland, and the war is to be attributed to their influence. The home Government, seeing in every direction the indication of a restless and aggressive spirit on the part of Russia and her agents directed against the security of the British empire in India, had instructed the Government to adopt vigorous measures for its protection; and Mr. M'Neill, the minister in Persia, strongly advised Lord Auckland to raise up a barrier in Afghanistan by subsidising and strengthening Dost Mahomed.

It was at this period of fermentation that Captain A.D. Burnes appeared at Cabul. In the East, the importance of 1837 a mission is measured by the value of the presents; and the magnificence of the gifts of Mr. Mountstuart Elphinstone in 1808 was not forgotten. When, therefore, Captain Burnes opened his treasury, consisting of a pistol and telescope for the Dost, and some pins and needles for the zenana, he and his embassy sunk at once into contempt. He found the influence of Persia paramount in Afghanistan. The Dost's brothers, the rulers of Candahar, were negotiating an alliance offensive and defensive with the Shah, and an envoy had arrived at their court to complete the treaty, together with an ambassador with robes and presents for the Dost. The passionate desire of his heart was the recovery of Peshawur, and he assured Captain Burnes that if he were permitted to hope for any assistance from the British Government, he would break off all intercourse with Persia, and send back the plenipotentiary from Candahar. But Lord Auckland had a morbid dread of giving offence to Runjeet Sing, and refused to listen to any proposal regarding Peshawur. Yet the Sikh ruler had offered to restore it to Dost Mahomed if he would pay tribute for it; and the Dost was prepared to hold it as a fief, sending the customary presents to Lahore; and there can be no doubt that if the cabinet Council at Simla had boldly met the question, and entrusted the settlement of it to Captain Burnes at Cabul, and to Captain Wade at Lahore, it would have been brought to an

Captain Burnes at Cabul.

early and satisfactory issue, and the Dost would have been secured as an ally; but from first to last a spirit of infatuation pervaded the Afghan policy of the Government. Captain Burnes had threatened the Candahar chiefs with the severe displeasure of the British Government if they persisted in cultivating the Persian alliance, and they dismissed the envoy without the usual ceremonies, on the assurance of Captain Burnes that he would protect them from the displeasure of the Persians, and, if necessary, subsidise their troops. Lord Auckland severely reprimanded him for having exceeded his instructions, and directed him to inform the rulers that he had held out expectations which his Government declined to sanction; and they lost no time in completing the treaty with Persia, which was ratified by the Russian minister at Teheran, who engaged to defend Candahar from every attack. The proposal of Captain Burnes was, however, highly approved of by the ministry in London.

After the receipt of Lord Auckland's unfavourable reply in 1836, Dost Mahomed despatched an envoy to solicit the emperor of Russia to protect him from the Sikhs. Captain Viktevitch was thereupon sent to Cabul with rich presents, and an autograph from the emperor, the authenticity of which has been questioned, but never disproved. He arrived in Cabul on the 19th December, and the Dost immediately visited Captain Burnes, and assured him that he desired no connection except with the English Government, and was ready to dismiss the Russian envoy summarily if any hopes were held out to him from Simla. Captain Burnes, on the one hand, dissuaded him from so imprudent a step, and, on the other, urged on Lord Auckland the importance of immediate and decided action in this neck-to-neck struggle between Russia and England at Cabul; but Lord Auckland replied that he must waive all hope of Peshawur, and be content with whatever arrangement Runjeet Sing might think fit to make. The Dost then stated that he should consider himself safe if the province were placed jointly in his hands and those of his brother, who governed it on behalf of Runjeet Sing; and Captain Burnes again importuned Lord Auckland to give a favourable hearing to his representations, assuring him that the Afghan ruler was so anxious to cultivate the friendship of England that the Russian envoy had not been acknowledged up to that time. This hope, however, was finally quenched by the letter which the cabinet

The Russian envoy.

A.D. 1837

of secretaries at Simla persuaded the Governor-General to address to Dost Mahomed. It was not only supercilious, but arrogant; every sentence in it was calculated to kindle a flame of indignation in the breast of the Afghan nobility, and Captain Burnes's mission became hopeless.

Retirement of Captain Burnes.

In the last resort, the Dost addressed a conciliatory letter to the Governor-General, imploring him, in language bordering on humility, to remedy the grievances of the Afghans, and give them a little encouragement; but he turned a deaf ear to every overture, and continued to require that he should reject the alluring offers made by Russia and Persia, while he himself offered nothing in return but good offices to prevent the farther encroachment of the Sikhs. It could scarcely have been unknown at Simla that Runjeet Sing had no more idea of marching to Cabul than to Pekin, and that the mere mention of the Khyber pass, as General Avitabile affirmed, gave the Sikh soldiers the colic. When the last ray of hope vanished, the Russian envoy was conducted with great parade through the streets, and received at the durbar with much distinction. Captain Burnes returned to Simla, and found a strong feeling of animosity against the Dost in Lord Auckland's advisers, who were irritated to perceive that, instead of meekly submitting to their dictation, he was sitting at the gate of India hesitating whether to accept their terms or the offers of their opponents, and it was resolved to march across the Indus and depose him, and to reinstate Shah Soojah on the throne. It was at first contemplated that an expedition should be organised to conduct him to Cabul, and that the British Government should contribute all the necessary funds, as well as a body of officers to discipline and command his troops, and a representative to accompany him. But it was soon apparent that, unless the Government of India engaged in the war as principals, it must end in a deplorable failure. It was accordingly determined to send a large British army into the unexplored regions of Central Asia, where all convoys of provisions, stores, and ammunition must traverse the states of doubtful allies, and thread long and dangerous mountain defiles, beset with wild and plundering tribes, to oblige the Persians to raise the siege of Herat, to drive Dost Mahomed from Afghanistan, and to place Shah Soojah in his seat. A tripartite treaty was negotiated and concluded by Mr. Macnaghten between the Government of India, Shah Soojah, and Runjeet Sing, who engaged to

A.D. 1838

contribute the aid of a body of troops on condition that the Shah should confirm his right to the possessions he had acquired beyond the Indus, and divide with him whatever sums he might be able to extort from the Ameers of Sinde. The expedition was undertaken chiefly under the advice of Mr. Colvin, though Sir John Hobhouse, the President of the Board of Control, subsequently claimed to share the responsibility of it, inasmuch as his letter, authorising it on the part of the ministry, crossed the letter from Simla announcing that it had been commanded. With the exception of the ministerial circle in Downing Street and the secretaries at Simla this preposterous enterprise was universally condemned. Mr. Elphinstone stated that "if 27,000 men "could be sent through the Bolan Pass to Candahar, and "we could feed them, we might take Cabul and set up "Shah Soojah; but it was hopeless to maintain him in a "poor, cold, strong, and remote country, among a turbulent "people like the Afghans." Lord William Bentinck considered the project an act of incredible folly. Lord Wellesley regarded "this wild expedition, 800 miles from our "frontier and our resources, into one of the most difficult "countries of the world, a land of rocks and deserts, of "sands, and ice, and snow, as an act of infatuation." The Duke, with prophetic sagacity, affirmed that "the conse-"quence of once crossing the Indus to settle a Govern-"ment in Afghanistan would be a perennial march into the "country." An attempt was made to justify the expedition in a manifesto dated at Simla the 1st October, one of the most remarkable documents in the Company's archives, unique for its unscrupulous misstatements and its audacious assertions. A single instance will suffice to stamp its character: it affirmed that the orders for assembling the army were issued in concurrence with the Supreme Council, whereas the Council, when required to place the proclamation on record, remonstrated on the consummation of a policy of such grave importance without their having had any opportunity of expressing their opinion on it. The immediate object was said to be to succour the besieged garrison of Herat, and to that memorable siege we now turn.

A.D. 1838

The siege of Herat.

The province of Herat, the acquisition of which had for many years been the one object of desire to the sovereigns of Persia, is the only route through which a large and well equipped army can advance from the north-west towards India, and is considered the gate of

Afghanistan on the west, as Cabul is on the east. All the materials for the equipment and maintenance of an army are to be found in great abundance, and the fertility of the soil has given it the title of the granary of Central Asia. The king, Kamran, was one of the worst specimens of an Oriental despot and voluptuary, and his minister, Yar Mahomed, though not devoid of courage and abilities, was justly described as "the greatest scoundrel in Afghanis-"tan." The king of Persia sat down before it on the A.D.
23rd November; the fortifications were crumbling away, 1837
and the town might have been carried by a vigorous assault on the first day. Its successful defence was owing to the exertions of one man. A few days before the commencement of the siege, a young officer of the Bombay Artillery, Lieutenant Eldred Pottinger, who had been sent to make researches in Central Asia, entered the town in the garb of a *syud*, or descendant of Mahomed, and resolved to remain and take part in the approaching struggle. His services were readily accepted by the king and the vizier, and the natural ascendancy of genius speedily gave him the chief direction of operations. The garrison was animated with a spirit of great resolution, and under his inspiration baffled all the assaults of the Persians for five months, though assisted by a regiment of Russians, who were styled deserters to save appearances. Mr. M'Neill, the English minister at Teheran, joined the Persian camp on
the 6th April, and, finding both parties inclined to accept 1838
his mediation, proceeded into the city to negotiate with Shah Kamran, and there was every prospect of an early accommodation; but, during his absence, the Russian minister who followed him from the capital in all haste had reached the Shah's encampment, and urged the continuance of the siege, and advanced funds for the support of the army. The aspect of affairs was immediately changed; the Shah gave a cold reception to the British minister on his return from the city, rejected the amicable arrangement he had made, and announced his resolution to renew the siege; and Mr. M'Neill retired to the Turkish frontier.

The siege raised.

The 24th June was fixed for a general assault. The works were attacked under the personal direction of Count Simonich, the Russian minister, and his engineer officers at five points; the assailants were repulsed from four of them, but at the fifth a practical breach was made in the defences, and the courage of the Heratees began to fail. Yar Mahomed withdrew from the carnage;

A.D. 1838 but Pottinger dragged him back to the breach, and urged on the defence with such irresistible energy that the Persians, when on the point of gaining the city, recoiled and fled, leaving 1,700 in killed and wounded. The siege was then turned into a blockade, and the inhabitants suffered the extremity of want. Meanwhile, two steamers were sent by the Government of India to occupy the island of Karrack, and they were magnified by rumour into a portentous squadron. Mr. M'Neill took advantage of the consternation created by this movement to send Colonel Stoddart to the Persian camp to assure the king that, if he did not relinquish his design, he would bring on himself the hostility of the British Government who had already sent an armament into the Persian Gulf. The king wanted only a decent pretext to raise the siege, which had cost him dear, and replied that to secure its friendship he was prepared to abandon it. He broke up his encampment on the 9th September, and retired with the loss of half his army and much treasure, and with the disgrace of having failed in an expedition which had been the talk of Central Asia for nine months. This memorable defence of Herat against 40,000 Persians aided by European engineers, stands side by side with the siege of Arcot, and reflects no little renown on the Anglo-Saxon youth by whose genius it was achieved, though he had never seen service, and possessed no knowledge of the art of war except what he had derived from books.

Persistence in the expedition.

The grand projects of Persia and Russia which had for two years agitated the public mind from the Caspian Sea to Cape Comorin were now quenched. The dangers which menaced the British possessions in India were at once dispelled. Russia was nowhere in Central Asia, and it was expected that the expedition to Cabul would be relinquished; but the infatuated Government at Simla determined to persevere.
1838 On the 9th November it was announced that, while the raising of the siege of Herat was a just cause for congratulation, the Government would still continue to prosecute the expedition with vigour. Of the reasons assigned, one was that the treaty with Runjeet Sing and with Shah Soojah bound us in honour to proceed with it; but, in the convention with the ruler of the Punjab there was no allusion to the march of a British army across the Indus, and the exiled monarch was particularly anxious to avoid the unpopularity of being carried to

Cabul on the shoulders of infidels. All he wanted was the Company's gold to enable him to secure the swords of the mercenary Afghans.

SECTION II.

LORD AUCKLAND'S ADMINISTRATION—THE AFGHAN WAR—SURRENDER OF THE DOST.

A.D. 1838

Meeting of Runjeet Sing and the Governor-General.

The army of the Indus, as it was designated, was assembled in November at Ferozepore, where there was a grand meeting between the Governor-General and the lion of the Punjab, then tottering on the brink of the grave, but still exhibiting in his countenance the calmness of design, while his single eye was still lighted up with the fire of enterprise. There were showy pageants, and gay doings, and the manœuvres of mimic warfare. As the army was no longer destined for Herat, its strength was reduced; and the Commander-in-Chief, who had consented to assume the command when it was to march into Central Asia, declined to head a diminished force simply to place Shah Soojah in the seat of a better man. The Bengal column started from Ferozepore on the 10th December 9,500 strong, with 30,000 camels and 38,000 camp followers. The force raised for Shah Soojah, and called his army, though commanded by Company's officers and paid from the Company's treasury, consisted of 6,000 men. The Bombay troops under Sir John Keane numbered 5,600, and the whole force amounted to 21,000. The political charge of the expedition was entrusted to Mr. Macnaghten, and he was styled the envoy. The direct route to Cabul lay through the Punjab; but Runjeet Sing, whom Lord Auckland styled our "ancient and faithful ally," declined to grant a passage through his dominions to a body of more than 50,000 men, and it became necessary to take a circuitous route of 1,000 miles down the Indus, and then across it up to Candahar and Cabul.

Coercion of the Ameers of Sinde.

This devious course had an eye also to the determination which had been formed to lay the Ameers of Sinde under contribution. The province had formerly been a dependency of Cabul, and had paid tribute whenever the Afghan sovereign was able to

A.D. 1839

enforce it. No revenue, however, had been paid for more than forty years, and the Ameers were to all intents and purposes independent; but they were now required to give twenty-five lacs of arrears to a sovereign who had been an exile for thirty years. Colonel Pottinger, the Resident, presented the demand, but was confounded by the production of two releases in full from all further claims of every description which Shah Soojah had written in two Korans and signed and sealed five years before, when he exacted three lacs of rupees of them; Lord Auckland, however, said that he did not consider it incumbent on him to enter into any investigation of this plea, and Mr. Macnaghten affirmed that, rather than allow the grand enterprise they were engaged in to be impeded by the opposition of the Ameers, it would be better to let 20,000 Punjab troops loose on their capital. It was likewise resolved to impose a subsidiary treaty on them for which they were required to pay three lacs a year; and, as they demurred to these demands, Mr. Macnaghten directed Colonel Pottinger to inform them that "neither the ready power to crush and "annihilate them nor the will to call it into action were "wanting, if it appeared necessary." Sir John Keane marched up with the Bombay army to the vicinity of Hyderabad, and the Bengal column was sent down to co-operate with him. Awed by these demonstrations, the Ameers submitted to necessity, signed the treaty, and sent in the first instalment.

Advance of the army.

The sepoys, notwithstanding their religious prejudices, crossed the Indus without hesitation, and planted the flag of England on its right bank; but the disasters of the army commenced as soon as it was across. The Bengal column pushed on in advance through the arid desert, 140 miles in length, of Cutch Gundava, which furnished little water and not a blade of grass. The camels died by hundreds, and the mortality among the draft cattle, on which the subsistence of the army depended, was portentous. After traversing this sterile waste the troops were six days getting through the terrific defiles of the Bolan Pass, where a small band might have brought the expedition to a deadlock. The flint stones lamed the camels; fatigue and the want of pasture disabled the artillery horses; the mountain paths were strewed with tents, equipages, and stores; and the rivulet which flowed at the bottom of the ravines was tainted with the carcases of animals. Emerging from this

pass the army entered the beautiful valley of Shawl; but the provisions found there were scanty, and starvation stared the army in the face. On the 6th April the Bombay A.D.
column and Shah Soojah's army joined the Bengal force at 1839
Qwetta, and Sir John Keane assumed the chief command. The troops were half mutinous for want of food, the loaf of the European soldier was diminished in weight, the native troops were reduced to a pound of flour and the camp followers to half that quantity, and the army was obliged to push on to Candahar. In the intervening space lay the Khojuk pass, scarcely less formidable than the Bolan, though of more limited extent. The batteries and field-pieces were dragged up and lowered down its tremendous precipices by the European soldiers, pressed by hunger, parched with thirst, and consumed by incessant fatigue. As Shah Soojah approached Candahar, the Barukzie chiefs, the brothers of the Dost, betrayed by their own officers who had been corrupted, fled to the west, and he entered the city on the 25th April.

Capture of Ghuzni.

The army, still on reduced rations, was obliged to remain inactive at Candahar for ten weeks to await the ripening of the crops. At a distance of 230 miles from the city and 90 from Cabul lay the renowned fortress of Ghuzni, from which Mahmood had marched eight centuries before to plant the standard of the crescent on the plains of India. Dost Mahomed's son, Hyder Khan, had been sent to strengthen the garrison and the fortifications and to provision the fort for six months. The parapet which rose sixty or seventy feet perpendicular above the plain, combined with the wet ditch, presented an insurmountable obstacle to any attack by mining or escalade. Sir John Keane had imprudently left his siege guns behind at Candahar, and the collapse of the expedition appeared inevitable. Happily, one of the gates had not been built up, and Captain Thomson, the chief engineer, convinced the Commander-in-Chief that the only mode of attack which presented any chance of success was that of blowing up the gate and forcing his way into the fortress. Under his direction, therefore, 900 lbs. of powder were packed up in bags and conveyed on a tempestuous night to the spot. The powder exploded; the barricade was shivered, and great masses of masonry and wood came toppling down. Colonel Dennie and the 13th Light Infantry rushed in with the storming party, and, after a fearful struggle over the *débris*, the English ensign was floating at daybreak over the proud citadel of Ghuzni.

The fall of Ghuzni, which left the road to Cabul open, bewildered Dost Mahomed, and he called his officers

Arrival at Cabul.

together, and with the Koran in his hand implored them to make one bold stand like brave men and true believers. "You have eaten my salt," he said, "for thirteen years; grant me one reqnest. "Stand by the brother of Futteh Khan while he makes "one last charge on these infidel dogs; he will fall; then "make your own terms with Shah Soojah." But there was neither spirit nor fidelity in them; and the Dost, seeing the struggle hopeless, parked his guns at Urgundeh and turned with a few followers to the region of the Hindoo Coosh. Captain Outram and nine other officers, animated by the ardent spirit of adventure, started in pursuit of him with a body of cavalry, and gave him no rest for six days and nights; but they were impeded at every step by the treacherous chief Hajee Khan, who accompanied them with several hundred Afghan horse, and on reaching Bameean they found that the Dost had passed beyond the limits of

A.D. 1839

Afghanistan. On the 7th August Shah Soojah, resplendent with jewels, was conducted with martial pomp through the city of Cabul to the Bala Hissar, the palace in the citadel; but there was no enthnsiasm. The inhabitants came to their thresholds to gaze not so mnch at the Shah as at the infidel soldiers parading their streets, on whom they poured a shower of maledictions. Three weeks later the Shah was joined by his son Timur, who had advanced on the direct route through the Punjab and Peshawur, with 4,000 raw recruits, paid by the Company, and under the direction of Colonel Wade. This expedition was accompanied by a contingent of 6,000 of Runjeet Sing's soldiers, to whom any movement into Afghanistan was odious, and they were repeatedly engaged in flagrant mntiny. As the force entered the Khyber, the Afreedies prepared, as usual, to oppose its progress; but Colonel Wade crowned the heights and turned their flanks, and by this masterly movement these terrible defiles were opened, probably for the first time, by steel instead of gold.

The object of the expedition—that of substituting a friendly for a hostile power in Afghanistan—was now ac-

Retention of the army.

complished, and the period had arrived when, according to the Simla manifesto, the British troops were to be withdrawn. Within a fortnight after

the entrance of Shah Soojah, however, Lord Auckland placed on record that "to leave him without the support of a "British army would be followed by his expulsion, which "would reflect disgrace on Government and become a "source of danger." It was determined, therefore, to leave a force of 10,000 men to maintain him on his throne; and, as the Duke had predicted, our difficulties began as soon as our military success was complete. General Willshire, who commanded the Bombay army, was instructed on his return to inflict a severe chastisement on Mehrab A.D.
Khan, the ruler of Belochistan, for having withheld supplies 1839
as the army advanced through his country; but as our troops had wantonly desolated the country in their march, and he had none to give, the proceeding was unjust and vindictive. The Belochees fought valiantly for their country and their chief; but the capital, Khelat, was stormed, and the Khan fell valiantly in its defence with eight of his principal officers.

Honours.

The expedition was as fertile in honours as it was barren in military achievements. It was a ministerial measure, condemned by the general voice of society in England and in India, and it was deemed politic to give as much *éclat* as possible to the first success. Lord Auckland was created an earl; Sir John Keane, who had done less than nothing, a baron with an annuity of 2,000*l*. Mr. Macnaghten, Colonel Pottinger, and General Willshire received baronetcies, and Colonel Wade a knighthood; but Captain Thomson, who had saved the expedition from an ignominious and fatal failure by blowing up the gate of Ghuzni, obtained nothing but a brevet majority and the lowest order of the Bath; and he abandoned the service.

Death of Runjeet Sing.

Runjeet Sing died as the expedition was leaving Candahar, on the 27th June, at the age of fifty-seven, the victim 1839
of excesses in which he had long been accustomed to indulge. He possessed the same creative genius as Sevajee and Hyder Ali. The edifice of Sikh greatness was exclusively his work, and he would doubtless have established a great empire in Hindostan if he had not been hemmed in by the Company's power. He succeeded to the leadership of a single tribe in the Punjab, when it was distracted with the contests of a dozen chieftains, and to the command of a body of matchlock horsemen. He bequeathed to his successor a great kingdom enriched with the spoils of its neighbours, together with an army 80,000 strong, with 300 pieces of

cannon, superior in discipline, in equipment, and in valour to any force ever before assembled under a native chief. He had the Oriental passion for hoarding, and left twelve crores of rupees in his treasury, of which he bestowed half a crore on the poor; the Koh-i-noor, which now adorns the diadem of England, he bequeathed to Jugernath. He was the only man in his country favourable to the English alliance, and during the expedition to Cabul placed the resources of his country at the disposal of the Government. The hostility of his ministers and officers broke out soon after his death, and so greatly augmented the perils of our position in Afghanistan, that Sir William Macnaghten urged Lord Auckland "to curb the Sings," as the Sikh chiefs were called, "and to macadamise the Punjab, and "annex Peshawur to the dominions of Shah Soojah."

A.D. 1840

Russian complaints against Khiva.

Soon after the occupation of Cabul, the Russophobia which distracted Sir William Macnaghten, Sir Alexander Burnes, and other British officers in Afghanistan rose to fever heat, on the announcement that a great Russian expedition was about to proceed to Khiva, the celebrated Kharism of early Mohamedan history. This country lies to the south of the sea of Aral on the banks of the Oxus, but, with the exception of the oasis of Merv, is a continuous waste, unrelieved by mountains, rivers, lakes, or forests, and with scarcely more than a million of inhabitants. For half a century the rulers had been in the habit of committing depredations on Russian caravans, attacking Russian posts, and kidnapping Russian subjects whom they held in slavery. The emperor determined on a military expedition to fulfil "the im-"perial obligation of protecting the lives and liberties of his "subjects;" but there was likewise a second motive. In his Simla manifesto Lord Auckland had stated that the object of the expedition was also "to give the name and just in-"fluence of the British Government its proper footing "among the nations of Central Asia." The ambitious spirit of Sir William Macnaghten was disposed to carry out this policy to an extent which startled even his own Government. He sent a military force beyond Bameean to depose an Oosbek chief and instal another, and alarm was spread through Turkestan. Major Todd, who had been sent as the representative of the Governor-General to Herat, was strengthening its fortifications, and had despatched one of his assistants to Khiva to offer the Khan the boon of British friendship. The envoy exceeded his instructions, and proposed an alliance, offensive and defensive, which Lord Auckland immediately disavowed. A mission was also sent to Bokhara.

Russian expedition to Khiva.

A.D. 1840

These simultaneous movements, military and diplomatic, aroused the jealousy of the cabinet of St. Petersburg, who resented any intrusion of the English Government into the politics of Central Asia, and the emperor ordered the Khiva expedition to advance without any delay, five months earlier than was originally intended. The manifesto which announced its despatch, after enumerating the injuries the Russians had sustained from the Khivans, adopted the language of Lord Auckland's proclamation, and stated that the expedition was also intended "to strengthen in that part of Asia the "lawful influence to which Russia had a right." The Russian journals affirmed without any disguise that the object of it was "to establish the strong influence of Russia "in Khiva, Bokhara, and Kokand, and to prevent the in-"fluence of the East India Company from taking root in "Central Asia." The two European nations destined to divide the predominant power in Asia between them, were at this time jealous of each other's progress, and were resorting to the fatal expedient of fitting out expeditions to counteract it. "If we go on at this rate," said Baron Brunow to Lord Palmerston, "the Cossack and the Sepoy "will soon cross bayonets on the Oxus." The Russian expedition proved a total failure. It moved from Orenburg in November on a march of 1,000 miles in the depth of winter, when the snow lay several feet deep on the ground, and not a blade of grass was to be found, and the general was obliged to retrace his steps after the loss of half his army. Subsequently Major Todd despatched Captain Shakespear to Khiva, who prevailed on the Khan to deliver up 400 Russian slaves, whom he conducted to Orenburg, but his interference was considered intrusive.

The Bala Hissar.

After the determination was formed to retain a British army in Afghanistan, the most important of all questions was the encampment of the troops at the capital. The Bala Hissar of Cabul stood on a hill, and completely commanded the city. It afforded accommodation for 5,000 troops, and, if well provisioned and supplied with military stores, could be held by 1,000 men against whatever force or skill the Afghans could bring against it. It was the key of Cabul, and the security of our position depended on our occupation of it. The Shah insisted on excluding the soldiers from it, that the privacy of his zenana might not be disturbed, and in an evil hour the envoy, contrary to his own better judgment, yielded to his importunity and the garrison was turned into cantonments in the plain, erected in the most exposed position that could be thought of. The whole of the Afghan policy from first to last was a tissue of folly, but the crowning act of insanity was the resignation of the Bala Hissar to the Shah's hundred and fifty women. The conviction daily became more confirmed, that he had no hold on the attachment of his subjects, and that it was the infidel aid on which he rested for support that was the chief element of his unpopularity. Its presence was regarded like a visitation of the plague. Many of the political officers were men of high honour and conciliatory manners, but there were others whose haughty and arrogant bearing created disgust, and whose unblushing licentiousness, which invaded the honour of the noblest families, raised a feeling of burning indignation. During the twenty-seven months of our occupation, the Government was a Government of sentry-boxes, sustained only by the sheen of British bayonets. The country was garrisoned, not governed, and we were reposing on a smouldering volcano. Within a few weeks of the occupation of Cabul, the highlanders in the Khyber massacred a large detachment of troops and carried off their baggage. The whole province of Belochistan rose in revolt and deposed the chief whom General Willshire had imposed on the people, and General Nott was obliged to march down from Candahar to restore our authority. But the chief cause of anxiety was connected with the movements of Dost Mahomed.

A.D. 1840

Movements of Dost Mahomed.

After his flight from Cabul, he accepted the hospitality of the Ameer of Bokhara, "the Commander of the Faithful," but the most atrocious tyrant in Central Asia, who soon after subjected him to a grievous captivity. Meanwhile his brother, Jubber Khan, after wandering from place to place with the females of his family, placed them under the protection of the British Government. The confidence thus shown in our honour and generosity by a people proverbial for perfidy, was no ordinary tribute to our national character. The Dost, having at length made his escape from Bokhara, approached Cabul and found himself at the head of 6,000 or 7,000 Oosbeks, with whom he resolved to cross the Hindoo Coosh, raise the war cry of the Prophet, and, gathering strength from the un-

popularity of Shah Soojah and his supporters, march in triumph to Cabul. But Brigadier Dennie encountered him with a mere handful of troops, and obtained a decisive victory over the host of Oosbeks. After this defeat Dost Mahomed moved into the Kohistan, or highlands north of Cabul, and the chiefs who had recently sworn fidelity to the Shah on the Koran, at once espoused his cause, but Sir Robert Sale attacked him with great success. He flitted about the hills for two or three weeks, and then came down into the Nijrow district in the vicinity of the capital, which was immediately thrown into a state of general ferment. The English officials were filled with A.D.
consternation, and guns were mounted in all haste on the 1840
citadel. On the 2nd November, Sir Robert Sale, who had been incessantly in pursuit of him, came upon him in the valley of Purwandurra; the heights were bristling with an armed population, but the Dost had only 200 horsemen with him. The 2nd Cavalry galloped down upon him, and he resolved to meet the charge manfully. Raising himself in his stirrups and uncovering his head, he called upon his troops, in the name of God and the Prophet, to aid him in driving "the accursed infidels" from the land. The cavalry troopers fled from the field like a flock of sheep, the European officers fought with the spirit of heroes, till three were killed and two wounded. Sir Alexander Burnes, who was on the field, sent a hasty note to the envoy to assure him that there was nothing left but to fall back on Cabul, and concentrate our force for its defence. The note was delivered to him the next afternoon as he was taking a ride, when to his surprise, Dost Mahomed suddenly presented himself, and dismounting, gave up his sword and claimed his protection. He had felt, he said "even in the "moment of victory that it would be impossible to con- "tinue the contest, and having met his foes in the open field "and discomfited them he could claim their consideration "without indignity." The Dost rode together with the envoy into the cantonment, where his frank manners and dignified bearing in the hour of adversity created a strong feeling of sympathy and admiration, which was in no small degree heightened by contempt for the puppet in the Bala Hissar. He was sent on to Calcutta, where he was treated by Lord Auckland with the greatest respect and consideration, and two lacs of rupees a year were assigned for his support.

SECTION III.

LORD AUCKLAND'S ADMINISTRATION—THE AFGHAN WAR—DESTRUCTION OF THE ARMY.

A.D. 1840 MAJOR TODD had been sent by Sir William Macnaghten to Herat to maintain the influence of the British Government and to improve the fortifications. Money was sent in great profusion from Cabul, but Yar Mahomed, the vizier, took great offence at the efforts made by the Major to suppress the execrable traffic in slaves, the curse of Central Asia, in which he himself was deeply implicated, and he offered to place the whole country under the control of the king of Persia. Incensed at this act of ingratitude and perfidy, Sir William Macnaghten urged the immediate annexation of the province to the dominions of Shah Soojah, but Lord Auckland was disposed to condone the conduct of the minister, and the supply of guns, muskets, ammunition, and money was renewed with such prodigality as to alarm the financial authorities in Calcutta. But this lavish expenditure only led to more audacious intrigues, and Yar Mahomed endeavoured to concert a plan with the Persian governor of Meshed for the invasion of Candahar. This renewed act of treachery exhausted Major Todd's patience, and he withheld the monthly subsidy till the orders of the Governor-General could be received. The minister then rose in his demands, and on the 8th February insisted peremptorily on the payment of two lacs for the discharge of his personal debts, and a further advance for the improvement of the fortifications, and an increase of the monthly stipend, or the immediate departure of Major Todd. The Major at
1841 once withdrew the embassy to the great mortification of Lord Auckland, who dismissed him from his political employ and remanded him to his regiment.

The political charge of the province of Candahar was entrusted to Major Rawlinson, and the military command
1840 to General Nott, an officer of sound judgment and great decision of character. He was prompt and successful in dealing with the revolts which were continually cropping up around him, but the freedom of his remarks was displeasing to Lord Auckland and to Sir William Macnaghten, and he was, unfortunately, refused the promotion which he expected on Sir Willoughby

General Nott and Major Rawlinson.

Cotton's retirement from the command at Cabul, and which, if it had been granted to him, would, in all probability, have averted the tremendous catastrophe of the ensuing November. The Dooranees who occupied the province lying between Candahar and Herat, and who were of Shah Soojah's own tribe, had hailed with delight the restoration of their own prince to the throne, but when their expectation of sharing the sweets of power was disappointed by the employment of European officers, they manifested a more rancorous hostility to him than any other tribe. Their chief, Akbar Khan, assembled 6,000 men on the banks of the Helmund in July, in six divisions, with a priest at the head of each and a banner inscribed "We "have been trusting in God; may He guard and guide us." He was vigorously attacked by Colonel Woodburn, and defeated; the confederacy was broken up, and all the chiefs made their submission with the exception of Akram Khan, whose indomitable spirit resisted every overture. In other countries he might have been considered a patriot; in Afghanistan he was regarded as a traitor. His feelings were well expressed in the Afghan remark, "We are con-"tent with blood, but shall never be content with a master." His retreat was betrayed for a bribe by one of his own tribe, and he was blown away from a gun by express orders from Cabul.

A.D. 1841

The Eastern Ghiljies.

The province lying to the north-east of Candahar was inhabited by the Ghiljies, a fine muscular race, expert in the use of military weapons, and able to bring 40,000 men into the field, but characterised by an intense ferocity of disposition. They were as jealous of their own independence as they were eager to conquer that of others. In time past they had carried their victorious arms to the capital of Persia, and exhibited their prowess on many a battle-field of India; nor had they ever bowed the neck to the rulers of Cabul or Candahar. Sir William had prevailed on them for an annual subsidy to abstain from infesting the highways and levying black mail, but their deep-rooted antipathy to the intruding foreigners became daily more apparent, and it was deemed necessary to strengthen the fortifications of Khelat-i-Ghiljie, a fortress lying in the heart of their territory. They determined to oppose this measure and advanced in great force to defeat it, when they were encountered by Colonel Wymer, who inflicted a signal defeat on them, after an obstinate conflict of five hours continued beyond sunset. Every *émeute* had now been put down, and Sir William Macnaghten was beginning to congratulate himself on the termination of all his difficulties, but Major Rawlinson assured him that the whole country was pervaded by a spirit of implacable hostility towards us, and that there would be a general outburst on the first favourable opportunity.

That opportunity was not far distant. The expense of garrisoning Afghanistan was beginning to tell on the finances of India. The army of occupation fell little short of 25,000 men, and the annual charge was computed at a crore and a half of rupees. All the treasure accumulated by Lord William Bentinck had been exhausted, the treasury was drained and the Court of Directors were filled with alarm. At the close of 1840 they communicated their views to the Government at Simla, and stated that as it was evident the restored monarchy could not be maintained without a large force, it was necessary to make a large addition to the army; but they should advise the entire abandonment of the country, with a frank avowal of the complete failure of our object. The circumstances of the period appeared to be more favourable to retirement than they had ever been. The Persian court was on the most friendly terms with us; the Russian expedition to Khiva had totally failed; Dost Mahomed and his family were state prisoners with us, and the revolt in Belochistan was completely quelled. Sir William Macnaghten had, moreover, stated that the noses of the Dooranee chiefs "had been brought "to the grindstone, and that Afghanistan was as quiet as "an Indian district, and its tranquillity was marvellous." Nothing could be more reasonable and politic than this advice, but the question of withdrawal was unfortunately left to the judgment of the Government of India—that is, to the decision of those who had advised the war, and they declared that to deprive the Shah of British support would be an act of "unparalleled political atrocity." There was no difficulty in persuading Lord Auckland that our troops ought not to be withdrawn before the authority of the Shah had been completely consolidated; whereas it was palpable to everyone but the envoy that his authority could never be sufficiently established while the "accursed in-"fidels," as we were universally termed, continued to garrison the country. It was therefore determined to remain in Afghanistan, to make no increase to the army, but to reduce the expenditure, and to open a new loan.

Resolution to hold Afghanistan.

A.D. 1841

A.D. 1841

Retrenchment and revolt.

The retrenchments were to be made by reducing the stipends of the chiefs, and, by that fatality which seemed to attend every measure connected with this unfortunate expedition, those which ought to have come last were taken up first. The eastern Ghiljies were the first to be summoned to Cabul, when they were informed that the exigencies of the State rendered the reduction of their allowances indispensable. The subsidies paid by us had been paid from time immemorial by every ruler of Afghanistan, and were regarded by the highlanders as a patrimonial inheritance. They were magnanimously indifferent to the politics of Afghanistan, and cared not who ruled as long as their franchise was not invaded. The stipends now reduced had, moreover, been guaranteed to them when we took possession of the country, and they had performed their part of the contract with exemplary fidelity. They had not allowed a finger to be raised against our posts, or couriers, or weak detachments, and convoys of every description had passed through their terrific defiles, the strongest mountain barriers in the world, without interruption. They received the announcement of the reduction in the beginning of October without any remonstrance, made their salaam to the envoy, and, returning to their fastnesses, plundered a caravan and blocked up the passes. The 35th Native Infantry, commanded by Colonel Monteith, which was under orders to return to India, was directed by the envoy to proceed "to the passes "and chastise these rascals, and open the road to India;" but he was attacked during the night and lost the greater portion of his baggage. Sir Robert Sale, commanding the brigade returning to India, who was directed to support the 35th, was vigorously assailed in the Khoord Cabul pass, and on reaching Tezeen, ordered a detachment against the fort of the Ghiljie leader, the capture of which would have inflicted a severe blow on the insurrection, but the wily chiefs contrived to cozen the political agent, and he was drawn into a treaty which conceded nearly all they desired. Their stipends were restored, and 10,000 rupees paid down, but the revolt, instead of being nipped in the bud, was strengthened by this display of weakness. While professing submission, they sent emissaries to raise the tribes in advance, and Sir Robert Sale was obliged to fight every inch of his way to Gundamuk, and on his arrival there, found his communication with the capital closed, and the whole country in a blaze of rebellion.

Sir William Macnaghten had been rewarded for his services in Afghanistan with the governorship of Bombay, and had arranged to leave Cabul in the beginning of November. Throughout the previous month, while the surface of society presented the appearance of an unruffled calm, a general confederacy, which embraced every chief of every tribe, had been organised for our expulsion. The envoy was warned by the most intelligent and experienced officers—Sir Alexander Burnes excepted—of the storm which was gathering, but he persuaded himself that the country was in a state of unprecedented repose, and that the rising of the Ghiljies was a local *émeute*. On the evening of the 1st November, Sir Alexander visited him to congratulate him on leaving the country in a state of such tranquillity. At that same hour, some of the confederates were assembled in a house in the city to arrange the plan of the insurrection, and at dawn on the 2nd November, the insurgents surrounded Sir Alexander's house in the city with loud yells. He instantly despatched a messenger to Sir William Macnaghten in the cantonments for aid, and harangued the mob from his balcony, offering large sums for his own and his brother's life, but they were thirsting for his blood. He was more obnoxious to the Afghan chiefs than any of the other British officers, some of whom had gained their esteem by their genial disposition and their high moral character. He was decoyed into his garden by a treacherous Cashmerian, and hacked to pieces, together with his brother. The insurgents then proceeded to assault the neighbouring house to which Captain Johnston, the paymaster of Shah Soojah's force, had been unwisely allowed to transfer his treasure, and plundered it of nearly two lacs of rupees, and burnt down the houses of the other officers. The mob did not originally consist of more than a hundred men, but the rich booty which had been obtained speedily augmented their number, and the whole city was soon in a state of wild commotion. The confederate chiefs had so little expectation of success, that they had their horses saddled for flight on the first appearance of British troops. They subsequently acknowledged that the slightest exhibition of energy at the commencement would have put down the insurrection at once; but no effort was made.

Murder of Burnes.

A.D. 1841

General Elphinstone who commanded the troops, was a gallant old Queen's officer, but utterly disqualified for this important and dangerous post by his bodily infirmities, and not less by his mental weakness and want of decision. On the retirement of Sir Willoughby Cotton, the Commander-in-Chief, Sir Jasper Nicolls, had recommended Sir W. Nott as his successor, but he had, as we have said, incurred the displeasure of the Governor-General by the freedom of his remarks on the perils of our position, and General Elphinstone was importuned to accept the appointment, though his tremulous and gouty handwriting gave the clearest evidence that he was wholly unfit to be placed in the command of an army in a country ripe for revolt. It is therefore impossible to exonerate Lord Auckland from a large share of the responsibility of the overwhelming calamity which ensued, and which is to be attributed solely to the incompetency of the officer whom he had selected. The envoy made light of the *émeute*, and said it would speedily subside, and the General was too happy to be spared the necessity of exertion not to acquiesce in this opinion. It was decided, however, that Brigadier Shelton's brigade, which was encamped on the heights of Sea Sung, should be ordered to the Bala Hissar, and that assistance should be sent, if possible, to Sir Alexander Burnes. No effort was made by either the political or military authorities to rescue him, though it might have been effected with perfect ease by a direct route only a mile and a half long, free from every impediment. At a crisis when moments were of inestimable value, hours were wasted in discussion with the Shah regarding the admission of Brigadier Shelton's force into the Bala Hissar, and when it was settled, he did nothing but cover the retreat of Colonel Campbell and a regiment of the Shah's Hindostanees, who had been sent to the rescue of Sir Alexander, but were driven back.

General Elphinstone.

A.D. 1841

On the evening of this first day of disaster General Elphinstone, instead of forming a vigorous plan of operations for the morrow, wrote to the envoy, "We "must see what the morning brings, and think "what can be done." Nothing, however, was done except a feeble attempt to penetrate the city with an inadequate force three hours after midday, but it was driven back by the thousands of armed men whom the success of the rising had brought into the city. Within thirty hours of the outbreak Sir William Macnaghten began to despond—as well he might—and despatched letters to General Nott and General Sale desiring them to come up immediately to his relief. The fatal error of having

Inactivity of the envoy and general.

A.D. 1841 given up the Bala Hissar and planted the cantonment in low ground on the plain, was now fully revealed. The ramparts were so contemptible that a pony might scale them, and they were so completely commanded by the neighbouring hills and forts that the troops could not move out without being exposed to a heavy fire. The commissariat stores, moreover, on which the existence of the army depended, instead of being lodged within the cantonment were deposited in a small fort, 400 yards distant, and guarded by eighty men. The supine general, instead of making a vigorous effort to secure them, allowed the enemy to undermine the fort; and the officer in charge of it, seeing no effort made to support him, was obliged to evacuate it, and men and officers looked over the walls of the cantonment with burning indignation, while a rabble of Afghans was employed unchecked, like a swarm of ants, in carrying off the provisions on which their hope of sustaining life depended.

General Sale received Sir William's order to return to Cabul at Gundamuk, but it was determined at a council of war that the force was in so crippled a state, and the intervening passes so completely blocked up by the insurgents, that any such attempt would result in its complete destruction, and it was determined therefore to push on to Jellalabad. General Nott at Candahar argued that his troops could not reach Cabul under five or six weeks; that beyond Ghuzni they would have to fight every inch of the way, and to wade through the snow, and would eventually arrive in such a condition as to be of little, if any, service. Three regiments were, nevertheless, despatched, but they returned on the first appearance of snow. Extraordinary efforts were now made at Cabul to obtain provisions from the neighbouring villages, and four days after the rising General Elphinstone informed the envoy that they had got temporarily, and he hoped permanently, over this difficulty, and, with 5,000 troops under his command, said, "Our case is not yet desperate; but it must be borne in mind that it goes very "fast." Sir William, seeing the honour and safety of the force in such keeping, felt himself constrained to open negotiations with the insurgent chiefs, and, through the moonshee, Mohun Lall, made them an offer of two, three, or even five lacs of rupees; but, as might have been expected, this fresh token of our weakness only served to increase their arrogance.

Generals Sale and Nott.

The utter incompetence of the general was hurrying the

garrison to destruction, but there appeared some faint hope of deliverance if Brigadier Shelton, who had remained in the Bala Hissar since the 2nd November, were associated with him in the command. He was an officer of great energy, distinguished for his courage and iron nerve, and his arrival on the 9th November raised the drooping spirits of the garrison. But it was soon apparent that his insupportable temper neutralised all his military qualifications. He might have secured the salvation of the force if he had cordially co-operated with the general, but the state of things was only rendered more desperate by the discord which his perversity created. There was yet one course which would have rescued the army from all its perils—an immediate retreat to the impregnable position of the Bala Hissar. Shah Soojah did not cease to urge this movement—which was equally advocated by the envoy and the general—but Brigadier Shelton pertinaciously resisted it on grounds positively absurd, and on his memory rests the ignominy of having sealed the doom of 15,000 human beings.

A.D. 1841

Brigadier Shelton.

There is little interest in dwelling on the long and melancholy catalogue of errors which followed close on each other, disgusting the officers, demoralising the men, and hastening the ruin of the force. On the 23rd November, the Afghans took up a position on the Behmaroo hills, which enabled them to inflict serious injury on the cantonment, and, at the earnest entreaty of the envoy, Brigadier Shelton went out with a considerable force to dislodge them. The chief who commanded their cavalry was killed, and the whole body was seized with a panic, and fled in disorder to the city. The envoy was standing by the side of the general on the ramparts, and importuned him to hasten out a sufficient force to improve the opportunity, but he languidly replied that it was a wild scheme. The enemy had time to recover their confidence and rushed back with redoubled fury, when the whole battalion of English soldiers abandoned the field and took to flight. The fugitives and pursuers were so mingled in the race that the Afghans might with perfect ease have captured the cantonments, but the chiefs drew off their men in the moment of victory. This defeat concluded all military operations; the disasters of these three weeks were justly attributed to the jealousies and the mismanagement of the two commanders, and all hope for the future was at an end; the army was demoralised, and a feeling of gloom and dismay pervaded the encampment.

Last engagement.

SECTION IV.

LORD AUCKLAND'S ADMINISTRATION—THE AFGHAN WAR—ANNIHILATION OF THE ARMY.

A.D. 1841 THE day after the disaster of the 23rd November, Shah Soojah again entreated the envoy to retire to the Bala Hissar, and he pressed it with increasing importunity on the military chiefs, but they persisted in rejecting the proposal, and the general, moreover, informed him in an official communication that it was no longer possible to maintain our position in the country. Sir William was therefore constrained to submit to the ignominy of holding a conference with the Afghan chiefs, but, finding us reduced to extremity, they haughtily demanded that the whole army should surrender at discretion with its arms and ammunition, and the negotiation was necessarily broken off. A week after, Akbar Khan, the ablest of Dost Mahomed's sons, a young soldier of great energy, but of a fiery and impetuous temper, arrived in Cabul and was at once accepted as the leader of the national confederacy. He was not slow to perceive that it was only necessary to cut off its supplies to extinguish the British force, and he immediately threatened with death all who should venture to furnish any provisions. The envoy, seeing the destruction of the force inevitable, renewed his entreaty to withdraw to the Bala Hissar, but the general again refused his concurrence. He then proposed that they should endeavour to obtain provisions from the country by their swords, but the imbecile commander replied that the only alternative now left was to obtain a safe conduct out of the country.

Negotiations.

Akbar Khan.

Starvation now stared the garrison in the face. On the 11th December, there was food left only for the day's consumption of the fighting men, and the envoy was obliged to make another effort to negotiate, and found himself constrained to submit to whatever terms the Afghans chose to dictate. They were sufficiently humiliating; the troops at Jellalabad, Candahar, Cabul, and Ghuzni were to evacuate the country, receiving every assistance of carriage and provisions; Dost Mahomed and his family were to be liberated; Shah Soojah was to be at liberty to remain on a pension, or to retire with the

Treaty of 11th December.

British force; the army was to quit Cabul within three A.D. days, and in the meantime to receive ample supplies of 1841 provisions, and four officers were to be given up as hostages. This is the most disgraceful transaction in the annals of British India. In extenuation of it, the envoy placed on record, that "we had been fighting forty days against "superior numbers, under the most disadvantageous cir-"cumstances, with deplorable loss of life, and in a day or "two must have perished of hunger. The terms I secured "were the best obtainable, and the destruction of 15,000 "human beings would little have benefited our country." But the position of the unhappy envoy is described still more accurately by Kaye in his classic history of the war in Afghanistan: "Environed and hemmed in by difficulties "and dangers, overwhelmed with responsibilities there was "none to share—the lives of 15,000 resting on his decision "—the honour of his country at stake—with a perfidious "enemy at his back, he was driven to negotiate by the "imbecility of his companions." The entire responsibility of this humiliating convention rests on General Elphinstone and Brigadier Shelton, than whom it would not have been easy to discover two men more disqualified for the posts they occupied, the one by bodily infirmity and constitutional imbecility, the other by almost incredible perversity of disposition. The brilliant success of Sir Robert Sale at Jellalabad shows how easily the position of the army of Cabul might have been rectified with the superior means and appliances at command, if it had been under an able commander.

Violation of the treaty.

It never, however, was the intention of the Afghans to fulfil the treaty, or to permit any European to escape. The Bala Hissar was evacuated on the 13th by the few troops in it; the forts around the cantonment were surrendered, and Akbar Khan received letters to the commandants at Jellalabad and other military stations ordering them to retire. The chiefs, moreover, were allowed to go into the magazines and help themselves to whatever stores they liked, while officers and men looked on in silent indignation. But the supplies furnished were so scanty as scarcely to appease hunger, and Akbar Khan and his chiefs not only continued to withhold supplies of carriage and provisions for the march, but rose in their demands, and insisted on the delivery of all the stores and ammunition of every description, and the surrender of all the married families as additional hostages. In these cir-

A.D. 1841 cumstances, Sir William directed his moonshee to open negotiations with other tribes, and inform them that if any portion of the Afghans declared to the Shah that they wished him to remain, he would break with the faithless Barukzies, the tribe of Akbar. It was at this critical juncture, when bewildered by the appalling crisis which was approaching, that Sir William Macnaghten received an unexpected message from Akbar, with a fresh proposal that the British force should remain till the spring; that Shah Soojah should retain the title of king, and that Akbar Khan should be appointed vizier, receiving from the British Government an immediate payment of thirty lacs, and an annual allowance of four lacs. In an evil hour for his reputation and safety, the envoy accepted these proposals in writing, and agreed to attend a meeting which was appointed for the next day.

General Elphinstone described the proposal as a plot, and endeavoured to dissuade the envoy from proceeding to the conference, but he replied in a hurried tone, "Let "me alone for that. Dangerous though it be—if "it succeeds, it is worth all risk. I had rather "suffer a hundred deaths than live the last six weeks over "again." At noon on the 23rd December he proceeded with three officers and about sixteen of his body-guard to the fatal meeting, 600 yards from the cantonment, where Akbar Khan had spread some horse cloths on the snow on the slope of the hill. They were no sooner seated than the officers were seized and placed each one on the saddle of an Afghan horseman and hurried off to the city. One of them fell off and was hacked to pieces; the envoy was shot dead by Akbar Khan, and the ghazees, or fanatics, rushed in and mutilated his body. Thus perished Sir William Macnaghten, the victim of an unwise and unjust policy, but as noble and brave an officer as ever fell in the service of his country. Throughout seven weeks of unparalleled difficulties, he exhibited a spirit of courage and constancy of which there is not another example in the annals of the Company. He was the only civilian at Cabul, and one of the truest-hearted soldiers in the garrison. He had served several years in the Madras army, and there can be little doubt that if he could have assumed the command of the force it would have escaped the doom that befell it.

Assassination of the envoy.

No effort was made from the cantonment to avenge the murder of the envoy, or even to recover his mangled re-

mains, which were dragged in triumph through the city. A.D. 1841
All eyes were now turned on Major Pottinger, who had come in wounded from Chareekar at the beginning of the insurrection, and had remained ever since unnoticed in the cantonment. He assumed the political post of envoy and called a council of war to consider the new terms on which the Afghan chiefs now agreed to grant the army a safe-conduct to Peshawur. They differed from those to which Sir William had given his consent only in the demand of larger gratuities to themselves. The hero of Herat recoiled from these humiliating concessions, and urged the officers to reject them with scorn and defiance. His energy might yet have saved the army, but the council would not fight, and the new treaty was accepted without a word of remonstrance. The confederate chiefs, as might have been expected, increased their demands, and required that all the coin and the spare muskets and every gun save six should be surrendered, and that all the married officers and their families should be left in the country. But letters were received at the same time from Jellalabad and Peshawur stating that reinforcements were on their way, and imploring the garrison to hold out. Dissensions were also reported among the Afghan chiefs, and the major seized the occasion of this gleam of sunshine to conjure the commanders to make one bold and prompt effort either to occupy the Bala Hissar, or to cut their way to Jellalabad; but Brigadier Shelton, the evil genius of the cantonment, declared that both courses were equally impracticable. The treaty was therefore completed, and small arms, guns, and waggons were given up amidst the indignant exclamations of the garrison. The ratification of the treaty by the seals of eighteen chiefs was received on the 4th January. It was dictated in a spirit of arrogance, and received in a spirit of humility, and violated without a blush.

Major Pottinger.

On the 6th January, 1842, the army, still 4,500 strong, with 11,000 camp followers, began its ominous retreat. As the snow lay ankle-deep on the ground, its salvation depended on the rapidity of its movements. If it had crossed the Cabul river before noon, and pushed on with promptitude, it might have escaped the dangers before it; but, through the mismanagement of the general the rear-guard did not leave the gate before the shades of night came on. The Afghan fanatics then rushed in and set the cantonments on fire, and lighted up this first night of horrors with the blaze. In the morning the spirit 1842

Retreat of the army.

A.D. 1842 of discipline began to wane, and the force was no longer a retreating army, but a panic-stricken and disorganised rabble. Safety was to be found only in speed, but by the unaccountable folly of the military authorities the troops were halted the second night at Bootkhak. The crowd of men, women, and children, horses and camels, lying on the snow in wild confusion, without food or fuel, or shelter, presented a spectacle of unexampled misery. Akbar Khan now made his appearance, and demanded fresh hostages for the protection, as he said, of the force as far as Tezeen, and they were surrendered. Between Bootkhak and Tezeen lay the terrific gorge of the Khoord Cabul, five miles in length, so narrow that the rays of the sun seldom penetrated its recesses. At the bottom of it ran an impetuous torrent, which the road crossed and recrossed twenty-eight times, and it was through this tremendous defile that the disordered mass of human beings pressed on with one maddening desire, to escape destruction. But the Ghiljies poured an incessant fire upon the crowd from every height with their unerring weapons that carried death to the distance of 800 yards, and 3,000 perished from their fire and the intensity of the cold. It was in this scene of carnage that delicate English ladies, some with infants in their arms, had to run the gauntlet of Afghan bullets amidst a heavy fall of snow.

Akbar Khan again appeared in the morning and offered a supply of provisions, and advised the general to halt. The whole force exclaimed against this insane proposal, but the general was deaf to all entreaties, and the perishing troops were constrained to sit down idle for a whole day in the snow. Akbar made an offer to take charge of the ladies and children, and convey them to Peshawur. They had scarcely tasted food since leaving Cabul; they were inadequately clad, and could obtain no shelter from the snow. Major Pottinger, who was Akbar's prisoner, felt that it would be impossible for them to survive these hardships, and, in accordance with his advice, Lady Macnaghten, Lady Sale, and nine other ladies, with fifteen children, and eight officers, were sent to Akbar's camp and rescued from destruction. On the morning of the 10th, the remainder of the army resumed its march, but, before evening, the greater number of the sepoys had disappeared. Panic-stricken and benumbed with cold, they were slaughtered like sheep by the remorseless Ghiljies, and a narrow defile between two hills was choked up with the dying and the dead; 450 European soldiers and a con-

Extinction of the army.

siderable body of officers yet remained, but the enemy took post on every salient point, blocked up every pass, and dealt death among their ranks. On approaching Jugdulluk a conference was held with Akbar, who continued to hang upon their rear, and he offered to supply them with provisions, on condition that General Elphinstone, Brigadier Shelton, and another officer, should be transferred to him as hostages for the surrender of Jellalabad. But this concession brought no respite from the ferocity of the Ghiljies, in whom the thirst for blood had overcome even the love of money, which was freely offered them. Akbar, having obtained possession of the persons of the ladies and the principal officers, abandoned the remnant of the army to their vengeance. At Jugdulluk, twelve of the bravest of the officers met their doom; and here the Cabul army may be said to have ceased to exist. Twenty officers and forty-five European soldiers contrived to reach Gundamuk, but they gradually dropped under the weapons of their foes, with the exception of one officer, Dr. Brydon, who was descried from the ramparts of Jellalabad, on the 13th January, slowly wending his way to the fort, wounded and exhausted, on his jaded pony, the sole survivor, with the exception of 120 in captivity, of 15,000 men.

A.D. 1842

Effects of the catastrophe.

The entire annihilation of this army was the severest blow which had been inflicted on the British power in India. Yet so strongly had its authority become consolidated that it did not produce any of those immediate demonstrations of hostility at the native courts, or any such fermentation in native society, as were visible on the destruction of Colonel Monson's force in 1804, or the failure in the Nepaul campaign of 1814, or even the sluggish progress of the army in Burmah in 1825. Lord Auckland, although overwhelmed by the magnitude of the calamity, was induced to issue a proclamation that "the Governor-General regarded the partial "reverse which had overtaken a body of British troops "in a country removed by distance and difficulties of "season from the possibility of succour, as a new occa-"sion for displaying the vigour and stability of British "power, and the admirable spirit and vigour of the British "Indian army." But after this spasm of energy he relapsed into a spirit of dejection, and, instead of considering how most effectually to restore our military superiority, the sole basis of our power in India, was prepared to leave it without vindication, and considered only how he could withdraw

A.D. 1842 General Sale from Afghanistan. Unfortunately, the Commander-in-chief was equally devoid of spirit; but Mr. —now Sir George—Clerk, the political agent in the Punjab, on hearing of the siege of the cantonment, hurried on the brigade which had been appointed to relieve the regiments returning from Afghanistan, but they were placed under the command of Colonel Wyld, and sent without cavalry or cannon. He crept through the Punjab at a slothful pace, and was thirty-five days in reaching Peshawur, whereas one of Runjeet Sing's European officers had accomplished the distance with his army in twelve days. The sepoys were eager to advance to the rescue of their fellow soldiers, but he lingered there until they were thoroughly demoralised by intercourse with the Sikh auxiliaries whom Runjeet Sing's successor had sent to co-operate with them, and who, on reaching Jumrood, and looking into the pass, turned round and marched back to Peshawur. Colonel Wyld then entered the pass without them, but the frail guns the Sikhs had lent him broke down on the first discharge; the sepoys lost heart, and allowed themselves to be ignominiously chased back, leaving their artillery in the hands of the Afreedies.

Lord Auckland was reluctant to send on a second brigade to relieve the army besieged in Cabul, but Mr. Clerk's energy overcame all objections, and a force of 3,000 men, including a corps of Europeans, crossed the Sutlej on the 4th January. It was happily under the command of General Pollock, an old artillery officer, who had campaigned with Lord Lake, and fought at Bhurtpore, in Nepaul, and in Burmah, and whose sagacity, caution, and decision of character eminently qualified him for the arduous task before him. The entire destruction of the Cabul force was announced on the 22nd January, and Mr. Clerk met the Commander-in-chief, Sir Jasper Nicolls, to discuss the measures necessary to meet the crisis. Sir Jasper stated that the only object now to be pursued was to withdraw Sir Robert Sale's force safely to India; but Mr. Clerk, in a spirit more worthy of a Briton, maintained that the national reputation and the safety of the empire imperatively required that the garrison at Jellalabad should be reinforced to march simultaneously with the Candahar force to the capital, and inflict a signal retribution on the Afghans on the scene of our late disgrace, and then withdraw from Afghanistan with dignity and undiminished renown. The energy of this appeal could

General Pollock.

not be resisted, and a third brigade was ordered to be held in readiness to join General Pollock; but Lord Auckland's last communication informed him that "his sole business "was to secure the safe return of our people and troops "detained beyond the Indus."

The arrival of Lord Ellenborough in Calcutta on the 28th February brought Lord Auckland's disastrous administration to a close. He wrote a benevolent minute on education, and he endeavoured to promote the interests of science, for which he had a natural turn; but his rule was comprised in a single series of transactions—the conquest, the occupation, and the loss of Afghanistan. His administration commenced with a surplus revenue of a crore and a half, and it closed with a deficit of two crores, and a large addition to the debt. The Tories contributed one inefficient Governor-General in Lord Amherst, and the Whigs another in Lord Auckland. The one wasted thirteen crores in the Burmese war; the other squandered an equal sum in the Afghan expedition.

A.D. 1842

Close of Lord Auckland's administration.

CHAPTER XIII.

SECTION I.

LORD ELLENBOROUGH'S ADMINISTRATION—ADVANCE OF THE ARMY ON CABUL.

LORD ELLENBOROUGH, who now assumed the charge of the Government, was a statesman of high repute, and an eloquent speaker, and had for several years taken a special interest in the affairs of India, more particularly during the discussion on the last charter. Like Lord Wellesley and Lord Minto, he had served an apprenticeship at the Board of Control, where he had acquired an ample knowledge of the principles and policy of the Indian administration. He was known to possess great energy and decision of character, and the community in India augured a happy relief from the weak and vacillating policy of his predecessor.

Lord Ellenborough.

General Pollock arrived at Peshawur on the 5th February,

A.D. 1842

and found the four regiments in a state of complete insubordination. Many of the sepoys had deserted their colours, and meetings were nightly held to encourage each other in the determination not to enter the Khyber Pass. Efforts were also made to debauch the regiments which the general had brought with him, but he put down these machinations with promptitude and energy. The officers manifested scarcely less reluctance to encounter the danger of the passes. Sir Robert Sale was importuning the general to hasten to his relief, but he felt that, with a force so completely demoralised, he could not advance without the certain risk of failure. Obliged as he was to wait for reinforcements, he devoted the months of February and March to the task of restoring the discipline, recovering the health, and reviving the confidence of his troops, which was strengthened in no small degree by the arrival of a regiment of dragoons and some horse artillery. Raja Golab Sing also came up and took the command of the Sikh contingent, and the masterly arrangements and resolute bearing of General Pollock at length overcame the dread with which the Sikhs regarded the Khyber, and secured the active co-operation of the raja. The Khyberees demanded an exorbitant sum for a passage through their defiles, and proceeded to block up the entrance of the pass with stones and branches of trees, while they covered the mountains on either side with their troops; but the plan adopted by General Pollock, of crowning the heights baffled all their efforts. At three in the morning of the 5th April the troops moved out of the camp in perfect silence and climbed up the rugged crags with great enthusiasm, and the dawn revealed their presence to the thunderstruck Afghans on the summit of their own hills. After a sharp conflict, they were seen to fly precipitately in every direction; the defence of the pass was abandoned, and it was opened to the long string of baggage which, including the military stores and the provisions for General Sale's force, extended two miles. No further obstacle was offered to the progress of the army, which reached Jellalabad on the 15th April.

General Pollock's advance.

Sir Robert Sale, reached Jellalabad on the 13th November, with provisions for only two days. The fortifications were in a state of complete dilapidation, and there were paths over the ramparts into the country. Immediately beyond the walls lay ruined forts and mosques, which afforded cover for assailants at the distance of only twenty or thirty yards, and the inhabitants, both in the

General Sale at Jellalabad.

town and country, were animated with feelings of bitter A.D.
hostility. The day after the arrival of the force, 5,000 of 1841
the armed population of the neighbourhood advanced with yells and imprecations to the walls, but were completely dispersed by Colonel Monteath. Captain Broadfoot, an officer of indomitable energy and fertile resources, who had accompanied the brigade with his sappers and miners, was appointed garrison engineer, and commenced the task of clearing and strengthening the fortifications. The whole of the 13th Foot was turned into a working party, a spirit of zeal and emulation was diffused through the garrison, and an indefensible mass of ruins was, in a short time,
converted into a fortress, proof against anything but siege 1842
artillery. On the 9th January a horseman rode up to the gate with the order to evacuate Jellalabad which General Elphinstone had written under compulsion. The officers replied that as Akbar Khan had sent a proclamation to the chiefs in the valley to destroy the force, they would await further communications from the general at Cabul. At the close of January a letter was received from Shah Soojah, as the ostensible head of the Afghan Government, demanding the evacuation of the town. At a council of war, the general and the political agent proposed to comply with the request, and the latter supported his advice to evacuate the place and return to Peshawur by the assertion that the Government of India had evidently abandoned the garrison to its fate, and that it was impossible for them to hold out much longer; to which Captain Broadfoot nobly replied, that even if their own Government had deserted them, they owed it to their country to uphold its honour at this crisis, and it was a duty from which nothing could absolve them. The majority of the council, however, agreed to adopt the views of the political agent, but with the understanding that if the next communication from the Shah and the chiefs at Cabul was equivocal, they should be at liberty to take their own course. The answer was clogged with requisitions which were deemed inadmissible; Captain Broadfoot reiterated his objection to a capitulation; the officers had recovered the tone of their minds, and a recent foray had supplied the garrison with 900 head of cattle; and, contrary to the advice of the general and the political agent, the majority voted against the renewal of negotiations.

On the 18th February a succession of earthquakes destroyed in a few hours the labours of three months. The parapets were prostrated, the bastions seriously injured,

A.D. 1842 and one of the gates was reduced to a heap of ruins. The damage was, however, repaired with such promptitude as to lead the Afghans to declare that the earthquake could not have been felt there. Soon after, Akbar Khan, who had been detained at Cabul by differences with the chiefs, arrived in the valley to take possession of the town, in accordance with the order of evacuation he had extorted from the British authorities at Cabul; but he found that the defences had been completed, and a store of provisions laid in; that he had not to deal with men like Elphinstone and Shelton, but with officers and men buoyant with animation and confidence. On the 11th March he advanced to the attack of the town, but the whole garrison sallied forth, and he was ignominiously driven from the field. He resolved, therefore, to turn the siege into a blockade, in the hope of starving the garrison into submission, as he had done at Cabul; and its situation began to be critical: the cattle were perishing for want of fodder; the men were on reduced rations of salt meat; the officers were on short commons; and the ammunition was running low. Akbar had been gradually drawing his camp nearer to the town, and it was now pitched within two miles of it. The general at length yielded to the importunity of Captain Havelock and his brother officers to relieve the force from its perilous position by a bold attack on the encampment of the enemy. The plan of the engagement provided that a simultaneous attack should be made in three columns, and that his army should be driven into the river, which was then an impetuous torrent. By some mistake, one column had to bear the brunt of the assault made by Akbar's splendid cavalry; but in the course of an hour he was driven from every point, and pursued to the river with the entire loss of his stores and equipment, and his camp was delivered up to the flames. He disappeared from the scene, and the neighbouring chiefs hastened to make their submission and to pour in provisions. General Pollock, on his arrival a week after, found the garrison, which had achieved its own deliverance, in exuberant spirits and robust health. One such day at Cabul would have saved the army.

Earthquakes.

Immediately after the outbreak at Cabul the chiefs despatched emissaries to raise western Afghanistan, and General Nott concentrated his force at Candahar, but the spirit of disaffection was irresistible. The Jaunbaz, the Shah's cavalry, as well as the chiefs of

Affairs at andha

A.D. 1842

his own tribe, threw off the mask and openly joined the insurgents, and even his own son placed himself at their head. After many weeks of preparation they moved down to attack Candahar, but were completely discomfited in an engagement which did not last more than twenty minutes. At length Mirza Ahmed, the ablest man in the country, and who had enjoyed the entire confidence of Major Rawlinson, went over to the hostile camp, and gave strength and organisation to the confederacy. The insurgents continued to hover round the city, and it was considered necessary to break up their camp. General Nott accordingly marched out on the 10th March, and was inveigled to a distance from the city, when Mirza Ahmed and the Shah's own son advanced at sunset to the Herat gate, where their emissaries had been employed for some hours in heaping up brushwood saturated with oil. As soon as it blazed up, the ghazees, or fanatics, maddened with drugs, rushed forward with hideous yells and imprecations. Amidst this scene of wild confusion, which was rendered more appalling by the darkness, Majors Rawlinson and Lane defended the gate with the greatest energy for five hours. Towards midnight the fury of the assailants was exhausted, and they retired, and Candahar was saved.

Disasters.

This brilliant success was counterbalanced by disasters. Ghuzni, after having stood a siege of four months, was surrendered to the Afghans, though under a different commander it might easily have been held till the garrison was relieved. General England, moreover, was advancing up to Candahar from the south with a convoy of provisions, ammunition, and money, and had reached Hykulzye when a body of 500 of his troops was suddenly assailed by a party of the enemy, who sprang up from behind a breastwork, four feet high, erected on a slight elevation, and a considerable number were killed. They recoiled at first from the shock, but soon recovered themselves, and were eager to be led on; but the panic-stricken general retreated in dismay to Qwetta, and actually began to throw up entrenchments.

Lord Ellenborough's proclamation.

On the 15th March Lord Ellenborough issued a proclamation, signed by himself and all the members of Council, stating that the course now to be pursued must have reference "to the establishment of our "military reputation by the infliction of some "signal and decisive blow on the Afghans which "may make it appear to them and to our subjects and

A.D. 1842 "allies that we have the power of inflicting punishment "upon those who commit atrocities, and that we withdraw "ultimately from Afghanistan, not from any deficiency of "means to maintain our position, but because we are satis-"fied that the king we have set up has not, as we were "erroneously led to imagine, the support of the nation." These noble sentiments were welcomed with exultation throughout India, but after a brief residence in Calcutta, he left the Council board and proceeded to the north-west; and, on hearing of the loss of Ghuzni and the repulse of General England and his precipitate retreat to Qwetta, announced to the Commander-in-Chief his determination to withdraw the troops from Candahar and Jellalabad at the earliest practicable period. He questioned whether "it would be "justifiable to put our troops forward for no other object "than that of avenging our losses and re-establishing our "military character in all its original brilliancy." General Nott was therefore directed to retire from Candahar after blowing up the gateways and demolishing the fortifications, and General Pollock was ordered to return to the provinces, except under certain contingencies.

Reply of Generals Pollock and Nott.

To this communication General Pollock replied that the withdrawal of the force at the present time would necessarily be construed into a defeat, and compromise our character as a powerful nation in Asia, and produce the most disastrous effect. The release of the prisoners was also, he said, an object not to be repudiated; but the want of cattle would effectually prevent his immediate retirement, and he might possibly be detained several months. By this dexterous suggestion he was enabled to evade the injunction to retire at once, and to wait the chance of another and more auspicious change in the versatile mind of Lord Ellenborough. General Nott and Major Rawlinson had, with no small difficulty, succeeded in maintaining anything like subordination in the province amidst the seething elements of revolt and anarchy, and any suspicion of retirement would have raised the whole country and rendered it impossible to obtain cattle or provisions without the employment of force. But General Nott replied promptly that the evacuation of the province should be effected in the best manner circumstances would admit, and thus gained a season of respite.

The order for the immediate evacuation of Afghanistan excited a burst of indignation throughout India. It was universally felt that to retire before our honour had been vindicated, or the prisoners rescued, would inflict a deeper stigma on the national character than the capitulation at Cabul, which might be considered one of the chances of war. With all the contempt Lord Ellenborough professed for public opinion, he could scarcely be indifferent to this unanimous expression of feeling, and he changed his mind again. On the 4th July, General Nott was assured, in an official communication, that the resolution of the Governor-General to withdraw the troops remained without alteration. On the same day, Lord Ellenborough wrote himself to the general, suggesting that it might possibly be feasible for him to withdraw from Afghanistan by advancing to Ghuzni and Cabul over the scenes of our late disasters; that this would have a grand effect upon the minds of our soldiers, of our allies, of our enemies in Asia, and of our own countrymen, and of foreign nations in Europe. It was an object of just ambition, but the risk was unquestionably great. A copy of this letter was sent to General Pollock, with the suggestion that he might possibly feel disposed to advance to Cabul and co-operate with General Nott. Both officers were too happy to obtain permission to move up to the capital and retrieve our honour, to think for a moment of the responsibility thus thrust upon them, and which the Governor-General, as the head of the state, should have had the courage to take on himself.

A.D. 1842

Lord Ellenborough's change of plan.

After the retreat of the army from Cabul, Shah Soojah was acknowledged as king, and allowed to reside in the Bala Hissar, but the insurgent chiefs engrossed all the power of the state. He sent repeated messages to Jellalabad declaring his unalterable attachment to the British Government, and asking for nothing but money, although he had contrived to save twenty lacs of rupees out of the sums lavished on him since he left Loodiana. To the Afghan chiefs he protested his constant fidelity to the national cause, and they desired him to demonstrate his sincerity by placing himself at the head of the army about to proceed to Jellalabad to expel General Sale. It was rumoured that he would be murdered or blinded by the Barukzies if he quitted the Bala Hissar, and he exacted an oath for his safety on the Koran, and descended from the citadel on the 5th April decked in all the insignia of royalty. He was shot dead on the road, and his body was rifled of the costly jewels he always carried about his person, and thrown into a ditch. It was rescued by his son, and

Shah Soojah.

A.D. interred with royal honours. Dissensions then broke out
1842 among the different chiefs, which ended in the complete ascendancy of Akbar Khan.

Of the British officers who were taken over as hostages, the greater number were entrusted to Zeman Shah, the only Afghan chief who never wavered in his attachment to the English during these scenes of perfidy. On the murder of Shah Soojah, he was constrained to transfer them to the high priest of Cabul, who sold them to Akbar Khan for 4,000 rupees. The captives, on being made over to him during the retreat, were conducted through the recent scenes of slaughter, amidst the mangled corpses which emitted the sickening smell of death, to a fort at Tezeen, and then over mountain paths, all but impassable, to Budeeabad, forty miles from Jellalabad, and were enabled to correspond with their friends in that town and to receive books and journals. On the approach of General Pollock they were conducted back for safety to Tezeen, where General Elphinstone sunk into the grave, a noble and brave soldier, endeared to all around him for his urbanity, but utterly unqualified for the arduous post which Lord Auckland had thrust upon him. On the 22nd May the captives were conveyed to a fort three miles from Cabul, where they enjoyed comparative freedom and comfort, and were permitted to interchange visits with their friends in the Bala Hissar. Meanwhile, Akbar Khan deputed one of the officers whom he held in captivity to General Pollock to propose the release of the prisoners on condition of his quitting the country without marching on the capital, threatening, in case of a refusal, to send them on to Turkestan and distribute them among the Oosbek chiefs. The proposal was peremptorily refused.

The hostages and captives.

The permission to march on Cabul was received with a shout of exultation at Jellalabad, but it was not before the middle of August that General Pollock was able to learn with certainty that General Nott had actually turned his face towards the capital. On the 20th of that month, 8,000 men, animated with a feeling of the highest enthusiasm, marched out of Jellalabad. At Jugdulluk the Ghiljies again appeared under the ablest of their chiefs, and with the flower of their tribes; but they no longer had a dispirited and fugitive soldiery to deal with, and in the battle which ensued the victory over them was in every way complete. The rout of the Ghiljies and the bold advance of General Pollock spread dismay at Cabul,

Advance of General Pollock.

A.D. 1842

and Akbar Khan, having put his threat in execution and sent the prisoners into Turkestan, moved down with all the chiefs and their levies to make one last effort to protect Cabul from the avenging foe. The two armies met in the valley of Tezeen, which had been the scene of a great massacre in January, and every height again bristled with matchlocks. The sepoy vied with his European comrade in driving the enemy from crag to crag, and dispersing them like a flock of sheep. Akbar fled from the field, leaving his troops to shift for themselves, and the British ensign was hoisted on the Bala Hissar on the 15th September.

Advance from Candahar.

General Nott evacuated Candahar on the 7th August. Owing to the admirable discipline maintained by the military and political chiefs, there had been no licentiousness on the part of the soldiery or officers to irritate the inhabitants, and they crowded around them and embraced them as they quitted the town. The army encountered no opposition of any moment on the route. The fortifications of Ghuzni were blown up, and the woodwork set on fire; and the flames of this ancient and renowned citadel, the cradle of Mahomedan power, lighted up the sky throughout the night. In it were deposited the gates of sandal wood of which Mahmood had despoiled the temple of Somnath eight centuries before, and Lord Ellenborough resolved to attach to his administration what he considered the merit of having restored them to India. General Nott was also instructed to bring away from the tomb of Mahmood "his club, which hung over it, and which, "together with the gates, would be the just trophies of his "successful march." The army reached Cabul the day after the arrival of General Pollock.

Rescue of the prisoners.

The first attention of General Pollock on his arrival was directed to the recovery of the prisoners whom Akbar Khan, on the 25th August, had hurried over the barren wastes and steep ascents of the Hindoo Coosh, many thousand feet above the level of the sea to Bameean, where they arrived on the 3rd September. Sir Richmond Shakespear, his military secretary, was therefore despatched after them with 600 horsemen. They were under the charge of Saleh Mahomed, who had been a native commandant in a local Afghan regiment, but deserted it in the previous year. On the 11th September, he called Captain Johnson, Captain George Lawrence, and Major Pottinger aside, and produced a letter from

A.D. 1842

Akbar Khan, directing him to convey the prisoners to the higher regions of the Hindoo Coosh, and deliver them to the Oosbek chief of Khooloom. At the same time, he exhibited a letter from Mohun lall, the moonshee in the service of the late envoy at Cabul, promising him, on the part of General Pollock, a gratuity of 20,000 rupees and an annuity of 12,000 rupees if he would restore the captives. "I know nothing," he said, "of General Pollock, "but if you three gentlemen will swear to me by your "Saviour to make the offer good, I will deliver you over "to your own people." The proposal was received with rapture, and the officers and ladies united in making themselves responsible by a deed for the funds.

Exertions of Major Pottinger.

Major Pottinger, by common consent, assumed the direction of their movements, and the hero of Herat was again in his element. He deposed the hostile governor of Bameean, hoisted another flag, and laid under contribution a caravan of Lohanee merchants passing through the country. He secured the Afghan escort consisting of 250 men by the promise of four months pay on reaching Cabul. He issued proclamations to the neighbouring chiefs to come in and make their obeisance, and granted them remissions of revenue. To prepare for a siege he repaired the fortifications, dug wells, and laid in a supply of provisions. On the 15th September a horseman galloped in with the cheering intelligence that Akbar Khan had been completely defeated, that the Afghan force was annihilated, and that General Pollock was in full march to Cabul. Major Pottinger and his fellow prisoners determined to return to Cabul without any delay. They bid adieu to the fort on the 16th, and slept that night on the bare rock, unconscious of fatigue or suffering. The next afternoon Sir Richmond Shakespear and his squadron was in the midst of them, and the anxieties of eight months were at an end. Two days after, the camp at Cabul was ringing with acclamations as the captives entered it, many of them wrapped in sheep skins. Never since the establishment of British power in India had so intense a feeling of anxiety pervaded the community as the fate of the prisoners excited, and the thrill of delight which vibrated throughout the country on the announcement of their safety may be more easily conceived than described.

The scattered remnant of the Afghan army was assembling in the Kohistan, the highlands of Cabul, under Ameenoolla, the most inveterate of our enemies, and it was deemed necessary to break up the gathering. A force was despatched against Istaliff, the chief town, which was considered the virgin fortress of Afghanistan, but it was captured with little loss. Chareekar, where the Goorkha regiment had been slaughtered, as well as several other towns which had taken a prominent part in the insurrection, were also destroyed. The object of the expedition had now been accomplished; Afghanistan had been reconquered, our prisoners recovered, and our military reputation restored to its former brilliancy; but it was considered necessary to leave some lasting mark of retribution on the capital. The great bazaar, where the mutilated corpse of the envoy had been exposed to the insults of the mob—the noblest building of its kind in Central Asia—was accordingly undermined and blown up. Notwithstanding the strenuous efforts of the officers to guard the gates, the soldiers rushed in from the camps of both generals, and for several days the city was subjected to the wild and licentious passions of men maddened by a remembrance of the indignities heaped on their murdered fellow-countrymen. The English colours were hauled down from the Bala Hissar on the 12th October, and the two armies turned their backs on Afghanistan. The family of Shah Soojah returned with the army to their former retreat at Loodiana. General Pollock halted at Jellalabad to blow up the fortifications, and the whole army at length reached the banks of the Sutlej.

A.D. 1842

Istaliff.

Lord Ellenborough received intelligence of the re-occupation of Cabul while residing at Simla in the house in which Lord Auckland had penned the declaration of war four years before, and he issued a proclamation announcing the termination of it. To give a dramatic effect to the proceeding, it was dated on the same day of the month with Lord Auckland's manifesto, though it was not issued till ten days later. It was universally censured for the unseemly reflections cast upon the preceding Governor-General. "Disasters," Lord Ellenborough said, "unparalleled in their extent, "except by the errors in which they originated, have in "one short campaign been avenged on every scene of past "misfortune." "The combined army of England and "India," he proceeded to say, "superior in equipment, in "discipline, and in valour, and in the officers by whom it "is commanded, to any force that can be opposed to it "in Asia, will stand in unassailable strength on its own "soil, and for ever, under the blessing of Providence,

Lord Ellenborough's proclamations.

A.D. 1842 "preserve the glorious empire it has won in security and "honour."

Lord Ellenborough had been in such a state of excitement ever since he assumed the government, that these inflated expressions excited little surprise, and the public only regretted that, with all his fine talents, he had so little ballast. The proclamation of the Gates appeared next, but it was ridiculed as a servile imitation of Bonaparte's proclamation of the Pyramids. "My friends and brethren," said the Governor-General in his address to the princes of India, "our victorious army bears the gates of the temple "of Somnath in triumph from Afghanistan, and the de- "spoiled tomb of Mahmood looks on the ruins of Ghuzni. "The insult of 800 years is avenged. To you, princes and "chiefs of Sirhind, of Rajwara, of Malwa, and of Guzerat, "I shall commit this glorious trophy of successful warfare. "You will yourselves, with all honour, transmit the gates "of sandal wood to the restored temple of Somnath." This quixotic address was designated by the Duke of Wellington a song of triumph, but by the community in India, native as well as European, it was considered the triumph of folly. The gates, which had been under the charge of General Nott, were placed on a waggon, covered with costly trappings, and brought in the train of the Governor-General to Agra. As the encampment moved on, hundreds of Hindoos prostrated themselves before the waggon, and made poojah, and presented offerings to it as to a deity. But the gates never moved beyond Agra, where they were consigned to a lumber room in the fort.

Lord Ellenborough had assembled a large army at Ferozepore, partly to overawe the Sikhs, and partly to get up a grand ovation, and there "at the foot of the bridge of

Meeting at Ferozepore.

"the Sutlej," amidst hundreds of elephants, which he had collected to do honour to the returning heroes, and which had been painted and decorated under his own immediate eye, he welcomed General Pollock with the captives, and General Nott with the gates. The officers were feasted in magnificent tents, decorated with flags bearing the names of their several victories, and the sepoys were regaled, as the Governor-General's notification ran, with their "favourite metoys," or sweetmeats. Including the regiments returning from Afghanistan, the camp at Ferozepore numbered 40,000 troops—an imposing and judicious display of military power after our recent disasters beyond the Indus. The Afghan prisoners in our hands were liberated. On taking leave of Dost Mahomed, Lord Ellenborough had the curiosity to enquire his opinion of us after all he had seen in India. "I have been struck," he replied, "with the magnitude of your resources and your "power, your armies, your ships, your arsenals; but what I "cannot understand is why the rulers of so vast and flourish-"ing an empire should have gone across the Indus to "deprive me of my poor and barren country." The surprise expressed by the Dost was equally shared by the community in England and in India; and here the curtain drops on the dark tragedy of Afghanistan.

A.D. 1842

On the 1st October Lord Ellenborough announced in his Simla proclamation that "the Government of India, con-"tent with the limits which nature appears to "have assigned to its empire, would devote all its "efforts to the re-establishment and maintenance "of peace," and he ordered a medal to be struck with the motto "Pax Asiæ restituta." Within six months he issued another proclamation, annexing the kingdom of Sinde to the Company's dominions. That country was divided into three principalities—upper, middle and lower Sinde, governed respectively by the Ameers, who were independent of each other. They had meekly submitted to the humiliation of the treaties enforced on them by Sir William Macnaghten in 1839, and, during the three years of the occupation of Afghanistan, their conduct had been marked by exemplary good faith. They permitted the free passage of our troops and stores, and supplied the steamers with fuel. After the Cabul force was annihilated, they still continued to furnish supplies and carriage, and it was solely by means of the 3,000 camels provided by them that General Nott was enabled to move on Cabul. Some of the chiefs, however, were emboldened by our reverses to manifest a spirit of hostility, and Major Outram, the Resident, brought charges against them, and advised a revision of the treaties. Lord Ellenborough replied that he was determined to inflict signal chastisement on any chief or Ameer who had exhibited hostile designs against us during the late events on a presumption of our weakness, but there must, he said, be the clearest proof of their faithlessness.

Conduct of the Ameers of Sinde.

Sir Charles Napier arrived in Sinde on the 9th September, invested with full diplomatic and military power. He was a soldier of distinguished reputation, and of extraordinary energy, but he came to his post

Sir Charles Napier.

A.D. 1842 with a violent prejudice against the Ameers. The investigation of the charges of disloyalty was referred to him by the Governor-General with the distinct injunction that he should not proceed against them without the most complete proof of their guilt. All the charges, except three, were at once dismissed, and the question of their delinquency turned upon the authenticity of a letter, which the best scholars in India said was exceedingly doubtful, but which Sir Charles, who was totally ignorant of the language, pronounced to be genuine, without calling on the Ameers for any explanation. The treaties of 1839, he affirmed, had been violated.

Major Outram had submitted to Lord Ellenborough, together with the charges he brought against some of the chiefs, the draft of a new treaty intended to substitute a cession of territory for the annual tribute, and to punish the disloyal Ameers by transferring a portion of their lands to the nabob of Bhawulpore. The treaty was received from the Governor-General by Sir Charles Napier on the 12th November, when Major Outram discovered that it prescribed the confiscation of more territory than had been originally intended, and deprived the Ameers of the cherished prerogative of coining money. He attributed this alteration to inadvertence, and requested Sir Charles to bring the subject to the notice of Lord Ellenborough. He thought fit, however, to detain the document ten weeks, and when it arrived at length with the Governor-General's instruction that the error should be rectified, the Ameers had been irretrievably ruined. Lord Ellenborough had distinctly ordered Sir Charles Napier not to act on the treaty till the Ameers had accepted and ratified it; but before they were allowed to discuss it, he sequestered the whole of the lands stated in the first and incorrect treaty, which belonged to the Beloch chiefs, the feudatories of the Ameers, and they were at once deprived of the means of subsistence.

The new treaties.

These violent and unjustifiable proceedings were prompted by the consummate villany of Ali Morad. The office of Rais was the highest dignity in Upper Sinde, and the turban was the symbol of it. It had long been enjoyed by Meer Roostum, then in his eighty-fifth year, who was venerated alike by the chiefs and the people and the British officers. The succession to this honour belonged by the usage of the country to his brother Ali Morad, but he was anxious to bestow it on his

Ali Morad's perfidy.

own son. To make sure of the turban Ali Morad insinuated himself, on the one hand, into the confidence of Sir Charles Napier and succeeded in poisoning his mind against Meer Roostum, and on the other, endeavoured to drive Meer Roostum into some overt act of hostility towards the British Government. Under his sinister influence, three haughty and menacing messages were sent by Sir Charles to the Meer, and when he sought an interview to afford an explanation, it was refused him and he was ordered to repair to his brother's fortress at Deejee. Soon after his arrival there, Ali Morad transmitted to Sir Charles a letter from his brother, stating that he had of his own free will resigned the turban, and his army, his forts and his country to him. Sir Charles was not without suspicion that the cession had been obtained by force or fraud, and he informed Ali Morad that it was his intention to see his brother in person on the subject. To prevent this interview, which would have been fatal to his scheme, he awoke his brother at midnight, and urged him to fly, as the English general was coming the next morning to apprehend him. The bewildered old chief rode off in haste to the camp of his relatives twelve miles distant, and Sir Charles immediately issued a proclamation to the Ameers and people of Sinde charging Meer Roostum with having insulted and defied the British Government, and announcing that he was resolved to maintain Ali Morad as the chieftain of the Talpoora family. Meer Roostum immediately sent his minister to assure Sir Charles that he had been placed under restraint by Ali Morad, that his seal was affixed to the deed by force, and that he had been prompted by him to fly. To this communication Sir Charles sent an arrogant reply. Soon after, he started on an expedition to Emamgurh in the desert, because it was considered the "Gibraltar of Upper Sinde," and he was determined to show the chiefs that "neither their deserts nor "their negotiations could intercept the progress of the "British army." The army traversed the desert for four days amidst great hardships, and finding the fort evacuated, blew it up with the powder contained in it. The Duke of Wellington pronounced it a great military exploit, but as Meer Mahomed, to whom the fort belonged, had never given any cause of offence to the British Government it was an act of wanton aggression. A.D. 1842

After having confiscated the lands in Upper Sinde and deprived Meer Roostum of his power and dignity, Sir

Charles Napier ordered the Ameers of Upper and Lower Sinde to meet Major Outram at Khyrpore, to discuss and sign the treaty, but as some of them did not attend, the conference was transferred to Hyderabad. Two days after, the agents of the Ameers of Lower Sinde arrived in the camp with their masters' seals, which they were authorised to affix to the treaty; and there would have been a peaceful solution of all differences if they had been permitted to do so. Sir Charles, however, refused them permission to execute the deed, and ordered them back to Hyderabad, and thus brought the combustible materials of the upper and lower divisions of the country together in that city.

Conference with the Ameers.

A.D. 1843

At the conference, the Ameers denied that they had infringed the treaty of 1839, and they repudiated the correspondence on which they had been condemned, and which they were not permitted to see. On the 12th February, they affixed their seals to the treaty, but assured the Major that the Beloche troops assembled at the capital were exasperated at the sight of the chiefs of Upper Sinde whom Sir Charles had deprived of their lands, and more especially of the venerable Meer Roostum, whom he had deposed, and that it was impossible to answer for their conduct. The confusion was increased by the approach of Sir Charles Napier and his army. As the Major was leaving the fort after the signature of the treaty, he was surrounded by a crowd of citizens and soldiers who poured curses on the British name, and he would have fallen a victim to popular fury, if the Ameers had not personally guarded him to the Residency. The next day a deputation from the Ameers waited on him, and stated that the Beloche troops were wrought up to such a state of desperation that they had ceased to be amenable to authority. For two days they continued to entreat him to retire from the Residency to a position of greater safety, but, with more chivalry than discretion, he refused to move. On the morning of the 15th February, three days after the signature of the treaties, masses of infantry came down on the Residency house, and Major Outram, after a gallant defence of three hours, withdrew to the armed steamer anchored in the river at the distance of 500 yards.

Conference at Hyderabad.

An appeal to arms now became inevitable. The Beloche troops flocked to the capital in augmented numbers when it was found that Sir Charles Napier persisted in advancing upon it after the treaty had been

The battle of Meeanee.

signed. On the morning of the 17th February he came in front of the Beloche army which was posted at Meeanee, six miles from Hyderabad, about 20,000 in number, while his own force did not exceed 2,700. The Beloches disputed every inch of ground, and, after fighting for three hours with desperate valour, retired gradually from the contest, leaving their camp and their artillery in the hands of the victor. Braver men never rushed on death, and never on any Indian battle-field had the gallantry of British troops and the generalship of a British commander been more conspicuous. No quarter was asked or given, and the loss of the enemy in killed and wounded was computed at 5,000, while on the side of the English the number did not exceed 257, of whom, however, nineteen were officers. A fresh body of 10,000 Beloche soldiers arrived the next day, and a similar number was hovering about in the neighbourhood, but the voluntary submission of the Ameers and the surrender of the fort, relieved Sir Charles from all anxiety. He entered Hyderabad on the 20th, and obtained possession of the accumulated treasures of the Talpoora dynasty, which, as usual, were at once distributed among the troops as prize-money. Lord Ellenborough on hearing of the victory of Meanee issued a proclamation, annexing Sinde, "fertile as Egypt," to the Company's dominions. The gallant Shere Mahomed collected together the scattered bands of Beloches to make another effort for the independence of his country. Sir Charles Napier, who had received reinforcements which raised his army to 6,000, found the Ameer encamped with 20,000 men at Duppa. The field was gallantly contested on both sides, but the victory was as complete as that of Meeanee, and the subjugation of the country was consummated.

A.D. 1843

The triumphs of the army in Sinde were contrasted with the pusillanimity exhibited at Cabul and created a feeling of just exultation in India, but it was damped by the conviction that the war was altogether indefensible. The elaborate vindication which Lord Ellenborough drew up of it only served to expose the weakness of his cause. His error lay in the overweening confidence he placed in Sir Charles Napier, who was always more under the influence of excitement than of reason, and who withheld much information which he was bound in honour to give. Sir John Hobhouse, the President of the Board of Control, justly observed that the conquest of Sinde would never have taken place if the Governor-General had been

Remarks.

in full possession of the real facts, and cognisant of Ali Morad's perfidy. But even before Sir Charles knew anything of that caitiff he wrote, "We only want a pretext to "coerce the Ameers . . . the more powerful Government "will at no distant period swallow up the weaker;" and he subsequently remarked, "We have no right to seize Sinde, "yet we shall do so, and a very advantageous, useful, and "humane piece of rascality it will be." The rascality is more obvious than the advantage, except to the captors, to whom it brought a rich harvest of prize-money, of which seven lacs fell to the share of Sir Charles Napier. On the finances of India it inflicted a loss of two crores and a half of rupees, in the course of fifteen years.

SECTION II.

LORD ELLENBOROUGH'S ADMINISTRATION—WAR WITH SINDIA—HIS RECALL.

A.D. 1843 THE annexation of Sinde brought its own retribution. It led to a relaxation of the bonds of discipline and loyalty of the native army, and afforded a premonition of that climax of mutiny which thirteen years after swept away the whole army. Sinde having become a British province, the sepoys ceased to be entitled to the extra allowance granted to them when on foreign service in an enemy's country, but they could see no reason why their pay should be curtailed because they had added a new kingdom to the dominions of their masters. In

Mutiny of native regiments.

A.D. 1844 February, the 34th Native Infantry refused to march to Sinde without the same allowance which had been granted to troops proceeding beyond the Indus. The 7th Bengal Cavalry and some Bengal artillery followed the example, and were marched back. The 69th and 4th, ordered in their stead to the frontier, refused to embark on the boats at Ferozepore, and the 64th mutinied at Loodiana, at Moodkee, and at Shikarpore. On none of these occasions was the authority of the state vindicated, or the spirit of discipline maintained. Finding it impossible to garrison Sinde with a Bengal force, the Government turned to the Madras army, and a regiment was sent to Bombay; but when the men found that the usual extra allowance was not to be granted, they also went into mutiny. The province was then made over to the Bombay Presidency, and satisfactory arrangements were made with regard to the pay of the sepoys.

The next event in the course of Lord Ellenborough's administration had reference to the affairs of Gwalior. Dowlut Rao Sindia died in 1827, and his widow Baeza bye adopted Junkojee, who died in 1843 without issue. In 1838 he had taken for his second wife Tara bye, who was thirteen years of age at the time of his death, when she adopted a boy of eight years, bestowing on him the title of Gyajee. The Gwalior cabinet was anxious that the government should remain with the existing ministry, but Lord Ellenborough, considering the extreme youth of the raja and his adoptive mother, deemed it prudent that the management of public affairs should be entrusted to a single individual. Of the two candidates who were presented to him he chose for regent the Mama Sahib, the uncle of the late raja, while the young queen and an influential party at court preferred Dada Khasjee, the hereditary chamberlain; and, finding their wishes disappointed, set every engine to work to thwart the measures of the regent and to embarrass the administration. To strengthen his authority, the regent betrothed the young raja to his own niece. The palace confederacy assured the queen that this alliance would undermine her influence, and ten days after the nuptials she informed the Resident that she had determined to dismiss the regent from her service. The Resident earnestly remonstrated with her on the folly of this proceeding, but she turned a deaf ear to his expostulations, and expelled him the country. The degradation of the minister who had been nominated and supported by the Governor-General placed the state in a position of antagonism to the British Government, and the Resident was instructed to retire from the court.

A.D. 1843

Affairs of Gwalior.

The great source of disquietude at Gwalior, however, was the state of the army, about 30,000 infantry, and 10,000 cavalry, not composed of Mahratta soldiers, but recruited chiefly from the martial population of Rajpootana, Oude, and other provinces, and commanded by officers of European descent. It was out of proportion to the necessities of the state, or to its revenues, of which it absorbed more than two-thirds. The ministers had made repeated efforts to reduce the number, but the troops would not permit a single corps to be disbanded. They were, moreover, always in arrears, which increased their arrogance. The

State of the army.

A.D. 1843 state had lost all control of the army. One regiment had recently committed great excesses in Malwa, and upon a strong remonstrance from the Resident the commandant had been summoned to appear at Gwalior alone, but he brought his whole corps with him, and overawed the court. Lord Ellenborough had pressed on the regent the indispensable necessity of dealing vigorously with the spirit of rebellion, but without any result.

On the expulsion of the regent the ranee assumed the ostensible management of affairs, and held durbars daily, though only thirteen years of age, but all real power was in the hands of the Dada, who had secured the influence of the zenana by lavish gifts of land and money. He was obnoxious to the most influential nobles, who formed an opposition party, and he could not venture to move about without the protection of a guard; to the British Government he manifested particular hostility, and expelled from office all who were favourable to it. The army, which was concentrated at the capital, was courted by both parties, and became more overbearing than ever, and the confusion in the state was rapidly approaching a crisis.

Confusion at Gwalior.

The ranee importuned the Resident to return to the court, but he informed her that until the Dada, the source of these complications, was removed from the public councils, there could be no restoration of friendly relations. This communication was received by the Dada, but withheld from her. Lord Ellenborough considered this a serious offence, and insisted on his being delivered up to the custody of the Resident, to which the ranee refused her consent. Three of the most influential of the chiefs, however, gained over one of the brigades, besieged the palace for three days and obtained possession of the person of the Dada, but he contrived to make his escape, and resumed the management of affairs, and began to make preparation to resist any adverse movement of the British Government.

On the 1st November, Lord Ellenborough recorded a masterly minute on the state of affairs at Gwalior. After referring to our position in India as the paramount and controlling power, and to the responsibilities connected with it, he passed in review the transactions of the year at Gwalior. The expulsion of the regent nominated with our concurrence, and the elevation of his rival, were an affront of the gravest character. An army of 40,000 men, with a numerous artillery,

Lord Ellenborough's minute.

lay within a few marches of the capital of the North-West Provinces, under the management of one who had obtained his post, and could only maintain it, in despite of the British Government. The events which had recently occurred at Lahore would not permit acquiescence in a policy suited only to a state of tranquillity. Within three marches of the Sutlej, there was an army of 70,000 men, confident in its own strength, proud of its various successes over its neighbours, desirous of war and plunder, and under no discipline or control. We were bound to take every precaution against its hostility, and no precaution appeared more necessary than that of rendering our rear and our communications secure, by the establishment of a friendly Government at Gwalior. Lord Ellenborough continued for two months to press the surrender of the Dada on the ranee, but still without success. He arrived at Agra on the 11th December, and finding that he had not left Gwalior, wrote to the ranee that he could neither permit the existence of an unfriendly Government in the territories of Sindia, nor permit it to remain without a Government able and willing to preserve the relations of amity with its neighbours. He had therefore ordered the British armies to advance, and would not arrest their progress until he had full security for the future tranquillity of the common frontier.

A.D. 1843

Communications with Gwalior.

Sir Hugh Gough, the Commander-in-Chief, was directed to commence his march to Gwalior, and the Dada was immediately sent in to the encampment of the Resident at Dholpore with a letter from the ranee, requesting that, as the wishes of the Governor-General had been complied with, the advance of the army might be countermanded. In his reply, Lord Ellenborough repeated his former remarks on the necessity of a strong Government at Gwalior to control its own subjects, and he required that the Gwalior army, which was to all intents and purposes master of the state it professed to serve, should be reduced, and the strength of the British contingent increased. The Cabinet, finding that the British army continued to move down to the Chumbul, the boundary of the two States, sent a deputation of the most influential chiefs to request that the ranee and the prince should be allowed to wait on the Governor-General in his present encampment. Lord Ellenborough replied that he could not wait their arrival, but they represented with greater importunity that the house of Sindia would be for ever disgraced, if, contrary to all precedent, the Governor-

A.D. 1843 General should cross the frontier before the head of the State had waited on him on British territory. As Lord Ellenborough continued inflexible, it was arranged that the meeting should take place twenty-three miles from the capital. The troops, however, would not permit the royal family to quit it, but marched out of Gwalior with acclamation, and informed the Resident that they were going to drive the English back across the Chumbul.

Battle of Maharajpore.

After waiting in vain for two days at Hingona for the royal party, Lord Ellenborough directed Sir Hugh Gough to advance to Gwalior. Sindia's army had taken up a strong position at Chounda, and Sir Hugh's arrangements were directed to this point; but during the night seven battalions with twenty guns of heavy calibre moved on unobserved to Maharajpore, and entrenched themselves, with their formidable batteries in front. The Commander-in-Chief and his staff considered the enemy a contemptible rabble, ready to fly on the first shot. The Adjutant-General said he should not have occasion for anything but a horse-whip. The march was described as a military promenade, and the Governor-General and the ladies of the chief officers were in the field on elephants. There had been no reconnaissance, and the enemy's change of position was not known. The troops advanced gaily to Maharajpore, where it was intended to breakfast, when a volley from the masked batteries gave the first intimation of their position. Sir Hugh was required to change his dispositions in haste, and the battle was justly characterised by the Governor-General as one in which everybody and everything was out of place. The British force numbered 12,000, that of the Mahrattas about 14,000. The siege train had been unaccountably left behind on the surrender of the Dada, and the light field pieces of the army were quickly silenced by the heavy ordnance of the enemy, and the troops were, according to the usual tactics of Sir Hugh, launched on the batteries, which were served with desperation as long as a gunner was left.
Dec. 29. The victory was at length achieved by the irresistible gallantry of our soldiers, of whom 1,000 fell killed and wounded. On the same day, another battle was fought at Punniar, of minor importance, which likewise ended in a victory.

These victories placed the kingdom of Sindia at the disposal of the Governor-General, but he left it entire, and simply curtailed its independence. The young ranee was deposed from the office of regent, and consigned to oblivion on an allowance of three lacs a year, and the administration was committed to a council of regency, who were required to act implicitly on the advice of the Resident. The turbulent army of the state was reduced to 9,000, and allowed only thirty-two guns. The British contingent was raised to 10,000, and became, in fact, a complete and compact little army of all arms, commanded by the officers of the Company, composed of high-caste brahmins and Rajpoots, men of athletic frames and high courage, and also of boundless presumption, as the Government found to its cost during the mutiny. 1844

New treaty.

Lord Ellenborough returned to Calcutta in March, and on the 15th June, India was astounded by the news that 1844 the Court of Directors had revoked his appointment. His correspondence with the India House had been marked by the absence of that deference to the Directors which was due to their high position in the empire, and it too much resembled his communications to them when he was dictator at the Board of Control; his proceedings had too often exhibited a contumacious disdain of their authority. He treated the civil service with undisguised contempt, and concentrated his sympathies on the army. He had contracted a fondness for military glory, and his administration presented only a succession of battles. The vagary of the Gates proclamation had exposed the Government of India to the ridicule of England and the contempt of Europe, and destroyed all confidence in the sobriety and soundness of his judgment. He appeared to the Directors to be without any definite principles of action, and they were in constant dread of the new embarrassments in which his eccentricities might involve them. They ceased to consider the empire safe in his hands; and in the teeth of ministerial remonstrances, more especially from the Duke, determined to exercise the power of recall which they had refused to renounce at the renewal of the charter. His removal was resented by the army he had caressed, with expressions bordering on disloyalty. The community in general, while duly appreciating his many noble qualities, the total absence of nepotism, the patriotic distribution of his patronage, his indefatigable industry, and his singular energy, still regarded the resolution of the Court of Directors as an act of unquestionable wisdom. He embarked for England on the 1st August, and the Sikh war was postponed for twelve months.

Recall of Lord Ellenborough.

Lord Ellenborough's attention was so completely absorbed in war and politics as to leave him little leisure or inclination for the moral, intellectual, or material improvement of the country, but there were some measures which deserve notice. It was during his administration that the police of the lower provinces was rendered more efficient by the establishment of the office of deputy magistrate, to which men of every class, creed, and caste were eligible; and also by an improvement of the pay of *darogas*, who held the comfort of the great body of the people in their hands. It was also under his government that state lotteries, which had become a prolific source of demoralisation, were abolished. To him also belongs the merit of having, under the advice of Mr. Wilberforce Bird, passed an Act for the total and immediate extinction of slavery.

Improvements in his administration.

SECTION III.

LORD HARDINGE'S ADMINISTRATION—THE PUNJAB—THE SIKH WAR.

A.D. ON the recall of Lord Ellenborough, the Ministry and the
1844 Court of Directors concurred in nominating his relative, Sir Henry—subsequently Lord—Hardinge, to succeed him. He had entered the army at an early age, and served in the Peninsula under the Duke of Wellington, and acquired a high reputation, more especially at the battle of Albuera, the success of which was ascribed to his skill and gallantry, and procured him from a great historical authority the commendation of being "the young soldier "with the eye of a general, and the soul of a hero." At Waterloo he was disabled by a severe wound. On his return to England he entered Parliament and was twice Secretary at War, and once Secretary for Ireland, and in these positions acquired much experience in the management of public affairs. It was his military qualifications, however, which recommended him for the government of India at a time when the right bank of the Sutlej was bristling with hostile bayonets and the Sikh army had ceased to be amenable to the control of the state. He was of the same mature age—sixty—as the Marquis of Hastings, and he entered upon his duties, as he said at the valedictory banquet,

Lord Hardinge.

with an earnest desire to establish his fame as the friend of peace, and not by means of conquest or the exhibition of military skill. But as in the case of his two predecessors, Lord Wellesley and Lord Hastings, these pacific intentions were destined to a speedy disappointment, and the most memorable events of his administration consist of the four battles fought within the period of fifty-four days.

From the period of his arrival the attention of Sir Henry Hardinge was anxiously fixed upon the storm then gathering in the Punjab, where the death of Runjeet Sing had been followed by unexampled anarchy and bloodshed. He was succeeded in July, 1839, by his imbecile son Khurruk Sing, whose young and gallant son Nao Nihal Sing, equal to his grandfather in talent and energy, managed the affairs of the State, but was obliged to share his authority with Dhyan Sing, the minister, a member of the Jummoo, or Dogra family, then one of the most influential in the Punjab. Golab Sing, the head of the house, was originally a running footman, who had attracted the notice of Runjeet Sing, and rapidly rose in his favour, and was endowed with the district of Jummoo. He was a Rajpoot and not a Sikh, and this circumstance, combined with the extraordinary power to which the family had risen, rendered them an object of envy and hatred. Khurruk Sing died prematurely of excess, and Nao Nihal his son, after performing his funeral obsequies, was killed by the falling of a covered gateway as he was returning to the city.

Revolutions in the Punjab. A.D. 1839

Shere Sing, the reputed son of Runjeet Sing, having gained over a portion of the army, marched to Lahore and seized on the government on the 14th January. He was shrewd and frank, but the slave of sensuality, and the vassal of the Jummoo family, whom he was unable either to shake off or to control. He rewarded the troops who had been the instruments of his elevation with an increase of pay, which served to sharpen their avarice and to increase their arrogance, and they proceeded to wreak their vengeance on all who were obnoxious to them. Shere Sing had made a request for British support, and so little idea had the Government of India of the strength of the Khalsa army that a force of 10,000 men was held in readiness to march to Lahore, to exterminate it. On receiving notice of this wild proposal, he simply drew his finger across his throat to signify the fate which would await him. If this force had crossed the Sutlej, the whole Khalsa army

Army of the Punjab. 1841

would have risen as one man, and hurled back the invasion. That army, with the exception of a few Mahomedans, consisted of a compact body of martial Sikhs, united by the strongest national and religious sympathies, proud of their past achievements, and haughty in the consciousness of their own superiority. When the iron sceptre of Runjeet Sing was removed, these Prætorian bands speedily became masters of the Punjab. The soldiers were individually obedient to their own officers, though they did occasionally tie the commandant up to a gun; but as a body their movements were regulated, not by the will of the sovereign or of the minister, but by the dictation of the army committees or *punches*, the Council of Five, who consulted nothing but the interests of the troops. Those who bestowed on them the greatest largesses were most sure of their support.

A.D. 1843 The year 1843 was marked by those convulsions to which Lord Ellenborough alluded in his minute of the 1st November, when he dwelt on the necessity of securing our rear by reducing the equally insubordinate army of Gwalior. The minister Dhyan Sing, finding his power on the wane, persuaded Shere Sing to recall Ajeet Sing, the head of one of the most powerful clans, whom he had banished. On his restoration to office, he invited Shere Sing to inspect some new levies which he had raised, and shot him dead on the parade. Ajeet Sing then assassinated Dhyan Sing, when his youthful son Heera Sing called on the soldiers to revenge these foul murders, and they proceeded to the citadel and put Ajeet Sing to death. Duleep Sing, then five years of age, the son of Runjeet Sing by the ranee Jhindun, was brought from the zenana and installed maharaja by Heera Sing, who took the post of minister, and attached the troops to his interest by an addition of two rupees and a half to their monthly pay. From this time, the army may be considered absolute master of the state.

Murder of Shere Sing.

The position of Heera Sing was unstable and perilous in the extreme. One of his uncles marched down to Lahore, from Jummoo to supplant him, but was defeated and slain. The Khalsa army, which supported his power, was also the great source of danger, which he endeavoured to lessen by distributing the regiments and raising levies in the highlands, but the *punches* would not permit a single corps to leave the capital without their concurrence. The success of his administration was due

Murder of Heera Sing.

chiefly to the genius of his tutor, the pundit Jalla, the priest of the Jummoo family, who was considered a man of such extraordinary ability that if he could have controlled the troops he might have established a dynasty of Peshwas at Lahore, but before his position was consolidated he endeavoured to reduce the power of Golab Sing, who succeeded Dhyan Sing as the ruler of Jummoo; he also sequestered the estates of some of the chiefs, and, more particularly, offended the ranee Jhindun and her brother by his supercilious deportment. She appealed to the army, A.D.
and Heera Sing and the pundit were obliged to fly, but 1844
were overtaken and killed, and their heads brought in triumph to Lahore. On the dissolution of the Government of Heera Sing the management of affairs fell into the hands of Jowaher Sing, the brother of the ranee, and of her favourite paramour, Lall Sing, a brahmin, who had nothing to recommend him but his comely person. The soldiers received a fresh augmentation of pay, and became so insubordinate that it appeared necessary to find some employment for them to prevent the total overthrow of the Government. They were therefore instigated to march to Jummoo and fleece raja Golab Sing, whom they brought down to Lahore and from whom they wrung more than a crore of rupees. To keep them from mischief at the capital they were then recommended to attack Moolraj, who had been allowed to succeed his father in the government of Mooltan, and from him they extorted eighteen lacs. Soon after, Peshora Sing, another of the sons of Runjeet, raised the standard of revolt, but was defeated and basely murdered by Jowaher Sing. He had always been popular with the people and the army, and the contempt which was felt for the wretched debauchee who occupied the post of minister was turned into indignation by this atrocity, and he was led out into the plain of Meean Meer and executed. After the loss of her brother, the ranee sat daily in durbar, and in the beginning of November appointed Lall Sing minister, and Tej Sing commander-in-chief. But the army, which had within the year humbled the two great feudatories of Jummoo and Mooltan, was now the sole power in the state.

The anarchy which reigned in the Punjab constrained 1845
the Government of India to make energetic preparations for the defence of the frontier. The cantonment at Ferozepore on the Sutlej which was inadequately garrisoned had been reinforced by Lord Ellenborough, but Sir Henry Hardinge found that the

Preparations on the frontier.

force assembled there, though amounting to 17,000 men, was not sufficient for its defence, still less for extensive operations if they should be forced upon us. He therefore gradually massed 40,000 men on the frontier, and in the stations below it, so imperceptibly as to attract no attention in our own provinces; and he likewise brought up from Sinde to Ferozepore the fifty-six large boats which Lord Ellenborough had wisely constructed to serve as a pontoon. It has been surmised that it was the assemblage of this large force on and near the frontier which roused the suspicions of the Khalsa army, and led them to anticipate our designs by the invasion of our territories. But since our discomfiture in Afghanistan had lowered our prestige, that army had twice marched down to the banks of the Sutlej and threatened to cross it. Considering, moreover, the distracted state of the Punjab Government, with the most efficient army ever collected under the banner of any native State, flushed with its past successes and panting for new triumphs, and utterly beyond control, the Governor-General would have been without excuse if he had not made the most ample preparations to meet a crisis which might turn up any day. The invasion was the work of the ranee—justly termed by Sir Henry Hardinge the Messalina of the north—and of Lall Sing and Tej Sing. They felt that the only chance of maintaining their authority in the Punjab was to involve the army in a conflict with the British Government; and it was they who launched the Sikh battalions on our provinces for their own security, and endeavoured to avert the plunder of Lahore by sending them across the Sutlej to plunder Delhi and Benares.

On the 17th November, the order was issued to cross the Sutlej. Major Broadfoot, the political agent on the frontier, urged the most prompt and energetic measures of defence, but Sir Henry Hardinge, still clinging to the hope of peace, directed him to send another remonstrance to the durbar, the only reply to which, however, was an order to commence the march without any further delay. Animated by a feeling of national and religious enthusiasm, 60,000 Khalsa soldiers, with 40,000 well-armed camp followers, and 150 guns of large calibre, crossed the Sutlej in four days, and by the 16th December, were encamped within a short distance of the fort of Ferozepore, which was held by Sir John Littler, one of the oldest and best officers in the service, with about 10,000 men and 21 guns. On the 11th December, preparations

A.D. 1845 The Sikh army cross the Sutlej.

had been made for a grand ball in the state tents of the A.D. 1845 Commander-in-Chief at Umballa, when information was received that the whole Sikh army had marched down to the Sutlej and was on the eve of crossing it. The ball was abandoned, and the night passed in preparing to march to the relief of Sir John Littler, who was enveloped by a force six times the number of his own. Hours were now invaluable, and the troops, heavily accoutred, performed a march never before attempted in India, of 150 miles in six days, through heavy sands, the most formidable of all roads, with little time to cook their food, and scarcely an hour for repose. On the 13th the Governor-General issued a declaration of war, and confiscated the districts belonging to the Sikh crown south of the Sutlej. The day after the Sikh army had crossed the river, a large portion of it pushed on to Ferozeshuhur and began to construct entrenchments of the most substantial character, leaving Tej Sing to watch the movements of Sir John Littler.

Battle of Moodkee.

Lall Sing's scouts brought him information that the Governor-General and the Commander-in-Chief were advancing with only a slender force, and he pushed on with 20,000 men and 22 guns to Moodkee, where he awaited their arrival under cover of the jungle. On the 18th December, the army had performed a fatiguing 1845 march of twenty-one miles over an arid plain; the troops were suffering severely from thirst; they had not broken their fast since the preceding night, and were preparing for a meal, when a cloud of dust rose up in front, and the roar of cannon announced the approach of Lall Sing's army. Sir Hugh Gough was taken by surprise, as at Maharajpore; and then came the first conflict between the sepoy of Hindostan and the Khalsa battalions of the Punjab, and the superiority of the Sikh, whom a high political authority had declared to be "a rabble demoralised by the absence of "every principle of subordination, and by its wretched "violence," became at once indisputable. One of our regiments turned round and sought the rear, and it was with difficulty the Commander-in-Chief and his staff could drag it to the front. Even a European corps was for a time staggered by the precision and rapidity of the enemy's fire, and in the confusion of the hour, one regiment fired into another; but victory declared on our side, though not without the loss of 900 in killed and wounded. For sixty years it had been the practice of the home authorities to unite the office of Commander-in-Chief with that of Governor-General, when he happened to be a military man, as in the case of Lord Cornwallis, Lord Hastings, and Lord William Bentinck. It was unfortunately omitted in the case of Sir Henry Hardinge, but after the miserable tactics exhibited at Moodkee, he placed his services at the disposal of Sir Hugh Gough, and magnanimously took the post of second in command, and thus restored in some degree the confidence of the troops.

A.D. 1845

Battle of Ferozeshuhur.

The army halted two days at Moodkee to take repose and bury the dead, and was reinforced by the arrival of two European and two native regiments, brought up by forced marches, through the indefatigable exertions of Sir Henry Hardinge. It started for the entrenched camp of the Sikhs at Ferozeshuhur on the morning of the 21st December, without provisions or tents. Sir John Littler was directed to join it at the computed hour of its arrival, and he moved out early in the morning, and evaded the notice of Tej Sing by leaving his camp pitched, his bazaar flags flying, and his cavalry pickets standing, and reached the main body with 5,500 men and 22 guns a few moments before noon. The Sikh entrenchment was in the form of a parallelogram, a mile in length and half a mile in breadth, with the village of Ferozeshuhur in the centre. The number of troops within it, commanded by Lall Sing, was estimated at 35,000, with 100 guns and 250 camel swivels. The batteries were mounted, not with ordinary field artillery, but with heavy siege guns, placed in position; the day was the shortest in the year, and with such an enemy to deal with as the Sikhs had proved themselves to be at Moodkee, every moment was of inestimable value; but three hours were strangely frittered away after Sir John Littler's arrival, and it was nearly four in the afternoon before the first shot was fired. Sir Charles Napier in his comments on the strategy of the day remarks that the attack should have been made on the two sides which were not protected by the tremendous guns immoveably fixed, but Sir Hugh Gough resolved to follow his usual practice of charging at once right up to the muzzle of the guns and carrying the batteries by "cold steel." He took the command of the right, Sir Henry Hardinge of the centre, and Sir John Littler of the left. It fell to Sir John to assault the strongest section of the enemy's position, where they had gathered the strength of their heaviest guns. His own field pieces were found to be of little, if any use, and his troops advanced gallantly up to the batteries, but were at once arrested by the overwhelming fire of the enemy. The 62nd Foot, mowed down by grape and round shot, was checked, and retired beaten, but not, in the eye of candour, dishonoured. The other divisions encountered an equally terrific resistance. To borrow the language of the historian of the Sikhs, "guns were dis-"mounted, and the ammunition blown into the air; "squadrons were checked in mid career; battalion after "battalion was hurled back with shattered ranks; and it "was not till after sunset that portions of the enemy's "position were finally carried. Darkness and the obstinacy "of the conflict threw the English into confusion; men of "all regiments and all ranks were mixed together. "Generals were doubtful of the fact, or the extent of their "own success, and colonels knew not what had become of "the regiments they commanded, or of the army of which "they formed a part." The Governor-General had five aides-de-camp killed and four wounded. He himself passed the night in moving from regiment to regiment, endeavouring to sustain the spirits and to revive the ardour of the men, and, instead of retiring to Ferozepore as he was advised to do, determined to renew the engagement the next morning, although there was only one weak division for the work which had baffled the whole army. At day-dawn he and the Commander-in-Chief collected the scattered soldiers of General Gilbert's division, attacked the batteries in reverse, and captured them after a feeble resistance. In the Sikh encampment during the night there had been stormy counsels and bitter recriminations; the military chest had likewise been plundered, and, through the cowardice or the treachery of the commander, the legions who had defended this Roman encampment with Roman courage were in full flight to the Sutlej. The British line halted as soon as it had cleared the works, and the two commanders were received with acclamation as they rode along the ranks. The cheers had scarcely died out when a cloud of dust announced the approach of a new enemy. This was Tej Sing, who, finding that Sir John Littler had eluded his vigilance, marched down to Ferozeshuhur on the morning of the 22nd, with 20,000 infantry, 5,000 cavalry, and seventy guns. He found that the entrenchment was lost, and the Sikh army in full retreat to the river, and after a brief cannonade, which at once dismounted our feeble artillery, withdrew to the Sutlej. He did not know that the British army, or what remained

A.D. 1845 21 Dec.

A.D. 1845 of it, was drooping from hunger, not having tasted food for thirty-six hours, and wholly without ammunition, and that, if vigorously attacked, the most brilliant courage could not have saved it from utter destruction. The British empire in India was again saved by a miracle. Our loss was 2,415 killed and wounded, including 103 officers. The battle of Ferozeshuhur was the most severe and critical the British army had ever fought in India. Never before had we encountered so resolute and so skilful an enemy; but it was the defect of our tactics and the deficiency of our ammunition, quite as much as the courage of the Sikhs, which for a time gave a character of equality to the struggle.

Battle of Alliwal.

The tide of invasion had now been stemmed, and of the 60,000 Khalsa soldiers who had poured down on the Company's territories twelve days before, not one remained in arms on the left bank of the Sutlej. But the two engagements had cost the army a fifth of its numbers and exhausted its ammunition, and it became necessary to bring up a large supply of stores as well as siege guns from the nearest depôt, which was at Delhi, 200 miles distant. The army was thus condemned to a season of inactivity, which the Sikhs attributed to timidity or to weakness, and Runjoor Sing crossed the river in force, and threatened the station of Loodiana. Sir Harry Smith was sent to cover it, but owing to his own obstinacy, he received a serious check at Buddewal which gave no little confidence to the Sikh commander; and it became necessary to make a vigorous effort to clear the left bank of the Sutlej of the enemy, and prevent an attack on the long convoy
1846 coming up from Delhi. General Smith's force was therefore raised to 11,000, and the two forces met at Aliwal, on the banks of the river. The hill men who defended it were speedily put to flight, but the Khalsa soldiers, men of true Sikh blood and mettle, stood their ground with unflinching courage, and it was not before their ranks had been thrice pierced by Colonel Cureton's cavalry, that they retreated to the river, in which many found a watery grave, leaving sixty-seven guns as trophies in the hands of the victors. This serious reverse disheartened the cabinet at Lahore. Lall Sing, the prime minister, was deposed for his incapacity, and Golab Sing was invited from Jummoo to open negotiations with Sir Henry Hardinge. He was informed that the Governor-General was prepared to acknowledge a Sikh sovereignty at Lahore, but not till the Khalsa army had been entirely disbanded. Golab Sing

informed him that it was impossible to control the movement of the troops, who continued to domineer over the public authorities, and the negotiation was broken off. A.D. 1846

While the Commander-in-Chief was awaiting the arrival of the train from Delhi, the Sikhs were transporting their forces across the Sutlej at the Hurrekee ford, where they erected one of the strongest works against which troops had ever been led in India. It consisted of a series of semicircular entrenchments, with the river for their base, the outer line being two miles and a half in circumference, surrounded by a deep ditch. The ramparts were defended by sixty-seven pieces of heavy ordnance and 35,000 Khalsa soldiers. A bridge of boats united the entrenchment with the encampment across the river, where heavy guns had also been planted to sweep the left bank. The long train of ordnance and stores coming up from Delhi marched into the camp on the 8th February, and raised the drooping spirits of the men. General Smith's troops also joined the army, and increased its strength to 15,000, of whom 5,000 were Europeans. The heavy ordnance was planted on commanding positions opposite the enemy's entrenchments, and opened upon them at seven in the morning of the 10th February. The Sikhs answered flash for flash from their powerful artillery, and at nine it was found that the cannonade had made no impression on their position; the ammunition, moreover, began to fall short, and, after having waited seven weeks for these guns, it was discovered that they were of little avail, and that the issue of the conflict must be left to the arbitrament of musketry and the bayonet. The attack was made in three divisions on three points, by Generals Dick, Gilbert, and Smith. Sir Robert Dick's division was the first to move up to the attack, and, charging home with the bayonet, cleared the ditch and mounted the rampart. The Sikhs perceiving that this was to be the principal point of attack, slackened the defence of the entrenchments elsewhere, and concentrated their guns on it. Fresh regiments were sent up to reinforce General Dick, but they were staggered and checked by the deadly fire of the Sikhs. The other two divisions were therefore ordered to make a simultaneous attack, which the enemy no sooner perceived than they immediately returned to the posts they had quitted, and from every foot of the entrenchment poured a withering fire of grape, round shot, and musketry. The most remarkable occurrence of the day was the charge of General Gilbert's division on the

Battle of Sobraon.

A.D. 1846 centre; his troops were repeatedly driven back, but their indomitable courage mastered the entrenchment, though not without the loss of 689 killed and wounded. The Sikh defences were at length pierced in all three directions. Tej Sing was among the first to fly, and either by accident or design, broke down the bridge after he had crossed it. The Khalsa soldiers, pressed on three sides into a confused mass, still continued to dispute every inch of ground till they were forced to the bridge, and, preferring death to surrender, plunged wildly into the stream, which had risen during the night and flooded the ford, and they perished by hundreds in their attempt to cross. The confusion, dismay, and carnage were such as had not been seen in India since the battle of Paniput. The loss on the side of the Sikhs was computed at 8,000, and the whole of their encampment, with all their artillery, standards, and stores fell to the victors. The loss on our side was 2,383 in killed and wounded, but the victory was complete. The conquerors, as they beheld the trenches filled with the bodies of their iron-hearted defenders, and the fords of the Sutlej choked up with thousands of corpses, and the river itself exhibiting in every direction the wreck of a great army, did not fail to pay a tribute of admiration to the gallantry and devotedness of the noble Khalsa legions.

The army enters the Punjab.

Major Abbot had been employed day and night in constructing a bridge of the boats which Sir Henry Hardinge had brought up from Sinde to Ferozepore, and it was completed the night before the battle. Sir Henry had been actively engaged in the field at Sobraon, and was severely injured by a fall from his horse, but as soon as the victory was assured, he rode twenty-six miles to Ferozepore to hasten the passage of the troops, and that night six regiments bivouacked in the Punjab. Three days after the action, the whole force, which, including camp followers, fell little short of 100,000 men, and 68,000 animals and forty pieces of artillery, crossed the river without a single casualty. On the line of march to the capital, a deputation from the Sikh cabinet, with Golab Sing at their head, waited on the Governor-General, but they were received as the representatives of an offending Government and their complimentary presents were declined. Soon after, the maharaja Dhuleep Sing came into the camp, and was dismissed with honour. On the 20th the citadel of Lahore was occupied by a British garrison, and the army was encamped on the plain of Meeanmeer.

The issue of the war had placed the Punjab at the disposal of the Governor-General, and he might have annexed it to the Company's dominions, but he did not consider it prudent to encumber the Government with the charge of a new kingdom. The morale of the army, moreover, was low, the season of heat and prostration was approaching, and the four battles had reduced his European strength to 3,000 men, while the remnant of the Sikh army still mustered 14,000, with forty pieces of cannon. He determined, therefore, to punish the Sikh nation for its wanton aggression without suppressing its political independence, and he simply deprived it of the possessions held south of the Sutlej and the province of Jullunder across it. The state was required to make good the expenses of the campaign, computed at a crore and a half of rupees, but the profligacy of the ministers and the rapacity of the soldiery had reduced the twelve crores left by Runjeet Sing to half a crore. Sir Henry Hardinge determined, therefore, to take over the province of Cashmere in lieu of the remaining crore, and Golab Sing, the powerful raja of Jummoo, stepped forward and offered to pay this sum on being constituted the independent monarch of Cashmere and Jummoo. The two provinces were, in fact, sold to him, but he merely received an indefeasible title to that which was already in his possession, and which we were not in a position to deprive him of.

A.D. 1846

Sir Henry Hardinge's arrangements.

The settlement of the Punjab was embodied in the treaty of the 9th March, which provided that the Khalsa army should be disbanded, that the military force of the state should be limited to 20,000 infantry and 12,000 cavalry, and that all the guns which had been pointed against British troops should be given up. Although the war had terminated in the total defeat of the Khalsa army and the dismemberment of the Punjab, the fact of our triumph was doubted in the native community, more especially as it was unwelcome. The natives had looked with a feeling of complacency on the growth of the new kingdom in the Punjab, the cradle of Hindooism, as the germ of a power destined to restore Hindoo supremacy throughout India. Sir Henry Hardinge considered it important to remove this feeling of incredulity, and to demonstrate that the power of Runjeet Sing was completely prostrated. A grand procession was accordingly formed of the 250 guns obtained from the Sikhs, which was conducted from Lahore to Calcutta with every demonstration of

Settlement of the Punjab.

A.D. 1846 military pomp. It was received at the stations and cantonments by the public functionaries with all honour, and its arrival in Calcutta was celebrated by a magnificent ceremonial. In England, the thanks of Parliament were moved to Sir Henry Hardinge, Sir Hugh Gough, and their brave companions by Sir Robert Peel and the Duke of Wellington, in speeches which enhanced their value in no small degree. Peerages were bestowed on the Governor-General and the Commander-in-Chief, and a baronetcy on the victor of Aliwal. To all the troops engaged in the campaign Lord Hardinge granted twelve months' full batta, without waiting for permission from home.

New arrangements in the Punjab.

At the earnest entreaty of the durbar, Lord Hardinge consented to leave a British force for the protection of the maharaja and the new government, but only to the end of the year; and Major Henry Lawrence, of the Bengal Artillery, was selected as the representative of the Government at the Lahore court. Lall Sing, the paramour of the ranee, was appointed prime minister. He was a man of low extraction, without any capacity for civil or military affairs, and his administration, which was both venal and oppressive, rendered him odious to the chiefs and the people. His treachery to the British government soon brought his career to a close. Cashmere had been made over to the raja Golab Sing, but the governor, Sheik Imam-ood-deen, at first hesitated, and then refused to surrender it. Major Lawrence considered it indispensable to extinguish the first spark of resistance, and at the risk of being blocked up by the snows of winter, marched with the utmost promptitude with a large force, consisting of 10,000 of the Sikh army which we had recently conquered, and a small detachment of British troops. The refractory chief was reduced to submission, and, in his own defence, produced a written order from Lall Sing to obstruct the transfer. A mixed commission of European officers and Sikh chieftains assembled to investigate the charge of treachery, which was fully substantiated, and, in spite of the tears of the ranee, he was banished from the Punjab and consigned to oblivion on a pension. At the close of the year, the Sikh cabinet and the most influential nobles assured Lord Hardinge that the withdrawal of the British force would inevitably lead to the resuscitation of the Khalsa army, and he yielded with great reluctance to their importunity. A new treaty was drawn up to which fifty-two chiefs affixed their seals, which provided that a council of regency, consisting of eight chiefs, should be constituted to act under the control and guidance of the Resident, that the various forts and cantonments should be garrisoned by British troops, for whose maintenance a sum of twenty-two lacs of rupees a year should be appropriated, and that the arrangement should continue for eight years during the minority of Dhuleep Sing. The government of the Punjab was virtually vested in Major Lawrence, an officer of artillery. A.D. 1846

For eight years the government in India had been incessantly engaged in war, or in preparations for it, and the armies of the three Presidencies had been augmented to the extent of 120,000 men. The pressure on the finances of the empire had been proportionately severe, and at the close of the Sikh war the expenditure was found to exceed the revenue by a crore and a half of rupees. In the course of the preceding twenty-six months, the three remaining independent armies—those of Gwalior, Sinde, and the Punjab—numbering 120,000 soldiers, had been extinguished, and their artillery, consisting of 500 pieces of cannon, had been transferred to our own arsenals. There was no longer any native military organisation in any province to oppose us, and the time appeared to have arrived when the strength of our own armies could be reduced without danger. Happily Lord Hardinge's long military experience both in the field and, as secretary-at-war, in the cabinet, enabled him to carry out this measure without in any degree impairing our military strength. Leaving the number of officers, European and native, without diminution, he curtailed the rank and file of the army by 50,000 men, and disbanded the police battalions, but he carefully avoided any mutilation of individual allowances. These arrangements resulted in a saving of a crore and a half a year, and the revenues of the two Sikh provinces which he had annexed left him a small surplus. Notwithstanding these material reductions, the security of the north-west frontier, the only point of danger, was more effectually provided for than ever, by allotting to Meerut and the stations above it 54,000 men and 120 guns. Equal wisdom and foresight were manifested in his arrangements for the peace of the Punjab. He did not expect that a country teeming with disbanded soldiers, the bravest and most haughty in India, who had revelled for seven years in military license, would be as free from disturbance as a district in Bengal. To provide for the prompt repression

Reduction of the army.

A.D. 1845 to 1848 of any insurrectionary movement, he organised three movable brigades, complete in carriage and equipment, consisting of infantry, cavalry, and artillery, to be held in readiness at Lahore, Jullunder, and Ferozepore to take the field at the shortest notice on the first appearance of an outbreak.

Other measures of improvement.

Lord Hardinge's attention during the forty-two months of his administration had been chiefly occupied in reducing the Khalsa armament, the construction of the Punjab administration, and the reorganisation of the army; but he found leisure to attend to the social and material improvement of the country. At the suggestion of Lord Auckland, the Court of Directors had given their sanction to the construction of the great Ganges Canal. The work was suspended under the pressure of war by Lord Ellenborough, but was resumed and pushed on with energy by his successor. It was during his incumbency that the memorable resolution was passed which held out the prospect of employment in the public service to the successful students in the Government educational institutions, and which thus gave the state the benefit of the talent it had assisted to develope. Education was as much a party question in India as in England, and this liberal measure, which was not universally approved, was not fully carried out for some years; but the merit of it belongs to Lord Hardinge's administration, and he was recompensed by a grateful address on the subject from the most influential native gentlemen in Calcutta. He gave a powerful impulse at an important crisis to the plan of Indian railways, then struggling into existence, which Lord Ellenborough had pronounced to be "all moonshine;" he prohibited Sunday labour in the public establishments, and gave our Hindoo and Mahomedan subjects a proof of our respect for the principles of our creed. Lord William Bentinck had abolished *suttees* throughout the Company's dominions, but they were still perpetrated in the native states, and on the death of the raja of Mundee, a principality in the vicinity of the Governor-General's residence at Simla, no fewer than twelve of his widows were burnt on the funeral pile. Lord Hardinge used all the influence of our paramount authority to induce the independent native chiefs to abolish the practice, and before his departure he had the satisfaction of receiving written assurances from twenty-four native princes and princesses that they were making strenuous efforts to meet his wishes; and a *suttee* is now as much out of vogue on the continent of India as a duel is in England. The distribution of his patronage was regulated by an exclusive regard to the public interests, and he was as free from the suspicion of nepotism as Lord Ellenborough. He secured the confidence of the community in India by his sterling sense, and by the rare combination of a kind and conciliatory disposition with decision of character and vigour of discipline. He left Calcutta on the 15th March, 1848, with the avowed conviction that it would not be necessary to fire another shot in India for seven years; yet so impossible is it to forecast the future in that hot-bed of revolutions, that before a twelvemonth had passed, the Punjab had revolted, and had been re-conquered, and converted into a British province.

CHAPTER XIV.

SECTION I.

LORD DALHOUSIE'S ADMINISTRATION—SECOND SIKH WAR.

A.D. 1848

Lord Dalhousie.

Lord Dalhousie landed at Calcutta and took his seat in council on the 19th January. He was in his thirty-sixth year,—the youngest of governors general. He had occupied a seat in the House of Commons before he succeeded to the family title, and in Sir Robert Peel's last cabinet enjoyed the post of president of the Board of Trade at the most busy period of its existence, when it was flooded with railway schemes. He entered upon the government of India without any of that acquaintance with its institutions and policy which Lord Wellesley, Lord Minto, and Lord William Bentinck had brought with them, but his natural genius soon caught the spirit, and mastered the details of the administration. The period of his rule, which extended to eight years, was crowded with transactions which will long continue to affect the happiness of the vast population of the empire, and may be considered one of the most memorable in its history. Waiving the chronological order of events, we shall distribute them under the three sections of military operations, annexations, and social and material improvements.

A.D. 1848 Within four months of his arrival, the note of war was again sounded in the Punjab. A small cloud appeared on the horizon over Mooltan, which in the course of six months overspread the country and brought on a conflict as arduous as that of 1845. Major—afterwards Sir Henry—Lawrence was constrained to visit England for the restoration of his health, and was succeeded by a civilian, Sir Frederic Currie, who was unhappily placed in circumstances which required the experience and the authoritative counsels of a military man, and the absence of which culminated in a general war. Moolraj took possession of the province of Mooltan, on the death of his father the governor in 1844, but his subordination to the authorities at Lahore was little more than nominal. Lall Sing, the principal minister, knowing that a large treasure had been accumulated by his father, demanded a crore of rupees as a *nuzzer*, or succession fine. It was compromised for a fifth of the sum, the payment of which, however, he contrived to evade until the establishment of a strong government at Lahore by Lord Hardinge, when it was adjusted, and he offered to resign the government, on the ground that it was intended to introduce new fiscal regulations, which were unpalatable to him. The durbar took him at his word, and sent Khan Sing to take over the government, and Sir Frederick selected Mr. Agnew, a civilian, and Lieutenant Anderson to accompany him, with an escort of about 350 Sikhs and a few guns. The party reached Mooltan on the 18th March.

Moolraj and Mooltan.

The next morning Moolraj waited on them to discuss the terms of his resignation, and asked for a general deed of acquittance, but Mr. Agnew insisted on the production of all the accounts of the previous six years. After much recrimination, Moolraj yielded to the demand, but he felt that he had been dishonoured in the eyes of his people, and he left the conference with a scowl on his brow. On the 20th the two officers proceeded to inspect the various establishments which were to be transferred to the new governor, but as they were leaving the fort they were struck down by assassins, and conveyed by their attendants to a fortified temple in the vicinity of the town in which they had taken up their residence. They defended it manfully until their Sikh escort proved treacherous, when the howling savages rushed in and hacked them to pieces, and presented their heads to Moolraj who, instead of affording them any

Murder of the officers.

assistance when they were attacked, had galloped off to his country residence. The next day he placed himself at the head of the insurrection and issued a proclamation summoning all the inhabitants of the province to rise and wage a religious war against the *feringees*, as the Christian foreigners were contemptuously termed. The emergency had now arisen for which Lord Hardinge had made provision by his movable columns, and there can be no doubt that if Major Lawrence had been the Resident at Lahore he would have marched down with promptitude and nipped the revolt in the bud, as he had extinguished the insurrection of Imam-ood-deen two years before in Cashmere. Sir Frederick, on hearing of the attack on the officers, ordered a large force to be prepared to proceed forthwith to Mooltan, but countermanded it when he learnt that they had been murdered, and referred the matter to the consideration of the Commander-in-Chief, who resolved to postpone all operations until he could take the field in person in the cold season. A.D. 1848

The Resident and the Commander-in-Chief had scarcely ceased to bandy arguments when Lieutenant—the late Sir Herbert—Edwardes, a young officer employed in the revenue settlement of the district of Bunnoo, across the Indus, animated with the spirit of Clive, determined to take the initiative in crushing the revolt. Without waiting for instructions from Lahore, he crossed the Indus with 1,200 infantry, 350 horsemen, and two guns; but having intercepted a letter, from which he learned that his men had agreed to sell his head and their services to Moolraj for 24,000 rupees, recrossed the river and raised other recruits free from the infection of treachery—"bold villains," he said, "ready to risk their own throats and cut those of "anyone else." He was soon after joined by a regiment of Musulmans, under Colonel Cortland, and by the troops of the raja of Bhawulpore, and fought an engagement with Moolraj and 8,000 Sikh troops at Kineyree on the 18th June, and defeated him. He importuned the Resident to support him, and preparations were made to despatch an adequate force, but Lord Gough again interposed his authority, because the season was not favourable, and the siege train had not moved from Cawnpore. Ten days after, Lieutenant Edwardes, who had received a reinforcement of 4,000 men, under Imam-ood-deen, whose fidelity however was doubtful, again attacked Moolraj at Suddoosain, but although his army now consisted of 11,000 Sikh soldiers, supported by

Lieutenant Edwardes.

A.D. 1848 eleven guns, he was completely defeated, and sought shelter with his fugitive troops within the walls of the capital.

Sir Frederick Currie now determined to lose no time in following up the successes of Lieutenant Edwardes, and took on himself the responsibility of ordering General Whish to proceed with 7,000 men and a battering train to Mooltan, and to this movement Lord Gough offered no opposition. Meanwhile, Lieutenant Edwardes was joined by a Sikh force, under Shere Sing, which the Lahore durbar had despatched, ostensibly to co-operate against Moolraj, but, in reality, to support him, and it was no secret at Lahore that they were thoroughly disaffected. The distance between Lahore and Mooltan is only 220 miles, but though General Whish had the convenience of water communication, he was thirty-nine days reaching his destination. During this procrastination Moolraj augmented his force and improved the defences of the fort, which was one of the strongest in the country. The battering train reached Mooltan on the 3rd September, but within a week after the batteries opened all operations were brought to a close. Shere Sing, who had joined General Whish's camp in conjunction with Lieutenant Edwardes, yielded to the importunity of his officers and men, and went over to the enemy with 5,000 troops on the 14th September. The general was obliged to relinquish the siege, and retire to a safe position in the vicinity of the town, adapted for the receipt of reinforcements, and there he threw up entrenchments, and was, in fact, besieged in his turn. Shere Sing immediately issued a proclamation, announcing a religious war, "under the auspices of the holy "Gooroo," against "the cruel *feringees*," and called upon all those who eat the salt of the maharaja to come forward and destroy them.

Despatch of General Whish.

During these proceedings events transpired at Lahore and elsewhere which disclosed the mine upon which we had been sitting. It was discovered that the maharanee, a woman of great ambition and indefatigable intrigue, had for some time been engaged at Cabul and Candahar, in Cashmere and in Rajpootana, in plotting against the British government, and that all the members of the Lahore cabinet, with the exception of two, were confederated with her. Sir Frederick Currie had by a skilful manœuvre obtained possession of her person, and transferred her to the Resident at Benares, the warder of the disinherited princes and princesses of India. The spirit

Spread of the revolt.

of revolt now began more openly to develope itself. Chutter A.D. 1848 Sing, the father of Shere Sing, the governor of the province of Hazara, on the left bank of the Indus, threw off the mask, and "devoted his head," as he said, "to God, and his arms to "the Khalsa." He opened a negotiation with Dost Mahomed and offered him the province of Peshawur on condition of his joining the crusade against the English. The proposition was too tempting to be resisted, and he readily agreed to join the insurgents with his contingent. Peshawur, which Chutter Sing thus sold to the Afghans, was under the political charge of Major—now Sir George —Lawrence, and was garrisoned by 8,000 Sikh troops, upon whose fidelity little dependence could be placed when the whole atmosphere of the Punjab was charged with treason. Owing to the influence the Major had obtained over them, they steadily resisted the importunities of Chutter Sing, but at length yielded to the seductions of Sultan Mahomed, the brother of Dost Mahomed, and the personification of Afghan perfidy. He was under the greatest obligations to Sir Henry Lawrence, who had released him from gaol at Lahore and restored his jageer. Under his instigation the troops assailed and sacked the Residency, and Major Lawrence and other English officers retired under the escort provided by him with the most solemn assurances of protection, but no sooner were they in his power than he sold them to Chutter Sing. The whole of the Punjab was now in a state of revolt; the veterans of Runjeet Sing, scattered throughout the country, were burning with impatience to meet the British battalions once more in the field, and recover their lost honour and restore the glory of their beloved Khalsa. The paltry outbreak at Mooltan, fostered by delay, had grown into a portentous war, and Lord Dalhousie had now to encounter the bravest soldiers in India, animated by a spirit of patriotic enthusiasm, but he was fully equal to the occasion. Through the great exertions of Sir George Clerk, the governor of Bombay, a body of 7,000 men was after much delay sent up the Indus to reinforce General Whish, and an addition was made of 17,000 to the strength of the Bengal regiments. On the 10th October, Lord Dalhousie proceeded to the scene of operations after having, at a farewell entertainment given him at Barrackpore, said, in the course of his speech, "Unwarned by precedent, uninflu-"enced by example, the Sikh nation has called for war, and, "on my word, sir, they shall have it with a vengeance."

A.D. 1848

Shere Sing was received with great mistrust by Moolraj, who wished him to desert the encampment of General Whish, but not to encumber him with his troops and his requisitions. Twenty-five days after his revolt, he left Mooltan and marched towards Lahore with 5,000 men, whose number was increased at every stage by the old soldiers of the Khalsa, and he had the audacity to burn a bridge of boats on the Ravee, the flames of which were visible from the cantonments. Lahore had been unaccountably left in a defenceless state for weeks after it was known that Shere Sing and his father were in the field with 15,000 troops, and he might have obtained possession of it if this fact had been known to him; but he moved on to Ramnuggur, on the Chenab. The grand army was at length assembled at Ferozepore early in November, and Lord Gough assumed command of it on the 16th. It consisted of four British and eleven native regiments of infantry, three noble regiments of British horse, with five regiments of native cavalry, and five corps of irregular horse. It was weak in infantry, but unusually strong in artillery. Lord Gough opened the campaign on the 22nd by marching down to Ramnuggur, where the main body of Shere Sing was encamped on the right bank, with his front protected by batteries mounting twenty-eight guns. He had boats on the river and the command of a ford, and had pushed a detachment across the river, which was at once driven back, when he opened an irresistible fire from his batteries planted on the high ground on the opposite bank, and the order was given to retire. One gun and two waggons, however, could not be extricated from the sand; but instead of spiking the one and blowing up the others, time was lost in endeavouring to rescue them. Several thousands of the enemy then rushed across the ford, while the batteries played on the British retiring force. Here the operations of the day should have terminated, but the Commander-in-Chief gave permission to Colonel Havelock, in command of the 14th Dragoons, an officer of Peninsular renown, to charge the Sikhs in the dry sandy bed of a river two miles wide; and in this contemptible cavalry skirmish his own life and that of the gallant Colonel Cureton were sacrificed.

Shere Sing and the grand army.

Any attempt to assail the position of Shere Sing in front would have been an act of infatuation, and Sir Joseph Thackwell was therefore despatched, with 8,000 horse, foot, and artillery, on the 1st December, to

Battle of Sadoollapore.

Wuzeerabad, thirty miles higher up the river, which he A.D. crossed the next day, and marched down twelve miles to- 1848 wards Shere Sing's encampment. That general, on hearing of this movement, at once withdrew his army from Ramnuggur, leaving Lord Gough to waste powder and shot on an empty entrenchment. The two forces met at Sadoollapore, where, after sustaining for two hours the incessant fire of the enemy without returning a shot till they were fully within range, General Thackwell's artillery opened on them with great effect, and their cannon began to slacken and then ceased. There remained only an hour of daylight, and, with the example of Moodkee and Ferozeshuhur before him, he wisely determined to postpone the attack till the morning. Under cover of the night Shere Sing retired with his tents, guns, and ammunition, and when General Thackwell put his army in motion in the morning to pursue him, he was already beyond reach. He retired from Sadoollapore with his artillery still entire, and the spirit of his troops unbroken, and took up a position of singular strength on the Jhelum, with his rear resting on that stream, his main body posted in ravines strengthened by field works, and his front covered by a broad and dense jungle. For six weeks our army remained inactive between the Chenab and the Jhelum, and, in the opinion of the first military authorities of the day, it would have done well to continue in this attitude till the capture of Mooltan had brought up to its aid the large division of troops engaged in the siege. This course was eventually taken, and brought the war to a glorious termination; but intermediately occurred the disastrous engagement of Chillianwalla.

On the 12th January the army advanced twelve miles to 1849 Dinjee, and on the following day to Chillianwalla, when it became evident that the Sikhs had quitted their strong entrenchments on the heights of Russool, and were ready to combat without the usual support of their bulwarks. Lord Gough had determined to defer the assault till a careful reconnaissance had been made the next day, and directions were given to mark out the ground for an encampment, when a few shots from some field-pieces the Sikhs had pushed forward dropped upon him. The spirit of defiance and antagonism at once overcame his sober judgment, and he issued orders for immediate action. The Sikhs began the engagement by a continuous peal of fire from a jungle so thick that nothing was offered as a mark for

Chillianwalla.

A.D. 1849

the British artillery but the flash and smoke of the enemy's guns. This cannonade lasted an hour or an hour and a half, according to different reports, and it was three in the afternoon with only an hour or two of daylight left, when the divisions were ordered to advance.

Of the two brigades of the infantry division of General Campbell — subsequently Lord Clyde — that of General Pennycuick was subject to a fearful repulse. The 24th Foot, which formed a portion of it, composed chiefly of young soldiers, advanced with such ardour that Shere Sing, to whom they were opposed, was on the point of retiring when he perceived them rushing breathless and panting, as he described it, like dogs in a chase, upon his guns. He poured a shower of grape into them, and, while shattered by its deadly effect, they were torn to pieces by a musketry fire from Sikh troops masked by a screen of jungle. The whole brigade was thrown into a state of confusion, and the most desperate efforts of the officers were of no avail to restore order. The colours of the regiment fell into the hands of the enemy, but not until 23 officers and 459 non-commissioned officers and men had been killed and wounded. General Campbell, who had been victorious in his front, came rapidly to the rescue, and snatched the victory from the Sikhs. General Gilbert's division succeeded by the most heroic efforts in putting the Sikhs to flight, but pursuit in a forest, where the men could not see twenty yards before them, was impossible. While they halted to collect their wounded, a body of Sikhs, who had turned their flank unperceived, opened fire on them, and they were rescued from destruction only by the field battery of Major Dawes. The struggle was terrific, and, to use the language of an eye-witness, it seemed as if the very air teemed with balls and bullets.

Movements of cavalry.

The adventures of the cavalry were most disastrous and humiliating. Lord Gough had brought four regiments into the first line, and they were thus opposed to an unapproachable artillery fire, and to entanglements in the recesses of the forest. The troops of artillery attached to the brigade were planted in the rear, and could not open fire from a single gun. The brigade was commanded by a superannuated general, who could not mount his horse without assistance, and who was irascible and wedded to ancient notions of cavalry manœuvres. As the line advanced it was broken up by clumps of trees and brushwood into numerous series of small sections doubled behind each other. In this state a small body of Sikh horsemen, intoxicated with drugs, rushed on the centre in a mass, and caused a sensation of terror among the native cavalry which nothing could counteract. Just at this crisis some one in the 14th Dragoons uttered the words "Threes about!" The regiment at once turned to the rear and moved off in confusion, and as the Sikh horse pressed on, it galloped headlong in disgraceful panic through the cannon and waggons posted in the rear. The Sikh horse entered the line of artillery with the dragoons and captured four guns. The shades of evening put an end to the conflict. The troops were half dead with fatigue and parched with thirst, but no water could be procured except at Chillianwalla, two miles distant, to which the Commander-in-Chief was obliged to withdraw the force. During the night, parties of Sikh troops and of the armed peasantry traversed the forest which had been the scene of combat, mutilating the slain and murdering the wounded, and rifling both. All the guns which had been secured during the engagement were carried off, with the exception of twelve, which had been brought into the camp.

A.D. 1849

Such was the battle of Chillianwalla, the nearest approximation to a defeat of any of our great conflicts in India. The Sikh army was not overthrown, but retired to another position three miles from the field. Four British guns were captured, the colours of three regiments were lost, the reputation of the British cavalry deplorably tarnished, while the character of Sikh prowess was proportionately elevated. The number of killed and wounded, including eighty-nine officers, was 2,446. The Governor-General officially pronounced it a victory, and it was announced by salutes at all the Presidencies; but he was anticipated by Shere Sing, who fired a salute the same evening in honour of his triumph. By the community in India it was considered a great and lamentable calamity. The intelligence of the combat was received in England with a feeling of indignation and alarm. British standards had been lost; British cannon had been captured; British cavalry had fled before the enemy, and a British regiment had been annihilated. These disasters were traced, and justly, to the wretched tactics of Lord Gough, and he was recalled, with the full approval of the Duke of Wellington, and Sir Charles Napier was sent out to supersede him.

Results of the battle.

SECTION II.

LORD DALHOUSIE'S ADMINISTRATION—SECOND SIKH WAR—ADMINISTRATION OF THE PUNJAB—THE BURMESE WAR—THE SANTALS.

THE conflict at Chillianwalla had so seriously crippled the infantry as to constrain Lord Gough to await the capture of Mooltan and the arrival of General Whish's force before he undertook any further operations. At Mooltan the advantages gained by the spirited exertions of Lieutenant Edwardes had been lost by the defection of Shere Sing. Moolraj regained possession of the province and of its resources, and was enabled to provision the fort and to improve its fortifications. General Whish, who had retired to a fortified position in the neighbourhood, was doomed to three months of inaction by the dilatoriness of the Bombay military authorities in forwarding reinforcements. The Bombay troops on their arrival raised his army to 17,000, with sixty four heavy guns, and he recommenced the siege on the 27th December. After clearing the suburbs, which was not effected without the loss of 300 men and seventeen officers, the batteries opened on the town, and for five days and nights the discharge from howitzers, cannon, and mortars never ceased. On the third day the fury of the combatants was for a few moments arrested by the explosion of a magazine in the town containing 400,000 lbs. of gunpowder, which shook the earth for miles and darkened the sky with smoke. After a brief pause the firing was renewed, the Bombay and Bengal artillery vying with each other and the enemy vying with both. On the 2nd January the city was stormed, and presented a melancholy picture of desolation; the buildings had crumbled under the storm of shot and shell, which had never been suspended for 120 hours, and the streets were strewed with the dead and dying. Moolraj continued to hold the citadel with about 3,000 troops for another fortnight, and he and his brave soldiers sustained the most terrific fire of ordnance, direct and vertical, which had ever been discharged in India within the same narrow limits. At length, when every roof but one had been demolished, and the incessant volleys became insupportable, the valiant chief surrendered at discretion, and on the 22nd January rode into the English camp, his chiefs and soldiers prostrating themselves before him in passionate devotion as he passed.

Siege of Mooltan.

A.D. 1848

1849

After the battle of Chillianwalla the Sikh and British troops lay encamped within a few miles of each other for twenty-five days; the one at Russool and the other at Chillianwalla. On the 6th February Shere Sing evaded Lord Gough and marched unperceived round the British entrenchments, and established his headquarters at Guzerat. The last brigade of General Whish's army having joined Lord Gough on the 20th February, the army moved up to that town. General Cheape, of the Bengal engineers, who had directed the siege of Mooltan with that professional skill and personal energy to which its success is to be attributed, joined the camp a week before the battle and assumed charge of the engineering department. With unwearied industry he applied himself to the duty of obtaining the most accurate information of the position of the enemy, the absence of which had produced the lamentable results of Maharajpore, Moodkee, and Chillianwalla. The army of Shere Sing, estimated at 50,000 men, with sixty pieces of cannon, was posted in front of the walled town of Guzerat, with the left supported on a streamlet, while the right was protected by the deep dry bed of the Dwara. Between them was a space of about three miles with two villages, loopholed and filled with troops. In all Lord Gough's battles he had trusted more to the bayonet than to his cannon, and the carnage had been severe. In the present case the principle was reversed. On the day preceding the engagement it was determined by the able engineer officers with the force that the artillery, in which no army in India had been so strong, should be brought into full play, and that the charge of the infantry should be reserved till the consistency of the Sikh army had been broken by the guns.

A.D. 1849

Arrangements of the battle of Guzerat.

The infantry divisions and brigades advanced in parallel lines with eighty-four pieces of cannon in front, and the cavalry on the flanks. The army, invigorated by rest and food, broke ground at half past seven. The morning was clear and cloudless, and the sun shone brightly on the extended lines of bayonets and sabres. The Sikhs, ever ready with their batteries, opened them at a long range. The British infantry was halted beyond their reach, and the artillery pushed boldly to the front and commenced a cannonade, of which the oldest and most experienced soldiers had never witnessed a parallel for magnificence and effect. The Sikhs fired with great rapidity, but it was manifest that neither human fortitude nor the

The battle of Guzerat.

A.D. 1849 best materials could withstand the storm which for two hours and a half beat on their devoted artillery; not a single musket was discharged before the fire of their formidable line had been subdued. The infantry then deployed and commenced a steady advance supported by their field batteries. The Sikhs fought with desperation, but the two villages were at length carried by the ardent courage of the British troops, and the whole Sikh line gave way and was pursued round the town by all the brigades of infantry. The cavalry, which had hitherto been kept in reserve, was then let loose, and onward they rushed, riding over and trampling down the flying and scattered infantry of the Sikhs, and converting the discomfited enemy into a shapeless mass of fugitives. It was not till half-past four, after they had advanced fifteen miles beyond Guzerat, that the cavalry drew rein, and by that time the army of Shere Sing was a wreck, deprived of its camp, its standards, and fifty-three pieces of cannon. The battle of Guzerat was one of the noblest achievements of the British army in India, and as it was gained by the judicious use of the arm in which the force had a preponderating power, it has justly been designated the "battle of the guns." The happy contrivance by which the Commander-in-Chief was restrained from interfering with the order of battle, and hurling the infantry, as usual, on the enemy's batteries, is well known.

The day after the battle Sir Walter Gilbert left the camp with 12,000 infantry, cavalry, and horse artillery, and pursued the relic of the Sikh army, now reduced to about 16,000 men, along the great high road of the Indus, with such rapidity as to allow them no breathing time, and they sent Major George Lawrence, who had been their prisoner since he left Peshawur, to make terms with the general. On the 12th March Shere Sing and Chutter Sing delivered up their swords to him at the celebrated monument of Manikyla, once considered a trophy of Alexander the Great; thirty-five subordinate chiefs laid their swords at his feet, and the Khalsa soldiers advanced one by one, and, after clasping their weapons, cast them upon the growing pile with a heavy sigh. It only remained to dispose of the Afghans whom Dost Mahomed had sent to co-operate with the Sikhs. The veteran Gilbert followed them across the Indus, with the buoyancy of youth, and chased them up to the portals of the Khyber, and, as the natives sarcastically remarked, "those who had

Pursuit of the Sikhs and Afghans.

"rode down the hills like lions ran back into them like "dogs." A.D. 1849

The battle of Guzerat decided the fate of the Punjab and finally quenched the hopes of the Khalsa soldiers. It was no ordinary distinction for that noble army to have met the conquerors of India successively at Moodkee, at Ferozeshuhur, at Aliwal, at Sobraon, at Chillianwalla, and at Guzerat; but after six such conflicts they resigned themselves with a feeling of proud submission to the power which had proved stronger than themselves, and there has never since been the slightest attempt at disturbance. The Punjab was now, by the indefeasible right of a double conquest, after unprovoked aggression, at the disposal of the British Government, and as there was not time for any reference to the Court of Directors, Lord Dalhousie annexed it to the Company's dominions, in a proclamation which stated that, "as the only "sure mode of protecting the Government of India from "the perpetual recurrence of unprovoked and wasting wars, "he was compelled to resolve on the entire subjugation of a "people whom their own government had long been unable "to control, whom no punishment could deter from violence, "and no acts of friendship could conciliate to peace."

Annexation of the Punjab.

On the 29th of March the youthful maharaja Duleep Sing took his seat for the last time on the throne of his father, and in the presence of the high British functionaries and the nobles of his court, heard Lord Dalhousie's proclamation read, and then affixed his initials to the deed which transferred the kingdom of the five waters to the Company, and secured to himself an annuity of five lacs a year. The British colours were hoisted on the ramparts, and a royal salute announced the fulfilment of Runjeet Sing's prediction that "the Punjab also would become red,"—in allusion to the colour which distinguishes the British possessions on the map of India. The jageers of the leaders of the rebellion were confiscated, and they retired into oblivion on small stipends. Moolraj, after a fair trial before a special court, was sentenced to imprisonment for life, but died within a short time. Lord Dalhousie was elevated to the dignity of a Marquis, the fourth marquisate bestowed on the Governors-General who had enlarged the Company's territories. The reproach of Chillianwalla was forgotten in the triumph of Guzerat, and Lord Gough received a step in the peerage.

Lord Dalhousie, having thus annexed the Punjab to the

A.D. 1849 to 1854

Administration of the Punjab.

Company's dominions, was determined to spare no pains to render our government a real blessing to the population. A noble field was presented for the construction of an administration free from the errors committed in other provinces in the infancy of our rule, and it was not neglected. A board was constituted with ample powers, at the head of which was placed Sir Henry Lawrence, one of the Company's great statesmen, a fit successor of Ochterlony, and Munro, and Elphinstone, and Metcalfe. With him was associated his brother Mr. John Lawrence, who was subsequently rewarded with the Governor-Generalship, and Mr. Robert Montgomery. A more efficient board it would have been difficult to construct even in India. The administration was formed on a new system, and entrusted to fifty-six officers, half of whom were military men and the other half civilians, the flower of the service, men of mature experience, or of noble aspirations for distinction. The system of government was well suited by its simplicity and vigour to the requirements of the country. For the voluminous regulations which lay like an incubus on the older provinces, a clear and concise manual adapted to the habits of a people who courted justice but dreaded law, was compiled by Mr. Montgomery, and comprised in a few sheets of foolscap.

The border tribes and disarmament.

The north-west boundary of the empire was now removed to the mountain range beyond the Indus, inhabited by tribes of highlanders, whose vocation, from time immemorial, had been to levy black mail. To protect the lowlanders from their raids, a chain of fortifications was established on the line, fully provisioned, and connected with each other by a series of roads. Nine regiments were especially raised for duty on these marches. Within six months of the conquest Lord Dalhousie disarmed the Punjab, and 120,000 weapons of every variety of form and character were surrendered. A military police, consisting of six regiments of foot and twenty-seven troops of horse, was organised. The ancient institution of the village watch, paid by the people and acting under local magnates, was revived in a more efficient form. As the result of these admirable arrangements, it was reported within three years that no province in India was more free from crime than the Punjab.

The vital question of the land assessment, on which the happiness, and, to a great extent, the loyalty, of the people in the East depends, was dealt with in a spirit of wisdom and liberality, and the egregious blunders committed in the A.D. older provinces were carefully avoided. The settlement was formed on a minute and accurate investigation; the land-tax was reduced in amount, and leases were granted, which in some cases extended to thirty years. The security of tenure and the moderation of the rent gave such encouragement to agriculture that more than 30,000 of the Khalsa soldiers exchanged the sword for the plough. Lord Dalhousie was likewise resolved to avoid the boundless irritation inflicted on the Gangetic provinces for half a century by dallying with the question of rent-free tenures; every case was carefully examined and satisfactorily and finally disposed of. The duties on the transit of merchandise from district to district and town to town—the great impediments of trade—were swept away, and the loss was compensated by the scientific selection of new taxes, four of which yielded a larger return than forty-eight of Runjeet Sing's clumsy imposts.

1849 to 1854

The revenue.

The Board of Administration likewise put down the sale of children, which was all but universal, and thus extinguished domestic slavery. Dacoity was rife when the Punjab came into our possession, but the Board took the field against the criminals with that exceptional energy for which the administration of this province has always been distinguished, and in the course of five years the country was more free from the crime than Bengal after eighty-five years of our rule. The thugs who had resorted to the Punjab, when driven out of Hindostan and the Deccan by Colonel Sleeman, were extirpated. Active measures were likewise adopted to eradicate the practice of female infanticide.

Slavery, dacoity, and thuggee.

Lord Dalhousie did not consider the conquest of the Punjab complete till it was intersected with military roads, and in the course of five years 2,200 miles were either completed or under construction. Of these the most important was that which united Lahore with Peshawur, a distance of 275 miles. It passed over more than 100 great bridges and 450 of smaller dimensions, and it penetrated six mountain chains; all these obstacles were overcome by Colonel Napier, since created Lord Napier of Magdala, to whose skill and energy the Punjab was indebted for those material improvements which gave it the appearance of a Roman province. Lord Dalhousie, moreover, considered that "of all works of improvement "which could be applied to an Indian province, works of

Roads and canals.

A.D. 1849 to 1854 "irrigation were the happiest in their effects on the physical condition of the people," and he directed all the canals excavated by former rulers, Mahommedan and Sikh, to be repaired, and others to be constructed with a liberal hand. The greatest of Colonel Napier's works of irrigation was the Baree Daoab canal, which with its branches extended to the length of 465 miles, equal, if not superior to, the longest European canal. Lord Dalhousie made the boon the more acceptable to the people by refusing to levy any water-rate, as he considered that the state was fully repaid by the increase of cultivation.

Result of these measures.

The government established in the Punjab was emphatically Lord Dalhousie's own creation. The administrative and executive talent employed in the improvement of it had never been equalled in any other province, but it was his genius which gave animation to the whole system. He traversed the country in every direction, and placed himself in constant and unrestrained communication with the public functionaries, who were thus enabled to prosecute their labours without official encumbrances. The administration embodied the maturity of our experience in the science of Eastern government, and rendered the Punjab the model province of India. By these wise and beneficent measures the nation which had recently been the great object of political anxiety became one of the chief elements of our strength. The brave soldiers who had shaken our power to its foundation at Ferozeshuhur and Chillianwalla enlisted under our banners, assisted in reconquering Delhi from the rebel sepoys, marched up the Irrawaddy to fight the Burmese, and aided in planting the English colours on the battlements of Pekin.

The second Burmese war.

1851 There was peace for three years after the conquest of the Punjab, and then came the unexpected and unwelcome war with the Burmese, who had been at peace with us for twenty-six years. In September the European merchants at Rangoon transmitted a memorial to the Government of India, complaining of various acts of oppression, sometimes accompanied with torture, which had been inflicted on them by the Burmese authorities, and stating that, unless they could obtain protection, they must quit the country and sacrifice their property. The Council in Calcutta—Lord Dalhousie being up the country—came to the conclusion that British subjects were entitled to British protection. Commodore Lambert,

commanding H.M. ship "Fox," who had recently arrived in Calcutta, was sent to Rangoon to investigate the complaints, and if they were substantiated, to forward a communication from the Government of India to the king demanding redress. The Ava cabinet replied that the offending governor should be removed, and that due enquiry should be made into the complaints of the merchants. The governor, however, left Rangoon with ostentatious parade, and his successor treated the British representative with studied insolence, and refused to appoint any day for an official audience. Captain Fishbourne therefore sent to A.D.
inform him that the deputation from the Government of 1852
India would wait on him at midday on the 6th January. He proceeded at the appointed time with his suite to Government House, but they were not permitted to enter it and were detained in the sun by the menials who declared that the governor was asleep and must not be disturbed, whereas he was all the time looking at them through the venetian windows, and enjoying their mortification. After waiting a quarter of an hour Captain Fishbourne returned and reported the treatment he had received to the Commodore. The mission had been entrusted to one of Cromwell's ambassadors, "a sixty-four gun frigate, which "spoke all languages and never took a refusal." The Commodore immediately proceeded down the river to establish a blockade, as he had been instructed to do, taking away with him a merchant vessel belonging to the king. On his way down a heavy fire was opened on him from the stockades below Rangoon on both sides the river, which the guns of the "Fox" demolished in a few minutes.

Proceedings of Lord Dalhousie.

Lord Dalhousie was at the time in the north-west provinces, and apprehending from the aspect of the negotiation that the Government was drifting into a war, hastened down to prevent it, and it was only till the third application for redress had been treated with contempt that he came to the determination to seek it by force of arms. "The Government of India," he said in his minute, "cannot consistently with its own "safety appear for one day in an attitude of inferiority, or "hope to maintain peace and submission among the num-"berless princes and people embraced within the vast "circuit of the empire, if for one day it give countenance "to a doubt of the absolute superiority of its arms and of "its continued resolution to maintain it." The Commander-in-Chief was in Sinde, and Lord Dalhousie was obliged to

A.D. 1852 become his own war minister, and he astonished India by the singular genius he displayed for military organisation. The task before him was one of no ordinary difficulty. It was the 10th February before the declaration of war was issued and the preparations for the campaign commenced, and it was of vital importance that Rangoon should be occupied before the rains came on in the beginning of May. He had two expeditions to despatch, one from Bengal and the other from Madras; the steamers were lying in the harbour of Bombay, and there was no telegraph; but his forethought anticipated, and his energy supplied, every requirement. He superintended every arrangement himself, and his aides-de-camp were incessantly employed in Calcutta in moving about from place to place to ensure promptitude and efficiency in every branch of preparation. The Tenasserim provinces were drained of cattle and provisions; bakehouses were erected on the coast, and steamers stationed to convey bread and meat to the camp. The framework of houses was constructed at Moulmein to afford shelter to the troops when the monsoon set in, and a convalescent depôt was established at Amherst, thirty miles below Rangoon.

The expeditionary force.

The land army amounted to 5,800 men, under the command of General Godwin, who had served in the first Burmese war, and it was strengthened by nineteen steamers carrying 159 guns and manned by 2,200 sailors and marines. On the arrival of the force in the Rangoon river, a flag of truce was sent up by a steamer to receive the reply of the king to the latest letter of the Governor-General, but it was fired upon, and the last hope of a peaceful solution of the difficulty vanished. The whole force took up a position in front of Rangoon on the 11th April. The great pagoda, the key of the enemy's position, had been fortified with great skill, and it was defended with more gallantry than the Burmese had exhibited in the former war; but nothing could withstand the fiery valour of our soldiers, and the British colours were planted on that noble temple after a short struggle. This was the first, and almost the only military operation of the campaign. The Burmese army was dispersed, and the people returned to their houses and resumed their occupations. The town was well supplied with provisions, and carpenters from Pegu hastened to erect the wooden houses. The health of the camp was little affected by the season; the river was crowded with shipping, and the port became a busy mart of commerce. But although General Godwin had a magnificent flotilla of steamers, and the complete command of the river, nothing could induce him to advance to Prome, and Lord Dalhousie was obliged to proceed to Rangoon in person, and insist on his moving up to occupy that important position; it was captured with the loss of only one man. A.D. 1852

The king refused to hold any communication with Lord Dalhousie, and he had now to consider the course he was to pursue. The inhabitants of Pegu were impatient to be released from the iron yoke of the Burmese, who had treated them with more than ordinary cruelty since they were conquered. They entreated to be taken under British protection, and Lord Dalhousie determined at once to accede to their wishes and to annex the province. In his minute on the subject he said, "In "the earliest stage of the present dispute I avowed my "opinion that conquest in Burmah would be a calamity "second only to the calamity of war; but I have been "drawn most reluctantly to the conclusion that no measure "will adequately meet the object which, in my judgment, "it is absolutely necessary to secure—the establishment of "our security now and its maintenance hereafter—except "the seizure and occupation of a portion of the territories "of the Burmah kingdom." The Court of Directors and the Ministry concurred in this opinion, and on the 20th December a proclamation was issued declaring that Pegu was henceforth to be considered a portion of the British dominions. No province has ever gained so much in so short a period by annexation. The export and import traffic has increased from a few lacs to nine crores; the people are happy and contented, and would consider a change of masters the greatest of calamities. The first Burmese war had entailed an expenditure of thirteen crores; the second cost a little over one crore.

Annexation of Pegu.

SECTION III.

LORD DALHOUSIE'S ADMINISTRATION—ANNEXATIONS.

THE confiscation of the Punjab and Pegu, like the annexations made during fifty years to the dominions of the Company from the territories of Mysore, Sindia, Nagpore, Holkar, and the Peshwa, followed the

Annexation policy.

A.D. 1848 fortune of war, and were the natural consequence of unprovoked hostilities; but the absorption of Satara, Nagpore, and Jhansi was based on the failure of heirs, and the assumed prerogative of the paramount power in India. They constitute what has been termed the "annexation "policy" of Lord Dalhousie, which has been compared to "the acts of brigands counting out their spoil in a wood, "rather than the acts of British statesmanship," and he has been stigmatised as "the worst and basest of rulers." To trace this policy to its origin, it is to be observed that, seven years before his arrival, the Governor-General and Council in 1841 recorded their unanimous opinion that "our policy should be to persevere in the one clear and "direct course of abandoning no just or honourable acces-"sion of territory or revenue while all existing claims of "right are scrupulously respected." Lord Dalhousie, soon after assuming the government, recorded his entire concurrence in the views of his predecessors, and said that "we were bound not to put aside or neglect such rightful "opportunities of acquiring territory or revenue as may "from time to time present themselves, by the failure of all "heirs of every description whatever, or from the failure of "heirs natural; but wherever a shadow of doubt can be "shown the claim should be at once abandoned."

Satara.

The principality of Satara, the first to which this principle was applied, was created by Lord Hastings in favour of the descendant of Sevajee on the absorption of the Peshwa's dominions in 1819, and endowed with a revenue of fifteen lacs a year. The raja died on the 5th April, 1848, without issue. He had repeatedly applied to the Resident for permission to adopt an heir, but had been informed that it was not in his power to grant it. Two hours before his death, a boy, previously unknown to him, was brought in by hap-hazard; the ceremony of adoption was performed with the usual rites, and a royal salute was fired. The adopted lad succeeded, as a matter of course, to the personal property of the raja, but the question arose whether he could succeed to the sovereignty without the sanction of the British Government. Sir George Clerk, the governor of Bombay, while admitting that the consent of the paramount power was required by custom, maintained that the Government could not object to it without injustice. His successor, Lord Falkland, concurred with the other members of government in taking an opposite view of the case. Mr. Willoughby, the ablest member of the Council, affirmed that the confirmation of the paramount authority in India was essential to the validity of an adoption, according to custom so ancient and so universal as to have all the effect of law, and he would not allow states which, like Satara, had lapsed to us, to be perpetuated by adoption. These conflicting opinions were submitted to Lord Dalhousie, and after a diligent examination of precedents and documents, he recorded his entire agreement with Mr. Willoughby's views, both on the general principle and on the policy to be adopted in this particular instance. The question was then referred to the decision of the Court of Directors, together with all the minutes recorded at Bombay and Calcutta. The Court, with the concurrence of the Board of Control, communicated for the guidance of the Government of India the principle on which they were to act: "By the general law "and custom of India, a dependent principality, like that "of Satara, cannot pass to an adopted heir without the "consent of the paramount power . . . and the general "interests committed to our charge are best consulted by "withholding it." A.D. 1848

About five years later a similar case turned up at Nagpore. 1853
It has been already stated that, in consequence of the treacherous attack of Appa Sahib on the Residency in 1817, the kingdom was forfeited, but Lord Hastings generously restored it to the royal family. The raja, who was childless, repeatedly resisted the earnest advice of the Resident to adopt a son, and died in 1853 without any heir or successor, lineal, collateral, or adopted. Lord Dalhousie recorded an elaborate minute on the subject, remarking, "We have not now to decide any question which "turns on the right of a paramount power to refuse con-"firmation to an adoption by an inferior. The raja has "died, and deliberately abstained from adopting an heir. "The state of Nagpore, conferred on the raja and his heirs "in 1818 by the British Government, has reverted to it on "the death of the raja without an heir. The Government "is wholly unfettered to decide as it may think fit;" and he came to the conclusion that "the gratuitous alienation "of the state of Nagpore in favour of a Mahratta youth was "called for by no obligation of justice or equity, and was "forbidden by every consideration of sound policy." The Court of Directors signified their entire concurrence in the annexation, and stated as the ground of their decision that Nagpore was a principality granted after conquest by the

Nagpore.

favour of the British Government to the late raja on hereditary tenure. He had left no heir of his body; there was no male heir who by family or hereditary right conld claim to succeed him; he had adopted no son; there was not in existence any person descended in the male line from the founder of the dynasty, and they had no doubt of their right to resume the grant.

A.D. 1854 The principality of Jhansi in Bundlecund was held by a chief as a tributary of the Peshwa, whose rights in the province were ceded to the Company in 1817, and Lord Hastings, to reward him for his fidelity, declared the fief to be hereditary in his family. He died in 1835, after having adopted a son, but Sir Charles Metcalfe, then governor of Agra, declared that in the case of chiefs who merely held lands or enjoyed revenues under grants such as are issued by sovereigns to subjects, the power which made the grant had a right to resume it on failure of heirs male. He therefore refused to acknowledge any right to bequeath the sovereignty by adoption, and bestowed it on a descendant of the first chief. He died in 1853, having adopted a son on his death-bed, and his widow, a woman of high spirit and great talent, demanded the succession for the lad. Colonel Low, one of the members of Council who had opposed the annexation of Nagpore, recorded in his minute "the native rulers of Jhansi were "never sovereigns; they were only subjects of a sovereign, "first of the Peshwa, and latterly of the Company; the "Government of India has now a full right to annex the "lands of Jhansi to the British dominions." Lord Dalhousie stated that, as the last raja had left no heir of his body, and there was no male heir of any chief or raja who had ruled the principality for half a century, the right of the British Government to refuse to acknowledge the present adoption was unquestionable. The Court of Directors took the same view of the case, and Jhansi was incorporated in their territories. During the mutiny the ranee took a fearful revenge by putting eighty-three Europeans, men, women, and children, to death in cold blood. To these three cases of annexation, that of Oude has been added to swell the condemnation pronounced on Lord Dalhousie's proceedings, though it was effected contrary to his advice, by the direct orders of the Cabinet and the Court of Directors. On these questions we leave the reader to form his own judgment from the facts which we have thus placed before him.

Jhansi.

It was during the administration of Lord Dalhousie, and

with his full concurrence, that the dignity and privileges A.D. 1853 of the nabob of the Carnatic were suppressed by the Government of Madras. The Carnatic was annexed to the Company's territories in 1801 by Lord Wellesley, who allotted a sum of about seven lacs of rupees a year for the support of the nabob and his household; but he distinctly excluded all allusion to heirs and successors. It was a personal settlement with a mediatized prince; the nabob enjoyed a titular dignity, received royal salutes, and was placed above law. Two nabobs in succession had left heirs at their death in 1819 and 1825, and the Government had allowed them to succeed to the title and the advantages attached to it. The last nabob died childless in 1853, and his uncle, Azim Jah, claimed the dignity and immunities and allowances attached to the nabobship. Lord Harris, the governor of Madras, pointed out in an elaborate minute that the Government was not bound to recognise a hereditary succession to this dignity, even of direct heirs, still less of those who were only collateral. He objected to the perpetuation of the nabobship, because it was prejudicial to the public interests that there should exist a separate authority in the town not amenable to law, which, combined with the vicious habits of the palace, encouraged the accumulation of an idle and dissolute population in the capital of the Presidency. The nabob's palace was mortgaged, and his debts amounted to half a crore of rupees. Lord Harris proposed that the annuities of the Arcot family should cease, that the Government should undertake to settle its debts and make a moderate allowance to the uncle. Lord Dalhousie fully concurred in these views, and the Court of Directors asserted that the rights of the family were restricted to the prince who signed the treaty in 1801.

Nabobs of the Carnatic.

The vexatious question of the Hyderabad contingent was 1853 brought to a satisfactory conclusion by the tact and resolution of Lord Dalhousie and the firmness and judgment of Colonel Low, the Resident at the Nizam's court. The origin of this force has been explained in a former chapter. It was over-officered and over-paid, and formed a severe tax on the revenues of the state, but the Nizam would not hear of its being reduced. Its allowances had repeatedly fallen into arrears, when it became necessary for the Resident to make advances from his treasury, which the Nizam acknowledged as a debt bearing interest. The territory of Hyderabad was sufficiently pro-

The Nizam and Berar.

A.D. 1853 ductive to provide for all the demands of the administration, but it was impossible to prevail on the Nizam to attend to business; his debts amounted to three crores, and the exorbitant interest he was obliged to pay, combined with the cost of a horde of 40,000 foreign mercenaries he persisted in maintaining, devoured his resources. The Nizam had from time to time made some payments towards the liquidation of the debt incurred for the contingent, but by 1853 it had again accumulated to half a crore of rupees. Lord Dalhousie's patience was exhausted by four years of evasion, and he determined to bring the question to an issue. He proposed the draft of a treaty placing the contingent on a definite and permanent footing, providing for its punctual payment, and effecting an equitable settlement of arrears by the transfer of territory yielding about thirty-six lacs a year, which was less than the annual claim on the Nizam by about six lacs. By this arrangement he was relieved from a debt of half a crore; but, however beneficial it might be to his interests, he manifested a strong reluctance to agree to it, and it was only on the importunity of his ministers, and more particularly through the influence of a favourite valet whom the ministers had bribed, that he was induced to give his consent to it. The districts which he ceded were those in West Berar, which Lord Wellesley had generously given his ancestor for the very equivocal assistance he had rendered in the war with the Mahrattas in 1803.

SECTION IV.

LORD DALHOUSIE'S ADMINISTRATION—OUDE—SOCIAL AND MATERIAL IMPROVEMENTS.

No province in India had suffered the affliction of misrule for so long a period as Oude, and it was to be traced to the presence of the British army, which effectually protected the ruler from the indignation of his subjects. The expostulations of Warren Hastings, of Lord Cornwallis, of Sir John Shore, and of Lord Hastings had been totally unheeded. In 1831 Lord William Bentinck assured the king, that unless prompt measures were adopted to reform abuses and to give the people the benefit of good government, the Company would assume the administration, and reduce him to the same condition as the nabob of

Chronic misrule in Oude.

Moorshedabad. This remonstrance produced a slight reformation, but it was transient. Twelve years after Lord Hardinge visited Lucknow and earnestly renewed the remonstrance, assuring the king that, unless these reformations were carried out within two years, the government of the whole country would be taken out of his hands.

Colonel Sleeman, who was soon after appointed Resident, was desired to make a tour through the country and ascertain whether any reform had been made in the administration. His report presented a dark record of crime and misery. The king maintained a superfluous army of 70,000 men, who received scanty and uncertain pay, and were driven to prey upon the people. Their foraging parties indiscriminately plundered the villagers of provisions, and brought away the roofs and doors of the houses for fuel. It was impossible to conceive a greater curse to a country than such a body of disorganised and licentious soldiery. There were 246 forts or strongholds in the country, with 476 guns, held by the higher class of landholders, chiefly Rajpoots. They had converted large tracts of the most fertile land into jungle, which became the haunts of lawless characters, who levied heavy imposts on all traders and travellers. Within sixteen miles of the capital one landholder had thus turned thirty miles of rich land into jungle, and erected four fortifications within the circle. The king, immured in his palace, was invisible except to his women, musicians, and buffoons. The favourite fiddler had been appointed chief justice; the chief singer was *de facto* king. Every officer on his appointment was required to pay heavy douceurs to the king, to the heir-apparent, to the minister, in fact, to whomever was supposed to have interest at court, and he reimbursed himself by extortions from the people. Colonel Sleeman—who was an impassioned foe to annexation—stated in his report that, notwithstanding his earnest desire to maintain the throne of Oude in its integrity, fifty years of experience had destroyed every hope that the king would carry out a system of administration calculated to secure life and property and to promote the happiness of the people. "He did not think that, with a "due regard to its own character as the paramount power "in India, and the particular obligations by which it was "bound by solemn treaties to the suffering people of this "distracted country, the Government could any longer "forbear to take over the administration," in perpetuity;

A.D. 1851

Colonel Sleeman's report.

A.D. 1855 making suitable provision for the dignity and comfort of the king. General Outram, who was equally desirous of maintaining, if possible, the few remaining states in India, was appointed Resident by Lord Dalhousie, and directed to make a thorough inquiry into the condition of the people. He stated that, not only was there no improvement, but no prospect of any, and that the duty imposed on the Government by treaty could no longer admit of its honestly indulging the reluctance hitherto felt of having recourse to the decisive measure of assuming the administration. He asserted that it was at the cost of 5,000,000 people, for whom we were bound to secure good government, that we were upholding the sovereign power of this effete and incapable dynasty.

Minute of Lord Dalhousie and the Council.

Lord Dalhousie drew up a comprehensive minute on the subject, in which he analysed the evidence which had been given during a long series of years of the gross and inveterate abuse of power in Oude, and the opinions which had been recorded, without exception, of our obligation to afford relief to the people. Were it not for the presence of our troops, he said, the people would long since have worked their own deliverance; inaction on our part could no longer be justified. But, he added, the rulers of Oude, however unfaithful to the trust conferred on them, have yet ever been faithful and true in their allegiance to the British power, and they have aided us as best they could in the hour of our utmost need. Justice and gratitude require that, in ameliorating the lot of the people, we should lower the dignity and authority of the sovereign as little as possible. The prospects of the people may be improved without resorting to so extreme a measure as the annexation of the territory and the abolition of the throne. "I do not therefore advise that Oude be "declared a British province." He proposed that the king should retain the sovereignty, that he should vest the whole of the civil and military administration in the hands of the Company, and receive an annual stipend for the support of his honour and dignity. Of the members of Council, Mr. —now Sir Barnes—Peacock coincided with Lord Dalhousie; Mr.—now Sir John—Grant, and governor of Jamaica, recommended the incorporation of Oude with the British territories; and General Low, who had opposed the annexation of Nagpore, and who had, moreover, been Resident at Lucknow, asserted that the disorders in the country were of such long standing, and so inveterate, that there was no

mode of maintaining a just government but by placing the A.D.
whole of its territory exclusively and permanently under the 1855
direct management of the East India Company.

Annexation of Oude.

Lord Dalhousie transmitted all these minutes, together with the reports of Colonel Sleeman and General Outram, to the Court of Directors, with whom, and with the Ministry, rested the decision of this great question. After earnest deliberation for two months, they came to the determination to overrule the advice of Lord Dalhousie, and to adopt what he had endeavoured to dissuade them from—the annexation of the territory and the
abolition of the throne; and thus ended the sovereignty of 1856
the king of Oude, on whom an annuity of twelve lacs of rupees a year was settled.

Administrative reforms.

Lord Dalhousie's administration was rendered not less memorable by his administrative reforms and by material progress than by its political results. There was no branch of the public service which his keen eye did not penetrate, and into which he did not introduce improvements, the value of which has been gracefully acknowledged even by his enemies. He had an insuperable aversion to what he described as the cumbersome and obstructive agency of boards, and he abolished them as far as possible, and invigorated each department by unity of control and responsibility. Though a civilian, there was no portion of the public service in which his reforms were more radical
and more beneficial than the army. He abolished the 1850
military board, and placed the multifarious duties which had been thrust upon it, and which it was never able to perform with efficiency, under the charge of single officers of large experience. The board had been weighted with the superintendence of all public works, and in no division had its failure been more palpable. Lord Dalhousie organised a public works department, with a separate
secretary, not only to the Government of India, but to each 1852
Presidency. The responsibility of management was vested in a chief engineer, assisted by a body of executive officers and subordinates. To secure the uninterrupted progress of public works, which had previously been prosecuted by spasmodic efforts, a schedule of those which were to be executed during each year was to be submitted to Government at the commencement of it.

The revenues of India were increased during Lord Dalhousie's administration from twenty-six to thirty crores.

A.D. 1848 to 1856

Revenues.

The wars in which the Government of India had been engaged with little intermission for ten years, had absorbed thirty crores, and entailed an annual deficit, which, however, ceased with the cause of it, and there was for a time the bright gleam of a surplus, but it was extinguished two years after by the mutiny. During the period of eight years now under review, the commerce of Bombay was developed to an extraordinary degree, and that of Calcutta was doubled, while the coasting trade was liberated from every obstruction, and rendered more safe by the erection of lighthouses along the coast.

1853 Postage.

The importance of conferring on the comparatively poor population of India the boon of cheap and uniform postage which had long been enjoyed in England, had been frequently discussed in a perfunctory manner. . Lord Dalhousie took up the question with his accustomed energy, and transmitted to Leadenhall Street the proposal of establishing a uniform rate of half an anna, or three-farthings, for every letter of a defined weight, irrespective of distance, though in some cases it even exceeded two thousand miles. The Court gave the same ready and liberal sanction to this plan as they had, indeed done to all his other great schemes of improvement. He likewise procured a reduction of the rate of postage between England and India, and took a national pride in an arrangement which he said "would enable the Scotch "recruit at Peshawur to write to his mother at John "O'Groat's house for sixpence."

The Ganges Canal.

The Ganges Canal was commenced long before Lord Dalhousie's arrival, but it was advancing at so sluggish a pace, that the sum expended on it from the beginning had not exceeded seventeen lacs of rupees. He pressed it forward with unabated ardour, allowing no financial pressure and no exigencies of war to interrupt its progress; and the sum appropriated to it in six years exceeded a crore and a half of rupees. The main stream
1854 was opened by Mr. Colvin, the lieutenant-governor of Agra, in March 1854. This gigantic undertaking which was designed and completed by the late Sir Proby Cautley, stands among the noblest efforts of civilisation. It nearly equals the aggregate length of all the lines of the four greatest canals of France, and is five times longer than all the main lines in Lombardy.

The system of railroads which is working a greater and more beneficial change in the social, political, and com-

mercial interests of India than has been known at any former period, is due to the exertions of Lord Dalhousie. The first railway was projected by Sir Macdonald Stephenson in 1843, and received great encouragement from Mr. Wilberforce Bird, when officiating as governor-general, and subsequently from Lord Hardinge, but the commercial disasters of 1846 and 1847, and the reluctance of English capitalists to embark in an unexplored field of enterprise in India, baffled the undertaking. The indefatigable zeal of Sir Macdonald succeeded at length in forming the East India Railway Company, and Sir A.D.
James Hogg, a member of the Court of Directors, prevailed 1848
on his colleagues, though not without great difficulty, to guarantee a rate of interest sufficient to raise the capital. Two short and experimental lines at Calcutta and at Bombay were sanctioned, but as numerous applications for similar concessions poured in upon the India House, the Court had the wisdom to refer them to the consideration of Lord Dalhousie, with the intimation of their wish "that "India should, without unnecessary loss of time, possess "the immense advantage of a regular and well-devised "system of railway communications."

Railroads.

The question could not have been placed in the hands of one better qualified to do justice to it. He had presided at the Board of Trade for several years during the most active period of railway enterprise, and had become complete master of the principles and details of railway economy. To this pre-eminent advantage he added large and comprehensive views of policy. In the elaborate minute he transmitted to the Directors on
the 20th April, 1853, which became the basis of the rail- 1853
way system of India, he expressed his hope that the limited section of experimental line hitherto sanctioned would no longer form the standard for railway works in India. A glance at the map, he said, would suffice to show how immeasurable would be the political advantages of a system of internal communication by which intelligence of every event should be transmitted to the Government at a speed fivefold its present rate, and enable the Government to bring the main bulk of its military strength to bear upon any given point in as many days as it now requires months. The commercial and social advantages of the rail were beyond all calculation. "A system of railways judiciously "selected and formed would surely and rapidly give rise in "this empire to the same encouragement of enterprise, the "same multiplication of produce, the same discovery of

Lord Dalhousie's minute.

A.D. "latent forces, and the same increase of national wealth that
1853 "have marked the introduction of improved and extended "communications in the various kingdoms of the Western "world. With the aid of a railway carried up to the "Indus, the risk involved in the extension of our "frontier to a distance of 1,500 miles from the capital "would be infinitely diminished. Peshawur would, in fact, "be reached in less time and with greater facility than "Moorshedabad, though only seventy miles distant from "Calcutta, in the days of Clive." He then proceeded to lay down a system of railways for the whole continent which should connect the Presidencies with each other and form the great trunk lines. He advocated the construction of the lines by public companies, sustained by a State guarantee and controlled, directly but not vexatiously, by the Government of the country, acting in the interests of the public on the principle for which he had contended, though in vain, when at the Board of Trade.

1852 Another boon conferred on India by Lord Dalhousie was the electric telegraph, created by the enterprising spirit of Mr.—now Sir William—O'Shaughnessy. After a series of experiments he succeeded in laying down a line from Calcutta to the sea at Kedgeree, which, by expediting the communication of intelligence, was found to be of eminent service during the Burmese war, when hours were invaluable. Lord Dalhousie lost no time in sending Mr. O'Shaughnessy to England with a letter to the Court of Directors, stating that the success of this experiment had added intensity to his desire to bring the various sections of the empire into communication with each other by telegraphic wires, and he made it his earnest personal solicitation that they would authorise the immediate construction of them. "Everything," he added, "moves faster nowadays all the world over, except the "transaction of Indian business." Happily Sir James Hogg occupied the chair at the India House, and he took the same interest in the promotion of the telegraph as he had done of the rail. The proposal was carried through the various official stages with such promptitude that, within a week of the arrival of Lord Dalhousie's communication, the despatch sanctioning the establishment of the telegraph was on its way to India. The wires have now been spread over the country, and have fully answered the hopes of the Governor-General, by increasing the security of the empire, and augmenting the facilities for governing it ten-

The Electric Telegraph.

fold. Even his most ambitious expectations have been realised by the progress of science. "It may yet be hoped," he wrote, "that the system of electric telegraphs in India "may one day be linked with those which envelope Europe "and which already seek to stretch across the Atlantic." Not only is the Government of India in daily communication with the home authorities, but on a recent occasion a complimentary message from the Governor-General at Simla to the President of the United States reached Washington and was acknowledged in three hours. It cannot, however, but be considered a fortunate, not to say a providential, circumstance that the submarine telegraph was not in existence before the conquest of India had been completed, and Peshawur had become the frontier station of the empire. Considering the inveterate repugnance of the Court of Directors and of the Board of Control to any increase of territory whatever, it is manifest that, if such facilities of communication had existed at a more early period, there would have been no Indian empire to govern.

Lord Dalhousie embarked for England on the 6th March, 1856. The population of the metropolis, moved by a feeling of admiration of the great ruler who had enlarged, consolidated, and improved the empire, crowded the plain to testify their regret at his departure. Eight years of incessant toil had exhausted his constitution, and, after a lingering illness of four years, he sank into the grave, on the 19th December, 1860, at the premature age of forty-eight. His administration forms one of the most important eras in the history of British India. His plans were always broad and comprehensive, and bore the stamp of solid improvement, and not of mere sensational innovation. With a clear intellect and a sound and independent judgment, he combined great firmness of purpose and decision of character. If he exacted the rigid performance of duty from those under him, he set them the example by his own intense application to public business, to which, by a noble devotion, he sacrificed leisure, ease, comfort, and even health. Every question that came before him was investigated with patience and diligence, and with a scrupulous desire to arrive at a right decision. He marshalled with great impartiality all the arguments on both sides of any subject, and adduced weighty reasons whatever the decision he formed, the soundness of which was rarely questioned by his colleagues or the public. Among the governors-general

A.D. 1856

Character of Lord Dalhousie's administration.

he stands on the same pedestal with Warren Hastings and Lord Wellesley, and his public character, like theirs, has had to pass through the ordeal of obloquy. It was twenty-seven years after the House of Commons had impeached Warren Hastings that the members rose in a body to pay spontaneous homage to his merits as he entered their chamber in 1813. It was thirty years before the Court of Directors, who had treated Lord Wellesley as a criminal, assured him that he "had been animated by an ardent zeal to promote "the welfare of India, and to uphold the interests and "honour of the British empire, and that they looked back "to the eventful and brilliant period of his government "with feelings common to their countrymen." Lord Dalhousie's acquittal may perhaps be longer delayed, but it is not the less certain. The only indictment against him is his annexation policy, as it is called, which was hastily pronounced to have been the cause of the mutiny; and it was inevitable that the feelings of indignation which its atrocities created should be in some measure transferred to the individual who was charged with having occasioned it. The great merits of his administration cannot, therefore, be fully appreciated till the voice of posterity has removed this reproach from it.

A.D. 1853

The Charter of 1853.

The Charter of 1833 expired in 1853, and a strenuous effort was made to wrest the government of India from the East India Company, but the Whig Ministry determined to continue it in their hands, not, however, as formerly, for any definite period, but until Parliament should otherwise ordain. The India Bill was introduced by Sir Charles Wood, the President of the Board of Control, in a lucid speech of five hours; which, considering that he came into office only five months before, a stranger to Indian affairs, exhibited no ordinary talent, and held out the prospect of an enlightened and vigorous administration, which was subsequently realised to the fullest extent. The chief modifications were three. The number of the Court of Directors was reduced from thirty to eighteen, and the elimination was effected by a most ingenious process of balloting, devised by the secretary, Sir James Melvill. Of the reduced number a certain proportion was to be nominated by the Crown. Under the old system, many of the most eminent of the public servants in India were excluded from the Direction on their return to England, owing to their invincible repugnance to a laborious and humiliating course of canvassing; but the Minister was now enabled at once to avail himself of their invaluable assistance. The government of Bengal and Behar, moreover, was entrusted to a separate Lieutenant-governor. The administration of these provinces, containing a population of more than fifty millions, and contributing one-third of the revenues of the empire, had down to this period been imposed on the Governor-general; and, whenever he was absent, which was generally one-half his time, it devolved on the senior member of Council, who sometimes happened to be a military officer rewarded for services in the field, and, in one instance, for reforming the Madras Commissariat. Under this anomalous system there had been no fewer than ten governors and deputy-governors of Bengal in the course of eleven years. Throughout this period of perpetual change and inevitable weakness the post of secretary was occupied by Mr.—now Sir Frederick—Halliday, and it was owing to his great local knowledge and experience, and to his sound judgment and diligence, that the administration exhibited any degree of energy or consistency. His eminent services were rewarded by the first appointment to the Lieutenant-governorship. By a third provision of the Charter, the patronage of the Civil Service was withdrawn from the Court of Directors to make way for the principle of unreserved competition.

A.D. 1853

CHAPTER XV.

SECTION I.

LORD CANNING'S ADMINISTRATION—THE MUTINY—MEERUT—DELHI—THE PUNJAB.

Lord Dalhousie was succeeded by Lord Canning, the thirteenth and last of the Governors-general of the East India Company, and the first viceroy of the Queen. His father, George Canning, was appointed governor-general in 1822, but did not embark. He himself had sat in the House of Lords for twenty years, and filled several offices of state, and had thus acquired a good store of official experience. At the valedictory banquet given to him by the Court of Directors

1856

Lord Canning governor-general.

he uttered these memorable expressions:—"I wish for a "peaceful time of office; but I cannot forget that in the sky "of India, serene as it is, a small cloud may arise no larger "than a man's hand, but which, growing larger and larger, "may at last threaten to burst, and overwhelm us with "ruin." The succeeding narrative will show how prophetic this enunciation proved to be. His administration was marked by a series of events of unexampled magnitude —the mutiny and extinction of an army of 150,000 sepoys, —the wholesale massacre of Europeans, men, women and children—the loss and recovery of the North-West provinces—the dissolution of the East India Company, and the annexation of the empire of India to the Crown.

A.D. 1856 Lord Canning landed in Calcutta on the last day of February 1856, and for a fortnight enjoyed the benefit of intercourse with Lord Dalhousie, who believed that India was in a state of profound tranquillity. As the year wore on, however, the elements of disquietude, though not of immediate danger, began to make their appearance. The deposed king of Oude was allowed to take up his residence in the suburbs of Calcutta, and his emissaries were actively employed in diffusing a feeling of hostility to the British Government in and around the metropolis. The chief commissionership of Oude had unfortunately been given to a civilian, Mr. Coverley Jackson, who was utterly unfit for such a post. Instead of labouring to reconcile the chiefs and people to a foreign rule, as Outram and Sleeman would have laboured to do, his time was passed in unseemly squabbles with his subordinates, and in sowing the dragon's teeth of rebellion among the proud aristocracy of the country by a wanton and disastrous interference with the tenures of their estates.

Appearances of disaffection.—Oude.

In the old Mahomedan capital of India, in which the royal family had been injudiciously permitted to keep up a mimic court, the proceedings of Government aroused a strong feeling of animosity. Contrary to the advice of some of the venerable members of the Court of Directors, the Board of Control had determined to remove the family from Delhi; and, on the death of the king Bahadoor Shah, to discontinue the royal title and immunities. From a feeling of deference to the strong remonstrances of the Directors who had opposed this measure, Lord Dalhousie had postponed taking action upon it, and it was left to the consideration of Lord Canning, who at once adopted the conclusion that the palace of

Discontent at Delhi.

Delhi, which was a mile in circumference and the citadel of a fortified town, and which was urgently required for military purposes, should be in the hands of the Government of the country. A communication to this effect was made to the king, who was likewise informed that his son Mahomed Korash would be recognised as his successor, but without the title of king. His young and favourite wife, Zeenut Mehal, was anxious to secure the succession for her own son, and resented his exclusion, and not less the loss of the regal dignity and privileges of the family. She set every engine at work to create a hostile excitement against the British Government in the Mahomedan community, not only of Hindostan, but also of the Deccan, and extended her intrigues to Persia, then at war with England. Rumours were at the same time disseminated that Lord Canning had arrived with orders from the Queen of England to enforce the profession of Christianity on the natives of India. There was likewise a prophecy abroad at the time that the Company's *raj*, or rule, was to last only a hundred years, and 1857 was the centenary of Plassy. This prediction was industriously propagated, and tended, as in other cases, to promote its own fulfilment, by creating an impression that the fate of the British Government was subject to the inevitable law of destiny. There can be little doubt that towards the close of 1856 the public mind had become unsettled, and that a vague apprehension of some portentous event was generally diffused through the community.

A.D. 1856

The native soldiery of India, whether under their native princes or under our own flag, had never been exempt from a spirit of insubordination. Sindia, Holkar, and the other Mahratta rulers had been repeatedly subject to coercion by their mutinous soldiers. Runjeet Sing declared that he dreaded his own victorious troops more than he feared his enemies. In the Company's army, from the first mutiny in 1764 at Buxar to the latest in 1850 at Shikarpore, there had been a constant succession of outbreaks more or less formidable. In 1856 there were two especial causes of annoyance calculated to disquiet the minds of men whom we had been accustomed to pamper. More than forty thousand of the sepoys were recruited from Oude, and with the view of attaching them to our service, they had enjoyed the privilege of having their lawsuits decided before others, on the production of a rescript from their commanding officers. This exclusive privilege, which gave

The native army.

A.D. 1856 them importance in their native villages, was lost on the annexation of the country, and it created a feeling of discontent. Moreover, only six of the Bengal regiments were enlisted for foreign service, and in 1856 Government promulgated an order that in future the services of no recruit would be accepted who did not engage to embark when required. The order was as reasonable as it was necessary, but it produced a deep feeling of dissatisfaction in every regiment. The Company's military service was considered both an honourable and an hereditary profession; but under the new rule the sons and nephews of the high-caste sepoys who were waiting for vacancies must either forego the service altogether, or defile their caste by crossing the "black water."

The greased cartridges.

It is questionable, however, whether the disaffection excited by the two royal families of Oude and Delhi, or even the discontent of the sepoys, would have culminated in the revolt of the whole army, and the barbarities which accompanied it, but for the unexpected incident of the greased cartridges, which proved a god-send to the enemies of Government. It had been determined to supersede the old infantry musket by an improved description of fire-arm with a grooved bore, which could not be loaded without lubricating the cartridge. Dumdum, in the neighbourhood of Calcutta, was one of the schools of musketry for instruction in the use of the Enfield rifle. Early
1857 in January 1857 a low-caste man employed in the magazine meeting a brahmin sepoy, asked him for a drink of water from his brass water-flask, and was refused on the ground of his caste; upon which he remarked that "high caste and "low caste would soon be on an equality, as cartridges "smeared with beef fat and hog's lard were being made up "at the magazine which all the sepoys would be compelled "to use." The alarm spread like wild fire among the sepoys at Dumdum and through the four regiments at Barrackpore. The emissaries of the king of Oude industriously circulated a report that, in prosecution of a long cherished design, the Government, under special instructions from England, had caused the cartridges to be greased with ingredients which would defile both Hindoos and Mahomedans, as a preliminary to their forcible conversion to Christianity. A frantic feeling of terror and indignation spread through the regiments, which was evinced by the incendiary fires which from night to night destroyed the officers' bungalows and the public buildings.

As soon as the excitement created by the rumour of the

greased cartridges became known to the Government in Calcutta active measures were taken to allay it. Telegraphic messages were despatched to all the stations up the country to issue the cartridges free from grease. At Barrackpore the sepoys were assured by General Hearsay, who had acquired great influence over them, that there was no cause for alarm, that the Government never had any design on their caste, that no greased cartridges had been issued, and that they might lubricate their own cartridges with bees' wax. But they were beyond the reach of reason, and it was found impossible to disabuse them. When it was demonstrated to them that there was no grease in the cartridges, they affirmed that the paper itself which had a glossy appearance, was polluted. The public post was laden with their letters, and in a few days every regiment throughout Hindostan was infected with the same feeling of alarm and passion. The little cloud was "growing larger and larger," and threatening to "burst and overwhelm the Government with ruin."

A.D. 1857

Endeavours to allay excitement.

At the time when the peril of the empire was thus in the extreme, the usual means of confronting it were wanting. India had been in a great measure stripped of the European force which was now urgently required to control an infatuated and infuriate native army. Regiment after regiment had been withdrawn from the country in spite of the remonstrances of Lord Dalhousie, who was constrained at length to inform Lord Palmerston that he could not be responsible for the safety of the empire if any more European troops were withdrawn; yet four more were sent to Persia after he had retired from the country. Instead of the safe proportion of one European to three native regiments, which the tradition of half a century had established, there was at this time, little more than a single regiment to ten native corps between Calcutta and Agra. Lord Lawrence indeed affirmed that, "if there had been 5,000 more Europeans, it "is certain that the mutiny would not have happened; "but the natives thought the country was quite denuded "of troops." When the crisis appeared imminent Lord Canning sent round to Rangoon for the 84th, and, on its arrival, ventured to bring down and disband the 19th, which had mutinied at Berhampore.

Paucity of European troops.

The month of April passed with little disturbance, but in great disquietude. It afterwards transpired that a general conspiracy had been organised throughout the

A.D. 1857 sepoy army, for the simultaneous revolt of every regiment at every station in Hindostan, on the evening of the last Sunday in May, at the hour of church service, when all the Europeans were to be massacred without regard to sex or age; but an unexpected transaction at Meerut led to a premature outbreak. It was the largest and most important military station in the North-West provinces, and also the head-quarters of the artillery, and any movement in it was sure to exercise a powerful influence at other stations. There the ordnance department had been employed in making up the greased cartridges under the eyes of the sepoys. The general excitement which pervaded the cantonment and the surrounding country was constantly fomented by fresh and more alarming rumours. It was asserted that the flour in the bazaars had been mixed up with ground bones, and that even the salt had been polluted. No lie was too absurd to be believed. It was manifest that the enemies of Government had taken advantage of the existing agitation to inflame the minds of the sepoys, and to convulse the country. Foremost among these conspirators in the North-West was Doondhoo Punt, commonly known as Nana Sahib, the adopted son of the ex-Peshwa Bajee Rao, who, during his residence at Bithoor, had received through his annuity an aggregate sum of two crores and a half of rupees, the greater portion of which he had bequeathed to the Nana. He had the effrontery to demand a continuance of the pension of eight lacs of rupees a year, which was necessarily refused him, and he vowed vengeance on the Government, and during the early part of the year was found travelling about in Oude and other districts sowing the seeds of revolt.

Open mutiny at Meerut.

The troopers of the 3rd Cavalry at Meerut, chiefly Mahomedans, were the first to break out into open mutiny. It was explained to them on parade that they were not required to bite the cartridges, but simply to pinch off the end; but of the ninety men to whom the cartridges were offered on the 24th April, eighty-five refused to touch them, and were ordered to be brought to a court-martial. The court was composed of fifteen native officers of artillery, cavalry, and infantry, and by the vote of fourteen the troopers were found guilty of disobedience of orders, and sentenced to hard labour for ten years. On the morning of the 9th May, in the presence of their fellow-soldiers drawn up on parade, their uniform was stripped

The 3rd Cavalry.

off their backs, and shackles affixed to their ankles. Some of them were the flower of the regiment, and had served the state in many campaigns, and they implored the general to have mercy on them, and not subject them to so ignominious a doom. To the feeling of alarm for their caste in the minds of the sepoys was now added a feeling of burning wrath as they saw their comrades marched off to gaol like the meanest felons. The whole transaction exhibited a spirit of incomprehensible infatuation on the part of the military authorities of the station as well as of the commander-in-chief.

A.D. 1857

The next day, Sunday, the 10th May, as the Europeans were proceeding to church in the evening, the native troops broke out. The troopers of the 3rd Cavalry hastened to the gaol, which was guarded only by sepoys, and liberated their companions. The infantry and the cavalry, the Hindoos and the Mahomedans, made common cause, and massacred all the Europeans without distinction of age or sex whom they could find. Half a century before Colonel Gillespie, with a regiment of dragoons and some galloper guns, had at once quelled the Vellore mutiny and saved the Deccan. The European force at Meerut consisted of a battalion of riflemen, a regiment of dragoons, and a large force of European artillery; and the exercise of similar promptitude would have saved Meerut at once, and checked the principle of revolt in its infancy. But the commander of the division, General Hewitt, was a superannuated officer, inert and imbecile, of unwieldy bulk, and the last man who ought to have been entrusted with the charge of so important a station at such a crisis. The night was passed in burning down the residences of the officers and Europeans, and the massacre of the Christians, without any attempt to check it. The women and children who sought refuge in the gardens were tracked out and shot amidst the yells of the mutineers. "The sweepings "of the gaols and the scum of the bazaars, all the rogues "and ruffians of Meerut and the robber-tribes of the "neighbouring villages, were let loose, plundering and "destroying wherever an English bungalow was to be "gutted and burnt."

The outburst of the 10th May.

In the morning it was found that the mutineers had started on the road to Delhi. Had the carabineers and the horse artillery been instantly despatched after them, they might have reached the city, only forty miles distant, in time to save the lives of the Euro-

Atrocities at Delhi.

A.D. 1857 peans there, and to hold the mutiny in check, even if they had not overtaken and cut up the mutinous regiments on the route; but the wretched Hewitt simply sent his cavalry out to reconnoitre. The 3rd Cavalry was speedily followed by the infantry, and being joined by the 38th, on duty in the city, began the work of destruction and murder. The commissioner, the chaplain and his daughter, and the European officers in the city were massacred. The Delhi bank was gutted and all its inmates slaughtered. The magazine, the largest in the North-West, with its vast supplies of gunpowder, was defended by only nine European officers and a few treacherous natives. The mutineers applied scaling ladders to the walls, and were streaming over them, when Lieut. Willoughby applied the torch to the train he had laid, and blew it up to prevent its falling into the hands of the enemy, and with it hundreds of the mutineers. None of these brave officers expected to survive the explosion, and the sacrifice of their own lives in the service of their country was an act of distinguished heroism; but four of them happily survived the catastrophe.

Proclamation of the king.

The city was now completely in the hands of the insurgents. The Europeans who had taken refuge at the main guard were shot down by volleys from the 38th. The cantonment which was immediately beyond the walls contained two sepoy regiments, who rose upon the officers, set fire to their houses, and turned the guns upon them. Some of them and their wives succeeded in making their escape, and many a tale is recorded of the heroic bearing of delicate ladies, some of them with children in their arms, as, under the burning sun of May, they sought refuge in the jungles or waded through streams with scanty clothing and little food. Meanwhile the European and East India women and children in the city, about fifty in number, were seized, and after five days of barbarous treatment, taken into a courtyard of the palace, when a rope was thrown round them to prevent their escape, and they were one and all murdered. Not a European was now left in Delhi. The sepoys then proceeded to offer the sovereignty to the king, which he formally accepted. An old silver throne was brought into the hall of audience, on which he took his seat, under a salute of twenty-one guns, and received public homage, and began to issue royal mandates.

The wire flashed down to Calcutta the portentous intelligence of the mutiny at Meerut, the loss of Delhi, and the establishment of a Mogul dynasty. Lord Canning immediately sent to Madras, to Ceylon, and to Bombay for every available European regiment. A steamer was despatched to intercept Lord Elgin on his mission to China, and entreat him to forward to Calcutta the European force which accompanied him, and orders were issued to despatch the troops returning from the Persian expedition to Calcutta as fast as they arrived.

A.D. 1857

Movements of Lord Canning.

The telegraph gave immediate notice of the crisis at Meerut to the officers in the Punjab. The number of European troops in the province was about 10,000, and of Sikhs 13,000, but they were outnumbered by the Hindostanee sepoys, all ripe for revolt. The strength of the Punjab consisted, however, not so much in the large collection of European soldiers, as in the body of able men in charge of the government. It was considered Lord Dalhousie's "pet province," and he had drained the older provinces of their best officers to enrich its establishments. Never since the introduction of British power into India had so large a number of statesmen and generals of the first order been collected together in the administration of any province. At the head of this galaxy of talent stood Sir John Lawrence, a tower of strength, with a genius for military organization, although a civilian, second only to Lord Wellesley and Lord Dalhousie; while among the foremost of his assistants were Robert Montgomery, Donald Macleod, Herbert Edwardes, Neville Chamberlain, and above all John Nicholson. But it is not easy to select any names without doing injustice to other distinguished men, civil and military, whose zeal, devotion, and energy achieved the success of which their country is justly proud. For the detail of their exploits the reader is referred to Kaye's standard "History of the Sepoy War." Cut off from all communication with the Government of India in the capital, they were constrained to act on their own judgment and responsibility; and when the vigour of their proceedings is contrasted with the official feebleness too visible in Calcutta, this isolation cannot but be considered a fortunate circumstance.

Proceedings in the Punjab.

In the cantonment of Lahore there were three regiments of native infantry and one of cavalry waiting only for the post to bring them information of the hostile movement at Meerut to follow the example. They were counterpoised by only one European regiment and two troops of European horse-artillery. Sir John

Sepoys disarmed at Lahore.

A.D. 1857 Lawrence was absent at Rawul Pindee, recruiting his health, and Mr. Robert Montgomery was at the head of affairs at the station when intelligence was received by wire on the 11th May of the revolt at Meerut, and on the 12th that Delhi was in the hands of the rebels, and it was resolved to deprive the regiments of their arms the very next morning. A ball had been fixed for the night of the 12th, and it was deemed advisable not to abandon it, lest a feeling of suspicion should be created in the minds of the sepoys. The officers moved from the ball-room to the parade, where the unsuspecting troops were drawn up as on ordinary occasions. The European regiments and the guns were suddenly wheeled into a commanding position, and the disaffected regiments, seeing that any attempt at resistance must be fatal to them, obeyed the order to pile arms, and Lahore was saved by the energy of Mr. Montgomery and Brigadier Corbett and Colonel Renney.

In the same spirit of promptitude the important fortress of Govindgurh which commanded Umritsir, the ecclesiastical capital of the Punjab, was secured. The great magazines of Ferozepore and Phillour, were in like manner saved from the mutineers, though not without difficulty. In the valley of Peshawur, across the Indus, there were about 2,000 European troops, and four times that number of native sepoys. The possession of it was considered essential to the security of the Punjab; and the officers in charge of it, Edwardes, Sydney Cotton, Chamberlain, and Nicholson, were equal to any emergency. At the first council which they held, Colonel Edwardes declared that "whatever gave rise to the mutiny, it had "settled down into a struggle for empire under Mahomedan "guidance, with the Mogul capital for its centre," and it was resolved to form a movable column of reliable troops, under a competent commander, to act wherever there was danger. On the 22nd, the four regiments of native infantry stationed there were taken by surprise as they were on the point of mutiny, and disarmed. This master stroke of policy produced a magical effect on the people and chiefs in the valley, which was enhanced soon after when a number of the fugitives of the mutinous 55th, which had been dispersed and cut up by Colonel Nicholson, were blown away from the guns on the Peshawur parade. At other stations, however, there was not the same prudence and success. Brigadier Johnson, another imbecile like Hewitt, allowed Loodiana to be plundered, and three regiments from Jullun-

Proceedings at other stations.

der and Phillour to escape with their arms to Delhi. The 14th at Jhelum was found to be ready for revolt, and a force was sent by Sir John Lawrence to disarm them, but the commandant disobeyed his instructions, and a fierce engagement ensued, in which the sepoys had the advantage and made their escape. The news of this transaction emboldened the disaffected regiments at Sealkote to rise on their officers, and, as usual, they threw open the gaol, plundered the treasury, gutted the houses of the European inhabitants, and marched on to Delhi, but retribution was not far off. Colonel Nicholson who had taken the command of the movable column, after having by his energy and skill disarmed three more regiments, marched with the utmost speed on the insurgents regardless of the insufferable heat, and completely routed them. All their baggage, and their ammunition, together with the spoils of Sealkote, fell into his hands and they fled, leaving 400 dead and wounded on the field. These energetic measures gave security for the time to the Punjab.

A.D. 1857

Within a month of the outbreak at Meerut there was scarcely a regiment between the Sutlej and Allahabad which had not revolted. The sepoys gravitated to Delhi as the seat of the new government, and the recapture of it became the more urgent as it became more arduous. Sir John and his associates directed their whole attention to the despatch of men and materials to the siege, but, with the means at his disposal and the local demands on them, the task appeared so difficult that he proposed to place Peshawur and the province lying beyond the Indus in the hands of Dost Mahomed, and thus obtain the valuable services of the European troops stationed there. The measure was strenuously opposed by Colonel Edwardes and his gallant companions, and referred to Lord Canning on the 10th June. His reply, "hold on at "Peshawur to the last," was dated the 15th July, but so completely had the communication between the Punjab and Calcutta been cut off that it was despatched by a steamer to Lord Harris at Madras to be telegraphed to Lord Elphinstone at Bombay, and sent on by him as best he could.

Proposal to abandon Peshawur.

SECTION II.

LORD CANNING'S ADMINISTRATION—THE MUTINY—LUCKNOW—CAWNPORE—ALLAHABAD.

A.D. 1857

Events at Lucknow.

THE post of Resident at Lucknow had been accepted by the great Sir Henry Lawrence in March 1857. The measures of his predecessor had fatally alienated the landed aristocracy, who were found to possess greater influence over the people than had been supposed, and whose opposition was therefore the more formidable. The city was filled with thousands of the starving soldiers and retainers of the old court seething with disloyalty, while the whole country was pervaded by the families of the 40,000 sepoys who were in a state of mutiny. There were nine native regiments of infantry and cavalry in the capital and its environs, containing about 7,000 men, and only 700 Europeans to hold them in check. The 7th cavalry was in a state of violent excitement, and had invited the 48th native infantry to join them in murdering their officers. On the 3rd May, on a bright moonlight night, Sir Henry Lawrence moved down unexpectedly with his Europeans to their lines, when they threw down their arms and fled. He then distributed his small force in such positions as to overawe the city and the native regiments, and laid in a store of provisions in a stronghold called the Mutchie Bhawan. On the night of the 30th May, however, five of the regiments broke out, and set fire to the cantonments and murdered their officers, in some cases with exceptional treachery. This became the signal for a general revolt at all the stations throughout the country, and by the middle of June every regiment in the province, as well as every police battalion, was in a state of mutiny. Sir Henry still held command of the city and the neighbourhood, but on the last day of the month he marched out to Chinhut to meet several thousand mutineers who were marching on it, when his native gunners cut the traces of their horses, threw the guns into a ditch, and rode away, and his little force was constrained to retreat with the loss of a sixth of its number, and, what was more disastrous, of the reputation which had hitherto held the city in awe. After this reverse he was obliged to contract his lines of defence within the Residency grounds. On the

General revolt of the army.

4th of July he expired of a wound he received from a shell which burst into his room two days before, and the state was deprived, at its greatest need, of the invaluable services of one of the most illustrious of its servants, beloved by the natives for his genial benevolence, and by his brother officers for his pre-eminent talent. On his death the command devolved on Brigadier Inglis, and he continued to sustain a close siege with unflinching energy for twelve weeks till he was relieved by Outram and Havelock. A.D. 1857

Death of Sir Henry Lawrence.

The large and important station of Cawnpore was garrisoned by three regiments of native infantry and one of cavalry under the command of General Wheeler, but unhappily he had only 200 European soldiers. With a mutinous feeling around him in every quarter, the month of May was passed in fear and anxiety, and he entrenched a spot about 200 yards square, and stored it with provisions sufficient to last 1,000 men for a month. Doondhoo Punt, the Nana Sahib, living at Bithoor, had been assiduous in fomenting the spirit of rebellion among the regiments, and on the 5th June they rose in mutiny, and after courteously dismissing their officers, plundered the treasury, opened the gaols, and marched off to Delhi. The Nana, whose object was to raise a Mahratta throne for himself and not to revive a Mogul dynasty, hastened after them and prevailed on them to return and clear the entrenchment of the *feringees*. The whole of the European population was crowded into the enclosure; the revolted sepoys laid close siege to it, and planted eleven guns of large calibre against it, which poured in an incessant shower of shot and shell. The miseries of the besieged have seldom, if ever, been exceeded in the history of the world, and the dauntless courage and the spirit of endurance they displayed have perhaps never been surpassed. The 23rd of June, the anniversary of Plassy, the day fixed by the prophets for the extinction of the Company's *raj*, was here, as elsewhere, marked by extraordinary exertions which, however, ended in so signal a defeat that the sepoys begged permission to remove their dead.

State of the Cawnpore garrison.

Three weeks had now elapsed since the investment of this slender fortification, and still this heroic band continued to repel every assault, and to inflict an almost incredible amount of slaughter on the insurgents, but their guns were becoming unserviceable, their ammunition was running low, and starv-

Desperate state of the garrison.

A.D. 1857 vation was staring them in the face; a stray dog was turned into soup, an old horse was considered a delicacy, and the well was nearly exhausted. It was impossible for human nature to hold out much longer, and General Wheeler at length agreed to the offer of the Nana to supply them with provisions and conveyances to Allahabad, on condition of his surrendering the entrenchment together with the guns and treasure. Little did the General dream that the incarnate fiend to whom he was entrusting his charge had on the 4th June massacred 130 men, women, and children who had escaped from the mutineers at Futtygurh in boats, and had been induced to land at Cawnpore. On the morning of the 27th June, the remnant of the garrison, together with the women and children, moved down, some on foot and some in vehicles, to the river which they found lined with the ferocious sepoys; and there was perpetrated one of the most diabolical acts of treachery and murder that the darkest page of human annals records.

Massacre at the ghaut.

No sooner had they embarked in the boats than Tantia Topee, acting for the Nana, took his seat on a platform, and ordered the massacre to commence. On the sound of a bugle a murderous fire of grape shot and musketry was opened on the boats from both sides of the river; the thatch of many of them was ignited by hot cinders, and the sick, the wounded, and the helpless women were burnt to death. The stronger women, many with children in their arms, took to the river, and were shot down one by one, or sabred by the troopers who dashed into the stream. A number of both sexes escaped to the shore, and the Nana issued his orders that not a man should be allowed to live, but that the women and children should be taken to the house which he occupied. There they were added to the captives he had previously made, and huddled together in one small room, fed on the coarsest food, subjected to every indignity, and taken out in couples to grind corn for his household. Of the entire garrison and the male European population of Cawnpore only four succeeded in making their escape in a boat which drifted down the river, and, after many hair-breadth escapes, were taken under the protection of a loyal Oude zemindar. On the 1st July the Nana was publicly proclaimed Peshwa with the ceremonies usual on such occasions. He then took his seat on the throne under a royal salute, and at night the town was brilliantly illuminated. But his triumph was of short duration; the avenging sword of Havelock was advancing to extinguish his career. A.D. 1857

The perilous condition of the garrisons of Lucknow and Cawnpore was the chief cause of anxiety to Lord Canning, and as the British troops entered the Hooghly they were pushed forward daily in such detachments as the scanty means of conveyance at his command would allow. Benares, the head-quarters of Hindooism, and always the most turbulent city in Hindostan, was likewise a source of disquietude, as the only European troops in the cantonment consisted of thirty gunners opposed to 2,000 native sepoys. It was owing to the cool courage and composure, and the skilful dispositions of Mr. Henry Tucker, the commissioner, and his associates, that an insurrectionary movement was warded off while small reinforcements came up from Dinapore. The first driblet from Calcutta, consisting of sixty Madras Fusileers under their gallant commander Colonel Neill arrived at Benares, then under the command of Brigadier Ponsonby, on the 4th June, and raised the European force to 250. Immediately before the arrival of the Colonel, the native regiment at Azimgurh, sixty miles distant, had mutinied, and obtained possession of seven lacs of rupees. The 37th at Benares was prepared to follow the example, and it was resolved in haste to disarm it, but the affair was grossly mismanaged, and presented a melancholy contrast to the masterly movements at Lahore and Peshawur, where the regiments were deprived of their arms without the loss of a single life. The sepoys fired upon the Europeans; Captain Olpherts's battery mowed down the sepoys and they fled towards the city. The work, however, was complete, though with an unnecessary sacrifice of life, and all further apprehension at Benares ceased.

Colonel Neill at Benares.

Colonel Neill, after having made a terrific example of all who were suspected of disaffection, and placed Colonel Gordon in command, moved up with all speed to Allahabad to save the fort, one of the largest and most important in the North West Provinces, which had been, unaccountably, left without a European garrison, and was at this time defended only by sixty invalids from Chunar, and by a portion of Brazier's Sikh corps. The 6th Native Infantry had offered to march to Delhi and fight the mutineers, and was drawn up on parade on the 6th June to receive the thanks of Lord Canning for its loyalty. The men sent up three cheers, and the European

Allahabad.

A.D. 1857

and native officers shook hands with each other. That same night, as the officers were seated at their mess, the perfidious sepoys rushed in and put them to death. In the number of the slain were eight unposted boy ensigns, fresh from Addiscombe, who had recently joined the regiment, and found a bloody grave on the threshold of their career. The prisoners in the gaol were then let loose, the houses of the Europeans pillaged and burnt, and the Europeans, men, women, and children, outside the fort butchered with every aggravation of cruelty. The telegraphic wires were cut, the rails torn up, and the engines, of which the sepoys had a superstitious dread, battered with cannon. The doors of the treasury, containing thirty lacs of rupees, were thrown open, and each sepoy is said to have carried off three or four bags of a thousand rupees each. The town with all its wealth was given up to plunder, and the king of Delhi proclaimed. The fort had been besieged for four days, when it was happily relieved by the arrival on the 11th of Colonel Neill, who had been directed by a telegram from Lord Canning to take the command at Allahabad. The handful of Europeans he brought with him was augmented by other detachments in succession, and he was soon enabled to re-establish the authority of Government in the city and surrounding districts, and to inflict a fearful retribution on the wretches who had been revelling in plunder and bloodshed, of which the gibbets in every direction bore ample testimony.

Massacre of the officers.

Major Renaud's column.

On the last day of June he sent on a detachment to succour Cawnpore, consisting of 400 Europeans, 300 Sikhs, 100 irregular cavalry; and two guns, under Major Renaud, who was ordered to inflict summary vengeance on all who were in any degree suspected of disloyalty, and who marched on for three days, leaving behind him traces of retribution in desolated villages and corpses dangling from the branches of trees.

Colonel Havelock's progress.

Colonel Havelock, the adjutant-general of the army, who had been the second in command in the Persian expedition, returned to Bengal on the conclusion of peace by way of Madras, and came up to Calcutta in the same steamer with Sir Patrick Grant, the Commander-in-Chief at Madras, who succeeded provisionally to the chief command in India on the death of General Anson. On the voyage Havelock had mapped out a plan of operations, and recommended the formation of a movable column, to proceed upwards from the lower provinces to the scenes of revolt. This column was placed under his command as Brigadier-General, with orders, after suppressing disorders at Allahabad, to lose no time in proceeding to the support of Sir Hugh Wheeler at Cawnpore, and Sir Henry Lawrence at Lucknow. He reached Allahabad on the 30th June, and soon after received unequivocal evidence that Cawnpore had fallen, and that the Nana was marching down with a large force and many guns on Allahabad. He clearly foresaw that if Major Renaud's little band had come in contact with the rebel sepoys, not a soul could have survived to tell the tale; and, contrary to the remonstrances of Colonel Neill, he ordered the Major to halt. Havelock could only muster 1,000 Europeans, 130 of Brazier's Sikhs, 18 volunteer cavalry, and 6 guns which he had improvised, and with this force he hasted to the support of Renaud, and overtook him at Futtehpore, and there he commenced his victorious career. The enemy, 4,000 strong, rushed down upon his army, but was soon seen to fly in dismay, leaving eleven guns with the victors. This was the first check the mutinous sepoys had received below Delhi, and it produced a most salutary impression. Three days after he again defeated them at Onao, and without a halt hastened on to the Pandoo river, where he again routed them, and was enabled to save the bridge, which they were preparing to blow up, and the loss of which would have fatally crippled his movements. The Nana's brother, who was in the field, galloped back in haste to Cawnpore, and gave him the alarming intelligence that the British commander had forced the bridge, and was in full march on the town. The monster determined to avenge himself on the helpless women and children, two hundred in number, who had been crowded together for many days in three narrow rooms. Among the captives there were four or five men, and they were brought out and despatched under the eyes of the Nana. A party of sepoys was then told off, and they poured volley after volley on the helpless victims through the venetian windows, but as the work of death did not proceed fast enough, Mahomedan butchers and other ruffians were sent in with swords and knives and other weapons to hack them to pieces. There the bodies lay through the night, and the next morning the dead and the dying were brought out, together with children alive and almost unhurt, and tossed indiscriminately into an adjoining well.

After this act of unparalleled villany, the Nana marched

A.D. 1857

A.D. 1857 out of Cawnpore with about 5,000 men to dispute Havelock's advance. The sepoys fought with the valour of desperation; but the admirable strategy of the commander, and the indomitable courage of the British soldiers, more especially the 73rd Highlanders, gave him a brilliant victory. The next morning the troops marched into Cawnpore, when the sight of the well choked with human victims told them that they were too late, but it inspired them with an unquenchable resolution to avenge this foul massacre. The rebel sepoys blew up the magazine and dispersed. The Nana fled to Bithoor, and then escaped with his females across the Ganges into Oude, when his palace was despoiled and destroyed.

Battle of Cawnpore.

Meanwhile Colonel Neill had arrived at Cawnpore with the recruits which Lord Canning had been pushing up, and Havelock confided the protection of the town to him, and moved on to the relief of Lucknow. The task before him was one of no ordinary difficulty. The whole of Oude was in revolt; the landed aristocracy was universally opposed to us, and an army of sepoys whom we had taught to fight was ready to dispute every inch of ground, while Havelock's force did not exceed 1,400 men. By the 25th July his troops had crossed the river by a bridge which had been erected under every disadvantage, and on the 29th he came up with the enemy at Aong, 12,000 in number, and thoroughly defeated them, capturing fifteen guns. He then pushed on to Busseerut-gunge, a walled village, from which the sepoys were driven with the loss of more guns, but as he had lost 150 men by cholera, wounds, and sunstroke, he was obliged to fall back to Munglewar. The sick and wounded were sent to Cawnpore and reinforcements were received from thence, which raised his force to 1,300, and on the 4th August he advanced a second time to Busseerut-gunge, now held by 20,000 Sepoys, whom he again defeated with heavy slaughter. But the cholera broke out afresh in his camp and his position became critical. A body of 4,000 sepoys had collected at Bithoor and threatened Colonel Neill; the famous Gwalior contingent, the finest native force in India, complete in every arm, had broken out into mutiny, and was said to have arrived at Culpee on the banks of the Jumna, forty-five miles from Cawnpore. The three native regiments at Dinapore had at length mutinied, and were reported to be advancing into Oude, and he felt that to move on to Lucknow with his slender force would not only

Havelock advances to the relief of Lucknow.

risk its destruction, but also the loss of Cawnpore and A.D. 1857
of the whole of the Doab. He determined wisely, to return to Cawnpore and await the arrival of reinforcements; but on reaching Munglewar he was informed by his scouts that a large force of the enemy was advancing against him which would not only have interrupted the passage of the river, but enabled them to report that they had chased him out of the country. He therefore turned back and inflicted a crushing defeat on them, and then crossed the river without molestation. On the 16th August he attacked the encampment of the rebels at Bithoor and put them to flight; and then the heroes of ten successful fights within five weeks rested on their oars, till they were reinforced from Calcutta.

Relief of Lucknow.

Through the month of August fresh troops poured into Calcutta by sea, and were rapidly drafted to Allahabad and Cawnpore. Sir James Outram, on his return from the Persian expedition, had arrived in Calcutta and was nominated chief commissioner in Oude, and appointed to the command of the Dinapore and Cawnpore divisions. Captain Peel had formed a naval brigade of 500 men from the sailors of his own frigate, the 'Shannon,' and of vessels in Calcutta, and the blue-jackets were for the first time sent into the interior of India. Sir James Outram reached Cawnpore with 1,400 men on the 16th September, and with the chivalrous generosity of his character determined to leave to Havelock the honour of accomplishing the relief of Lucknow, for which he had so nobly toiled, and to accompany him as a volunteer. Since the death of Sir Henry Lawrence, Brigadier Inglis had been incessantly engaged in repelling the assaults of the enemy, but the force at the Residency was now reduced to 350 Europeans, and 300 natives, whose loyalty was beginning to waver under the fatigues and the casualties of the siege. The brigadier informed Havelock that it was not possible for him to hold out much longer, and it became necessary to push on without delay. The relieving force, consisting of 2,500 men, nearly all British, met with little impediment till it reached the Alum-baug in the vicinity of Lucknow, which was mastered on the 23rd September. On the morning of the 25th the bugles sounded the advance into Lucknow, and the army, instead of advancing through two miles of streets of loophold houses filled with sepoys, skirted the city canal, till it reached the Kaiser-baug, a royal palace strongly fortified and garrisoned, and here the most severe struggle of

A.D. 1857 the day occurred. The troops had been fighting without intermission since the morning, and the shades of evening were coming on, but under the impression that the garrison was in extremity, Havelock deemed it advisable to penetrate to the Residency that night, and pushed on through streets where, as he said, every house formed a fortress. The toils of the day, however, were forgotten when the garrison sent up a shout of gratulation as they entered the gate and brought the anxieties of three months to a close. The loss in killed, wounded and missing was very severe, amounting to 464, among whom, to the great regret of the army, was numbered Colonel Neill, who fell in the arms of victory before he had enjoyed the opportunity of adding to his richly-deserved renown as a gallant soldier, the higher reputation of a general.

SECTION III.

LORD CANNING'S ADMINISTRATION—THE MUTINY—DELHI—LUCKNOW—CENTRAL INDIA.

TO TURN now to the siege and recovery of Delhi. General Anson, the Commander-in Chief, was at Simla when intelligence of the mutiny at Meerut and the occupation of Delhi by the insurgent troops reached him, and he immediately ordered the three European regiments in the hills to proceed to Umballa, where he joined them, but was seized with cholera and expired on the 27th May. The command of the column then devolved on Sir Harry Barnard and he proceeded towards Delhi. In obedience to the reiterated orders of General Anson, General Hewitt had at length sent a detachment from Meerut to join it, and the united force met the rebels posted on the Hindun and twice defeated them, and a week after encountered them at Budlee-ka-serai, about six miles from Delhi, and obtained a still more complete victory, capturing all their guns, stores, and baggage. The army then took up a commanding position on the ridge overlooking Delhi, the site of the old encampment. The fortifications of the city had been greatly improved and strengthened, and it was now held by a large force of well-trained soldiers, fighting with a halter round their necks, who had the command of an almost unlimited supply of guns and military stores from our own arsenal. The impossibility of wresting from them a city

The siege of Delhi.

seven miles in circumference by the weak force under General Barnard was self-evident, and it was suggested to relinquish the siege for the present and employ the European force assembled before it in protecting other stations, and restoring the authority of Government; but Lord Canning would not listen to the proposal. He felt that Delhi had become the rallying point of revolt, the capital of a Mogul dynasty, and that it was impossible to restore confidence in our power while it continued in the hands of the enemy. The retirement of the army would, in his opinion, give an irresistible impulse to the spirit of rebellion, and render its suppression all but impossible. A.D. 1857

On the 5th July Sir Harry Barnard was carried off by cholera, and the command devolved on General Wilson. The British force was established on the ridge on the 10th June, but during the fourteen succeeding weeks, though Delhi was considered to be in a state of siege, it was in reality the cantonment which was besieged by the enemy. The force was too weak in men and guns to do more than defend its own position, and for every shot fired from our batteries the sepoys responded four-fold. Few days passed without an assault on the cantonment, and that on the 23rd June, the anniversary of Plassy, was marked by extraordinary vigour, as the day fixed for the dissolution of the Company's *raj*; but in this, as in every other encounter but one—and they numbered more than thirty—the sepoys were driven back into the city with ignominy. Their loss was indeed always heavier than that of the British force, but their numbers were constantly swelled by the accession of fresh regiments of rebels which gravitated to Delhi as to the common centre of the revolt, while the reinforcements from the Punjab were, for a time, few and far between. While, moreover, they had no lack of guns and stores, the ammunition in the British camp required to be husbanded with great care.

Position of the forces at Delhi.

Meanwhile, Sir John Lawrence was actively engaged in raising additional regiments of Sikhs, who were loyal to the core. There was an old Khalsa prophecy that they should one day enjoy the plunder of Delhi, and they now hailed with passionate ardour the prospect of realising it, and enlisted under our banner by thousands. The disbandment of the regiments and the extinction of the Sealkote mutineers by Brigadier Nicholson, enabled Sir John to redouble his efforts to reinforce General Wilson. Nothing could exceed the skill and energy with

Reinforcements from the Punjab.

A.D. 1857

which he organised and despatched the detachments in succession. It was at length found possible to dispense with the services of the Brigadier's movable column, 2,500 strong, in the Punjab, and it was sent down to Delhi and reached the cantonment on the 14th August, and imparted fresh courage to the exhausted troops. The Brigadier had preceded it by a week, and was welcomed in the camp with a feeling of homage as if he had been the very god of war.

Assault and capture of Delhi.

The great siege train, which occupied a line of thirteen miles, was wending its way from Ferozepore, and the revolted Neemuch brigade, always considered the flower of the sepoy army, which was now in Delhi, was sent out with eighteen guns to intercept it, as it was feebly guarded by the last detachment which Sir John could spare. Brigadier Nicholson marched out to encounter this force, and obtained a complete victory. The train entered the camp on the 3rd September, and the erection of batteries within breaching distance was pushed on with vigour. For a week fifty guns and mortars poured an incessant stream of shot and shell upon the walls and bastions, and on the 13th the breaches were reported practicable. At three on the morning of the 14th the assault was delivered on four points. Brigadier Nicholson, who led the attack, drove the enemy before him, but, to the infinite regret of the whole army was mortally wounded in the arms of victory. The other columns, with one exception, were equally successful, but the resistance of the enemy was desperate, and the operations of this the first day entailed a loss in killed and wounded of sixty-six officers and 1,104 men. The troops had made a lodgment within the walls, but the sepoys continued to dispute every inch of ground, and it was six days before all the important and defensible posts within the vast circle of the city were captured. For several days an uninterrupted fire had been kept up on the well-fortified palace. On the 20th the gates were blown up and the troops rushed into it, but the king had fled to the tomb of Humayoon, a few miles to the south of the city. The next day Captain Hodson proceeded to the tomb and dragged him, together with his favourite wife, who had been one of the chief instruments in stirring up the revolt, and her son, to the palace, where they were lodged as prisoners. The following day he went in search of the two sons and the grandson of the king, and as an attempt was about to be made to rescue them shot them dead on the spot with his own hand. Several months after the king was tried by a military commission in the imperial palace and found guilty of having ordered the murder of forty-nine Christians at Delhi, of having waged war upon the English Government, and urged the people by proclamation to subvert it. Lord Canning determined to spare his life, but sentenced him to be transported to Burmah ; and thus ended the royal house of Baber three hundred and thirty-two years after he had ascended the Mogul throne.

A.D. 1857

The total number of killed and wounded during the siege was 3,537, a heavy return of casualities, but the reduction of the city broke the neck of the rebellion. Oude and Rohilcund were still in revolt; the Gwalior contingent, 10,000 strong, was still in open arms, and Central India was in possession of the mutineers, but so completely had the revolt been identified with the possession of the ancient capital that the capture of it satisfied the country that the star of Britain was again in the ascendant, and that the final extinction of the mutiny was only a question of time. All the machinations in the Punjab, which the protraction of the siege had fostered, were dispelled. The rebel army was deprived of its organization by the loss of its citadel, while the British Government was daily gaining strength by the arrival of the regiments brought by sea. The liberation of the force engaged in the siege of Delhi likewise proved the salvation of the neighbouring city of Agra. It was attacked by the Neemuch and other mutineers on the 6th July, but owing to the incompetence of Brigadier Polwhele, the European troops sent against them were foiled, and retreated to the fort, where for nearly three months between 5,000 and 6,000 people of all rank, ages, and colours were shut up. At the beginning of October a large body of rebels came down and threatened it, when the young Brigadier Greathead, who had been sent from Delhi to clear the Dooab of the mutineers with his flying column, received an express from the fort, and after a forced march of forty miles in twenty-eight hours, drove off the enemy, with the loss of their guns, stores, camp and 500 in killed and wounded.

Result of the capture of Delhi.

The garrison of Lucknow had been relieved by Outram and Havelock, but their force was too weak to escort the women and children to Cawnpore, still less to recover a city garrisoned by a large rebel army with an abundance of military stores. The Residency was again in a state of close blockade but well supplied with provisions and able to await the arrival

Sir Colin Campbell's march to Lucknow.

A.D. 1857 of reinforcements with little risk or inconvenience. The attention of the enemy was chiefly devoted to the construction of mines, which they carried on to an extent which Sir James Outram affirmed had no parallel in modern warfare. Sir Colin Campbell, who had been appointed Commander-in-Chief in succession to General Anson, hastened to Cawnpore with the reinforcements which had reached Calcutta, accompanied by Captain Peel of the "Shannon." He started on the 9th November with a body of 5,000 men and 30 guns, and on the 14th advanced against the enemy's entrenchments, but so determined was the opposition he encountered at the various strong positions they had fortified, that he was three days forcing his way to the Residency. The Secunder-baug, indeed, a large enclosure, was breached and stormed by the Highlanders, when every soul within it perished and 2,000 bodies were carried out and buried. By the masterly arrangements of Sir Colin the relieved garrison, together with the women and children, were withdrawn with such skill as not to attract the attention and the assaults of the enemy, but Havelock, worn out with toil and exposure, was attacked by diarrhœa and sunk under the disease, a Christian hero and general of the highest stamp.

Disaster of General Windham.

General Outram was left at the Alum-baug with a sufficient force to keep open the communication with Cawnpore and to maintain our footing in Oude, and Sir Colin Campbell hastened back to Cawnpore, the defence of which had been entrusted to General Windham, with more than 2,000 men, and was just in time to save him from a fatal calamity. The Gwalior contingent, which had finally broken into open mutiny in the middle of October, crossed the Jumna and marched down, 20,000 strong, to Cawnpore to join the Nana. General Windham moved out to meet them, without suspecting their numbers, and was at first successful, but his force was handled without any skill, and, finding himself outflanked by the enemy, he retreated in hot haste to the entrenchment, with the loss of his equipage. The sepoys obtained possession of the town, and for two days he had to sustain an unequal contest with a body of the ablest of the mutineers ten times his own number, flushed with recent success, animated by the presence of the Nana, and commanded by Tantia Topee, the only native general created by the mutiny. General Windham must have suffered the fate of General Wheeler, if he had not received timely succour by the arrival of Sir Colin, who reached the Ganges in time to save the bridge of boats, the destruction of which would have been irreparable. After having safely despatched the sick and the wounded, the women and the children to Allahabad, he marched out against the rebel force, now swelled to 25,000 men with 40 guns. Captain Peel's sailors, handling their 24-pounders like playthings, did fearful execution, and the skilful dispositions of Sir Colin, and the valour of his troops, inflicted a crushing defeat on the rebels, who were pursued for fourteen miles and loss of all their guns—the arm in which they were strongest. The total loss on the side of the British army amounted only to 99.

A.D. 1858

We turn now to the pursuit of the rebels in Central India. While the task of extinguishing the mutiny at Delhi fell to Sir John Lawrence, and that of recovering Cawnpore and Lucknow to Lord Canning, the work of stamping out the revolt in Central India was undertaken by the Madras and Bombay Presidencies. A column of Madras troops was assembled at Nagpore and moved on to Jubbulpore, and a Bombay column advanced to Kotah. They constituted the Central India Field Force, and comprised about 6,000 troops, of whom 2,500 were Europeans. General Stuart, commanding one brigade, proceeded to relieve Mhow, which had been besieged since the commencement of the mutiny, and then captured Dhar, and defeated a body of 5,000 mutineers at Mundisore. Having thus cleared the southern districts of the rebels, he advanced to Indore. There Sir Hugh Rose, on the 15th December, assumed the command of the whole force, and started for Sehore, where he inflicted summary vengeance on the insurgents, and moved on to Saugor, and relieved a body of Europeans who had been cooped up for several months. On the 21st March he proceeded to Jhansi, the little principality in Bundlecund which Lord Dalhousie had annexed five years before, as stated in a former chapter.

Campaign in Central India.

The ranee, a woman of extraordinary energy but of unmatched vindictiveness, took advantage of the mutiny to recover the independence of her principality and to satiate her revenge. The sepoys stationed there rose in mutiny on the 4th June and assailed the Europeans, who took refuge in the fort, but were induced to surrender upon a promise of protection made under the most solemn oaths; but the whole body, seventy-five in number, were immediately bound together, the men in one row, and their

Capture of Jhansi.

A.D. 1858 wives and children in another, and butchered under the immediate direction of the ranee. She assembled 10,000 men for the defence of the town, which was surrounded by a wall of solid masonry from six to twelve feet thick and from eighteen to thirty feet in height. After Sir Hugh had invested it for nine days, a body of 20,000 men, including that portion of the Gwalior contingent which had escaped from the sword of Sir Colin at Cawnpore, advanced under the command of Tantia Topee to the relief of the ranee. Without slackening fire on the town, Sir Hugh moved out to meet them on the 1st April with 1,200 men, of whom only 500 were British, and drove them in dismay across the Betwa, which gives its name to the engagement, with the loss of 1,500 men and all their guns. The assault on the town was renewed with redoubled vigour; every street was fiercely contested; no quarter was asked or given; and the palace was stormed and sacked.

The ranee, after making her last stand in the fort, fled to Calpee, the head-quarters of the Gwalior contingent, and the rallying point of the mutineers west of the Jumna, where they had established foundries for casting cannon, and collected military stores of every description. Sir Hugh advanced towards it, when the martial ranee who took her share in the command, riding in male attire at the head of her own body guard, came out with Tantia Topee and 20,000 men to meet him at Koonch, but they were signally defeated. The general then marched on to Golowlee within five miles of Calpee where he was again attacked by the entire force of the enemy, but was again victorious and became master of Calpee, with the vast military stores the rebels had accumulated from the plunder of various cantonments. He considered the revolt in Central India extinguished by the capture of their citadel, and resolved to break up the army, which was prostrated by insupportable heat, and issued a valedictory order to the troops, congratulating them on "having "marched more than 1,000 miles and taken more than 100 "guns, on having forced their way through mountain "passes and intricate jungles and over rivers, and cap-"tured the strongest forts, and beat the enemy, no matter "what the odds, wherever they had met him, without a "single check, and restored peace and order to the "country."

Capture of Calpee.

But there was still work for his exhausted troops. Nothing appeared more remarkable during the course of

A.D. 1858

Capture of Gwalior by the rebels.

this revolt than the rapidity with which the insurgent sepoys rallied after a defeat, and presented a new and more formidable array. Tantia Topee, after his defeat at Koonch, proceeded to Gwalior to organise a conspiracy against Sindia. The troops driven from Calpee hastened to join him, and within a week a force of 18,000 mutineers was embodied in the cantonment at the capital. Sindia's able minister, Dinkur Rao, advised him to await the arrival of the troops which were marching down from Agra, but his ardent spirit led him to attack them with his household troops, about 8,000 in number, who either joined the rebels or withdrew from the field, and on the 1st of June he fled to Agra. The rebels then took possession of the capital, and supplied themselves with stores and ammunition from the royal arsenal, and, with the far-famed Gwalior artillery, plundered the treasury of half a crore of rupees, distributed six months' pay to each sepoy, and then proclaimed Nana Sahib, Peshwa.

Recovery of Gwalior.

Sir Hugh, on receiving intelligence of this astounding event, resumed the command he had laid down, and hastened on to Gwalior without a moment's delay, though the heat was 130° in the shade; and on the morning of the 16th June, though the troops were exhausted with marching all night, attacked the sepoys at once, and chased them with heavy loss from the cantonment. The next day, Brigadier's Smith's column came up from the westward, driving the rebels before him, and it was in his last charge that the valiant ranee, who had taken a share in every engagement since she left Jhansi, was killed by a hussar who was ignorant of her sex. On the 18th, the whole of the enemy's entrenchments and positions were stormed and fifty guns captured, and they sought refuge in flight; but a compact body of 6,000 with a splendid field artillery retired in good order from the field, when Brigadier Napier hastened after them with 600 cavalry and six field guns, and, dashing into the midst of their ranks, put them to utter rout. With this brilliant action the campaign was brought to a close, and Sindia remounted his throne amidst the acclamations of his subjects.

SECTION IV.

LORD CANNING'S ADMINISTRATION—THE MUTINY EXTINGUISHED.

A.D. 1858 During these operations, which completely crushed the mutiny in Central India, Sir Colin Campbell was employed in extinguishing it on the east of the Jumna. His first object was to clear the Dooab, lying between that river and the Ganges. Towards the end of November, Colonel Seaton left Delhi with a movable column and marched downwards, while General Walpole moved upwards. The sepoys were beaten in every encounter, and the power of the nabob of Futtyghur, who had assumed independence early in the mutiny, was annihilated. By the end of December the authority of the Company was re-established throughout these districts, and Sir Colin Campbell found himself at the head of 10,000 troops at Futtygurh. The mutiny was now confined to the two provinces of Rohilcund and Oude, but Sir Colin, whose movements would have been more successful and satisfactory if they had been less tardy, wasted two months idly in this neighbourhood.

The Dooab cleared of rebels.

Meanwhile, General Franks was organising a force at Benares, which eventually amounted to 6,000 men, to clear the lower portion of Oude of the rebel bands, and in his triumphant progress defeated them at every stage. Jung Bahadoor, the regent, but in reality the ruler, of Nepaul, marched down with a body of 9,000 hardy Goorkhas to assist the British Government in the reconquest of Oude, and on two occasions defeated the insurgents with great slaughter. Sir James Outram, who had been left in command at the Alum-baug, had been twice assailed by the rebel army and population of Lucknow, and had dispersed them though six times his number. At length, on the last day of February, Sir Colin Campbell saw his force, consisting of 18,277 horse, foot, and artillery, Europeans and Sikhs, across the Ganges, and on the 5th March was encamped at the Dilkoosha outside the fortifications of the city, where he was joined by the army of General Franks and Jung Bahadoor. The siege opened on the 6th. The defence was the most obstinate our arms had ever encountered in India, not excepting even that of Delhi. The rebels were animated by

March into Oude.

the presence of the begum of Oude, a woman of indomitable A.D. 1858
energy, who had been the soul of the insurrection and had prevailed on the chiefs and sepoys to recognise her son as king. During the time lost at Futtygurh, the mutineers had availed themselves of the opportunity of improving the defences of the city, and the extraordinary industry displayed by them had seldom been equalled, and never surpassed, in India. Every outlet had been covered with a work, and barricades and loopholed parapets had been constructed in every direction. The various buildings formed a range of massive palaces and walled courts of vast extent, and they had been fortified with great skill. It was not till after ten days of incessant fighting that the recovery of the city was complete; but by some mismanagement on the part of one of the British commanders, Sir Colin was deprived of the full fruit of victory by the escape of the greater part of the mutineers, together with their leaders. The number of killed and wounded throughout the siege did not exceed 900. It was impossible to restrain the victorious soldiers from the rich plunder of the city, of which, however, the largest share fell to the Goorkhas, who returned to Nepaul with some thousand cartloads of spoil.

Confiscation of the land in Oude.

On the capture of Lucknow, Lord Canning, on the 31st of March, directed Sir James Outram, the chief commissioner, to issue a proclamation confiscating the proprietary right of every estate in Oude, with the exception of six zemindarees. Sir James earnestly remonstrated against the injustice, as well as the impolicy, of a measure which confounded the innocent with the guilty, and could not fail to retard the peaceful settlement of the kingdom. The proclamation was repudiated in England by a spiteful and sarcastic despatch from Lord Ellenborough, then President of the Board of Control, but Lord Canning was, in the meanwhile, induced to mitigate the severity of the order, and to entrust large discretionary powers to Mr.—now Sir Robert—Montgomery, the successor of Sir James Outram, who had been raised to Council. He concluded a fresh settlement with the Talookdars, the proudest aristocracy in India, upon a moderate rental, and gave them the advantage of a new and Parliamentary title to their estates, and, moreover, endeavoured to attach them to the interests of the Government by appointing them honorary magistrates.

Bareilly the capital of Rohilcund was held by Khan Bahadoor Khan, a descendant of Hafiz Ruhmut, of the days

A.D. 1858

Operations in Rohilcund.

of Hastings, who had proclaimed his independence in the early stages of the mutiny, and put two judges to death under the mimic forms of European justice. In the town were collected the begum of Oude, the Nana, Prince Feroze, and the other chiefs and rebels who had escaped from Lucknow, and three columns were sent against it. One column, 6,000 strong, with light and heavy artillery under Brigadier Walpole came upon a petty fortification, fifty miles from Lucknow, consisting of nothing but a high loop-holed wall and a ditch, held by about 400 men. Instead of shelling them out, the commander, contrary to the express injunctions of Sir Colin Campbell, determined to carry it by assault, but the assailants were driven back with the loss of 100 men, among whom was Brigadier the Hon. Adrian Hope, "the most "gallant and best beloved soldier in the army," the idol of his own Highlanders, who invoked malisons on the Commander. By the beginning of May, the columns under the personal command of Sir Colin closed upon Bareilly, which was speedily captured with all its stores and ammunition; but the prize was again lost; the rebel chiefs, with the bulk of their armed followers, made their escape. They were followed up by Sir Hope Grant, and a body of 16,000 posted in a jungle at Nabob-gunge was attacked and defeated, but the indefatigable begum rallied her forces anew on the Gogra, where she was again assailed and routed. She was hunted from post to post down to the Raptee, where, although hemmed in on every side, she made her escape across the river, together with the remaining leaders and their followers, and got away safe into the Nepaul territory. Jung Bahadoor did not refuse permission to Lord Canning to pursue the fugitives, and thousands perished under British weapons and from the malaria of the *teraee*. The mutiny was virtually at an end, though in some districts bands of rebels continued for several months to maintain a show of resistance. The Nana and his brother died in the jungles of Nepaul during 1859; the begum found a peaceful asylum at Katmandhoo; Prince Feroze made his way through Oude and joined Tantia Topee in Central India, where he was moving about with the remainder of his troops and a large amount of treasure, baffling the various columns which were in pursuit of him. He was at length betrayed by his most trusty companion, and was seized on the 7th April while asleep in the jungle, and tried and executed at Sepree. With the exception of the ranee of

Jhansi and the begum of Oude, he was the only great leader whom the rebellion produced, and the extraordinary energy and valour he displayed might have entitled him to a more lenient penalty; but, for the monster who had taken his seat on a stage and directed the diabolic massacre at the ghaut of Cawnpore, there could be no compassion. On the 8th July 1859, peace was proclaimed by Lord Canning throughout India; and on the 12th October he made a royal progress through the provinces, receiving the homage of chiefs and nobles. On the 3rd November he held a durbar at Cawnpore, with a display of magnificence well suited to captivate the native mind, and to demonstrate the restoration of British power. All the loyal chiefs were collected at that brilliant assembly, and as the representative of the Queen who had assumed the sovereignty of India, he decorated them with dresses of honour and titles of distinction.

A.D. 1859

The mutiny has been attributed by different writers to a variety of causes—to the annexations during Lord Dalhousie's administration; to the rapid introduction of improvements, such as the rail and the telegraph, which bewildered the native mind; to the spread of English education and European science, which were undermining Hindooism and disquieting the orthodox; and to a national revolt against British authority. On the other hand, Sir John Lawrence asserted, "The mutiny had "its origin in the army itself; it is not attributable to any "external or antecedent conspiracy whatever, although it "was taken advantage of by disaffected persons to compass "their own ends; the approximate cause was the cartridge "affair, and nothing else." But we live too near this stupendous event, and the excitement it created is as yet too fervid, to admit of a calm judgment of its origin, which must be left to the unruffled determination of posterity when it has ceased to be a party question. To assist that decision, it may be remarked that the conduct of the people, even in the most disturbed districts in the north-west, was eminently neutral. The agricultural, the mercantile, and the industrial population, made no demonstration in favour of the revolt. There was no insurrection where there were no sepoys; the Sikhs, and more particularly the rajas in the Cis Sutlej states, rendered the most essential service in quelling the insurrection; the princes in Rajpootana were perfectly loyal; Sindia, Holkar, the begum of Bhopal, and the nabob of Rampoora, sided with the British Government; the Nepaul cabinet sent down 9,000 troops to its aid. In

Cause of the mutiny.

A.D. 1858 the south, the Gaikwar, the inhabitants of the annexed provinces of Satara and Nagpore, the Nizam and his great minister Salar Jung, the great Mahratta feudatories and the nobles of Mysore, were faithful in their allegiance to the British Government. These princes do not appear to have ever entertained a doubt of its triumph even when, before the reduction of Delhi and Lucknow, its fortunes appeared desperate. They were not ignorant that for twenty-five centuries from the period of the great war celebrated in the Muhabharut downwards, India had been the constant theatre of revolutions, and the insurrection which now threatened the existence of the British Government appeared to come in the usual order of events. The confusion, moreover, which ensued on the temporary eclipse of its authority, in the rapid rise of various aspirants for power in Hindostan—the king of Delhi, the Nana, the begum of Oude, the nabob of Futtygurh, the nabob of Bareilly, who would have proceeded to fall upon each other and revive the anarchy of former days when the British power was extinct, rendered these princes the more anxious to maintain it as the guardian of peace and order.

Extinction of the East India Company.

The mutiny was the death-warrant of the East India Company. England was astounded by the announcement of a revolt which threatened the dissolution of the empire, and of the atrocious massacres which accompanied it. The responsibility of the outbreak was at once cast on the Company, though for more than seventy years no political or administrative measure had been executed without the full concurrence of the Ministry. During this period the President of the Board of Control had carried more weight in the government of India than the Chairman of the Court of Directors; but the one was before the public, the other behind the scenes. The argument on which the Court of Directors had endeavoured, half a century before, to justify the precipitate dismissal of Lord William Bentinck after the Vellore mutiny, was now applied with fatal effect to themselves on the occasion of a larger mutiny—"As the misfortunes which "happened under your administration placed your fate under "the government of public events and opinions which the "Court could not control, so it was not in their power to "alter the effect of them." In December 1857 Lord Palmerston informed the Court of Directors that a Bill for placing India under the direct authority of the Crown would shortly be laid before Parliament. Mr. John Stuart

Mill was instructed by the Directors to draw up a petition to Parliament pleading their services, denying that the mutiny was owing to their mismanagement, and deprecating so fundamental a change in the government while the mutiny was still raging. It was one of the ablest state papers in the language, but nothing could withstand the popular outcry. Mr. Baring, on presenting the petition to the House of Commons, moved as an amendment to Lord Palmerston's Bill, that "it is not at present expedient to legis-"late for the government of India," but it was rejected by 318 to 173, whereas the continuance of the government of India in the hands of the Company was voted without a division only five years before. While Lord Palmerston's Bill was passing through Parliament, the Conservatives came into power, and it fell to the lot of Lord Stanley to carry through the Bill which extinguished the Company. On the 1st September 1858, the Court of Directors met for the last time in their council chamber in Leadenhall Street, and, as their last act of administration, gracefully voted an annuity of 2000*l.* a year to Sir John Lawrence, who had been the instrument of saving the empire now transferred to the Crown.

A.D. 1858

Character of the Company.

The East India Company was incorporated by Queen Elizabeth in the year 1600, but its political existence is to be dated only from the battle of Plassy in 1757, and closed, after the lapse of a hundred years, with the revolt of the army. During this century it created an empire greater than that of Rome, and at the period of its dissolution transferred the government of 150,000,000 of subjects to its sovereign. There is no record in history of so brilliant a career, nor is there any instance of power so extensive and so rapidly acquired, with so few causes of regret on the score of political morality. Notwithstanding its errors and its shortcomings, it may be safely affirmed that no foreign dependency has ever been administered in a spirit of higher energy, or greater benevolence, or by a longer succession of great men. But its mission was accomplished, and the anomaly of continuing the government of so vast a domain with such an agency was daily becoming more obvious; and even without the crisis of the mutiny, the termination of its trust could not have been far distant.

On the 1st November 1858, the Queen's proclamation, translated into the various languages of India, was promulgated throughout the continent with every demonstra-

A.D. 1858 tion of official pomp. It announced that Her Majesty had at length assumed the government of India, which had hitherto been conducted by her trustees, the Honourable the East India Company; that all treaties, dignities, rights and usages should be faithfully upheld, that the public service should be open to all her subjects without distinction of caste or creed, and that while the Government was a Christian Government no one should be molested or benefitted on account of his religion. The proclamation was cordially welcomed by the princes and people of India. The *ikbal*, or good fortune, of the Company to which they had paid homage for a century expired with the mutiny which exposed its weakness. Its name was associated with one of the greatest calamities which had befallen India. British authority had been re-established by the armaments sent by the Queen, and it was expedient that she should assume the sceptre of India. The introduction of an entirely new policy after such a convulsion was eminently calculated to tranquillize and reassure the public mind. The natives of India, moreover, have from the earliest ages paid deference to the principle of royalty, and a feeling of pride and satisfaction was diffused through the country in being considered the subjects of a sovereign, and not of a farmer, in which light the Company was now viewed.

The Queen's proclamation.

SECTION V.

EPITOME OF EVENTS SUBSEQUENT TO 1858.

THE century occupied in the conquest of India terminated with the suppression of the mutiny and the annexation of the empire to the Crown of Great Britain. The record of subsequent events belongs to a new epoch in the history of British India, upon which it is not advisable to enter in the remainder of the space necessarily prescribed for this compendium, and we therefore bring it to a close with a brief reference to the chief transactions of the period extending to the death of Lord Mayo.

1859 At the renewal of the charter in 1853, the Supreme Council, which had been invested with the power of imperial legislation, was enlarged by the addition of one member from each Presidency and lieutenant-governorship, and two of the judges of the Supreme Court. A more important alteration was made upon the transfer of the government to the Crown; the two judges of the Supreme Court were excluded, and the Governor-General was instructed to summon additional members, not exceeding twelve, to the Council when engaged in making laws. One half the number was to consist of non-official members, who might be either Europeans or natives, and the natives thus for the first time obtained a voice in the deliberations of the state. The earliest members of Council were the raja of Putteala, the raja Dinkur Rao, and the raja of Benares, all of whom had been exemplary in their allegiance to the Government during the mutiny. Similar Councils were attached to the Governments of Bengal, Madras, and Bombay, with the same admixture of the native element.

The suppression of the mutiny was mainly due to the A.D. 1859
assistance derived from the annexation of the Punjab, but the full value of this reservoir of soldiers of exemplary courage, and untainted with the high-caste prejudices of the sepoys, was not fully developed till the war in China came on. The merit of having ventured to enlist their services only three years after they had shaken the empire at Ferozeshuhur belongs to Lord Dalhousie, who called down a regiment from the Punjab to supply the place of the sepoy regiment which had refused to embark for Rangoon. The example was followed by Lord Canning, and a large contingent of Punjabee troops was sent on the expedition to China, who assisted in planting the British standard on the battlements of Pekin.

The transfer of the establishments of the East India 1859
Company to the Crown carried with it the transfer of their European troops, in number about 24,000. But though this made no change in the position or prospects of the men, they protested against being handed over from one service to another without being allowed a voice in the matter, and a feeling of dissatisfaction was manifested by a large number, and a spirit of insubordination in one corps. Lord Canning offered their discharge and a passage to England to all who objected to the exchange. The soldiers felt no objection to the royal service, but they looked for a small bounty, similar to that which the royal troops were accustomed to receive when, upon the expiration of their time, they enlisted into other regiments. The expectation was perfectly reasonable, but it was imperiously and injudiciously denied them, and 10,000 demanded their discharge. The state was thus not only subjected to a heavier

payment for their passage than the small bounty would have amounted to, but lost the invaluable services of a body of seasoned and veteran European soldiers. Contrary, moreover, to the advice of some of the most eminent Indian statesmen, it was resolved to abolish the local European army, the value of which had been insisted on by Lord Cornwallis and by all his successors. The Indian navy, as it was termed, a small squadron of armed schooners belonging to the Company, and which was employed in maintaining the police of the Indian seas, was at the same time abolished, and the duty entrusted exclusively to the royal navy.

A.D. During the year 1859 the indigo districts in Bengal were
1859 disturbed by the refusal of the ryots to cultivate indigo for the planters. The cultivation had never been remunerative, but they were bound to it by advances forced on them, and by contracts to which they were often obliged to affix their mark without knowing their contents. Having once received advances, they found they could never be released from the planter's books. The lieutenant-governor of Bengal, on his return from Dacca, was assailed by thousands of men and women, who lined the banks for a whole day's journey, crying to him for justice. To meet the difficulty, the Government passed an Act, inflicting a penalty for a breach of the contracts of the year, and appointing a commission to investigate the complaints of the ryots. They were fully substantiated, and Sir Charles Wood refused to sanction the proposal which had been made to consider the non-performance of a civil contract by a ryot the ground of a criminal prosecution.

1860 The mutiny had augmented the debt by fifty crores, and the annual expenditure, owing to the increase of the military charges, had risen from thirty-three to fifty crores, while the annual deficit amounted to ten crores. The financial department had always been the weakest point of the Government. India had produced eminent statesmen, and diplomatists, and generals, and administrators, but not one Chancellor of the Exchequer. Sir Charles Wood resolved to supply this deficiency by adding a financial member to the Executive Council, and selected for this post Mr. James Wilson, one of the secretaries of the treasury in London, who had an especial genius for finance. He revised the customs on scientific principles, and laid on an income-tax for five years as an exceptional impost to meet the charges entailed by the mutiny, and he imposed a license duty; at the same time he remodelled the currency, and withdrew the privilege of issuing bank notes which had been granted in their charters to the banks of Bengal, Madras, and Bombay, and established a State paper currency. By the taxes thus imposed, and the retrenchments which were effected, the deficit was extinguished in less than three years. Mr. Wilson's career was unhappily cut short by death before his financial reforms were completed.

Mr. Macaulay had drawn up a penal code in 1837, which A.D.
was bandied about for twenty years from one commission 1860
to another, and, having at length received its final modification, became law in 1860. At the same time, the Legislative Council passed an admirable code of civil and criminal procedure, which substituted simplicity and expedition for the complicated and tardy forms of pleading, which had previously impeded the course of justice. Lord Elphinstone, the governor of Bombay, who had rendered great service to the state during the insurrection, by repressing every hostile tendency at that Presidency, and by organising the force which quelled the mutiny in Central India, returned to England in this year with his constitution seriously impaired by the labours and anxieties of his post, and sunk into a premature grave.

The Nizam who had remained firm in his loyalty to 1860
Government during the mutiny was rewarded with honours, and with the more substantial boon of three of the provinces which he had assigned to meet the payment of the contingent and to satisfy other obligations, as well as with the remission of the balance of his debt to the extent of half a crore of rupees. The principality of Shorapore, which had been confiscated for the treason of the raja, was likewise transferred to him.

The whole machinery of judicature was remodelled 1861
throughout the country during the latter period of Lord Canning's administration. The Supreme and Sudder Courts were amalgamated, and a High Court established at each Presidency, consisting partly of English barristers, and partly of the Company's judges. A native lawyer of eminence was likewise placed on the bench, with no little honour to himself and great gratification to the country; and thus was the baneful ostracism of Lord Cornwallis abolished by the admission of natives to the distinction of making and administering the law, upon a footing of perfect equality with Europeans. At the same time Small Cause Courts, with a simple procedure, were established in

the provinces, and the recovery of small debts and demands rendered more easy.

A.D. 1862 The death of Lady Canning hastened the departure of Lord Canning, whose health had been greatly affected by six years of unexampled care and toil. He embarked in March 1862, but did not survive his arrival in England more than three months. His administration forms the most memorable period in the history of British India. No governor-general ever had to pass through a season of such profound anxiety, or to encounter so momentous a crisis. If he was slow and dilatory in his movements in circumstances in which Lord Dalhousie's foresight, promptitude, and energy would have been invaluable, yet he never lost heart or confidence, and his equanimity in the most appalling circumstances has never been exceeded and rarely equalled.

1863 Lord Elgin, who had brought affairs in China to a successful issue, was appointed to succeed him, and reached Calcutta on the 12th March, but died at Dhurmsala, in the Himalayas, on the 20th November in the ensuing year. His brief tenure of office afforded no opportunity for the display of his talents. It was, however, marked by a Mahomedan conspiracy against the British Government, fomented by Wahabee fanatics, which burst forth at Sitana, across the Indus, on the Afghan frontier. A large force, under the command of Brigadier Chamberlain, consisting of two European and six native regiments, was pushed forward into the fastnesses in which the whole army of Akbar had been exterminated two centuries before; but it was not only held in check but vigorously assailed by the irreconcilable highlanders. The Brigadier was disabled by wounds, and the position of the army became so critical that the Council in Calcutta, contrary to the remonstrance of the Commander-in-Chief, was on the point of withdrawing the troops from what appeared to them a bootless warfare in the mountains, a step which would have brought all the wild tribes down upon the Punjab. Happily Sir W. Denison, the governor of Madras, arrived in Calcutta at this juncture to officiate as governor-general, and ordered the campaign to be prosecuted with vigour, and it was brought to a satisfactory close by the end of 1863.

1864 The Ministry in England were filled with alarm at the prospect of a new Mahomedan outburst, and of the risk associated with it, and they at once offered the governor-generalship to the man to whom the salvation of the empire during the mutiny was mainly due, and who was, moreover, personally acquainted with the condition of that turbulent frontier. Sir John Lawrence arrived in Calcutta on the 12th January 1864, and found the "Umbeyla campaign," as it was called, terminated. Four years after, there was another of the chronic outbreaks of these untameable barbarians, but it was at once suppressed by the timely march of a brigade.

The civil war in America interrupted the supply of cotton A.D.
with which the looms of England had been fed, and it 1864
became necessary to look to India for a substitute. The price accordingly rose to a rare amount, and the exports increased two and three hundred per cent., but as they greatly exceeded the imports from England, the article was paid for in coin. During the continuance of the American war the imports of the precious metals into India amounted to more than seventy-five crores of rupees and poured riches into the lap of the cultivators, such as neither they nor their ancestors had ever dreamt of. The influx of wealth was poetically described by the metaphor that the ryots made the tyres of their cart-wheels of silver.

The unexpected increase of prosperity at Bombay arising 1865
from the export of cotton, created a perfect mania of speculation. The most preposterous schemes were brought forward, and met with ready acceptance, and the shares of the companies rose fifteen and twenty-fold. The Bank of Bombay lent itself to these wild projects without scruple, and when the bubble burst was driven into the bankruptcy Court, the first bank associated with Government which had ever been subject to such disgrace.

Sir John Lawrence found the Government of Bengal 1864
involved in disputes with the wild tribes of Bootan. On the conquest of Assam, the tract of cultivated land lying at the foot of the hills, called the Dooars, was annexed, but a trifling annuity was paid to the chief by way of compensation and to keep the tribes quiet, but it did not restrain them from making inroads into the plains, plundering the villages, and kidnapping its inhabitants. The subsidy was accordingly withheld, and the inroads were multiplied, and the Hon. Ashley Eden was sent as an envoy to the Bootan capital by the Government of Bengal. It was an imprudent act, and met with its reward. Mr. Eden was subject to every indignity from the barbarians, and signed an ignominious treaty under compulsion, resigning the Dooars to the chief. The consequence was a declaration of war; the foe was contemptible, yet one fort was retaken; the country was unhealthy, and the force was found to be inadequate.

A second campaign was undertaken the next year, with a larger force, and though the troops suffered to a fearful extent from the climate, the Bootanees were obliged to succumb. The treaty made with them, however, assigned them an annuity of 25,000 rupees for the Dooars. The
A.D. whole transaction, from first to last, was unfortunate, and
1865 proved that the existing Government of Bengal was equally as incompetent in war as in diplomacy.

1866 The year 1866 was marked by a desolating famine in Orissa. The total failure of the rains in the preceding year had given a premonition of its approach, but the Government of Bengal took no precautionary measure, and continued indifferent until the visitation arrived, and it was too late in the season to send succour by sea. The calamity was mitigated by the exertions of Lord Harris, the governor of Madras, but the number of victims was moderately estimated at three quarters of a million, and the event has left a deep stain on the reputation of the Bengal authorities.

1865 One of the most important legislative measures of Sir John Lawrence's administration had reference to the tenancy question in the Punjab and in Oude. He was anxious to protect the rights of the hereditary cultivators against the encroachments of the landholders, whether zemindars or talookdars. A great outcry was raised against the Acts which were of his creation, as being calculated to unsettle the engagements which had been made with the talookdars, and to revive disaffection. It was found, on enquiry, that the ryots in Oude for whose benefit the Government had incurred the greatest risk, had joined their old talookdars during the mutiny, in spite of the oppression under which they had groaned, and that there was in fact no class to whom the term of hereditary cultivators could be applied. The question was discussed with great earnestness, and no little acrimony, and it was silenced rather than settled by Sir Charles Wood's despatch, desiring the local authorities "to take especial care, without sacrificing the just rights of others, to maintain the talookdars of Oude in that position of consideration and dignity which Lord Canning's Government contemplated conferring on them."

1867 The affairs of Mysore were brought to an issue during the administration of Sir John Lawrence. Lord William Bentinck, as already stated, was constrained, by the insufferable misrule of the raja to assume the government of the country, and grant the raja a suitable pension. The administration was placed in the hands of General Cubbon, one of the Company's great statesmen, under whom Mysore reached a state of unexampled prosperity. The raja petitioned Lord Hardinge to restore the government to him. The question was referred to General Cubbon, who reported that every improvement which had been made had encountered the strenuous opposition of the raja, and that the transfer of the government to him would be fatal to the prosperity of the people; the request was therefore declined. A similar application was made to Lord Dalhousie, to Lord Canning, to Lord Elgin, and to Sir John Lawrence, and it was emphatically refused. Sir Charles Wood upheld the decision of the five Governors-General. The raja then proceeded to adopt a son, and demanded that he should be acknowledged the heir to the throne. In the creation of the principality in 1801, Lord Wellesley had expressly excluded all reference to heirs and successors, and limited the enjoyment of the crown to the raja, on whom he had bestowed it as a personal gift. But in 1867, the Conservative Secretary of State for India reversed the decisions of all the public authorities in India, and recognised the adopted son as the future heir of the throne, to whom the administration of the country is to be consigned on his coming of age.*

Dost Mahomed, who had faithfully maintained his en- A.D
gagements with the British Government, died in 1863, and 1868
a struggle for the crown immediately commenced in his family. His son, Shere Ali, whom he had nominated his successor, mounted the throne and was soon driven from it, but at length succeeded in recovering it. During these intestine struggles, Sir John Lawrence maintained a strict neutrality, and avoided any interference in the contests, which were desolating the country. His policy was by some applauded as masterly inactivity, and it might possibly for a time have been a prudent course, but the rapid development of events in Central Asia, and the progress of Russian influence have rendered the maintenance of it impracticable.

Sir John's administration was marked by great attention
to works of irrigation, and immediately before the expira- 1868
tion of his term of office he drew up a minute detailing those which had been completed and planned for all the Presidencies. These works would have required an expenditure of many crores of rupees, but as the finances exhibited an annual deficit, the complete canalization of India was necessarily postponed to a more auspicious period.

* He does not attain his majority until February 1881.

A.D. 1868 Sir John Lawrence on his return to England was rewarded for his pre-eminent services to India by his elevation to the peerage.

Lord Mayo was appointed his successor, and landed in India in the beginning of 1868; and one of his first acts was to modify Sir John Lawrence's policy of non-interference in the affairs of Afghanistan. The Ameer Shere Ali was invited to an interview, and, on the 29th March, was received with great distinction and pomp at Umballa, when not only was his position as the ruler of the nation recognised, but he was gratified with a subsidy of twelve lacs a-year, and a supply of arms. Lord Mayo rendered himself popular with the native chiefs by his graciousness, and with the European community by his princely hospitality. The most noted feature of his administration was the projection of a system of railways, embracing 10,000 miles, to be constructed by the State, and not by the agency of guaranteed companies. He fell by the dagger of an assassin, in January 1872, at Port Blair, on the Andamans, to which he was paying an official visit.

1872 On the death of Lord Mayo, Lord Napier, the Governor of Madras, succeeded by law to the supreme administration, until the appointment, early in 1872, of Lord Northbrook. The new Viceroy possessed a large official experience, having been Under-Secretary in various departments at home, and his qualities as a statesman were soon tested by the alarming progress of Russia in Central Asia. To a demand by the Khivans for assistance, Lord Northbrook replied that, where just claims were made by a great European power like Russia, a less civilized nation was bound to comply with them, and that he could not guarantee any aid from England. As the Russian Government had specifically stated that their only object was the redress of grievances, and that there was no intention on their part to retain any Khivan territory, it was difficult to see why England should interfere.

1873 The threatened expedition against Khiva took place in the spring of 1873, and resulted in the complete success of the Russians. Their army, under General Kauffmann, marched almost unmolested through the country, and occupied the capital without serious resistance. The Khan surrendered, and agreed to all the demands which were forced upon him by the Russian General, including a complete submission to the Czar's authority, which virtually deprived him of independence. After this fresh advance, an agreement was concluded between the English and Russian Governments, that the latter should abstain from interference with the boundaries of Afghanistan as fixed by England; and subsequent events showed the wisdom of this arrangement.

In India itself the dread of famine caused great anxiety. The failure of the autumn rains in Bengal and Behar had so materially injured the rice crops, that scarcity was imminent unless precautionary measures were taken. Determined to avoid the miseries of Orissa in 1866, Sir George Campbell, the Lieutenant-Governor of Bengal, an active and vigorous administrator, had purchased large quantities of grain, and organized relief works in anticipation of the impending dearth; while in all his efforts to surmount the difficulties he foresaw, he received the approval and support of the Viceroy and home authorities.

The year 1874 opened with gloomy prospects, and the distress soon assumed large proportions. Not only the late crop of 1873, but the April crop which followed, proved failures, and the Government found it necessary to supply far larger quantities of rice than they had calculated upon, and to face transport difficulties which impeded the distribution of food. All obstacles were, however, overcome by Sir Richard Temple, the successor of Sir George Campbell, who displayed rare administrative ability, and, by his energy and the skilful use of the means at his disposal, battled with the famine till the plentiful rains in June put an end to all anxiety, and enabled those who had been relieved by Government during the scarcity, to return to their occupations. Some idea may be gathered of the gigantic nature of the task of conveying food to the famine districts, when it was found to require 100,000 carts and 200,000 bullocks to carry the grain from the railway to the depots; and in addition to these, 2000 camels and 9000 horses were needed to take supplies into the more inaccessible parts of the interior; while over 2300 boats and 10 steamers transported the grain by water, on the Ganges and other rivers. Lord Northbrook, moreover, determined to utilize the public distress by employing the sufferers on two great public works—the extension of the Soane Irrigation Canal, and the construction of the Northern Bengal Railway. The number of people engaged in these and local relief works when the distress was at its height, was estimated at 1,770,000; and the cost to the Government of the relief operations alone, was nearly £7,000,000.

A.D. 1874

In Afghanistan affairs had assumed an unsatisfactory position. The Ameer, Shere Ali, having banished his eldest son, Yakoob Khan, induced him to return to Cabul, and then imprisoned him. The ostensible cause of this act of treachery was the report that Yakoob was intriguing for the surrender of Herat to Persia; the real reason was the desire of the Ameer to secure the succession for a younger and favourite son, Abdullah. This son died before the question was settled, and by the recent accession of Yakoob to the throne vacated by his father, it would appear that he had retained his hereditary position, in spite of the deceit practised on him.

A.D. 1874 The corrupt and vicious administration of Mulhar Rao, the Gaikwar of Baroda, had repeatedly called forth the remonstrances of those in authority, and the hesitation of the Government to recognise a son he affirmed to be legitimate, had increased his irritation against them. Colonel Phayre was the British Resident at Baroda, and while these disputes were at their height, an attempt was undoubtedly made to take his life by poison. It was alleged that this act was instigated by the Gaikwar, and a
1875 Royal Commission was therefore formed to inquire into the matter. This Commission was composed of three native princes—the Maharajahs of Gwalior and Jeypore, and Rajah Sir Dinkur Rao—and three English officials—Sir Richard Couch, the President, Sir Richard Meade, and Mr Philip Melville. Although the proceeding was simply an inquiry for the information of Government, it was conducted in the same manner as an English trial, and the Gaikwar was defended by an advocate—Mr Serjeant Ballantine—specially sent out from London on his behalf. In the result the Court was divided in opinion, the native princes expressing doubts as to the guilt of the accused, the English entertaining none. The practical decision, therefore, rested with the Viceroy, who, with the sanction of the home authorities, declared the Gaikwar to have forfeited his throne,—though the measure was afterwards stated to be more an act of political necessity than a judicial sentence. A young prince of the Kandeish branch was chosen to succeed him, and educated for his post by one of the most able of native statesmen under British supervision; but no alterations have been made in any of the existing treaty arrangements.

The Governor of Madras, Lord Hobart, died on the 27th April 1875. He was an able and conscientious administrator, who did much to promote the welfare and prosperity of the community, and initiated during his tenure of office the construction of an artificial harbour for Madras, and a scheme for draining the town. He was succeeded by the Duke of Buckingham and Chandos.

An event of national importance—the visit of the Prince A.D.
of Wales to India—took place towards the close of this year. 1875
Leaving England on the 11th October, the Prince, after stopping a few days at Athens, proceeded to Cairo, where he invested the Viceroy's eldest son, Prince Tewfik, with the Order of the Star of India, and landed at Bombay on the 8th November. The reception that greeted him was most enthusiastic; and throughout his tour everything tended to show the gratification of the natives at the royal visit. At Madras, where he was magnificently entertained by the Governor, he exchanged visits with the Maharajahs of the Presidency; and on New-Year's Day 1876, he presided over 1876
an investiture of the Star of India, which was held at Calcutta on a sumptuous scale. He then proceeded up the country, entered Delhi in state, through five miles of soldiery, and received an address from the native municipality of that ancient capital of Hindostan. Opportunities were afforded him of studying the native principalities, by his visits to Nepaul, to the Maharajahs of Puttiala and of Gwalior, and to Holkar at Indore; and when he embarked at Bombay, on the 13th March, he expressed, in a letter to Lord Northbrook, the sincere pleasure as well as instruction which he had derived from his first visit to India.

Some difficulties had meanwhile arisen between the Viceroy and the Secretary of State. The Government of India passed, on the 5th August 1875, an edict known as the Tariff Act. It revised the whole system of customs in India, and abolished export duties, but confirmed the import tax on manufactured cotton goods, and imposed an additional tax on raw cotton of the finer sort. Lord Salisbury at once not only expressed his dissent from, and desired the repeal of, these two provisions of the Act, but he also strongly censured the Indian authorities for passing so important a measure without reference to the Home Government. Lord Northbrook defended his position with skill and dignity, and on his retirement from office, on the 4th January 1875, his services were rewarded with an earldom. His successor, Lord Lytton, although he had distinguished himself in literature and diplomacy, had not hitherto held any important administrative trust. The obnoxious cotton duties were repealed by degrees; but, on the other hand, the new Viceroy adopted a conciliatory tone towards the natives of India, and endeavoured to diffuse the same through Anglo-Indian society.

A.D. 1877 A year had not elapsed since the Prince of Wales's visit to Delhi, when it again became the scene of a grand ceremonial. Parliament having decided that her Majesty the Queen should assume the imperial title of Empress of India, an assemblage of native chiefs and princes took place at Delhi on the 1st January 1877, when the new dignity was proclaimed by the Viceroy, amidst the most enthusiastic demonstrations of loyalty. The presence of so many native and British officials afforded an opportunity of holding a conference on the important legislative and fiscal matters which pressed at this time; while many concessions were made, rewards for past services granted, and pensions augmented. One most important act was the release of some 16,000 prisoners, whose cases had been carefully inquired into by Sir Edward Bayley; and to him must be attributed the beneficial influence this salutary measure exercised upon the minds of the natives of India.

Still, this splendid ceremony did not produce the entire political effect that might have been expected. Men's minds were too full of the prospects of the famine, which threatened to devastate the presidencies of Bombay and Madras, and even to penetrate into some of the neighbouring states. These fears were only too soon fulfilled: the rainfall of the previous year had more or less failed, while the spring and summer rains of 1877 were poor and irregular, and the dearth could no longer be averted. But Indian authorities had grown wise by sad experience, and the means previously used in Bengal to distribute supplies, and organize relief works, were everywhere adopted. In spite of all efforts, however, it was afterwards stated in the House of Commons that no less than 1,350,000 lives had been lost; and it was not until autumn was well advanced that the officials in the famine districts ceased to require help. England had liberally assisted their efforts by sending them nearly half a million of money; and the generous and noble manner in which she took up the cause of her impoverished subjects in Asia, did much to unite the two nations, and to frustrate any evils arising from supposed Russian designs. In view, however, of the terrible frequency of famines in India, the Finance Minister, Sir John Strachey, brought forward a proposal, advocating an additional tax, the proceeds of which were to be set aside to form a sinking fund for future emergencies; and the measure in due course received the sanction of Government.

Jung Bahadoor, the virtual sovereign of Nepaul, whose services during the Mutiny are elsewhere noticed (see p. 516), died this year. Although he strictly excluded Europeans from his territory, he invariably maintained an amicable policy towards the Indian Government, and the loss of so steady a friend on the frontier was severely felt.

The tribes on our north-west boundary, always turbulent, now showed signs of aggression, and it was evident that strong measures were required to repress them, one of them, the Jowakis, having, within the short space of a week, made no less than four incursions into British territory. In their last expedition, they attacked a body of the 22d Regiment, and killed and wounded some of the soldiers. A small field-force, however, was sent against them, which soon put down all resistance, and quiet was again restored along the border.

In April 1878 the Government received orders from home to despatch a force of 7000 native soldiers to Malta. Such an event as the employment of sepoys in Europe was without precedent in our annals; but the disturbed state of affairs in the East, which originally caused the movement, becoming by diplomatic arrangements more tranquil, the troops were recalled after a few months' absence. A.D. 1878

Our relations with Cabul had meanwhile become most precarious. The Ameer, Shere Ali, was offended by our occupation of Quettah; this, and various other alleged grievances, caused the failure of a conference at Peshawur between his agent and our representative, Sir Louis Pelly, and were doubtless among the motives which induced him to receive a Russian embassy at Cabul. A counter-embassy, under General Chamberlain, was promptly despatched by Lord Lytton; but on the 21st September 1878, it was turned back at Ali Musjid, the first Afghan fortress in the Khyber Pass, by the commandant, who, acting under orders from Shere Ali, refused to allow the Mission to proceed. A native envoy, Gholam Hassan Khan, who had previously been sent to sound the Ameer on the subject of the embassy, returned with an unsatisfactory answer; and the Viceroy thereupon despatched an ultimatum to Shere Ali, with the assurance that hostilities would be commenced, if he did not accede to the English demands before the 20th November. An evasive reply was received, and war was at once declared.

General Sir Samuel Browne was directed to move upon the capital with a large body of troops by the Khyber Pass. His forces advanced on the 21st November, but their march was checked at Ali Musjid. The capture, however, of that important fortress, and the evacuation of Jellalabad by the Afghans, followed in quick succession; and our troops soon afterwards encamped outside the town for the winter, without encountering any serious opposition.

General Roberts, who commanded the 2d brigade, advanced into Afghanistan by the Khurum Valley, and met with a sharp resistance at the Peiwar Pass, the occupation of which the enemy valiantly but unsuccessfully opposed; while General Stewart—in charge of the other battalion—after an unprecedented march of nearly 400 miles over most difficult country, joined the forces of General Biddulph at Takht-i-pul, the junction of the Khojak and Gwaja passes; and, with the exception of a slight encounter with the native cavalry outside Candahar, they took possession of that city unmolested. Desultory fighting followed in the neighbourhood, as well as in the Khost Valley, with General Roberts. The hill-tribes also were unceasingly active; but a further advance of the army into the country was not deemed necessary.

At the first approach of the British troops, Shere Ali had fled from Cabul to Mazar-i-Sharif in Balkh, where he endeavoured to obtain assistance against us; but his death
A.D. there on 21st February 1879 prevented his schemes from
1879 being carried out, and closed his checkered career. His son, Yakoob Khan, succeeded in making good his title to the throne, and was acknowledged by the Indian Government; but he at first refused to negotiate with them, until threatened with an advance of the army on Cabul. He then agreed to meet our emissary, Major Cavagnari, at Gandamuk, half-way to the capital, where, after some diplomatic delays, a treaty of peace, offensive and defensive, was concluded on the 25th May 1879, one of the principal articles of which was the permanent residence of an English Minister at Cabul.

Major Cavagnari, who had been knighted for his services in the late campaign, was appointed our Envoy—a post which he was eminently fitted to fill, from his long experience and great tact in dealing with the half-civilized nations on our north-west frontier. But he and his mission had hardly entered Cabul, when Yakoob Khan warned him that his life was in danger; to which he replied, "that if he were killed, there were many more in India ready to act as his successors." A few weeks, however, passed quietly, and confidence seemed to be fairly established, when the massacre of the gallant Cavagnari and his brave associates, and the burning of the Embassy on the 3d of September, rudely destroyed all hopes of peace. The Afghans had a third time broken faith with us, and avenged their wrongs, fancied or real, on our representatives; and a British army once more advanced, burning with indignation, to exact retribution for the murder of their countrymen. General, now Sir Frederick, Roberts lost no time in marching on Cabul, which he occupied on October 12th, after a struggle at Char-Asiab. Yakoob Khan, who had previously fled to the British camp, was declared to have forfeited the throne, and made a prisoner of State; and it was announced that the future government of the country would be decided after the advice of the Sirdars had been taken, and order had been restored. A fresh rising of some of the hill-tribes and mutinous soldiers in November caused great alarm, which was increased by the cessation of communications with General Roberts, and he was compelled to evacuate his post and establish his troops at Sherpur, a high cantonment outside and commanding the capital. But he succeeded in holding his own. General Gough advanced to support him, and the close of the year saw the British troops again victorious possessors of Cabul. With subsequent events there, and the future prospects of this great question—the government of Afghanistan—it is not proposed to deal.

On the 31st December 1879, the East Indian Railway ceased to be an independent body: the English Government, by virtue of an Act of Parliament, took the same into their own hands, this being the first instance of the exercise of the Imperial powers to purchase the Indian railways.

INDEX

ADDENDA.